THE TEACHING OF THE CATHOLIC CHURCH

CONTENTS OF THIS VOLUME

See page v for Analytical List of Contents

The TEACHING of the CATHOLIC CHURCH

A Summary of Catholic Doctrine

arranged and edited by

CANON GEORGE D. SMITH, D.D., Ph.D.

Volume II

NEW YORK

THE MACMILLAN COMPANY

1955

NIHIL OBSTAT: EDVARDVS CAN. MAHONEY, S.T.D.
CENSOR DEPVTATVS

IMPRIMATVR: E. MORROGH BERNARD
VICARIVS GENERALIS

WESTMONASTERII: DIE X IVNII MCMXLVII

Ninth Printing 1955

PRINTED IN THE UNITED STATES OF AMERICA

ANALYTICAL LIST OF CONTENTS

XIX—THE MYSTICAL BODY OF CHRIST

By the Right Rev. Mgr. Canon E. Myers, M.A.

XX—THE CHURCH ON EARTH

By Dom Aelred Graham, O.S.B., S.T.L.

XXI—THE SACRAMENTAL SYSTEM

By the Rev. C. C. MARTINDALE, S.J.

XXII—THE SACRAMENT OF BAPTISM

By the Rev. JOHN P. MURPHY, D.D., Ph.D.

XXIII—THE SACRAMENT OF CONFIRMATION

By the Rev. G. D. Smith, D.D., Ph.D.

XXIV—THE SACRAMENT OF THE EUCHARIST

By the Rev. G. D. Smith, D.D., Ph.D.

XXV—THE EUCHARISTIC SACRIFICE

By the Rev. B. V. Miller, D.D., Ph.D.

XXVI—SIN AND REPENTANCE

By the Rev. E. J. Mahoney, D.D.

XXVII—THE SACRAMENT OF PENANCE

By the Rev. H. Harrington, M.A.

XXVIII—EXTREME UNCTION

By the Rev. J. P. Arendzen, D.D., Ph.D., M.A.

XXIX—THE SACRAMENT OF ORDER

By the Very Rev. Mgr. Canon C. Cronin, D.D.

XXX—CHRISTIAN MARRIAGE

By the Rev. E. J. Mahoney, D.D.

XXXI—DEATH AND JUDGEMENT

By Abbot ANSCAR VONIER, O.S.B.

XXXII—PURGATORY, OR THE CHURCH SUFFERING

By Dom J. B. McLAUGHLIN, O.S.B.

XXXIII—ETERNAL PUNISHMENT

By the Rev. J. P. Arendzen, D.D., Ph.D., M.A.

XXXIV—THE RESURRECTION OF THE BODY

By Dom Justin McCann, O.S.B., M.A.

XXXV—HEAVEN, OR THE CHURCH TRIUMPHANT

By the Rev. J. P. Arendzen, D.D., Ph.D., M.A.

XIX

THE MYSTICAL BODY OF CHRIST

§ I: THE HOLY CATHOLIC CHURCH

OUR purpose in these few pages is to emphasise the truth that when we profess our belief in the Holy Catholic Church we make an act of faith in a great mystery of the Christian Revelation.

The Church the Mystical Body of Christ

The Church is more than a religious society whose purpose is the worship of God, more than a society different from all others because it was founded by God, more than a depository of grace and revealed truth. The Church herself is supernatural in her nature and essence, since she is the Body of Christ, living with the life of Christ himself, with a supernatural life. From the " fulness of Christ "[1] all his members are filled, so that the Church herself is " the fulness of him who is wholly fulfilled in all."[2] Hence the mystery of the Church is the very mystery of Christ himself.

Our act of faith in the great mystery of Christ's Church means far more than belief in a wonderful world-wide organisation of millions of men, united as no other group of men has ever been in belief, in practice, and in central government; it means that there circulates throughout the Church the life of grace which Christ came to bring into the world, linking together the members of the Church under Christ their Head with such a closeness of union that Head and members form a unique reality: the mystical Body of Christ. Our act of faith in the Church is an act of faith in Christ ever active in our midst, ever speaking, ever teaching, ever guiding, ever sanctifying those who are one with him, through the organism he has willed should exist in the world.

Visible and invisible elements in the Church

The negation of the visible character of the Church of Christ, and of its hierarchical constitution, has led to such stress being laid upon the visible, tangible aspects of the Church that those who are not Catholics have come to think of it in terms of its external organisation and of its recent dogmatic definitions, and not a few Catholics, concentrating their attention upon the argumentative, apologetical, and controversial side of the doctrine concerning the Church, have been in danger of overlooking theoretically—though practically it is impossible for them to do so—the supernatural, the mysterious, the vital, the overwhelmingly important character of the Church as the divinely established and only means of grace in the world, as the Mystical Body of Christ. Practically the doctrine of the supernatural life, of sanctifying grace, of the development of the spiritual

[1] Col. ii 9 ff. [2] Eph. i 23.

life, has safeguarded these deep truths; though even there individualism has asserted itself to the detriment of the collectivism of Christian activity. The stress laid by St Paul on the edification of the body of Christ, on the benefit the whole derives from the perfection of the members, has tended to be passed over where the social value of the contemplative life is not appreciated.

It is in and through the Church that Jesus Christ has willed to effect the salvation of mankind. From the beginning that Church has been a complex entity, and its history is filled with incidents in which men have concentrated upon some one essential element of its constitution to the exclusion of another equally essential element, and have drifted into heresy. The Church has its visible and its invisible elements, its individual and its social claims, its natural and its supernatural activities, its adaptability to the needs of the times, while it is uncompromising in vindicating, even unto blood, that which it holds from Christ and for Christ.

The development of the doctrine of the visible Church and of the authority of its visible head upon earth has been very marked. The persistent rejection of these revealed truths demanded their reiterated assertion and their vigorous defence. No thinking man can overlook the fact of Catholicism: there stands in the midst of the world a body of men with a world-wide organisation, and a carefully graded hierarchy, with a well-defined far-reaching process of teaching, law-making, and jurisdiction. The Vatican Council teaches us that "God has instituted the Church through his only-begotten Son, and has bestowed on it manifest marks of that institution, that it may be recognised by all men as the guardian and teacher of the revealed Word; for to the Catholic Church alone belong all those many and admirable tokens which have been divinely established for the evident credibility of the Christian faith. Nay, more, the Church itself, by reason of its marvellous extension, its eminent holiness, and its inexhaustible fruitfulness in every good thing, its Catholic unity and its invincible stability, is a great and perpetual motive of credibility, and an irrefutable witness of its own divine mission. And thus, like a standard set up amidst the nations, it both invites to itself those who do not yet believe, and assures its children that the faith which they profess rests on the most firm foundation." [1]

In that teaching the interplay of the visible element and the invisible element is set forth most clearly; and so it has been from the days of Our Lord himself.

His parables and his teaching on his Kingdom make it clear that it is an organic and social entity, with an external hierarchical organisation, aiming at bringing all men into such an attitude of mind and heart that the just claims of God his Father are recognised and honoured on earth, and hereafter in the heavenly kingdom in which alone Christ's ideal will be perfectly achieved. On earth the seed

[1] *Dogm. Const. De Fide*, iii.

is sown, the grain of mustard seed becomes the mighty-branched tree; the leaven works in the paste and raises it; even now we must needs enter in if our lot is to be with the elect; this, then, is the Kingdom preached by Christ and his followers.

On earth the kingdom of heaven is likened to a man that sowed good seed in his field, but while men were asleep his enemy came and over-sowed cockle among the wheat;[1] again it is "like to a net cast into the sea, and gathering together all kinds of fishes";[2] again it is likened to ten virgins—the wise and the foolish. Members of the Kingdom may give scandal and be rejected, they may be persecuted and falter before the deceptions of Antichrist. No doubt the Kingdom is life and spirit, and "the true adorers shall adore the Father in spirit and in truth."[3] But it is also clear that Christ's Kingdom is seen and known and persecuted, and subject to the vicissitudes of human movements.

Now it was precisely the visible organised body of men that Saul the persecutor knew, when he was "consenting to the death" of Stephen, a deacon of the organised Church, and when he "made havoc of the Church," imprisoning its members; when he set forth from Damascus, "breathing out threatenings and slaughter" against them. In later years he recalls that he was "according to zeal, persecuting the Church of God";[4] "that beyond measure I persecuted the Church of God and wasted it."[5] "For I am the least of the Apostles . . . because I persecuted the Church of God."[6]

The relation between them

Our Lord has willed that his Church should be what it is, and that it should be the instrument of salvation for all. He might have willed otherwise: he might have dealt with individual souls as though no other individual souls existed, by direct and immediate action, without taking into account the actions, the reactions, and the interactions of souls upon one another; without the realities underlying the Mystical Body; he might have ensured the preservation of his doctrine by direct revelation to individual souls; he might have willed that his followers should have been unknown in this world and known only to him, linked without knowing it in the invisible, mysterious life of grace—with no external sign of communion.

But that was not his will. He has taken into account the normal workings of our nature and he has supernaturalised them. Our individuality is respected, our social nature is respected too. Man is essentially a dependent being: dependent upon others for his life and its preservation, yearning for the company and the help of others. And so too in the supernatural life: the personal love of Our Lord for each one of us does not deprive us of the supernatural help, support, and sympathy of those with whom we are united in Christ, in his Church. Under the headship of the successor of Peter, the

[1] Matt. xiii 24 ff. [2] Matt. xiii 47. [3] John iv 23.
[4] Phil. iii 6. [5] Gal. i 13. [6] 1 Cor. xv 9.

Christ-founded Church teaches, safeguards and sanctifies its members, and their co-ordinated, directed prayers and efforts combine to achieve the purpose for which Christ founded his Church—by mutual help and intercession and example.

Man is a sense-bound creature and the appeal of sense is continuous. Our Lord has taken our nature into consideration. The merely invisible we can accept on his authority. But he has given us a visible Church, with recognisable rules and laws and doctrines and means of sanctification, in which man is at home. We accept Our Lord's gift to us with gratitude and strive to avail ourselves of its visible and invisible character. He has willed that as individuals we should be united with him by sanctifying grace, and that at the same time we should be united to one another with a unique collectivity, an unparalleled solidarity, which is the reality designated as the Mystical Body of Christ. And he has further willed that all the members of that Mystical Body should be members of the visible, organised hierarchical society to which he has given the power of teaching, ruling, and sanctifying. That visible Church is to be the unique indefectible Church which is to last until the end of time, and in its unity to extend all over the world.

The analogy of Body and Soul is used of the Church of God, and may be useful in emphasising the relative importance of the two essential elements of the Church. Our Lord wills that all should have life and should have it more abundantly : we have that life when we form part of the Mystical Body of Christ by supernatural Charity. All the *merely* external elements of Church membership will be insufficient unless the purpose of that external organisation is achieved : life-giving union with Christ. It is for that purpose alone that the visible Church exists.

§ II : THE DOCTRINE REVEALED

The teaching of Christ

Our Lord's prayer for the unity of his Church stands out very vividly. " Holy Father, keep them in thy name whom thou hast given me, that they may be one as we also are. While I was with them I kept them in thy name. Those whom thou gavest me I have kept, and none of them is lost but the son of perdition." [1]

That last prayer of Our Lord, embodying his last wish, embodies also his abiding, effective will. He had told his apostles that " I am the true vine and my Father is the husbandman. Abide in me and I in you. As the branch cannot bear fruit of itself unless it abide in the vine, so neither can you unless you abide in me. I am the vine, you are the branches ; he that abideth in me and I in him, the same beareth much fruit, for without me you can do nothing." [2] When he sent his Apostles on their mission, he told them : " He that receiveth you receiveth *me*." [3] " He that heareth you heareth *me*.

[1] John xvii 11-12. [2] John xv 1-5. [3] Matt. x 40.

He that despiseth you despiseth *me*, and he that despiseth me despiseth him that sent me."[1] And in the picture Our Lord gives us of the last judgement (Matthew xxv 31 to 40) he identifies himself with his followers, and declares that "as long as you did it to one of these my least brethren, you did it to *me*."

The teaching of St Paul

When St Paul was struck down on the way to Damascus he heard a voice saying to him "Saul, Saul, why persecutest thou me?"[2] Who said "Who art thou, Lord?" and he, "I am Jesus, whom thou persecutest." Saul was persecuting the Church of God; Our Lord identifies himself with that persecuted Church: in persecuting the Church Saul was persecuting Christ himself. Thus at the very outset of his Christian career, St Paul learned that truth which was to affect the whole of his teaching, the truth of the union of Christ with his Church, a union so close, so unique, so unparalleled, that he uses one imaged expression after another to try to bring home to his hearers a fuller realisation of the supernatural reality which had been revealed to him. He uses the analogy of the human body, of the building, of grafting, to render more vivid the truth he wants Christians to understand. Christ is the Head of his Church, and "he hath subjected all things beneath his feet and hath given him for supreme *Head* to the Church, which is his body, the fulness of him who is wholly fulfilled in all."[3] And again, "the husband is the head of the wife, as Christ too is *Head of the Church*, himself being the saviour of the body."[4] And speaking of the visionaries of Colossa, he emphasised their "not holding fast by the *head*, for from this [which is Christ] the whole body, nourished and knit together by means of the joints and ligaments, doth grow with the growth that is of God."[5] And again in the Epistle to the Ephesians,[6] "Rather shall we hold the truth in charity and grow in all things unto him who is the Head, Christ."

Christ, then, is the Head of the Church, which is his body; the Church is the fulness of Christ, made up of head and members. "You are [together] the body of Christ, and severally his members." The body of Christ, like the human body, presents a variety of structure, but "now there are many members yet one body."[7] And there is a variety of functions which cannot be exercised in isolation. "The eye cannot say to the hand 'I have no need of thee'; nor again the head to the feet 'I have no need of you.' Nay, much rather, those members of the body which seem to be weaker are [still] necessary. . . . [Yea] God hath [so] compounded the body [as] to give special honour where it was lacking, that there may be no schism in the body, but that the members may have a common care for each other. And if one member suffereth, all the members suffer therewith. If a member be honoured, all the members rejoice therewith. Now you are [together] the body of Christ, and severally

[1] Luke x 16. [2] Acts ix 4. [3] Eph. i 22-23.
[4] Eph. v 23. [5] Col. ii 19. [6] iv 15. [7] 1 Cor. xii 20.

his members." [1] Those varied gifts have their place in the Church, "and himself 'gave' some as Apostles, some as prophets, some as evangelists, some as shepherds and teachers for the perfecting of the saints in the work of the ministry unto the building up of the body of Christ." [2] Again, "to one through the Spirit is granted utterance of wisdom, to another utterance of knowledge according to the same Spirit; to another faith in the same Spirit; and to another, gifts of healings [still] in the same Spirit; and to another, workings of miracles; to another, prophecy, [divers] kinds of tongues, and to another interpretation of tongues." [3]

Yet in spite of this variety of gifts and endowments, all must tend to perfect unity. "For all you who were baptised into Christ have put on Christ. In him is neither Jew nor Greek, neither slave nor free, neither male nor female; for ye are all one person in Christ Jesus." [4] "For the perfecting of the saints in the work of ministry unto the building up of the body of Christ till we all attain to the unity of the faith and of the full knowledge of the Son of God, to the perfect man, to the full measure of the stature of Christ . . . thus . . . rather we shall hold the truth in charity, and grow in all things into him who is the Head, Christ. From him the whole body, welded and compacted together by means of every joint of the system, part working in harmony with part—[from him] the body deriveth its increase unto the building up of itself in charity." [5]

Without going into exegetical detail, the truth that St Paul is trying to express is clear: that there is the very closest possible relation between the members of the Church and the Head of the Church, so close that together they may be looked upon as one person, and that there is an ever-growing, intimate compenetration of members and head; the working of the members together with their Head constitutes the fulness of Christ; and in order that this universal fulness of grace should be diffused, our effort and our collaboration is called for: Christ is only his whole self by the unceasing working of his members. The gifts they severally receive have no other purpose than to foster this increase, and in the working out of Christ's scheme, the head is not the whole body, though it may be the focus of the whole vital influence. Merely to say that Christ is the Head is not fully to define Christ. "God hath given him for the supreme head to the Church, which is his body, the fulness of him, who is wholly fulfilled in all." [6]

In these many passages we are faced by a reality which goes beyond any mere moral influence, any relation of the merely moral order. The influence of Christ upon his members is a real, a vital influence, the nature of which we have to bring out more clearly. St Paul, in speaking of Christ as Head of the Church, is speaking of Christ as he now actually is. No longer the suffering Son of God

[1] 1 Cor. xii 20-27. [2] Eph. iv 11-12. [3] 1 Cor. xii 8-11.
[4] Gal. iii 27. [5] Eph. iv 12-16. [6] Eph. i 22.

making his way in the midst of men, but Christ triumphant, inseparable from the fruits of his victory, from those whom he has redeemed, whose redemption is realised by their incorporation with him; so that in virtue of their union with Christ they share in his merits and in his glory.

A twofold solidarity

To the solidarity of human nature in Adam, with its Original Sin and consequent evils, God has willed to contrast a more glorious restoration, a triumphant solidarity of supernaturalised creation transcending the limits of time and place and uniting all "in Christ," whether Jew or Gentile, so that "through him we both have access in one Spirit to the Father."[1] That is the great "Mystery of Christ,"[2] bringing together mankind in one city, one family, one temple, one body under the headship of Christ, "recapitulating" all in Christ, so that all who are justified should think and act as members of the Body of Christ, having the closest possible relations as individuals with Christ their Redeemer, and through him and in him, with their fellow Christians. Relations so close that the merits of Christ become theirs in proportion to the degree of their identification with him, and the merits of all avail unto all for the achieving of Christ's purpose, the application of his merits to the salvation of mankind.

This great Mystery of the identification of Christ and the faithful in the mystical body of which he is the head and they are the members dominates the mind of St Paul. Christ is the head, the Source of its corporate unity; the indwelling of his Spirit is the source of its spiritual activity.

"It seems to be true, speaking quite broadly, that where the Apostle refers to Christ's Mystical Body, whether *à propos* of the whole Church or of the individual, he is thinking primarily of external organisation, and when he refers to the indwelling of the Holy Spirit, primarily of inward sanctification. The doctrine of the Mystical Body, like that of the Kingdom in the Gospels, has its internal and external aspect."[3]

St Paul teaches us that it is by Baptism that we enter upon our "new life" "in Christ Jesus," when we die to sin, and are crucified with Christ and, "putting on the Lord Jesus,"[4] become one with him, identified with him, incorporated in him, members of his body and members of one another.

The Fathers

The doctrine of the Mystical Body of Christ is one which has stood out quite clearly from the very beginning. It has not undergone development. The sacred writers have simply made known to us the reality revealed to them. This being so, it will be unnecessary to quote at any length the teaching of the Fathers on this most important point. A few indications will suffice.

St Irenaeus is familiar with the idea that the Churches scattered

[1] Eph. ii 18.
[2] Eph. iii 4.
[3] Lattey, *Westm. New Test.*, Vol. iii, p. 247.
[4] Rom. xiii 14.

throughout the world form a unique community; and that social reality corresponds to a mystical reality, for the Church is the grouping of the adopted sons of God, the body of which Christ is the Head, or is simply "the great and glorious body of Christ," which Gnostics divide and seek to slay.[1] For Tertullian all the faithful are members of one same body, the Church is in all those members, and the Church is Jesus Christ.[2] St Ambrose, explaining the teaching of the Epistle to the Ephesians, gives as the motive of the charity we must have for one another, our close union with Christ, as we form only one body, of which he is the Head.[3]

The teaching of St Augustine is so full that it might well fill a volume. The Church is the body of Christ and the Holy Ghost is the soul of that body; for the Holy Ghost does in the Church all that the soul does in all the members of one body; hence the Holy Ghost is for the body of Jesus, which is the Church, what the soul is for the human body. Therefore if we wish to live of the Holy Ghost, if we wish to remain united to him, we must preserve charity, love truth, will unity, and persevere in the Catholic faith; for just as a member amputated from the body is no longer vivified by the soul, so he who has ceased to belong to the Church receives no more the life of the Holy Spirit.[4] "The Catholic Church alone is the body of Christ . . . outside that body the Holy Spirit gives life to no man . . . consequently those who are outside the Church have not the Holy Spirit."[5] "His body is the Church, not this Church or that Church, but the Church throughout the whole world; . . . for the whole Church, consisting of all the faithful, since all the faithful are members of Christ, has in Heaven that Head which rules his body."[6] In his *De Unitate Ecclesiae* (2), he tells us that "the Church is the body of Christ, as the Apostle teaches.[7] Whence it is manifest that he who is not a member of Christ cannot share in the salvation of Christ. The members of Christ are bound together by the union of charity, and by that self-same charity they are united to their Head, who is Christ Jesus." In the *De Civitate Dei*,[8] he emphasises the union of the souls of the departed with the Church which is the Kingdom of Christ. The members of the Church alive on earth are one with the departed; hence the commemoration of the departed at the Eucharist, and hence again the practice of reconciling sinners on their death-bed and baptising the dying. Hence again the commemoration of the martyrs who bore witness to the truth unto death, and who now reign in Christ's kingdom. To that Church of God belong also the just of all ages, and also the angels of God, for the angels persisted in their love of God and in their service

[1] *Contra Hær.*, iv 33, 7.
[2] *De Pœnitentia*, X.
[3] Letter 76, No. 12.
[4] Sermons 267, 268.
[5] St Augustine, Letter 185, section 50.
[6] *Enarrationes in Psalmos* lvi 1.
[7] Col. i 24.
[8] xx 9.

of God.[1] St Augustine thus explains the binding force of the Church of God: "Our Lord Jesus Christ, who suffered for us and rose again, is the Head of the Church, and the Church is his body, and in his body it is the unity of the members and the union of charity that constitute its health, so that whenever a person grows cold in charity he becomes a sick member of the body of Christ. But he who exalted our Head is also able to heal our infirm members, provided only they have not been cut off by undue weakness, but have adhered to the body until they were healed. For whatever still adheres to the body is not without hope of healing; but if he should be cut off from the body his cure is impossible." [2] "It is the Holy Spirit that is the vivifying force in the body of Christ." [3]

§ III: THE DOCTRINE EXPLAINED

The term

In view of the confusion that exists to-day in the use of the term "mystical" it may be well to give some account of its various meanings in ancient and modern literature.[4] Etymologically it is akin to "mystery"; both words spring from the Greek μύω: to close the lips or the eyes, lest words should reveal or eyes see what is hidden. Thus in pre-Christian literature it is used of pagan cults, indicating a religious secret bound up with the "mysteries," which were closed to all but the initiated. Nevertheless it is sometimes used colloquially of non-religious secrets.[5]

The Christian uses of the term are manifold. We find the word commonly connected with the celebration of the Christian mysteries, especially of Baptism and the Eucharist. Whatever was concerned with the administration of the Sacraments, or their explanation, was "mystical." Even to-day we speak of the "mystical oblation," the "mystical sacrifice," the "mystical cleansing." It is easy to see, therefore, how the word "mystical" was used so frequently to designate the sacrament, or the outward sign of inward grace. It is also used in the sense of "symbolical" or "allegorical." Hence the "mystical meaning of Scripture" is the spiritual, figurative, or typical meaning, as distinct from the literal or obvious meaning. The mystical sense of Scripture is that hidden meaning which underlies the simple statement of events. Again the word "mystical" is applied to the hidden reality itself. The sacred writer often sets forth the truth in allegories, comparisons, and figures of speech; thus St Paul teaches us that the faithful are members of the organism

[1] *Enchiridion* lvi; Sermon, 341, 9. [2] Sermon 137, 1

[3] Sermon 267, 4. The patristic teaching will be found set out at length in Petavius, *De Incarnatione*, Bk. XII, c. 17, § 8; in Thomassinus, *De Incarnatione*, Bk. VI, c. 7-9; in Kirsch, *The Doctrine of the Communion of Saints in the Ancient Church.*

[4] *Cf.* Prat, *Theologie de St Paul*, ii (10th Ed., 1925), p. 467.

[5] *Cf.* Cicero *ad Attic.*, vi 3.

of which Christ is the Head, and of which the faithful form the body. This is what we have come to speak of as the " mystical body of Christ."

A further development of those earlier meanings is the application of the term to the hidden and mysterious realities of the supernatural order. In this sense the secrets of grace in the souls of men, supernatural communications with God, are " mystical." In a more restricted sense it is used of the spiritual life of faith and sanctifying grace with its striving after perfection through prayer and mortification : the " mystical life." But in the strictest and technical sense it is applied to the state of infused contemplation.

What may be designated as the post-Christian or non-Christian senses of the term are not easy to analyse. But in a philosophical religious sense the term is used of any teaching which admits the possibility of reaching " the fundamental principle of things " otherwise than by the normal use of the human faculties. A linked meaning takes us away even from that vague religious sphere into the realm of thought inaccessible to ordinary minds dependent on intuition, instinct, or feeling. A still more vague use of the term is the fashionable craze for designating anything that is secret, or in any way connected with worship, with sentiment, with dreams, with the indefinable, the invisible, as " mystical."

It may not be without interest to note that the term " mystical body " which is used by commentators on the scriptures and by theologians to designate the body of Christ, put before us so vividly by St Paul and by the early Fathers, does not actually occur in the New Testament, nor yet in the patristic writings. The two words " mystical body " are actually combined by St John Chrysostom, when he is speaking of the Blessed Eucharist.[1] And that patristic use of " mystical body " for the Eucharist persisted in Rabanus Maurus (died 856) and in Paschasius Radbertus (died 851). The latter's book on the Body and Blood of the Lord has a chapter (7) on the uses of the term " body of Christ," where " mystical body " is still confined to the Blessed Eucharist. Alexander of Hales, who died in 1245, in his *Universæ Theologiæ Summa*,[2] treating of the grace of Christ and his Headship of the Church, uses the words " mystical body " of the Church. The same use is found in William of Auvergne (died 1249) in his *De Ordine*,[3] and in Albert the Great (1206-80). All three authors use the term quite as a matter of course, and it would seem to have been in common use in the early thirteenth century.

Albert the Great explains the term " Mystical Body," applied to the Church, as the result of the assimilation of the whole Church to Christ consequent upon the communion of the true Body and

[1] Homily on the resurrection of the dead, n. 8, Gaume edition, Paris 1834, p. 56 C.

[2] Edition 1622, Vol. 2, p. 73.

[3] Opera, vol. 1, p. 545.

Blood of Christ in the Eucharist; so that the true Body of Christ under the appearance of bread became the symbol of the hidden divine reality.

Meaning of the Mystical Body of Christ

What, precisely, then, is meant by the Mystical Body of Christ? [1] It is obvious that the Church is not the natural Body of Christ. On the other hand it is more than merely morally the Body of Christ, *i.e.*, the union between its members and Christ is not merely the union of ideas and ideals—there is a much closer connection between Christ the Head and his members, constituting a unique entity, which, because of its close connection with the Word Incarnate, is designated by a unique name: the Mystical Body of Christ—a body in which the members, living indeed their natural life individually, are supernaturally vivified and brought into harmony with the whole by the influence, the wondrous power and efficacious intervention of the Divine Head. That Invisible Head ever abides, the members of the Mystical Body come and go, but the Body continues to exercise its influence in virtue of the vivifying power from on high animating its members, and that with such persistence and consistency, with such characteristic independence of action transcending the powers of the individual members, that we may speak of it as a Person, as Christ ever living in his Church, which is his Body, inasmuch as we are the members of which he is the Head.

What makes Christ's Mystical Body so very different from any mere moral body of men is the character of the union existing between Christ and the members. It is not a mere external union, it is not a mere moral union: it is a union which, as realised in Christ's Church, is at once external and moral, but also, and that primarily, internal and supernatural. It is the supernatural union of the sanctified soul with Christ, and with all other sanctified souls in Christ. Now, given the nature of the human soul, its individuality, its immortality, it is clear that the union of our soul with Christ in his Mystical Body excludes the conversion of our soul into the Divine Substance, excludes any identification of man with God, any confusion or a co-mingling of the Divine and human natures. In that union there is not and cannot be equality or identity, but there is a likeness, a supernatural likeness between our soul and Christ the Head of the Mystical Body.

Vital influence of Christ

With Christ we form one Mystical Body, whereof he is the Head and we are the members. A unique Body indeed, not a physical body, not a merely moral body, but a Mystical Body without parallel in the physical or moral order. As our Head, Christ exercises a

[1] The principles of St Thomas utilised in this section will be found: *Summa Theol.*, III, Q. viii; III *Sent.* Dist., 13; *Quæstiones Disput.*: de Veritate, Q. xxix, art. 4 and 5; *Compendium Theologicæ*, Cap. 215; and also St Thomas's *Commentary on* 1 *Cor.*, chap. xii, lect. 3; *Commentary on Eph.*, chap. i, lect. 7 and 8; chap. iv, lect. 4 and 5; *Commentary on Col.*, chap. i, lect. 5.

continuous, active, vitalising, interior, and hidden influence, governing, ruling, and raising his incorporated members. So that from Christ as Head comes the Unity of that Body, its growth, the vitality transmitted throughout its members. The life and increase of that Body is obtained by the operations of each of the members according to the measure of the vitalising influence which each one receives from the Head.[1]

That is the internal influence he exercises through his grace in our souls. There is, moreover, the external influence he exercises through his visible Church.

It is by the grace of Christ that we are united to Christ our Head, and Christ is the source of all our grace in the present dispensation. Not, indeed, that we are to conceive that the very grace which existed in his human soul is transferred to ours—that would be absurd ; but he is the source of our grace inasmuch as in the Divine Plan of Redemption he *merited* grace for us, and is the efficient instrumental Cause of grace, since as Man he taught the truth to men, he founded his Church and therein established the power of jurisdiction, teaching authority, and Holy Orders, and in particular because he instituted the sacraments, whereby grace is produced, and he gives to those sacraments all the efficacy they possess. This causality of Christ, this active influence exercised by Christ, the Church never loses sight of, ever directing her petitions to God : Through Jesus Christ our Lord.

Our chief concern at present is, however, not so much with the active influence exercised by Christ, as with the effect which is thereby produced in men by Christ, produced by the Head upon the members of the Mystical Body.

Likeness of members to Head

In virtue of our incorporation in Christ, we are united to Christ, and that union consists *in the supernatural likeness* established between our soul and Christ : for unity of souls is as we have seen obtained by likeness. Now that likeness is manifold. There is, first of all, *a real and physical* (not material) *likeness*, attained by the justified soul, inasmuch as the sanctifying grace, the infused virtues and the gifts of the Holy Spirit which are bestowed upon it, are of the same species as those which inhered in and were infused into the human soul of Christ : they differ, of course, in degree, inasmuch as in Christ they exist in the supreme degree. In the faithful soul this sanctifying grace, with its retinue of virtues and gifts, may, of course, be increased by meritorious good works, and thus the likeness to Christ increases. From that physical likeness there follows *moral likeness* also. For being informed, being vitalised by the same supernatural life, we are disposed to the same supernatural activity as Christ himself : that is to say, the infused supernatural habits dispose the soul to the same operations, freely performed, as those

[1] *Cf.* the scriptural texts quoted above, pp. 663–664 : Col. ii 18-19 ; Eph. i 22-23 ; iv 15-16 ; v 23.

elicited by Christ: the Christian by acting in accordance with those virtues, imitates or follows Christ. We are thus united to Christ in thought and word and deed, striving to look at all things as Christ himself would have looked at them, to speak of all as Christ would have spoken, to behave to all as Christ would have behaved—thus becoming "other Christs." Christ became the living standard of holiness, the divine example which we strive to reproduce in ourselves.

Union with Christ by charity

Besides that union of our soul with Christ through supernatural likeness, we must recall the union consequent upon supernatural cognition and love, a most intimate union. Christ is known to his followers by Faith, he is loved by Charity: how deep may be that knowledge, how intense, how ardent that love, how efficacious and vivifying may be the influence thus exercised by Christ is to be seen in the lives of the Saints. It is clear that here exists true friendship, the mutual love of benevolence of Christ for the Faithful, of the Faithful for Christ. But this friendship not only exists between Christ and each of the faithful, but also mutually amongst the faithful themselves. The love whereby the Christian loves Christ is supernatural charity, the primary object of which is God himself, as he is himself Infinite Goodness itself. But the secondary object of that theological charity is every single one of our neighbours, inasmuch as he is actually or potentially a sharer in the Divine Goodness. And so by loving Christ, we wish happiness to ourselves and to our neighbours; by the virtue of hope we hope it for ourselves and for others; and finally, by performing works of mercy, we co-operate in procuring for one another sanctification in this life and eternal happiness in the next. And all this meets in due subjection and obedience to the Vicar of Christ, who in this world rules and governs the Mystical Body of Christ. Hence arises the Communion of Saints, which is the communication of good things amongst all the members of the whole Church: militant, suffering, and triumphant.

And thus the life which animates the Mystical Body of Christ consists in (1) the unity of souls by likeness to Christ, and (2) the unity of souls by knowledge and love and consequent co-operation.

Christ lives in the Church

What confronts the world and the powers of evil at every moment of the world's history is not merely the resolute will of strenuous and righteous men banded together in the most wonderful organisation the world has ever known: behind that will, behind that organisation, is the will and power of Christ working through his grace, reproducing in every age supernatural effects of virtue, arousing in every age similar opposition from all, of whatever type or character, who are not in the fullest harmony with Christ our Lord. Of the undying character of that hatred, that virulent, active hostility, there can be no doubt, and in the world there is one Body alone upon which all anti-Christians, and not a few professing Christians, can agree to concentrate their destructive energies: surely the very abnormal character and persistency of that attack, reproducing in its varying phases every phase of opposition to Jesus Christ himself, is a strong corroboration of the well-founded character of the claims of the Catholic Church, that she and she alone is the Mystical Body of Christ, that in and through her alone Christ still lives and speaks to the world.

It is this silent, supernatural influence radiating from Christ indwelling in his Church which is the real explanation of that wonderful unity of faith which characterises the genuine Catholic Church: which, as the priest speaks to the people, brings forth acts of faith from the hearts of his hearers, which, when Catholics are gathered together at a Eucharistic Congress, causes every heart and mind to be in complete, entire, and helpful harmony with every Catholic mind and heart throughout the entire universe. It is that same silent influence which accounts for the self-sacrifice and generosity of Christ's servants, manifesting itself in identical ways in cloister and home, in modern and ancient times, although no external communication has taken place between Christ's faithful ones.

Holy Ghost the soul of the Mystical Body

The soul of the Mystical Body is the Holy Spirit: he is the inspiring, the animating principle. He indwells in the Church and in each one of the faithful, he is the internal force giving life and movement and cohesion. He is the source of the multiplicity of charismata manifesting the vitality of the Body.[1] From him proceeds even the smallest supernatural act, for "no one can say 'Jesus is Lord,' save in the Holy Spirit.

"The Holy Spirit is the spirit of Christ, in him he is and through him he is given to us. His work is to achieve unity, unity among men, and with God."[2]

Jesus in his mortal days was "full of the Holy Ghost,"[3] "and of his fulness we all have received."[4] "But the Paraclete, the Holy Ghost, whom the Creator will send in my name, he will teach you all things, and bring all things to your mind, whatsoever I shall have said to you."[5]

"But if any man hath not the Spirit of Christ, that man is not of Christ."[6] "And because ye are sons, God hath sent forth the Spirit of his Son into our hearts, crying Abba, Father!"[7]

Baptism, which incorporates us into the Mystical Body, gives us too the principle of our unity and activity: "For as the body is one and hath many members, and all the members of the body, many as they are, form one body, so also [it is with] Christ. For in one Spirit all we, whether Jews or Greeks, whether slaves or free, were baptised into one body; and were all given to drink of one Spirit."[8]

This common teaching was set forth by Leo XIII in 1897 in his Encyclical *Divinum illud munus* on the Holy Ghost: "Let it suffice

[1] Rom. xii 4-11. [2] St Cyril of Alex., Com. on John xvii 20-21.
[3] Luke iv 1. [4] John i 16. [5] John xiv 26.
[6] Rom. viii 9. [7] Gal. iv 6. [8] 1 Cor. xii 12-13.

to state that as Christ is the Head of the Church, the Holy Spirit is the soul of the Church."

§ IV: THE MYSTICAL BODY AND REDEMPTION

The Fall and Redemption

THE record of God's dealings with man makes clear a two-fold contrast between grace and unity on the one hand and sin and discord on the other. God's grace has ever been the great unifying factor, uniting God with man and man with his fellow-men. Sin separates man from God and from his fellow-men. The purpose of Christ's coming into the world was to rid it of discord and unite it with God in the grace-union once more. His supreme prayer for his followers was "that they all may be one, as thou, Father, in me and I in thee; that they also may be one in us . . . that they may be one as we also are one. I in them and thou in me; that they may be made perfect in one."

In the mystery of the Redemption by the Word Incarnate we see the relation of fallen man to God changed to man's advantage; he has been redeemed, saved, reconciled, delivered, justified, regenerated; he has become a new creature. The significance of the Redemption from the point of view of our subject lies in this, that the Redemption of man is analogous to his Fall. All men, deriving their human nature from Adam, had inherited from him the stain of original sin, and thus the whole human race in one man had been set at enmity with God. Just as man's Fall had been corporate, so his reconciliation was to be corporate too. For the fatal solidarity with Adam which had resulted in death and sin was to be substituted a new and salutary solidarity whereby all men, born in sin of the first Adam, might be regenerated to the life of grace in the new Adam, Jesus Christ. Our lost rights to supernatural development in this world, and to a vision of God after the time of probation, have been restored to us through the supernatural action of Christ's human nature, hypostatically united to the Word of God. Christ is the Spokesman of mankind, the Representative Man, the Second Adam, carrying out for our sakes what we could not carry out for ourselves, giving to God that glory and adoration, that worship, thanksgiving, and reparation, which the Man-God alone could give. In virtue of our solidarity with him we share in the results of his activity, and our share will be the greater in the measure in which we more and more completely identify ourselves with Christ, "put on Christ," become "other Christs."

St Thomas on redemption and the Mystical Body

It is in terms of this solidarity of man with Christ, in terms of the Mystical Body formed by mankind united with its Head, that St Thomas, as follows, sets forth the doctrine of the Redemption, and of the application of its fruits:

"Since he is our Head, then, by the Passion which he endured from love and obedience, he delivered us as his members from our sins, as by the price of his passion: in the same way as if a man by the good industry of his hands were to redeem himself from a sin committed with his feet. For just as the natural body is one, though made up of diverse members, so the whole Church, Christ's Mystical Body, is reckoned as one person with its Head, which is Christ." [1]

" Grace was in Christ not merely as in an individual, but also as in the Head of the whole Church, to whom all are united as members to a head, who constitute one mystical person, and hence it is that Christ's merit extends to others inasmuch as they are his members; even as in a man the action of the head reaches in a manner to all his members, since it perceives not merely for itself alone, but for all the members." [2]

" The sin of an individual harms himself alone; but the sin of Adam, who was appointed by God to be the principle of the whole nature, is transmitted to others by carnal propagation. So, too, the merit of Christ, who has been appointed by God to be the head of all men in regard to grace, extends to all his members." [3]

" As the sin of Adam reaches others only by carnal generation, so, too, the merit of Christ reaches others only by spiritual regeneration, which takes place in baptism; wherein we are incorporated with Christ, according to Gal. iii 27: *as many of you as have been baptised in Christ have put on Christ;* and it is by grace that it is granted to man to be incorporated with Christ. And thus man's salvation is from Grace." [4]

" Christ's satisfaction works its effect in us inasmuch as we are incorporated with him as the members with their head, as stated above. Now the members must be conformed with their head. Consequently as Christ first had grace in his soul with bodily passibility, and through the Passion attained to the glory of immortality: so we likewise, who are his members, are freed by his Passion from all debt of punishment, yet so that we first receive in our souls *the spirit of adoption of sons* whereby our names are written down for the inheritance of immortal glory, while we yet have a passible and mortal body: but afterwards, *being made conformable* to the sufferings and death of Christ, we are brought into immortal glory, according to the saying of the Apostle,[5] *and if sons, heirs also: heirs indeed of God,* and joint heirs with Christ; yet so if we suffer with him, that we may also be glorified with him." [6]

" Christ's voluntary suffering was such a good act, that because of its being found in human nature, God was appeased for every offence of the human race with regard to those who are made one with the crucified Christ in the aforesaid manner." [7]

" The head and members are as one mystic person; and there-

[1] III, Q. xlix, art. 1.
[2] III, Q. xix, art. 4.
[3] III, Q. xix, art. 4, ad 1.
[4] III, Q. xix, art. 4, ad 3.
[5] Rom. viii 17.
[6] III, Q. xlix, art. 3, ad 3.
[7] III, Q. xlix, art. 4.

fore Christ's satisfaction belongs to all the faithful as being his members. Also in so far as any two men are one in charity, the one can satisfy for the other, as shall be shown later." [1] "But the same reason does not hold good of confession and contrition, because the satisfaction consists of an outward action for which helps may be used, among which friends are to be computed." [2]

"As stated above,[3] grace was bestowed upon Christ, not only as an individual, but inasmuch as he is the Head of the Church, so that it might overflow into his members; and therefore Christ's works are referred to himself and to his members in the same way as the works of any other man in a state of grace are referred to himself. But it is evident that whosoever suffers for justice' sake, provided that he be in a state of grace, merits his salvation thereby, according to Matt. v 10. Consequently Christ by his Passion merited salvation, not only for himself, but likewise for all his members." [4]

On Baptism and incorporation

The fruits of the Redemption, therefore, are applied to individuals inasmuch as they are incorporated into the Mystical Body of Christ. Now the means which Christ has instituted for this incorporation are the sacraments, and in particular Baptism, the sacrament of regeneration. Hence in the teaching of St Thomas concerning this sacrament we are able to see again the far-reaching importance of the doctrine of the Mystical Body.

"Since Christ's Passion," he writes,[5] "preceded as a kind of universal cause of the forgiveness of sins, it needs to be applied to each individual for the cleansing of personal sins. Now this is done by Baptism and Penance and the other sacraments, which derive their power from Christ's Passion."

Even those who lived before the coming of Christ, and therefore before the institution of the sacrament of Baptism, needed, if they were to be saved, to become members of Christ's Mystical Body. "At no time could men be saved, even before the coming of Christ, unless they became members of Christ: 'for there is no other name under heaven given to men, whereby we must be saved.' [6] Before Christ's coming men were incorporated into Christ by faith in his future coming, and the seal of that faith was circumcision." [7]

Treating the question whether a man can be saved without Baptism, St Thomas allows that where actual Baptism is absent owing to accidental circumstances, the desire proceeding from "faith working through charity" will in God's providence inwardly sanctify him. But where you have absence of actual Baptism and a culpable absence of the desire of Baptism, "those who are not baptised under such conditions cannot be saved, because neither

[1] Supplement, Q. xiii, art. 2.
[2] Q. xlviii, art. 2, ad 1.
[3] Q. vii, art. 1, ad 9; Q. viii, art. 1, ad 5.
[4] Q. xlviii, art. 1.
[5] III, Q. xlix, art. 1, ad 4.
[6] Acts iv 12.
[7] Rom. iv 11. III, Q. lxviii, art. 1, ad 1.

sacramentally nor mentally are they incorporated in Christ, through whom alone comes salvation."[1] He emphasises the same truth when speaking of men who are sinners in the sense that they will to sin and purpose to remain in sin. These, he says, are not properly disposed to receive Baptism: "'For all of you who were baptised into Christ have put on Christ'; now as long as a man has the will to sin, he cannot be united to Christ: 'for what hath justness in common with lawlessness.'"[2]

The reason why the effects of the Passion of Christ are applied to us in Baptism is that we are a part of Christ, we form one with him. "That is why the very pains of Christ were satisfactory for the sins of the baptised, even as the pains of one member may be satisfactory for the sins of another member."[3] Indeed, the effects of the Passion of Christ are as truly ours as if we had ourselves undergone the Passion: "Baptism incorporates us into the Passion and death of Christ: 'If we be dead with Christ, we believe that we shall also live together with Christ';[4] whence it follows that the Passion of Christ in which each baptised person shares is for each a remedy as effective as if each one had himself suffered and died. Now it has been seen that Christ's Passion is sufficient to make satisfaction for all the sins of all men. He therefore who is baptised is set free from all liability to punishment which he had deserved, as if he himself had made satisfaction for them."[5] Again, "the baptised person shares in the penal value of Christ's Passion as he is a member of Christ, as though he had himself endured the penalty."[6] "According to St Augustine," he writes in article 4 of the same question, "'Baptism has this effect, that those who receive it are incorporated in Christ as his members.' Now from the Head which is Christ there flows down upon all his members the fulness of grace and of truth: 'Of his fulness we have all received.'[7] Whence it is evident that Baptism gives a man grace and the virtues."

Body and Soul of the Church

From this explicit teaching it is clear that there is only one Body of Christ, and it is by Baptism that we are incorporated in it. Consequently we must be very careful in using the well-known distinction of the "body" and "soul" of the Church.

Every man validly baptised is a member of Christ's Mystical Body, is a member of the Church. Now it may well happen that adverse external circumstances may prevent a man's character as an incorporated member of the Church being recognised, and the absence of such recognition may involve the juridical denial of all that it involves. In the eyes of men he may appear to have broken the bond uniting him to the Church, and yet, because of the supernatural faith, and the persistent loving life of grace, whereby he seeks in all things to do the will of God, his union with the Church

[1] Rom. iv 11. III, Q. lxviii, art. 2. [2] 2 Cor. vi 14.
[3] III, Q. lxviii, art. 5, ad 1. [4] Rom. vi 8.
[5] Q. lxix, art. 2. [6] *Ibid.*, ad 1. [7] John i 16.

really continues : *spiritually* he remains a member of the Church, he belongs to the body of the Church. He may, all the time, through error, be giving his external adhesion to a religious society which cannot be part of the Church. But at heart, by internal and implicit allegiance, he may be a faithful member of the Church.

Evidently, if the Church is the Mystical Body of Christ, then to be outside the Mystical Body is to be outside the Church, and since there is no salvation outside the Mystical Body, there is no salvation outside the Church. But, as we have seen, a man's juridical situation is not necessarily his situation before God.

The use of the term " the Soul " of the Church as distinct from " the Body," in the sense that Catholics belong to the Body and the Soul, and non-Catholics to the Soul only, and therefore may be saved because of their good faith, does indeed convey an element of truth, but not the whole of it. The continual stressing of the " good faith " of those who are unfortunately out of visible communion with us, does seem to undermine the traditional horror of heresy and of heretics, replacing it by a horror of " heresiarchs " ; it seems to put a premium on muddle-headedness, and to reserve the stigma of heresy for the clear-headed ones. After all, the malice of heresy lies in the rending of the Body of Christ : what our Lord meant to be one, heretics, even material heretics, divide. They may be in good faith—and that good faith will at some moment lead them to see what they had not seen before—but the fact remains that their error or ignorance, however inculpable, retards the edification of the Body of Christ. Even the claims of Charity should not blind us to the importance of growth in the knowledge of objective truth, as contrasted with the limitations of error, however well-meaning it may be.

In this matter the advice of St Paul to the Ephesians is relevant : " With all humility and mildness, with patience supporting one another in charity, careful to keep the unity of the Spirit in the bond of peace. One body and one Spirit, as you are called in one hope of your calling. One Lord, one Faith, one Baptism." [1]

The notions of Redemption, Baptism, and the Mystical Body are combined by the Apostle in the following magnificent passage : " Christ also loved the Church and delivered himself up for her, that he might sanctify her, purifying her in the bath of water by means of the word, and that he might present her to himself a glorious Church, not having spot or wrinkle or any such thing, but holy and without blemish. . . . Surely no man ever hated his own flesh, nay, he doth nourish and cherish it, even as Christ the Church, because we are members of his body." [2]

[1] Eph. iv 2 ff.

[2] Eph. v 25-27, 29.

§V: THE SACRIFICE OF THE MYSTICAL BODY

Redemption and sacrifice

THE Catholic doctrine of Redemption is inseparable from that of Sacrifice, for it was by his sacrifice on Calvary that Christ achieved our Redemption. "Christ, being come an high-priest of the good things to come, by a greater and more perfect tabernacle, not made with hands, that is, not of this creation: neither by the blood of goats or of calves, but by his own blood, entered once into the Holies, having obtained eternal redemption. For if the blood of goats and of oxen . . . sanctify such as are defiled, to the cleansing of the flesh, how much more shall the blood of Christ, who by the Holy Ghost offered himself unspotted unto God, cleanse our conscience from dead works, to serve the living God? And therefore he is the Mediator of the New Testament: that by means of his death for the redemption of those transgressions which were under the former testament, they that are called may receive the promise of eternal inheritance." [1]

Such being the intimate connection between Redemption and Sacrifice in the economy of our salvation,[2] it is not to be wondered at if the doctrine of the Mystical Body finds its clearest illustration and most practical application in the Catholic teaching concerning the sacrifice of the Mass.

The Mass the sacrifice of the Mystical Body

The central fact of human history is the Redemption, wrought, in accordance with the divine plan, by the life-work of Christ, and culminating in the supreme act of self-oblation made by his human will in manifestation of his love of his Father. The sacrifice which Christ offered to his Father on the Cross is the one perfect act of worship ever offered by man to God. But Christians have never regarded that sacrifice simply as an event of the past. They have been ever mindful of the command he gave his followers to do as he did in commemoration of him, "showing the death of the Lord until he come," [3] "knowing that Christ, rising again from the dead, dieth now no more, death shall have no more dominion over him." [4] Christ as he is to-day is Christ triumphant with the fruits of his victory, with the faithful in whom his Spirit dwells and works. The same sacrifice which Christ offered on Calvary is unendingly renewed in the sacrifice of the Mass. The sacrifice is Christ's; the victim is Christ; the priest is Christ. The only difference lies in the absence of actual blood-shedding on the Calvary of the Altar. The Mass is the sacrifice of the Mystical Body of Christ.[5]

That the whole Church has a sacerdotal character is clear from several passages of the New Testament. Baptism, which made us sons of God, members of the Mystical Body, gave us an indelible

[1] Heb. ix 11.
[2] See Essay xiv: *Christ, Priest and Redeemer, passim.*
[3] 1 Cor. xi 26.
[4] Rom. vi 9.
[5] See Essay xxv in this volume: *The Eucharistic Sacrifice.*

character : " But you are a chosen generation, a kingly priesthood, a holy nation." [1] " Jesus Christ . . . who hath loved us and washed us from our sins in his own blood, and hath made us a kingdom and priests to God and his Father." [2] " Be you also as living stones built up, a spiritual house, a holy priesthood, to offer up spiritual sacrifices, acceptable to God by Jesus Christ." [3] Together with our Head, through the ministry of the priests who have the power of consecrating, we co-operate effectively in the offering of the sacrifice in the measure of our supernatural importance in the Mystical Body.[4]

Christ, Head and Members, offers the sacrifice

It would be a pitiable mistake to think of the Body and Blood of Christ in the Mass as a dead offering. It is a living offering and is offered by the living Christ. Christ is the priest of the Mass. It is Christ who celebrates the Mass, and he celebrates it with a warm and living Heart, the same Heart with which he worshipped his Father on Mount Calvary. He prays for us, asks pardon for us, gives thanks for us, adores for us. As he is perfect man, he expresses every human feeling ; as he is God, his utterances have a complete perfection, an infinite acceptableness. Thus when we offer Mass we worship the Father with Christ's worship. Our prayers being united with his obtain not only a higher acceptance, but a higher significance. Our obscure aspirations he interprets ; what we do not know how to ask for, or even to think of, he remembers ; for what we ask in broken accents, he pleads in perfect words ; what we ask in error and ignorance he deciphers in wisdom and love. Thus our prayers, as they are caught up by his Heart, become transfigured, indeed, divine.

Hence by God's mercy we do not stand alone. In God's providence the weakness of the creature is never overwhelmed, unaided, by the omnipotence of God. In particular the Catholic is never isolated in his prayers, in his pleadings with God. He is a member of the divinely instituted Church, his prayers are reinforced by the prayers of the whole Church, he shares, in life and in death, in that amazing combination of grace-aided effort and accumulated energy known as the Communion of Saints. But especially is the Catholic strong when he pleads before God the perfect sacrifice of Christ. Simply as a member of the Church, as a member of Christ's Mystical Body, every Catholic has a share in the sacrifice offered by Christ as Head of his Church, a share in the supreme act of adoration thereby offered to God. And that partaking in the offering of the Sacrifice is as real and as far-reaching as is the Mystical Body itself.

Christ, Head and Members, the victim

Christ, head and members, offers the sacrifice, but Christ, head and members, offers himself, and we, in union with our Head, are victims too. St Paul has told us that we are " heirs of God, and joint heirs with Christ, if, that is, we suffer with him, that with him we may also be glorified." [5] We must share in his sufferings if we would

[1] 1 Peter ii 9. [2] Apoc. i 5. [3] 1 Peter ii 5.
[4] *Cf. The Eucharistic Sacrifice*, pp. 902 ff. [5] Rom. viii 17.

share in his salvation. And in his epistle to the Colossians,[1] St Paul stresses the importance of our privilege : " Now I rejoice in my sufferings on your behalf, and make up in my flesh what is lacking to the sufferings of Christ, on behalf of his body, which is the Church, whereof I am become a minister." So that as we are members of the one body, our sufferings, our prayers, our sacrifices, " may further the application to others of what Christ alone has secured for all." [2] " The Church," says St Augustine,[3] " which is the body of which he is the head, learns to offer herself through him." " The whole redeemed city, that is, the congregation and society of the saints, is the universal sacrifice which is offered to God by the High Priest." [4]

" I exhort you therefore, brethren," writes St Paul,[5] " by the compassion of God, to present your bodies a sacrifice, living, holy, well-pleasing to God, your spiritual service." Since we are members of Christ our sufferings, united with the offering of Christ, acquire a value in the carrying out of Christ's purpose in the world which they could never have of themselves. Our mortifications, our fastings, our almsdeeds are seen to have a range of effective influence in the Mystical Body, however trifling they may appear in themselves. The Lenten Fast is no mere personal obligation : the Church calls upon her children to do their share in furthering the interests of Christ in the world, insists that they should not be merely passengers in the barque of Peter, but should " pull their weight " ; for they too have benefited and are benefiting from the fastings and prayers of God's holy servants throughout the world. The call to reparation on behalf of others is bound up with the privileges we enjoy through our solidarity with our fellow-members of the Mystical Body.

The sacrificial attitude of mind

Every sacrifice is the external expression of an internal sacrificial attitude of mind, whereby we submit all that we have and all that we are to the divine will, that in all things it may be accomplished. In every sacrifice the victim is offered in place of him who offers it, as a means of expressing as adequately as possible the perfection of his submission to God. Now we have seen that our union as members of Christ's Mystical Body with the Victim offered to God in the Mass, unites us with our High Priest both as offerers and as offered. Hence, from our solidarity with the priesthood and the victimhood of Christ there follows as a necessary corollary the duty in Catholics of cultivating the sacrificial attitude of mind.

When the pursuivants were thundering at the door of the house of Mr. Swithun Wells in Gray's Inn Lane on the morning of All Saints' Day, 1591, as the priest, Edmund Genings, stood at the improvised altar and offered the Sacrifice of the Mass, there could be no mistake about the sacrificial attitude of mind of the small group of faithful present on that occasion. All had suffered for the

[1] i 24. [2] Lattey *in loc.* [3] *De Civ. Dei*, x 20.
[4] *Ibid.*, 6. [5] Rom. xii 1.

privilege of worshipping God as he would be worshipped in his Church, and had refused to conform to the observances of the Established Church. With calm deliberation they took their lives and fortunes in their hands, and offered them up to God in union with the redeeming sacrifice of Christ himself. The working out of God's will was to them as mysterious as it is to us. But their duty to God was clear, and the danger they ran was clear ; but they commended themselves into the hands of God, and prayed that his will might be done. The spirit inspiring them shines out in Mr. Swithun Wells' reply when in prison he answered, " That he was not indeed privy to the Mass being said in his house, but wished that he had been present, thinking his house highly honoured by having so divine a sacrifice offered therein," and the Justice told him that though he was not at the feast, he should taste of the sauce. On 10 December, 1591, he won the crown of martyrdom.

If we compare the attitude of mind of the small group of devoted Catholics who were gathered round the martyr's altar with the attitude of those indifferent Catholics who under the most favourable conditions content themselves with deliberately conforming to the very minimum of the Church's requirements, we can see that there is room for many gradations in the intensity of the worship of God in the Holy Mass. Better perhaps than any technical definitions the example of our Catholic forefathers can teach the lesson so many of us have to learn.

Our lives are spent in the midst of men who, however religious-minded they may be, have lost all idea of sacrificial worship : the Great Christian Act of Sacrifice is no longer the centre of their religious observance. At times one may wonder whether the influence of atmosphere does not affect the less-instructed of the faithful. Our people have a firm and deep belief in the Real Presence of Our Lord in the Blessed Sacrament, but it often happens that they have a less clear perception of what the Sacrifice means. At times one hears the question, " Why is it that when Our Lord is already present in the Tabernacle, such a great manifestation of reverence should surround the Consecration ? " a question which shows how little it is realised that at the Consecration Our Lord comes offering himself as our Victim, bearing our sins, offering himself to his Eternal Father for us. Such a thought makes the Sacrifice real and living to us, and moves us to offer ourselves up with him, to be ready to suffer what we can for him who suffered and died for us.

§ VI: THE MYSTICAL BODY AND HOLY COMMUNION

Union with Christ consummated by Holy Communion

THE end of all sacrifice is union with God ; and the end of the Sacrifice of the New Law is union with God through and in Jesus Christ ; a union which is consummated by Holy Communion, wherein those who have offered the sacrifice partake of the sacred Victim. It is evident, therefore, that the Sacrament of the Eucharist, as well as the Eucharistic Sacrifice, the Mass, is intimately bound up with the doctrine of the Mystical Body. In fact, the Eucharist is the Sacrament of the Mystical Body of Christ.

Nature of this union

How close this connection really is may be seen from the study of three well-known texts of the Gospel of St John: "Abide in me and I in you. As the branch cannot bear fruit of itself unless it abide in the vine, so neither can you unless you abide in me. I am the vine, you the branches; he that *abideth in me, and I in him*, the same beareth much fruit, for without me you can do nothing."[1] "That they all may be one, as *thou*, Father, *in me, and I in thee*; that they also may be one in us . . . *I in them, and thou in me;* that they may be made perfect in one."[2] "Except you eat the flesh of the Son of man and drink his blood, you shall not have life in you; he that eateth my flesh and drinketh my blood hath everlasting life. . . . He that eateth my flesh and drinketh my blood *abideth in me, and I in him.* As the living Father hath sent me and I live by the Father; so he that eateth me the same also shall live by me."[3]

The comparison of these three passages not only brings out in a striking manner the nature of the union that Christ wills should exist between himself and the faithful—and among the faithful themselves—but also shows what Christ intends to be the primary and chief cause of that union. The union for which Christ prayed is a union of life, a communion of supernatural life, of the divine life of grace and charity, that union which, as we have seen, knits together the members of the Mystical Body, as the branches are united with the vine. It is a union so intimate that those who are united may be truly said to be *in each other*; a union so close that Christ does not hesitate to compare it with the union existing between his Father and himself: "as thou, Father, in me, and I in thee." Now the union between Christ and his Father is a union of nature and life. "He that seeth me," he had said to Philip, "seeth the Father also. Do you not believe that I am in the Father and the Father in me? . . . Yet a little while, and the world seeth me no more. But you see me; because I live, and you shall live. In that day you shall know that I am in my Father, and you in me, and I in you. . . . If any one love me . . . my Father will love him, and we will come to him and make our abode with him."[4] The members of Christ, therefore, are united with their Head and with each other by the communication of the life of grace and charity, which, as St Peter tells us, is nothing else than a participation of the divine nature.[5]

[1] xv 4-5. [2] xvii 21-23. [3] vi 54 ff. [4] John xiv 9 ff.

[5] *Cf.* 2 Peter i 4. *Cf.* also 1 John iv 7: "Everyone that loveth is born of God and knoweth God"; *ibid.*, 15-16: "Whosoever shall confess that Jesus is the Son of God, God abideth in him, and he in God. . . . He that abideth in charity abideth in God, and God in him."

The sacrament of the Mystical Body

What is the chief means whereby this life of grace is to be communicated to the members of his Body? The answer is found in the third of the texts quoted above: "He that eateth my flesh and drinketh my blood abideth in me and I in him. As the living Father hath sent me and I live by the Father; so he that eateth me, the same also shall live by me." The Sacrament of Our Lord's Body and Blood is the divinely appointed means for incorporation into his Mystical Body. The Eucharist, in other words, is not only the Sacrament of Christ's true Body; it is also the Sacrament of his Mystical Body. Hence St Paul writes: "The cup of blessing which we bless, is it not fellowship in the blood of Christ? The bread which we break, is it not fellowship in the body of Christ? We many are one bread, one body, for we all partake of the one bread." And commenting on these words of the Apostle St Augustine says: "The faithful know the body of Christ if they do not neglect to be the body of Christ. Let them become the body of Christ if they wish to live by the Spirit of Christ; and therefore it is that St Paul, explaining to us the nature of this bread, says, 'We being many are one bread, one body.' O sacrament of piety! O symbol of unity! O bond of charity! He who wills to live has here the place to live, has here the source of his life. Let him approach and believe, let him be incorporated, that he may receive life." [1] "Be what you see," he writes elsewhere,[2] "and receive what you are. . . . He who receives the mystery of unity and does not hold the bond of peace, does not receive the mystery for his profit, but rather a testimony against himself."

Hence also St Thomas, dealing with the sin of unworthy Communion, having pointed out that the Eucharist signifies the "Mystical body, which is the fellowship of the Saints," writes: "He who receives this sacrament, by the very fact of doing so signifies that he is united to Christ and incorporated in his members: now this is effected by charity-informed faith which no man can have who is in mortal sin. Hence it is clear that whosoever receives this sacrament in a state of mortal sin is guilty of falsifying the sacramental sign, and is therefore guilty of sacrilege." [3]

The Eucharist and Baptism

The intimate connection of the Sacrament of the Eucharist with the Mystical Body may be clearly illustrated by the teaching of St Thomas on the necessity of the Eucharist for salvation.[4] It has been seen in a preceding section that Baptism is the Sacrament of incorporation in the Mystical Body, and hence for infants the actual reception, and for adults at least the desire, of this sacrament is indispensable for salvation; for outside the Mystical Body of Christ none can be saved. Now to assert that Incorporation is the proper effect of the Eucharist would seem at first sight to contradict the

[1] *In Joan.*, tr. xxvi 13.
[2] Sermon 272.
[3] III, Q. lxxx, art. 9.
[4] See Essay xxxiv: *The Sacrament of the Eucharist*, pp. 877–879.

undoubted truth that Baptism is the " gate of the Sacraments " and, alone, is necessary for salvation. St Thomas solves the difficulty by pointing out that the Eucharist is the source of the efficacy of all the other Sacraments, these being subordinated to the greatest of them all. " This Sacrament," he writes,[1] " has of itself the power of bestowing grace ; nor does any one possess grace before receiving this sacrament except from some desire thereof ; from his own desire in the case of the adult ; or from the Church's desire in the case of children." If this desire in adults is a sincere one, as it should be, and the baptised person is faithful to the promptings of the Holy Spirit, he will complete what is expected of him and receive the Blessed Sacrament :

" The effect of this sacrament is union with the Mystical Body, without which there can be no salvation ; for outside the Church there is no entry to salvation. . . . However, the effect of a sacrament can be had before the actual reception of the sacrament, from the very desire of receiving it ; hence before the reception of this sacrament a man can have salvation from the desire of receiving this sacrament. . . . From the very fact of being baptised infants are destined by the Church for the reception of the Eucharist, and just as they believe by the faith of the Church, so from the intention of the Church they desire the Eucharist, and consequently receive its fruit. But for baptism they are not destined by means of another preceding sacrament, and therefore before the reception of baptism infants cannot in any way have baptism by desire, but only adults. Hence infants cannot receive the effect of the sacrament (of baptism) without the actual reception of the sacrament. Therefore the Eucharist is not necessary for salvation in the same way as Baptism." [2]

And elsewhere : [3] " There are two ways of receiving this sacrament, namely, spiritually and sacramentally. Now it is clear that all are bound to eat it at least spiritually, because this is to be incorporated in Christ, as was said above (*i.e.*, in the passage just quoted). Now spiritual eating comprises the desire or yearning for receiving the sacrament. Therefore a man cannot be saved without desiring to receive this sacrament. Now a desire would be vain, except it were fulfilled when opportunity presented itself."

Union of the faithful

But it would be a mistake to regard the Eucharist as having its effect merely in the individual soul that receives it. All that has been said hitherto about the solidarity of the members of Christ forbids any such restricted view. The Eucharist has far-reaching effects passing beyond the mere individual to the masterpiece of divine Love, the sanctification of mankind ; bringing all men under the Headship of Christ, uniting soul with soul, and souls with Christ, until all the elect in Heaven and in Purgatory are one in Christ with his faithful on earth ; so that all work together to achieve his Fulness :

[1] III, Q. lxxix, art. 1, ad. 1.

[2] III, Q. lxxiii, art. 3.

[3] III, Q. lxxx, art. 11.

" for the perfecting of the Saints in the work of ministry, unto the building up of the body of Christ, till we all attain to the unity of the Faith and of the full knowledge of the Son of God, to the perfect man, to the full measure of the stature of Christ . . . thus . . . we shall hold the truth in charity, and grow in all things unto him who is the Head, Christ." [1]

§ VII: THE COMMUNION OF SAINTS AND ITS CONSEQUENCES

Meaning of the term

THE term " Communion of Saints " seems to have been first inserted in the baptismal creeds in the South of Gaul; and it is to be understood as the South Gallic writers of the fifth and sixth centuries understood it; giving the word " Saints " the normal meaning which it still holds to-day: the Elect, those who have attained the end for which they were made, in the Kingdom of God. The term " communion " is used in the abstract sense and means a spiritual benefit conferred in the Church, or the Mystical Body of Christ. " And so the addition ' the Communion of Saints ' signifies the inward spiritual union of the faithful as members of Christ's Mystical Body with the other members of this Body, especially the elect and perfectly just, whose participation in the heavenly kingdom of God is absolutely certain, and through whose intercessions help may be given to the faithful still wayfaring on earth." [2]

Veneration of the Saints

In venerating the Saints of God and especially the Mother of God, we give them due honour because of the supernatural excellence we recognise in them as derived from God himself through the merits of Jesus Christ. It is therefore to the honour and glory of God that is ultimately directed all the veneration paid to his servants. Strictly speaking a like honour might be paid to saintly men and women while they are still living on this earth. It is, however, the custom of the Church not to venerate the just until she has declared by infallible decree that they are in definitive enjoyment of their eternal reward in heaven. In English we are accustomed to speak of " honouring " or " venerating " the Saints, while the cult of " adoration " is reserved for God alone. This distinction—for the rest, a convenient one—may be regarded as roughly corresponding to the Latin theological terms *dulia*: the honour paid to the Saints, and *latria*: the worship paid to God alone.

Mary is particularly honoured because of the special greatness of the favours she received from God. She is what God made her, and as such we recognise her. All her graces on earth and her glory in heaven are celebrated in relation to her unique privilege: her Divine Maternity. By reason of her unique supernatural

[1] Eph. iv 12-15.

[2] Kirsch, *The Doctrine of the Communion of Saints in the Ancient Church* (Tr. McKea), 268.

excellence the special veneration which we pay to her is called "hyperdulia."

In honouring her and the Saints of God the Church would have us celebrate with veneration their holiness which they owe to the merits of Jesus Christ; obtain their prayers—which avail only in so far as by the divine ordinance they intercede in virtue of the grace they have received from Christ the Head of the Mystical Body, and in view of his merits; and finally set before ourselves the example of their virtues, the exercise of which is due to the grace of God through which they were united to the Mystical Body, and so imitated the model of all virtues, Jesus Christ himself. The veneration of the Saints is thus directed to the glory of God, who is wonderful in his Saints, and therefore in his Saints is duly honoured.

So eminently reasonable is this practice, so perfectly in accord with the doctrine of the Mystical Body, that we are not surprised to find that from the earliest times Catholics have paid honour to the Saints. We may see it especially in the commemoration of the Martyrs. Thus when Faustus the Manichean objected to the practice St Augustine replied: "Faustus blames us for honouring the memory of the martyrs, as if this were idolatry. The accusation is not worthy of a reply. Christians celebrate the memory of the martyrs with religious ceremony in order to arouse emulation and in order that they may be associated with their merits and helped by their prayers. But to none of the martyrs do we erect altars as we do to the God of the martyrs; we erect altars at their shrines. For what bishop standing at the altar over the bodies of the martyrs ever said 'We offer to thee, Peter, or Paul, or Cyprian?' What is offered (*i.e.*, the sacrifice) is offered to God who crowned the martyrs, at the shrines of the martyrs, so that the very spot may remind us to arouse in ourselves a more fervent charity both towards them, whom we can imitate, and towards him who gives us the power to do so. We venerate the martyrs with the same love and fellowship with which holy men of God are venerated in this life . . . but the martyrs we honour with the greater devotion that now, since they have happily gained the victory, we may with the greater confidence praise those who are blessed in their victory than those who in this life are still striving for it." [1]

Intercession of the Saints

With regard to the intercession of the Saints let it suffice to note with St Thomas that "prayer may be offered to a person in two ways, either so that he himself may grant it, or that he may obtain the favour from another. In the first way we pray only to God, because all our prayers should be directed to obtaining grace and glory, which God alone gives, according to the Psalmist (83): 'The Lord will give grace and glory.' But in the second way we pray to the angels and Saints, not that through them God may know our petitions, but that through their prayers and merits our petitions

[1] *Contra Faustum*, l. 20, c. 21.

may be effective. Hence we read in the Apocalypse [1] that, 'the smoke of the incense of the prayers of the saints ascended up before God from the hand of the Angel.' And this is manifest also from the method which the Church uses in praying; for we ask the Trinity to have mercy upon us; but we ask the Saints to pray for us." [2]

Relics and images

Closely associated with the veneration of the Saints is the honour paid to their relics and images. The principle underlying the veneration of relics is thus set out by St Thomas: "It is manifest that we should show honour to the saints of God *as being members of Christ*, the children and friends of God and our intercessors. Wherefore in memory of them we ought to honour every relic of theirs in a fitting manner: principally their bodies which were temples and organs of the Holy Ghost dwelling and operating in them, and as destined to be likened to the body of Christ by the glory of the Resurrection. Hence God himself fittingly honours such relics by working miracles at their presence." [3]

A similar reason justifies the veneration of their images. The images recall the Saints to our minds, and the reverence we pay to them is simply relative, as the images themselves, considered materially, have no virtue in them on account of which they should be honoured. The honour paid to them passes to the rational persons, the Saints, whom the images represent. The purpose of the practice is explained by the second Council of Nicaea in its decree concerning sacred images: "that all who contemplate them may call to mind their prototypes, and love, salute and honour them, but not with true 'latria,' which is due to God alone. . . . For honour paid to the image passes to the prototype, and he who pays reverence to the image, pays reverence to the person it depicts." [4]

Indulgences

A final application of the doctrine of the Mystical Body may be found in Indulgences.[5] The matter is explained by St Thomas as follows:

"The reason why indulgences have value is the unity of the Mystical Body, in which many of the faithful have made satisfaction beyond what was due from them. They have borne with patience many unjust persecutions, whereby they might have expiated many temporal punishments if they had deserved them. The abundance of those merits is so great as to surpass all the temporal punishment due from the faithful on earth, and that particularly owing to the merit of Christ. That merit, although it operates in the Sacraments, is not limited to the Sacraments in its effectiveness: but its infinite value extends beyond the efficacy of the Sacraments. Now, as we have seen above,[6] one man can make satisfaction for another. On

[1] viii 4.
[2] II, IIæ, Q. lxxxiii, art. 4.
[3] III, Q. xxv, art. 2.
[4] Denzinger, 302.
[5] *Cf.* Essay xxvii: *The Sacrament of Penance*, pp. 976–980.
[6] Q. xiii, art. 2.

the other hand, the Saints, whose satisfactory works are superabundant, did not perform them for some one particular person (otherwise without an indulgence he would obtain remission) but in general for the whole Church, according to the words of St Paul,[1] 'I rejoice in my sufferings on your behalf, and make up in my flesh what is lacking to the sufferings of Christ, on behalf of *his Body, which is the Church.*' And so these merits become the common property of the whole Church. Now the common property of a society is distributed to the different members of the society according to the decision of him who is at the head of the society. Consequently, as we should obtain the remission of the temporal punishment due to sin, if another had undertaken to make satisfaction on our behalf, so too do we obtain it when the satisfaction of another is applied on our behalf by him who has authority to do so." [2]

§ VIII: CONCLUSION

ONE of the most striking phenomena of the present development of the Church's life in the course of the last few years is the appeal made to the minds of the faithful by the doctrine of the Mystical Body. Books are being published in every tongue setting out its implications, especially in its bearing on the practice of frequent Communion, and of assisting at Mass.

The time is ripe for it. For as far as the Church at large is concerned, Protestantism is of the past, however much it may linger on in these islands. It has left us a legacy for which future generations will be grateful. The last four hundred years have witnessed a remarkable development in the working out and clear formulation of the revealed teaching concerning the Church, and more particularly of the teaching concerning the *visible* headship of the Church. The great disadvantage of the controversial treatment of any doctrine is that it involves the stressing of the controverted point to a disproportionate extent, and there is a consequent lack of attention paid to other truths. Not that those other truths are entirely lost to sight—the remarkable correlation of revealed truths, each involving and leading up to the others, which so impressed Newman, is sufficient to prevent such an oversight: but the truths which are not actually under discussion attract less attention and study, and consequently what is involved in them is not made fully explicit nor is the connection which actually does exist between them always clearly seen.

Now Catholics and Protestants alike agree that Christ is the Head of the Church—the struggle arose and has continued on the question as to whether the Pope, as Christ's Vicar on earth, was the visible Head of the Church. But even that argument was largely verbal: since the very constitution of the Church was in dispute, and the

[1] Col. i 24. [2] *Summa Theol.*, III, Suppl., Q. xxv, art. 1.

character of the Headship differed fundamentally as conceived by both sides. That point, however, remained in the background, and did not attract the attention it deserved.

A second obstacle stood in the way of the development of the doctrine of Christ's Headship of the Mystical Body—involving, as it does, the full Catholic doctrine of Sanctifying Grace.

Baianism, Jansenism, and Cartesianism are all bound up with erroneous or heretical teaching concerning sanctifying grace. The influence of Cartesianism was particularly disastrous on the philosophical setting of Catholic teaching: its rejection of the distinction between substance and accidents cut away the basis of the traditional treatment of sanctifying grace and the virtues, and not a few eighteenth-century theologians took to the simple method of ignoring the supernatural accidents of the soul as mere mediæval subtleties, and that unfortunate attitude of mind made its influence felt well into the nineteenth century. This statement admits of easy historical verification: consult the text-books in use in theological seminaries in the early nineteenth century and you will be amazed at the indifference or, at least, the astonishing reserve with which the all-important doctrine of sanctifying grace is treated. Actual grace and all the interminable controversies to which it gave rise absorb all their energies. A sad practical result followed: the clergy being insufficiently instructed in these important doctrines were incapable of instilling them into the faithful, of bringing them to realise what the supernatural life is, and so were unable effectively to resist the onset of naturalism. The heavy penalty of this neglect is now being paid in many Catholic countries on the Continent.

Fortunately, happier days have dawned. These anti-Protestant polemics, necessary as they may be, do not absorb all our energies, and the stimulating and consoling truths of our supernatural life and destiny are being studied more and more, so that we may hope for a fuller development of the truths involved in Christ's Headship of his Mystical Body.

We know that the Church is a perfect society; we analyse all that that statement involves, we realise the Church's complete and entire independence of the State within her own sphere. We have defended every detail of her visible organisation against non-Catholic assault. But let us be on our guard against imagining that because we have grasped every element of her visible and of her moral constitution which Christ willed should be in order that his Church might utilise all that is best in man's human nature—that we understand Christ's Church through and through. For there still remains the most potent element of all in the supernatural constitution of the Church, that divine, all-pervading, all-guiding and directing influence interiorly exercised by Christ upon every individual member, and upon all the members collectively, bringing the individual soul into harmony with himself, and with all faithful souls, so that, as St Paul wrote to the Ephesians :[1] " We may in all things grow up in him, who is the Head, even Christ. From whom the whole Body, being compacted and fitly joined together, by what every joint supplieth, according to the operation in the measure of every part, maketh increase of the Body unto the edifying of itself in charity."

We have to strive to realise more vividly Christ's living influence in the world to-day, and the need in which we stand of it, to realise, too, the wonderful way in which Our Lord meets this need by making us, and preserving us as members of his Church, members of that Mystical Body of which he is the Head.

EDWARD MYERS.

[1] iv 15-16.

XX

THE CHURCH ON EARTH

INTRODUCTORY NOTE

THE purpose of this essay is to give a brief but comprehensive outline of the nature and constitution of the community of believers founded by our Lord Jesus Christ, the Christian Society with which the Catholic and Roman Church affirms her substantial identity. What is chiefly aimed at is not an apologetic defence of the Church, or even a direct vindication of her claims against those who would challenge them, but to explain the import which Catholics themselves attach to the words of the Creed: *Credo in . . . unam sanctam catholicam et apostolicam Ecclesiam.* The sources for such an exposition are the official pronouncements of the Church herself, as formulating the deliverances of Scripture and Tradition. Accordingly these will be generously drawn upon, personal comment and reflection being reduced to a minimum. Among the documents of the Church's teaching authority, Pope Pius XII's great Encyclical *Mystici Corporis Christi* [1] now holds a place of first importance: it is a magisterial restatement of traditional doctrine in the face of the divided Christendom in which we live, and should clarify much of the contemporary confusion about the nature of the Church. From this treatise, for it is nothing less, the following pages draw their main inspiration. The preceding essay has dealt with "The Mystical Body of Christ" considered in its inner life. Here we shall be concerned to show, what is in fact one of the objects of the Encyclical, how the inner mystery of the Mystical Body is inseparably linked with the concrete juridical structure of the Catholic Church.

PART I

THE CATHOLIC CHURCH: THE SOCIETY OF THE REDEEMED

§ I: CORPORATE FALL—CORPORATE REDEMPTION

Remote origins of the Church

THE Church of Christ did not come suddenly into existence, unheralded and unannounced, during the lifetime of our Lord. It has its roots deep in the past, not only in the previous history of Judaism, but in the remote origins of the human race, when Adam

[1] 29 June, 1943. All references are to the marginal numbers in Canon G. D. Smith's translation for the Catholic Truth Society.

fell from grace and with him his whole progeny. Our first parents were not, however, left without the hope of ultimate redemption; the evil one who had compassed their downfall would finally be crushed; [1] someone was to restore what was lost and, as we gather from subsequent prophecy, a new people would be born endowed with a life of undreamt of fulness. The connection which exists between the Church and the sinful state of man, due to Adam's disobedience, is of capital importance to understand, for it provides the key to the Church's *raison d'être*. Just as there is little evidence to suggest that the Son of God would have become incarnate had Adam not offended, so the Catholic Church as we know it would never have appeared in history but for man's being cut off from God, and at odds with his fellows, through the primal disaster of sin.

The fact of sin

Nevertheless, "where sin abounded, grace did more abound." [2] Sin has worked itself out in all manner of rebellion and human selfishness, but its first result, so far as Adam was concerned, was to deprive him of that state of holy innocence and integrity which he was intended to transmit to posterity. The sons of Adam were thereby robbed of God's adoptive sonship and the participation in the divine nature which should have been theirs and became instead "children of wrath." [3] This was the calamity which, first and foremost, Christ came to undo.[4] The Son of the Eternal Father took to himself a human nature, innocent and stainless, becoming as it were a "second Adam"; for from him the grace of the Holy Spirit was to flow into all the children of our first parent. Through the Incarnation of the Word men would regain their lost inheritance, become brethren according to the flesh of the only begotten Son of God, and so themselves receive the power to become the sons of God. Thus, by the great redemptive act on the Cross, not only was the Father's outraged justice placated, but an immense treasury of graces was merited for us, his kindred. These heavenly gifts might have been bestowed upon us directly; but God's plan was that they should be distributed by means of a visible Church in which we, being united together, should co-operate with him in his redemptive work. "As the Word of God vouchsafed to use our nature to redeem men by his pains and torments, in a somewhat similar way he makes use of his Church throughout the ages to perpetuate the work he had begun." [5]

Mankind, broken away by its own act from its Creator and Lord, bereft of a divine inheritance, turned in upon itself, no longer united but disintegrated and atomised, each man for himself and no man for his brother—such was the tragic state of things from which Christ came to set us free. And, in this very act of liberation, he restored

[1] Genesis iii 15. [2] Romans v 20. [3] Ephesians ii 3.

[4] *Cf.* Encyclical *Mystici Corporis Christi* (hereinafter designated *MCC*), 12. [5] *Ibid.*

what was lost and raised us to a supernatural destiny surpassing in splendour all human conception. "For God so loved the world, as to give his only begotten Son: that whosoever believeth in him may not perish, but may have life everlasting." [1] Nor did he will to bring salvation simply by his physical presence on earth, to serve as a gracious memory for the ages to come; or even by the great act of redemption achieved on the Cross, considered as a climax to a life to which there was to be no sequel. The Second Person of the Blessed Trinity was to remain united to humanity, and his saving work continue, until the end of time. There was never again to be a day when man should find himself in the condition of "having no hope of the promise and without God in this world." [2] The human race was to be transformed, born anew, integrated and reunited to God through the Church.

The Incarnation

By the Incarnation a single human nature was taken up into union with God in the Person of Christ our Lord. Jesus is the Son of God by nature. The manhood of Christ is perfect and undiminished; but in Person he is none other than the Word of God himself. But he is also "the firstborn amongst many brethren"; [3] he wills that, so far as may be, we should share his divine sonship. Whereas he is the Son of God by nature, we are meant to become the sons of God by adoption. It was to enable us to be admitted as it were into his family that he lived and died. "But as many as received him, he gave them power to be made the sons of God, to them that believe in his name." [4] The plan he devised for carrying out this project was to continue the Incarnation through the centuries; not simply in its effects but, so to say, in its very substance. This prolongation of the Incarnation is but another name for the Church. So we find the great incarnational principle—viz., the pouring out upon the world of what is divine and spiritual through the medium of material elements—verified in every aspect of the Church's life.

The Mystical Body of Christ

From this we should be able to understand why the Holy, Catholic, Apostolic, Roman Church, to employ her official title, rejoices in proclaiming herself "the Mystical Body of Jesus Christ." [5] For she is animated by his life, co-operates with him, declares his message and distributes the fruits of his redemption; in a very real sense she suffers with him, just as one day she will triumph with him, when her supreme task of perpetuating his work throughout the ages has been accomplished.

§ II: CHRIST THE FOUNDER OF THE CHURCH

The Church born from the death of Christ

THE Mystical Body, which is the Church, took its rise from the death of Christ on Calvary. "By his death on the Cross he made void the Law with its decrees and fastened the handwriting of the Old

[1] John iii 16. [2] Ephesians ii 12.
[3] Romans viii 29. [4] John i 12. [5] *MCC* 13.

Testament to the Cross, establishing the New Testament in his blood which he shed for the whole human race."[1] So centuries before it had been foretold; so in fact it was fulfilled.[2] By the Incarnation itself our Lord had become Head of the whole human family; but it is in virtue of his saving death that he exercises in all its fulness his Headship of the Church.[3] "It was by the victory of the Cross that he merited power and dominion over all nations."[4] All the graces which through the centuries were to be poured out upon the Mystical Body were won for it by this supreme act of atonement. At that moment the Church, like a second Eve, a new "mother of all the living,"[5] was born from the Saviour's side.

Three successive stages in the formation of the Church

But without prejudice to Christ's sacrificial death as being the decisive factor, we may yet distinguish three stages in the formation of the Mystical Body. Though the Church, as a juridical institution, had no proper existence before the death of Christ, nevertheless, during his public ministry, he had outlined its constitution, described what were to be its functions and powers, and prepared the organs through which these were to be exercised. "For while he was fulfilling his function as preacher he was choosing his Apostles, sending them as he had been sent by the Father,[6] that is to say, as teachers, rulers and sanctifiers in the community of believers; he was designating him who was to be their chief, and his own Vicar on earth;[7] he was making known to them all the things which he had heard from the Father;[8] he was prescribing Baptism[9] as the means by which believers would be engrafted into the Body of the Church; and finally, at the close of his life, he was instituting at the Last Supper the admirable sacrifice and the admirable sacrament of the Eucharist."[10]

This preparatory work, as we have said above, was ratified by the redemptive act on the Cross. At that moment "the veil of the Temple was rent in two from the top even to the bottom,"[11] the Old Law was abolished and the Messianic Kingdom on earth came into being. The Church, thus brought to birth, was, so to say, formally constituted on the Day of Pentecost, when the Holy Spirit animated the organism of the Mystical Body, infusing each of its organs with his own power and endowing the whole with life, vigour and abiding fruitfulness.

Thus, within the limits of the New Testament writings, we can discover three successive states of Christ's Church: (*a*) an inchoative, or initial period, during the lifetime of its Founder, when

[1] *MCC* 28.
[2] *Cf.* Hebrews viii 8 ff.
[3] *Cf. MCC* 29.
[4] St Thomas, *Summa Theologica*, III, Q. xlii, art. 1.
[5] Genesis iii 20.
[6] John xvii 18.
[7] Matthew xvi 18-19.
[8] John xv 15; xvii 8, 14.
[9] John iii 5.
[10] *MCC* 26.
[11] Matthew xxvii 51.

he announced and prepared the Kingdom of God;[1] (*b*) its foundation, beginning with the death of Jesus, by which the Old Law was done away with and the new Messianic Kingdom, the Church, instituted; (*c*) its definitive existence with the coming of the Holy Spirit at Pentecost when the Church, both as a collectivity and in its individual members, became instinct with divine power, and began as a social organism the new life which was to continue "even to the consummation of the world."[2]

§ III: THE RELATION BETWEEN CHRIST AND THE CHURCH

Christ the Head of the Church

"RATHER we hold the truth in charity, and grow in all things unto him who is the Head, Christ. From him the whole body, welded and compacted together by means of every joint of the system, part working in harmony with part—(from him) the body deriveth its increase, unto the building up of itself in charity."[3]

We shall now pass briefly in review the chief points of the Catholic doctrine concerning the relationship between Christ and the Church,[4] and consider in greater detail (below, § VIII) the manner in which his Headship is exercised through his Vicar, or visible representative, the Pope, who, together with the Bishops, rules the juridical society which is the Church on earth.

It will help us to understand how Christ is the Head of the Church if we paraphrase St Thomas's teaching on the point.[5] As

[1] The notion of "the Kingdom (perhaps, more accurately, the *Rule*) of God" is extremely rich. We find three aspects of it foreshadowed in the prophetical teaching: (i) a Kingdom that was national and at the same time universal; reigning over Israel as his chosen people, God was to extend the Kingdom to the Gentiles; (ii) a spiritual Kingdom in which the moral qualities of justice and peace were to flourish; (iii) an eschatological Kingdom, in the sense that its perfection was to come after a judgement in which the wicked were to be separated from the just. In continuity with, and development of, this doctrine, our Lord announced a Kingdom that was to be (i) no longer national but universal, embracing all peoples and times; (ii) external and social, but at the same time internal and spiritual; (iii) present, but also future and eschatological, when the good should be separated from the bad. We may note, for it is sometimes overlooked, that theologians do not identify *tout court* the Catholic Church with the Kingdom of God. The Church is the Kingdom of God *on earth*. *Cf.* Schultes, *De Ecclesia Catholica*, p. 41: "Nevertheless the Kingdom of Heaven (*i.e.* of God) and the Church founded upon Peter are not wholly identical. For the Church founded on Peter belongs to this world and this life: for it is founded on Peter, a mortal and terrestrial man, who will bind and loose 'on earth'; —but the Kingdom of Heaven will exist when time is at an end and for all eternity."

[2] Matthew xxviii 20.

[3] Ephesians iv 15-16 (Westminster Version).

[4] Briefly, because the matter, which is of paramount importance, has been dealt with more fully elsewhere. See Essay xix, pp. 667 ff.

[5] *Summa Theologica*, III, Q. viii, art. 1, "Utrum Christus sit caput Ecclesiae."

the whole Church is one Mystical Body by a similitude with man's natural body, each of whose members has its appropriate activity (as St Paul teaches in Romans xii and 1 Corinthians xii), so Christ is called the Head of the Church by a parallel with the human head. This Headship may furthermore be considered under three aspects, viz., from the point of view of order, perfection and power. To take the first, order: we note that, beginning with what is highest, the head is the principal part of a man; it is thus that we call the source or origin of anything its "head." Considered in this way, Christ has the chief place, by reason of his soul's nearness to God; he is pre-eminent in God's grace to such a degree that all others receive grace in virtue of his. This is what is implied in St Paul's words: "For whom he foreknew, he also predestinated to be made conformable to the image of his Son: that he might be the firstborn amongst many brethren." [1] Secondly, in the hierarchy of perfection: St Thomas points out that, whereas in the head we find located all the interior and exterior senses, in the other parts of the body there is only the sense of touch. Similarly in Christ, as distinct from the inferior members of the Mystical Body, we find the fulness and perfection of grace.[2] Finally, with reference to power: just as the control of the other parts of the body resides in the head, so Christ rules over the Church's members by the influence of grace. "And of his fulness we all have received." [3]

Christ's influence upon the Church

In virtue of this pre-eminence our Lord "reigns in the minds and hearts of men, bending and constraining even rebellious wills to his decrees." [4] He takes charge both of the individual soul, by reason of his intimate presence within it, and of the whole Church, enlightening and strengthening her rulers in the faithful discharge of their high office. It is by his power that the fruits of holiness are brought forth in the Church, as made manifest in the lives of the saints, with a view to "the building up of the body of Christ." [5] Whenever sin is resisted, whenever a soul grows in holiness, whenever the Church administers her sacramental rites, "it is he himself who chooses, determines, and distributes graces to each 'according to the measure of the giving of Christ.'" [6]

His love for the Church

Of Christ's love for the Church it should be almost superfluous to speak, for it is but another aspect of his love for redeemed humanity. "Christ is the Head of the Church. He is the saviour of his body." [7] In the illuminating words of Pius XII: "the loving knowledge with which the divine Redeemer has pursued us from the first moment of his Incarnation is such as completely to surpass all the searchings of the human mind; for by means of the beatific vision, which he enjoyed from the time he was received into the womb of the Mother

[1] Romans viii 29.
[2] *Cf.* John i 14.
[3] John i 16.
[4] *MCC* 37.
[5] Ephesians iv 13 (Westminster Version).
[6] *Ibid.* iv 7; *MCC* 49.
[7] Ephesians v 23.

of God, he has for ever and continuously had present to him all the members of his mystical body, and embraced them with his saving love."[1] Nor does that love ever grow less; our Saviour continues his redeeming work from his state of heavenly glory: "Our Head," says St Augustine, "makes intercession for us; some members he receives, some he scourges, some he cleanses, some he consoles, some he creates, some he calls, some he calls again, some he corrects, some he renews."[2]

The Holy Spirit and the Church

Moreover, as the greatest pledge of this love, Christ has given us his own Spirit, the Paraclete, to be the life-force, the very "soul" of the Mystical Body. Again, it is impossible to state this doctrine more clearly than in the words of Pope Pius XII. Speaking of "the Spirit who proceeds from the Father and the Son, and who in a special manner is called the 'Spirit of Christ' or the 'Spirit of the Son,'"[3] he continues, "For it was with this Spirit of grace and truth that the Son of God adorned his soul in the Virgin's immaculate womb; he is the Spirit who delights to dwell in the Redeemer's pure soul as in his favourite temple; he is the Spirit whom Christ merited for us on the Cross with the shedding of his own blood; the Spirit whom he bestowed upon the Church for the remission of sins, breathing him upon the Apostles.[4] And while Christ alone received this Spirit without measure,[5] it is only according to the measure of the giving of Christ and from the fulness of Christ himself that he is bestowed upon the members of the Mystical Body.[6] And since Christ has been glorified on the Cross his Spirit is communicated to the Church in abundant outpouring, in order that she and each of her members may grow daily in likeness to our Saviour. It is the Spirit of Christ which has made us adopted sons of God,[7] so that one day 'we all, beholding the glory of the Lord with open face, may be transformed into the same image from glory to glory.'"[8]

The Church modelled on Christ

Where love does not find a likeness it tends to create it. So it is with the union between Christ and the Church. The Word, in taking flesh, assumed our human nature; this he did in order that his brethren according to the flesh might be made "partakers of the divine nature."[9] We were to be made conformable to the image of the Son of God,[10] renewed according to the likeness of him who created us.[11] Thus all Christians have as the object of their lives the imitation of Christ, the shaping of their thought and conduct in response to his Spirit. So, in fact, the Church, as Christ's Mystical

[1] *MCC* 75.
[2] *Enarr.*, in Ps. lxxxv 5, Migne, *P. L.* xxxvi, 1085; quoted from *MCC* 57.
[3] Romans viii 9; 2 Corinthians iii 17; Galatians iv 6.
[4] *Cf.* John xx 22.
[5] *Cf.* John iii 34.
[6] *Cf.* Ephesians i 18; iv 7.
[7] *Cf.* Rom. viii 14-17; Gal. iv 6-7.
[8] 2 Cor. iii 18; *MCC* 54.
[9] 2 Peter i 4.
[10] *Cf.* Rom. viii 29.
[11] *Cf.* Col. iii 10; *vide MCC* 44.

Body, models her life upon his. "Following in the footsteps of her divine Founder, she teaches, governs and offers the divine sacrifice. Again, when she practises the evangelical counsels she portrays in herself the poverty, the obedience, and the virginity of the Redeemer. And again the manifold Orders and institutions in the Church—so many jewels with which she is adorned—show forth Christ in various aspects of his life: contemplating on the mountain, preaching to the people, healing the sick, bringing sinners to repentance, and doing good to all. No wonder, then, that during her existence on this earth she resembles Christ also in suffering persecutions, insults and tribulation." [1]

Co-operation between Head and members

Finally there follows, as a consequence, the need for co-operation between Head and members. The Bridegroom and the Bride, which is the Church, must be of one mind. Our Lord invites—in a sense, he needs—our working together with him in the building up of the Mystical Body. We could not have affirmed a truth so audacious were it not for St Paul's reminder that the head of the body cannot say to the feet "I have no need of you." [2] That we depend utterly upon Christ our Head is clear enough: "Without me you can do nothing."[3] But he has also condescended to make us joint-agents with him in the carrying out of the great redemptive plan. "By one and the same means," says Clement of Alexandria, "we both save and are saved." [4] God need not have arranged it thus; for he lacks nothing of self-sufficiency; but in the divine liberality of One who "emptied himself, taking the form of a servant," [5] he has chosen this method for the greater glory of his Church.

The most striking example of this co-operation with Christ is the part played by the Blessed Virgin in man's redemption. "She, the true Queen of Martyrs, by bearing with courageous and confident heart her immense weight of sorrows, more than all Christians filled up 'those things that are wanting of the sufferings of Christ, for his Body which is the Church.'" [6] Within the sphere of Church government our Lord's appointment of a Vicar, or representative, on earth is a conspicuous witness to his design of delegating divine responsibility to a merely human agent. But, even in his personal capacity of direct and invisible ruler of the Church, Christ has honoured us by requiring our co-operation. "Dying on the Cross, he bestowed upon his Church the boundless treasure of the Redemption without any co-operation on her part; but in the distribution of that treasure he not only shares this work of sanctification with his spotless Bride, but wills it to arise in a certain manner out of her labour. This is truly a tremendous mystery, upon which we can never meditate enough: that the salvation of many souls depends upon the prayers and voluntary mortifications offered for that in-

[1] *MCC* 45. [2] 1 Cor. xii 21. [3] John xv 5.
[4] *Strom.* vii 21. Migne P.G. IX, 413; quoted from *MCC* 57.
[5] Phil. ii 7. [6] Col. i 24; *MCC* 110.

tention by the members of the Mystical Body of Jesus Christ, and upon the co-operation which pastors and faithful, and especially parents, must afford to our divine Saviour." [1]

§ IV: THE CHURCH: A VITAL ORGANISM

Diversity of function

"For as in one body we have many members, but all the members have not the same office: so we, being many, are one body in Christ; and every one members one of another." [2] The oneness of the Church does not consist in a universal sameness but, as we might have expected in a creation so beautiful as to merit the title of "Bride of Christ," [3] in a manifestation of unity in variety. There is subordination of function, diversity of office. This is most clearly to be seen in the doctrinal, sacrificial and juridical work of the Church, wherein she inherits our Lord's triple rôle of prophet, priest and king. It is evident also in the grades of the ecclesiastical hierarchy, bishops, priests and deacons, lawfully exercising their power of orders in virtue of their communion with the Pope, Vicar of Christ and successor to St Peter. But the rich and manifold life of the Mystical Body has multifarious patterns. Members of the religious orders and congregations, whether contemplative or active, or aiming at an apostolate which issues from contemplation, testify to its abundant fruitfulness. So too do the Catholic laity, more especially in their work of co-operation with the pastors of the Church. There are states of life holier than others: the episcopate, for example, as compared with the condition of the layman in the world; likewise do the religious vows offer to a select few instruments of perfection which are denied to the majority. But, in the last resort, "the Spirit breatheth where he will"; [4] the ultimate criterion is not official status but the measure of charity in the individual soul.[5] By this test the mother of a family may be more closely united to God than Pope or Bishop, a man or woman immersed in "worldly" duties than the monk or cloistered nun.

"To every one of us is given grace, according to the measure of the giving of Christ." [6] Thus there is a profound mystery, as well as a natural fittingness, in the variety of place and function proper to each member of the Mystical Body. We do not know, or, at best,

[1] *MCC* 42. Canon Smith, p. 13 in his C.T.S. pamphlet *Some Reflections on the Encyclical Mystici Corporis Christi*, has pointed out how Pius XII "condemns a quietism which attributes all activity exclusively to the grace of God (*MCC* 86) and on no fewer than ten occasions insists upon the necessity of our energetic co-operation"; viz. 13, 16, 17, 42, 59, 85, 86, 88, 97, 98. Very strikingly, on the subject of reunion, the Pope himself asks for the co-operation of the faithful, "that most effective aid," to the end that "all of us may be one in the one Church which Jesus Christ founded"; Encyclical *Orientalis Ecclesiae Decus*, 9 April 1944. C.T.S. translation *Rome and the Eastern Churches*, 39-40.

[2] Rom. xii 4-5.
[3] *Cf.* Apocalypse xxi 1-6; xxii 17.
[4] John iii 8.
[5] *Cf.* 1 Cor. xiii.
[6] Ephesians iv 7.

can but dimly discern the rôle for which we are cast ; hence we have no material for passing judgement on one another, still less for mutual jealousy. St Paul was at pains to make this clear : " God hath set the members, every one of them, in the body as it hath pleased him." [1] A fact which provides us with the chief motive for neighbourly charity. We are being invited to rejoice in, to show good will towards, our neighbour simply for being what he is and doing what he does. Our evil actions apart, we each make our distinctive contribution by being our own best selves and behaving accordingly. The doctrine of the Mystical Body excludes any enforced or rigid conformity to a single pattern. It teaches us to appreciate other people in their very differences from ourselves ; we are left with no grounds for assessing the worth of others, as we are all too prone to do, merely by our own individual standards.

The Sacraments

The vital channels of this life of grace and charity are the Sacraments of the Church. These visible signs, effecting what they signify, minister to our spiritual needs progressively from the cradle to the grave. By Baptism we are reborn from the death of sin into the living membership of Christ's Body, the Church, and invested with a spiritual power enabling us to receive the other sacraments. Through Confirmation we are strengthened in the faith and gain spiritual maturity ; it has been well described as " the sacrament of Catholic action," as it fits us to defend the Church, conferring on us the privileges and duties of a soldier of Jesus Christ. To enable us to recover from the sins into which we may have fallen after Baptism we have been given the sacrament of Penance. Supreme among them all is the Eucharist, the sacrament *par excellence* of the Mystical Body, whereby we are continually nourished and united ever more closely with its Head. Lastly, to console us in mortal sickness, there is the comfort of Extreme Unction. Sometimes, if God so wills, it effects the restoration of bodily health ; always it ministers a supernatural balm to the wounded soul and prepares it for entry into heaven.

So much for our needs as individuals. For the benefit of the Church's social life our Lord instituted the two sacraments of Matrimony and Holy Order. Through the first the parties in marriage minister to each other the graces needful for their state. By this means is sanctified the whole process by which the Christian community gathers increase. The mutual love between man and wife is raised to the supernatural level of divine charity and the welfare of their offspring, especially in regard to that religious education which is of such moment to the growth of the Mystical Body, is safeguarded. Holy Order, finally, " consecrates to the perpetual service of God those who are destined to offer the Eucharistic Victim, to nourish the flock of the faithful with the Bread of Angels and with the food of doctrine, to guide them by the divine commandments

[1] 1 Cor. xii 18 ; but see whole passage 14-21 and 27.

and counsels, and to fortify them by their supernatural functions."[1] Thus the whole sacramental system is designed to ensure the prosperity of the Mystical Body on earth, to enable it to grow and gather strength "unto the measure of the age of the fulness of Christ."[2]

§V: THE VISIBLE CHARACTERISTICS OF THE CHURCH

The Church a visible society

JUST as all men of good will who came into contact with our Lord were able to know him for what he was, the Son of the living God,[3] so it must be equally possible for them to recognise his Church as a divine institution. For the claims of the Church upon the world's attention are no less imperative than those of Christ himself. Indeed it is the Church's boast that she is, in her very constitution, "a perpetual motive of credibility and unassailable witness to her own divine mission."[4] Whence it follows that she must be a society visible to all as an unmistakable concrete fact. Not that we shall be led to expect the sort of visibility proper to a building or landscape; rather must we look for certain marks or notes characteristic of the Church whereby she can be clearly and definitely apprehended by the mind for what she is. Thus, for example, when we hear of a book entitled "The History of the English People," though it may suggest to the imagination no very clear-cut picture, we know that its subject-matter is nothing vague and intangible; it is a reality as intelligible in its own order, as susceptible of scrutiny, as anything which comes within the range of sense observation. So it is with the Church. She is "a city seated on a mountain,"[5] challenging men's gaze, proclaiming her own authenticity to those who will pause to examine.

Hostility to this doctrine

Curiously enough, this claim of the Church to be a visible society has proved a stumbling-block to many. In the Middle Ages the Fraticelli thought they had discovered two Churches, one "carnal," the other "spiritual," while Wycliff and the Hussites vigorously opposed the notion of a Church that could be visible. In the same line of thought lies Luther's restriction of the Church to the Communion of Saints, and Calvin's to the number of the predestined. All these theories were devised to justify the repudiation of traditional Christianity as embodied in Catholicism. Analogous to them is the modern antithesis between "the religion of authority" and "the religion of the spirit"; likewise the familiar distinction drawn by idealists between the "institutional" and "mystical" elements in religion.

The Church and mysticism

It is not to our present purpose to discriminate the amount of truth which lies concealed in these fundamental aberrations. All

[1] *MCC* 19. [2] Ephesians iv 13. [3] *Cf.* Matt. xvi 16.
[4] Vatican Council: Constitution *de fide catholica*, cap. 3; Denzinger, 1794. [5] Matt. v 14.

heresy is an isolating of a part of the Christian inheritance and setting it in opposition to the whole, a principle which is conspicuously verified in every attempt to concentrate attention on the hidden riches of the Church to the exclusion of what is visible. But it is worth remarking that there is an all but ineradicable tendency in certain minds, not least among the loftier and more intellectual, to show devotion to the spiritual by contempt for the material. The Manichean dualism, reproduced in a different form in the Platonic and neo-Platonic philosophical tradition, which has deeply influenced sections of Christian thought, bears striking witness to this. There is evidence of it also in the widespread contemporary interest in "mysticism," as divorced from Christian faith and worship. The neo-mystics professedly inveigh against "established Christianity," which is alleged to have "failed," but in fact their revolt is against the Incarnation itself. Now, as to the intellectuals in St Paul's day, the notion of a God who so loved sinners as to identify himself with them in visible humanity is "foolishness." [1]

The Catholic Church, though she gives scope to the highest aspirations of mysticism, provided it is based on an acknowledgement of sin and the need for salvation, is concerned with the eternal welfare of all mankind, not of a select group. And men in the mass need to approach the things of the spirit through the medium of what they can see and hear and touch. So the Church comes before them, as did Christ himself, with evidence which testifies to divinity, in lineaments recognisable by all who have eyes to see. As our Lord pointed to his life's work in proof of the validity of his claims, [2] so

[1] 1 Cor. i 18 ff. One of the objects of the Encyclical *Mystici Corporis Christi* was the refutation of this error; *cf.* 9, 62, 63. "We therefore deplore and condemn also the calamitous error which invents an imaginary Church, a society nurtured and shaped by charity, with which it disparagingly contrasts another society which it calls juridical. Those who make this totally erroneous distinction fail to understand that it was one and the same purpose—namely, that of perpetuating on this earth the salutary work of the Redemption—which caused the divine Redeemer both to give the community of human beings founded by him the constitution of a society perfect in its own order, provided with all its juridical and social elements, and also, with the same end in view, to have it enriched by the Holy Spirit with heavenly gifts and powers. It is true that the Eternal Father willed it to be the 'kingdom of the Son of his love' (*Col.* i 13), but he willed it to be a true kingdom, one, that is, in which all believers would yield the complete homage of their intellect and will, and with humble and obedient hearts be likened to him who for us 'became obedient unto death' (Phil. ii 8). Hence there can be no real opposition or incompatibility between the invisible mission of the Holy Spirit and the juridical office which Pastors and Teachers have received from Christ. Like body and soul in us, the two realities are complementary and perfect each other, both having their origin in our one and the same Saviour who not only said, as he breathed the divine Spirit upon the Apostles: 'Receive ye the Holy Ghost' (John xx 22), but also enjoined aloud: 'As the Father hath sent me, I also send you' (xx 21); and again: 'He that heareth you heareth me' (Luke x 16)"—*MCC* 63; see also 64-66.

[2] John x 25.

does his Mystical Body exhibit to the world the distinctive qualities of unity, holiness, catholicity and apostolicity as warranting her divine origin.

The Church's unity

UNITY.—To speak of the Church as the Body of Christ is to proclaim her unity, her undividedness. No truth was dearer to the heart of St Paul than this: "We, being many, are one body in Christ."[1] This oneness was not simply a unity of ideals and aspirations, or even that union in charity for which our Lord prayed at the Last Supper,[2] indispensable though that is if we are to be wholly united to him; rather was it a surrender to the complete "mind of Christ."[3] The Church was one because her most sacred rite was one,[4] because her Lord, her faith, her baptism was one.[5] The Church worshipped "One God and Father of all";[6] hence her unity was not a prospect set before her to be realised in the remote future; it was a mark of her constitution from the beginning. The unity promised by Christ was that proper to the society of his followers, to be manifested visibly in the unanimous profession of one faith, the performance of one act of worship, the acceptance of one system of government.

Both the divine and human elements in the Church alike demand her unity. She comes from the Triune God, the one and the true, in whom disunion is unthinkable, and shares in a manner the oneness of the life of the Godhead. This life is given to us through grace, faith, hope and charity, created gifts emanating from the depths of the Blessed Trinity and raising us up to a supernatural union with God. On the other hand, the unity of the human race, the whole of which is intended to be incorporated into the Mystical Body, demands a Church that is manifestly one and undivided. Moreover, the fact that there is no approach to God save through Christ, that he is the "one mediator of God and men,"[7] reinforces the need for unity. He is the only door to God's sheepfold;[8] we cannot hope to please the Father except in so far as he sees us in his Son.

The Church's holiness

HOLINESS.—No less evident a mark of the Church than her unity is the note of holiness. Christ's sanctifying mission demands that the organised society, which is its instrument, should share in the sanctity of its Founder. We have express evidence that, in its consummated state at least, he willed it to be "a glorious Church, not having spot or wrinkle,"[9] and that he himself sanctified it for this very purpose.[10] The Holy Spirit, who is the living source of holiness, had been promised to it for ever.[11] Sanctity means the dedication of ourselves and all our actions to God; it implies freedom from sin and impurity and the possession of grace, whereby the whole direction of our lives is brought into harmony with the divine

[1] Rom. xii 5. [2] John xvii 21. [3] I Cor. ii 16.
[4] I Cor. x 17. [5] Ephesians iv 5. [6] *Ibid.* 6.
[7] I Tim. ii 5. [8] John x 1. [9] Ephesians v 27.
[10] *Ibid.* vv 23-30. [11] John xiv 16-17.

commandments. Accordingly the Church presents herself to the world as the fellowship in which this happy state of things may be realised. Her claim is that, on the authority of our Lord himself and as informed by his Spirit, she teaches what is holy both in doctrine and in conduct, that she offers the means whereby this may be put into practical effect, and that, despite the exceptions which prove the rule,[1] her teaching conspicuously bears fruit throughout her membership.

The fact that the Church proclaims the Gospel of Christ is in itself sufficient proof of the holiness of her teaching. From him she was given her mandate [2] and the promise of the Spirit's guiding presence.[3] Our Lord himself claims to have received his doctrine from the Father and to teach only within the limits of that commission. "When you shall have lifted up the Son of Man, then shall you know that I am he and that I do nothing of myself. But as the Father hath taught me, these things I speak." [4] This message thereafter passed into the keeping of his Body, the Church, as witness St Paul's complete assurance on the point: "As we said before, so now I say again: If anyone preach to you a gospel, besides that which you have received, let him be anathema. . . . For I give you to understand, brethren, that the gospel which was preached by me is not according to man. For neither did I receive it of man: nor did I learn it but by the revelation of Jesus Christ." [5]

Moreover, by means of her sacramental system, the Church effectively produces in her members the holiness which she preaches. She cleanses them from original guilt by Baptism, strengthens them by Confirmation, absolves them by Penance, and crowns these and other instruments of grace with the Holy Eucharist, the supreme sacrament and sacrifice of the Mystical Body, containing the living presence of Christ himself. This is the method by which the Saviour "who gave himself for us" fulfils for each individual his plan "that he might redeem us from all iniquity and might cleanse to himself a people acceptable, a pursuer of good works." [6] In this people, which is the Church, we find realised the fruits of the Spirit, the source of sanctity: "charity, joy, peace, patience, benignity, goodness, longanimity, mildness, faith, modesty, continency, chastity." [7] With justice does the Vatican Council attribute to the Church "a marvellous holiness, an inexhaustible fecundity in all good things." [8]

The Church's catholicity

CATHOLICITY.—The Fathers of the Council referred also to the "wonderful propagation" and "Catholic unity" [9] of the Church.

[1] It need hardly be said that the Church's sanctity does not imply universal sinlessness. There is no incompatibility between this doctrine and the ready admission of "the lamentable tendency of individuals towards evil, a tendency which her divine Founder suffers to exist even in the higher members of his mystical Body." *MCC* 64; *cf.* 65, 66.

[2] Matt. xxviii 19-20; *cf.* Luke x 16.

[3] John xiv 16.

[4] John viii 28.

[5] Gal. i 9, 11-12.

[6] Titus ii 14.

[7] Gal. v 22-23.

[8] Denzinger, 1794.

[9] *Ibid.*

Not only is she one and undivided, but her unity is conspicuously diffused throughout all mankind. Hence she possesses a universality by which she appears as a constituted society in every part of the world. The Church's catholicity [1] was to pass gradually from the sphere of legal right to that of accomplished fact, as conditioned by the circumstances of time and place in which she finds herself. That the Church was intended to grow to full stature, not suddenly but by a process of gradual development, is clearly indicated by our Lord's parables of the mustard seed [2] and the leaven. [3] But it is no less clear that this catholicity, far from arising as it were by an accident of history, was part of the divine plan from the beginning. The whole scheme of the redemption demands it; all division of nation against nation, free man against slave, is to be transcended. "There is neither Jew nor Greek: there is neither bond nor free: there is neither male nor female. For you are all one in Christ Jesus." [4] To this objective the Apostles had been directed from the outset of their ministry: "Go ye into the whole world and preach the gospel to every creature." [5] And forthwith they set out to achieve it: "But they going forth preached everywhere: the Lord working withal, and confirming the word with signs that followed." [6]

The Church's apostolicity

APOSTOLICITY.—As a consequence of this Apostolic mission there follows, as a property and distinguishing characteristic of Christ's Mystical Body, its identity and continuity with the Church of the Apostles. In express words he built it upon the rock-foundation of the twelve,[7] and pre-eminently of Peter.[8] Whence there is to be looked for in the Church a legitimate, public and uninterrupted succession of pastors, heirs, as it were, of the Apostles, and in agreement with them in faith, worship and Church government. This condition of things is implicit in our Lord's manifest desire that his Church should remain substantially as he had founded it "even to the consummation of the world." [9] Indeed such a continuity is

[1] The phrase "Catholic Church" first appears in St Ignatius of Antioch († 117), *Epistle to the Smyrnaeans* viii 2—"wheresoever Christ Jesus is, there is the Catholic Church." The word "Catholic" is Greek (καθ' ὁλόν) and means "universal," or, literally, "according to the whole." Whence it follows that the Church can be called "Catholic" in a variety of senses: with reference to, first, *place*, inasmuch as she is diffused throughout the world; secondly, *time*, because she will always exist; thirdly, *peoples*, having members of every tribe, nation and tongue; fourthly, *conditions of men*, for neither masters nor slaves, neither wise nor foolish, are excluded from her fold; fifthly, *doctrine*, in that she possesses the entire teaching of Christ in its unimpaired truth; sixthly, *the means of salvation*, because, as the whole of Christ's Passion operates within her, she possesses a remedy against the spiritual ills of all men; seventhly, *the obligation and necessity of embracing the Church* which bears upon all, as she is the divinely appointed means for their salvation. *Cf.* Schultes, *De Ecclesia Catholica*, p. 179.

[2] Matt. xiii 31-32. [3] *Ibid.* 33.

[4] Gal. iii 28. [5] Mark xvi 15. [6] *Ibid.* 20.

[7] Matt. xviii 18; John xx 21. [8] Matt. xvi 18; John xxi 15-17.

[9] Matt. xxviii 20.

demanded by the Church's oneness. To have departed from its original constitution would mean that the unity of the Mystical Body had been broken ; that which St Paul regarded as an impossibility—the " division " of Christ [1]—would have come about.

Thus we see that each of the properties of the Church emanates from the first and most evident of them all, its oneness. Catholicity is, so to say, the diffusion throughout the world of the Church's unity, a witness to the divine efficacy and power within her. Holiness demonstrates the world-wide fruitfulness of the life of the Church, disclosing her as the effective instrument of men's salvation. Apostolicity, in making clear the line of continuity with the primitive Church, points at the same time to her divine origin. Whence we catch a glimpse of the immense significance of the words of the Creed wherein we proclaim our faith in *unam, sanctam, catholicam et apostolicam Ecclesiam.*

§ VI : MEMBERSHIP

" FOR in one Spirit were we all baptised into one body, whether Jews or Gentiles, whether bond or free." [2] We have now to examine the conditions for membership of Christ's Mystical Body. What is it that makes us " fellow citizens with the saints and domestics of God " ? [3] Not a few erroneous answers have been given to this question. The Donatists in the fifth century, for example, maintained that only the " just "—or, as we should say nowadays, those in a state of grace—belonged to the Church. Others, notably Wycliff and Hus, have limited Church membership to the predestined ; nor do Luther and Calvin, in this respect at least, seem to have held a different view.

The conditions of membership

Pius XII has reaffirmed in the clearest language what are the conditions for membership of the Church. " Only those are to be accounted really members of the Church who have been regenerated in the waters of Baptism and profess the true faith, and have not cut themselves off from the structure of the Body by their own unhappy act or been severed therefrom, for very grave crimes, by the legitimate authority." The Pope then cites the words of St Paul to the Corinthians with which this section opens and continues : " Hence, as in the true communion of the faithful there is but one Body, one Spirit, one Lord, and one Baptism, so there can be only one faith; and therefore whoever refuses to hear the Church must, as the Lord commanded, be considered as the heathen and publican. It follows that those who are divided from one another in faith or government cannot be living in the one Body so described, and by its one divine Spirit." [4]

[1] I Cor. i 13. [2] I Cor. xii 13. [3] Ephesians ii 19.

[4] *MCC* 21. The following is the Latin text of this highly significant passage : In Ecclesiae autem membris ii soli annumerandi sunt, qui regenerationis lavacrum receperunt veramque fidem profitentur, neque a Corporis compage semet ipsos misere separarunt, vel ob gravissima admissa a legitima

That it is through the reception of Baptism that we "put on Christ"[1] is the Church's constant teaching,[2] and the Code of Canon Law[3] lays it down that it is precisely by this means that we become a "person" in the Church with all the rights and duties of Christians. By Baptism we are incorporated in Christ and made his members; we attain a state of grace and become the adopted sons of God, all our sins being remitted, both that which we inherit from Adam and those of which we are personally guilty. Furthermore Baptism imprints on the soul a "character"—described by St Thomas as a "spiritual power"[4]—which provides us as it were with a title to the reception of the other sacraments.

Sin does not exclude from membership

Sinners, as such, are not deprived of their membership of the Church.[5] It is true that, having lost baptismal innocence, they are now but imperfectly incorporated in Christ; for, though they retain supernatural faith and the baptismal character, they lack the sanctifying grace and charity which give full and living membership. They are, so to say, "putrefied" members, but, as long as they are on earth, not beyond revivification from the Church's inexhaustible treasury of graces. That our Lord did not wish to exclude sinners from membership of his Mystical Body is clearly indicated by his own words. "They that are in health need not a physician, but they that are ill"[6] . . . "For I came not to call the just, but sinners."[7] The parables of the lost sheep and the prodigal son offer a moving illustration of the same point.[8]

Excommunication, apostasy, heresy, schism

Nevertheless the melancholy possibility must be envisaged of those who may have "cut themselves off from the structure of the Body by their own unhappy act or been severed therefrom, for very grave crimes, by the legitimate authority."[9] In other words, the Church, as being a perfectly constituted society, has the right for grave reasons of excluding from membership. She may pass sentence of, or lay down conditions which involve, excommunication. This carries with it the deprivation of rights and privileges enjoyed by those in communion with the faithful.[10] But such a juridical penalty does not wholly nullify membership of the Church, still less does it necessarily imply the final condemnation before God of the

auctoritate seiuncti sunt. Etenim "in uno Spiritu," ait Apostolus, "omnes nos in unum corpus baptizati sumus, sive Iudaei, sive gentiles, sive servi sive liberi" (1 Cor. xii 13). Sicut igitur in vero christifidelium coetu unum tantummodo habetur Corpus, unus Spiritus, unus Dominus et unum Baptisma, sic haberi non potest nisi una fides (*cf*. Eph. iv 5); atque adeo qui Ecclesiam audire renuerit, iubente Domino habendus est ut ethnicus et publicanus (*cf*. Matt. xviii 17). Quamobrem qui fide vel regimine invicem dividuntur, in uno eiusmodi Corpore, atque uno eius divino Spiritu vivere nequeunt.

[1] Gal. iii 27.
[2] Denzinger, 696, 895.
[3] *Codex Iuris Canonici*, can. 87.
[4] III, Q. lxiii, art. 2.
[5] *MCC* 22.
[6] Matt. ix 12.
[7] Mark ii 17.
[8] Luke xv.
[9] *MCC* 21.
[10] C.I.C. can. 2257-2267.

excommunicated person. Certain sins—viz., apostasy, heresy and schism [1]—of their nature cut off the guilty from the living Body of Christ. Apostasy is a form of spiritual suicide, being the complete and voluntary abandonment of the Christian faith which one once professed. Heresy, objectively considered, is a doctrinal proposition which contradicts an article of faith; from the subjective point of view it may be defined as an error concerning the Catholic faith, freely and obstinately persisted in by a professing Christian. Schism consists in a refusal of subjection to the Vicar of Christ, the Pope, in whose office the source of the Church's visible unity is embodied, or a withdrawal from communion with the faithful subject to him. It can hardly be denied that those who take up any of these positions —most evidently is this the case with the deliberate apostate—sever themselves by their own act from membership of the Church.

Non-Catholics in good faith

The necessity of belonging to the Catholic Church in order to obtain salvation is a dogma based on the words of our Lord himself: "Go ye into the whole world and preach the gospel to every creature. He that believeth and is baptised shall be saved: but he that believeth not shall be condemned." [2] But here we must remark briefly upon the position of non-Catholics in good faith.[3] Even such authorities as Suarez and the theologians of Salamanca, writing at a time when, and in a country where, Catholicism reigned supreme, were prepared to allow that there could be heretics and infidels so untouched by Christian influences as to experience no doubt about the truth of their own religious tenets.[4] The possibility of a sincere adherence to error is clearly recognised by the Church. Pope Pius IX has declared that, taking into account all the circumstances of time and place in which individuals might find themselves, as well as of their capacity to understand, it would be presumptuous to set limits to the possibilities of invincible ignorance of the true Church.[5] The recognition of this fact, however, can do nothing to attenuate the Church's often repeated teaching that it is necessary for all men to belong to her explicitly.[6]

The "soul" and "body" of the Church

It has sometimes been argued that non-Catholics in good faith may be said to belong to the *soul*, as distinguished from the body, of the Church. In the previous essay it has been pointed out that this is not an entirely satisfactory way of viewing the matter, as the distinction in question is not free from ambiguity. It lends itself to the false antithesis between an "invisible" and "visible" Church,

[1] Can. 1325, § 2.

[2] Mark xvi 15-16.

[3] That is to say, the much misunderstood doctrine of *extra Ecclesiam nulla salus*: "no salvation outside the Church." For the meaning of "good faith" see the article "Bonne Foi" in the *Dictionnaire de Théologie Catholique*, tome ii, cols. 1009-1019.

[4] Suarez, *De Fide*, disp. XVII, sect. ii, n. 6; Salamanticenses, *Cursus theologicus dogmaticus*, tr. XVII, disp. ix, n. 9.

[5] Denzinger, 1647.

[6] Denzinger, 423, 468, 714, 1646-1647, 1716 and 1717.

and suggests that one might belong to Christ's Mystical Body without being incorporated, simultaneously and in the same degree, in the visible Catholic Church—which is impossible. Moreover, the "soul" of the Church, according to tradition, is the Holy Spirit, by whose power the Mystical Body is animated.[1] Although, from a slightly different viewpoint, we may also consider the created effects of the Spirit's activity—viz., the vital organism made up of grace, the theological virtues and the gifts of the Holy Spirit—as being the source of the Church's supernatural life,[2] and to that extent her "soul." But limitations of space preclude a detailed examination of the relevance of this doctrine to the position of non-Catholics in good faith. Here we shall be content to summarise the generally accepted teaching on a question of great theological difficulty.

Membership by desire

The whole tenor of the Church's official documents makes it clear that, apart from two cases, it is necessary for salvation to belong explicitly (*in re*) to the Catholic Church. The two exceptions, wherein membership of the Church by desire (*in voto*) suffices, are the following: (i) In the event of the impossibility of Baptism, which is always necessary for membership, being effectively received. Since, according to the teaching of the Council of Trent (Session VI, cap. iv),[3] the desire for Baptism (contained in the act of charity) can suffice for the soul's regeneration, it is clear that the desire for membership of the Church, which is made effective by this sacrament, can likewise suffice. And this holds good both for catechumens, who are prevented from receiving the sacrament owing to some insuperable obstacle, and for converts from heresy whose antecedent Baptism may be uncertain and who are impeded by the like extremity from the actual reception of the sacrament. (ii) The Church teaches no less clearly that actual membership of the Catholic Church is not necessary for the salvation of those in invincible ignorance of her true nature. This is stated expressly in the consistorial allocution *Singulari quadam* of Pius IX, 9 December 1854,[4] and in his Encyclical to the Italian Bishops, 10 August 1863.[5] It follows therefore that in this case also to belong to the Church *in voto* suffices for salvation.[6]

Necessity of belonging to the Church explicitly

But, when rightly understood, these seeming exceptions serve to emphasise rather than diminish the universal urgency of full and explicit membership of the Catholic Church. "We invite them all," writes Pope Pius XII,[7] alluding to the whole non-Catholic world, "each and everyone, to yield their free consent to the inner stirrings of God's grace and strive to extricate themselves from a state in which they cannot be secure of their own eternal salvation; for, though they may be related to the Mystical Body of the Redeemer by some unconscious yearning and desire, yet they are deprived

[1] *Cf. MCC* 55. [2] *Ibid.*, 56.
[3] Denzinger, 796. [4] *Ibid.*, 1647. [5] *Ibid.*, 1677.
[6] *Cf.* art. "Église" in *D.T.C.*, tome iv, cols. 2166-2167.
[7] *MCC* 102.

of those many great and heavenly gifts and aids which can be enjoyed only in the Catholic Church. Let them enter Catholic unity, therefore, and joined with us in the one organism of the Body of Jesus Christ, hasten together to the one Head in the fellowship of most glorious love. We cease not to pray for them to the Spirit of love and truth, and with open arms we await them, not as strangers but as those who are coming to their own father's home."

PART II

THE JURIDICAL STRUCTURE OF THE CHURCH

§ VII: PRELIMINARY: THE AUTHORITY OF THE CHURCH

The inner life of the Church and its outward structure inseparable

We must now consider how Christ rules the Church visibly through his Vicar, the Pope, and the Bishops in their respective dioceses. Nor shall we lose sight of the fact that "in the first place, in virtue of the juridical mission by which the divine Redeemer sent forth his Apostles into the world as he himself had been sent by the Father,[1] it is indeed he who baptises through the Church, he who teaches, governs, absolves, binds, offers, makes sacrifice."[2] Although it must be admitted that "the structure of the Christian society, proof though it is of the wisdom of the divine Architect, is nevertheless something of a completely lower order in comparison with the spiritual gifts which enrich it and give it life,"[3] we have seen how complete is the error of those who would detach the inner mystery of the Mystical Body from the outward framework of the Church.[4] Both are so closely connected that it is impossible truly to love the one without loving the other;[5] they are as integral to the Church as body and soul to man, as divinity and humanity to Christ, who is the Head and Pattern of his Church.[6]

Powers conferred by Christ on his Church

To enable the Church to carry out Christ's commission of leading mankind to salvation she has been vested by him with a threefold power, corresponding to his own office of Prophet, Priest and King: that of teaching, her *doctrinal* authority; that of order, her *ministerial* authority; that of government, her *jurisdictional* authority. We may note in passing that some theologians make further subdivisions within these three powers and arrange them differently,[7] while others point out that they are fundamentally reducible to two, that of order and that of jurisdiction.[8] But the classification here given[9]

[1] John xvii 18; xx 21. [2] *MCC* 52. [3] *Ibid.* 61.
[4] *Cf.* p. 685; *cf. MCC* 63. [5] *Ibid.* 91.
[6] *Ibid.* 62. [7] Schultes, *op. cit.*, pp. 329-332.
[8] Billot, *De Ecclesia Christi* (tome i, editio 5), pp. 339-342.
[9] *Cf.* Tanquerey, *Synopsis Theologiæ Dogmaticæ* (tome i, editio 23), p. 552.

perhaps lends itself to the clearest treatment in the space at our disposal. Further, as the power of order, which is concerned directly with the sanctification of the Church, is discussed elsewhere in this volume,[1] there remain for our consideration only the Church's (*a*) doctrinal authority and (*b*) jurisdictional authority.

(*a*) *Doctrinal Authority*

The infallible magisterium of the Church

The doctrinal authority, or *magisterium*, with which Christ has equipped his Church includes all the rights and privileges necessary for the effective teaching of divine revelation and guarding intact the deposit of faith. He has willed that the human race as a whole should acquire God's truth, not by individual inspiration, nor by the private interpretation of Scripture, but by attending to the living voice of the Church. Hence, as a corollary, he has ensured that that voice shall not err; in other words, he has endowed his Church with the gift of infallibility. This infallibility extends, in principle, to the tradition of Christian belief (*faith*) and the manner of life (*morals*); it is concerned with what men must believe, and what they must do, if they are to be saved.

As, however, the Church derives her teaching on these points from the original deposit, "the faith once delivered to the saints,"[2] she must know how to preserve her sacred trust from contamination by "philosophy and vain deceit, according to the tradition of men, according to the elements of the world and not according to Christ."[3] That is to say, the teaching Church (*Ecclesia docens*) may pass an infallible judgement, not only upon truths of revelation, but on matters so intimately connected with those truths that, were an authoritative decision upon them lacking, men's hold upon revelation itself would be endangered. Such activities as the formulation of creeds, the public condemnation of errors, the prohibition of certain books as dangerous to faith and morals, are all functions of the Church's doctrinal magisterium. It is by the same authority that she sends out missionaries, both to the faithful and to unbelievers, that she opens her schools and, in general, supervises with such vigilance the education of the young.

The nature of infallibility

But, as it has often been misunderstood, we must examine in greater detail the meaning and extent of the Church's infallibility. We recall that it has for its object all the truths, collectively and individually, which are formally contained in the sources of divine revelation; indirectly it bears also upon such other truths as are necessary for our knowledge so that the deposit of revelation may be safeguarded. Be it noted that infallibility is a gift, a *charism*, bestowed upon the Church, the effect of which is to exclude the possibility of error from her teaching with regard to faith and morals. It implies

[1] Essay xxix: *The Sacrament of Order*.
[2] Jude 3.
[3] Col. ii 8; *cf.* 1 Tim. vi 20.

the assistance of the Holy Spirit, and so may be called a supernatural grace ; [1] its function, however, is not, as such, to sanctify the Church or her individual members, but to ensure that she does not teach false doctrine. Infallibility should further be carefully distinguished from *revelation* and *inspiration*. Revelation is the new manifestation of truth by God. Scriptural inspiration implies a divine prompting of the sacred author in the very act of writing, so that what results is literally the "word of God," even though what is contained in it need not always be a revelation. Or, to put the matter another way : revelation belongs exclusively to God ; inspiration is a joint divine-human act, the writer playing the rôle of God's instrument ; infallibility, as being proper to the Church and the Roman Pontiff, concerns a human activity wherein God is neither revealer nor inspirer, but in which he assists (*Deo adiutore*).

In the popular mind it is *Papal* infallibility which most arrests attention. But it should be remembered that, when the Pope defines infallibly, he does so as the mouthpiece or organ of an infallible Church. Technically, he may use his official prerogative without first consulting the Church ; nor do his decrees depend for their validity upon the Church's subsequent ratification ; but he cannot be thought of as defining doctrine *apart* from the Church—for "he enjoys that infallibility with which the Divine Redeemer willed *his Church* to be endowed." [2] Infallibility, then, belongs fundamentally to the Church, and to the Pope in his capacity of visible Head of the Church. In harmony with the doctrine of the Mystical Body of Christ, it is a gift bestowed upon Head and members. Thus the Church enjoys not only an *active* infallibility in teaching, but also a *passive* infallibility in believing.

The scope of infallibility

The *direct object* of the Church's infallibility includes, in addition to the revealed truths, such matters as the drawing up of the official Creeds or Symbols, the determination of the terms to be employed in dogmatic canons and definitions, the manner of interpreting Scripture and Tradition, the decision as to what is to be included in the Canon of Scripture, the condemnation of heresy. All these are but instruments for the expression and clarification of revealed truth ; were the Church deprived of them her doctrinal authority would be nullified and without effect. Accordingly they form an indispensable part of the Church's teaching office.

We must now briefly summarise the implications of what theologians call the *indirect object* of infallibility. This covers *inter alia* matters which, strictly speaking, are the concern of the natural philosopher, but error in which would undermine the rational structure on which faith is built ; *e.g.* the spirituality of the soul, which is the natural foundation for its immortality and future life. On occasion the Church, without stigmatising a proposition harmful

[1] *Gratia gratis data ; cf.* I-II, Q. 111, art. 1.
[2] Denzinger, 1839.

to faith and morals as *heretical*, will attach to it a censure such as, *proximate to heresy*, *erroneous in faith*, *false* ; in so doing she judges infallibly, for she thus defines, though negatively, a truth as closely affecting divine revelation.

Dogmatic facts fall likewise within the scope of this infallibility. These concern such information as is necessary for our knowledge if our belief in dogma itself is to be safeguarded ; *e.g.* the legitimacy of a Pope, the oecumenicity of a General Council. Clearly, were there uncertainty on such points, we should have no guarantee of the authenticity of doctrinal definitions emanating from these sources. Similarly the Church can decide infallibly whether a given book, objectively considered, contains orthodox or heterodox doctrine—and this without prejudice to what the author *meant* to say. Thus the Fathers at Nicaea condemned the *Thalia* of Arius, and Innocent X certain propositions from the *Augustinus* of Jansen. The moral precepts of the Church, as affecting the conduct of all the faithful, are backed by her infallibility; so also is the Church's definitive approval of the various Religious Orders. Though what is here guaranteed is the essential goodness of what is proposed, the fidelity with which a given religious rule reflects the evangelical counsels, but not necessarily its suitability for all times and places ; since this is a matter, not of infallibility, but of practical prudence. In the same connection the Church exercises her infallibility in the solemn canonisation of saints. For it is unthinkable that the lives of those whom the Church upholds as models of heroic sanctity should be other than she declares them to be.

We have yet to touch upon a subject which, after the original deposit of faith itself, first engages the attention of the Church's doctrinal authority, viz., *theological conclusions*, sometimes called *truths virtually revealed*. They are propositions not formally contained in, but deduced from, divine revelation. Often the mind reaches them by means of a reasoning process, or syllogism, of which one premise is known by faith, the other by reason. For instance, that " God will render to each according to his works " is a truth formally revealed. With this I may connect the thought : " God can only so act on the supposition that man is free," and draw from these two statements together the inference : " Therefore man is free." This is a theological conclusion. Some famous examples of truths arrived at in this way are the following : " Christ never lacked efficacious grace " ; " Christ is impeccable " ; " Christ's knowledge is immune from error." Now these conclusions fall within the scope of the Church's infallibility. In a matter so closely connected with the deposit of faith, involving also the whole process of the development of dogma,[1] it is imperatively demanded that the Church should have the deciding voice ; without it her teaching authority

[1] See Essay i, *Faith and Revealed Truth*, pp. 33-5.

would be gravely deficient. Finally, we should note that infallibility in this connection guarantees that the truth in question is in fact virtually [1] revealed, but it says nothing about the validity of the arguments by which the mind may have deduced it. The charism of infallibility safeguards, not the reasoning processes of theologians, but what the Pope and Bishops, as custodians of divine revelation, teach to the faithful throughout the world.

(*b*) *Jurisdictional Authority* [2]

In addition to her authority to teach men the way of salvation the Church has been given effective power to guide them along its course. The right to rule, no less than the right to teach, is an integral part of her saving mission. So Christ very clearly laid it down: "As the Father hath sent me, I also send you." [3] "Whatsoever you shall bind upon earth shall be bound also in heaven." [4] "Going therefore, teach ye all nations . . . *teaching them to observe all things whatsoever I have commanded you.*" [5] We shall see more clearly how this power of rulership is exercised when we come to consider the functions of the Pope and the Bishops, in whom it is chiefly vested. For the moment we may note that the practical government of the Church falls under three heads: the authority which she possesses is legislative, judicial and coercive.

Legislative authority

The Church's *legislative authority*, as its name implies, means that she has power to make laws binding in conscience, for the general good of the Christian community. It includes also the right to impose precepts; that is, to apply the law to individuals in the form of a command. Every properly constituted society must, from the nature of the case, be able to legislate for its members. Least of all can this right be denied to the Church, which is a divine society organised for the most vitally significant of purposes: the eternal salvation of mankind. Nor may it be objected that the words of Christ and the precepts of the Gospel should be sufficient without any further commandments being added. It is true that the fundamental principles of the Christian law are to be found in these sources; but the Church has been promised the assistance of the Holy Spirit in adapting, interpreting and developing these for the benefit of the

[1] Or *mediately*, as distinguished from immediately (*i.e.* formally), revealed. The theologians further distinguish, within the sphere of formal or immediate revelation, between what is *explicitly* and what is *implicitly* revealed. But this complex, though highly important, subject cannot be pursued further here. *Cf.* Schultes, *Introductio in historiam dogmatum*, pp. 99-115; 166-179; F. Marin-Sola, *L'Evolution homogène du Dogme Catholique*, I, pp. 61 *et seq.*

[2] The Church's jurisdictional authority, strictly speaking, includes her doctrinal authority; for she teaches by divine *right* (*ius*). We here use the term in its more restricted sense of *power of rulership* (*potestas regendi seu regiminis*); to be distinguished again from the power of order.

[3] John xx 21. [4] Matt. xviii 18. [5] Matt. xxviii 19-20.

faithful according to the diversity of time and place. Confident of the divine guidance, she has exercised this prerogative from the beginning, *e.g.*, in the decrees of the apostolic assembly at Jerusalem with regard to the Mosaic observance,[1] as also in the so-called "Pauline privilege."[2] So the Church has continued to act through the ages, assured that her charism of infallibility will protect her from enacting what is contrary to Christ's Gospel.

Judicial authority

As a consequence of the Church's power to legislate there follows her *judicial authority*. This may be defined as the right, and duty, of deciding definitively in a given case the true meaning of her own laws, and of the conformity, or non-conformity, of the actions of her subjects with the law. Our Lord himself gave an indication of the exercise of this sort of power[3] with reference to wrong-doing among the faithful. The offending brother is first to be corrected privately, then, if he refuse to amend, the case is to be brought before the Church. Ecclesiastical authority must next pronounce judgement. Should the guilty party refuse to abide by it, there is the appropriate sanction: he is to be regarded "as the heathen and the publican." St Paul acted as judge in this way in the case of the incestuous Corinthian,[4] and he gives explicit advice to Timothy as to the correct procedure.[5]

Coercive authority

Again, as an inevitable corollary to the foregoing powers, we find the Church possessed of *coercive authority*. In fact, the words of our Lord just quoted and the behaviour of St Paul illustrate the Church's judicial and coercive powers operating together. What is here meant is not that the Church can bring direct physical compulsion to bear upon her subjects, but that she has the right to punish them when they offend against her ruling. Unpalatable as this doctrine may be to the mind of the modern man, living as he does in a world contemptuous of all ecclesiastical authority, it is nevertheless bound up with the Church's function of government. It is only the counterpart, on a higher plane, of the right of civil society to attach to its laws the sanction of a penalty for their infringement. Canonical punishment normally consists in the wrongdoer being deprived by legitimate authority of some spiritual or temporal benefit.[6] Excommunication is an example of a spiritual penalty, the imposition of fasting of a temporal. The object of such punishment, it need hardly be said, is not any arbitrary exercise of power, but the correction of the delinquent and the restitution of the order of justice broken by his offence. St Paul's second Epistle to the Corinthians shows him conscious of the possession of coercive authority as here understood.[7]

With the power of the Church in temporal affairs we shall deal

[1] Acts xv 28 ff.
[2] 1 Cor. vii 12 ff.
[3] Matt. xviii 15 ff.
[4] 1 Cor. v 3.
[5] 1 Tim. v 19.
[6] C.I.C., can. 2214-2219.
[7] 2 Cor. xiii 10; *cf.* x 6.

more fully when we come to consider her relations with the State. Here it will suffice to note that those directly subject to the Church's *potestas regiminis* are baptised persons; for these only, as we have seen, are in the proper sense of the word members. Finally, it should be borne in mind that governmental authority was given directly and immediately by Christ to the Apostles and their successors, and not to the Church as a whole or to the collectivity of the faithful. In other words, this power is now vested in the Bishops, who are not delegates of the Church's members, but appointees of God. The constitution of the Church is thus not democratic,[1] but hierarchic, its pastors deriving their office from above, not from below. To this must be added, as a qualification, the principle of monarchy, inasmuch as the fulness of authority was given solely to Peter, Prince of the Apostles, and to his successors, the Bishops of Rome.

§ VIII: THE POPE: VICAR OF CHRIST[2]

IT is the belief of Catholics that our Lord promised to Peter a primacy of jurisdiction over his Church,[3] a primacy which he actually conferred after his resurrection;[4] they hold, moreover, that it was given, not to Peter alone, but to the successors in his office and that it is vested for all time in the Roman Pontiff, who is the visible Head of the Church. No article of the Christian faith is more fully substantiated in Scripture and Tradition than this. Our present task, however, is not to set out exhaustively the evidence for the doctrine,[5] but briefly to explain its meaning.

St Peter's primacy

Let us recall the words of the principal Petrine text: "And I say to thee: That thou art Peter (Aramaic: *kepha*), and upon this rock (*kepha*) I will build my church. And the gates of hell shall not prevail against it. And I will give to thee the keys of the kingdom of heaven. And whatsoever thou shalt bind on earth, it shall be bound also in heaven: and whatsoever thou shalt loose on earth,

[1] Though there is a very real element of democracy in the appointment to the chief offices of the Church: the Pope and the Bishops, not being hereditary officials, are drawn from all nations and every condition and walk of life. Election by voting has also its part in the procedure.

[2] "Moreover it is absolutely (*omnino necessarium est*) necessary that there should be the supreme Head, visible to all, effectively directing the mutual co-operation of the members to the attainment of the proposed end; and that visible Head is the Vicar of Jesus Christ on earth. For just as the divine Redeemer sent the Paraclete, the Spirit of Truth, to undertake in his name (John xiv 16, 26) the invisible guidance of the Church, so he gave mandate to Peter and his successors, representing his person on earth, to conduct also the visible government of the Christian commonwealth." *MCC* 69.

[3] Matt. xvi 18-19.

[4] John xxi 15 ff.

[5] This has been compendiously done in, *e.g.*, Dieckmann, *De Ecclesia*, I, pp. 285-319.

it shall be loosed also in heaven."[1] Our Lord here makes known his will in a series of three metaphors whose meaning, clear enough to us, would be still clearer to listeners familiar with Old Testament Scripture and the teaching methods of the Rabbis. He first compares his Church to a building of which Peter is to be the foundation; he next employs the comparison suggested by "the keys," which will be handed to Peter as a sign of his power over Christ's house; finally comes the reference to "binding and loosing," a symbol of the moral nature of the office, which is furthermore backed by a divine sanction.

The comparison of the Church to a *house*—that is, *of Israel*—is derived from the Old Testament and occurs frequently in the New.[2] Equally scriptural is the idea of a *foundation* to the building.[3] To the strength of this foundation the house owes its firmness and stability, enabling it to withstand rain, wind and floods, "for it was founded upon a rock."[4] Similarly it is from its foundation that the unity of the house arises, the walls, roof and whole structure being bound together in one single edifice in virtue of the rock on which it is based. All this illustrates the relation between the Church and Peter. He who was Simon is given the rôle of foundation to the building erected by Christ; hence he receives the name of "Peter," which means "rock." By him the new House of Israel is to be unified and stabilised so that nothing, not even "the gates of hell,"[5] symbol of all that is opposed to Christ's Kingdom, can prevail against it.

[1] Matt. xvi 18-19. The gospel text, of course, is in Greek, the words respectively for "Peter" and "rock" being πέτρος and πέτρα. M.-J. Lagrange (*Saint Matthieu*, pp. 323-324) comments as follows: "Πέτρος n'existait pas comme nom propre ni en grec, ni en Latin, et ne peut pas être dérivé du latin *Petronius*. C'est donc un nom nouveau qui paraît dans l'histoire. Le nom commun πέτρος signifiait pierre, et πέτρα rocher. Mais πέτρος convenait mieux pour un homme, et πέτρα convenait mieux comme fondement de l'Église. En araméen, on ne pouvait réaliser cette élégance. Nous savons par le N.T. que Simon était nommé Cephas dans l'Église primitive (John i 42; Gal. i 18; ii 9; 1 Cor. ix 5 etc.) . . . On comprend donc très bien . . . que Jésus ait pu dire et Ma. écrire: Tu es Cépha et sur ce Cépha je bâtirai mon Église, et que le traducteur grec ait gardé en meme temps πέτρα qui répondait mieux à la situation, et πέτρος qui avait prévalu en grec comme nom masculin."

[2] *Cf.* Acts ii 36; vii 42; 1 Tim. iii 15; Heb. iii 6.

[3] See especially Eph. ii 19 ff.; *cf.* iii 17; Col. i 23; 1 Cor. iii 10.

[4] Matt. vii 25. An interesting text, showing our Lord himself using "rock" in the same sense as in xvi 18. *Cf.* Luke vi 48.

[5] Matt. xvi 18. See the striking corroboration of this text in Luke xxii 31-32: "And the Lord said: Simon, Simon, behold Satan hath desired to have you (plural), that he may sift you as wheat. But I have prayed for thee (singular), that thy faith fail not: and thou, being once converted, confirm thy brethren." We may note the parallels: Satan hath desired you—the gates of hell; I have prayed for thee—I will build upon this rock; confirm thy brethren—Peter the stabilising force in the Apostolic college. *Cf.* Dieckmann, *op. cit.*, p. 313.

His primacy continued in the Pope

"Feed my lambs. . . . Feed my lambs. . . . Feed my sheep."[1] So the promised primacy was conferred in the words of the risen Christ. He who had spoken of himself as the "good shepherd,"[2] who desired that there should be "one fold and one shepherd,"[3] was handing over the sheepfold to Peter's care; for he himself was to ascend to the Father.[4] True, he was only withdrawing his visible presence; he would still take care of his own as their chief pastor; hence the commission: "Feed *my* sheep." But Peter had become shepherd of the flock of Christ in the same way as he was the foundation of his Church. Christ remains, in the words of the selfsame Peter, "the prince of pastors,"[5] but he now acts as the Lord's representative, his Vicar, and he, together with the rest of the Apostles under his leadership, is a true pastor of souls.[6] Nor can it be argued that this pastoral office was to terminate with the death of Peter. For the Kingdom of God was to endure until the end of ages.[7] Accordingly, unless the gates of hell were to prevail, there could never come a time when Christ's sheepfold would be deprived of its shepherd, his Church of its rock foundation.

Primacy of jurisdiction

When, four centuries later, the Fathers at the Council of Chalcedon, on receiving the *Tome* of Leo, acknowledged its author as "the interpreter of Peter,"[8] they summarised in a phrase the traditional belief of Christians in the position of the Pope. It is true that in an earlier age the great Patriarchs and Bishops acted with less frequent reference to Rome than is now the case, but they were none the less fully conscious of their subordination to the Apostolic See, "mother and mistress of all the churches."[9] In the Middle Ages the conspicuous exercise of the power inherent in their office by such pontiffs as Gregory VII and Innocent III was, in effect, no more than the Church's assertion of the primacy of the spiritual over the temporal order. In modern times the breakdown of Christendom at the Reformation and the disruptive influence of the various National Churches, together with the development of easy and rapid communications, has indeed produced a highly centralised ecclesiastical organisation hitherto unknown. But this "ultramontanism," as it has sometimes not very happily been called, serves only to emphasise the primacy, not merely of honour, but of jurisdiction, which belongs to the Pope in virtue of Christ's commission to St Peter. The Pope's rulership over the Church is thus not simply directive, it is wholly authoritative (*potestas iurisdictionis*); moreover, it concerns, in addition to faith and morals, matters of

[1] John xxii 15-17. [2] John x 11. [3] *Ibid.* 16; *cf.* xi 52 ff.
[4] John xx 17; *cf.* xiv 1 ff.; xvi 28; xvii 4 ff.; viii 21 ff.
[5] 1 Peter v 4 (lit. "chief shepherd"); *cf.* ii 25.
[6] *Cf.* Matt. xviii 18; ix 36-38.
[7] Matt. xxviii 18-20; *cf.* xiii 38 ff.; xiii 47 ff.
[8] *Synodal Letter to Leo;* No. 98 in the collection of Leo's letters; P.L. 54, 951-960. *Cf.* Hefele, *History of the Councils* (Eng. trans. vol. 3), p. 429 ff.
[9] Denzinger, 999.

discipline and government as they affect the Church in every part of the world.

Papal infallibility

The Church's doctrinal and jurisdictional authority, which we have briefly examined, is vested also in the Roman Pontiff. It is with regard to the first of these, as touching the Pope's office as teacher, that he enjoys the charism of infallibility. On this point it will suffice to quote the words of the Vatican definition: "We teach and define it to be a dogma divinely revealed that the Roman Pontiff, when he speaks *ex cathedra*, that is, when acting in his office of pastor and teacher of all Christians, by his supreme Apostolic authority, he defines a doctrine concerning faith or morals to be held by the whole Church, through the divine assistance promised him in Blessed Peter, he enjoys that infallibility with which the divine Redeemer willed his Church to be endowed in defining doctrine concerning faith and morals; and therefore such definitions of the said Roman Pontiff are irreformable of themselves, and not from the consent of the Church."[1]

The Pope's non-infallible teaching

Every word of this pronouncement was weighed and debated by the Fathers of the Vatican Council. It should be studied with equal care by those who would grasp the Church's teaching on Papal infallibility. Much of the hostility to which it has given rise has its source in ignorance or misunderstanding of the scope and limitations clearly indicated in the definition itself. An *ex cathedra* definition is one in which the Pope employs the fulness of his apostolic authority to make a final and irrevocable decision (*definit*) on a question of faith or morals, with the clear intention of binding all the faithful to its acceptance, as involving, directly or indirectly, the deposit of faith. It will be obvious that this does not necessarily include the normal teaching authority by which he is frequently addressing the faithful, either directly or through the medium of the Roman Congregations. Teaching of the latter kind, though it is to be received with all reverence, does not enjoy the charism of infallibility. The Holy Father may speak, for example, merely as Bishop of Rome; or, as Pope, he may give instruction to only a section of the universal Church; or again, he may address the whole Church, but without the intention of defining anything as of faith. In none of these activities does he enjoy, within the terms of the definition, immunity from error. The same may be said of the occasions when the Pope expresses his mind *motu proprio*, *i.e.* by initiating a question himself, or, it may be, in response to queries submitted to him by others. Teaching which is; technically, non-infallible may be imparted in Pontifical Decrees and Instructions and in Encyclical Letters, for all of which the Pope is the responsible author. His authorisation of the decisions of the Roman Congregations, notably that of the Holy Office and, of equal authority within its prescribed limits, the Biblical Commission, is not to be regarded in the light of a solemn definition.

[1] Denzinger, 1839.

To these decisions, on account of their great weight, a respectful internal assent is demanded of the faithful ; but they are not necessarily irreformable and have not the sanction of infallibility behind them.

The Pope's jurisdictional authority

Of the Pope's legislative, or jurisdictional, authority it will be enough to remark that all the power of rulership possessed by the Church is vested in his office ; adding that while he is subject to none, save God himself, all the members of the Church, not excluding the Bishops, are subject to him. He may appoint and depose Bishops and send Legates, with authority delegated by him, wherever he deems fit. In a word, his jurisdictional authority is supreme. But, though authoritarian and absolute within its own sphere, the Papal power cannot be fairly described as arbitrary or despotic. The Pope is as subject as the least member of the faithful to the prescriptions of the divine and natural law ; from these he can dispense neither himself nor any member of his flock. His jurisdictional authority is such that the canons and positive laws of the Church have no coercive sanction in respect of his actions, but they have for him their directive force none the less ; and he is bound to use his great powers with the charity and prudence of one ever conscious of his grave responsibility before God. To enable him to do so—how otherwise could he hope to succeed ?—he enjoys the assistance of the Holy Spirit, as a guarantee that his rulership will be "unto edification and not unto destruction."[1]

The Pope representative, not successor, of Christ

Finally, be it remembered that nothing we have said concerning the successor of St Peter militates against the supreme power over the Church exercised by Christ himself. He is the Head of the Church in his own right ; Peter and his successors only in virtue of the power received from him. Thus the Pope is the *Vicar* (*i.e.* representative), not the successor, of Christ. Christ is Head as Redeemer and Mediator of all men ; "and therefore," writes Pius XII, "this Body has only one principal Head, namely Christ, who, continuing himself to govern the Church invisibly and directly, rules it visibly through his personal representative on earth."[2] Christ is the Head of all men throughout all time,[3] the successor of Peter only of those living under his Pontificate. Christ is Head alike of the Church militant on earth, suffering in Purgatory, and triumphant in Heaven ; the Pope's headship is concerned only with the Church militant. The Pope, as visible Head, rules the Church visibly ; but Christ, though hidden, rules it still, bringing to bear upon his Mystical Body all those unseen influences, of grace and light and strength, which can emanate only from the Incarnate Son of God and his life-giving Spirit.

[1] 2 Cor. xiii 10. [2] *MCC* 38.
[3] *Summa Theologica*, III, Q. viii, art. 3.

§ IX: THE BISHOPS: SUCCESSORS OF THE APOSTLES

Christ's commission to his Apostles

An account will be found elsewhere in this volume of the institution of the Ecclesiastical Hierarchy and the origins of the Episcopate.[1] Here we shall be concerned, not with the power of Order, but with the jurisdiction proper to the Bishops of the Church as successors to the Apostles. For they collectively received from Christ a commission no less explicit than that given to their head, Peter. "Amen I say to you, whatsoever you shall bind upon earth shall be bound also in heaven: and whatsoever you shall loose upon earth shall be loosed also in heaven."[2] "Going therefore, teach ye all nations . . . teaching them to observe all things whatsoever I have commanded you. And behold I am with you all days, even to the consummation of the world."[3]

The Bishops' powers

"Therefore the Bishops are not only to be regarded as more eminent members of the Universal Church, by reason of the truly unique bond which unites them to the divine Head of the whole Body . . . but each of them is also, so far as his own diocese is concerned, a true Pastor, who tends and rules in the name of Christ the flock committed to his care."[4] The Bishops possess, within the limits of the dioceses assigned to them, jurisdiction in the fullest sense, *i.e.* as including doctrinal and jurisdictional authority. It should be noted that they are not merely the Pope's delegates, as, for example, are Apostolic Vicars in missionary countries; their jurisdiction is *proper* (*i.e.* belonging to them *ex officio*) and *ordinary* (*i.e.* not delegated). Thus, as the episcopacy was a method of government instituted by Christ, it would be against the constitution of the Church for their authority so to be superseded as to be reduced to vanishing point. On the other hand the Roman Pontiff's supremacy implies that the exercise of the Bishops' powers may be controlled by him, either by limitation, or extension, or, in a particular case, by their total removal.

Here also it may be explained that no Bishop, with the exception of the Pope, has, by divine law, any jurisdiction over his episcopal brethren. The episcopacy itself was instituted by Christ but, St Peter alone excepted, all the Apostles ranked as equals. Patriarchates, now little more than honorific titles, and archbishoprics have their origin in ecclesiastical law; their authority descends to them from that of Peter and his successors. It was found to facilitate the government of the Church to raise certain Bishops to a higher rank and give them, within prescribed limits, powers of delegating faculties to others; but they exercise these powers, not in virtue of their own episcopacy, but as sharing in the governing authority of the Apostolic See. Even the Cardinals, as such, have no powers

[1] Essay xxix.
[2] Matt. xviii 18.
[3] *Ibid.*, xxviii 19-20; *cf.* Acts x 40-42.
[4] *MCC* 40.

distinct from those proper to the Holy See, *i.e.* the Pope. They are his counsellors and assistants in the government of the Universal Church ; to them also pertains the negotiation of such business as must be done while the Roman See is vacant, notably the supervision of arrangements for the election of the succeeding Pontiff ; but the cardinalate, unlike the episcopate, is not of divine institution.

Other prelates in the Church

Abbots and Superiors of Religious Orders, though they may exercise a quasi-episcopal power in respect of their own subjects, do not belong to the hierarchy of jurisdiction in the Church as instituted by Christ. Nor, strictly speaking, can parish priests claim this privilege ; though in the past a case has been made out for them. True, they have the power of Order by divine right and the indelible sacramental character ; they may possess also, under the Bishop, ordinary jurisdiction over a portion of the faithful for the preaching of the word of God and the administration of the sacraments, but not for making laws or passing judgements in the external forum. Their historic function is that of assistants to the Bishop. They clearly share in the exercise of his pastoral office, but they are not pastors in the sense that he is, nor do they possess his jurisdiction. Parish priests are not to be thought of as holding the same relation to the Bishops as the latter have to the Pope. Their rights and privileges, though carefully legislated for in Canon Law,[1] are, according to the divine constitution of the Church, of a far more subordinate kind. The prerogatives of the Bishop, as successor to the Apostles, are inalienable.[2]

The Bishops' doctrinal authority

In virtue of the commission received from Christ it belongs to the Bishops to feed their flocks with the word of God ; that is to say, they have *doctrinal authority* over their own subjects. The subject-matter of this is proportionately the same as that of the Roman Pontiff's magisterium, viz., divine revelation and matters connected therewith. Accordingly, within their respective dioceses, they have the duty of supervising the teaching and defence of Christian doctrine, of proscribing errors, of prohibiting books and periodicals dangerous to faith and morals. As the Bishops individually, however, are not graced with the charism of infallibility, they do not normally take responsibility for decisions of great doctrinal moment ; here the procedure is to refer the matter to the Holy See or to an Oecumenical Council. None the less, Bishops are authentic masters and judges in matters of faith, and their teaching is to be presumed sound until the contrary is proved. Should doubt arise as to a Bishop's orthodoxy, the question is to be settled, not by his subjects, but by an appeal to the Roman Pontiff.

[1] C.I.C., can. 451 *et seq.*

[2] These remarks apply in their full import to residential Bishops who rule a diocese : *vide* can. 334 ; not to *titular* Bishops, who exercise no jurisdiction in the diocese (*in partibus infidelium*) whose title they bear : *vide* can. 348.

But whatever be the possibility of individual Bishops falling into error, the Bishops collectively, *i.e.* the body of the episcopate, whether dispersed throughout the world in union with the Pope, or assembled under the presidency of the Pope in General Council, are infallible teachers of Christ's doctrine. Of General Councils we shall speak in the next section. But, apart from these, the Bishops' infallible doctrinal authority is exercised explicitly when, for example, they unanimously accept as the rule of faith the decrees of a particular Council; or in giving an identical response to a question proposed by the Pope; or by agreeing in the repudiation of some error. Implicitly the Bishops may testify infallibly to the truth of a doctrine by the fact that they unanimously allow it to be taught in their dioceses, since it is the duty of Bishops to oppose and forbid teaching that is untrue.

Their jurisdictional authority

Their *jurisdictional authority* runs parallel with, or rather, is involved in, their office as pastors of the flock. They *rule* their subjects in both the internal and external forum. Accordingly they may legislate within their own dioceses in matters pertaining to faith, worship and Church discipline. They are also judges in the first instance and may inflict canonical penalties on delinquents. But, as has already been said, the Bishops exercise both their doctrinal and jurisdictional authority in dependence upon the Roman Pontiff; he may impose limits on their powers even within their respective dioceses, as well as reserve special matters to his own competence. Bishops, it need hardly be said, may lay down nothing contrary to the decisions of the Holy See; nor have they, as individuals, any power of legislation over the Universal Church.

Pastors of souls

Lastly, what has been said of the gravity of the Pope's personal responsibility before God applies with no less force to the Bishops. If the most eloquent description of his office is that of "the servant of the servants of God" so, proportionately, should it be theirs. They, as he, must be mindful of the dignity of their calling; but as upholding the honour of the Church, not as a claiming of personal prestige. Being true pastors of souls, they look for their model, not to the autocracy and despotism of secular monarchy, but to the "Good Shepherd" who lays down his life for the sheep.[1] Notwithstanding the respect that is rightly paid them, like him they come "not to be ministered unto, but to minister." [2] If the Bishops can appeal for their great authority to the mandate given by our Lord to the Apostles,[3] they have received from him instructions no less clear as to the spirit in which it is to be exercised: "You know that the princes of the Gentiles lord it over them and they that are the greater exercise power upon them. It shall not be so among you: but whosoever will be the greater among you, let him be your

[1] John x 14-15. [2] Mark x 45.
[3] Matt. xviii 18; xxviii 18-20.

minister. And he that will be first among you shall be your servant." [1]

§ X: COUNCILS OF THE CHURCH

Councils in the Church

A Church Council may be defined as a legitimate assembly of the Pastors of the Church for judging and legislating in matters of doctrine and ecclesiastical discipline. Such a council is described as *provincial* when there are present at it the bishops of a single province, under the presidency of its Archbishop or Metropolitan; *plenary* (at one time called *national*) when composed of the bishops of one kingdom or nation; *general* or *oecumenical* (from the Greek οἰκουμένη meaning "the inhabited world") when representing the Universal Church, with the Roman Pontiff presiding, either personally or through his representative. The decrees of provincial and plenary councils are not, of themselves, infallible; they may, however, become embodied in the rule of faith, if they are so regarded by the Bishops throughout the world, or are ratified by the Pope with his full teaching authority; as happened, for example, with the decrees of the plenary council of Carthage (418) and the second council of Orange (529).

Oecumenical or General Councils

The decrees of a General Council, on the other hand, are an infallible witness to the Catholic rule of faith. For a council to rank as oecumenical [2] a number of conditions must be fulfilled, of which the most important is its confirmation by the Roman Pontiff. The convoking of such a council belongs to the Pope, as the supreme ecclesiastical authority; though this condition, with regard to certain of the early eastern councils, has been waived, or rather supplied by a subsequent ratification or the use of a legal fiction analogous to a *sanatio in radice*.[3] Thus the first general councils at Nicaea (325) and Constantinople (381) were summoned by the Emperor, but received the hall-mark of oecumenicity by the Roman Pontiff's approbation. This procedure did not conflict with the present state of the law as violently as might be supposed. There existed at that date an interconnection between secular and religious affairs the closeness of which we can scarcely realise to-day. The unity of the Church, then practically conterminous in its visible extent with the Empire, was a vital interest to the Roman Emperor; hence he was not acting

[1] Matt. xx 25-27.

[2] There have been twenty Oecumenical Councils (of which only the first seven are recognised by the Greek schismatics): Nicaea I (325), Constantinople I (381), Ephesus (431), Chalcedon (451), Constantinople II (553) and III (680-681), Nicaea II (787), Constantinople IV (869-870), Lateran I (1123) and II (1139), III (1179), and IV (1215), Lyons I (1245) and II (1274), Vienne (1311-1312), Constance (1414-1418), Florence (1438-1445), Lateran V (1512-1517), Trent (1545-1563) and Vatican (1869-1870).

[3] *Cf.* Billot, *op. cit.*, p. 718. The phrase means "a validation from the beginning"; that is to say, the Council gains a retrospective legalisation by the Pope's recognition of it.

entirely beyond his rights in assembling the Bishops with a view to preserving that unity, especially as it lay with the civil authorities to keep open communications and generally to provide facilities for such a gathering. Nor did he interfere in the strictly ecclesiastical deliberations of the conciliar Fathers, even though he may have been given the place of honour among them. Due deference was always paid to the Papal Legates, and neither the Emperor nor the assembled Bishops were in doubt as to the need of having the Council's decrees ratified by the Roman Pontiff.

Those who take part

Those summoned to an Oecumenical Council, and having a deliberative vote, are [1] the Cardinals of the Holy Roman Church, whether or not they be Bishops ; Patriarchs, Primates, Archbishops, residential Bishops, even if not yet consecrated ; Abbots and Prelates *nullius* ; [2] the Abbot Primate, the Abbot Superiors of Monastic Congregations, and the chief Superiors of exempt religious orders of clerics. Titular Bishops also have a deliberative vote when called to a Council. The expert theologians and canonists who always attend are there in an advisory capacity, not as judges and witnesses in matters of faith. The Pope, as sole superior to all the Bishops, is the only president of the council, a presidency which he may exercise by means of Legates ; with him the decision rests as to what is to be discussed and its order of treatment, likewise of transferring, suspending or dissolving the Council ; should he die while it is in session, its deliberations are automatically suspended pending the orders of the succeeding Pontiff for their resumption.

Conciliar decisions

Nor is it necessary that all the Bishops of the Catholic world should attend a Council in order to make it oecumenical. This is a practical impossibility and it suffices that the whole Church, morally speaking, should be represented. A completely unanimous decision is not required. In the event of dissension arising, the final judgement lies with that portion of the Council adhering to the Roman Pontiff, since he is the Head of the Church and protected from error by the gift of infallibility. But if the decision is to be conciliar, and not simply Papal, the Bishops siding with the Pope, even though a minority, must be morally representative of the universal Church. Confirmation by the Roman Pontiff, as has already been said, is an indispensable condition of the oecumenicity of a Council ; for a gathering of Bishops, no matter how numerous, could not, if separated from the Head, represent the Church as a whole. By the same principle, it is within the Pope's power to ratify some, but not all, of the Bishops' decisions ; as instanced at Chalcedon, when Pope Leo repudiated its 28th Canon concerning the prerogatives of the See of Constantinople.

[1] C.I.C., can. 223.

[2] I.e. *nullius diocesis*, " of no diocese " : ruling over territory, with clergy and people, not enclosed in any episcopal diocese (can. 319). Twelve Benedictine Abbots—among them the Abbots of Monte Cassino, Subiaco and St Paul's outside the Walls—enjoy this privilege.

The function of a General Council

In conclusion, it should be remembered that Papal infallibility does not, as is sometimes imagined, render the calling of a General Council superfluous. Such an assembly is not indeed absolutely necessary for the government of the Church, but there are occasions when it may be both advisable and highly beneficial. The Pope, being neither the recipient of private revelation nor divinely inspired, is morally bound to employ all available human means in his investigations; accordingly, he is much helped in discovering the content of the deposit of faith by consultation with the Bishops, who aid him in this way, as well as acting as judges of whatever may be decided. In matters of Church discipline the advantages of taking counsel with the pastors of souls from all parts of the world are too obvious to need emphasis; it is in this way that the needs of the faithful in the various countries can be understood and their case legislated for. Furthermore, although the authority of a Council is essentially the same as that of the Pope, there is an impressiveness about decisions issuing from such an assembly more arresting to men's minds than that of a single voice, however exalted. But it is vain to attempt to place the Catholic episcopate in opposition to the Roman Pontiff; the specious appeal of the Gallicans, and of many a heretic before them, from the decision of the Pope to some future General Council is subversive of the divine constitution of the Church. The Church's infallible teaching authority is vested in the body of Bishops joined with the Pope, and in the Pope himself. It is idle to seek to separate the two.

§ XI: CHURCH AND STATE

The teaching of Leo XIII

"Let every soul be subject to higher powers. For there is no power but from God." [1] All authority, whether ecclesiastical or civil, has for its final sanction the divine law. But, as the main object of the State's existence differs from that which is the chief concern of the Church, we must distinguish a duality of function. Pope Leo XIII has restated for the benefit of modern society the principles which should determine the relations between Church and State. "The Almighty, therefore, has appointed the charge of the human race between two powers, the ecclesiastical and the civil, the one being set over divine, the other over human, things. Each in its kind is supreme, each has fixed limits within which it is contained, limits which are defined by the nature and special object of the province of each, so that there is, we may say, an orbit traced out within which the action of each is brought into play by its own native right." [2] Though both Church and State come from God, they are to be dis-

[1] Rom. xiii 1.

[2] Encyclical "*Immortale Dei,*" 1 November 1885: translated as "The Christian Constitution of States" in *The Pope and the People* (1929 edition), p. 51.

tinguished by the diversity of ends each has in view, a distinction which is the basis of the difference of powers enjoyed by each.

The sphere of the Church's authority

As we have gathered from the foregoing pages, the reason for which the Church exists is man's sanctification and eternal felicity. "Whatever, therefore, in human things is of a sacred character, whatever belongs either of its own nature or by reason of the end to which it is referred, to the salvation of souls, or to the worship of God, is subject to the power and judgement of the Church. Whatever is to be ranged under the civil and political order is rightly subject to the civil authority. Jesus Christ has himself given command that what is Caesar's is to be rendered to Caesar, and that what belongs to God is to be rendered to God." [1] Among things "of a sacred character" there obviously fall such activities as the preaching of the Gospel, the administration of the sacraments, the celebration of divine worship, the final judgement with respect to the morality of human acts. Besides these and the like indisputably spiritual functions, there are other matters, in themselves temporal but consecrated to God by reason of the uses to which they are put, which are subject to ecclesiastical authority; *e.g.* Church buildings and all articles set apart for divine worship, as well as the sources of income appropriated to the upkeep of God's ministers.

"Mixed matters"

But in actual practice the division between the respective provinces of Church and State is not absolute and clear-cut; there is a "mixed" category, pertaining to the Church from one point of view, to the State from another. The marriage contract and education are conspicuous examples of this. Marriage is a sacrament, and as such pertains exclusively to Christ's Church; but it is also a social contract, and under this aspect the State rightly takes cognisance of it. Education, fostering as it does the growth and development of a free individual human person, potentially or actually a member of Christ's Mystical Body, must always be among the chief preoccupations of the Church. But the State, responsible in large measure for the welfare of its future citizens, may also legislate within the sphere of education, provided that in doing so it does not override, but rather respects and reinforces, the freedom and spiritual interests of those chiefly concerned. More particularly is the State within its rights in using its powers to ensure that the benefits of the best education should not be withheld from any member of the community capable of profiting by them. In furthering justice in one department, however, the State must guard against perpetuating, or aggravating, injustice in another. Thus, for example, the State is beyond question exceeding its powers in determining that the adequate financial assistance, needful for the educational reforms which it imposes, shall be made conditional upon the acceptance of a religious syllabus offensive to the consciences of a large number of

The authority of the State

[1] *The Pope and the People*, p. 52.

its citizens. This is to trespass upon the rights of the Church, a usurpation by Caesar of the things that are God's.

The business of the State is to foster the common good of its citizens, to provide for their temporal well-being. But, as man is so constituted that he cannot be happy even in this world unless his heart is set on his final end, which is God, the State cannot disregard these supra-temporal aspirations ; it must, at least indirectly, encourage whatever may assist their realisation. Directly, however, the State is concerned with promoting the public good by legislation in the interests of the political, social and private rights of its citizens. The application of its laws to particular cases and the settlement of individual claims and counter-claims are subject to the State's judiciary. Determining the effects of civil contracts, the punishment of law-breakers, the imposition of taxes, preparation for national defence, subsidising the arts and sciences—these are the activities which properly engage the attention of the State. Nor can the State be fairly accused of undue interference with personal liberty when it reinforces the moral law with positive statutes ; for example, by forbidding blasphemy and public indecency. Propaganda in favour of philanthropic endeavour and personal unselfishness and, in general, the fostering of an intellectual and moral atmosphere favourable to the practice of the natural virtues, especially justice and mutual well-doing, fall likewise within the legitimate province of the State.

Power of the Church in political and social orders

In none of these matters has the Church the right of direct interference. Occasion might arise, however, when she must speak her mind even here. For the political and social orders, *in so far as they fall under the moral law and the judgement of human conscience*, are subject to the authority of the Church. This supremely important principle is not seldom overlooked : most often by those who resent the subjection of their political and social actions to any higher tribunal ; though it is by no means unknown for the representatives of the Church to offend against it, for example, in advocating merely personal views on political and social questions by an illegitimate appeal to alleged " Catholic principles." The Bishops, it should be noted, are not qualified by their office to criticise the military strategy of a war, or express their views as to what the political and economic arrangements of a peace-settlement should be ; but they may, as pastors of their flocks and witnesses to the Gospel, pronounce upon the justice, or otherwise, of the issues involved.

Political elections, as such, are no concern of bishops and priests, save in their capacity as private citizens ; it is in fact their duty to remain strictly impartial, so as not to prejudice their position as spiritual guides to every section of their flock ; but if a political party, or individual candidates, are advocating measures opposed to the Church's interests, then the faithful may be reminded of where their duty lies. Again, ecclesiastical authority is not empowered to sit in judgement upon purely economic questions of supply and demand, though clearly it may use its influence, let us say, to ensure that the workers are not deprived of a just wage. Thus many human situations can arise upon which the episcopate is entitled to give guidance, without being charged with "interference" in matters outside its sphere.

Harmony between Church and State

These considerations should make clear both the distinction between Church and State, and the need for their harmonious co-operation. "When political government (*regnum*) and ecclesiastical authority (*sacerdotium*) are agreed," writes Ivo of Chartres, "the world is well ruled and the Church flourishes and bears fruit. But when they disagree, not only do less important interests fail to prosper, but those of the greatest moment fall into miserable decay." [1] It is obvious that civil authority can, and should, while keeping within its due limits, facilitate the mission of the Church. The making of good and just laws, the respecting of its citizens' conscientious rights, especially in regard to religion, the preservation of peace and order effectively assist the growth of God's Kingdom on earth; just as their contraries, social injustice, the absence of religious liberty, discord and anarchy constitute so many hindrances. Similarly, though at a much deeper level, the Church contributes within its own order to the well-being of the State: by inculcating respect for authority, fostering the observance of civil laws, upholding the moral standard and encouraging the practice of the social virtues.[2]

Concordats

It is beyond the scope of these pages to enter into the detailed relations of the Church with the modern State. Liberal democracy on the one hand, and the various forms of totalitarianism on the other, have given rise to a new set of problems, emphasised by the complete secularisation of politics and an attitude towards religion ranging from sceptical indifference to fanatical hostility; but the principles of their solution remain the same. The Church will always claim the right to judge of politics in their ethical and religious bearings; but she will never descend into the political arena or allow herself to be identified with any human polity. If her own prerogatives are infringed she will make known her protest, not indeed on account of mere prestige, but lest she prove unfaithful to her mission. In situations where the ideal is unobtainable, she will tolerate much that is imperfect for the sake of the good that may be preserved. It is thus that, without compromising her message, she comes to terms, by means of a *concordat*, with governments in many ways opposed to her own interests. Such a diplomatic instrument is a treaty between the Holy See and a secular State touching the

[1] Epistle 238; *P.L.* 162, col. 246.

[2] For the benefits conferred by Christianity on the State, see Pope Leo's Encyclical already quoted; *op. cit.*, pp. 53-56.

conservation and promotion of the interests of religion in that State. The extreme flexibility whereby the Church, in this way or by tacit agreement, can effect a *modus vivendi* with almost any political régime is a proof, not of unprincipled opportunism, but that she is committed to none. Here, as in many other of her activities, she may appeal for her mandate to the example of the Apostle Paul: "I became all things to all men, that I might save all." [1]

EPILOGUE

Indefectibility of the Church

By way of concluding our brief survey of the juridical structure of Christ's Mystical Body, which is the Catholic Church, we may note that it possesses the property described by theologians as *indefectibility*. The Christian Society, of its nature "far more excellent than all other associations of human beings, transcending them as grace transcends nature and as things immortal transcend all things that pass away," [2] is destined to survive until the end of time. "Unbelievers", says St Augustine,[3] "think that the Christian religion will last for a certain period in the world and will then disappear. But it will remain as long as the sun—as long as the sun rises and sets; that is, as long as the ages of time shall roll, the Church of God—the true body of Christ on earth—will not disappear." The reason for this power of survival lies, not in the Church's juridical elements, but in the indestructibility conferred upon her by the abiding presence of the Holy Spirit and of Christ himself.[4] The visible hierarchy, the elaborate Church organisation, being inseparable from human imperfections, though a part of our Lord's plan from the beginning, have not in themselves the stuff of immortality. This they derive from the sources of grace and divine life within, the hidden riches of the Mystical Body which constitute the veritable "Mystery of the Church." [5]

No one has put this point more forcibly than Pope Pius XII, in words that refute for ever the charge that Catholic Christianity oppresses the free life of the spirit under the weight of ecclesiastical formalism: "For although the juridical grounds upon which also the Church rests and is built have their origin in the divine constitution given her by Christ, and although they contribute to the achievement of her supernatural purpose, nevertheless that which raises the Christian society to a level utterly surpassing any order of nature is the Spirit of our Redeemer, the source of all graces, gifts and miraculous powers, perennially and intimately pervading the Church and acting in her. Just as the framework of our mortal

[1] I Cor. ix 22.
[2] *MCC* 61.
[3] *In Psalm.* lxx, n. 8.
[4] John xiv 16; Matt. xxviii 20.
[5] The title of an invaluable little book by Père Clérissac; it comprises an admirable series of meditations on the Church.

body is indeed a marvellous work of the Creator, yet falls short of the sublime dignity of our soul, so the structure of the Christian society, proof though it is of the wisdom of its divine Architect, is nevertheless something of a completely lower order in comparison with the spiritual gifts which enrich it and give it life, and with him who is their divine source." [1]

The Church lives by the Holy Spirit

It is by the Spirit within that the Church lives; it is by our correspondence with that Spirit that the Church grows, speaking metaphorically, to "the fulness of Christ." [2] While Christ and his members can never constitute physically one person, as some have mistakenly supposed,[3] there is yet a profound sense in which the final consummation of the Mystical Body will realise, as St Augustine saw, "the whole Christ," *totus Christus*. "It is due also to this communication of the Spirit of Christ that all the gifts, virtues and miraculous powers which are found eminently, most abundantly and fontally in the Head, stream into all the members of the Church and in them are perfected daily according to the place of each in the Mystical Body of Jesus Christ; and that, consequently, the Church becomes as it were the fulness and completion of the Redeemer, Christ in the Church being in some sense brought to complete achievement." [4]

The will of Christ fulfilled in the Church

So it is that the Catholic Church remains, now as ever, the ultimate hope of the world. She is the one supra-national force able to integrate a civilisation fast dissolving in ruins. Outside her visible communion there may be "broken lights," half truths of authentic Christianity; but only within the fold can men respond to the full and objective will of Christ. Fittingly we may end with the memorable words of St Augustine:[5] "Let us love the Lord our God; let us love his Church; the Lord as our Father, the Church as our

[1] *MCC* 61. Thus we are enabled to see how the overflowing richness of the Church's inner life can find expression in a great variety of rites and formularies. We may note in this context, and indeed on the whole subject of the reunion of Christendom, the significant words of the same Roman Pontiff: "We would have this to be known and appreciated by all, both by those who were born within the bosom of the Catholic Church, and by those who are wafted towards her, as it were, on the wings of yearning and desire. The latter especially should have full assurance that they will never be forced to abandon their own legitimate rites or to exchange their own venerable and traditional customs for Latin rites and customs. All these are to be held in equal esteem and honour, for they adorn the common Mother Church with a royal garment of many colours. Indeed this variety of rites and customs, preserving inviolate what is most ancient and most valuable in each, presents no obstacle to a true and genuine unity. It is especially in these times of ours, when the strife and discord of war have estranged men's hearts from one another nearly all the world over, that all must be impelled by the stimulus of Christian charity to promote union in Christ and through Christ by every means in their power." Encyclical *Orientalis Ecclesiae Decus*; C.T.S. trans., 27.

[2] Eph. iv 13. [3] *MCC* 85. [4] *MCC* 77.

[5] He is alluding to the schism of Donatus.

Mother. . . . What doth it profit thee not to offend the Father, who avenges an offence against the Mother ? What doth it profit to confess the Lord, to honour God, to preach him, to acknowledge his Son, and to confess that he sits on the right hand of the Father, if you blaspheme his Church ? Hold fast, therefore, O dearly beloved, hold fast unswervingly to God as your Father, and the Church as your Mother." [1]

AELRED GRAHAM, O.S.B.

[1] *Enarratio in Psalm.* lxxxviii, sermon ii, n. 14 : quoted from Leo XIII's Encyclical *Satis cognitum*, 29 June, 1896.

XXI

THE SACRAMENTAL SYSTEM

§ I: MAN'S APPROACH TO GOD

Composite nature of man

SINCE these essays make one work, and follow one another in a definite order, I might assume that readers of this one have read those that come before it, and therefore, the one that treats of the nature of Man.

However, I must be forgiven if I recall the essential point of that essay. Man is not an Automaton, nor an Ape, nor an Angel. By this I mean, a man is not just a piece of mechanism, like a steam-engine; nor yet is he merely an animal, that has but instinct and cannot think nor choose. Nor yet is he an angel, for angels are simply Minds—they have no bodies: "a spirit hath not flesh nor bones as ye see *me* having," said our Lord, when after the Resurrection the Apostles thought they were seeing a ghost. Man is Body-Soul. He is flesh-and-blood, *and* mind. Mind means the power of thinking, and the power of choosing. And in Man, Mind works along with the brain in a way which we need not here discuss, provided we remember it; and when I say "brain," I include all the rest that man's living body involves—the nervous system, the senses, the instincts. Therefore, whenever the ordinary living man feels, he also thinks; and when he thinks, his imagination and his emotions and his nervous system, and in fact all that is in him, respond and become active at least in some degree.

Therefore when you are dealing with man, it is quite useless to try to separate him into two, and pretend he is either just a body, or just a mind. This essay will show that God, according to the Catholic Faith, does not do so: but first, it is worth seeing that man, when he has dealt with God, or has sought to get into touch with him—in a word, to "worship" him—has always acted in accordance with this double nature of his: or, on the rare occasions when he has tried to do otherwise, has got into grave trouble.

I speak, of course, of the normal man behaving normally, and not of morbid, nor of mystical states; and, of course, I am speaking of man in this life, and not in the next.

Man's knowledge of God

From what I have said, you will see that man cannot so much as *think* of God as if man were merely Mind. He has to use his brain, and when he does this, he makes pictures with his imagination —even to-day, after all our training, we make some sort of picture to ourselves when we say the word "God." Even the Scriptures are full of phrases that represent God as though he were like ourselves—our Lord's eternal exaltation in heaven is described as

" sitting down at the right hand of God," " not," as the Catechism reminds us, " that God has hands." He is a Spirit: but we, being men, have to picture him to ourselves somehow. As a matter of fact, the human mind has always risen to the thought of God from the experience of material objects—that is, of course, save in the case of direct and special revelations: but these are abnormal and I am speaking only of the normal. For example, a quite uneducated man, call him a " savage " if you like, is quite able to rise from the spectacle of limited, changing things to the notion of that great Cause which must be at the back of them.

That he can do so is defined by the Vatican Council, though of course that Council does not say that all men as it were hatch the notion of God from what they see around them or that they do it in the same way, or successfully. In fact, experience shows that though the most simple man can quite well use the sight and touch of things in order to reach a notion of a God who made them, and keeps them, and arranges them, yet he can quite well go on to misuse his mind on the subject, and make many a mistake about it. For example, if he sees a violent storm, or a raging mountain fire, or volcano, he will very easily proceed to say that the God who is responsible for this must be not only powerful, but cruel or destructive. The fact remains that he has got, by means of his mind, to the thought of God, by way of his senses; and then has proceeded, also because of what he sees and feels, to use his mind awry, and to draw deductions that careful training would show him to be unwarranted.

Let us therefore keep to this conclusion—When a man so much as begins to think about God, he always starts from something that touches his senses, and he can never altogether exclude the fact that he is Body as well as Mind, and in his life never will so exclude it. Nor should he. It is quite useless to try to pretend you are something that you are not, and God does not mean you to try. Why should he? If he has made you a man, he does not wish you to behave as if you were something quite different, like an ape, or like an angel. Some men practically behave like the former, and you call them " sensualists." A minority of students and over-cultured persons would like to behave as if they were just minds—you call them " intellectualists." Each sort is lop-sided. You are sometimes tempted to think that the latter sort is in the greater danger. For the sensualist may always pull himself up—human nature does not take kindly to a complete collapse into animalism. But the man who despises material things is quite likely to experience a sudden fatigue, to give up, and to suffer a " reaction," and become extremely greedy for the good things of life. If he does not, he is none the less quite out of touch with ordinary men and women.

Worship

Now when a man is very convinced of anything, he always wants to *do* something about it. If he is a simple person, he probably does it at once, and rather noisily. With education, he may behave with greater restraint: but if he never tends to *express* himself, as we say, he is probably a languid and colourless person. If children are pleased, they jump and dance. When a man feels in good form, he sings in his bath. When he is in love he wants to kiss the girl he loves; and, in short, he wishes to do something exterior to give vent to the interior state of his feelings. So when men have been convinced of the existence of God, they have always done and said things to reveal the fact. They feel how small they are compared to him—they fall flat on the ground, or kneel. They feel he is good and great and takes care of them—they sing hymns or gesticulate or even dance. Above all, when they feel that everything, and themselves in particular, belongs to him, they have invariably tended to show this outwardly—usually by "giving" him something, to prove that they recognise his right to everything. Men interested in fields, will offer him field-produce: in orchards, fruit: in flocks, a sheep or goat or ox. This has gone so far that they feel they ought to offer him something which represents *themselves* even more adequately, and you find instances of men killing their eldest son, or mutilating themselves so that the "life-blood" flows. Why "killing"? It seems fairly clear that men, by destroying the "gift" they offer to God, are trying to prove to themselves, and even to show to God, that they truly recognise that he deserves the whole of the gift, and that nothing is kept in reserve: and that they must never take it back, because they have in reality no "right" in it at all. They will also feel the need of expressing outwardly what they think in their minds and picture with their imaginations, and so they make images, and surround these images with signs symbolical of the homage they want to pay to the invisible God. They will do all the things that occur to them; and everything that their senses or imagination can suggest does occur to them. They will burn sweet spices: they will light bright fires: they will sing and dance, and they will collect coloured flowers or stones or anything else that strikes them. And above all, since man is "social" and lives together in groups, of which he feels the unity very acutely, men will tend to do all these things in common, and make social acts of them.

This is what I mean by worship—any and every piece of human homage paid to God: and while it is quite true that the supreme and only necessary homage is that of the mind, whereby we know God, and the will, whereby we love him and choose to subordinate ourselves to him, yet man rightly tends to express himself exteriorly, and "cult" or "worship" has always, in accord with complete human nature, contained an exterior, material element.

It is well to see that neither in the Old nor the New Testament has exterior cult been disapproved of, any more than the use of our brains concerning God and the things of God has been rebuked.

It is perfectly clear from what I have said that just as a man can make all sorts of mistakes when he starts thinking about God, so he can make mistakes about the ways in which God likes to be worshipped. For example, the human sacrifices and mutilations I mentioned above are not really an apt way of expressing the completeness of our response to God's all-inclusive claim. So what you will find in the Old and New Testaments is a progressive check upon inadequate *ways* of showing your worship of God, but you will not find that the exterior worship is in itself condemned. The Hebrews inherited from their pagan ancestors a number of forms of worship, and picked up a number more during their sojourns among pagans. When Moses gave them their Law, he abolished many of these, and regulated others, and above all taught a true knowledge of God's nature and attributes so as to prevent a wrong meaning being given to the acts of worship they still used. The one thing that was absolutely forbidden was, the making of images of God for the *eye*. It was too easy for men to attach a wrong value—a " person-value," so to say, to such images. But the Hebrews still went on talking about God in terms that suit the imagination, for they were not abstract philosophers : and as late as you like in Hebrew history, ritual is very minute and exact, and even increasingly so in some ways. As to the New Testament, I say no more than this, so as not to anticipate : Our Lord shows perfectly well that he recognises the duty of expressing exteriorly our interior worship, if only because in the Our Father he provided his disciples with a form of words ; and what he rebuked was, not exterior actions, but the idea that exterior actions were good enough without interior dispositions, or, hypocrisy in the carrying out of such actions, for example, in order to win esteem, and not to worship God. And he himself, in the Garden of Gethsemani, allowed his body to reveal the agony of his mind, by falling prostrate, and lifted his eyes to heaven when giving thanks, and raised his hands when he blessed the Apostles, and by the use of clay cured the blind man, and by the use of formulas—like the very term " Father " as applied to God—sanctioned our drawing help from customary things of sense, and pictured heaven as a feast.

This leads me to my second point : the first has been, that man by his very nature tends to worship as well as think about God by means of his knowledge and experience of created things, and that God has not prohibited him from doing so.

§ II : GOD'S DESCENT TO MAN

I WANT now to go much further than this, and say that God not only as it were puts up, reluctantly, not to say disdainfully, with this sort of worship from the men whom he has made, but spontaneously deals with them in accordance with their whole nature, in which the material element plays so great a part.

God reveals himself through visible things

After all, God is himself the Author of nature. He could quite well, had he chosen, have created nothing but angels. (Even had he done so, the angels would have had to worship him, as in fact they do, in accordance with *their* nature.) However, he not only created this visible universe, but created Man in particular, and continually thrusts nature into his eyes and on to his attention so that to worship God by means of nature and in nature is the very suggestion, so to say, of God himself. St Paul[1] insists that men had no excuse for not knowing and worshipping God, since "what is invisible in God is (none the less) ever since the foundation of the world made visible to human reflection through his works, even his eternal power and divinity"; and to the Lystrians[2] he preaches a charming little sermon to those simple-minded pagans about how God has never left himself without sufficient witness, by means of his ceaseless gifts of rain and sun, of harvests and happiness. As I said, the nature of pagan notions about God, and worship of God, could easily degenerate; but the root of the matter is there, and was supplied by God himself.

Catholics hold, no less than the Protestant tradition does, that God revealed himself freely and specially to the Hebrews. From the first, we read how God revealed himself and worked through what struck the senses—objects, like the Burning Bush, the Pillar of Fire, the Glory over the Ark—in a sense, through the symbol of the Ark itself: phenomena, like the storm upon Mount Sinai: events, like the Plagues of Egypt. The rules for sacrifice and ritual were not just tolerated by God, but sanctioned positively by him: and, altogether, the Old Testament dispensation was so made up of material things intended to be used spiritually in a greater or a less degree, that the Prophets had to spend much more time in recalling the Jews to interior dispositions of soul than in exhorting them to be true to the details of the Law. I add, that God chose to reveal himself by means of writings—the Old Testament religion is a "book-religion"—and again, through men: prophets, priests and kings. And all this was essentially social: the People was held together not only by its worship of One and the selfsame God, but by tribal and national and family ceremonies, from what concerned marriage right up to the great festivals like the Pasch, the Day of Atonement, and Pentecost.

The Incarnation

Concerning the manifold reasons for, and nature of, the Incarnation, this volume already contains an essay. Let me then say here only one thing: It establishes once and for ever, and in fullest measure, the principle that God will not save human nature apart from human nature. The material side of the transaction of our Saving might have been minimised. God might have saved us by a prayer, a hope, by just one act of love. He might have remained invisible to eye, inaudible to ear. But he did not. He took our

[1] Rom. i.

[2] Acts xiv.

human nature—the whole of it. Nothing that is in us, was *not* in him. Jesus Christ was true God, and true Man. In him was that two-fold nature, in one Person. And indeed, in his human nature was that double principle that is in ours—there was body, and there was soul. In Jesus Christ are for ever joined the visible and the invisible; the Infinite, and the created, limited thing that man is: Man, in short, and God. Since, then, the Incarnation, no one can possibly criticise a religion because it is not wholly "spiritual." We are not wholly spiritual: Christ is not wholly spiritual. The religion that we need, the religion that he gives, will not be totally unlike what we are, and what he is. Christ did not treat us as though we were stones: nor yet, as if we were angels. He became Man, because we are men; and *as* men he, perfect Man, will treat us.

The work of salvation incarnational: the sacraments

You expect that a man's work will be characteristic of him. When therefore you observe that the whole method of our salvation was an incarnational one, wherein the Spirit operates in and by means of the flesh, you will expect to see this work itself out in detail. You see that it does so, first, in the massive fact of the sort of Church that Christ founded. The Church, existing as it does upon this earth for the sake of men who live on the earth and not for disembodied souls, still less for angels, is so constructed as to suit the situation. It is visible, yet invisible. It has its way in, and its way out. It has quite definite frontiers. It has a perfectly unmistakable form of government. Of the structure of the Church, this volume has also spoken. I need therefore not dwell on it, any more than I need upon the Incarnation itself. I need but add, that the nature of its Founder being what it is, and the nature of the Church being what it is, and our nature being such as we have described it, you cannot possibly be surprised if what goes on within the Church is in keeping with all the rest. The object of the Church being the salvation and sanctification of ourselves, the method of the Church will include and not disdain a material element. Even beforehand, we might have expected this, nay, felt sure that it would be so. In the concrete, this method will turn out to be, normally, the Sacramental System. This is what we have to study.

Let me but add, that we should be glad that this is so. Had our Lord given us a wholly "spiritual" religion (if such a thing is conceivable), we might have reproached him for neglecting those bodies of ours, which minister to us so much good pleasure, and provide for us such grave difficulties. We might have grieved that he had done nothing for our social instinct, that always, in every department, forces us to create some social unit or other. Again, knowing ourselves all too well, we might have felt that the ideal, just because so disembodied, would prove to be beyond us: we would be sure that the weight of our bodily humanity would sooner or later drag us down. After all, we must eat and drink: men marry: they mingle with their fellows—if we can in no way co-ordinate all this with what is spiritual, catch it up, use it, see how it is legitimate and can be made of value—we are practically being asked to despair of human life. On the other hand, if we see that no part of human nature is neglected by our Lord, we are, as I said, not only grateful but most humbly grateful, seeing that what has so often supplied material for sin is judged, by Christ, as none the less able to be given a lofty task, the sublimest duty—that of co-operating with Grace, nay, being used by Grace and in its interests. And once and for all, we see that God scorns nothing that he has made: that Jesus Christ was Man, not despising nor hating his manhood; that his Church understands, as he does, all that is "in man"; and that as the Eternal Son of God assumed a human nature, never to lay it down, so too in our very bodies, and helped by bodily things, we are to enter into that supernatural union with God through Christ, wherein is to consist our everlasting joy.

§ III: THE SACRAMENTAL SYSTEM

When we read the earliest documents relating to the Christian Church, we find Christians at once using all sorts of religious *behaviour*. They do not only pray, or propound a moral code—you find them being dipped in water: meeting for common meals of greater or less solemnity: "laying hands" on one another: maintaining the institution of marriage: anointing sick persons with oil: not eating certain sorts of foods: paying attention to certain days, such as that of the New Moon, and also the first day of the week, and sometimes adopting quite strange rites, like putting honey upon the lips of children or even adults.

Early developments

These rites did not all stand upon the same footing. Some were prohibited: some were tolerated or kept within certain bounds (like the observance of special days): some were regarded as quite exceptionally solemn, and were imposed officially. Looking at the matter from outside, you see, on the whole, that what these last-named had of special about them was, that Christ himself had instituted them, or at least his Apostles officially imposed or used them: and that they implied something beyond themselves, and even produced certain results in the soul. No one, for example, professed to suppose that Christ had ordered the observance of the New Moon: though placing honey on the lips of a child, or milk, might signify something spiritual, no one quite claimed that it produced any special result in the child's soul. On the other hand, you will hear expressions such as that we are "saved by means of the Bath of New Birth" (Titus iii 5): that the Holy Spirit, or Grace, is given "by means of the laying-on of hands" (2 Tim. i 6; Acts viii 18). And marriage is spoken of as a "mighty symbol" (Eph. v 25).[1]

[1] The word "*musterion*," here translated as "symbol," is explained below, p. 741.

It is easily seen that there was much here that might induce confusion, and even abuses, and needed clearing up. Indeed, the confusion is often manifest. Some people urged that it was better not to marry at all: others acted as though Christianity had abolished all restrictions upon whom you married. Some began to make life intolerable by introducing all sorts of food-restrictions; others went freely to pagan feasts. Some seemed to think that the "bath of New Birth" was meant to give you even bodily immortality: others that you could bathe in it vicariously, on behalf of those who had already died. Some turned the meals, taken in common, into an occasion for creating social cliques, and quite failed to see in the meal that which it stood for or signified—to put it at the lowest, for Paul makes clear that as the ceremony to which it was but a preface proceeded, there was more in it than just a noble or pure idea: the "Lord's Body" itself was to be discerned therein, to be fed upon as he had ordained, with vast consequences to those who thus received it. Hence even the preface to this, with its signification of union in charity, was being travestied by these social schismatics.

We must not be surprised that these Christian rites were not, at first, exhaustively explained, nor perfectly understood by all. Very little, in Christian doctrine, was or could be immediately stated in an adequate formula: even in the simpler matter of issuing orders, it was at once found that questions were asked, and interpretations had to be given. Thus, the Apostles decreed that meat that had been used in a pagan sacrifice must not be eaten. "What," asked the Christians, "are we to do when marketing? what, when invited to dinner? How can we tell whether the meat in the butchers' shops, or offered at table, has come from a pagan temple or not?" Such questions needed answering whenever they arose. So with dogma. The Christians knew that they worshipped Christ as God. "How then," some of them asked, "could he have been also man? He could not. His humanity must have been merely apparent—he was a ghost-man." "No," said the Church, "he was true man." Already St John has to make this point. Thereupon the pendulum swung back. "Then he cannot have been true God—his sonship can have only been one of adoption, not of nature. He must have been 'divine,' not God." "No," insisted the Church, "he was true God too." Questions and answers continued till the theology of the Incarnation, as we say, was worked out—the complete *theory* and the proper official expressions in which the dogma was to be stated were provided. The same sort of process is seen in regard of these pieces of ritual behaviour that the Christians carried through. It will be clear that I am not remotely suggesting that what we now know as the Seven Sacraments did not exist from the beginning, and exist in substance just as they do now: but, if I may say so reverently, the first Christians needed desperately to *use* our Lord Jesus Christ himself, rather than speculate about him—though the time came and came soon when they had to do that, and did it: and somewhat in the same way they were baptised, married, confirmed, went to Communion, but had no "covering formula," so to call it, to apply to all these transactions precisely from what we call the "sacramental" point of view.

Signs

You first see coming to light the notion that certain transactions are "signs"—they visibly represent something you do not see—an idea, or an event. Washing with water is a very natural symbol of spiritual purification; sharing in a common meal naturally symbolises social unity, and, indeed, the breaking of bread could well represent the sacrifice of Christ himself: oil had always stood for a symbol of health and well-being. Hence the word "mystery" began very soon to be used by Christians of their rites, and the Latin word "sacramentum" after a while began to be used as a translation of "mystery." But be careful about these words. "*Musterion*" originally only meant something "shut up," and then, something which had a meaning concealed within it, and then, just a "secret." The pagan rites known as "Mysteries" consisted in ceremonies of a symbolical sort, wherein religious impressions were made on the minds of the participants—for example, the solemn exhibition of an ear of corn represented the presence of a god: an elaborate dance or procession represented the progress of a soul in the underworld, and so forth. What the devotee had learnt or experienced was to be kept a dead secret. "Mystery," then, in this original sense has nothing to do with the word technically used now to mean a Truth in itself surpassing human intelligence, and needing to be revealed by God, and even so, not fully intelligible to our natural powers of thinking. Similarly, "sacrament" meant at first no more than a "holy thing," or rather, a "religionified" thing, so to say. It was first applied to money deposited by litigants in some religious place, or forfeited by the loser and given to religious purposes. It came thus to mean any solemn engagement, and in particular the military oath. As equivalent (very roughly: the Latins were not skilful in finding equivalents for Greek words) to "mystery," it meant little more than that what it was applied to was more sacred than its mere external nature would lead you to suppose.

But you see at once that this notion of "sign" extends so widely as to cover almost anything; similarly, almost any religious performance could be called a "holy thing," and indeed the word "sacrament" for a long time was applied to all sorts of religious activities—the Lord's Prayer was a sacrament in this sense. We ourselves apply the word "mystery" not only in the technical sense, but, for example, to the incidents commemorated in the Rosary, because they were material occurrences with profound significations. The notion then admits of much further definition.

It is at once clear that some "significant" transactions stood out as quite special because they had been instituted by Christ himself.

He said: "Go, baptise in the Name of the Father and of the Son and of the Holy Ghost." He said: "Do this in commemoration of me." Yet even this would not be sufficient as a definition of certain special transactions; for Christ told his Apostles to "Wash one another's feet," for example. Here is an obvious symbol, and it was instituted by himself, and the institution is duly observed from time to time in the Church even now. Yet it stood on quite a different footing, for instance, from baptism. But why did it do so?

Causes

Because it became clear that some of these signs were instituted by Christ to produce certain results in those who used them, and by no means ordinary results of a moral or devotional sort, such as the looking at a pious picture might do, or even what I have just quoted—the Washing of Feet. Our Lord says definitely that Baptism is necessary for salvation (Mark xvi 16); that to enter the Kingdom of Heaven you *must* be born again by water as well as by the Holy Spirit (John iii 5); and St Paul (quoted above) says we are "*saved* by means of the bath of New Birth." When, after baptism, hands are laid on the newly baptised, or when they are laid on those set apart for the Christian ministry, the Holy Ghost, and Grace, are said to be given "by means" of this laying-on of hands.

We see then that there exist in the Church certain material transactions, such that they stand as signs of something spiritual, and also, somehow cause and confer and contain what they signify, and that these efficacious signs were in some sense instituted by Christ himself. There is one more preliminary remark to be made.

The Sacramental System

I have called this essay *The Sacramental* "*System.*" This implies that Christ has not as it were instituted "sacraments" casually, but according to a principle; and that the sacraments are not thrown haphazard into the Church, but form an orderly series: not only that their existence is governed by an *idea*, but that an idea rules, no less, their number and their nature, gives them coherence and a unity. The idea that governs their existence has already been sufficiently, perhaps, explained. I therefore merely recall that it involves the doctrine that matter is not bad, nor to be despised, but can be, and is, made use of by God and by Christ and by the Church in the work of our sanctification. The opposite to this would be the doctrine that matter, or the body, or the visible world at large *is* somehow bad, and this doctrine was best seen in the sect of the Manicheans—a curious sect, Persian in origin, but made up as time went on of all sorts of ideas and practices. As a matter of fact, the notion has always existed in some shape side by side with the true Catholic one, which is, that nothing that God has made is bad, nor has it become bad since and because of the Fall. Right down to our own day, a false Puritanism has existed: the Middle Ages saw many strange versions of it, involving strange results, such as, that food, marriage, and in fact anything to do with the physical life of man, was bad, owing to his fallen state, or even to the essential badness of matter. It is no part of my duty to go into this here ; but you will see at once that the Sacramental System opposes this definitely. No part of God's creation is bad : every part of it can be used by God for the most spiritual purposes. The results, on the other hand, of the false doctrine have been very bad indeed. Men, by dint of thinking that matter and the body were bad, have developed a sort of insane hatred of them, and have gone so far in their desire to be rid of them as even to commit suicide. Or again, since they saw that they had not the strength thus to inflict pain and denial upon themselves consistently, they took refuge in the notion that their body was not really part of themselves at all, but that the real " self " resided somehow inside the body, like a jewel in an ugly and filthy case or shell ; and so they said that it could not really matter what their body did, because it was not really " they." They could then allow the body to indulge in every kind of debauchery, while still maintaining that their soul, or " self," was living a lofty and holy life. The sacramental doctrine of the Church prevents both these disastrous notions taking root amongst us. Even were the body no more than the shell of the soul, it has to be treated with extreme respect, and kept holy and pure, because it contains so precious a thing. But it is more than the soul's shell : along with the soul it constitutes " man " : and so, body must be saved no less than soul, and by means of bodily or material things the living man is approached and may be helped as well as by spiritual things. We thank God that this is so : were it not, we might despair.

When I said that the sacramental " system " also implies that the actual Sacraments can be arranged in an " order " of an intelligible sort, I meant that they could be thought of by us, in proportion as we understand them better, in that sort of way. Thus, there is obviously such a thing as *natural life*—the life by which we all of us live by dint of being born and not having yet died. In the essay on Grace you have seen that God has freely willed to make to man a " free gift " (which is what the word Grace really means), namely, a supernatural life which is in no way due to him nor can be earned by him, but which involves a far greater happiness and well-being for him if he lives by it. Now just as a man requires to be born in order to live at all, so must he have a " new birth " if he is to begin to live by this " new life." This New Birth is given by the first Sacrament, Baptism. After a while, boys and girls begin to " grow up " : they take stock of their position and responsibilities : also, their bodies and their minds change in many ways, and their human nature may be described as being " completed." They also require not a little strengthening, body and mind, during this period. In many ways the Sacrament of Confirmation may be regarded as fulfilling a like " completing " function in the supernatural life : it does not give that life, but it completes and establishes it, and St Thomas compares it to adolescence. As life proceeds, it is normal for men and women to go even further in the completing of their human life, by joining another life to their own in marriage. The Church does not substitute anything for human marriage, but it so infuses grace into and through the Christian marriage contract as to raise it to the dignity of a Sacrament, and a supernatural element enters into this great human crisis-in-life. Within the Christian Church, however, men may be called to consecrate their lives to the immediate service of God as priests. This choice and vocation are of such overwhelming importance, and so unlike anything else, that we are not surprised to see that Ordination, in the Catholic Church, is a Sacrament too, not merely a setting aside of a man for a special duty. But for the proper maintenance of any part of life, appropriate food has to be given : for the maintenance and development of the supernatural life it will be seen that there is in the Church a unique and a uniquely appropriate food, the Eucharist. Again, a man may fall sick : he thereupon requires doctoring : there is in the Church a Sacrament instituted precisely for the purpose of healing even the gravest sicknesses of the soul, which are all due to sin. But after all, no human life lasts for ever upon this earth : men die. When death is imminent, or probable, in how great a need does the spirit stand ! for the body and its brain can now no more assist it. At such an hour the supernatural life, too, runs its grave risks ; and the " Last Sacraments " are there to succour it.

Thus it will be seen that the Sacraments can all be thought of under the heading, or general idea, of " Life " and its needs. In this way their unity of purpose and order in action can be clearly seen, and more easily appreciated and remembered.

I have now to enter with somewhat more detail into the Catholic teaching concerning the various elements that make up a " Sacrament."

§ IV: THE THEOLOGY OF THE SACRAMENTS

It used to be said that the Sacraments, as Catholics understand them, were medieval inventions. Research showed that St Augustine, who died in 430, taught a fully " sacramental " theology. He was therefore said to be the guilty innovator. Finally it is clear that well before his time, in fact from the beginning, the Church contained the *fact* and, better than that, the *use* of those things which we now call Sacraments.

The Sacraments are signs

That the Sacraments always included and could not but include the element of " sign," " symbol," is evident. The water used in baptism symbolised at once the washing away of spiritual stains : also, as St Paul saw, it symbolised (especially when the candidate for baptism was often, though not always, *immersed* in the baptismal water) the complete passing away of the " old man," the merely natural man, and the emergence of the New Man, the supernatural self. The " bath " is a " bath of second and new birth." The Eucharistic meal symbolised forthwith a unity among Christians, in charity, which any common meal, taken among men, naturally symbolises even in our Western world, and still more in the Eastern one. The Bread, one loaf of many grains, symbolised that mystical Body of Christ which the Church is. And the Breaking of the Bread, the Sacrifice of Christ upon the Cross ; and again, the participation of all in that one Bread, the fellowship of Christians in Christ himself. The wine, again, so manifestly symbolised Christ's Blood outpoured in sacrifice, that the heresy of the Aquarians, who wished to use water instead of wine, stood condemned, if for no other reason, because the " sign " provided by the wine thus disappeared. The " imposition of hands," used in Confirmation and in Ordination, was even more obviously a sign of the giving of the Holy Ghost when the metaphor of " God's Right Hand," meaning that same Holy Ghost, was more in use than it is now. The hand, issuing from clouds, so common in ancient days, was at once recognised as meaning the Holy Spirit ; when the priest to-day, at the Blessing of the Font, plunges his hand into the water, this symbolises the same thing—the infusion of the Holy Spirit. Oil, used in Confirmation, Ordination, and in the Sacrament of the Sick, also carried an obvious symbolical value both to Jewish and ex-pagan converts. For, among the Jews, the olive had always gone along with the vine and the fig-tree as a symbol of prosperity, and oil had been poured on those who were consecrated to kingship and so forth, in sign of the gift of the richness of God's blessing. Among the Greeks, its use by athletes at once connected it with the idea of suppleness and strength. Marriage, even natural marriage among pagans, had always been fenced about with ceremonies expressive of union, even when that union was far rather one of possession by the man than of true union between two. But the very event of a marriage, necessarily expressing itself outwardly, enabled St Paul to present it as the sign and symbol of a far higher union, that between Christ and his Church, and indeed the metaphor of Espousal as applied to the union between God and the chosen people, or God and the individual soul, was quite ancient and familiar. Finally, the whole concrete behaviour of penitent and priest could not but express, exteriorly, the spiritual events of forgiveness and restoration to grace.

Naturally enough, those Sacraments which were not only most necessary, but whose institution was most vividly described in Scripture, and whose material element was most obvious, such as water, bread and wine, were most dwelt upon by early writers ; and, again naturally enough, the idea of their symbolic character was chiefly worked out in a place like Alexandria, where people tended to see signs in almost everything, and attached symbolical values to the most concrete historical events. The Latin world was far less inclined to look below the surface of things, yet here too from the beginning the " sign " value of Sacramental transactions is perfectly clear.

St Augustine, who was very fond of working out the notion of God's " traces " in nature—even in connection with such doctrines as the Holy Trinity—naturally elaborates the meaning of " signs " in general. He says that a " sign " is a thing which, because of its outward form which it thrusts upon the senses, makes something else, by its own nature, come into the mind. A Sacrament, then, he says, is a " sacred sign of a spiritual object." It is a natural object that evokes the idea of, because picturing, a spiritual object. Of course he says much more than this ; but we are keeping close to the " sign-element " in Sacraments.

As the Middle Ages began to dawn, it was seen that men were insisting rather upon the " mystery-element " in Sacraments, *i.e.*, of the hiddenness of what was in them, rather than on the manifesting of the spiritual and invisible by the material and visible. But the balance soon swung back, or rather, reached a good equilibrium—in Sacraments was seen *both* the outward sign, *and* the inward thing that was symbolised. The thing by its nature was " secret," because invisible ; but it was meant to become visible by means of what signified its presence.

Matter and form of Sacraments

I might perhaps just mention here that you may often read the phrase " the *matter* and the *form* " of the Sacraments. This is a philosophical notion that need not really delay us. In practice it means that the exterior element in the Sacraments can be seen as consisting of two parts, one more general, like the water in baptism —for water can stand for all sorts of things, as oil can, or bread—and the other more specifical and more accurately expressing what the general symbol really stands for in the circumstances ; this second part consists of words or their equivalent actions : thus " I baptise thee " shows for what, precisely, the water is being used, and what, in consequence, it symbolises : something more is required than the mere fact of meeting and living together, to show that a man and woman really mean to be husband and wife. And so for the rest.

These philosophical terms, derived from Aristotle, have been found useful, so as to make clear what are the essential elements of the sacramental sign, *i.e.*, what is necessary for the validity of the *sacrament*.

So far, then, it is at least clear how foolish are they who talk about Catholic Sacraments as " meaningless bits of ritual " and so forth. They include ritual ; but since they are essentially and from the nature of the case *signs*, they cannot possibly be " meaningless."

The Sacraments are causes

We have, however, insisted that the Sacraments are a very special sort of " sign." They are *not* mere pictures. The essence of the matter is seen in phrases like : " you are saved *by means* of the bath of New Birth." " The grace which is in thee *by means of* the imposition of my hands." If I decide to become a Christian, and then go through a ceremony to show that I have acted on my decision, that ceremony is a sign of my decision, but need not be anything else. If I went to Holy Communion, and it made me remember the Passion, and this memory touched my heart, my act of Communion might well count as a " commemoration " of the Passion, which occasioned my having religious sentiments, but it still would not be more than an exterior commemoration, even symbolical, of a past event, such as my touching my hat when I pass the Cenotaph, which may well fill me with affectionate or patriotic emotions and resolves. Nay, even though *on the occasion* of my doing this or that, God gives me grace, the thing that I do remains merely the occasion of that gift. Thus I might do a kind act to a sick man, and on occasion of this God might bless and help me. But the doing of that act would not be a Sacrament. You see then the difference between a sign which is a mere representation of something else; and a sign of something invisible which is the mere occasion of my obtaining that invisible thing; and a sign which is that *by means of which* I obtain the invisible thing it symbolises. It is in this last sense that the Sacraments are Signs.

Since the perfectly definite " by means of " so clearly to be read in the Scriptures, and the almost violent description of the effects produced by good or bad Communions, given by St Paul (1 Cor. xi), there could be no doubt as to the *work done* by the Sacramental Signs, which become, as Origen says (about 250 A.D.), symbols which are the " origin and fount " of the invisible thing they symbolise. The notion became clear precisely by way of that double nature of man on which we have already insisted. The Sacrament was one thing, and yet it reached and affected both elements in man, the invisible spiritual soul no less than the body. When these very early writers asked themselves *how* this might be, they contented themselves on the whole by answering: " By means of the Spirit or Power of God, working in " the water, and so forth. The fact that a Sacrament is an efficacious symbol, as we now say, was then clearly realised well before Augustine. Cyprian, indeed, insists that the Eucharist at once symbolises, and *is*, the Sacrifice of Christ; it is a representation which contains the reality. In Augustine, the notion of efficacy is so strong that he keeps saying that in the Sacrament it is Christ who acts; Christ who washes; Christ who cleanses. But it could still be argued that Augustine does not make clear the difference between a divine action *on the occasion* of a sacramental rite carried through and a divine action so bound to the rite that it is done through and by means of it. But you can see from an examination of his whole mind that if you had asked him directly this question: Am I given grace by means of the Sacrament? he would have answered: Yes. But as language became ever more exact, keeping pace with thought ever more accurate, the nature of the bond between the divine action and the sacramental sign become perfectly clear. Hugh of St Victor (*c.* 1140) says: A Sacrament is a corporal or material element, set forth exteriorly to the senses, which by its similarity portrays, and by its institution means, and by blessing contains, some invisible and spiritual grace. While Peter Lombard (*c.* 1150) says even more clearly: A Sacrament is properly so called because it is the sign of the grace of God, and the expression of invisible grace, in such a way as to be not only its image, but its cause.

What perhaps helped more swiftly than anything else to make this nature of a Sacrament—"efficacious sign"—quite clear, was a series of three questions: What exactly is it that is done to us by our using a Sacrament? Who can administer a Sacrament? if not just anyone, how far does the effect of the Sacrament depend on the person of its minister? and how far do my personal dispositions enter into the affair? does the good result obtained from using a Sacrament depend upon *me*? Many details of the answers to be given to these questions belong to other essays which deal with the Sacraments severally. Here I need do little more than get at the various principles involved, illustrating them by allusion to the several Sacraments rather than examining each Sacrament separately.

Causes of Sanctification

The answer to the first question—What does the (due) use of a Sacrament bring about in me? was easily and immediately answered—Sanctification. Baptism was from the very words of Christ seen to be absolutely necessary if the soul was to be saved at all. But salvation comes through grace and only through grace. Therefore sanctifying Grace is what is given through the use of the Sacraments. I need but add one point here. This grace is, quite simply, a divine life infused into the soul—a supernatural union with God. Grace then is always and everywhere one and the same thing. But Grace may be given to a soul in which grace is not—as to the unbaptised, or again, to those who by mortal sin have lost grace; or, more grace may be given to those who already possess grace. There may be the first infusion of Grace, or the restoration of Grace, or the ever renewed intensification of Grace. Already, then, you can see that though the gift be, in all the Sacraments, one and the same thing, yet it may be given in various circumstances, and in fact is variously given according to the circumstances of those using the various Sacraments—for example, Baptism, Penance, or Confirmation. However, this is not the only difference between Sacraments. Marriage and Ordination, for example, are not just means of providing more grace to people who happen to be going to get married or be ordained. They are meant to provide them with grace *because* they are going to be married or ordained; that is, grace so acting as to help them in their circumstances—to sanctify them precisely *as* married people or as priests. That is, grace is given not just in general, but in view of the state upon which its recipients are entering or in which they live and need special assistance. Baptism gives the first grace of all which unites a man to God through Christ: Confirmation establishes him in this: Penance restores a man to that supernatural life if he have lost it: the special needs of the married or of the clergy are obvious; so, too, are those of the sick: all our life through we have need of more and more grace, especially in difficult moments, and we gain it supremely through Holy Communion. This special grace is called "sacramental grace," to distinguish it from "sanctifying" grace at large.

Christ the author of the Sacraments

The fact that the whole existence of the Sacraments, and of each Sacrament, is concerned with the giving of Grace, involves a point so important that it may be touched on here. It is, that the Sacraments were instituted by Christ. Historically, this fact became emphasised for the very reason that we have been giving. It was because the Sacraments give grace that men saw, and insisted on, the fact that they were instituted by Christ; it was not because they were instituted by Christ that men concluded they gave grace. Both ways of looking at the thing can be true; but the former was the way in which men first and chiefly looked at it. The Sacraments give grace. But Grace is only given by God through the merits of Jesus Christ. Therefore if the gift of Grace is so annexed to the Sacraments as to make them (anyhow in the case of baptism) an instrument of salvation, they must have been of divine institution: but since everything in the Church, that is essential and substantial, was created by Christ himself upon earth, therefore the Sacraments were instituted not just by God, but by the God-Man, Christ.

Not that such a statement settles a variety of subsidiary questions, any more than the definition of the Council of Trent does, which simply states that the Sacraments were "all of them instituted by Jesus Christ"; and even the Modernist errors condemned by Pius X can be grouped under the general notion that it was not Christ who instituted the Sacraments in *any* real sense, but that they grew up under pressure of circumstances, either in the time of the Apostles or even after it, and began by being mere rites of various sorts, quite different in nature from anything we have been talking about.

This clumsy notion is as alien to facts as would be the idea that for a Sacrament to have been instituted by Christ, it was necessary for Christ personally and in so many words to institute it just as it is at present carried out in the liturgy of the Church. The earlier writers of the Church did not go into details on the subject: no one ever disputed that Baptism and the Eucharist were instituted by Christ in person and in a form from which the Church must never recede. But it was usually through something else that the point was reached and the fact asserted—I mean, for example, it was the habit of the Gnostics to appeal to a kind of inner light, as settling truth and right, which drove an Irenaeus to insist that the proper guardian of truth was the episcopate, whose origin was Christ himself by way of the Apostles, though Ignatius had already been clear enough on the subject.[1] But when it began to be thought that the administration of the Sacraments or at least their " matter and form " must always remain, and have remained, unchanged in every way, then writers were either forced to assert that Christ had so instituted them in person, or, since that would be very difficult and in fact impossible to show, that he need not have instituted them in person at all, but that, for example, the Holy Ghost, not Christ, instituted Confirmation, and a Church council in the ninth century instituted Penance (so Alexander of Hales, *c.* 1245). In this department, Dominican and Franciscan schools of thought seem to have clashed not a little, the Franciscan ones going too far away from the doctrine of institution by Christ himself—St Bonaventure, for example, allowing that Confirmation and Unction might have been instituted either by the Apostles or immediately after their death, though by divine authority. There was, however, current the idea that Christ might have instituted the Sacraments quite generally, and no more—that is, have appointed the divine effect, leaving the method of its obtaining to the arrangement of his Church. The real point is reached when one sees that a man can be described as " instituting " a thing whether he does so in detail, or whether he initiates a thing only " in the rough," and leaves the working out of it to others.

Take the case of Confirmation. You could, conceivably, imagine Christ saying : " When a man has been baptised, lay your hands on him and anoint him with oil, saying certain words : this sign will produce grace in him, such as to ' confirm ' him and ' complete ' his baptism." Or, " When a man has been baptised, he will require to be ' confirmed ' : do this by some suitable sign." Though the Council of Trent has defined that all the Sacraments were instituted by Christ, which settles for us that they were not merely invented by the Apostles, nor merely grew up under pressure of circumstances, yet that Council does not state in what way exactly they were instituted by Christ. It does not, to start with, follow that they were *all* instituted in the *same* way. But it would never be admitted by a Catholic theologian, and should not be asserted by any historian, that Christ merely gave the Apostles some vague hint that there were to be transactions of a sacramental sort in his Church, and then left them to do what they thought best in the matter. Apart from all other considerations, a historian would, I think, see that the older Apostles were so very conservative—and among them all, perhaps, St James the most conservative—that they would never have started anything at all unless they were quite sure that Christ meant them to do exactly that. Hence since no one ought to dispute that Baptism and the Eucharist were instituted immediately and explicitly by Christ himself ; and since the Apostles immediately began to confirm and to ordain ; and since it was precisely St James who promulgated

[1] Irenaeus fl. about 140-200 ; Ignatius, † 107.

what was to be done in the way of anointing the sick; and since it was St Paul (who positively piqued himself on not being an innovator) who declares the sacramental value of Christian marriage; and given Christ's assertion that those sins which the Apostles remitted were remitted, and those that they retained were retained—with the necessary consequence that they would be called upon at times to remit and to retain sins—we are right to be morally certain, historically, that the Apostles had Christ's direct order to do, in substance, all those things which we now know as the administration of the Sacraments.

Historically, then, we can show that all the Sacraments can be connected up with something that Christ said; and a foundation for the assertion that he instituted them can be found in his own words: the general behaviour and temperament of the Apostles bear out that herein they acted on some sort of mandate received from Christ in person: precisely in what way he gave it, save in the case of Baptism and the Eucharist, we cannot ever know. What further is certain is that the Church cannot substantially alter anything that he instituted, though in what precisely the substance of the material element of the Sacrament, by his order, consists, again can be matter for discussion. What the Church has the perfect right to do is to ordain that a Sacrament has now to be administered in such and such a way, under pain of its being illicitly or even invalidly administered. Thus the Church can add conditions to the administering of the Sacraments, but she cannot subtract anything in them that is of Christ's ordaining and has been substantial in them from the beginning.

The Sacraments and pagan mystery-cults

Our purpose is rather the explanation of Catholic doctrine than the refutation of false doctrines. It is however so often said, nowadays, that St Paul practically invented the Sacraments by introducing into certain current practices quite new ideas, that this theory has to be glanced at. I might notice, in passing, how far things have travelled since the time when the Sacraments were called "medieval accretions." So thoroughly "sacramental" is the earliest Church seen to have been, that no one short of St Paul is appealed to as the originator of Sacraments. Paul therefore is said to have borrowed religious terms and notions from the "mystery-cults" of the contemporary pagans. These mystery religions involved the exercise of a great deal of magical ritual (magic is spoken of briefly below) and the recitation of formulas, so that the "initiate," as he was called, became on the one hand much impressed by the uncanny spectacles he had seen, and, on the other, was convinced he now was guaranteed to escape the dangers in the next world which were calculated to befall one who found himself there without some such magical preliminary. In more philosophical forms of these cults, a good deal of allegory was introduced, and a more philosophical initiate might maintain that in some sense he was incorporated with the god in whose honour the mystery was celebrated. Indeed, the god's history might be enacted during the celebration by means of a symbolical dance or other piece of ritual. Briefly: Paul knew of, as did everyone, the existence and general nature of mystery-cults, and once or twice remotely alludes, with contempt, to them. The rule observed by himself, St John, and early Christians in general, with regard to pagan forms of worship, was to keep from all contact with them: their abhorrence of them was almost ferocious. Paul does *not* use any of the characteristic words of the mystery-religions; he insists that he introduced nothing into the Christian creed or code that was new—save, if you will, the emphasis laid by him on the truth that non-Jews were to be admitted as freely into the Church as Jews were, and that none of them had to observe the Jewish ritual. The mysteries moreover were expensive affairs, and reserved for a small minority who were pledged under secrecy to reveal nothing that they experienced; Christianity on the other hand was for all. Christianity was a doctrine; there was no doctrine in the mysteries—they affected not the intelligence, but the imagination and the nerves. The whole method and effect of the mysteries was "magical"—you recited the due formula, performed the proper programme, and the effects occurred automatically. There was nothing moral about the mysteries, the purity you there gained was merely a ritual one—in the concrete the celebration of the mysteries was anything but pure: one writer has called them a mixture of shambles and brothel. If anyone imagines that Paul is going deliberately to borrow or even unconsciously to absorb anything from such a source, with which to improve the Faith to which he had turned, we abandon such a critic as foolish, or, as determined to discover at any and every cost some non-Christian source for the Christian Sacraments.

The minister of the Sacraments

The Sacraments therefore receive their efficacy from Christ. What then is the rôle played by the "minister" of the Sacrament? for after all you cannot baptise nor confirm nor ordain nor anoint nor absolve yourself, nor can a layman at any rate consecrate the Eucharist; and though the man and the woman are the ministers, each to the other, of the sacrament of Marriage, yet each does require the other, and obviously cannot administer that Sacrament to himself by himself.

Again, the rôle of the minister in the administration of Sacraments did not come up on, so to say, its own merits, but, because of the claim of heretics to administer the Sacraments equally with the orthodox. This claim seemed so horrible to certain groups, or to fierce-tempered individuals like the African Cyprian that, on the grounds that where the Church was not, the Holy Spirit was not, and where he was not, nothing of a sanctifying nature could exist, and therefore not the Sacraments, they denied to heretic ministers the power to administer any Sacrament whatsoever validly. This dispute will be found explained, and the course it took, in the pages of this volume dealing with the Sacrament of Baptism. But behind that dispute existed the universally admitted certainty, that a proper minister is necessary in the case of each and every Sacrament, and the dispute really turned upon the question—Who *was* the proper one ? It was, all admitted, the " word " of the proper minister that made the bread to be Christ's Body, that made the water to be no mere water, but baptismal water. This conjunction of the word with the thing, so that a moral whole was created, supplied that due material element through which the Spirit of God could act. But the minister was not ever regarded simply as a man. Had he been so regarded, certainly much might have turned upon his moral or mental dispositions. But he was definitely regarded as representing, in his person, the Church ; and the Church was the continuation of Christ, and the dwelling-place of his Spirit. Therefore, albeit it was a man who spoke the words, Christ spoke through them—" Christ cleanses."

It is therefore certain that the moral condition of the minister of the Sacrament does not interfere with its validity on its own account. The mere fact that his soul has sin in it, does not render him useless as an instrument in the hands of the Church and of Christ, for the " making " of the Sacrament. It is desirable, in every way, that a priest, for example, should be a holy and even a cultured man. But the fact that he is immoral, or boorish, cannot affect the Sacrament as such. Certainly a devout priest will obtain, by his holiness and the fervour of his prayer, additional grace for those on whose behalf he administers a Sacrament ; but this is a consideration exterior to the essence of the Sacrament itself. Similarly, two people who intend to get married and go through the marriage ceremony in proper circumstances, may, if they be frivolous, obtain little enough actual grace, but they will be truly married, and have administered to one another the Sacrament. It is very important even here to distinguish between a valid Sacrament and a fruitful one.

The intention of the minister

Is there, then, no way in which the minister can interfere with the validity of the rite he accomplishes ? Certainly, but only one—that is, by not " intending " to accomplish a Sacramental rite at all, even though he goes through the ritual quite scrupulously. Illustrate this as follows. If an unbaptised person says to me : I do not intend to become a Christian, but I wish you would show me how people are baptised. And if I were to answer : Very well. I do not intend to baptise you ; but were I to do so, this is how I would do it—and proceeded to pour the water, pronouncing the words. I did not mean to baptise the person, and the person did not intend to be baptised ; therefore I did not baptise him despite the complete performance of the ritual. After all, this is the merest common sense. In just the same way, if a woman, for example, is forced to go through a marriage ceremony, and does so, but does not intend that her submission to the rite should mean a real marriage, married she is not. Observe what a denial of this would imply. It would mean that a woman could be married off, willy nilly, like a head of cattle. All civilised persons would reject so barbarous a notion.

However, just what sort of intention must the minister have? He must have "the intention of doing what the Church does." The Council of Trent, while defining that intention was necessary, did not settle whether a purely external intention of doing the rite properly sufficed, or whether some deeper kind of intention was needed too. It is at least certain that the minister need not personally believe that the Church's doctrine is true: provided he intends to do what the Church does, whatever that may be, he does do it. Of course, if the minister intends, positively, to do something different from what the Church does, he has not the requisite intention: I mention this, because while the ordaining bishops in the days of the Protestant revolution in this country would undoubtedly have said that they meant to do what Christ did when ordaining, and therefore, what his true Church did, yet they meant definitely *not* to create sacrificing-priests in the old sense; therefore they did not create them. Add to this that by changing the rite they showed that they had not the slightest intention of making priests in the old sense. So, owing to this lack of due intention (as well as for other reasons), the old sort of priest was not made. The traditional sort of Order was no more given.

Dispositions of the recipient

This leads us to the final question, How far do the dispositions of the recipient of the Sacrament affect its work in his soul? The question was most urgently asked when the Reformers began to say that nothing *save* the dispositions of the recipient mattered. There could be two extremes—one, where the action of the Sacrament would be described as purely mechanical; carry the rite through, and then, whatever be your interior dispositions, its effect is produced; this would be the extreme of "magic": the other extreme would involve (as among many of the Reformers it actually did) the assertion that the minister and the form of administration mattered nothing at all; all that mattered was the faith of the recipient: this would be complete subjectivism. Anyhow the question, so far as Catholic doctrine goes, has already been half answered above. If the subject to whom the sacramental rite is administered does not in any sense intend to receive the Sacrament, he does not receive it. I say, "in any sense," because there can be such a thing as a virtual intention: the recipient may be distracted at the moment and not think about what he is doing; or (in the case, for example, of Penance and the Eucharist) the action may have become so customary that he does what he does without reflecting on the nature of his action at all. However, were you to interrupt, and ask him what he intends to be doing, he would answer that he means to be getting absolved, or to be receiving Communion. He has therefore a virtual intention, and validly, so far as that is concerned, receives the Sacrament in question. Even an habitual intention—an intention once made and never retracted—suffices for the valid reception of any Sacrament except Penance and Matrimony, which, by reason of their special nature, require at least a virtual intention in their recipients.

The special question of Baptism being given to children is treated of in the essay upon that Sacrament. Enough here to say that the will of the Church, and in a sense of the parents or sponsors, creates a social solidarity such that the child, embedded therein, can be answered for by that will.

Obstacles to grace

But the real problem arises when a man approaches a Sacrament with such dispositions as to present an obstacle to grace. Such obstacle, in the case of the "Sacraments of the Living,"[1] would be *conscious* mortal sin; in the case of the "Sacraments of the Dead," *unrepented* mortal sin. The question is particularly important for those Sacraments which cannot be repeated—*i.e.*, Baptism, Confirmation, Order and Matrimony (which cannot be repeated, at any rate, while the matrimonial bond persists). If I approach these sacraments with an obstacle to grace, yet desiring to receive the Sacrament, I am indeed validly baptised, confirmed, ordained, or married, but, I cannot actually receive grace (which is the union of the soul with God), since I am all the while resolving to be disunited from him. What then happens? Theologians teach that the grace of the Sacrament is produced in my soul when I remove the obstacle set by my evil will.

Effects "ex opere operantis"

Does this then mean that the whole of the effects of the Sacraments are achieved within me if I merely interpose no obstacle of evil will to those effects? Is grace given *wholly* "ex opere operato," as they say—by means of the work *done?* the mere subjecting myself to a certain rite? By no means. There is also the effect which comes "ex opere operantis," which means, through the effort I myself put into the transaction. If I approach a Sacrament without an obstacle to grace indeed, yet dully, Grace will no doubt reach me: but if I approach it with, so to say, an appetite, Grace will be appropriated and assimilated by me far more richly. All our Christian religious life, and our sacramental life most certainly, is in reality co-operative. The special feature about Christ's activity is, that it always comes first—the very impulse to seek or desire a Sacrament or any other good thing comes from God before it exists in our own heart; and that it creates, and creates what is supernatural, whereas our own best efforts, unaided, cannot create more than what is commensurate to them, that is, what is natural. I cannot lift myself up by the hair of my own head.

[1] The Sacraments of the Living are those which presuppose the state of grace in the recipient—*i.e.*, all the sacraments except Baptism and Penance, which two are called Sacraments of the Dead.

The Character

Three Sacraments, then, produce an effect such that they cannot be repeated. They impress upon the soul what is called a "Character," or seal. The sacramental "Character" is not grace, but is a separate effect produced in the soul by the three sacraments of Baptism, Confirmation, and Order. They place my soul for ever in a special relation to Christ, and I cannot be replaced in it. I am for ever a baptised, confirmed, or ordained person. Even apostasy cannot alter this fact. Even though, by my evil will, I prevent the Sacrament from producing grace within me, yet I cannot prevent it from producing this "Character," if I will to receive the Sacrament validly at all. The theory of the Sacramental Character followed on the Church's consistent practice of not re-baptising, re-confirming, re-ordaining anyone who had properly been baptised and the rest. The controversies on this matter concerned, not the principle, but the concrete question whether so and so had been properly baptised, and the rest. I think that further discussion of these points, and of allied speculations, is now unnecessary.

The Sacraments and "magic"

Certain critics of the Catholic Faith and practice are never tired of denouncing the Sacraments as pieces of "magic." It is seen by now how wrong at every point they are. A magical transaction would be of the following nature. I repeat a formula, or perform an act, like "Open Sesame!" or, sticking pins into a wax figure of my enemy, either without knowing why, or merely because someone whom I consider to know why tells me to. Automatically, an effect takes place, such as a door opening, or the sickness and death of my foe. All I have to do is to carry my part through with mechanical accuracy. In the use of a Sacrament, first of all, the rite *means* something: it is a sign. Further, I use that rite because *Christ*, the Son of God, appointed it and told me to use it. Further, I do so, not because there are any mechanical consequences attached to it, but because it is the cause in me of Grace, a purely supernatural thing of which God alone is the origin and giver. Again, he who administers to me that rite, does not do so in any private capacity, nor because he has the key to certain spells or pieces of esoteric knowledge, but because he acts as the Church's minister, and she acts in him, and Christ acts in her. Finally, whether or no the Sacrament be fruitful in me depends on my intention and will, wholly or in part. Hence at no point do a magical transaction and a sacramental transaction coincide.

Synopsis of the teaching of the Council of Trent

Before concluding, it may be of service to summarise the teaching of the Council of Trent, our classical source of information, upon the Sacraments in general. That Council denounces those who should say that the Sacraments of the New Law were not, all of them, instituted by Christ, or, that they are more, or fewer, than the seven often enumerated above. That any of these is not a true and proper Sacrament. That these Christian Sacraments differ in no way from Old Testament Sacraments save in their ceremonial. (Observe, that this implies that there were Sacraments under the Old Law, but that they were different from ours. The main differences are, that the Old Testament Sacraments were indeed Signs instituted by God, but that they looked forward to and promised the Grace of Christ, yet did not impart it : in so far as they were efficacious signs, they effected not a moral, but a legal and ritual purity.) The Council proceeds to denounce anyone who says that the Seven Sacraments are all of them on an equal footing, so that none is in any way nobler than another (clearly Baptism, an absolutely necessary Sacrament, is on a different footing from Marriage or Ordination, since no one is obliged to get married or ordained). That the Sacraments of the New Law are not necessary for salvation, but superfluous, and that without them or the desire of them a man obtains the grace of justification from God by means of faith alone. Not, the Council adds, that all the Sacraments are necessary for each and every man. The allusion to the " desire " for a Sacrament alludes primarily to " baptism by desire," which is explained in the essay on Baptism : briefly, it means that if a man does not know of Baptism, he can (by means of an act of perfect charity, that is, of love of God for his own sake, and of detestation of sin for his sake, with the implied readiness to do all that God might command him, if he knew it) obtain grace and salvation. Similarly, if he knows of Baptism, and wishes for it, and cannot obtain, *e.g.* anyone to baptise him, or water, he can cleanse his soul from sin, as I have just explained. The " faith " alluded to by the Council means faith as Protestants conceived of it, *i.e.* trust. The Council further denounces one who should say that Sacraments exist only in order to nourish faith in the recipient. That they do not contain the Grace that they signify, or do not confer that grace upon those who interpose no obstacle, as though they were merely external signs of grace or justice, received by means of faith, or were mere marks, as it were, of the Christian profession, whereby believers might be distinguished from unbelievers. Or that Grace is not always given, and to all, so far as God's action goes, even if the Sacrament be duly received ; but only sometimes, and to certain persons. (This regards the false Protestant doctrines of predestination, according to which God so predestines certain souls to hell, that no matter what they desire and do, they are not given Grace.) Or that Grace is not given through the Christian Sacraments " ex opere operato," but that sheer trust in the divine promise suffices for the obtaining of Grace. That the three Sacraments, Baptism, Confirmation, Order, do not impress a " character " on the soul, that is, a spiritual and indelible sign, so that these three Sacraments cannot be reiterated. Or that all Christians have power to celebrate and administer all the Sacraments. That the intention at least of doing what the Church does is not required in the ministers when they celebrate and impart the Sacraments. That a sinful minister, who observes all the essential elements in the celebration or imparting of a sacrament, yet does not celebrate or impart it at all. Finally, that the traditional Catholic rites, wherewith the Sacraments are surrounded, can be despised, omitted, or altered at the whim of any and every pastor.

As for the errors of Modernism, condemned by Pius X, which concern the Sacraments, I have sufficiently indicated their general character. Those which touch upon the nature of Sacraments at large are, that the opinions concerning the origin of Sacraments, entertained by the Fathers of the Council of Trent and doubtless colouring their dogmatic decisions, are very different from those which are now rightly admitted by those who study the history of Christianity. That the Sacraments took their rise from the Apostles and their successors who interpreted some idea or intention of Christ according to the suggestion or impulse of circumstances. That the aim of Sacraments is merely to recall to men's minds the ever-beneficent presence of the Creator.

How such doctrines fly in the face of the traditional Catholic dogma concerning the Sacraments must by now be clear.

§ V: RECAPITULATION

TURNING our eyes back, then, to those brief records of the life of Christ that the four Gospels are, we see that the Eternal Son of God was sent to redeem our race, and to elevate it to an unthinkably lofty state of union with its God, and was sent to do all this as Man, and by means of his manhood. We see that no thing that was in man did he despise: no human element did he fail to make his own. He did not, if I dare say so, just verify in himself the definition of "man," but in every way he lived as man in this our world of human men and women and of all material things. In his teaching he constantly helped himself, and his hearers, by using the things he saw around him for the conveying of his doctrine; and submitted himself not only to the rich and meaningful ritual of the Law, and was circumcised, and went to the Temple feasts, and observed the Pasch, and so forth, but spontaneously, for his own reasons, sought for and carried through an action that in his case seems to us almost uncalled-for. He was baptised by John. Thus Christ our Lord was human, and lived as man among men, and used all simple and human things during his life, and caught them up into his own spiritual life, and wove them into his teaching.

Hence we are not surprised to find him saying that we too, his disciples, are to be dipped in water; salvation is to come, not just to him who "believes," but to him who believes and is baptised. If we are surprised at anything herein, it is at the sudden increase of solemnity that invests his words when this topic of baptism arises. When after his resurrection he sends forth his Apostles to that world-wide, world-enduring work that he came to inaugurate, he bids them not only to baptise, but to do so in a manner that involves the invocation of the whole of the Most Blessed Trinity—the Father, the Son, and the Spirit, are all knit into this tremendous act ; and into it, you would say, all that is, is taken up—man's new birth, that transforms him from being child of earth into son of God, takes place by means of " water and the Spirit," the two in conjunction and co-operation : the new World of Grace is definitely seen in mysterious parallel with that first creation, when the Spirit of God was borne over the face of the watery abyss and earth took shape and the world grew into life.

Along with this, at the most solemn hour of all, when he was about to leave the house where for the last time before his Passion he had eaten with the men he loved and chose, he orders them to do what he has just done—to take bread, to bless and break it—to take wine, and to bless it—and then to partake in what has been blessed, because it is his Body and his Blood—Himself. What should be the consequences of entering thus into himself, and receiving himself into us, if not the living by an intertwined life, his and ours ? We become " one thing " with him, even as he with the Father is " One Thing." And if indeed it be true that without the New Birth by water and the Spirit, we cannot be said to live at all from the Christian point of view, so, in his words in the synagogue of Capharnaum, he insists and re-insists that without this eating of his Flesh and drinking of his Blood, we cannot maintain that new life, still less develop it and bring it to its consummation.

There is another moment of exceptional solemnity—when, breathing on his Apostles, he tells them that they now possess the Holy Ghost, and adds that the sins they remit, are remitted, and the sins that they retain, are likewise retained. Elsewhere, doubtless, he definitely wishes his Apostles to give a special, healing, Christian care to the sick ; and certainly he insists that the old permission for divorce, dating from Moses, was now to be regarded as over and done with, and indeed become impossible, for it is God, he says, that joins the hands and lives of those who marry.

Sometimes, then, by solemn declarations, sometimes by gentle hints and suggestions, amplified, it may be, in unrecorded parts of his instruction during those Forty Days after his resurrection when he must have fulfilled his intention of telling them the " many things " that earlier they " could not bear," or, perhaps, left just as hints to men whom his Spirit was going to guide into using even his hints aright—well, by grave asseverations, or by quiet suggestion, he prepared the Apostles for their work, and started them off on that career which was to be theirs, and which was to continue itself in all the Church's history.

Pentecost comes : the Spirit is given, and the Apostolic Age of the Church's history begins. From the outset we see that there is one Gate into that Church—Baptism. " Here is water ! What hinders me from being baptised ? " asks the convert officer. Without the slightest question, Baptism follows upon conversion. This mighty action is installed upon the very highest plane : there is One Baptism just as there are one Faith, one Lord, one God. Into the baptismal laver we descend, just the men to whom our mothers gave life : we come forth therefrom, a New Creation, new-born, Christ-men : our lives are hid in Christ, and in us, Christ lives. And forthwith after Baptism we see the Apostles again without discussion " laying hands " upon the new Christian, and at once the Holy Ghost is given ; and similarly, when men are set apart for the Christian ministry, hands are laid upon them, the Holy Ghost descends, and a permanent gift exists within the man by means of this imposition of hands, so that it can be invoked, and stimulated by the will of him who has received it, for it is always there.

Marriage, too, is declared by Paul to be a mighty " mystery," or symbol : henceforward it is not to be thought of save in terms of Christ and of his Church, between whom Grace has achieved an ineffable espousal ; and James, manifestly initiating nothing but setting order in and explaining a rite already familiar and authoritative, bids the sick to be anointed so that sins be forgiven them, and they be saved. And even in life, men can be (as St Paul's action with regard to the incestuous Corinthian proves) cut off from the body of the Church, handed over to Satan, and thereafter, on the Apostle's own terms, reinstated.

Finally, yet with paramount dignity, the Breaking of Bread is established among Christians, and Paul leaves us in no doubt as to its meaning. It involves a real participation in the life and sacrifice of Christ, such that the soul, that shares in that Feast unworthily, becomes guilty in regard of the Body and Blood of Christ himself, and sickens to its death. The Eucharist is, in a unique sense, what it signifies.

The Apostles passed : the Christians of the Early Church continued happily—heaven-wise happily in their human-wise tragic conditions—living their Christian life ; living in company with Christ, and experiencing his presence, experiencing too those overwhelming gifts of the Spirit that were so necessary in days when there was no other accumulated experience such as we have, of what Christianity means and can do for men ; and using in all simplicity the practices that they had been taught to use. For a while there was little enough speculation, though even from the outset they began to draw conclusions—sometimes exaggerated and mistaken ones, as when it seems pretty clear that some of St Paul's converts were so impressed by the " life " which they had understood was given by Baptism, that they were surprised and almost shocked when a convert died so much as physically, and anyway, felt sure that there must be some method of baptising, by proxy, those who had already died but would, they felt certain, have wished for baptism had they lived.

Others soon enough were to surmise that Communion—that " medicine that makes immortal "—must confer even bodily incorruption ; and others, again, began to wonder whether the Holy Ghost did not somehow actually take up his dwelling in the baptismal water, and whether the reality in that water were not somehow similar to that veiled beneath the Eucharistic Bread. It will be noticed that all the mistakes lie on the side of *reality*, not of understatement, so very far were they from imagining that the Sacraments were mere ways of suggesting pious thoughts, of evoking faith, and so forth, or that the virtue of the Sacrament was wholly in the well-disposed recipient.

Naturally, the two all-important Sacraments, Baptism and Eucharist, the necessary ingress into the Christian Life, and the unutterably precious " daily bread " of the living soul, were what immediately and outstandingly occupied the minds of those who had, after all, constantly to make use of the latter when once they had made the vitally necessary use of the former. Naturally, too, I suppose, it was in the Latin half of the Empire—Africa, at any rate—that attention was first notably given to the Sacrament of Penance—that rectification of violated Law. The Romans always understood Law better than the Greeks did ; and the lawyer Tertullian, the first Christian thinker who wrote in Latin, began according to his temperament to think this topic out. Doubtless that same temperament, hard and even ferocious at times, caused him to err in his views of the merciful Sacrament : still, he rendered great services to those who were, more accurately, to follow him. At first it may seem strange that along with Penance, Confirmation claimed his more close attention. Yet not strange ; for Tertullian, personally, and like all good Roman men, was a soldier, and in the vigorous Sacrament he detected something that harmonised with his idea of what a Christian, militant in this antagonistic world, ought to be.

Not much later, another African, Cyprian, again rendered great service to the better elucidation of the Sacraments of Baptism and of Order, because the tendency of his compatriots to split off into a mere nationalist church, forced his attention to all that concerned unity and schism ; and so passionate was his abhorrence of the latter, that inevitably he tended to deny to heretics and schismatics powers that they actually possessed, or could possess, those, that is, of ordaining and baptising. Here then the question of who was the due minister of these or of other Sacraments began to get aired, and again, of Intention ; and again, the fact of the non-repetition of Baptism, Confirmation, and Order, if once it could be shown that they had been properly conferred, struck out the clear notion of the sacramental Character or Seal ; while the deaths of unbaptised martyrs brought into the open the idea of baptism of blood, and by desire. Even the tremendous importance seen to belong to the Blessing given by the minister of a Sacrament, to the material element used in it, made a remote preparation for that theory of "matter and form" in Sacraments that was to have so great an historical importance later on.

Thus little by little the thing that Christians had always possessed and serenely made use of, came to be better understood, more clearly described and defined, shielded against abuse, linked up with other parts of the Christian Faith and practice, and to take its place within that mighty system of Theology that the ages are still bringing towards perfection.

The colossal figure of St Augustine dominated the imagination of the centuries that succeeded him: he did not complete the theology of the Sacraments; but scattered up and down his works may be found practically all the elements that were to compose it. It was he, perhaps, that brought into prominence the action of Christ himself in the several Sacraments, and who developed the notion of Character, and again, of that revival of Grace of which we spoke, when an obstacle placed by the human will in the way of the fruitful effects of a validly administered Sacrament was at last removed. This cleared up most usefully the problem which confronted those who observed that heretics of a manifestly rebellious sort were ordaining priests, who themselves continued rebellious and ill-disposed. They had felt it was all or nothing—either these ordinations were valid, and then it looked as if a contumacious rebel could confer grace upon another contumacious rebel; or, that the ordination was not valid at all, and must be repeated when the heretic was converted. In its measure this problem had affected Confirmation too and even Baptism. However, the explanation that a Sacrament could indeed be valid and therefore produce the Character, although grace was excluded so long as the obstacle remained,[1] solved the difficulty, which returned however, when in the bad centuries of Europe the reformation of incontinent clergy which had obtained its ecclesiastical position by simony had to be thought of. The practical question of whether these men had to be re-ordained when they repented could be solved along Augustinian lines without much difficulty.

As I said, the theology of St Augustine contained in itself practically all the elements of a complete treatise upon the Sacraments. Not much was left to do but to co-ordinate them. When therefore all the elements which compose a Sacrament in the strict sense were set before the eyes, it was easily enough seen that seven rites, and no more nor less, contained them all. Hence we are not to be surprised when we find that a writer so far forward in the Church's history as Peter Lombard (*c.* 1150) was the first definitely to catalogue the Sacraments as Seven. Other rites were seen to approximate to them, and to contain some but not all of the requisite elements,

[1] There are theologians who suggest that *all* the Sacraments give grace that revives when an obstacle, set by sinful will, is removed.

and could be called with greater or less accuracy Sacramentals, but not Sacraments.

I think it may safely be said that after the Middle Ages little more that was constructive in sacramental theology was done. Certain points were cleared up—the distinction between the *opus operatum* and the *opus operantis* was made explicit; the kind of causality brought into play when a Sacrament was described as "causing" Grace was thought out, and so forth. Since then what has really happened has been that the history of the several Sacraments has been far more closely studied, and the Catholic theory has been defended against attacks far more vigorous and definite than the old ones were. For of course the religious revolution of the fifteenth and sixteenth centuries, with its claim to reinstate Christ in the position from which the cultus of Saints, ritual, sacerdotalism, the Papal authority, and so forth were said to have dislodged him, did all that it could to discredit the Catholic doctrine with regard to Sacraments in particular. If you had to find one word in which to crystallise the Catholic sacramental tradition, I think it would be "Efficacy." The Sacraments are, as we see, efficacious of themselves. It was this that the Reformers attacked. A Sacrament was an absolutely inert thing. They could not eliminate all the Sacraments (as a matter of fact, the Quakers did, as the Salvation Army to-day also does), but they got rid of five out of the seven, and then stripped the two that remained of any intrinsic value or force. The whole "work" was done by the recipient. He arrived with that trust in God to which the word "faith" was attached, and on the grounds of that faith, good was accomplished within him. At least this much credit has to be given to the Reformers—they believed in certain fundamental things, such as sin and grace, forgiveness and salvation, to which modern creeds pay practically no attention at all. None the less, the Reformation was the immediate ancestor of that scepticism which to-day pervades almost everything religious, and has succeeded in making modern non-Catholics forget, above all, anything connected with the dogma of the Supernatural as such. But, as we saw, the Sacraments have no meaning save on the Supernatural plane.

Catholics may well be grateful for the institution by our Lord Jesus Christ of those Seven Sacraments that we have been speaking of. We have had once or twice to look aside from the Catholic doctrine to those alien systems, or that alien chaos, that confronts all that we mean by the Sacramental System. We can afford to smile when non-Catholics talk of "meaningless" or "magical" rites, and we need not retort with gibes of "subjectivism," for not only are all gibes, directed even to the most mistaken of honest and sincere men, out of place, but they have practically come to be off the point, for, save among Catholics, there is to-day very little theory about Sacraments at all, and less and less use of them or of their substitutes.

As always, this doctrine carries us back to the love of God for man. Why, unless God had loved us, should he have willed so much as to offer us the gift of Supernatural Life, and why, save again because he loved us, should he have willed to restore to us that life, once our race had lost it through sin ? Well, he did decree to restore us to the place from which the race, in Adam, had fallen ; and that restoration was not to be done as it were in some technical way, as though, for example, God taught us just how to make a "good act of contrition," and thereupon pronounced us once again his sons. The redemption and restoration of mankind was to be done through God's eternal Son taking our human flesh so as to knit up our nature with his divine nature into one person, Jesus Christ. This torrential invasion of God's love makes any sacramental doctrine we may proceed to tell of quite "natural," since never can the Sacraments catch up, in their tender intimacy, with that tremendous and total approach of God in human guise. Or is there a way in which one of them, at least, so catches up ? I suggest it in a moment. At any rate, God has entered our world as man, and in a sense Christ himself can be called the Supreme Sacrament, since his humanity veils, yet is the vehicle of, his invisible divinity, and through that Humanity the eternal God energises and does his work in our souls if we but make use of him.

But, after all, Jesus Christ our Lord no longer treads this earth. He has left it, and "sits ever at the right hand of the Father." Yet would he not leave us desolate and without himself. In that visible-invisible Society which the Church is, he continues himself, and in the Church lives and teaches and rules and gives life to the world.

But that Church, like her Head, has never preached some chill doctrine of the salvation of our souls such that we must think that our bodies are of no interest or value. We are and ever hereafter shall be true men, body-soul, however much our bodies shall be perfected and exalted by glory. And in many ways, though in seven chief and special ways, Grace, that is the germ of glory, reaches us, and all of these ways most mercifully take into account our bodies as well as our souls. Simple elements are taken up by Christ, and are made the visible part in those transactions through which we appropriate salvation. For ever, henceforward, Water must be regarded by us with awe and affection, since Christ has used it in his Sacrament of Baptism. Drowning and barren water has become that which washes from us all spiritual stain, and that from which we ascend, new-born sons, to God. He takes that ancient gift of Oil, in which our forefathers saw so many hints of the richness and grace of God, and anoints and consecrates us by its means—anoints our youth, that it may be strong for God and joyous in God ; anoints the men who are to be priests, the royal priests, of God Most High ; anoints too those sick who stand in such special need of consolation and spiritual power. Is there not a quite special tenderness in the fact that the Sacrament of Marriage takes—not, this time, some non-human element, but the human action and will of two human beings who should love one another and who desire to join in building up that true vital cell of the full human life, which a home is ? The contract that these two freely enter upon is the very stuff of God's Sacrament ; and, again a special delicacy of his goodness, it is these same two, the man and the woman, who are ministers of this Sacrament, and give to one another the Grace of Christ. For my part, I cannot but see once more in the Sacrament of Penance a great revelation of the gentle " homeliness " of our Lord, since here too he refrains from introducing some alien material on to which the divine forgiveness may descend and in which it may operate. Here too the material element in the Sacrament consists in human acts—in the acts of that very penitent who might be thinking that he was not so much as worthy to enter into the house of his Father, nor lift up his head in the presence of his offended God. No. God calls him to his side, bids him confess his sins, and then uses the acts of contrition and resolution, as of confession, nay, uses the very sins themselves that the penitent has spread forth before him as that wherein his healing Grace may work.

But it is the Eucharist beyond which the inventiveness of God's humble love could not proceed. God takes, once more, the simple elements of Bread and Wine, and, this time, not only becomes as it were their partner in the sacramental work, but, leaving only their appearance for the sake of our poor senses, transubstantiates their reality into his most real Self, so that the Gift here is the Giver ; the means have become the End. We are given, not a memory, not a hope ; not a metaphor, not an instrument, but himself.

We shall then be wise to practise *living* as it were upon this Sacramental principle. We shall seek ever to look below the surface. We shall see in all nature traces of God's presence and of his power. We shall reverently anticipate, as it were, the Church, by creating " sacramentals " for our own use, by seeking to see God in all things, and above all in our fellow-men, by worshipping him there—for there indeed and of necessity he is—and by drawing thence his reward, which is grace, love, and truth. But this is matter for our private devotion ; and though we are wise to keep that devotion in the framework, so to say, of the Church's sanctioned ideas, yet we shall be wisest of all to recall continually those great Sacraments that we have received and can receive no more—Baptism, that opened every grace to us : Confirmation, that established in us that Christian Character owing to which we can call on the Indwelling Spirit, as by right, to succour us : and above all we shall be wise and acting rightly if we make the maximum of use of the two great Sacraments of Penance and of the Eucharist, wherefrom we draw sure and certain healing if we are sick, even if we are spiritually sick to death, and increase of soul's health and strength if, as God grant, there be life in our souls and sin be absent from them.

Finally, we shall pray for those who know nothing of these Sacraments : we shall pray that all men and women now alive may make those acts of faith and contrition upon which all the rest of the spiritual life is built (for they involve, too, charity), and we shall ask that as many as possible may pass from the realm of desire and what is but implicit, to the full, conscious, deliberate and most joyous appropriation of all the riches of our God.

C. C. MARTINDALE, S.J.

XXII

THE SACRAMENT OF BAPTISM

§ I: INTRODUCTORY

Baptism shown to be a Sacrament

OUR Blessed Saviour, after his Resurrection from the dead and just before his Ascension into Heaven, told his Apostles to teach all nations, baptising them in the name of the Father, and of the Son, and of the Holy Ghost.[1] To what was he referring when he told them to baptise in the name of the Father, and of the Son, and of the Holy Ghost? He was referring to a sacramental rite which he himself had instituted. Let us briefly demonstrate this simple fact.

That he was referring to a rite which he had instituted is perfectly clear to anyone who reads the New Testament, wherein the baptism of Christ is often contrasted with the baptism of John; the basis of this contrast being that the baptism of John, which is inferior to that of Christ, is to give place to the baptism of Christ; for John came baptising in preparation for the Messias, in order that he might be made manifest in Israel.[2] It was this baptism, then, his own baptism, that he ordered his Apostles to administer. Clearly, therefore, he was referring to a rite which he himself had instituted. But was this rite a sacramental rite?

That it was a sacramental rite is equally clear from many passages in the New Testament. The reader will already know what a Sacrament is from the essay on the Sacramental System in this volume: he will know that it is a rite which not only signifies some specific Grace, but which of its intrinsic power produces that Grace in the soul of the person to whom it is administered. Our Blessed Lord's own words enable us to see in what his baptismal rite is to consist, when he tells Nicodemus that unless a man be born again of *water* and the Holy Ghost he cannot enter into the Kingdom of God;[3] and when he tells his Apostles to *baptise in the name of the Father, and of the Son, and of the Holy Ghost*. We have then a rite of washing with water which is done in the name of the three Divine Persons, a rite which signifies something, namely, a spiritual cleansing. Nor less evident is it that this rite not only signifies a cleansing Grace, but that it also produces in the soul the Grace which it thus signifies. In the first place, it is a rite that regenerates man; for Christ tells us that by it a man is born again. Secondly, this regeneration which begins a new life in the soul ensures the salvation of the baptised person; for St Paul tells us that Christ saved us by the laver of regeneration and renovation of the Holy

[1] Matt. xxviii 19. [2] John i 31. [3] John iii 5.

Spirit.[1] Again, baptism not only produces this new life in us, but it kills sin in us, as St Paul tells us that all who have been baptised are dead to sin.[2] Further, this baptism creates in us a new relation towards God, making us the children of God,[3] and it incorporates us in the Church of Christ.[4] These points we shall go into in more detail when we are speaking of that effect in the soul which we call the sacramental Grace of baptism; our one object just now being to show the reader that the Sacred Scriptures clearly, and indeed abundantly, demonstrate to us that the baptismal rite instituted by Christ is a sacramental rite; that is to say, it is an exterior sign that produces in the soul the Grace it signifies, a Grace that cleanses the soul of sin and begins its supernatural life.

What is thus shown to us in the Sacred Scriptures is repeated in the most unmistakable way in the tradition of the Church from the earliest times. We may dispense with all quotations from tradition on a matter so obviously true and so generally admitted. From this point of view the position of the Sacrament of Baptism is somewhat unique; for there is no Sacrament the existence of which is so generally admitted outside the Church. Its existence is recognised by all the Christian sects, and the errors into which they fall concerning this Sacrament arise, as a rule, indirectly. Thus, they may fall into error concerning Grace, which undermines the whole sacramental system; or they may fall into error on the Divinity of Christ, which undermines the whole body of revealed truth. In such partial and total collapses baptism is inevitably involved in the general ruin, but it is rarely singled out in an isolated way as the object of direct attack. Let us, therefore, pass on to a full explanation in the next section of what baptism is; reserving for subsequent sections the question of its necessity, its minister, and its subject.

§ II: THE SACRAMENT OF BAPTISM

At the outset, let us observe that when we speak of a Sacrament we mean one or more than one of three things that are perfectly distinct. First of all, we may mean just the exterior rite or "Outward Sign," as it is called, made up of actions and words which constitute the *matter* and *form* of the Sacrament, and known to theologians as the "Sacrament only." Secondly, we may mean the Grace produced in the soul by the Sacrament, which is known to theologians as "The Thing." Thirdly, we may mean another effect produced by the Sacrament which is quite distinct from Grace, and means a title or disposition in the soul to receive sacramental Grace; which title or disposition is necessarily and infallibly connected with the outward sign. The reader will readily understand

[1] Titus iii 5.
[2] Rom. vi 11.
[3] Gal. iii 26-27.
[4] 1 Cor. xii 13; Acts ii 41.

what this title or disposition means from the following illustration: Let us suppose that a man is married in the state of mortal sin. It is clear that he cannot receive any sacramental Grace from matrimony while he is in that state, and that not only does he receive no Grace by being so married, but he even adds the sin of sacrilege to his already burdened soul. None the less, he has been validly married and has received the Sacrament just as truly, as far as validity is concerned, as if he had been in the state of Grace. Later on he repents and has his sins forgiven. Now, at the moment in which his sins are forgiven, the Sacrament of Matrimony immediately produces its effect of Grace in his soul. How is this to be explained? Simply in this way, that the valid reception of the Sacrament of Matrimony entitled him to receive sacramental Grace, but this effect was held up owing to the obstacle of sin in his soul. The moment that obstacle is removed he receives the Grace.[1] Therefore, in every Sacrament there is an effect upon the soul distinct from Grace, which, as we have said, is a title or disposition to receive Grace; and which is known to theologians as "The Thing and the Sacrament." In putting a full explanation of baptism before the reader in this section we shall adopt this threefold division, and the reader will find this method of great assistance in obtaining an orderly and simple idea of all that is meant by baptism. Not to harass him with theological terms which may be unfamiliar, we shall call these three things respectively:

1. The Sacrament.
2. The Grace.
3. The Character.

1. The Sacrament

In this section we are speaking of the rite or the outward sign. What does it consist in? It is an exterior washing of the body under a prescribed form of words. The remote *matter* of the Sacrament is water, and the proximate *matter* is a washing of the body with water. The *form* is this: "I baptise thee in the name of the Father, and of the Son, and of the Holy Ghost"; or, as with the Greeks, "The servant of God is baptised in the name of the Father, and of the Son, and of the Holy Ghost." Let us now explain this *matter* and *form* in greater detail.

The matter

The Matter.—The remote matter of this Sacrament is water. That this is so is shown by Christ's words to Nicodemus, when he says that water is necessary for producing the regeneration that is to give a new life to man. There can be no doubt but Christ is speaking literally here and not in any symbolic way. For we find that after the Ascension of Christ water is always used in the administration of this Sacrament. Thus, the deacon Philip baptises the

[1] See pp. 755, 762 and n.

eunuch of Candace, Queen of the Ethiopians, as soon as they come to some water.[1] Moreover, the universal teaching and practice of the Church leave us in no doubt on this point. The author of the work *The Doctrine of the Twelve Apostles*, written about the year 100, tells us that candidates for baptism are either to be plunged in flowing water, or, failing that, in the still water of a pool, etc. If one has not enough water for this purpose, then the water may be poured three times on the head. From the writings of the Fathers of the Church it is clear that any attempt to abolish the use of water or to introduce customs at variance with Apostolic tradition were vigorously put down by the Church as being destructive of the very Sacrament itself. For instance, we find the Fathers, from the second century, inveighing against heretics like the Gnostics and Quintillians, who wish to dispense with the use of water, owing to their tenet that water was a source of evil, as it was something material; all matter, according to them, being something evil in itself. Other quaint practices, such as the use of sand, or a mixture of oil and water, or fire, instead of water, were at once condemned.[2]

The Blessing of water

Though water of any kind was used for the administration of this Sacrament, the custom of blessing the water is of very great antiquity, and soon became universal in the Church. And very naturally so, because the water which is used in baptism is raised by the work of the Holy Spirit to the dignity of an instrumental cause of our regeneration, and as such is fittingly hallowed by a blessing. We find this custom frequently referred to by the Fathers, and we have to-day a prayer of very great antiquity in our Liturgy—deriving from the writings of the Fathers, and of St Ambrose in particular—which is used for the blessing of the water in the baptismal font on Holy Saturday and the Vigil of Pentecost. As it is very long, we shall quote but a portion of this beautiful prayer:

"May this holy and innocent creature (the water) be free from all the assaults of the enemy, and purified by the destruction of all his malice. May it be a living fountain, a regenerating water, a purifying stream: that all those who are to be washed in this saving bath may obtain, by the operation of the Holy Spirit, the grace of a perfect purification. Therefore I bless thee, O creature of water, by the living God, by the true God, by the holy God, by that God who in the beginning separated thee by his word from the dry land, whose Spirit moved over thee. Who made thee flow from the fountain of Paradise and commanded thee to water the whole earth

[1] Acts viii 38.

[2] We might remind the reader at this point that when he finds, as he will frequently find throughout this essay, quotations from the Fathers, these quotations are not given as if the isolated testimony of a single Father here and there were sufficient evidence for an argument from tradition, but simply as examples of the customary belief and practice of the Church, which is the real argument from tradition.

with thy four rivers. Who, changing thy bitterness in the desert into sweetness, made thee fit to drink, and produced thee out of a rock to quench the thirst of the people. I bless thee also by our Lord Jesus Christ his only Son: who in Cana of Galilee changed thee into wine by a wonderful miracle of his power. Who walked upon thee dry-foot, and was baptised in thee by John in the Jordan. Who made thee flow out of his side together with his blood, and commanded his disciples that such as believed should be baptised in thee, saying: Go, teach all nations, baptising them in the name of the Father, and of the Son, and of the Holy Ghost. Do thou, Almighty God, mercifully assist us that observe this command: do thou graciously inspire us. Do thou with thy mouth bless these clear waters: that besides their natural virtue of cleansing the body, they may also be effectual for the purifying of the soul."

The proximate *matter* is the washing of the body with water. In what way is this washing to be done? It may be in any of these three ways: immersion of the body in water; infusion or pouring of water on the body; and sprinkling of the body with water. Something must now be said of each of these.

Immersion

Immersion.—Many people, including some Catholics, believe that baptism by submerging the body in water was the only method followed in the early Church. Such a belief is quite groundless. One might say, indeed, that such immersion was common; but it was probably just as customary for the candidate to stand in water, perhaps up to the thighs, and then have water poured over him; and infusion and sprinkling were known and used, most probably from the very beginning. What we have already quoted from *The Doctrine of the Twelve Apostles* shows that pouring and sprinkling were recognised as valid proximate matter, and many other quotations to the same effect might be given. It is very interesting to note that some of the baptisms recorded in the New Testament were given in circumstances in which baptism by submersion of the body would have been awkward and therefore improbable; as when St Paul baptised his gaoler and the gaoler's family,[1] or when three thousand, converted by St Peter's sermon, presented themselves all together for baptism. Again, the fact that St Paul stood up in the house of Ananias in order to be baptised [2] has sometimes been taken to mean that he was not baptised by a submersion of his body in water.

Where baptism was given by submerging the body, this was usually done three times. The custom of submerging the body once only appears to have arisen in Spain. It was looked upon askance for some time, not as if it interfered with the validity of the baptism, but simply as being against the ordinary use. Pope St Gregory the Great informed Leander, Bishop of Seville, who had consulted him on this point, that such a method was valid, but that in Rome it was customary to give three immersions, to signify the

[1] Acts xvi 33. [2] Acts ix 18.

three days' burial of Christ;[1] the whole Liturgy being based on the text of St Paul in his Epistle to the Romans,[2] where he shows that our baptism represents the death of Christ. The second method of immersion, where—as we have said—the candidate stood in water up to the thighs and then had the water poured over him, is represented to us in the very interesting and valuable pictures discovered in the Catacombs, which prove that this method of baptising is very ancient and suggests that it was very common.

Infusion

Infusion.—Baptism administered by pouring water on the head while the candidate did not himself stand in the water was recognised as valid at all times, but was not much used, as far as we can gather, except in cases of necessity, such as the scarcity of water or the sickness of the candidate. The same may be said of sprinkling. Infusion, however, grew in popularity, and eventually, as everybody knows, supplanted all other methods in the Roman rite. Baptism of the sick was known as "clinical" baptism. It was probably very common indeed during the fourth century, at least from the peace of Constantine, owing to the deplorable custom that arose of postponing one's baptism until the last moment. This custom was largely due to a desire to have all guilt and punishment remitted at the opportune time of one's last illness; but it was also due to the seriousness with which baptism was regarded, and the clear realisation of the high standard of life that would be demanded of any baptised person.

It is important to note, in connection with baptism by infusion or sprinkling, that the proximate matter must always be a washing *of the body*. The body may be said to be washed when there is an infusion or sprinkling of water on some principal part of it, such as the head or the breast. Could one say that the body was washed if the water was poured or sprinkled on the hand only or the foot? One could not answer definitely. Certainly, if baptism were so administered owing to necessity, it would be obligatory to baptise conditionally later on, if the opportunity of doing so presented itself.[3]

The form

THE FORM.—The form of the Sacrament of Baptism is this: "I baptise thee in the name of the Father, and of the Son, and of the Holy Ghost." Or, as among the Greeks, "The servant of God is baptised in the name of the Father, and of the Son, and of the Holy Ghost." Are all these words in the form necessary for the validity of the Sacrament?

Beyond doubt, the words expressing the act of washing are necessary. Thus, the act of washing would not be expressed if the words "I baptise thee" or "The servant of God is baptised" were omitted. Again, the express and distinct invocation of each Person of the Blessed Trinity is necessary. The command of Christ that men should be baptised in the name of the Father, and of the Son,

[1] P.L., tome lxxvii, col. 498.
[2] Chap. vi.
[3] See p. 790.

and of the Holy Ghost, puts this beyond all question. When St Paul met some of the disciples of Christ at Ephesus, who had not heard of the Holy Ghost, he immediately asked them: What baptism have you received ?—much as to say: If you have received the baptism instituted by Christ you could not have failed to have heard of the Holy Ghost, as each Person of the Blessed Trinity is invoked. Occasionally one sees certain texts quoted from the Acts of the Apostles (ii 38, vii 12) in which baptism in the name of Jesus Christ is mentioned, as if these texts showed that baptism could be given in the name of the Second Person of the Blessed Trinity only, and not in the name of all three. But this contention is really frivolous. For it is clear that these texts have absolutely no reference to the form of baptism, but simply to the Sacrament which Christ instituted, and which he commanded his Apostles to administer (as he commands us to do all things) in his name. It is the baptism of Christ that must be distinguished from the baptism of John, a distinction all the more necessary in the beginning, when many of those baptised by John were still alive. Thus—to refer again to a text alluded to above—in chap. xix of the Acts we read: "Paul . . . came to Ephesus and found certain disciples. And he said to them: Have you received the Holy Ghost since ye believed? But they said to him: We have not so much as heard if there be a Holy Ghost. And he said: In what then were you baptised? Who said: In John's baptism. Then Paul said: John baptised the people with the baptism of penance, saying that they should believe in him who was to come after him, that is to say, in Jesus. Having heard these things, they were baptised in the name of the Lord Jesus Christ."

The evidence supplied by ancient liturgical books gives us a striking proof of the universal agreement in the Church as to the form of baptism. Were our Church not a Divine institution, it would certainly appear remarkable that the same form should be given everywhere; especially when we consider that we have ancient liturgical evidence on this point in the following rites: Roman, African, Ambrosian, Gallican, Mozarabic, Celtic, Alexandrian, Syrian, and Byzantine. Even among heretics this form of baptism was, as a rule, rigorously adhered to; so that St Augustine tells us that it is easier to find heretics who do not baptise at all than to find heretics who, in baptising, do not invoke the three Persons of the Blessed Trinity.[1]

2. The Grace

We have now to speak of that effect of baptism which we call Grace. This grace, as the sacramental rite shows, is a cleansing. "Christ," says St Paul, "cleanses his Church by the laver of water."[2] This cleansing grace is a full renovation by which a man is freed

[1] *De bapt. cont. Donat.*, vi 25, 47. [2] Eph. v 26.

from all stain of sin and born to a new spiritual life. We must now explain the meaning of the terms we use, and make clear everything that they imply.

By the stain of sin we mean here both the guilt of sin and all the punishment, whether temporal or eternal, that is due to it. By being born to a new life we mean the reception of habitual Grace, the infused theological and moral virtues, and all the gifts of the Holy Ghost.

St Paul, in the sixth chapter of his Epistle to the Romans, uses these words : " Know you not that all we who are baptised in Christ Jesus are baptised in his death ? For we are buried together with him by baptism unto death : that as Christ is risen from the dead by the glory of the Father, so we also may walk in newness of life. Knowing this, that our old man is crucified with him, that the body of sin may be destroyed, to the end that we may serve sin no longer. For he that is dead is justified from sin. Now, if we be dead with Christ, we believe that we shall live also together with Christ. Knowing that Christ, rising again from the dead, dieth now no more. For in that he died to sin, he died once ; but in that he liveth, he liveth unto God. So do you also reckon that you are dead to sin, but alive unto God, in Christ Jesus our Lord."

From these magnificent words of the Apostle it is clear that baptism reproduces in us, as it were, the death and resurrection of Christ. We share through baptism in the death of Christ, because our " old man " is crucified with him ; that is to say, baptism destroys in us all the sin that defiled our souls. In the same Epistle [1] St Paul says that there is nothing to condemn in those that are in Christ Jesus. That is to say—for such is the interpretation of these words given by the Fathers of the Church, the theologians, and the Council of Trent—baptism exonerates us completely before God, since there is neither guilt nor debt of punishment in the souls of the baptised. More explicitly, whether it be a question of original sin or actual sin, baptism not only delivers us from eternal loss, but also remits all temporal punishment due to actual sin, and entitles us to eternal life. It does not, of course, mean that we cannot sin again, for our salvation will depend on our fidelity to the obligations we have undertaken in baptism ; but it means that as regards all sin that has gone before, Christ has saved us by this laver of regeneration and renovation of the Holy Spirit.

Taking the words of Christ, in which he speaks of our being born again through baptism, in conjunction with the words of St Paul, we find that baptism has not merely the effect of destroying sin in us, so that sin is as dead in us as the body of Christ was dead upon the Cross—and in what more forcible way could the power of baptism over sin be described ?—but it also causes a new birth in the spiritual order, which begins a new life, corresponding to the

[1] viii 1.

Resurrection of Christ. Everyone, then, who is baptised, at no matter what period of his life, is beginning this new life, is completely innocent, and a newly-begotten infant, without guile, in the sight of God. The life of sin is at an end, and the life of innocence has begun. This life, as the reader can learn from the essays on grace in this volume, involves an infusion of habitual grace, a title to actual graces in the future, an infusion of the theological and moral virtues, and all the gifts of the Holy Ghost. Again, this life begun by baptism establishes us in new relations towards God, as St Paul tells us when he says, in his Epistle to the Galatians : " You are all children of God by faith in Jesus Christ. For as many of you as have been baptised in Christ have put on Christ." [1] One must also bear in mind that every single passage in the New Testament dealing with the effects of justification might be quoted, at least indirectly, as descriptions of the effect of baptism, because that Sacrament is the source and origin of it all.

That very word *Justification* is in itself a complete summary of the effect of baptism. By it the soul is adjusted towards God in a supernaturally perfect and complete relation of innocence and favour. Sin is gone and the soul can rejoice, in peace and serenity, in that unhindered intimacy with God to which grace has raised it.

3. The Character

The effect of sacramental grace can be hindered by a lack of due dispositions in the recipient ; but there is another effect, distinct from grace, which—as we have mentioned before—is necessarily and infallibly produced in the soul, as it cannot be separated from the outward sign or rite. This effect is the title to receive grace. Now in three of the Sacraments this effect is known as a Character, and Baptism is one of these three ; the others being Confirmation and Holy Order. The reason why this effect is called a Character in the case of these three Sacraments is that, in addition to the title to grace which they confer, they assign one, in the divinely ordered parts or hierarchy of the Church, to a particular state, which has definite duties and rights attached to it. To what does baptism assign one ? To the state of membership in the Church, membership of the Mystical Body of Christ, which is the Church. Whoever is baptised, then, has all the duties and rights of a member. By what process does baptism make one a member ? By causing one to be born in the Church, and into the Church ; for this is the meaning of Christ's words to Nicodemus. Now, it is clear that, in virtue of this Character, the Sacrament of Baptism cannot be repeated, and that anyone who is baptised must always and unalterably belong to the Church. If a man had been born in England nothing could ever alter that fact ; and so it is—though we need not push the

[1] iii 26, 27.

example to the point of lameness—with anyone who, being baptised, is born in the Church. As a member one is obliged by all the duties of Christian life, and entitled to all the graces (such as the reception of other Sacraments) that flow from the inexhaustible treasury of the Church.

Nor let the reader suppose that all this applies only to those who have received baptism at the hands of Catholics. It applies to anyone who has received the Sacrament of Baptism, whether he received it at the hands of Catholic or heretic, man or woman, believer or infidel. For, as we have said more than once—and it is no harm to repeat it several times—the Character of baptism is necessarily and infallibly received whenever baptism is validly administered, as this effect cannot be separated from the outward sign. It may well be, as with large heretical bodies, that the Church cannot enforce her rights over all that belong to her, and it may equally well be that, prudently weighing what is ultimately best for mankind, she may not wish to enforce these rights. Yet she always has those rights; for they are, and must be, co-extensive with that portion of the human race that is marked with the Character of baptism.

That baptism has this effect of making one a member of the Church is clearly put before us in the Sacred Scriptures. We have already referred to Christ's words that entry into the Kingdom is by baptism. Again, we are told in the Acts of the Apostles that those who received the word of Peter were baptised, and there were *added* in that day about three thousand souls; that is to say, there were added to the Church by means of baptism. But probably this truth could not be put in more forcible terms than those St Paul uses, when he says that in one spirit we were all baptised into one body.[1] We need not dwell on the tradition of the Church concerning this fact, beyond saying that there is no tradition more clearly or explicitly before us, and that the entire Liturgy of Christian Initiation is based upon it.

§ III: THE NECESSITY OF BAPTISM

Indispensable for salvation

THERE are two ways in which a Sacrament may be necessary for salvation. It may be necessary as a means, or it may be necessary as the fulfilment of a precept only. Now, in saying that baptism is necessary for salvation, we mean that it is necessary as a means of salvation; so that, without it, it is impossible to go to Heaven. That being so, it is obvious that baptism is also necessary as the fulfilment of a precept, as we are bound to do whatever is indispensably necessary for our salvation.

It is a fact that is easily demonstrated. Habitual grace, which is the root principle of eternal life, is an absolutely indispensable means of salvation. Now, every soul is originally deprived of this

[1] 1 Cor. xii 13.

habitual Grace through the sin of our first parents; and, in the case of adults, it may be doubly deprived owing to the presence of grave actual sin. It is, then, indispensably necessary for salvation that the soul be spiritually regenerated or born again to this life of which it is deprived; and it is baptism, as we have seen in the previous section, that effects this regeneration.

At this point the reader should avoid any confusion of mind that may arise from his knowledge of the existence of the Sacrament of Penance. It must be perfectly clearly understood that if, after baptism, one has had the misfortune to fall into grave sin, it is the baptismal Character and nothing else that entitles one to avail of God's mercy in the Sacrament of Penance. For this Character entitles us to the advantages that arise from being a member of the Church. Once we have received the baptismal Character, Satan can never again have the same power over us, and can only make us soil our feet, as it were. If Christ had not washed us we should have no part with him; but since he has washed us we need but to wash our feet, and be clean wholly again. In saying this we do not wish to detract in any way from the fact that mortal sin after baptism is both a destruction of our new life and the gravest infidelity to our baptismal obligations. Indeed, we find that in the early Church, ever since the neophytes had heard the ringing words of Paul, it was regarded as a catastrophe that anyone should sin after baptism; so much so that many of these early converts never went to Confession, for there was no need of it, and it is doubtful if many of them even reflected on the fact that they might make use of the admitted power of the Church to forgive post-baptismal sin.[1] Our point is simply to stress the fact that it is fundamentally and originally to the great baptismal Character that we owe all spiritual graces and blessings.

Christ himself tells us that we must receive this spiritual regeneration through baptism, and that without it we cannot save our souls. He says to Nicodemus: "Unless a man be born again he cannot see the Kingdom of God."[2] When Nicodemus asks him: "How can a man be born when he is old? Can he enter a second time into his mother's womb and be born again?" Christ explains his meaning, without in any way diminishing its force, declaring solemnly: "Unless a man be born again of water and the Holy Ghost, he cannot enter into the Kingdom of God."

Heresies on this point

Naturally, what Christ had said so clearly the Fathers of the Church repeated, as occasion arose. Such occasions did arise through various heresies, which the Fathers were obliged to combat. There were the Cainites and the Quintillians in the second century, who held that faith alone was sufficient for salvation and that baptism was not necessary; there were the Manicheans, from the third century onwards, who regarded water as something evil in nature,

[1] *Cf.* Essay xxvii, *The Sacrament of Penance*, pp. 965, 967. [2] John iii 3 *sq.*

and as such quite unsuited as a means of salvation; there were the Massalians, who regarded it as useless; and there were the Pelagians, against whom St Augustine wrote, who regarded it as unnecessary. These latter, not recognising the existence of original sin, inevitably regarded baptism as of no real necessity, but admitted its utility for the remission of actual sin and for facilitating one's access to the Kingdom of Heaven.

The Fathers

These and all other errors on the necessity of baptism were resolutely condemned as soon as ever they showed themselves, as the Church always regarded baptism as of absolute necessity. In the controversy between St Cyprian and Pope St Stephen on the question of rebaptising heretics (of which more in a later section),[1] it is taken for granted by all parties that baptism itself is absolutely necessary for salvation. Again, St Irenaeus says that Christ came to save all through himself—that is, all who are born to God again by him, infants and little ones, children, youths and adults.[2] Tertullian points out to us that while the words "Teach all nations, baptising them," etc., show us that baptism is necessary as a precept, the words "Unless a man be born again," etc., show its necessity as a means.[3] St Ambrose tells us that without baptism faith will not secure salvation, as the remission of sin and special graces come only through baptism.[4] St Augustine regards it as a principle that admits of no dispute that no unbaptised person is without sin, and baptism therefore is necessary for his salvation.[5] This is true, he tells us, even of persons who practise virtues and walk in the way of a relative perfection. Even if one has given his possessions to the poor, is better instructed in the truths of faith than the majority of baptised persons, and is careful not to be vain on that account and not to despise baptism, but is not yet baptised—then all his sins are still upon him, and unless he comes to saving baptism, where sins are loosed, in spite of all his excellence, he cannot enter into the Kingdom of Heaven.[6] Moreover, in his controversy with the Pelagians, St Augustine lets us see that he regards the baptism of infants as necessary, owing to the stain of original sin upon their souls.

No substitute for Baptism

At this point the reader may have a difficulty. It can be put in this way: Is it not true that Mary Magdalen was a saint from that moment in which Christ forgave her because she loved much? And yet we are not aware that she was then baptised. Is it not true that the Holy Innocents did not receive the Sacrament of Baptism? Also, that some of the canonised saints were only catechumens, and so forth? Now, it will promote tidiness and clarity of thought if we deal with this difficulty by proposing to ourselves these two questions, and by answering them: First, Has Christ instituted any other positive means of regeneration besides baptism, either by way

[1] See pp. 785 ff.
[2] *Cont. haer.*, i 22, n. 4.
[3] *De bapt.*, 12.
[4] *De myst.*, iv 20.
[5] *Cont. litt. Petil.*, l. ii, n. 232.
[6] *In Ioa.*, tr. iv. 13.

of addition to or exception from the law of baptism? Secondly, Is it not possible that, from the very nature of things which precedes all positive law and is allowed for in positive law, it might happen that a person could receive justification without the actual reception of the *Sacrament* of Baptism?

We answer the first of these questions in the negative. We cannot admit any other means of salvation positively instituted by Christ, for the very good reason that his positive law has provided one means and only one. If, therefore, any theories are advanced on the question of salvation which involve the recognition of some means of salvation positively instituted by Christ, other than baptism, such theories must immediately be rejected as at least erroneous. Attempts of this kind have been made from time to time. The best known is that of the theologian Cajetan, who expressed the opinion that in the case of infants dying in the mother's womb, the prayers of the parents could secure the justification and salvation of the children. He thought that a blessing of the child in the womb, given in the name of the Blessed Trinity, would secure this. This opinion was regarded with great disapproval by the theologians of the Council of Trent, and though it was not actually condemned, Pope Pius V ordered that it should be expunged from the works of Cajetan. A somewhat similar view was held by Gerson, Durand, Bianchi, and others. Even St Bonaventure seems to have nodded; for he says that an infant would be deprived of grace if unbaptised, unless God made it the object of some special privilege.[1]

The fundamental error of all such views is that they introduce, without warrant of any kind from Revelation, a second means of salvation positively instituted by Christ. They demand the recognition of what we might call a pseudo-Sacrament. If, for instance, such a rite as blessing an infant in its mother's womb is sufficient for its justification, then we must admit a pseudo-Sacrament positively instituted by Christ, by way of addition to or exception from the law of baptism which he has made. To admit this is gratuitous, as it is not mentioned by Christ, and it is erroneous, as it is plainly against the universality of the words of Christ.

We must conclude then that infants dying in their mother's womb do not enjoy the Beatific Vision in Heaven. At the same time they do not suffer from what is called the pain of sense. According to St Thomas, they enjoy a real happiness which consists, not indeed in that vision of God which grace alone makes possible, but in the natural love and knowledge of God.[2]

Two equivalents

We answer our second question in the affirmative. It can happen that a person receives justification without actually receiving the Sacrament of Baptism. And it can happen in one of two ways: either, 1, by Martyrdom, or 2, by Charity. Let us take them

[1] *In IV Sent.*, I iv, dist. iv.
[2] *In IV Sent.*, I ii, dist. xxx, Q. II, art. 2, ad 5.

separately, giving exact explanations of the words we use, and showing that each of them amounts to baptism.

Martyrdom

By martyrdom we mean suffering death for the cause of Christ. We must first make this important proviso: to have the merit of martyrdom it is not necessary that one should be an adult, knowing the teaching of Christ and acting with deliberation. It is sufficient that one should simply suffer death for the cause of Christ. Now, the cause of Christ may mean something concerning the Person of Christ; as when the Holy Innocents were put to death by Herod, in the hope that Christ might be among the victims of the general slaughter. Or it may mean something concerning the religion and faith of Christ, as with the majority of the martyrs. Or, finally, it may mean something concerning a virtue which is specially enjoined by the law of Christ; as when St John the Baptist was beheaded for defending the virtue of chastity.

Having made clear what we mean by the cause of Christ, we may say that two conditions are necessary for true martyrdom. The first is that the person guilty of inflicting death persecutes Christ in one or other of the three ways mentioned above. The motive for which the persecutor acts is not of the slightest importance as far as martyrdom is concerned, provided that it is *because of their Christianity* that the victims are made to suffer. Thus we are told by Tacitus that Nero's first persecution of the Christians was simply in order to make the public believe that the Christians, and not he, were guilty of the burning of Rome.[1] His motive was the purely personal one of averting suspicion from himself, yet his victims were none the less martyrs, as it was because they were Christians that they were made to suffer.

The second condition is that the person who is killed dies by allowing himself to be killed. If one were killed simply through being overcome by superior force, in spite of the stoutest resistance that one was capable of, it could scarcely be called martyrdom, as it would not conform to the type of Christ, who as a lamb was led to the slaughter.[2] The Church has never shown any disposition to canonise all those who lost their lives in the Crusades. Crusaders may be said to have suffered for the cause of Christ, but the element of being meekly led to slaughter was decidedly to seek.

Perhaps one ought to mention a question that is discussed a good deal to-day. Could we say that those who lost their lives during the Great War, and who discharged their exalted duty from motives that referred to Christ, are entitled to the name of martyr? It is hard to see how they can be entitled to that name. For one thing, they did not suffer for the cause of Christ, as they were put to death, not for being Christians, but because they belonged to this or that nation. Again, they did not submit to death, but were overcome by force. If we admit to the merit of martyrdom all those who bear

[1] Tacitus, *Annal.*, l. 15, n. 44. [2] Isa. liii 7.

their death from Christian motives, then it is hard to see how any good Christian can be excluded. For any good man might suffer his last illness and accept his death from Christian motives. It is true that the word martyrdom can be used in a certain broad sense of all those whose motives Christianise their death ; but they cannot be called martyrs in the strict sense of the word. Certainly, we may believe that anyone who accepts death that comes to him in the discharge of duty, from some Christian motive, may immediately be admitted to Heaven. It would be very rash to disbelieve it, since Christ has said that greater love than this no man hath, that a man should lay down his life for his friend.[1] One might, therefore, regard death in such circumstances as a proof of baptism of Charity or Desire—of which more anon.

Is it necessary, for true martyrdom, that the motive which prompts one to give one's life should be perfect charity or love of God ? It is not. It is sufficient that one should accept death for any motive of Holy Faith, such as the fear of Hell, the hope of Heaven, and so on.

Having determined with precision what we mean by martyrdom, we must show that it is equivalent to baptism. This is put beyond doubt by the words of Christ : " He that shall lose his life for me shall find it." [2] It is also shown by the constant teaching of the Church. We find, for instance, that the cult of the Holy Innocents is of the greatest antiquity. Their feast is to be found in the Leonine Sacramentary, which is one of the oldest liturgical books we possess, and it is also found in the Gelasian Sacramentary, which is the most important of the early liturgical books of the Latin rite. Besides, the Fathers of the Church affirm this truth in the most unmistakable way. St Cyril of Jerusalem says : " If a person has not been baptised he cannot be saved, always excepting martyrs, who receive the kingdom without water. Our Saviour, who redeemed the world through the Cross, sent forth blood and water from his pierced side ; so that in time of peace men might be saved by water, and in time of persecution by their own blood." [3] St Augustine says that those who die for confessing Christ without being baptised have their sins forgiven by their death, just as much as if they had been washed in the sacred font of baptism. And if Christ said that unless a man be born again of water and the Holy Ghost he cannot enter into the Kingdom of Heaven, he also said : " He that shall lose his life for me shall find it." [4] St Augustine tells us, too, that he who prays for the martyrs commits an outrage against them.[5] St Cyprian asks us : " Can the power of baptism be greater or stronger than the confession a man makes by confessing Christ before men, and being baptised in his own blood ? " [6]

[1] John xv 13.
[2] Matt. x 39.
[3] *Catech.* 3, n. 10.
[4] L. 13 *de civ. Dei*, c. 7.
[5] *Serm.* 17 *de verbis apost.*
[6] *Ep. ad Iubaian.*, n. 21.

Martyrdom, then, is baptism. How does it compare with the Sacrament of Baptism ? It is less and greater. It is less, because it is the Sacrament alone that confers the Character. It is greater, because it not only justifies the soul, but it removes—as the Sacrament does not—the possibility of the soul ever being stained again by sin, and places it in the white stole of radiant sanctity in the presence of God. The martyrs are those who have come through a great tribulation, and have washed their stoles and made them white in the Blood of the Lamb.[1]

Charity—Baptism of desire

We have said that Charity, or Desire, as it is just as frequently called, is another form of baptism. And here, again, let us define what we mean by the word, and then show how it is equivalent to baptism.

We may say quite briefly that charity is an act of the love of God because he is infinitely good in himself, or an act of perfect contrition—that is, contrition arising from the motive of the love of God. In an adult sinner charity will always imply the presence of contrition ; for no sinner could love God unless he was sorry for his sin.

Now, an act of charity always and necessarily contains a desire for the Sacrament of Baptism, hence the expression Baptism of Desire. The reason why it must contain this desire is that an act of the love of God must contain a desire of conforming to his will in every way. Therefore, since it is God's will that we should receive the Sacrament of Baptism, this act must contain the desire for baptism. But this desire may either be implicit or explicit, and each alternative requires our careful consideration.

The desire is explicit, for example, in a catechumen who is instructed in all the essential truths of faith, who is actually preparing to be baptised, and is well disposed in every way. If, however, a catechumen were well instructed, and yet his baptism had to be postponed because he was unwilling to give up something grievously sinful in his life, we could not say that he had baptism of desire, as it is evident that he has not charity. It is implicit in anyone who makes an act of the love of God, and, through invincible ignorance, does not know of the necessity of sacramental baptism. This might happen in a country like England to people who are not baptised. They might easily know sufficient of the truths of faith to make an act of the love of God, and yet be in ignorance of the true necessity of baptism, which they would not, therefore, explicitly desire. Might it not also happen to heathens who had never heard of Christ ? It might, if we suppose that these heathens have in some way obtained the necessary minimum knowledge of Revelation, and are capable of a salutary faith and hope in God. For it is very important to understand that when we speak of charity, we do not mean just any kind of love of God above all else, such as the natural love of a creature for its Creator. Charity is essentially a love of friendship

[1] Apoc. vii 14.

(Our Blessed Lord does not call us servants, but friends), which implies an intimate communication with God, such as is only possible in a supernatural order. The existence of this supernatural order can only be known through Revelation. Charity, therefore, cannot exist without at least the knowledge of the principal truth of Revelation, which St Paul describes for us in his Epistle to the Hebrews, when he says: "He that cometh to God must believe that he is, and is a rewarder of them that seek him." How heathens have in some way received or can in some way receive this minimum knowledge of revealed truth it would be outside the scope of this essay to enquire.[1]

That charity infallibly justifies man, obtaining remission of all sin and infusion of grace, is evident from the words of Christ: "He that loveth me shall be loved of my Father; and I will love him and will manifest myself to him."[2] Again: "If any one love me he will keep my word. And my Father will love him: and we will come to him and will make our abode with him."[3] And again, when the lawyer answered Christ's question, saying: "Thou shalt love the Lord thy God with thy whole heart, and with thy whole soul, and with all thy strength, and with all thy mind," our Blessed Lord rejoined: "This do, and thou shalt live."[4] No portion of the Sacred Scriptures makes it clearer to us that this charity is the love of friendship than the writings of St John, who tells us once directly, and in numerous passages equivalently, that charity is of God, and every one that loveth is born of God.[5]

In these passages of the Sacred Scriptures there is not, as is evident, the least suggestion that there should be any explicit knowledge of the need of the Sacrament of Baptism. In patristic times we find abundant proof of the sufficiency of charity where the desire of baptism is explicit. We may quote, as an example, the famous funeral oration of St Ambrose over the Emperor Valentinian, who died as a catechumen. He says that he had heard people expressing regret that the Emperor was not baptised. He points out that the Emperor had the intention of being baptised, and had asked him, St Ambrose, to baptise him. Will he not then receive the grace which he desired and obtain what he asked for? Did he not court unpopularity on the very day before his death, by putting Christ before men on the question of the pagan temples? If he had the spirit of Christ, did he not receive the Grace of Christ? If the martyrs are cleansed in their blood, then so is he in his good-will and piety.[6]

Could we say that the Fathers recognised charity as equivalent to baptism where the desire for baptism was only implicit? They did not develop this point for us, with the exception of St Augustine,

[1] See Essay xvii, *Actual Grace*, pp. 608-610.
[2] John xiv 21.
[3] John xiv 23.
[4] Luke x 27, 28.
[5] 1 John iv 7.
[6] *De ob. Valen. cons.*, n. 51.

who may be said to have defended the sufficiency of charity without any explicit reference to baptism. In discussing the question of the salvation of the Penitent Thief, he is not altogether satisfied with St Cyprian's contention that he died a martyr, but seems more disposed to attribute his salvation to his faith and the conversion of his heart. It is true that St Augustine afterwards expresses uncertainty about the whole question of the Penitent Thief; but, quite independently of this question, he recognises faith and the conversion of the heart as a means of justification; [1] basing his argument on the text of St Paul: "For with the heart, we believe unto justice; but with the mouth, confession is made unto salvation." [2] The development of this point after St Augustine was but slow, yet always inclining towards the acceptance of charity with the implicit desire as sufficient. To-day it is the opinion of all theologians. It is, of course, always understood that charity with the explicit desire exists only if there is the intention of receiving the Sacrament when possible; and that charity with the implicit desire exists only when the ignorance of the Sacrament and of its necessity is invincible and therefore inculpable.

How does charity compare with the Sacrament of Baptism? It is something less. For, though it is sufficient for justification, it does not give the Character which comes from the Sacrament, and it does not necessarily remit all debt of temporal punishment. We say it does not necessarily remit all debt of temporal punishment; but we do not deny that an act of charity might be so perfect as to secure this end as well.

Summary

To sum up: apart from martyrdom, the Sacrament of Baptism, either in reality or in desire, is necessary for salvation. Martyrdom and charity, or baptism of desire, we recognise as equivalent to baptism as regards their essential effects. Any other way of receiving justification, such as that invoked by Cajetan, we reject. Let us suppose that the State were to make some law to the effect that to obtain certain rights and privileges the taking of a certain oath were necessary. It is conceivable that these rights and privileges might be granted to people who did not take this oath because, for some excusable reason, it was not in their power to do so, but who had otherwise given indisputable and even extraordinary proof of their loyalty. On the other hand, it is not conceivable that they would receive these rights and privileges simply because they had employed some rite of their own, other than the oath which the State had sanctioned. In the same way—using the example for what it is worth—we recognise that Almighty God accepts the giving of one's love and the giving of one's life on the part of those for whom the actual reception of the Sacrament itself is not possible. But we can never admit that he would recognise some positive rite as an alternative to the law of sacramental baptism which he has sanctioned.

[1] L. 4 *de bapt.*, c. 22.

[2] Rom. x 10.

§ IV: THE MINISTER OF BAPTISM

ALL that has to be said about the minister of baptism can be summed up in these two statements: First, anyone, man or woman, baptised or unbaptised, can validly administer the Sacrament of Baptism. Secondly: while all can administer this Sacrament validly, only priests (and bishops, of course) are the ordinary lawful ministers of it; others being lawful ministers only in cases of necessity. In the first statement, then, we deal with the valid administration of baptism, and in the second with its lawful administration. Let us examine each of these statements in detail.

Valid minister, anyone

We say that anyone can validly administer this Sacrament. Is it possible to establish this truth from the Sacred Scriptures alone? In the full ambit of our assertion, no. The chief argument, therefore, must come from the tradition of the Church. But we can say this much: that the Scriptures make it clear to us that others besides priests and bishops can administer this Sacrament, and that the position of baptism in this respect, as compared with the other Sacraments, is unique.

It is, of course, certain that the Apostles baptised, as they were commanded by Christ to do. Very probably St Paul baptised less than any of the other Apostles, as he tells us that his work was to preach the Gospel rather than to baptise.[1] Yet he certainly administered baptism on different occasions. We are told, for instance, in the Acts of the Apostles, that he baptised his gaoler and all the gaoler's family; and at Corinth he baptised Crispus and Caius and the household of Stephanas.[2] But it is clear from the Scriptures that not only the Apostles, but even a deacon could baptise. For Philip, who was only a deacon, baptised Simon the Magician, a number of people in Samaria, and the eunuch of Queen Candace.[3] More interesting still is the baptism of St Paul himself, as it is probable that Ananias, who baptised him at Damascus, was only a simple layman.[4] It is true, of course, that Ananias did this in obedience to a command that came directly from Christ himself, and the incident cannot, on that account, be claimed as an indication of any general custom. The conclusion, therefore, which we are entitled to draw from the evidence of the Scriptures is this: that the administration of baptism is not on a par with the other Sacraments, as we find that not only priests, but deacons, and possibly the faithful laity, can baptise. As to whether heretics or infidels can validly baptise we cannot say on the authority of the Scriptures, and must, therefore, seek our information from tradition. Let us briefly follow this interesting question in its historical setting.

The teaching of the Fathers of the Church on this question of valid ministry may be stated in this way: apart from the solemn

[1] 1 Cor. i 17.
[2] *Ibid.* i 14, 16.
[3] Acts viii.
[4] *Ibid.* ix 18.

administration of baptism, and when it is not possible to have recourse to the clergy, any baptised person can administer this Sacrament.

A constitution attributed to Pope St Victor (189-198), authorises the administration of baptism in case of necessity, in any place whatsoever, by a Christian to a pagan who has previously recited the symbol of faith. St Cyril of Jerusalem tells us that baptism can be conferred by the ignorant as well as by the learned, by slaves as well as by freemen.[1] Clearly, though he is speaking of Christians, St Cyril is not speaking of the clergy alone, as they would not come under the category of the ignorant. St Jerome tells us that though neither a priest nor a deacon can ordinarily baptise without chrism and the mandate of a bishop ; yet, if necessity arises, even laymen can baptise.[2] We need not multiply quotations on a point that is so often stated by the Fathers. No doubt there was some dissent, but the general Catholic custom and conviction was clear and emphatic. It was, however, always recognised that a person baptised in such circumstances of necessity by a layman should present himself, as soon as possible, to a bishop, for the imposition of hands and the Sacrament of Confirmation. None the less, should anyone die who had been baptised by a layman, and had not been confirmed, his salvation was regarded as secure. The reader may be puzzled as to the urgency of Confirmation ; it simply arose from the fact that originally Confirmation—and, for that matter, Holy Communion—followed immediately after baptism, the rite of initiation embracing all three Sacraments.

Validity of heretical baptism

So far we have shown that the Fathers held that the faithful could baptise. But what of heretics ? To answer this question we must briefly review the controversy on the point in patristic times.

Towards the end of the second century, when the heretical sects were becoming discredited, many of their members, moved by grace, sought to be reconciled to the Catholic Church. On what conditions were they to be admitted to the Catholic Church ? If they had originally been Catholics who had lapsed into heresy the question was readily answered : they were obliged to do penance, often for long periods of time, and were reconciled to the Church. But suppose that they had never been Catholics, and had received baptism at the hands of heretics ? The general custom was to admit them to the Church after the imposition of hands, and not to baptise them again ; provided, of course, that the heretical sect from which they came had preserved the correct rite, or, as we should say, the matter and form of the Sacrament. In certain localities, however, it was thought that they should be rebaptised. This custom was followed in Proconsular Africa at the beginning of the third century. How did it arise ? Very probably from the erroneous

[1] *Cat.*, xvii 35. [2] *Dial. cont. Lucif.*, 9.

view of Tertullian that the baptism administered by heretics differed from that administered by Catholics. Since then there is but one baptism [1] and that the baptism given by Catholics, anything differing from it cannot be baptism at all, and therefore heretics do not validly baptise. This doctrine had been sanctioned by a local council of the bishops of Proconsular Africa and Numidia under Agrippinus, Bishop of Carthage, and a contemporary of Tertullian.

The position thus taken up was bound to lead to trouble before long, and matters came to a head under St Cyprian, who was made Bishop of Carthage, probably in the beginning of the year 249. He, like St Augustine, had been converted from a life of pleasure, and had become distinguished for his zeal in defending Catholicity and defeating heresy. But, unlike the great Augustine, he allowed his zeal to flourish at the expense of his better judgement and discretion. Being asked by a certain Magnus if it were necessary to re-baptise members of the Novatian sect who wished to be reconciled to the Church, he replied with emphasis in the affirmative. In 255 he was asked a similar question by eighteen bishops of Numidia. Again Quintus, a bishop of Mauritania, asked him this question, and from one source or another he was continually consulted on this particular point. His answer was always the same: such people should always be re-baptised. Cyprian even expressed astonishment that any of his colleagues should admit heretics to the fold without first re-baptising them; preferring—so he said—to do honour to heretics rather than to agree with him.

At a council of the bishops of Proconsular Africa and Numidia in the autumn of 255 it was declared that baptism administered by heretics was null and void. Cyprian himself informed the Pope, St Stephen, of this decision. Stephen, invoking the tradition of the Apostles, condemned the African custom and proclaimed the validity of baptism administered by heretics. He further threatened to break off ordinary relations with the recalcitrant African bishops if his decision was not accepted. Whether he ever put this threat into effect is not known. Apparently the question of excommunication never arose, as alarums and excursions of this kind between Rome and Africa were not uncommon, and it was not customary to resort to excommunication. Stephen's decision, however, was not accepted, and two further councils in Africa, in the spring of 256 and on September 1 of the same year, in which the error was adhered to, made matters worse rather than better. There is nothing to show that Cyprian ever came to any agreement with Stephen, who was martyred on August 2, 257, shortly after the first edict of Valerian. But the fact that Cyprian immediately resumed relations with the successor of Stephen, Pope Sixtus II, would show that there had been no complete rupture between the Holy See and Africa. Cyprian himself was martyred on September 14, 258, being beheaded

[1] Eph. iv 5.

at the gates of his episcopal villa, and being the first bishop of Africa to win the martyr's crown.

His error, however, did not die with him, but continued to create, not indeed an open breach, but a divergence between Rome and Africa. But the truth is great and it gradually prevailed. Thus, the Council of Arles in 314 declares that baptism conferred by heretics is valid, provided they administer it correctly as the Catholic Church does, and with the invocation of the Blessed Trinity. Again, a canon added to the Council of Constantinople in 381 declares that baptism administered by certain heretics, such as the Arians, Novatians, and others, is valid; whereas that administered by the Eunomians, Montanists, and Sabellians is invalid; because the latter do not administer the Sacrament correctly with the formula of the Blessed Trinity. Finally, the victory of Rome was for ever assured by the writings of St Augustine, who developed the entire theological doctrine of this Sacrament to such an extent that he left little indeed to be completed by his successors.

So much for this very brief historical outline of this controversy. Let us now ask, To what error in doctrine was the behaviour of Cyprian due? Undoubtedly to this, that he did not distinguish between validity and lawfulness in the administration of a Sacrament. He did not realise that, though it may be unlawful to administer baptism in certain circumstances, yet it may be quite validly done in spite of that. We say that he did not realise this; for one could scarcely say that he positively did not know it. Quite early in the controversy one Jubaianus had put the situation neatly to him, by pointing out a distinction between the unlawfulness of the minister's action and the validity of what he did. It is not a question, said Jubaianus, of *who* did a thing, but of *what* he did. Cyprian replies that such baptism cannot be recognised as valid, as what is done is *illicit*. His otherwise admirable zeal kept him from reflecting that an action may be illicit and yet be valid.

We sum up the teaching of the Fathers, as shown by the history of the controversy, in this way: the valid administration of baptism depends on the use of the correct rite. If this is followed, heretics can baptise validly as well as others. If they mutilate this rite they do not administer baptism. In other words (the words of the Schoolmen), if you intend to administer the baptism of Christ and use the right matter and form you do administer it; if you destroy either the matter or the form you do not administer it.

Even the unbaptised can baptise

So far we have shown that the Fathers taught that any baptised person, be he one of the faithful or a heretic, can validly baptise. But can those who are not themselves baptised administer this Sacrament? The Fathers do not answer this question, which to them was academic rather than practical. But they give us, very clearly, the lines on which the answer is to be found, by their insistence that the validity of baptism does not depend on the minister or the kind of person he may be, but on the fact that, wishing to administer the baptism of Christ, he uses the correct rite. St Augustine indeed raises the question in a speculative way. Though he does not dogmatically answer it, he gives his opinion very strongly: anyone who follows the rite instituted by Christ administers baptism validly.[1] After the Fathers, this question was gradually developed, and by the time of St Thomas it was universally held by theologians that anyone, man or woman, baptised or unbaptised, could validly baptise. It must, of course, be clearly understood that a right intention, that is, an intention of doing what the Church of Christ does, is always necessary for the validity of the Sacrament.

Why did our Blessed Lord confer this power of baptising, not upon his priests alone, but upon the whole world? No doubt, as St Thomas tells us, because it is due to the great mercy of God that he should make it easy for men to obtain whatever is absolutely necessary for their salvation. Now—always prescinding from martyrdom—the actual reception of the Sacrament of Baptism is absolutely necessary for the salvation of infants, and the actual or desired reception of it is absolutely necessary for the salvation of adults, and for the remission of all debt of punishment. Therefore our Blessed Lord has given this power to all; assigning water as the matter of the Sacrament, in order that we might have an agency of salvation that is easily found.

The second part of this subject need not detain us long. We have shown that anyone can validly baptise. We have now to show that this power must not be used indiscriminately. Let us insist, however, that whether lawful or illicit the baptism is always valid, so long as the minister who intends to baptise uses the correct matter and form.

Ordinary lawful minister, priest or bishop

That the ordinary lawful minister of baptism is a priest or bishop arises simply in this way: only those who have received a special authorisation from Christ to administer the Sacraments to others are the ordinary lawful ministers of them. Now, it is only priests who have this special authorisation. From what does this special authorisation come? It comes from the Character imprinted on their souls by the Sacrament of Holy Order, which deputes them to the administration of sacred things to others, making them, as St Paul has it, dispensers of the mysteries of God.[2] Could a deacon administer this Sacrament solemnly? By a special commission from a bishop he could do so, but not otherwise. His position is not that of a priest, because the office proper to the diaconate is not to administer the Sacraments solemnly to others, but to assist the priests when they are engaged in doing so.

The solemn administration of this Sacrament, then, is reserved to the clergy, and in no conceivable circumstances could anybody else administer baptism *solemnly*—that is, in its official liturgical

[1] *De bapt. cont. donat.*, vii 53, 102.

[2] 1 Cor. iv 1.

setting. The reason for this is that the solemn administration of a Sacrament implies that one is acting in virtue of a special authorisation from Christ, such as comes only through the Sacrament of Holy Order ; in virtue of an office which is proper to the state in which the Character of Holy Order places one. The administration of baptism by the laity is, as it were, unofficial, and therefore can never be solemn or ceremonial. It is therefore called private baptism.

Unofficial action, however, in things divine as well as human, is often lawful in matters of great urgency. On this account it is lawful for anyone to baptise in case of necessity. Such necessity arises when a priest cannot be had, and the salvation of a soul may depend on baptism here and now. This we have already shown from the traditional teaching of the Church. The passages we have quoted in order to prove that anyone can baptise are also passages which demonstrate that it is only in circumstances of necessity that it is lawful for people, other than priests, to do so. It is important to note that, when necessity arises, it is not only lawful but obligatory to baptise. The obligation arises from the fact that if baptism is not given under such circumstances a soul is deprived of salvation. When a priest cannot be had, then, it is lawful and obligatory to baptise an infant in danger of death, or an adult in similar danger, who has faith and contrition and wishes to be baptised. In the case of infant baptism a parent ought not to baptise if some other person is available, and a woman should not baptise if a man can be had.

Some instructions

Before concluding this section we must mention a few points which it may be useful and even necessary for a section of our readers to know.[1]

1. No infant should be baptised in its mother's womb, as long as there is a probability of its being born alive.

2. If, in childbirth, the head of the infant emerges, and the infant is in imminent danger of death, it must be baptised on the head.

3. If some other member, such as the hand, emerges, and a similar danger exists, the infant must be baptised conditionally on that member ; the person who baptises saying : " If thou art capable of being baptised, I baptise thee in the name of the Father, and of the Son, and of the Holy Ghost." The reason why the conditional clause is inserted is that we cannot be sure if the washing of such a member as the hand is a true washing *of the body*. Should the infant (so baptised conditionally) be born and live, it must be baptised conditionally in this way : " If thou art not baptised, I now baptise thee," etc. Should the baptism administered previously not have been true baptism, owing to the absence of a washing *of the body*, it is now made certain. The necessity for the condition expressed in the words, " If thou art not baptised," arises from the fact that

[1] See *Codex Iuris Can.*, c. 746.

we must not attempt to repeat the administration of this Sacrament. However, unless a new necessity arose, this second conditional act would be done by a priest.

4. If a pregnant mother dies, and the fœtus is extracted, it should be baptised if alive; if there is doubt as to its being alive, it should be baptised conditionally—" If thou art capable," etc.

5. A fœtus baptised in the womb should be baptised conditionally after birth—" If thou art not baptised," etc.; this conditional act would, unless a new necessity arose, be done by a priest.

6. All abortions, at whatever period of pregnancy they may occur, should be baptised if they are alive, and should be baptised conditionally (" If thou art capable ") if there is doubt of their being alive.

7. The way to administer baptism is this: The person who baptises, intending to administer this Sacrament, pours some water on the forehead of the person to be baptised, saying at the same time (the action accompanying the words): " I baptise thee in the name of the Father, and of the Son, and of the Holy Ghost." It is correct, though not necessary for the validity, to give a name when baptising, thus: " John, I baptise thee," etc.

8. Those who have been baptised by the laity should be brought, as soon as possible, to church, to have the ceremonies supplied by a priest.

§ V: THE SUBJECT OF BAPTISM

We have already seen that baptism is necessary for all. In speaking, then, of the subject of baptism here, we are simply dealing with the conditions requisite for the reception of this Sacrament. It will be convenient to divide this section into two, corresponding to the answers to these two questions: 1. What condition is required for the valid reception of baptism? 2. What conditions are required for the lawful reception of baptism?

Conditions for valid reception

For valid baptism no further condition is requisite on the part of the adult subject than the intention of receiving this Sacrament. Needless to say, no conditions whatsoever are necessary for valid baptism on the part of infants. So long, then, as an adult has the intention of being baptised he is validly baptised. Any wrong dispositions on his part cannot interfere with the validity of the Sacrament. Even though he may, owing to these wrong dispositions, be guilty of sacrilege, he is none the less validly baptised.

Conditions for lawful reception

What conditions are required for the lawful reception of this Sacrament? Baptism, as we have seen, is a Sacrament which destroys all sin and all consequence of sin in our souls, and which bestows upon us a new life. Now, this destruction of sin and birth to a new life obliges us to a renunciation of Satan and to faith in the teaching of Christ. For we could not live according to this new life unless we had been cleansed from original sin, unless we were determined not to sin, and unless we knew and believed in the teaching of Christ. Again, actual sin and its consequences in our souls could not be destroyed unless we repented of them. It is clear, then, that the two conditions attaching to the lawful reception of baptism are these : faith and the renunciation of Satan. Let us now see how these conditions must be fulfilled in every kind of circumstance.

For an adult sinner the conditions necessary for the lawful reception of baptism are faith and repentance. Let us explain our terms. By an adult sinner we mean one who, in addition to inheriting original sin, has also been guilty of actual sin. By faith we do not, obviously, mean the virtue of faith possessed as a principle of activity arising from habitual grace (for baptism is the means to this habitual grace), but simply an act of faith to which the aspirant to baptism is assisted by actual graces from God, preparing and disposing him for the habitual grace that is to come from baptism. By repentance we mean that, in the case of an actual sinner, the renunciation of Satan must inevitably include contrition for the actual sins of which he has been guilty. Nor, unless one would deny the great efficacy of this Sacrament, is it necessary that the contrition should be perfect. Imperfect contrition is quite sufficient for the reception of this Sacrament, as it is for the reception of the Sacrament of Penance. Let it be noted, however, that contrition is required as a part of the Sacrament of Penance ; the acts of the penitent being the *matter* of the Sacrament, without which the Sacrament cannot exist. In baptism, on the contrary, contrition is required as a disposition only : the *matter* of the Sacrament being the washing of the body with water, so that the absence of contrition would make the reception of baptism unlawful, but it would not invalidate it.

The teaching of Scripture and Tradition

That these dispositions of faith and repentance are necessary for adult sinners is shown to us in the Sacred Scriptures. Our Blessed Lord joins faith and baptism together, saying that whoever *believes* and is baptised will be saved.[1] Again, the eunuch said to Philip : " See, here is water : what doth hinder me from being baptised ? " And Philip said : " *If thou believest* with all thy heart, thou mayest." [2] Moreover, when the multitude, moved to compunction by Peter's words, ask him what they shall do, he replies : " *Do penance*, and be baptised every one of you in the name of Jesus Christ, for the remission of your sins." [3] Again, it is the most obvious of truths that, throughout our Lord's teaching, there is this insistence on the conversion of the heart as a necessary condition for admission to his Kingdom.

These two conditions were recognised and insisted upon by the Church from the earliest times. The whole system of the catechumenate, in which aspirants to baptism were prepared, is based upon these two ideas : that they must know the teaching of Christ and believe in it, and that they must repent of their sins. The gradual

[1] Mark xvi 16. [2] Acts viii 36, 37. [3] Acts ii 38.

understanding of the faith that came through the instructions of the catechumenate brought these aspirants to a realisation of the unhappy state to which sin had brought their souls. This realisation, when they did not resist the working of grace, led them to a detestation of sin, to a readiness to renounce it, and a longing for the holy way of life to which the grace of baptism would raise them; the aspirants being helped still further by the exorcisms of the Church, through which Satan is expelled from their souls, and forced to give way to the Holy Spirit. The enlightenment, too, that comes through faith gives them a new taste for the things of the Spirit and a detestation for the works of darkness. In the solemn administration of baptism to-day these renunciations of Satan, profession of faith, and exorcisms, are embodied in one beautiful liturgical act. It would be very interesting to explain all this beautiful liturgy in detail, but, unfortunately, it would take us outside the modest scope of this little essay. We shall, therefore, confine ourselves to a summing up of what we have said on the necessity of these conditions of faith and repentance by the following words from the Council of Trent:

"Men are prepared for justification in this way: aroused and sustained by divine grace, led to believe from what they have heard, they turn to God freely, believing in the truth of the Divine Revelations and promises, and believing especially that God justifies the sinner by his grace, through the work of Redemption by Jesus Christ. Then, as they know that they are sinners, they pass from the fear of Divine justice, which oppresses them for their good, to a consideration of the mercy of God; they are raised to hope, confident that, for the sake of Christ, God will help them; and they thus begin to love him as the source of all justice. In this way they begin to turn from sin with hate and detestation; that is, by that sort of repentance that is necessary before baptism. Finally, they form a resolution to be baptised, to commence a new life, and to keep the commandments of God."

The "revival" of baptism unworthily received

But suppose that an adult sinner does not so repent, and is yet baptised? He is certainly validly baptised, but he can receive no grace from the Sacrament which he has received. Can he ever receive grace from his baptism? He certainly can; for the baptismal Character which he has received entitles him to sacramental grace, as soon as the obstacle of sin in his soul is removed. When is this obstacle removed? Fully to answer this question, we must consider three hypotheses.

First, let us suppose that he received baptism, without repenting, in good faith—that is, not knowing or suspecting that such repentance was necessary for its lawful reception. And, let us further suppose, that he has committed no grave sin since being baptised. In such circumstances he receives the grace of the Sacrament the moment he makes a simple act of repentance, as by doing so he removes the only obstacle in his soul. Secondly, let us suppose that he receives the Sacrament without repenting, in good faith as before, but that since receiving it he has been guilty of grave sin. In this case he must go to Confession, and the moment he is absolved each Sacrament produces the effect of grace proper to it in his soul. But in this case it is to be noted that all temporal punishment attached to sin is remitted by baptism only as regards those sins committed before baptism ; the temporal punishment due to the sin committed after baptism not being affected by that Sacrament. Thirdly, suppose that he is baptised in bad faith—that is, knowing that he ought to repent and yet not doing so. He then receives no sacramental grace until he has been to Confession. This case differs from the second, because he actually committed a sacrilege in being baptised. Now, when he is absolved, is the temporal punishment due to this sin of sacrilege removed by baptismal grace ? Not so, because it belongs to the period after baptism. Certainly, in the order of time it is simultaneous with baptism, but, in the nature of things, it is really after baptism, as it impedes that ultimate effect of baptism which is grace. In each of these hypotheses, it may be well to point out, the Sacrament of Penance does not produce the sacramental grace of baptism, but simply removes the obstacle of sin, thus allowing baptism to reach its ultimate effect.

Is it necessary that along with repentance one should confess one's sins and have satisfactory works imposed ? Certainly not. The confession of sin is necessary for one who, being a member of the Church through the baptismal Character, falls into sin and becomes thereby subject to the judicial and merciful power of that Church to which he belongs. Satisfactory works cannot be necessary, for he who is baptised dies to sin as Christ died to redeem us. We cannot, then, without detracting from the efficacy of the Passion and death of Christ, recognise any consequence of sin remaining in the soul of the baptised.

Infant baptism

So much for the adults. And now what of infants ? Before speaking of any conditions relating to their baptism, let us ask this question : is it right to baptise them at all ? There is no direct answer to this question in the Scriptures, but there is no mistaking the directness of the answer supplied from tradition. Origen spoke truly in saying that the Church received this custom from the Apostles.[1] Even those who, like Harnack, deny the apostolicity of this custom, are none the less obliged to admit that it was a widespread custom in the time of Tertullian, who was born about the year 160. We have said that there is no direct answer in the Scriptures, but let us not forget that St Paul tells us that the grace of Christ abounds much more than the sin of Adam.[2] If it were not possible for infants to be baptised, and thereby be released from the effect of Adam's sin, it could scarcely be said that the grace of Christ abounded more than the sin of Adam, which was universal in its effect on mankind.

[1] *In Rom.*, l. v, 9.

[2] Rom. v 15.

There is one objection to the baptism of infants which we ought to answer here. It may be put in this way: it does not seem possible that infants could receive the virtues of Faith, Hope, and Charity, and the moral virtues too, since they are incapable of making acts of Faith, Hope, and Charity, and of performing moral acts. Therefore it does not seem possible that they could receive the Sacrament of Baptism. Again, they cannot prepare themselves by faith and the renunciation of Satan, and consequently cannot be disposed for the reception of this Sacrament.

We answer the first of these difficulties (which are really not very profound, but have troubled people here and there since the time of Tertullian) as follows: an act and the source or principle from which it arises are not the same thing. The act of seeing is not the same thing as the sense of sight; the act of willing is not the same thing as the will; an intellectual act is not the same thing as the intellect, and so forth. These sources of activity can exist and, of course, do exist even when they are not active. If it were true that an infant could not receive these virtues as the sources or principles of activity of the supernatural life that is given it in baptism, simply because it cannot as yet make use of them, then it would be equally true that infants could not be human beings, since they cannot perform intellectual acts or moral acts. The principles, then, or sources of supernatural activity are there, and will become active coincident with the activity of the reason and the will, as soon as the development of the child permits it.

To the second objection there are several irrefragable answers. The first is that the objection implies a misunderstanding of the nature of a Sacrament. A Sacrament, of its inherent power, produces an effect upon the soul when there is no obstacle placed in its way by the person to whom it is administered. An infant cannot place such an obstacle.

Again (and this brings us back to the main subject of this section), as regards the obligations of baptism, the obligation to live according to faith and to renounce the devil, we may say at first that nothing can be more erroneous than to think that obligations cannot exist without the consent of the human will. At the same time the Church in divine things, as the State in human things, can and does insist on the guaranteeing of these obligations in the case of infants. We have seen that baptism obliges one to live according to faith and to renounce sin. These obligations, as we have stated in the beginning of this section, the Church cannot waive. We are, therefore, in a position to state the situation with regard to the baptism of infants as follows: wherever the discharge of these obligations can be guaranteed, not according to absolute certainty, but according to human frailty, it is both lawful and obligatory to baptise infants. In what circumstances can we say that such a guarantee exists?

It exists for all infants who are about to die; for they cannot, from the nature of the case, ever abuse the Sacrament they are about to receive, or forfeit the grace, the virtues, and the gifts that it confers. Again, children of Christian parents must be baptised, as must also children of infidel parents who are abandoned by these parents; the act of abandonment meaning that the parents have forsaken their natural rights.

God-parents

By whom is this guarantee to be given? By the god-parents,[1] who, by professing faith for the infant and promising to renounce Satan on its behalf, guarantee that the child will live according to the obligations of baptism, and according to the life and virtues that are now conferred upon it. If the parents bring the child up well, the god-parents will have nothing to do. If the parents neglect their spiritual duties towards the child, the god-parents must seek to remedy this omission by whatever zeal and prudence may suggest. Let us add, lest an important point of doctrine should be misunderstood, that as the child grows up the obligation of living a good life according to faith arises from the Sacrament itself, from the baptismal Character, and not from its accepting what the god-parents have promised for it. On that point it has no choice. A little practical information on the subject of god-parents may be useful.[2]

1. One god-parent is sufficient. There may not be more than two, and if there are two they may not both be of the same sex.

2. Parents may not be god-parents.

3. God-parents must be Catholics. An excommunicated Catholic could not act as a god-parent.

4. They ought to be chosen by the parents.

5. They must touch the infant at baptism, either by holding or putting a hand on it, or by raising it from the font or from the hands of the minister immediately after baptism. This they must do in person or by proxy.

There are also two conditions necessary in order that one may lawfully act as a god-parent.

1. God-parents should not be under thirteen years of age, unless the minister of the Sacrament, for some good reason, allows a younger to act.

2. They should know the rudiments of faith.

Both the minister of the Sacrament and the god-parents contract spiritual relationship with the person baptised. When a god-parent acts by proxy, it is, of course, the god-parent and not the proxy who contracts the spiritual relationship. If baptism is given privately, owing to necessity, and no god-parent has been assigned, the person who acts as god-parent later on when the ceremonies are being supplied does not contract spiritual relationship.

What of the insane? If they are incurably insane they are to be baptised as infants, and nothing is required of them. God's mercy

[1] *Codex Iuris Can.*, c. 769. [2] *Ibid.*, 765, 766.

is manifest here, inasmuch as those whose condition is most pitiable of all in this life are certain of happiness in the next. If, however, their insanity is intermittent, it is necessary that they should have had at some time the intention of receiving baptism, and should have, as far as they are capable, the dispositions required in ordinary adults.

Are there any infants for whom these guarantees cannot be given ? Yes, the children of unbelievers. It would not be lawful to baptise them, as they would be brought up, if not to hate, at least to disbelieve in the teaching of Christ, and most probably to follow a mode of life inconsistent with the Christian conscience. Nor would it be lawful to withdraw these children by force from their parents, and bring them up in the faith against their parents' wish. For the parents by natural law have the care of their own children, and this law would be violated by such compulsion. Wrong must never be done that good may come of it. Suppose a child of infidel parents had been thus unlawfully baptised. In that case the child belongs to the Church, the natural right of the parents yielding to the divine right of the Church which the baptismal Character establishes. Whether or no the Church would insist on her rights would depend on what prudence would have to say to the merits of the individual case.

§ VI: SUMMARY

In this summary we shall review each of the preceding sections quite briefly, pointing out concisely to the reader what he must believe.

§ I.—Of what has been said in this section we must believe that baptism is a Sacrament, and that it was instituted by Christ. The Council of Trent (which deals exhaustively with baptism in its Seventh Session) has defined that all the Sacraments are of Divine institution, and that baptism is one of the seven Sacraments.[1]

§ II.—Before putting before the reader what he must believe in this section, we must take the precaution of calling his attention to the system by which we have divided it. We have divided it into three sections, adopting the system of distinguishing between the " Sacrament only," " The Thing," and " The Thing and the Sacrament." Now, we must impress upon the reader that he is not bound to believe that these three elements are to be found in every Sacrament ; for theologians are not in agreement on the point. We make use of it, none the less, because it is held by some of the greatest theologians, and because it enables us to put information before the reader in a tidy and orderly way. The one thing about which all theologians are agreed and which the reader must believe (on this particular point) is that whenever the Sacrament of Baptism is validly received the baptismal Character is given. Let us now

[1] Denz., 844 *sq.* (1913 ed.).

point out what one must believe with regard to the different points touched upon in this section.

We are bound to believe that true and natural water is necessary for this Sacrament. Anyone who asserts (as Luther somewhat vulgarly does in his *Table Talk*) that other substances, such as milk, beer, etc., could be used instead of water, would certainly sin against the faith. Still more would one sin who denied that water was necessary at all, maintaining that Christ only spoke in a figurative way when he mentioned water. Are we bound to believe that washing (proximate matter) is necessary? We are. No Council of the Church, it is true, has defined this point for us; but that is simply because the need of such definition has not arisen. To deny the necessity of washing would be to contradict the Scriptures, which speak of baptism as a laver or washing, and would undermine the Scriptural meaning of the word *baptism* itself; for it simply means a washing.

What of the form? We must believe that the expressions signifying the act of washing and the invocation of the three Divine Persons are necessary. Thus, the Council of Florence (1438-1445), in its famous decree for the Armenians, says that the form of baptism is, "I baptise thee in the name of the Father, and of the Son, and of the Holy Ghost"; or, "The servant of God (so-and-so) is baptised in the name of the Father, and of the Son, and of the Holy Ghost"; or, "So-and-so is baptised at my hands in the name of the Father, and of the Son, and of the Holy Ghost."[1] The seeming indirectness of the two latter forms does not militate against their correctness, because, since the principal cause from which baptism derives its efficacy is the Blessed Trinity, the function of the minister is sufficiently indicated in these forms. The assertion of the Council of Florence is not to be taken as a definition of faith, as the entire decree for the Armenians is intended as a practical direction and not as a definitive declaration. It is, however, of the highest authority, as coming from an Oecumenical Council. Nor are there wanting other important documents on this subject. Among thirty-one propositions condemned by the Holy Office under Alexander VIII, on December 7, 1690, is the following: "Baptism conferred in this way 'In the name of the Father, and of the Son, and of the Holy Ghost,' and without the words 'I baptise thee,' is valid."[2] Again, Pope Pelagius I (556-561), in his letter to Gaudentius, Bishop of Volterra, says that if it is truly shown that certain heretics have been baptised only in the name of the Lord, without the slightest hesitation they are to be baptised in the name of the Blessed Trinity.[3] We have, then, the Council of Florence directing us on the whole form of baptism, and Alexander and Pelagius directing us on each part of it respectively.

[1] Denz., 696. [2] *Ibid.*, 1317. [3] *Ibid.*, 229.

As regards the effects of baptism, we are bound to believe the following: that it remits sin, both actual and original, and all temporal punishment due to sin; that it gives grace and sanctification, virtues and gifts; that it makes us the adopted children of God; that it gives a Character to the soul; makes us members of the Church; and that it cannot be repeated. We are, moreover, bound to believe that baptism produces all its essential effects in infants as well as in adults.

The Council of Trent has made many definitive assertions on the effects of baptism, which we need not go into here, as they are primarily assertions against Luther and others, whose errors are so out of fashion to-day that the reader is not likely to encounter them. Thus, the Council anathematises those who assert that the mere act of recalling one's baptism rids one of sins, or that the grace given by baptism cannot be lost.

§ III.—We must believe—always excepting the martyrs—that the Sacrament of Baptism in reality or in desire (Charity) is necessary as a means of salvation; and we shall act very prudently in believing that the implicit desire, where nothing more is possible, is sufficient.

We must also believe that martyrdom is a means of justification and salvation. This has not formally been defined by the Church, but a denial of it would amount to a denial of our Lord's words: "He that shall lose his life for me shall find it"; and it would also amount to a contradiction of the teaching and practice of the Church, as shown in the writings of the Fathers, of the theologians, and in the Sacred Liturgy.

What if one were to hold the opinion of Cajetan? One would certainly be guilty of grave error. For, though the Council of Trent refrained from censuring the opinion of such a great theologian, it was ordered that this opinion should be expunged from his works.

§ IV.—We are bound to believe that priests are the ordinary ministers of baptism; and that, in case of necessity, the laity can and ought to administer this Sacrament; that women as well as men, and heretics, can administer it. Are we bound to believe that the unbaptised, or infidels, can administer this Sacrament? Yes, inasmuch as it would be rash to go against the opinion of all theologians to-day, who maintain that if an infidel had the intention of doing what the Church does, and used the correct outward sign, he would baptise validly. We might mention here that all converts in England to-day, coming from the various sects, are baptised conditionally. The principle of the validity of baptism as administered by heretics is not at stake here, as the precaution of conditional baptism is taken lest, through carelessness, the outward sign might not be correctly used. That such carelessness might arise is all the more likely from the fact that, outside the Catholic Church, there is no clear theological teaching on the nature of the Sacraments and the way in which they cause Grace. What of the intention of the ministers of baptism among the sects? Most probably it is a correct intention; for we may presume that they intend to do what Christ wishes us to do, unless (through an acute prejudice against the Church, which must be of very rare occurrence) they deliberately excluded the intention of doing what the Catholic Church does. In such an event, of course, the baptism would be invalid, as a person who will not do what the Church (which is the Mystical Body of Christ) does, will not do what Christ wishes us to do.

§ V.—We are obliged to believe that baptism can and ought to be given to infants as well as to adults. We are bound to believe that infants can and do receive grace and virtues at baptism. We are also obliged to believe that for lawful baptism adults must repent of their sins, and that they must believe. The words quoted from the Council of Trent above, p. 793, make this very clear to us. Also, we have a very interesting and important document in the letter of Innocent III to Humbert, Archbishop of Arles, in 1201, in which he points out how original sin and actual sin are washed away by baptism. We must understand, he tells us, that sin is of two kinds, original and actual. Original sin is contracted without our consent, and actual is committed with our consent. Original sin, therefore, which is contracted without consent, is washed away without consent (baptism of infants); but actual sin, which is committed with our consent, is not forgiven without our consent (need of repentance for adult sinners).

We introduced what we had to say about baptism with the observation that there is no Sacrament the existence of which is so generally admitted by all. Let us conclude by observing that there is no Sacrament concerning which all questions of importance have been settled from such an early date.

In fact, in the course of this essay we have found but two questions of importance that were not decisively settled in patristic times. These are: first, the question of the sufficiency of the implicit desire for baptism of Charity; and, secondly, the question of the validity of baptism administered by the unbaptised. And even in these two questions the principles on which a solution should be found were laid down. To whom do we principally owe this wonderful theological development in patristic times? It is not a departure from that sense of proportion which the enthusiast should be careful to observe in historical matters, to say that we owe it to the great St Augustine. His genius for seizing the fundamental principle to be relied upon in the solution of a difficult point, and his remarkable precision in stating a case theologically, are all the more praiseworthy when we remember that he had not, as the Scholastics had later on, the inestimable service of that handmaid of the theologian—the Aristotelian philosophy.

But Augustine was also indebted to his predecessors. When he was born, November 13, 354, the catechumenates had already been in existence for over a century and a half. In these catechumenates the aspirants to baptism were tried and instructed, and all the ceremonies and prayers accompanying the immediate preparation of those chosen for baptism embody the whole of the Church's teaching on baptism; not indeed expressed in theological terms, but expressed in her liturgical prayer, which is the spontaneous utterance of her teaching and her truth. Tertullian, who was born about 160, was himself, in all probability, a catechist in the school for catechumens at Carthage. So intense was the interest in baptism in his day that his writings not only contain frequent references to it, but show a development of the subject in such maturity that there is an entertaining air of modernity about them. How shall we explain this intense interest, to which the early development of the theology of this Sacrament is due?

We must remember that while baptism means the same for us as it did for Christians in every age, it is probably hard for us to realise the wonderful joy and the unexpected hope that this Sacrament brought to the pagan world of old. To a world that had largely begun to despair of itself there came the assurance, on the authority of a Church claiming to be and every day proving itself to be divine, that no matter what men had done, no matter how old they were, no matter how ineradicable their vices had seemed to be, their past could be completely wiped out and God himself would take them as his friends, enabling them to begin a new life with him and to persevere in that life with fidelity; the only obligation on their part being to prepare themselves by faith and repentance for the wonderful graces of baptism. This assurance, and the proof of the mysterious efficacy of baptism in the lives and the deaths of the early Christians, brought such a new happiness and confidence into the world that it led to the greatest reformation of society that the world has ever seen; a reformation so great, indeed, that it is inexplicable without recourse to a miracle of the moral order.

The writings of the Fathers are a witness to this wonderful reformation of society, but nowhere is it more vividly brought before us than in the Liturgy of Christian Initiation. Through the enlightenment of mind and the reform of his will that has resulted from his hearing the word of God, the neophyte is given a new taste for heavenly wisdom to replace the folly of sin, and an odour of sweetness to replace the foulness of Satan. This much results from the opening of his ears. But the power of Satan, who would try to wrest from the neophyte the good dispositions to which he has been brought, is offset by the great exorcisms of the Church. He turns to the west, the region of darkness and the setting sun, and for ever renounces Satan and all his works and pomps; then he turns to the east, the region of light and the rising sun, and solemnly makes his profession of that faith through which he is saved. Finally, he is baptised, and, when the rite of his Confirmation and first Holy Communion is finished, he is for ever admitted to a land that is flowing with the milk and honey of God's abundant Grace. All these things are represented and effected by the ceremonies and prayers of initiation, of which baptism is the focal point. These prayers and ceremonies are so full of a chaste joy, of a new and wonderful hope, that they recover for us, with a vividness that is extraordinary, the iniquity of the pagan world and the wonder of its reformation through Holy Baptism. Even the inscriptions in the ancient baptisteries bring this hope and joy before us. We may well believe that many a poor sinner, so happy and so repentant, read through the inscription in the baptistery of the Lateran, and perhaps repeated the last two lines again and again :

> " Nec numerus quemquam scelerum, nec forma suorum
> Terreat, hoc natus flumine salvus erit."

Which we may translate freely :

" Let no one be terrified by the number or the nature of his sins ; he who is born of these waters will indeed be holy."

JOHN P. MURPHY.

XXIII

THE SACRAMENT OF CONFIRMATION

§ I: THE SACRAMENT OF MATURITY

Confirmation the complement of Baptism

As Baptism is the sacrament of supernatural birth so Confirmation is the sacrament of supernatural maturity. The baptised are mere infants in the life of grace, *modo geniti infantes* ;[1] the confirmed are adults, they have reached the status of Christian manhood. Confirmation thus confirms or perfects the life which Baptism has bestowed, and for this reason is called in Christian tradition the consummation, the perfection, or the complement of Baptism, and in the early stages of the Church was administered immediately after Baptism itself.

Conferring, not full supernatural growth

But if the notion of maturity is to convey accurately the peculiar meaning and effect of Confirmation it must not be understood in the sense of completed supernatural growth. Full growth in the life of grace means Christian perfection, it means the attainment of the greatest possible likeness to Christ through the perfect exercise of the Christian virtues. In this sense the attainment of maturity is, quite literally, a life's work ; for of no man can it be said, so long as life lasts, that he has reached the full stature of sanctity or achieved that particular degree of holiness which God has assigned to him for his measure. In the performance of his task he has the valuable aid of the sacraments, each of which has its appointed part to play in the process of sanctification, but there is no one sacrament which of itself confers the seal of accomplishment. It is not in this sense that Confirmation perfects the work of Baptism.

Nor the power of growth

Nor must we allow ourselves, in assigning the place which Confirmation holds in the sacramental system, to usurp functions for it which belong to other sacraments ; in particular we must not ascribe to it effects which Baptism already suffices to produce. Thus, we might perhaps be tempted to suppose that, Baptism being the sacrament of birth or infancy, it is for Confirmation to supply that vital strength which will enable the infant life to develop. This, however, would be to belittle the efficacy of Baptism. It is true that the soul newly baptised is supernaturally an infant. But this does not mean that it has received only and barely that minimum which is needed to make it supernaturally alive. Just as the child newly born to the life of this world receives by the natural process of generation all those intrinsic vital powers by the development of which he will grow to manhood, so the newly baptised Christian possesses already

[1] 1 Peter ii 2.

every inherent supernatural power by the development of which he can grow to perfection. Endowed with sanctifying grace, infused virtues, gifts of the Holy Ghost, he has within himself all the inner principles or springs of supernatural life and activity. It is not, therefore, as conferring the power of growth that Confirmation perfects the work of Baptism.

Nor supernatural nourishment

Supernatural growth does indeed call for supernatural nourishment. But to provide this is, again, not the function of Confirmation but rather of the Eucharist, instituted by Christ for the very purpose of giving us his own true Flesh and Blood as our spiritual food. If, therefore, among the sacraments there is one to which the supernatural growth of the soul is especially to be attributed, it is surely this. "All those effects," writes St Thomas, "which material food and drink produce in regard to bodily life are produced in respect of the spiritual life by this sacrament: it sustains, it gives increase, it repairs loss, it gives delight." [1]

Nor, specifically, the power of resistance to temptation

Nor, finally, would it seem to be the specific purpose of Confirmation to strengthen the life of the soul by arming it against the agents of destruction as such, by enabling it to resist the devil, the world, and the flesh, which are the enemies of the supernatural life of grace. For this also is a function which belongs properly to other sacraments. In the first place it belongs to the Eucharist which, besides "nourishing and strengthening those who live by the life of him who said, 'He that eateth me the same also shall live by me,' serves also as an antidote to deliver us from the sins which we daily commit and to preserve us from those sins which kill the soul." [2] And the same effect is also produced by those sacraments (Penance and Extreme Unction) whose purpose is not only to repair the ravages of sin but also to forearm the soul against temptation by the sacramental graces which are proper to each.

But the power to fulfil one's public duty as a Christian

We are thus forced to conclude that the maturity which Confirmation bestows is not to be understood merely in terms of vital vigour or development. It is in some other characteristic of adult age that we must find an analogy to illustrate the special effect of this sacrament. What else, apart from the mere fact of physical and mental growth, distinguishes the adult from the child? Surely it is the sense of public responsibility. "In childhood," says St Thomas, "a human being is an individualist; he lives, as it were, only for himself. But when he reaches the full vigour of manhood he begins to exert his activity upon others." [3] The child, naturally and legitimately, is an individualist; he is himself the only object of his own solicitude and of the loving care of all who surround him. And this is quite right and proper. Nature bids a child direct all his powers and energies to his own self-development, to the nourish-

[1] *Summa Theol.*, III, Q. lxxix, art. 1.
[2] Council of Trent, sess. xiii, cap. 2.
[3] *Summa Theol.*, III, Q. lxxii, art. 2.

ment of his little body and the exercise of his little limbs, to the preservation of his life against the dangers that beset it especially when it is young and tender, to the education and training of the physical and mental powers which are to bring him to his full stature as an individual human being. A child's responsibilities are all for himself. It is only when he reaches manhood that he must take his place as a citizen and shoulder his burden as a member of society.

The child in the life of grace

Something of the same sort is true of the Christian in his supernatural life. His baptismal endowments are intended for his spiritual status and growth as an individual. "In Baptism," says St Thomas, "a man receives power for those actions which concern his own salvation, in so far as he lives his own life." [1] This does not mean that he is an isolated unit, entirely self-contained, and able to grow in grace independently of any relations with his fellow men. The Christian life is essentially a life of union, of union with God and of union with one's neighbour. The Christian, whether confirmed or not, is bound by the paramount duties of charity, charity towards God and towards men ; indeed it is upon his observance of the first and greatest commandment, and of the second which is like to it, that his continuance in the state of grace and his progress in the spiritual life essentially depend. He has his duties of justice towards others, and in all his dealings with his fellow men he is bound by the code of the moral virtues. He has the duty, moreover, in virtue of his baptism, of guarding his supernatural life against hostile influences, conformably with the solemn injunction laid upon him when he was born to grace : "Receive this white garment and see thou keep it without stain unto the judgement seat of God."

The adult in the life of grace

And yet he remains only a child in the supernatural order until the moment comes in which, so to speak, he takes the *toga* of public life in the Church. And this is the stage marked by the Sacrament of Confirmation. Ever since his baptism he has been a member of the Church, a son of God, a citizen of the City of God, and has enjoyed all the privileges of that status. But it is only in Confirmation that he receives the charge and the strength also to shoulder its responsibilities, to fulfil those obligations in the eyes of the world which rest upon him, not merely as a son of God, bound already by his Christian duties towards God and men, but as a mature and officially accredited citizen of the one holy, catholic, and apostolic Church.

The duty of bearing witness

A summary indication of the responsibility which Confirmation imposes is so important for the understanding of what follows that it must be given at once. It is described briefly by Christ himself in the words which he used to his Apostles before he ascended into heaven : "You shall be witnesses unto me." [2] It is the bounden duty of each spiritually mature and adult member of the catholic and apostolic Church to be a witness. The Church is the authentic

[1] *Summa Theol.*, III, Q. lxxii, art. 5. [2] Acts i 8.

witness to Jesus Christ on earth, and every responsible citizen of this City of God shares in that divinely appointed function of the Church, according to the place which he occupies in the organism of the Mystical Body of Christ. This is surely the deep significance of that gift of tongues which in the primitive Church, both on the day of Pentecost and on other occasions, gave external proof of the coming of the Holy Spirit. " The Holy Ghost descended upon them, and they spoke with tongues " ; as though to say, they were confirmed and they bore witness. And not only did they bear witness, but they bore witness in the tongues of every nation under heaven, because they were members of a Church not only apostolic but catholic also. As St Augustine aptly observes, in Jerusalem the universal mission of the Church had already begun, and the Pentecostal tongues were but a symbol to foreshadow the reality of a Church which would in fact, and not merely in figure, preach the gospel throughout the world. And if the Mystical Body of Christ is a witness, he argues, then every member of it is a witness too. " I, too," he exclaims, " I, too, speak with the tongues of all nations. Am I not in the Body of Christ, am I not in the Church of Christ? If the Body of Christ speaks with the tongues of all nations, then the tongues of all nations are mine." [1]

The strong and perfect Christian

Such is the glorious task to which Confirmation calls the Christian and for which it endows him. Already truly a member of the Church, he now becomes a spokesman of the Church, of the Church who, " like a standard set up unto the nations, calls to herself those who have not yet believed, and at the same time gives assurance to her own children that the faith which they profess reposes on the firmest of foundations." [2] Proudly conscious of his citizenship, he testifies to the world that he is indeed a follower of Christ and an upholder of his faith, ready if need be to die as a soldier in its defence. In Baptism the life of grace appears as a white garment to be kept pure and unspotted from the stains of the world ; in Confirmation the faith is raised aloft as a flying banner, under which we march as " strong and perfect Christians and soldiers of Jesus Christ."

The Sacrament of the Holy Spirit

Confirmation is called pre-eminently the Sacrament of the Holy Ghost. And it is fitting that to this Divine Person, in whom the eternal processions of the Godhead find their culmination, we should attribute in a particular way the seal of sanctification which sets the finishing touch of maturity to the making of the Christian. This " appropriation " [3] reflects the words of Christ himself, who consistently assigns this perfective function to the Holy Spirit whom he would send, and it finds its firm support in the Acts of the Apostles, where this complement of Baptism is commonly called " the gift of the Spirit " or " the coming of the Holy Ghost."

[1] *Enarr. in psalm.* cxlvii 19.
[2] Vatican Council, *De fid. cath.*, cap. 3.
[3] For the meaning of this term, see Essay iv, *The Blessed Trinity*, p. 137.

It may be useful, however (though not necessary to those who have studied earlier essays in this work),[1] to observe that the confirmed are not receiving the Holy Spirit for the first time. Wherever there is an outpouring of sanctifying grace there is the mysterious presence of the Trinity in the soul, and an invisible mission of the Son and the Holy Ghost. Already in Baptism the three divine Persons have taken up their abode in the soul, already the Holy Ghost dwells therein as in his temple. Consequently, if Confirmation is called the Sacrament of the Holy Spirit *par excellence* it must be because the peculiar effect of this sacrament—to create official witnesses to God's truth—is one which is in a special way associated with the third Person of the Blessed Trinity. And that this is indeed the case it must now be our object to show.

§ II: THE SPIRIT OF TESTIMONY

" Qui locutus est per prophetas "

In the Nicene Creed the Church professes her belief in the Holy Ghost " who spoke through the prophets " (*qui locutus est per prophetas*) ; and if by prophets we understand, as we should, not merely those who foretell future events but all those who deliver God's message to men, who bear witness to divine truth, we shall see that there is a close connection between this article of the Creed and the Sacrament of Confirmation.

In the prophets of old

This special function of the Holy Spirit is revealed to us already in the Old Testament. We are told how the Spirit rested upon the seventy elders so that they prophesied ; [2] Samuel assures Saul, the king of Israel, that the Spirit of the Lord will come upon him and he will prophesy ; [3] and it is to the same Spirit that Micheas attributes the power in which he speaks. " I am filled with strength," he says, thanks to " the Spirit of God." [4] And we are even given an indication that the time will come when the Spirit of testimony will no longer be the privilege of a favoured few, but will be granted to all. " It shall come to pass after this," the prophet Joel proclaims in God's name, " that I will pour out my Spirit upon all flesh, and your sons and your daughters shall prophesy." [5]

In the immediate heralds of the Messias

But as the moment approaches which the Scriptures call the fulness of time, when the promises of the Old Testament are at last to be fulfilled, and when God, having in times past spoken to men by the prophets, is about to speak to them by his own Son,[6] then the Spirit of testimony becomes more and more active and is poured out in special abundance upon the immediate heralds of the Messias. The opening chapters of St Luke's Gospel tell us the story of this busy activity of the Holy Spirit in all those who are associated with the infancy of the divine Redeemer. The same Spirit who comes

[1] See Essay v, *The Holy Ghost*, pp. 161 ff.
[2] Numbers xi 25.
[3] 1 Kings x 6-10.
[4] Micheas iii 8.
[5] Joel ii 28 ; *cf.* Essay v, p. 144.
[6] *Cf.* Heb. i 1.

upon Our Lady to operate in her the miraculous conception of the Son of God,[1] fills the heart of Elizabeth so that she bears testimony to Mary as the Mother of her Lord and utters those inspired words, "Blessed art thou among women and blessed is the fruit of thy womb," with which the Church still salutes the Mother of God.[2] The same Spirit fills the soul of the Precursor, so that he leaps in the womb of his mother to bear witness to Mary's unborn Child.[3] Zachary is moved by the Holy Ghost to chant his canticle in praise of the coming Saviour ;[4] and it is under the same inspiration that Simeon greets the Redeemer who is to be for the fall and the resurrection of many in Israel, and that in prophecy he associates Mary with the redemptive sufferings of her Son.[5]

In the Saviour himself

But it is in Jesus himself, the true Christ, anointed by God with the oil of gladness (*i.e.* with the Holy Spirit) beyond his fellows,[6] in Jesus, who came into the world that he might give testimony to the truth,[7] that the Spirit of testimony pre-eminently exerts his power. From the moment in which the Son of God became incarnate in his Virgin Mother's womb, the Holy Spirit with all the plenitude of his supernatural gifts and graces took up his abode in the most holy soul of Christ, and to that fulness of grace and truth, which was the rightful heritage of the Word Incarnate, nothing could be added. If he is said to have grown in grace it is only because the hidden treasures of his soul became more and more manifest as men came to know him for what he was. And so, when the time came at which he must be shown forth before men as the Son of God, in complete possession of all the secrets of the Father and charged with the mission of revealing them to mankind, a special manifestation took place. After he had been baptised by John in the Jordan "the heaven opened and the Holy Ghost descended in bodily shape, as a dove, upon him. And a voice came from heaven : Thou art my beloved Son."[8] It was the Spirit of testimony openly displaying himself in the King of the prophets. His work of bearing witness to the truth was about to begin.

Jesus anointed to preach the gospel

The deep significance of this visible manifestation of the Spirit at the beginning of Our Lord's public life did not escape the inspired vision of St Peter, who ascribes to the assistance of the Holy Spirit the power with which Jesus fulfilled his mission of preaching. "You know the word," he said at Caesarea after the conversion of Cornelius, "which hath been published through all Judea ; for it began from Galilee after the baptism which John preached : how God anointed Jesus of Nazareth with the Holy Ghost and with power."[9] And lest we should have any doubt that it is indeed the Spirit of testimony who speaks also in Jesus, we have his own words to the people of Nazareth : "The Spirit of the Lord is upon me," he proclaims,

[1] Luke i 35. [2] Luke i 41-42. [3] Luke i 44.
[4] Luke i 67. [5] Luke ii 25-35. [6] Heb. i 9 ; *cf.* Ps. xliv.
[7] John xviii 37. [8] Luke iii 21-22. [9] Acts x 37-38.

quoting the words of the prophet Isaias; "for he hath anointed me to preach the Gospel."[1] No wonder that the Fathers have seen in that striking scene enacted by the river Jordan a prefigurement of the Christian sacraments of Baptism and Confirmation.

The Apostles sent to continue the work

For the mission of preaching the Gospel which Christ had received from his Father was not to be completed with his earthly life. His Apostles were to continue the work: "As the Father hath sent me, so I also send you . . . going teach ye all nations."[2] The task of bearing witness to the truth had cost the Saviour his Passion and Death, and only the power of the Spirit had sustained him against the torrent of hatred which had greeted his message. It was not to be an easy task for the Apostles either. "The disciple," he warned them, "is not above his master, nor the servant above his lord. It is enough for the disciple that he be as his master and the servant as his lord. If they have called the goodman of the house Beelzebub, how much more them of his household?"[3] Their mission would not be one in which they would be welcomed with open arms: "Behold I send you as sheep in the midst of wolves. Beware of men; for they will deliver you up in councils and they will scourge you in their synagogues. And you shall be brought before governors and kings for my sake, for a testimony to them and to the Gentiles."[4]

Promise of the Spirit to the Apostles

The Apostles were to be under no illusions, therefore; they must be prepared to meet the same opposition as their Master. But were they to undertake their mission unaided? Was that Spirit of testimony who had spoken through the prophets of old, through Zachary, Elizabeth, the Baptist, Simeon, who had anointed Jesus himself for the preaching of the Gospel, was this Spirit to be withheld from them? Our Lord reassures them immediately. "When they shall deliver you up," he tells them, "take no thought how or what to speak; for it shall be given you in that hour what to speak. For it is not you that speak but the Spirit of your Father that speaketh in you."[5]

Their need of the Spirit

Their need of the Spirit is shown clearly when we consider their conduct before they received it. They did not lack faith in their Master, nor loving devotion to him; what they needed was the courage to proclaim their faith and loyalty in the face of scornful opposition. The behaviour of Peter may be taken as typical of them all. He had so boldly professed his faith at Caesarea when there were no enemies of Christ at hand;[6] together with the other Apostles he had clung to his Master when so many of the other disciples "went back and walked no more with him";[7] in the enthusiasm of his loyalty he had declared: "Although all shall be scandalised in thee, I will never be scandalised. . . . Yea, though I should die with thee, I will not deny thee."[8] But none knew better than the Master

[1] Luke iv 18.
[2] John xx 21 with Matt. xxviii 19.
[3] Matt. x 24-25.
[4] Matt. x 16-18.
[5] Matt. x 19-20.
[6] Matt. xvi 16.
[7] John vi 67-70.
[8] Matt. xxvi 33, 35.

himself how frail were such resolutions when unconfirmed by the Spirit of testimony, and therefore we must surely read a divine tenderness in the words of warning which he addressed to Peter: "Amen I say to thee that in this night before the cock crow thou wilt deny me thrice." [1] As the event proved, it needed only the taunting of a serving maid and the questioning of a few casual by-standers to overwhelm a courage which was as yet not firmly established in the Spirit.[2]

They are warned to await the Spirit

So well did Jesus know their weakness that, even after he had risen from the dead and so afforded them ocular proof of his glorious triumph, he still warns them that they must not attempt to begin their mission of bearing witness until they have received the needful strengthening of the Spirit. In his last discourse before ascending into heaven he shows them that they have now every ground for firm faith in him: "Thus it is written," he says, "and thus it behoved Christ to suffer and to rise again from the dead the third day; and that penance and remission of sins should be preached in his name unto all nations, beginning at Jerusalem. And you are witnesses of these things." But then, as though bidding them beware of a self-reliance which had already betrayed them, he adds: "I send the promised one from my Father upon you; *but stay you in the city till you be endued with power from on high.*" [3] And again, as St Luke tells us more clearly in the Acts of the Apostles, "He commanded them that they should not depart from Jerusalem, but should wait for the promise of the Father, which you have heard (saith he) by my mouth. . . . You shall receive the power of the Holy Ghost coming upon you, and you shall be witnesses unto me in Jerusalem and in all Judea and Samaria, and even to the uttermost part of the earth." [4]

The promise fulfilled at Pentecost

On the day of Pentecost Our Lord's promise was fulfilled: "When the days of Pentecost were accomplished, they were all together in one place. And suddenly there came a sound from heaven, as of a mighty wind coming; and it filled the whole house where they were sitting. And there appeared to them parted tongues, as it were of fire, and it sat upon every one of them. And they were all filled with the Holy Ghost, and they began to speak with divers tongues, according as the Holy Ghost gave them to speak." [5]

[E]xternal phenomena and inner working of the Spirit

It is important both in this, the first instance of the giving of the Holy Ghost in the Christian dispensation, and in others which are related by St Luke, to distinguish between what is incidental and what is essential in the effects of his outpouring; and if, in what precedes, we appear to have stressed unduly the terms in which the Spirit was promised by Christ and the need in which the Apostles stood of his strengthening grace, it has only been in order that we may now more clearly perceive wherein lies the essential fulfilment

[1] Matt. xxvi 34. [2] *Ibid.*, 69-75.
[3] Luke xxiv 46-49. [4] Acts i 4, 8. [5] Acts ii 1-4.

of the promise. We must not allow ourselves to be blinded to the interior workings of the Spirit by undue attention to his outward manifestations. These have their importance, and for St Luke, whose chief object is to explain the rapid spread of the Christian Church, they have a very great importance indeed. That the first communication of this divine power which was to renovate the world should be accompanied by unmistakable proofs of its presence, that the invisible Spirit should make himself seen in the brightness of fire, heard in the sound of a mighty wind, felt in the shaking of the earth;[1] that the Apostles themselves, and also the first members of the infant Church, should exhibit to the world outward and manifest signs (the gift of tongues, the working of wonders, the casting out of devils)[2] as proofs of the Spirit that worked within them—all this appears natural and appropriate when we remember that Pentecost is not only the "Confirmation" of the Apostles but also the first solemn promulgation of the Christian Church; and it would be strange if these phenomena did not assume great prominence in the story.

Essential effect of the coming of the Spirit

But if we were to see, as some have been led to see, in these visible portents the sole or the chief effect of the gift of the Spirit, we should be forgetting the principal purpose for which that gift was promised. The Spirit whom Christ had promised to send from the Father was to supply in them what had hitherto been so conspicuously lacking, namely, the courage to bear witness to Christ; if they were to be baptised with the Holy Ghost not many days hence, if they were to receive his power coming upon them, if they were to be endued with power from on high, if they were to postpone the inauguration of their mission until they had received that power, it was in order that they might be enabled thereby "to speak the word of God with confidence."[3]

Therefore the essential working of the Spirit of testimony is within the hearts of the Apostles, and its outward showing is to be seen not in the working of miracles or the speaking with tongues, but in the new courage with which they now proclaim their message and which presents so marvellous a contrast with their former timidity. Peter, who not long before had denied his Lord at the word of a serving wench, now lifts up his voice before the whole people of Jerusalem, telling them how God had raised Jesus from the dead, "whereof all we are witnesses."[4] "Let all the house of Israel know most certainly," he cries, "that God hath made this same Jesus whom you have crucified both Lord and Christ."[5] Apprehended by the officers of the temple, he boldly preaches Jesus to the Jewish authorities; "filled with the Holy Ghost," he proclaims the power of Jesus of Nazareth whom they had put to death;[6] charged by

[1] Acts iv 31.
[2] *Cf.* Acts viii 15-18; xix 2-6; iv 30-31; vi 5-8; viii 7.
[3] Acts iv 31.
[4] Acts ii 32.
[5] *Ibid.*, 36.
[6] Acts iv 1-10.

them not to speak at all nor teach in the name of Jesus, he joins with the other Apostles in making that solemn declaration which has been the motto of the Christian martyrs ever since: "We ought to obey God rather than men."[1] The power of the Spirit of testimony makes itself felt so irresistibly within them that they are constrained to bear witness to God's truth: "We cannot but speak the things which we have seen and heard."[2] And with their shoulders still smarting from the scourges, they come forth from the council "rejoicing that they are counted worthy to suffer reproach for the name of Jesus."[3]

Could the promise of Christ have been more manifestly fulfilled? "They will scourge you in their synagogues. . . . But when they shall deliver you up it shall be given to you in that hour what to speak. For it is not you that speak but the Spirit of your Father who speaketh in you."

All the faithful must bear the burden of witness

But the burden of witness lies not only upon the chosen twelve; it lies upon the faithful also, all of whom are called, each in his own way, to bear witness to the faith of Jesus Christ. It was not only to the Apostles but to all his followers that Jesus said: "Everyone that shall confess me before men, I will also confess him before my Father who is in heaven. But he that shall deny me before men, I will also deny him before my Father who is in heaven."[4] To preach the gospel by word of mouth will not be the task of everyone, but none is exempt from the obligation of so living that he may be recognised by the world for a disciple of Christ. "So let your light shine before men," he says, "that they may see your good works and glorify your Father who is in heaven."[5]

The task of witness will be hard

And for the faithful too the task of bearing witness to Christ will be a hard one. If their Christian conduct brings upon them the hatred of a hostile world, this is only the price that must be paid by all the prophets, by all who give testimony to God's truth: "Blessed are ye when they shall revile you and persecute you and speak all that is evil against you, untruly, for my sake. Be glad and rejoice for your reward is very great in heaven; for so they persecuted the prophets that were before you."[6] They will be hated and reproached and their name will be cast out as evil for Christ's sake.[7] St John tells the Christians of the first century not to wonder if the world hated them;[8] he has in mind the words which Christ had intended for all believers: "If the world hate you, know that it hath hated me before you. If you had been of the world, the world would love its own; but because you are not of the world, but I have chosen you out of the world, therefore the world hateth you."[9] This is why the Prince of Peace himself had to proclaim that he came not to bring peace but the sword, and why he, who is the Author of

[1] Acts v 28-29. [2] Acts iv 20. [3] Acts v 40-41.
[4] Matt. x 32-33. [5] Matt. v 16. [6] *Ibid.* 11-12.
[7] *Cf.* Luke vi 22. [8] 1 John iii 13. [9] John xv 18-19.

the commandment to honour father and mother, imposes upon his disciples one of the hardest tests of all: "He that loveth father or mother more than me is not worthy of me." [1]

The Spirit promised to all the faithful

But if every Christian must bear the burden of witness, we shall expect also that for every Christian there will likewise be a share in the outpouring of the Spirit by which Apostles are strengthened for their task. And so indeed it is. Christ promises that the Father "will give the good Spirit to them that ask him"; [2] and it is of this same Spirit of fortitude that St John bids us understand the mysterious words of Christ in the temple: "He that believeth in me . . . out of his belly shall flow rivers of living water." "Now this" (the evangelist explains), "he said of the Spirit which they should receive who believed in him; for as yet the Spirit was not given, because Jesus was not yet glorified." [3] The same reassurance is given to the early Christians by St Peter: "Dearly beloved," he writes, "think not strange the burning heat which is to try you, as if some new thing happened to you. . . . If you be reproached for the name of Christ you shall be blessed; for the Spirit of glory, which is the Spirit of God, resteth upon you." [4] And it is of this universal promise that he understands the prophecy of Joel when he preached to the people of Jerusalem on the day of Pentecost: "It shall come to pass . . . I will pour out of my Spirit upon all flesh." To receive this precious gift they need not belong to the chosen twelve. "Do penance," he tells them, "and be baptised every one of you in the name of Jesus Christ for the remission of your sins. And you shall receive the gift of the Holy Ghost. For the promise is to you and to your children and to all that are far off, whomsoever the Lord our God shall call." [5]

The Spirit granted to all the faithful

Already in the primitive Church we begin to see the promise fulfilled. Even the first Pentecostal outpouring, it would appear, was not reserved to the Apostles alone. St Luke's account leads one to suppose that, besides Mary the Mother of Jesus and the Apostles, the whole of the little Christian community (about one hundred and twenty souls) were present in that upper room when the Holy Ghost "came upon every one of them, and they were all filled with the Holy Ghost." [6] Thereafter the activity of the Holy Spirit is widespread throughout the infant Church. "We are witnesses," exclaims St Peter, "and so is the Holy Ghost, whom God has given to all that obey him." [7] A new outpouring fills the faithful when the Jewish authorities begin their persecution, "and they speak the word of God with confidence"; [8] the seven deacons are filled with the Holy Ghost, [9] and under his inspiration Stephen, first fruits of the Spirit of Christian martyrdom, confounds the Jews and with his dying

[1] Matt. x 34-37. [2] Luke xi 13. [3] John vii 38-39.
[4] 1 Peter iv 12, 14 (according to the Greek text).
[5] Acts ii 16, 38. [6] Acts i 13-15; ii 3-4.
[7] Acts v 32. [8] Acts iv 31. [9] Acts vi 3.

breath bears witness to Jesus whom he sees standing at the right hand of God.[1] Under the guidance of the same Spirit Philip the deacon evangelises the Samaritans,[2] upon whom the Apostles Peter and John subsequently confer the Holy Ghost by the imposition of hands;[3] Paul is no sooner converted than he is filled with the Spirit;[4] Cornelius, in whose person the Gentiles are called to the Church, receives the Holy Ghost even before he is baptised;[5] the same Spirit is poured out upon all the converts from paganism;[6] and the disciples of Ephesus, as soon as they have been baptised in the name of the Lord Jesus, also receive the Holy Ghost by the imposition of the hands of St Paul.[7]

What Joel had foretold was indeed coming to pass: the Holy Spirit who had spoken by the prophets of old, who had enlightened the immediate forerunners of the Redeemer, who had anointed Jesus himself for the preaching of the Gospel, who had been given with overwhelming evidence to the Apostles and the first disciples on the day of Pentecost—this same Spirit of testimony was being poured out "upon all flesh."

§ III: THE SACRAMENT IN SCRIPTURE

A Sacrament of Confirmation antecedently probable

THE information already gleaned from the Scriptures, combined with a consideration of the general plan by which Christ has provided for the needs of his Church, would lead us to expect that he has instituted a Sacrament of Confirmation. Supernatural gifts are by their very definition entirely gratuitous; man has no claim to them and God is under no absolute obligation to bestow them. Still less is the Author of grace, should he see fit to bestow such gifts, in any way restricted as to the means he may choose for communicating them. Nevertheless the Christian dispensation of the supernatural is marked by a regular and harmonious arrangement which presents many analogies with the natural order, for both nature and supernature are equally the work of that Wisdom which "reaches from end to end mightily and orders all things sweetly."[8] We are thus often able in some measure, by means of what theologians call the analogy of faith, to surmise in advance what the divine dispositions are likely to be.

The sacramental system

Now among the graces given to men are some which we may call particular graces: that is to say, supernatural aids rendered necessary by particular circumstances which are not the common lot of all Christians and are not involved in the ordinary life of the Church. That such graces will never be lacking to those who need them we may be certain; but we should not expect God to have

[1] Acts vi 5, 10; vii 55.
[2] Acts viii.
[3] Acts viii 14-17.
[4] Acts ix 17.
[5] Acts x 44.
[6] Acts x 45, 47; xi 15, 17; xv 7-9.
[7] Acts xix 1-7.
[8] Wisdom viii 1.

established permanent and regular channels for their bestowal. There are other graces, on the contrary, which we may call normal; normal because they form part of the usual equipment of the Christian, or are designed to meet common emergencies, or are required for the government and administration of the Church. For such needs God has provided by the institution of the sacraments: birth, nourishment, healing, wedlock, government and social welfare, all these ordinary features of our natural life have their counterpart in the supernatural economy, and the respective graces are available in a marvellously devised sacramental system.[1] It would therefore be surprising if this divinely established scheme did not include a sacrament for the bestowal of that grace, promised to all Christians, which enables them to confess their divine Master before men.

Let us examine our earliest sources, then, to see whether there existed in the primitive Church a rite or ceremony designed for the normal bestowal of what we have come to call, for convenience sake, the Spirit of testimony. I say, for its normal bestowal, because only such a rite can be regarded as truly sacramental, that is, as permanently instituted by Christ for the sanctification of the faithful.

Abnormal conditions of the primitive Church

But when we turn to the Acts of the Apostles, our chief inspired source of information about the primitive Christian community, we are immediately confronted with a difficulty. It is the difficulty of finding traces of the normal in the midst of conditions which are very far from normal indeed. Allusion has already been made to the emphasis which is laid upon the extraordinary in St Luke's narrative, an emphasis which is explained by the purpose of his writing. Primarily interested as he is in describing the overwhelming impact of the divine Spirit upon the world, it is no wonder that he writes chiefly of those challenging manifestations whereby the Spirit of testimony was compelling the attention of men to the first beginnings of Christianity, and thus makes little mention of the regular pastoral work of the Church which, for the rest, had scarcely yet begun. A study of the Acts accordingly reveals two types of "Confirmation"; the extraordinary or supra-sacramental, which appears with greater prominence, and the normal or sacramental, of which the indications are casual and rare.

Supra-sacramental Confirmation: e.g. Pentecost; the case of Cornelius

To the first category belongs certainly the descent of the Holy Ghost on the day of Pentecost; the occasion called for an overwhelmingly manifest and direct intervention of divine power. Another extraordinary communication of the Spirit is that which was made to Cornelius and his companions. Here, too, was a crisis demanding abnormal measures. A new stage in the development of the Church (the admission of the Gentiles) was about to begin, and it had required a vision from God to overcome St Peter's hesitation in embarking on it. And so, while he is still instructing Cornelius and his company, and before he has baptised them, the Spirit of

[1] See Essay xxi, *The Sacramental System*, pp. 743-744; *cf.* pp. 73-74.

testimony intervenes with a special portent to endorse his action. " While Peter was yet speaking, the Holy Ghost fell upon all them that heard the word. And the faithful of the circumcision, who came with Peter, were astonished for that the grace of the Holy Ghost was poured out upon the Gentiles also. For they heard them speaking with tongues and magnifying God." [1] Neither Peter nor the converts from Judaism who were with him could have any further doubt. " Can any man forbid water," he exclaims to his companions, " that these should not be baptised, who have received the Holy Ghost as well as we ? " [2] And when, on returning to Jerusalem, he is required to justify his extraordinary action to those " of the circumcision," he appeals again and again to this manifest sign of the divine approval.[3]

The normal procedure : the Samaritans

And now here, to compare, and also in some measure to contrast, with these extraordinary outpourings of the Spirit, are two instances in which the same grace is conveyed by what has every appearance of being a normal sacramental rite. The first is the Confirmation of the Samaritans. Among the providential results of the persecution of the Church at Jerusalem was the dispersal of many members of the new community among the neighbouring districts, with the consequent preaching of the Gospel over a wider field. Philip the deacon found scope for his zeal in the province of Samaria, where he made many converts to whom he administered the Sacrament of Baptism. St Luke thus relates how they received also the Sacrament of Confirmation : " When the Apostles who were in Jerusalem " (where they had stayed despite the persecution) " had heard that Samaria had received the word of God, they sent unto them Peter and John. Who, when they were come, prayed for them that they might receive the Holy Ghost. For he was not as yet come upon any of them, but they were only baptised in the name of the Lord Jesus. Then they laid their hands upon them, and they received the Holy Ghost." [4]

A comment of St Cyprian

The incident bears all the marks of a normal procedure ; it is just as though a modern bishop, being informed that a great number of converts had been received into the Church in one of the parishes of his diocese, immediately sets out (with his auxiliary) to make a visitation and to confirm them. Already, some seventeen centuries ago, St Cyprian has remarked upon the similarity between this incident and the ordinary administration of a diocese in third-century Africa : " Exactly the same thing happens with us to-day," he writes ; " those who have been baptised in the Church are presented to the bishops of the Church so that by our prayer and the imposition of our hands they may receive the Holy Spirit." [5]

Simon Magus and the efficacy of the rite

Curiously enough Simon Magus, who was an admiring witness of these scenes in Samaria, has unwittingly and providentially

[1] Acts x. [2] Acts x 47. [3] Acts xi 15, 17 ; xv 7-9.
[4] Acts viii 1-17. [5] *Ep.* 73.

afforded us a valuable testimony to the sacramental efficacy of the imposition of hands: "When Simon saw (St Luke tells us) that by the imposition of the hands of the Apostles the Holy Ghost was given, he offered them money saying: Give me also this power, that on whomsoever I shall lay my hands he may receive the Holy Ghost."[1]

The disciples at Ephesus

The second description of the ordinary method of conferring the Holy Ghost occurs in connection with a group of twelve believers whom St Paul found at Ephesus. Here is St Luke's account of the incident: "It came to pass that Paul . . . came to Ephesus and found certain disciples; and he said to them: Have you received the Holy Ghost since you believed? But they said to him: We have not so much as heard whether there be a Holy Ghost. And he said: In what then were you baptised? Who said: In John's baptism. Then Paul said: John baptised the people with the baptism of penance, saying that they should believe in him who was to come after him, that is to say, in Jesus. Having heard these things, they were baptised in the name of the Lord Jesus. And when Paul had imposed his hands upon them, the Holy Ghost came down upon them; and they spoke with tongues and prophesied."[2]

Taking it for granted that the Ephesians in question had already received Christian baptism,[3] the Apostle asks whether they have been confirmed; clearly he expected that they would have been, for the giving of the Holy Ghost was the normal complement of the Christian rite. No, they had not received the Holy Ghost; they had not even heard of his existence. St Paul's surprise disappears, however, as soon as he learns that they had been baptised only with John's baptism, which was not followed by the rite of conferring the Spirit. He thereupon gives them Christian baptism, and once more we are told of the ordinary ceremony which follows: he imposed hands upon them and they received the Holy Ghost.

Always essentially the same grace

But, whether ordinarily or extraordinarily bestowed, the gift is always the same. The Prince of the Apostles is himself our witness that the grace given to Cornelius and his companions when the Holy Spirit came upon them, was exactly the same grace as that which the Apostles and the first disciples had received on the day of Pentecost: "He gave them the Holy Ghost as to us," he says, "and put no difference between us and them. . . . He gave them the same grace as to us."[4] Moreover, this grace, given in common both to Apostles and to converts from paganism, is in its turn the same grace as that which the Apostles had power to convey by the imposition of hands. Of this St Peter again gives us the proof, for on the very

[1] Acts viii 18. [2] Acts xix 1-7.

[3] The phrase "since ye believed" means "since you received Christian baptism"; *cf.* Rom. xiii 11: "Now our salvation is nearer than when we believed," *i.e.* than at the time of our baptism.

[4] Acts xv 7-9; xi 15-17; *cf.* above, pp. 813-814.

day of Pentecost he promises to the people of Jerusalem that, if only they will do penance and be baptised in the name of Jesus Christ, they will receive that gift of the Holy Ghost of which they had just witnessed the stupendous effects.[1] The circumstances of its bestowal might be different, the outward phenomena accompanying it might vary, such phenomena might even be completely absent, but the essential effect is identical in all : an outpouring of the Spirit of testimony, enabling those who received it to " speak the word of God with confidence." [2]

The grace of the Spirit distinct from the grace of Baptism

But if Baptism must be received before the gift of the Spirit can be granted, it is not by Baptism itself that the gift is conferred. This is made plain in St Luke's account of the Confirmation of the Samaritan disciples. " The Holy Ghost," he writes, " was not as yet come down upon any of them, but they were *only* baptised in the name of the Lord Jesus." The same is seen in the case of the Ephesians who received the Spirit, not immediately upon being baptised, but only after Paul had laid his hands upon them.[3] We may draw the same conclusion, that the grace of the Spirit is distinct from the grace of Baptism, if we consider the Confirmation of the Apostles themselves. For it cannot be doubted that these, already before Pentecost, had received the ordinary effects of Baptism, if not the sacrament of Baptism itself. Whatever view be held as to the moment in which Baptism was instituted by Our Lord—whether, as some maintain, at the time of his conversation with Nicodemus, or when he was baptised in the Jordan, or even, as a few theologians have held, when, after his Resurrection, he entrusted to his Apostles the commission of baptising and preaching the Gospel—it is certain that already at the Last Supper the Apostles were cleansed from original sin and endowed at least with the equivalent of the baptismal character when they received the Sacrament of Holy Order.

Complementary to the grace of Baptism

But the two graces, though so evidently distinct from each other, are shown throughout the Acts of the Apostles to be most closely associated. The words of St Peter to the people of Jerusalem, " Be baptised every one of you . . . and you shall receive the gift of the Holy Ghost " ; the prompt action taken at Jerusalem to ensure that the Samaritans should quickly receive the Holy Spirit after they had been baptised ; the surprise of St Paul at the unconfirmed condition of the twelve Ephesians whom he supposed already to have received Christian baptism ; and even the solicitude of St Peter to baptise Cornelius and his companions as soon as possible after they had already (by a unique inversion of the normal order) received the Holy Spirit—all this is evident proof that the one grace is normally called for by the other. It is proof in fact—since the exceptional case of Cornelius may be legitimately disregarded—that the gift of the Spirit is the ordinary complement of the Sacrament of Baptism.

[1] *Cf.* Acts ii 38. [2] Acts iv 31.
[3] *Cf.* Acts viii 16 ; xix 5, 6.

The special outlook of St Luke

So close, indeed, is the connection which appears in St Luke's narrative between Baptism and the gift of the Spirit, that some have been led to suppose that this gift is nothing else than the effect of Baptism itself. The above considerations show that this is an error. But it is perhaps allowable to suggest that in the eyes of the author of the Acts the gift of the Spirit is so important, that the previous grace of Baptism appears in his account as little more than a preliminary to the gift which is its normal complement and crown. With an outlook which is primarily missionary and apostolic, his thought is not arrested to consider the sublime privileges which Baptism confers—divine sonship, the indwelling of the Trinity, heirship to eternal life—in a word, all those consoling aspects of justification upon which St Paul enlarges in his epistles. Rather he hurries on to the thought of the splendid mission which falls to every member of the catholic and apostolic Church, and therefore to that gift of the Spirit which makes the Christian a valiant witness of the faith and a bearer of the good news of salvation to those who have not yet received it.

The grace of the Spirit conferred by a special rite and by a special minister

Finally, this grace of the Spirit, distinct from the grace of Baptism and complementary to it, is exhibited in the Acts of the Apostles as being normally communicated by a special rite, employed by a special minister. The explicit and clear accounts of the Confirmation of the Samaritans and of the Ephesians leave us in no doubt as to the rite employed: it is the imposition of hands. Moreover, in both these instances, the only two which we can with certainty consider as representing the normal procedure, the ministers are Apostles. Philip the deacon, who had converted and baptised the Samaritans, had apparently not been qualified to confirm them; it is difficult to understand otherwise, especially when we consider the close connection between Baptism and its complement, why he should not have done so.[1] In the absence of any certain evidence to the contrary we are therefore justified in concluding that the ordinary minister of this rite, not only *de facto* but also *de jure*, was an Apostle.[2]

Thus within a year of the day of Pentecost we find already existing in the Church a special rite, distinct from that of Baptism, the administration of which appears to be reserved to the Apostles, and whose effect, also distinct from that of Baptism, is a special outpouring of the Spirit enabling the recipient to be a confident witness of the faith of Jesus Christ.

This is the Sacrament of Confirmation.

[1] See Acts viii 12, 16.

[2] But see below, p. 831 and n. 5.

§ IV: THE SACRAMENT IN TRADITION

Confirmation and martyrdom

THE precious benefits conferred by the Sacrament of Confirmation were fully seen during the first three centuries of the Christian era; for this was pre-eminently the period of martyrdom, that is to say, the period of witness. To suffer and die for the name of Christ is the sovereign profession of faith, it is that most perfect testimony which Christ foretold would be asked of his followers. It is the highest testimony that can be rendered to Christ both as being the supreme proof of devotion to his cause,[1] and also as being the most perfect reproduction of the suffering and dying Christ which the Christian can exhibit in himself.[2] The Apostles had led the way, setting the seal of their own blood upon their heroic witness, and that same Spirit of testimony which fortified them in their own ordeal, and which they had communicated to others by the imposition of hands, is passed on by the Sacrament to others in turn, raising up a numberless band of martyrs throughout the world: not only among bishops and priests, but also among men and women of the laity, of every condition and degree, and even among children of the tenderest age—until the very earth became saturated with that martyrs' blood which, in the words of Tertullian, is the seed of the Church.

The rudimentary age of sacramental theology

This fact, that the witness of the Church in the first three centuries of her existence is written so large in the blood of her children, may account to some extent for the relative scantiness of other contemporary records. It is further to be borne in mind, when searching for early allusions to the sacraments, that these are primarily things to be administered and received, not to be talked or written about; and that, consequently, such written records as we possess of this period are found to deal, not so much with the rites and ceremonies of the Church with which the faithful might be presumed to be familiar through their daily practice, as rather with those particular doctrines of the faith which the rise of heresy or the conditions of the time brought into prominence. Add to this the fact that the precise theological language of to-day (including even such common words as "sacrament" and "confirmation" in the modern connotation) was only just beginning to be formed, and it will be appreciated that the sparse and often merely incidental allusions to the sacraments which we do find in early writings lack that fulness and lucidity to which our own books of instruction have accustomed us, and that, in consequence, the task which faces the student of early sacramentary theology is by no means an easy one.

Two distinct questions

It will be somewhat simplified in the present instance, however, if we carefully distinguish, and try to answer separately, what are really two quite different questions. It is one thing to ask whether the Church has consistently, from the earliest times of which we have

[1] John xv 13.   [2] *Summa Theol.*, III, Q. lxvi, art. 11.

sufficient record, observed a special sacramental rite, recognisably distinct from Baptism and complementary to it, and conceived as bestowing a special outpouring of the Holy Spirit. This is simply to ask whether the Church has always administered the Sacrament of Confirmation. But it is another thing to ask whether that sacramental rite has remained at all times and in all places entirely unaltered. This is to ask what constituted the essence of the Sacrament of Confirmation during the early centuries of the Church. The first question is easy, and all theologians are agreed upon the answer to be given to it. The second question is very complicated and difficult, and there is still much discussion among theologians as to its solution. Let us consider the easy question first.

I

The Sacrament of Confirmation in Tertullian

Among the earliest descriptions we possess of what must certainly be recognised as the Sacrament of Confirmation is one which occurs, significantly enough, not in a work devoted to the study of this sacrament, but in a small treatise written by Tertullian about the year 200 in refutation of a certain woman who rejected the Sacrament of Baptism. We cannot reproduce it here in full ; Tertullian's description of the rite of Christian initiation, as practised in Africa at the end of the second century, is interspersed with allegories and scriptural allusions which are not strictly relevant to our purpose. But enough of it must be cited to show the relation, and the distinction, between Baptism itself and the rite of Confirmation which immediately succeeds it ; enough also to provide some material which will be of use when we come to deal with our second question.

Through Baptism, he writes, " man receives anew that Spirit of God which he had first received when God breathed upon him, but had afterwards lost through sin. Not that we obtain the Holy Spirit in the waters (of Baptism), but being cleansed . . . in the water we are made ready for the Holy Spirit. . . . Thereafter, when we have come forth from the font, we are anointed thoroughly with a blessed unguent ; this in accordance with the ancient practice, whereby men were anointed unto the priesthood from that very same horn from which Aaron was anointed by Moses. Since Christ takes his name from chrism, *i.e.* unguent, this unguent which gave the Lord his name has become spiritualised ; for he was anointed with the Spirit by God the Father, as we are told in the Acts (iv 27). . . . So on us likewise, though it is upon the flesh that the oil streams, it confers a spiritual benefit ; just as the physical act of Baptism, whereby we are immersed in the water, has the spiritual effect of delivering us from sin. *After this, the hand is laid upon us invoking and inviting the Holy Spirit by the* (prayer of) *blessing.* Human ingenuity can summon air (*spiritum*) into water, and by the application of hands thereon is able to animate the conjunction of the two with a spirit of clear sound.[1] Shall not God, then, also be able on his own instrument (*i.e.* man) to play the sublime melody of the Spirit through the medium of consecrated hands ?" [2]

Whatever be the significance of the rite of anointing upon which Tertullian comments at such length, it is impossible not to see in the words I have italicised a clear description of that same rite which is now familiar to us from our study of the Acts of the Apostles. "Peter and John . . . prayed for them that they might receive the Holy Ghost . . . for they had only been baptised. . . . Then they laid hands upon them, and they received the Holy Ghost." A comparison of the words of Tertullian with those of St Luke leaves no doubt that both are referring to a rite additional to Baptism and distinct from it, a rite which conveys a grace of the Holy Ghost not conveyed by Baptism : the Holy Spirit, Tertullian tells us explicitly, is not obtained in the waters of Baptism ; but it *is* given by the imposition of hands.

St Cyprian

We have already quoted a passage from a letter of St Cyprian, Bishop of Carthage, written some fifty years later than the above, in which he tells us that it was still the custom in Africa to confer the gift of the Holy Ghost by the imposition of hands,[3] just as it had been conferred upon the Samaritans by the Apostles Peter and John. Having occasion in another circumstance to refer to this sacrament, he writes : "It is not by the imposition of hands, when he receives the Holy Ghost, that a man is regenerated. He is regenerated in Baptism, in order that, being now born, he may receive the Holy Ghost. . . . He cannot receive the Spirit without first existing to receive him. But the birth of Christians is in Baptism." [4] Again the distinction is clearly made between two different rites, having two different effects : the Sacrament of Baptism which regenerates, and the sacrament which confers the Holy Spirit, and which is administered by the imposition of hands. It will be remarked also in this passage how St Cyprian, besides stressing the distinction between the two sacraments, points to the intimate connection between them.

St Jerome

It is interesting to compare with St Cyprian's description of bishops imposing hands upon those who had previously received only the Sacrament of Baptism, the following statement of St Jerome, made more than a hundred years later : "Know you not," he writes, "that it is the custom in all the churches that upon those who have been baptised hands should afterwards be imposed, that the Holy Spirit may thus be called down upon them ? Where is this written, you ask ? In the Acts of the Apostles. But even if there were no scriptural authority for it, the agreement of the whole world on this matter would have the force of a precept. . . . It is also the custom

[1] Tertullian alludes to the hydraulic organ.
[2] *De baptismo*, cc. 5, 6, 7, 8.
[3] See p. 816.
[4] *Ep.* 74.

that, in the case of those who have been baptised by priests or deacons in districts far away from the greater cities, the bishop should go out and lay hands upon them to invoke the Holy Spirit upon them."[1]

St Cyril of Jerusalem

Turning now to the Church in the East, we find some interesting instructions on the Sacrament of Confirmation given by St Cyril of Jerusalem (about the year 348) to his neophytes. "In the time of Moses," he writes, "the Spirit was given by the imposition of hands; St Peter also grants it by the imposition of hands; and upon you also who are to be baptised this grace will be bestowed. But I do not tell you how; for I do not want to anticipate the opportune time."[2] When he comes to describe the ceremony in which the Spirit is conferred, however, he says nothing about the imposition of hands; he speaks only of an anointing with chrism: "To you, when you came up from the font of sacred water, an anointing was given, the antitype of that chrism with which Christ was anointed. . . . Christ, however, was not anointed by men with a physical oil or unguent; the Father, in constituting him the Saviour of the whole world, anointed him with the Holy Spirit. . . . But you are anointed with a real unguent, and so become sharers and fellows with Christ. See that you do not regard this as a mere material and common unguent. For just as the bread of the Eucharist is no longer ordinary bread after the invocation of the Holy Spirit, but the Body of Christ, so too this holy unguent is no longer a mere common unguent after the invocation. It is the treasury of the gifts of Christ and the Holy Ghost, causing its effect by the presence of the divinity within it. It is smeared as a symbol upon your forehead and the other senses. But while the body is being anointed with the visible unguent, the soul is quickened by the holy and life-giving Spirit. . . . It is a spiritual amulet for the body and a saving protection for the soul."[3]

It would appear then that in the East, at any rate in the fourth century, the most prominent feature of Confirmation was an anointing with chrism, for the context of Cyril's discourse makes it impossible to understand this anointing as anything else than the rite which confers the gift of the Spirit. The prevalence of this practice in the East is corroborated by the terms, strongly suggestive of Confirmation, which were used in the East for blessing the chrism about this time:

The Sacramentary of Serapion

"O God . . . we beseech thee . . . to work a divine and heavenly operation in this oil, that the baptised who have been anointed therewith in the saving sign of the Cross of thine only-begotten Son—that Cross through which Satan with every hostile power has been cast down and overthrown—may, having been regenerated and renewed by the waters of regeneration, be made also partakers of the gift of the Holy Spirit and, being confirmed in

[1] *Adversus Lucif.*, n. 9.
[2] *Catech. myst.*, xvi.
[3] *Catech. myst.*, iii.

this seal, may remain 'steadfast and immovable,' unharmed and inviolate."[1]

Innocent I

And here, finally, is an authoritative pronouncement of Pope Innocent I, at the beginning of the fifth century: "That only bishops have the power either to confer the sign of the Cross or to give the Holy Ghost, is shown not only by the custom of the Church, but also by that passage of the Acts of the Apostles where we read that Peter and John were sent to give the Holy Spirit to those who had been baptised. For priests . . . when they baptise may anoint the baptised with chrism (only however with chrism consecrated by the bishop) but they may not sign the forehead with the same oil, this being reserved to the bishops only, when they confer the Holy Spirit."[2]

Confirmation always administered in the history of the Church

This strictly limited selection of texts suffices to show that the early centuries of the Church were quite familiar with a special rite, distinct from Baptism, which conferred the Holy Ghost; and they could be multiplied with very much greater abundance from the writings of the fifth and succeeding centuries, from liturgical books, and from the decisions of councils. The net result of these is to prove clearly that, from the time of Tertullian at the very latest (and therefore by presumption from a much earlier date) until the present day, a sacrament which we cannot but recognise as the Sacrament of Confirmation has been regularly administered by the Church.

Heresies concerning Confirmation

And, in fact, if we except the Novatians of the third century, whose custom of not receiving this sacrament appears to have been due merely to the example of their founder and not to any theological conviction, no heresies seem clearly to have denied the sacramental status of Confirmation before that of the Reformers of the sixteenth century. These, generally speaking, admitted that it was a harmless but useless ceremony instituted by the Church. Calvin and others suggested that it was originally introduced into the Church as a public act by which Christians, when they reached adolescence, endorsed or "confirmed" the undertakings made formerly on their behalf by their sponsors in Baptism; a view which, besides finding no grounds whatever in historical documents, strangely overlooks the long-standing custom of administering Confirmation to infants.[3] The Council of Trent, in its definitions on Confirmation, contented itself with condemning these various doctrines of the Reformers.[4]

II

History of the "proximate matter" of the Sacrament

We pass now to our second historical question which, although its complexity makes a complete survey quite impossible here, is so important that it cannot be entirely omitted. Briefly, it concerns

[1] *The Sacramentary of Serapion*, n. 25.
[2] *Ep. ad Decentium.*
[3] See below, p. 833.
[4] Sess. vii, *de Conf.*

the essentials of the rite of Confirmation as administered during the early centuries, and especially the gesture used in the sacrament, or what is technically called its proximate matter. It is quite certain that the anointing of the forehead with chrism forms an essential element in the Sacrament of Confirmation as administered to-day, whether in the Western or in the Eastern Church. Has it been so always and everywhere?

What is generally admitted

So far as the East is concerned there is abundant evidence that, at the latest from the fourth century, and probably also from an earlier time, anointing with chrism has been regarded as alone constituting the essential matter of the sacrament. In the West there is equally no question that, since the thirteenth century, theologians have commonly considered this anointing to be at least an essential part, if not the whole essence, of the sacramental matter; indeed this view seems to have begun to prevail even three centuries earlier. It is furthermore established, especially by the evidence of Innocent I's letter quoted above,[1] that an anointing—whether regarded as essential or not—accompanied the administration of Confirmation in the Church of Rome as early as the fourth century, and that this practice spread rapidly to the other churches of the West. Finally, in the West, unlike the East, the imposition of hands continued for a long time, and has continued even to the present day, to be mentioned, side by side with the anointing, as an element in the rite of this sacrament.

The early centuries: Imposition of hands

The controversy, then, turns chiefly on the practice of the Church, especially in the West, during the first three centuries. The very few texts which we have cited, whether from the Scriptures or from the writings of the Fathers, are of course totally inadequate as a basis for a considered judgement. But, precisely because they have been selected for that purpose, they do at any rate suffice to show why the controversy exists. The relevant passages of the Acts speak only of prayer and the imposition of hands as the means by which the gift of the Spirit was bestowed. It is likewise to the imposition of hands that Tertullian ascribes the giving of the Holy Ghost after Baptism. St Cyprian points to the bishops of his day as employing exactly the same rite, the imposition of hands, as had been used by Peter and John when they confirmed the Samaritans; and St Jerome, writing towards the end of the fourth century, assures us (though admittedly he may have in mind only the West) that the same custom existed all over the world. There is enough evidence here to make at least a *prima facie* case for the imposition of hands as having been the essential matter of Confirmation in the West from the time of Tertullian until the time of St Jerome.

Or anointing?

But the evidence, as may be observed even from a reading of some of the passages cited above, is one-sided; and scholars who on theological grounds are loth to admit that a rite which the Church

[1] See p. 824.

of God has for so many centuries regarded as essential to Confirmation found no place in its primitive administration, are not slow to urge other grounds which appear to favour a confirmational anointing from the earliest times. They point to the post-baptismal anointing which Tertullian describes and which he explicitly associates with the interior anointing of the soul of Christ by the Holy Spirit, and they appeal to numerous passages of the early Fathers, showing beyond all doubt that Baptism was consistently followed by an anointing to which the giving of the Holy Spirit was attributed as its proper effect. They remind us of Tertullian's celebrated "caro ungitur ut anima consecretur; caro signatur ut et anima muniatur"[1] ("the flesh is anointed that the soul may be consecrated, the flesh is marked with the sign of the cross that the soul may be fortified"), and of St Augustine's clear statement that "the sacrament of chrism . . . is sacred among the class of visible signs, as is Baptism itself."[2] As for the practice of the Apostles themselves, they urge that the fact that no anointing is mentioned does not prove that none took place,[3] and they interpret certain scriptural texts which mention anointing[4] as being likely allusions to the Sacrament of Confirmation.

The post-baptismal anointing

Both sides are thus seen to have their reasons, and it is clearly beyond the scope of this essay to attempt to adjudicate between them. But it is only fair, perhaps, to admit that the conclusions reached by the most recent scholars do not entirely favour the view which sees in the ancient post-baptismal anointing a part of the rite of Confirmation. It appears more likely to have belonged to the baptismal rite which precedes than to that of Confirmation which follows, and would thus correspond, not to the anointing now employed in Confirmation, but to another anointing of the head with chrism which, still in the ceremonies of Baptism as administered to-day, follows immediately after the essential rite of that sacrament. This ceremony, though not essential to the effect of Baptism, was regarded by the Fathers as extremely important, because it was the literal "christening." It was, indeed, as Tertullian explains,[5] an external sign which symbolised the anointing of Christ by the Holy Spirit; but it symbolised also the inner anointing of the Christian himself which took place in Baptism, and by reason of which he became another Christ. St Isidore of Seville sets forth the significance of this ceremony in the following words: "Since Our Lord, the true king and eternal priest, has been anointed by God the Father with the heavenly and mystic unguent, it is now not only priests and kings, but the whole Church that is anointed with chrism, for the whole Church is member of the eternal king and priest. It

[1] *De resurr. carnis*, c. 8.
[2] *Contra lit. Petilian.*, lib. 2, cap. 104.
[3] *Cf.* St Thomas, *Summa Theol.*, III, Q. lxxii, art. 4, ad 1.
[4] *E.g.* 2 Cor. i 21; 1 John ii 20, 27.
[5] See p. 821.

is for this reason, because we are a priestly and royal people, that after we have been washed in baptism we are anointed in order that we may bear the name of Christ."[1] St Augustine expresses the same thought more briefly: "In the Acts of the Apostles we are told that God anointed our Lord Jesus Christ with the Holy Spirit; not with visible oil, but with the gift of grace, which is signified by that visible unguent with which the Church anoints the baptised."[2]

The Holy Spirit in Baptism and in Confirmation

For it is important to remind ourselves that the sanctifying action and presence of the Holy Ghost is not restricted to the Sacrament of Confirmation. It is indeed here that he is poured out with special abundance, and with an effect which both the promise of Christ himself and the constant usage of the Scriptures authorised the Fathers in ascribing so particularly to the Third Person of the Blessed Trinity, that Confirmation came to be called *par excellence* "the gift of the Spirit." This is why it became usual to say, after the example set by the Acts of the Apostles, that those who had only been baptised had not yet received the Spirit, or that in Baptism the Spirit is not given (*i.e.* is not received or given in the technical sense of Confirmation); and it is in this sense that we must understand Tertullian, for example, when he says that the Holy Spirit is not given in the waters of Baptism.[3] But the same Fathers who extol the action of the Spirit in Confirmation are equally, and even more, lyrical in singing the praises of the Holy Spirit who, just as he once moved over the waters so that they brought forth living creatures, now moves over the waters of Baptism so that they bring forth living Christians;[4] and who, having once wrought the birth of the Son of God in the womb of Mary, now daily operates the birth of God's adopted sons in the baptismal font.[5] Quite certainly, the Fathers who said that we do not receive the Spirit in Baptism had no intention of denying that in this sacrament we receive the adoption of sons, and therefore also that Spirit of adoption in whom we call God our Father.[6]

A natural development

Moreover, wherever there is question of the Holy Spirit, the thought and the mention of anointing are not far away. The prophets, Christ himself, and the Apostles have justified the conception of the Holy Spirit as a divine unguent, sanctifying, healing, strengthening; it thus soon became natural for the early Christians to speak of every outpouring of the Spirit as a spiritual unction,

[1] *De eccl. off.*, lib. ii, cap. 26, 1-2.

[2] *De Trin.*, xv, 46. St Augustine's "sacramentum chrismatis" is therefore not a peremptory argument. He is accustomed to use the word *sacramentum* in a wide sense to mean any sacred sign, including what we should nowadays call a "sacramental." In the passage quoted he may therefore well have been referring to the anointing which forms part of the baptismal ceremony, and which he might be comparing with the essential rite of Baptism: "sicut et ipse baptismus."

[3] See above, p. 821.

[4] Tertullian, *De baptismo*, c. 4.

[5] Leo the Great, Serm. 25, cap. 5.

[6] *Cf.* Rom. viii 15.

and for the Church, guided by the same Spirit, to use oil or chrism in her sacramental rites to symbolise it.[1] In the ceremony of Baptism the use of chrism seems to have been introduced at an early stage: the thought that Christians are "born again of water *and the Holy Ghost*"[2] must soon have suggested the addition of an anointing to the essential rite of washing. Confirmation, pre-eminently the sacrament of the Holy Ghost, called even more clamorously for the use of chrism to symbolise the new anointing of the soul by the Spirit, and in the East we soon find this ceremony accompanying and even, at any rate to all appearance, supplanting the imposition of hands as the essential matter of the sacrament. And the historical evidence appears to indicate a similar, though more gradual, development of the sacramental rite in the West and throughout the Church.[3]

The question of "immediate institution"

Such, I say, is the process which historical research would appear to suggest. Nevertheless the difference of opinion still existing among experts forbids any peremptory statement on the facts of the matter. It still remains possible that anointing was used in Confirmation universally and from the beginning. If this is so, the facts of history present no difficulty to those theologians who would apply a very rigid interpretation to the doctrine that Christ instituted all the sacraments "immediately."[4] In this view, Christ would have instructed his Apostles to use chrism (and a certain form of words) as a means of conveying the gift of the Spirit, and this method of administration, admittedly with slight modifications, would have been followed perpetually throughout the Church until the present day.

A less restricted view

But such a narrow and restricted understanding of the doctrine of "immediate institution" is by no means imposed by the teaching authority of the Church. Indeed, the progress of historical science and the closer acquaintance with Christian antiquity which is its result are causing a broader interpretation of it to find increasing favour with theologians. This version, while attributing to Christ alone the institution of the sacrament in its "substance" (*i.e.* while holding that Christ alone gave instructions that a suitable rite should be chosen by means of which he would bestow a particular grace), suggests that he left power to his Church to determine the essential details of some rites and to make such changes as the conditions of the time, the utility of the faithful, and reverence to the sacrament

[1] *Cf.* Isaias lxi 1; Luke iv 18; Acts x 38; Heb. i 9. [2] John iii 5.

[3] The development may have been assisted by the desirability of distinguishing the rite of Confirmation more clearly from that of Holy Order.

[4] The Council of Trent defined only that Christ instituted all the sacraments (sess. vii, can. 1). But it is the common teaching of theologians that he instituted them all immediately, *i.e.* himself, and not by giving a mandate to his Apostles to do so. The extent to which the immediate institution of the sacraments implies the immediate determination of the elements of the sacramental rite is a matter of controversy among theologians. See Essay xxi, *The Sacramental System*, pp. 749–750; cf. pp. 1054–1055.

itself might render necessary or expedient.[1] It is obvious that, so understood, the doctrine that Christ alone is the author of the sacraments has nothing to fear from any purely material alteration in certain sacramental rites which historical evidence may authorise, and even oblige, us to admit.

The institution of Confirmation

For that Christ did in fact institute the Sacrament of Confirmation becomes certain when once we have shown that Confirmation is a Sacrament. Our study of the promise of the Spirit, made by Christ to all who should believe in him, fulfilled in the Apostles and the first disciples at Pentecost, and fulfilled also in all the faithful when he was given to them by a special rite and as a normal part of their initiation, reveals the existence of a permanent sign which is a cause of grace. But of such a sanctifying rite we know that Christ alone, the source of all sanctification, can be the Author. In this sense we may say with St Thomas that he instituted Confirmation by the very fact that he promised it.[2]

§ V: THE ADMINISTRATION OF THE SACRAMENT

The rite in the West to-day

THE rite of Confirmation, as administered in the Western Church to-day, consists of the following main elements: (*a*) The bishop, stretching forth his hands towards the candidates, prays that God may send forth his Holy Spirit with his sevenfold grace upon them. (*b*) Having moistened the thumb of his right hand with chrism, he confirms each one of them, saying: "I sign thee with the sign of the Cross" (saying which, he places his right hand on the head of the candidate, makes the sign of the Cross with his thumb on his forehead, and then proceeds): "and I confirm thee with the chrism of salvation. In the name of the Father, and of the Son, and of the Holy Ghost. Amen." (*c*) He then gives the confirmed person a light blow on the cheek, saying, "Peace be with thee." (*d*) Then follow an antiphon, some versicles, a concluding prayer, and the bishop's blessing.

Essential rite: the anointing with the accompanying words

Theologians now commonly teach, and the doctrine must be regarded as certain, that the essential rite in this ceremony is that which is described under *b*. The Council of Trent appears to have had no intention of defining what are the essential elements of the sacrament, but it is probable that in condemning the teaching of certain Protestants who regarded it as "an insult to the Holy Ghost to ascribe efficacy to the sacred chrism," the Fathers of the Council had in mind the accepted theological opinion that the anointing with chrism constituted the sacramental "matter."[3] This doctrine, universally held by the scholastics of the Middle Ages, had already received what must be admitted to be at least a very high sanction

[1] *Cf.* Council of Trent, sess. xxi, *De communione*, cap. 2.
[2] *Cf. Summa Theol.*, III, Q. lxxii, art. 1, ad 1.
[3] Sess. vii, can. 2 *de Conf.*

in Pope Eugenius IV's famous Decree for the Armenians at the Council of Florence, which declared (using the words of St Thomas) that "the matter of this sacrament is chrism composed of oil . . . and balsam . . . blessed by the bishop," and that "the form consists of the words, 'I sign thee, etc.'"[1] This pronouncement derives an added significance from the fact that the object of the Council of Florence was to settle certain differences of doctrine and practice between East and West; the mention of anointing alone as the matter of Confirmation would therefore seem to indicate that the practice of the Western Church on this point did not differ from that of the East, where the anointing had been considered as the essential action in the sacrament from time immemorial.

There have been theologians, even since the Council of Trent, who have seen the essential rite of Confirmation in the ceremony described under *a*, being influenced therein by some of the historical considerations mentioned above, according to which the imposition of hands would seem to have been the sole essential matter of the sacrament during the first three centuries. This opinion, however, has received little encouragement from certain official decisions which, in cases where Confirmation has been administered without this preliminary ceremony, have declared it unnecessary to repeat the rite even conditionally.[2]

Is the anointing also an imposition of hands?

But, granting that the essence of the sacrament consists in the anointing, together with the accompanying words, there remains a difference of opinion among theologians whether the act of anointing is to be considered as *merely an application of chrism*, or as simultaneously and virtually *an imposition of hands*; and the latter view, although hardly any trace of it is to be found among the scholastics of the thirteenth century, seems to be favoured by the majority of theologians to-day. Here, too, historical reasons are primarily invoked: the imposition of hands is so consistently associated with Confirmation in the early centuries, that it is not easy to suppose that it has entirely disappeared from the rite as used in the West to-day. And we must confess that the opinion which regards the anointing as also a virtual imposition of hands derives a certain support from the instructions given in the Code of canon law, where we read: "The Sacrament of Confirmation is to be conferred by the imposition of the hand together with the anointing with chrism on the forehead, and by the words prescribed . . ."; and also: "The anointing is not to be done with any instrument, but with the hand of the minister laid properly upon the head of the candidate."[3] These injunctions certainly seem to imply that the contact of the minister's hand with the head of the candidate is an essential part of the sacra-

[1] *Cf.* Denzinger, 697; on the authority of this decree, see Essay **xxix**, *The Sacrament of Order*, pp. 1052, 1058.

[2] *E.g.* Holy Office, 22 March 1892.

[3] Cnn. 780, 781, § 2.

ment: in other words, that the anointing is at the same time an imposition of hands.

The rich symbolism of this rite

It would be hard to imagine a rite more appropriate and more rich in significance than this. While oil alone is already the divinely revealed emblem of the fulness of the Holy Spirit and of the virile strength which this sacrament bestows, the addition of the fragrant balsam is an eloquent symbol of the purpose for which the Spirit comes in Confirmation: namely that we may become the good odour of Christ, spreading abroad the knowledge of the faith as a perfume diffuses its sweetness.[1] The anointing is made in the form of a Cross, to signify the standard under which the new soldier of Christ is to fight, the standard by which (as we have already read in an early Sacramentary) "Satan with every hostile power is cast down and conquered."[2] And it is upon his forehead that he bears the Cross, intimating that he must have no shame in professing the name of Christ, and be prepared to suffer any ignominy or persecution that the open confession of his faith may involve. The words of the bishop as he administers the sacrament summarise its meaning and effect with a truly inspired simplicity: "I sign thee with the sign of the Cross, and I confirm thee with the chrism of salvation; in the name of the Father, and of the Son, and of the Holy Ghost."[3] There is an echo of mediæval chivalry, too, in the light blow on the cheek (a ceremony which appears to have been introduced into the rite in the twelfth century), dubbing the candidate a true knight of Christ.

Ordinary minister: the Bishop

As knighthood is conferred by the king, so enrolment in the army of Christ is appropriately reserved to the ordinary competence of its appointed leaders. And in fact the Church teaches that the bishop alone is the ordinary minister of Confirmation.[4] The Acts of the Apostles show that Philip, a deacon, was not able to administer this sacrament; but whether it was in virtue of their priestly or their episcopal character that the Apostles conferred the Holy Ghost it is not easy to determine on scriptural grounds alone. At any rate there is no undisputed instance in the primitive Church of its being bestowed by any one of lower rank than an Apostle.[5] However that may be, during the first three centuries the administration of this sacrament, both in the East and in the West, was certainly reserved

[1] *Cf.* 2 Cor. ii 14. [2] See above, p. 823.

[3] The use of this form can be traced back, at least in some parts of the West, to the seventh century. In the East the form consists simply of the words, "The seal of the Holy Spirit." This form, the legitimacy and validity of which have always been recognised, at least tacitly, by Rome, is of very great antiquity.

[4] Council of Trent, sess. vii, can. 3 *de Conf.*

[5] It has been suggested that Ananias conferred the gift of the Spirit on St Paul when he laid hands on him (Acts ix 17-18). But this passage of the Acts is by no means clear, and has occasioned much discussion among exegetes.

to the bishop. Perhaps this fact alone would not suffice to show that the reservation was *de jure*: the three Sacraments of Baptism, Confirmation, and the Eucharist at that time formed successive stages in one solemn ceremony of initiation at which the bishop presided, and it was in fact to him that the neophyte, after being immersed in the baptismal font, was led to receive the Holy Spirit by the imposition of hands. What is more significant is that in those cases in which (whether for reasons of ill-health or other causes) the candidate had received Baptism from a deacon or a priest, he was always brought to the bishop to receive the Sacrament of Confirmation.[1]

Difference of practice between East and West

When parishes came to be formed, however, and the spread of Christianity caused some of the functions hitherto performed by the bishop to be entrusted to priests, a difference of practice in regard to Confirmation begins to show itself between the Eastern and the Western Church. In the East it soon became the ordinary custom for priests to confirm immediately after Baptism. But in the West it was, and has remained until the present day, a privilege reserved to the bishop to be the ordinary minister of Confirmation. As early as the beginning of the fifth century we find Pope Innocent I speaking of the exclusive right of bishops to confirm as an established fact, and appealing in proof of it to the Acts of the Apostles;[2] and again and again throughout the centuries instances recur in which ecclesiastical authority has had to resist the pretensions of priests in the West to usurp this function. The reason usually given is that assigned by Pope Innocent I: that priests do not possess the fulness of the priesthood.[3]

Priests as extraordinary ministers

On the other hand the Church also teaches that, as extraordinary minister, the priest can confer this sacrament. This is shown by several undoubted facts, in particular by a number of past and present instances of priests being empowered by the Holy See to confirm; by the present discipline of the Church which, besides communicating this power to certain priests by special indult, allows it *ipso jure* to certain dignitaries enumerated in the Code of canon law;[4] and by the more significant fact that the Church recognises, subject to some exceptions, the validity of the Confirmation administered by priests of the Eastern communities, whether uniate or dissident. Clearly, then, by indult, delegation, or dispensation of the Holy See (the terms seem in this matter to be used indiscriminately in ecclesiastical documents) a priest becomes able to confirm validly.[5]

[1] See the statement of St Jerome above, pp. 822–823.

[2] See above, p. 824.

[3] *Cf.* Denzinger, 98, where the relevant paragraph of Innocent's letter is given in full.

[4] Can. 782, § 3. See *Additional Note* below, p. 838.

[5] It is to be noted, however, that the chrism used must be that blessed by the bishop. See Council of Florence (Denzinger, 697).

A theological problem

This fact gives rise to a theological problem which cannot be fully discussed here. It is asked whether the inability of a priest to confirm validly without the commission of the Holy See is due to a lack of the power of order or to a lack of jurisdiction. Authors differ on this question, described by Pope Benedict XIV as one of "great difficulty and complexity." [1] We must be content to state briefly an answer, given by Billot, which appears to meet the difficulty in a satisfactory way. According to this theologian the character of the priesthood includes the power to confirm; but by divine ordinance the valid exercise of that power is made conditional upon a commission received from the Head of the Church. Thus the fact that the Church acknowledges as valid the Confirmation administered by priests in the East does not make them *ordinary* ministers of the sacrament; it implies only a tacit commission formerly granted to them by the Holy See.[2]

Recipient of Confirmation

Turning our attention now to the recipient of Confirmation, we may say briefly that *only* the baptised, and *any* baptised person not already confirmed, can receive it validly. Previous Baptism is obviously necessary, because the baptismal character is required for the valid reception of any other sacrament, and it is especially manifest in the case of a sacrament which is exhibited to us in the sources of revelation as the complement of Baptism itself. Nor is its valid reception a privilege reserved to any class or section among the baptised, for it has been abundantly shown that the gift of the Spirit is intended by Christ to be given to all.

Infant Confirmation valid

That even infants are capable of receiving Confirmation is sufficiently proved by the custom, common in the Church in early times, of administering it to them immediately after Baptism, a custom which persisted in the West until the twelfth or thirteenth century, is allowed to continue to the present day in certain parts of it,[3] and still prevails throughout the East. This sacrament is by no means useless to infants, for, as St Thomas remarks, "the age of the body is no prejudice to the development of the soul, and even children can attain the perfection of spiritual maturity. Thus many of these, through the strength of the Holy Spirit which they have received, have fought valiantly for Christ even to the shedding of their blood." [4]

[1] *De syn. dioec.*, lib. 7, c. 8, n. 7.

[2] Billot, *De Sacramentis*, I (ed. 5), p. 309. A further indication of the importance which the Church attaches to the doctrine that the priest is not the ordinary minister of this sacrament, but that he administers it validly only in virtue of the delegation of the Holy See, may be seen in the latest edition (1925) of the Roman Ritual. It is here laid down that, in the event of a priest administering Confirmation by special indult, he shall preface the ceremony by publicly warning the faithful that only the bishop is the ordinary minister of this sacrament, and by reading aloud, in the vernacular, the decree of delegation in virtue of which he is about to administer it as extraordinary minister. *Cf. Congr. de Sacr.*, January 1934.

[3] Especially in Spain and parts of South America.

[4] *Summa Theol.*, III, Q. lxxii, art. 8, ad 2.

But the reasons for which the Church has seen fit to modify her practice in this matter, as well as certain other considerations affecting the reception of Confirmation, will be more conveniently set forth when we have given some account of the effects of the sacrament, for which we have reserved the following, which is also the concluding, section of this essay.

§ VI: THE EFFECTS OF THE SACRAMENT

The sacramental character

CONFIRMATION is one of those three sacraments concerning which the Council of Trent has defined that they "imprint a character on the soul, that is, a spiritual and indelible sign, by reason of which they cannot be repeated."[1] And this truth finds expression in the traditional name given to this sacrament, "the seal of the Holy Spirit," and preserved in the form of words with which it is still administered to-day in the East.[2]

The early Fathers were fond of using comparisons to illustrate the meaning of the sacramental character, and, although they commonly had in mind the Sacrament of Baptism (always more prominent in their thoughts than Confirmation, as indeed it still is in ours), yet they serve to show us what they conceived the function of this sacramental effect to be. Here, for example, is a striking illustration used by St Basil: "None will recognise whether you belong to us or to the enemy unless you prove by the mystic signs you wear that you are really one of us, unless the light of the Lord's countenance is sealed upon you. How will an angel come to your help, how will he deliver you from your enemies, unless he recognises the seal that is set upon you? How can you say, I belong to God, unless you bear marks to distinguish you?"[3] And here is another, used by St John Chrysostom: "As a special mark is branded upon sheep, so the Spirit is set upon the faithful. It is thus that, if you desert your ranks, you become conspicuous in the sight of all."[4]

The character of Confirmation

The sacramental character thus appears as a spiritual modification of the soul, whereby the recipient is marked out officially and definitively for a particular status or condition in the Church of God. In the theology of St Augustine it gains prominence as an effect which is inevitably produced by the valid Sacraments of Baptism, Confirmation, and Holy Order, and which no sin can subsequently obliterate; it is for this reason that the sacrament conferring it can be administered only once and for all. St Thomas Aquinas summarises the teaching of Tradition when he sees in the character a spiritual power, conferring on the recipient a particular official capacity or competence in the practice of the Christian religion.[5] And with this general definition, applied to the Sacrament of Con-

[1] Sess. vii, *De sacr. in gen*, can. 9.
[2] *Cf.* above, p. 831, n. 3.
[3] *Hom. in S. Bapt.*, n. 4.
[4] *In 2 Cor.*, hom., 3, n. 7.
[5] *Summa Theol.*, III, Q. lxiii, art. 2.

firmation, we are brought back once more to the point at which our study of this sacrament began; for the character of Confirmation, the first and direct effect of its administration, makes the Christian an official witness to the truth of the Christian faith.

Therefore, as the official donning of the military uniform confers upon the citizen the public right and duty to fight in defence of his country, so the reception of this character gives to the Christian the publicly recognised right and duty to defend the faith of Christ and the Church. "Analogy with the life of the body," writes St Thomas, "shows that the activity of an adult differs from that of the new-born child. Therefore in Confirmation we receive the spiritual power to perform certain sacred actions different from those for which we are empowered by Baptism. In Baptism a man receives power for those actions which concern his own salvation, in so far as he lives his own life. But in Confirmation he receives power for those actions which concern the spiritual combat against the enemies of the faith." [1]

The grace of Confirmation

But with the character of Confirmation is intimately connected that further and most precious gift, by reason of which this sacrament is called pre-eminently the gift of the Holy Spirit. When a soldier has been arrayed in his uniform he is given arms to fight with. And so the character of Confirmation brings with it that special outpouring of the Spirit, that most abundant increase of sanctifying grace, which endows the soul with the militant vigour of spiritual manhood. The soul is already in the state of grace, but the Holy Ghost comes now to fill up its measure, to pour out in greater fulness the virtues and the gifts of the Spirit: gifts of wisdom, understanding, counsel, fortitude, knowledge, piety, fear of the Lord [2]—all those invaluable endowments, in short, which it had first begun to possess in Baptism—and conferring in addition that sacramental grace which, as St Thomas explains, adds to sanctifying grace in general a special help towards the particular effects for which the sacrament is intended: [3] in this case, therefore, a supernatural disposition for the courage and fortitude which will be demanded by the task of professing and defending the faith. "The effect of this sacrament," we read in the Council of Florence, "is that the Holy Spirit is given us *unto strength*, as he was given to the Apostles on the day of Pentecost, that is to say, in order that the Christian may boldly confess the name of Christ." [4]

[1] *Summa Theol.*, III, Q. lxxii, art. 2.

[2] The prayer which precedes the essential rite of Confirmation is to be understood, therefore, not as asking for the first infusion of the sevenfold grace of the Spirit, but as beseeching God to increase it. *Cf. Summa Theol.*, III, Q. lxxii, art. 11, ad 3. On the gifts of the Holy Ghost, see Essay xviii, *The Supernatural Virtues*, pp. 654-658.

[3] *Summa Theol.*, III, Q. lxii, art. 2; Q. lxxii, art. 7, ad 3.

[4] *Cf.* Denzinger, 697.

The fruitful reception of the Sacrament

With so rich a store of grace available for him in this sacrament, it becomes a matter of the highest importance that the candidate should receive it worthily. This complement or consummation of Baptism presupposes that he who receives it is already in the state of grace ; if he were not he would belie the meaning of a sacrament instituted by Christ for the purpose of bringing to maturity the life of grace already existing in the soul, and thus falsifying the sacred sign would obstruct its sanctifying effect. He would still receive the character, nevertheless, since nothing can prevent the seal of the Holy Spirit from being imprinted by the valid sacrament. He would thus be in the unhappy condition of a Christian soldier unarmed.[1] But the state of grace is only the very least that is required in the candidate in order that he may receive the grace of this sacrament ; an appreciation of the great reverence which is due to the gift of the Holy Ghost will inspire him with the resolution to bring to its reception the best possible dispositions of mind and heart, so that he may receive its fruits in greater abundance.

The age at which Confirmation should be administered

It is such considerations as these that have caused the Church to change her discipline in regard to the age at which Confirmation should be administered. That the sacrament confers its spiritual benefits even on those who receive it before they have attained the use of reason, the Church maintains now as she has always taught, and therefore she does not forbid its administration to infants if they are in danger of death ; [2] for, as St Thomas points out, " children who die confirmed will receive on that account a greater glory in heaven, inasmuch as they have thus received a greater measure of grace on earth." [3] Nevertheless, the urgent reason for which Baptism is regularly administered as soon as possible after birth does not hold in the case of Confirmation, since this sacrament is not an indispensable means of salvation. The Church therefore prescribes that as a rule Confirmation should not be administered until a child has reached the use of reason, that is, about the age of seven years.[4] In this way greater reverence towards the sacrament is ensured, since the candidate is able to approach it as he should, fully instructed (so far as his age permits) in the faith which he is to profess and concerning the nature and effects of the sacred rite he is receiving, and capable, by means of his own enlightened dispositions, of deriving from it the greatest possible benefit to his soul. It is, moreover, in

[1] On the question of what constitutes an obstacle to grace in the case of sacraments of the living, and on the " revival " of the sacrament when such obstacle has been removed, see Essay xxi, *The Sacramental System*, p. 755.

[2] Can. 788. See also *Additional Note*, p. 838. Theologians admit also other urgent cases in which Confirmation may be anticipated.

[3] *Summa Theol.*, III, Q. lxxii, art. 8, ad 4.

[4] Can. 788. Even in those parts of the West where the ancient custom of Infant Confirmation is allowed to continue (see above, p. 833, n. 3) the Church requires the faithful to be instructed concerning the common law of the Church. *Cf. Congr. de Sacr.*, 30 June 1932.

keeping with the function of this sacrament, which confers the fulness of the Holy Spirit, that children should receive it before they make their first Communion.[1]

CONCLUSION

All that we have seen concerning the history of this sacrament —the importance which Christ himself attached to the promise of the Holy Spirit, the marvellous effects of courage and fortitude which the gift of the Spirit produced in the Apostles and in the early community of Christians, the fruits of martyrdom which it bore during the first three centuries and has indeed continued to bear throughout the history of the Church, the vital function which it is destined to fulfil in the life of every Christian—all this more than suffices to show that no one can neglect it with impunity. Christ has imposed upon every one of his followers the high duty of bearing witness to him in the world, and because, as he himself has foretold, this duty will prove also to be a heavy burden he has provided the grace of Confirmation to form an integral part of our supernatural equipment.

Martyrs who bear witness to Christ by the shedding of their blood are never lacking in the Church ; these are the finest fruits of the Spirit of testimony. But there is a wider sense in which we may say that the age of martyrdom is never past. The life of the Church and her members is a martyrdom that never ends. Our Lord's prophecy that the world would hate his disciples has been too manifestly fulfilled in history to leave any doubt whether it will find fulfilment also to-day. The world changes, for better or for worse. But the spirit of the world remains always the same, and it is against this spirit that the changeless Church of Christ, animated by the Holy Spirit of God, must wage endless war, and therein bear witness to her Founder.

The teaching of the Catholic Church runs counter to the spirit of the world, because it knows no compromise with error ; and every Catholic is a martyr, a true witness to the faith of Christ, when he refuses to yield one iota of revealed truth for the sake of amity and peace. The moral law of the Catholic Church runs counter to the spirit of the world, because it knows no compromise with sin. Every Catholic is a martyr, a true witness to the law of Christ, when he refuses dalliance with evil. Here, in its simplest terms, is the conflict of Christians with the world, here is their abiding witness to Christ. The Master has told them : " If you had been of the world, the world would love its own ; but because you are not of the world,

[1] *Cong. de Sacr.*, 30 June 1932. Nevertheless the fact of not having been able to be confirmed previously must not be considered as debarring children from making their first Communion, if they have reached the years of discretion. Cf. *ibid.*

but I have chosen you out of the world, therefore the world hateth you." Their conflict with the spirit of the world is a proof that they are disciples of Christ; and so the soldier of Christ who fights, is at the same time the witness who bears testimony to his Master. Here is the public responsibility which Confirmation imposes, and for which it equips us. Clergy and laity, men and women of every rank, condition, or degree, will fulfil it in different ways, but in all it will be the same Spirit of testimony who speaks. "They were all filled with the Holy Ghost and they spoke with divers tongues, according as the Holy Ghost gave them to speak." The manifold ways in which the Christian life can be lived in this world are so many divers tongues in which we can proclaim that we are the disciples of Christ.

ADDITIONAL NOTE

On the Extraordinary Minister of Confirmation

Since this essay was completed the Holy See has considerably extended the field in which a priest may act as extraordinary minister of Confirmation. In accordance with a Decree of the Congregation of the Sacraments, dated 14th September, 1946, and taking effect on 1st January, 1947,[1] parish priests or their equivalent (not, however, their curates or assistants) are empowered by a general indult of the Apostolic See to administer this Sacrament, as extraordinary ministers, to the faithful within their own territory when they are truly in danger of death by sickness, and when the bishop of the diocese, or other bishop in communion with the Holy See, is not available. The reason of this measure is to ensure that the grace of Confirmation, which, though not necessary for salvation, is yet of great spiritual profit to the soul and a means of greater glory in heaven, may not be denied to the many infants, children and adults who, being in danger of death by sickness, might never be able to obtain it if the Church insisted upon the exact observance of the common law in regard to the ordinary minister of this Sacrament.

G. D. SMITH.

[1] *A.A.S.* XXXVIII, 1946, pp. 349–358.

XXIV

THE SACRAMENT OF THE EUCHARIST

§ I: INTRODUCTORY

Sacrifice and Sacrament

By sacrifice man offers himself and his life to God, his sovereign Lord and Creator ; by the sacraments God gives himself, he gives a participation of his own divine life, to man. In sacrifice a stream of homage flows from man to the eternal Source of all being ; by the sacraments grace, sanctification, descends in copious flood upon the souls of men. This twofold stream, from God to man and from man to God, flows swift and strong in the Eucharist, sacrament and sacrifice. As the culminating act in the life of Jesus Christ on earth was the sacrifice which he offered on Calvary to his eternal Father, so the central act of Catholic worship in the Church, the mystical body of Christ, is the Eucharistic sacrifice, the Mass, which he instituted to be a perpetual commemoration and renewal of it. Likewise, just as it was through the sacred humanity of Christ that God mercifully designed to transmit to us the divine life of grace, so the sacrament of the Eucharist, which truly contains that living and life-giving humanity, holds the principal place among the sacraments instituted by Christ for our sanctification.

Truly, really and substantially present upon the altar under the appearances of bread and wine, Christ our High Priest offers himself, the infinite Victim, to his Father through the ministry of his priests. This is indeed a sacrifice unto the odour of sweetness, in which Christ, God and man, offers to his Father an infinite adoration, a prayer of unbounded efficacy, propitiation and satisfaction superabundantly sufficient for the sins of all mankind, thanksgiving in a unique manner proportionate to God's unstinted generosity to men. And then, as if it were in munificent answer to this infinitely pleasing gift which through Christ man has made to God, there comes God's best gift to man : the all-holy Victim, divinely accepted and ratified, is set before men to be their heavenly food. Through Christ we have given ourselves to God. Through Christ God gives his own life to us, that we may be made partakers of his divinity. The victim of the Eucharistic sacrifice, offered to man under the form of food, is the august sacrament of the Eucharist.

" This sacrament," we read in the Catechism of the Council of Trent, " must be truly said to be the source of all graces, because it contains in a wonderful way Christ our Lord, the source of every heavenly gift and blessing and the author of all the sacraments ; this sacrament is the source from which the other sacraments derive whatever goodness and perfection they possess." The unique place which the Eucharist occupies among the sacraments was clearly indicated in the early liturgy, and may still be seen even in the practice of the Church at the present day. It was the custom in the early centuries of the Church to administer the sacraments of Baptism and Confirmation on the night of Holy Saturday just before the Easter Mass. The reconciliation of sinners with the Church by Penance took place on Maundy Thursday during the celebration of the Sacrifice. The sacrament of Matrimony—as well as Holy Order—has always been, and still is, solemnly administered during Mass; and it is during the Mass of Maundy Thursday that the oil used in Extreme Unction is consecrated. All the sacraments, therefore, in their administration are closely connected with the Eucharist, the source from which all derive their efficacy.

Hence hardly anything that we might say to stress the importance of the Eucharist would be an exaggeration. The Eucharist is the centre of the Christian life as Christ is the central figure of the Christian religion. The priests of the Church are ordained, not primarily to preach the gospel, not merely to comfort the sick with the consoling truths of religion, not merely to take the lead in works of social improvement, but to offer the sacrifice of the Mass, to consecrate the Eucharist. If Catholics in the past—and in the present, too—have thought nothing in art, riches, and architecture too beautiful to lavish upon their churches, it is because the Catholic Church is the house of the king of kings, the home of Christ, truly present in the sacrament of the Eucharist. If Catholics, even the poorest, are ready to deprive themselves even of the comforts of life in order to support their clergy, it is because they believe that at all costs the sacrifice of the Mass must continue to be offered, the sacrament of the Eucharist, the food of Christian souls, must ever be administered. Devotion to the Eucharist is not an incidental pious practice of Catholics; it is of the very essence of the Catholic life.

The fundamental doctrine of the Eucharist is that Christ is truly, really, and substantially present therein, and to the doctrine of the Real Presence much of this short essay will be devoted. When once this has been grasped, the rest follows as a matter of course; the effects of the sacrament, its necessity, its constitutive elements, the reverence due to it, the Eucharistic practice of the Church, all this is but a necessary consequence of the stupendous truth that as a result of the words of consecration the living body and blood of Christ are present in this sacrament under the appearances of bread and wine.

Since at the present day—and it has ever been so—non-Catholics commonly use Catholic terms, giving them a meaning which is entirely subversive of Catholic truth, it will be well, before examining its scriptural and traditional foundation, to explain what is meant by the Catholic doctrine of the Real Presence. It will then be shown that this doctrine, as defined by the Council of Trent and taught by the Church to-day, is none other than the teaching of Christ himself and his Apostles, none other than the Eucharistic dogma which has been handed down to us infallibly by the Tradition of the Catholic Church. Necessarily involved in the doctrine of the Real Presence is the dogma of Transubstantiation, to which special attention will be devoted, because here we reach the heart of the Eucharistic mystery, and in this unique and wonderful conversion of the substance of bread and wine into the Body and Blood of Christ is to be found the root of all that theologians tell us concerning the mysterious manner of Christ's presence in the Eucharist. The remaining sections will deal with the sacrament considered formally as such, with its reception and its effects.

§ II: THE EUCHARISTIC DOGMA

The teaching of the Council of Trent summarised

THE reader who has studied with attention the other essays of this work will have observed that, generally speaking, in the history of the doctrines of the Catholic Church three stages may be distinguished. There is first a period during which the truth is in serene and undisputed possession; then follows a period of discussion when the truth is attacked by heretics, a period which usually culminates in a solemn definition of the Church by which the meaning of revelation is put beyond all possibility of misunderstanding. The doctrine of the real presence had indeed been attacked before the sixteenth century, but never had it been so fundamentally and categorically denied as it was by the heretics of the Reform. Already St Paul had pointed out that the Eucharist is the symbol and the cause of ecclesiastical unity;[1] St Ignatius of Antioch appealed on the same grounds to the Docetists of the first century to avoid schisms, and "to use one Eucharist, for one is the flesh of our Lord Jesus Christ and one the chalice unto the communion of his blood; one is the altar, and one its bishop together with the priests and deacons."[2] It is not surprising, therefore, that the great schism of the Protestants should have been inaugurated by a vehement attack upon the sacrament of our Lord's Body and Blood. The Council of Trent[3] in condemning the errors of the Reformers has given us a clear and unequivocal statement of the Eucharistic dogma, which we cannot do better than reproduce here, with appropriate commentary.

"In the first place the holy Synod teaches . . . that in the precious (*almo*)[4] sacrament of the holy Eucharist, after the consecration of the bread and wine, our Lord Jesus Christ, true God and true man, is truly, really and substantially contained under the species of those sensible things." The three words, "truly, really and substantially," are used by the Council with a definite purpose of rejecting three Protestant views concerning the presence of Christ in

[1] I Cor. x 17.
[2] *Ad Philadelph.*, chap. iv.
[3] Session xiii.
[4] Literally: nourishing.

the Eucharist. Zwingli held that his presence was only figurative: "Just as a man about to set out on a journey might give to his wife a most precious ring upon which his portrait is engraved, saying, 'Behold your husband; thus you may keep him and delight in him even though he is absent,' so our Lord Jesus Christ, as he departed, left to his spouse the Church his own image in the sacrament of the supper." [1] As opposed to this figurative presence, the Council describes the presence of Christ as *true*. Others taught that Christ is present by faith; the sacraments, they held, have no other effect than that of arousing faith in Christ, especially, however, the Eucharist, since it is a memorial of what Christ did on the last night before his death. The Council excludes this view by calling the presence of Christ *real*, *i.e.* independent of the faith of the recipient of the sacrament. Finally Calvin taught that Christ is present in this sacrament virtually, that is, inasmuch as he exercises his sanctifying power in the Eucharist. As against this doctrine the Council teaches that Christ is *substantially* present in this sacrament.

The faith of the Church in the real presence of Christ in the Eucharist rests upon the words which he used at the Last Supper, words which have ever been interpreted by Catholic Tradition in this sense. "For thus all our forefathers, as many as were in the true Church of Christ, who have treated of this most holy Sacrament, have most openly professed, that our Redeemer instituted this so admirable a sacrament at the Last Supper when, after the blessing of the bread and wine, he testified in express and clear words that he gave them his own very Body and his own Blood." From the words of Christ it follows not only that his presence in the Eucharist is real, but also that it is permanent. The body and blood of Christ are contained in this sacrament not only in the moment in which it is received by the faithful but independently of its administration. "The most holy Eucharist," we read in Chapter III of the Decree, "has indeed this in common with the rest of the sacraments, that it is a symbol of a sacred thing, and is a visible form of an invisible grace; but there is found in the Eucharist this excellent and peculiar thing, that the other sacraments have then first the power of sanctifying when one uses them, whereas in the Eucharist, before it is used, there is contained the Author of sanctity. For the Apostles had not as yet received the Eucharist from the hand of the Lord, when nevertheless he himself affirmed with truth that what he presented to them was his own body." The permanence of the presence of Christ is thus asserted by the Council against the error of Luther who, although he admitted the real presence, held that it began and ended with the reception of the sacrament by the faithful.

But from the fact that the Eucharist is called the sacrament of the Body and Blood of Christ it should not be concluded that only

[1] *De vera et falsa religione.*

his body and blood are contained therein. In this sacrament are present the living body and blood of Christ; therefore also his soul which gives them life, therefore also the divine nature which is indissolubly united with his sacred humanity. "This faith has ever been in the Church of God, that, immediately after the consecration, the veritable Body of our Lord and his veritable Blood, together with his soul and divinity, are under the species of bread and wine; the Body indeed under the species of bread and the blood under the species of wine by the force of the words; but the body itself under the species of wine and the blood under the species of bread, and the soul under each, by the force of that natural connection and concomitance by which the parts of our Lord 'who hath now risen from the dead, to die no more,' are united together; and the divinity furthermore on account of the admirable hypostatic union thereof with his body and soul. Wherefore . . . Christ whole and entire is under the species of bread and under any part of that species; likewise the whole Christ is under the species of wine and under the parts thereof."

What then has become of the bread, over which the words of consecration have been pronounced? Has the body of Christ mysteriously united itself with the bread and the wine? Has Christ permeated these substances with his own? Is he present in the bread or with the bread? The Council answers these questions in the negative. Luther taught the doctrine of consubstantiation or impanation, according to which the bread remains together with the body of Christ in the Eucharist. The Catholic doctrine—no less certain, no less a dogmatic truth than that of the real presence itself—is that the substances of bread and wine no longer remain after the words of consecration; they have been converted into the substance of our Lord's body and blood. Of the bread and wine there remain only the appearances, the species. "And because Christ, our Redeemer, declared that which he offered under the species of bread to be truly his own Body, therefore it has ever been a firm belief in the Church of God, and this holy Synod now declares it anew, that by the consecration of the bread and wine a conversion is made of the whole substance of the bread into the substance of the body of Christ our Lord, and of the whole substance of the wine into the substance of his blood; which conversion is suitably and properly called by the holy Catholic Church transubstantiation."

Hence wherever bread and wine are duly and validly consecrated, there is truly, really and substantially present the living Christ, the same Christ as was born of the Virgin Mary, who suffered and died for us, who now sits in Heaven at the right hand of the Father. "For these things are not mutually repugnant, that our Saviour himself always sits at the right hand of the Father in Heaven, according to his natural mode of existing, and that nevertheless he is in many other places sacramentally present, by a manner of existing which, though we can hardly express it in words, we can yet conceive, our understanding being enlightened by faith, and ought most firmly to believe to be possible to God."

In these few sentences the Council sums up the whole essence of the Catholic teaching concerning the mystery of the Eucharist. By virtue of the words of consecration the bread and wine cease to be bread and wine and, while still retaining the appearances of these, are changed into the body and blood of Christ. All else that theologians tell us of the mysterious presence of Christ in this sacrament is but a consequence of these fundamental truths, that Christ is truly, really and substantially present, and that he becomes present by the conversion of the substance of bread and wine into the substance of his body and blood, a conversion which is called by the Church Transubstantiation.

§ III: THE EUCHARIST IN SCRIPTURE

The Promise of the Eucharist

THE sixth chapter of the gospel of St John relates a discourse of our Lord which we may well call the preparation of his disciples for their first communion. It was the day following the two miracles of the feeding of the five thousand and the walking of Christ upon the lake of Galilee, and the Jews, impressed by the wonders they had witnessed, had come in search of Jesus. Addressing his hearers in the synagogue at Capharnaum, Jesus began by upbraiding them for their unworthy motives in seeking him: "You seek me not because you have seen miracles but because you did eat of the loaves and were filled." The Jews had seen in the miracles of Christ, not a proof of his divine mission, but merely a source from which they might derive earthly profit and advantage. Christ would have them seek him for their spiritual nourishment, for "the meat which endureth unto life everlasting, which the son of man will give you." This is the theme which he then proceeds to elaborate throughout his discourse: a heavenly food which would give everlasting life.

The idea of receiving food from heaven was not unfamiliar to the Jews, who well remembered the story of the manna that their fathers had eaten in the desert. This, however, had been merely a type of the true bread that Christ himself had come to give. The manna had fed the Jews only; the bread of Christ would give life to the world. But it was useless for the Jews to ask for this food unless they had faith in Christ; like all the sacraments, the Eucharist could produce no effect, could not give the divine life which is its fruit, unless the recipient believed in what he was receiving. The Jews had seen many miracles worked by him and yet they did not believe that he was what he claimed to be. Did they not know his parents, Mary and Joseph? How could they believe that he had come down from heaven? But the knowledge that his hearers were so ill-disposed to believe him does not prevent Christ from explaining still more definitely the nature of the heavenly food that he promises them. "The bread that I will give is my flesh for the life of the world." The food that was to give eternal life was nothing else than his own body which was to be offered in sacrifice for the sins of the world. At these words the scepticism of his hearers becomes open disbelief. "How can this man give us his flesh to eat?" But their incredulity only calls forth a reiterated and still more explicit statement; it is as if Christ were determined to leave no loophole for misunderstanding: "Amen, amen, I say unto you; unless you eat the flesh of the son of man and drink his blood you shall not have life in you. He that eateth my flesh and drinketh my blood hath everlasting life, and I will raise him up at the last day. For my flesh is meat indeed and my blood is drink indeed. He that eateth my flesh and drinketh my blood abideth in me and I in him. As the living Father sent me, and I live by the Father, so he that eateth me the same also shall live by me. This is the bread that came down from heaven. Not as your fathers did eat manna, and are dead. He that eateth this bread shall live for ever."

There could no longer be any doubt that Christ meant what he said; here was no metaphor, no parable; Christ intended to give his own flesh and blood as food and drink. "Many therefore of his disciples, hearing it, said, This saying is hard, and who can hear it?" Reading their thoughts, Jesus returns once more to the earlier subject of his discourse, the necessity of faith: "Therefore did I say to you, that no man can come to me unless it be given him by my Father." And his hearers then divided into two parties; some of them "went back, and walked no more with him"; the twelve Apostles remained, and, as at Caesarea Philippi, so here too it was Peter who made the great profession of faith: "Lord, to whom shall we go? Thou hast the words of eternal life. And we have believed and have known that thou art the Christ the Son of the living God." St Peter seems to have had in mind the profession of faith that he had made on the previous occasion; he had then acclaimed Jesus as the "Son of the living God"; now he proclaimed his faith in the sacrament by which chiefly the Son of God proposed to infuse into the souls of men that divine life which should make them the adoptive sons of God. It is not merely of immortality, not merely of the unending existence of the soul, or indeed of the immortality of the risen body that he is thinking when he says that Christ has the words of eternal life. St Peter's words are an answer to Christ's declaration: "As the living Father sent me and I live by the Father, so he that eateth me the same also shall live by me. . . . The words that I have spoken to you are spirit and life." The life which is the fruit of this living bread is the life which the Son of God lives, the life of God himself, the life which, when shared by man, is called sanctifying grace.

Hence the discerning reader may find in this discourse of Christ a complete treatise upon the aim and purpose of the Incarnation. God sent his only begotten Son into the world that he might offer in sacrifice his "flesh for the life of the world," and the life that he came to give—or rather to restore—to the world is none other than a finite participation of the divine life which he, the Son of God, lives in common with the Father, the divine life of grace which had been given originally to mankind in Adam and by him had been lost. The fruits of that sacrifice were to be communicated to us principally through the sacrament of the Eucharist, in which we should eat his flesh and drink his blood, receiving as food that same living body which was to be the Victim of the sacrifice.

The Last Supper

The promise thus made was fulfilled at the Last Supper. The moment had arrived to which during the whole of his life he had been looking forward with loving anticipation, the moment in which, about to give himself as a sacrifice for the sins of the world, he would institute this sacrament as the great pledge of his love: "With desire I have desired to eat this pasch with you before I suffer."[1] The scene is described, with slight variations, by the three synoptic evangelists and by St Paul in his first epistle to the Corinthians. This is the account given by St Paul: "The Lord Jesus, the same night in which he was betrayed, took bread and giving thanks, broke, and said: Take ye and eat; this is my body which shall be delivered for you; this do for the commemoration of me. In like manner also the chalice, after he had supped, saying: This chalice is the new testament in my blood; this do ye, as often as you shall drink, for the commemoration of me."[2]

As, just a year previously, in preparing his disciples for their first communion, he had left no room for doubt as to the meaning of his words—"my flesh is meat indeed and my blood is drink indeed"—so here his words leave no possibility of misunderstanding. Wishing to indicate that he was giving his own flesh and blood to his Apostles under the form of food and drink, he could not have expressed himself more clearly. The sentence, "this is my body," is one upon which it is impossible to make any commentary without weakening its force. Searching in my mind for words more simple, more convincing, I can find nothing but circumlocutions, which would convey the same meaning only at the cost of long and involved explanations. Those who have related the incident have not thought it necessary to give any such explanation; feeling that any amplification of the words of Christ, far from clarifying, would only obscure their meaning, they have left them to speak for themselves. And if the writer of these lines consulted merely his own inclination he would do likewise. Nevertheless the attacks which have been made by Protestants consistently for the last three hundred years upon the literal interpretation of the words of Christ seem to call, if not for an express answer, at least for some remark.

[1] Luke xxii 15. [2] 1 Cor. xi 23-25.

The language of the decrees of oecumenical councils is usually measured and calm. But the attempts of the Protestants to interpret the words of institution in a figurative sense seem to have aroused in the Tridentine Fathers a holy indignation: "(Christ) testified in express and clear words that he gave them his own very Body and his own Blood; words which—recorded by the holy Evangelists and afterwards repeated by St Paul, whereas they carry with them that proper and most manifest meaning in which they were understood by the Fathers—it is indeed a crime the most unworthy that they should be wrested, by certain contentious and wicked men, to fictitious and imaginary figures of speech."[1]

And indeed it is difficult to see how the literal meaning of the words of Christ can be evaded. The solemnity of the occasion, the words used, the absence of any warning that a metaphor was intended, the very feebleness of the metaphor—if metaphor it was—all conspire to exclude the figurative sense of the words "this is my body." It is true that Christ had often used figures of speech, but they had either been so obviously such as to need no explanation, or else Christ had carefully explained them lest the Apostles, simple-minded men, should be misled.[2] Nor was the occasion one which called for ambiguity; on the contrary, it was precisely the moment for plain speaking. It had been necessary for him in the early days of his ministry to shroud his meaning under the form of parables, both to adapt himself to the minds of his hearers and in order to give an opportunity to men of good will to come and ask him to explain. But he was now at the last evening of his life on earth; he was surrounded, not by the suspicious Pharisees and Sadducees, but by his own faithful Apostles whom he trusted, to whom he spoke no more in parables, but plainly.[3] If they failed to grasp his meaning now, they could not learn it from him on the morrow; for then he would be no more with them. He spoke plainly because he was instituting a new Testament, a new Law; and a testament, a covenant, is not formulated in figurative language. The Old Testament had been ratified by the blood of victims, and Moses had sprinkled the people with it; the New Testament was ratified by the blood of Christ, of whom those victims had been but a type. Was the reality

[1] As an example of the lengths to which certain Reformers were prepared to go, the following incident is instructive. Zwingli, the protagonist of the figurative interpretation, had been holding a public discussion with a Catholic on the question at Thuringen. That same night, he relates, "I dreamed that I was again disputing with him, when suddenly there appeared to me an adviser, whether he was white or black I do not remember, who said to me: 'Answer him, thou fool, that it is written in Exodus: It is the phase, *i.e.* the passing of the Lord.' Immediately awaking I jumped from my bed, verified the passage, and later delivered a discourse before the assembly which effectively removed any doubts that had remained in the minds of pious men." *Subsidium Eucharistiæ.*

[2] *Cf.* Matt. xvi 11; John iv 32.

[3] *Cf.* John xvi 29.

to be less perfect than the figure, the shadow more real than the substance? It was therefore the real blood of Christ which the Apostles reverently drank, the blood which was shed for the remission of sins; it was the true body of Christ which they ate, the body which was given for them, the flesh that was given for the life of the world.

If this were a treatise of apologetics it would be my duty here to show that according to sound hermeneutical principles the words of Christ at the Last Supper cannot but be taken literally, and that the figurative interpretation put upon them by the Protestants is out of the question. This has been done exhaustively by Cardinal Wiseman in his well-known lectures on the Eucharist,[1] so fully indeed that authors who have dealt with the subject subsequently have been able to do little but repeat the unanswerable arguments which he there sets forth. But the theologian, as distinct from the apologist, has another method of discovering the meaning of the words of Scripture. It has been shown elsewhere in these essays that the Church is the custodian of Scripture, and not merely of its letter but also of its sense.[2] Hence the theologian as such does not treat the books of Scripture as a merely human document. If he wants to know the meaning of a particular passage he does not rely only upon his own understanding; he appeals to the living teaching of the Church; for him the sense of Scripture is the sense in which it has always been interpreted by the Catholic Church. We may therefore base our literal interpretation of the words of Christ upon the fact that the Fathers of the Church have always thus understood them, a fact which will become abundantly apparent in the following section.

The gospel of St John makes no reference to the institution of the Eucharist, and the epistles contain only brief and sparse indications of Eucharistic doctrine and practice. Nor is this surprising. St John seems to have had as one of his objects in writing his gospel to fill the lacunæ left by the other evangelists; hence, having related fully the promise of the Eucharist, he thinks it unnecessary to add another account of its institution to the four already existing, the more so as the story must have been so familiar to his readers because it was embodied in the celebration of the Eucharist itself.

The teaching of St Paul

As for the epistles, these, as is well known, were never intended to be theological treatises but were written to meet the various demands of the moment, and thus are hortatory rather than expository both in style and content. Nevertheless it happened on two occasions that St Paul made incidental reference to the Eucharist; once in connection with idolatry and again in connection with the behaviour of certain of his converts at Corinth during the Eucharistic assemblies. The Christians of Corinth, surrounded as they were by pagans and idolaters, many of them their own friends and relatives, had many

[1] See especially Lectures v and vi.

[2] Essay i, *Faith and Revealed Truth*, pp. 30–1.

difficulties to contend with, and not the least among them was the question of meats which had been offered to idols. St Paul gives them some practical advice on the matter in the eighth and tenth chapters of his first epistle to them. Evidently they must not take part in the sacrificial banquets of the pagans ; this would be equivalent to the sin of idolatry. Might they buy in the market meats which had been used in pagan sacrifices and eat them privately at home ? St Paul answers in effect that they might do this so long as all danger of scandal was eliminated. But the interest of the matter from our point of view lies in the reason which St Paul gives for prohibiting their attendance at the sacrificial banquets of the pagans. It was the belief of the pagans that by partaking of the sacrificial gifts they were put in communion with the divinity—in truth, as St Paul rather sardonically remarks, " with devils." How then, St Paul asks, can Christians dare to take part in these banquets, when in the Eucharist they have a sacrificial banquet wherein they are made partakers of the body and blood of Christ ? It is to be remarked that he does not say simply that by drinking of the cup and partaking of the bread Christians are put into communion with *God* or with *Christ* ; this is what we should have expected, to preserve the parallelism with the pagan sacrifices ; to receive the Eucharist, according to the Apostle, is to be united with *the body and blood* of Christ. " The chalice of benediction which we bless, is it not the communion of the blood of Christ ? And the bread which we break, is it not the partaking of the body of the Lord ? . . . You cannot drink the chalice of the Lord and the chalice of devils ; you cannot be partakers of the table of the Lord and of the table of devils." [1] It need hardly be remarked that this passage, besides indicating the doctrine of the real presence, contains an evident proof of the sacrificial character of the Eucharist.[2]

St Paul makes another interesting, though again an incidental, reference to the Eucharist in reproving the Corinthians for certain abuses which had crept into the Eucharistic gatherings.[3] He takes the opportunity of impressing upon them the reverence with which this most holy sacrament should be received, and of warning them of the dire penalties attending a sacrilegious reception. The solemnity of the terms in which this admonition is expressed can hardly be understood except in the light of the real presence of the body and blood of Christ in the Eucharist. Having reminded them, in the words above related, of the manner in which Christ had instituted the Eucharist, he goes on : " For as often as you eat this bread and drink the chalice, you shall show forth the death of the Lord, until he come. Therefore whosoever shall eat this bread or drink the chalice of the Lord unworthily shall be guilty of the body and of the blood of the Lord. But let a man prove himself, and so let him eat

[1] 1 Cor. x 16-21. [2] See *The Eucharistic Sacrifice*, pp. 883–884.

[3] 1 Cor. xi 18 *seq.*

of that bread and drink of the chalice. For he that eateth and drinketh unworthily eateth and drinketh judgement to himself, not discerning the body of the Lord." Here, as in the passage previously quoted, it may be remarked that the sacrilegious communicant is not only said to be guilty of irreverence to the person of Christ who instituted this sacrament, but is said to be guilty of the body and of the blood of the Lord. He who receives unworthily will be punished because he fails to discern in this sacrament the body of the Lord. If the Eucharist is nothing else but a symbol of the body and blood of Christ surely the words of St Paul are excessively severe.

We may sum up the teaching of Scripture regarding the sacrament of the Eucharist quite briefly and simply. Christ, having previously promised his disciples to give them his own flesh as food and his own blood as drink, at the Last Supper took bread and gave it to his disciples telling them that it was his body, and took wine and gave it to them telling them that it was his blood. Neither in the account of the promise nor in that of the institution of the sacrament is there anything to indicate that Christ spoke figuratively; on the contrary, the circumstances, the power and the wisdom of Christ himself, the manner in which his words were understood by his hearers, all point to the literal meaning of those words as the only possible interpretation, an interpretation which is confirmed by the manner in which St Paul speaks of the Eucharist, and which appears in the constant teaching of the Church from the earliest times. "When the Lord," writes St Cyril of Jerusalem, "has said of the bread 'This is my body,' who shall dare to doubt? And when he has asserted and said, 'This is my blood,' who shall ever doubt that it is indeed his blood?" [1]

§ IV: THE EUCHARIST IN TRADITION

NOT the least noteworthy feature of the Eucharistic literature of the early centuries is its extraordinary abundance; so that it is impossible to convey in this small space any but a very inadequate idea of the complete teaching of the Fathers of the first three or four centuries on this all-important dogma. Yet the very familiarity of Catholics with the Eucharist prevented them from giving us in their writings the clear and explicit testimony to their belief which to-day—from a controversial point of view, at any rate—would be so valuable and interesting. References to the Eucharist we find in great abundance; but set treatises on the subject are very rare. In fact, with the exception of the Catechetical instructions of St Cyril of Jerusalem—and to a certain extent the Apology of St Justin—I know of no writings in the very early centuries professedly devoted to a doctrinal exposition of Eucharistic belief. Nevertheless those numerous passages in which the Fathers refer incidentally to Eucharistic

[1] *Catech.* xxii 1.

doctrine, treating it as well known and not requiring explanation, by the very absence of the intention to instruct become all the more instructive. So accustomed were the early Christians to frequenting the Holy Sacrifice and to receiving Communion, so intimately did the Eucharist enter into their daily lives, that their pastors did not deem it necessary to write books to teach them what must have been so familiar to them from their daily practice.

St Ignatius of Antioch

Already in the sub-apostolic age we find St Ignatius of Antioch arguing from the Eucharist to the necessity of unity in the Church. " See that you use one Eucharist," he writes,[1] " for one is the flesh of our Lord Jesus Christ, and one is the chalice unto the communion of his blood ; one is the altar, and one the bishop together with the priests and deacons." The argument is that of St Paul in his first epistle to the Corinthians : [2] in the Eucharist you all partake of the one body of Christ and of his blood, you all assist at one and the same sacrifice ; hence you should be one among yourselves. But here, as also in St Paul, the argument loses all its force unless the Eucharist is really and truly the one body and blood of Christ. Still more clearly is belief in the real presence implied in the martyr's epistle to the Smyrnæans [3] where, writing of the Docetists who denied the reality of the human nature of Christ, he says : " They abstain from the Eucharist and the prayer [*i.e.* probably the Eucharistic prayer or the Canon of the Mass] because they do not believe that the Eucharist is the flesh of our Saviour Jesus Christ which suffered for our sins and which the Father in his bounty raised up again." Clearly then, Catholics, as opposed to the Docetists, did believe that the Eucharist is the very body and blood of Christ.

St Justin

Still more explicitly does St. Justin state the doctrine of the Real Presence when in his account of the celebration of the Eucharist he writes : " We do not receive these as ordinary food or ordinary drink ; but, as by the Word of God Jesus our Saviour was made flesh, and had both flesh and blood for our salvation, so also the food which has been blessed (lit., over which thanks have been given) by the word of prayer instituted by him, and from which our flesh and blood by assimilation are nourished, is, we are taught, both the flesh and blood of that Jesus incarnate. For the Apostles in the accounts which they wrote, and which are called gospels, have declared that Jesus commanded them to do as follows : ' He took bread and gave thanks and said : This do in commemoration of me ; this is my body. And in like manner he took the chalice and blessed it and said : This is my blood, and gave it to them alone.' " [4] There can be no doubt of St Justin's meaning. He is explaining the doctrine of the Eucharist to pagans, not to Christians who might be presumed to have some previous knowledge of the subject, and therefore if the Eucharist

[1] *Ad Philadelph.*, chap. iv. [2] x 16. [3] vii 1.

[4] St Justin's account is quoted more fully in Essay xxv, *The Eucharistic Sacrifice*, pp. 890–892.

were deemed to be nothing more than a mere symbol of the body and blood of Christ, the writer would certainly have made this clear. But of the symbolic meaning there is no indication whatever. St Justin says quite simply that the Eucharistic bread and wine are not mere bread and wine (" ordinary food "); they are the body and blood of Jesus Christ who became man for our salvation. In fact we may find more than a hint of the doctrine of Transubstantiation in the comparison made between the Incarnation and the Eucharist. Just as the Word of God is so mighty that he could unite a human nature to the divinity, so the words that he instituted at the Last Supper have the virtue of making the bread and the wine his own flesh and blood.

St Irenaeus Many pertinent passages might be quoted from the *Adversus Hæreses* of St Irenaeus in which this great controversialist uses the Eucharistic dogma to refute the tenets of the Gnostics. These held that matter was essentially evil. How could this be so, asked St. Irenaeus, if Christ used bread and wine in the Eucharist, elements which, " perceiving the word of God (*i.e.* through the power of God's word) become the Eucharist, which is the body and blood of Christ ? "[1] But the references to the Eucharist are so scattered that it would be impossible to quote them here at all adequately. One passage, however, is especially remarkable because of its similarity with that of St. Justin above quoted : " The bread that is taken from the earth, perceiving the invocation of God, is no longer ordinary bread, but the Eucharist, consisting of two things, an earthly and a heavenly."[2]

Tertullian The temptation to idolatry which was a constant menace to Christians by reason of their close contact with pagans caused the Fathers of the third century to reiterate the warning already given by St. Paul[3] against desecrating the Eucharist. So Tertullian has some very strong remarks about those Christians who engaged in the manufacture of idols ; he speaks of the scandal caused by the sight of a Christian " passing from the idols to the church, from the shop of the enemy to the house of God, raising up to God the Father the hands that are mothers of idols . . ., applying to the Lord's body those hands that give bodies to demons. Nor is this enough. Grant that it be a small matter that from other hands they receive what they contaminate, but those very hands even deliver to others what they have contaminated : idol-makers are admitted even into the ecclesiastical order. O wickedness ! Once did the Jews lay hands upon Christ ; these mangle his body daily. O hands to be cut off ! Now let them see if it is merely by similitude that it was said : ' If thy hand scandalise thee, cut it off.' What hands deserve

[1] v 2, 3.

[2] iv 18, 5. The earthly element seems to be the appearances of bread which remain, and the heavenly element the body of Christ present under those appearances.

[3] 1 Cor. ch. viii and ch. x.

more to be cut off than those in which scandal is done to the body of the Lord!" [1]

St Cyprian is no less vehement about the Christians who had fallen into idolatry during the fierce persecution of Decius (251). While he praises the fortitude of the many confessors of the faith, saying that "the noble hands that had been accustomed only to perform the works of God had resisted the sacrilegious sacrifices of pagans, the lips which had been sanctified with heavenly food, after the body and blood of the Lord, turned in disgust from the touch of things profane and the leavings of idols," he laments at the same time that many of those who had fallen into idolatry expected immediately, without having done penance, to be allowed to receive Communion: "Returning from the altars of the devil they approach the sacred thing of the Lord (*sanctum Domini*) with filthy and stinking hands; still belching the deadly food of idols, with their very breath still giving evidence of their crime . . . they assail (*invadunt*) the body of the Lord. . . . Violence is done to the body and blood of the Lord, and greater violence now with their hands and with their lips than when they denied the Lord." [2] *St Cyprian*

Evidence of early belief in the dogma of the Real Presence may be seen also in the outward reverence with which the sacrament was received. Origen thus impresses upon the faithful the need of reverence for the word of God: "You who are accustomed to assist at the divine mysteries know how, when you receive the body of the Lord, you hold it with every precaution and veneration lest any of the consecrated gift should fall. For you believe, and rightly believe, yourselves guilty if through your negligence any of it should be dropped. If you—justly—use such care to preserve his body, do you consider it a lesser sin to neglect his word?" [3] A detailed description of the manner in which the Eucharist was received in the fourth century is given us by St Cyril of Jerusalem: "In approaching, therefore, come not with thy wrists extended or thy fingers spread, but make thy left hand a throne for the right, as for that which is to receive a King. And having hollowed thy palm, receive the body of Christ, saying over it 'Amen.' Then having carefully sanctified thine eyes with the touch of the holy body, partake of it, taking heed lest thou lose any portion thereof; for whatever thou losest is evidently a loss to thee as it were from one of thine own members. For tell me, if any one gave thee grains of gold, wouldst not thou hold them with all carefulness, being on thy guard against losing any of them and suffering loss? Wilt thou not then much more carefully keep watch that not a crumb fall from thee of what is more precious than gold and precious stones? Then after thou hast partaken of *Origen; St Cyril of Jerusalem*

[1] *De Idololatria*, 7.

[2] *De lapsis*, chap. xv. Chapters xxv and xxvi contain other striking passages concerning the Eucharist.

[3] *In Ex.*, hom. xiii, 3.

the body of Christ draw near also to the chalice of his blood ; not stretching forth thine hands, but bending, and saying with worship and reverence 'Amen,' hallow thyself by partaking also of the blood of Christ. And while the moisture is still on thy lips, touch it with thy hands and hallow thine eyes and brow and the other organs of sense. Then wait for the prayer and give thanks to God who has accounted thee worthy of so great mysteries." [1]

With the Catechetical Instructions of St Cyril, from which this passage is taken, we enter into a new category of Eucharistic literature. In the works which have been quoted hitherto reference is made to the Eucharist only incidentally and indirectly ; but St Cyril intends expressly to instruct his catechumens on the great sacrament which they are shortly to receive for the first time, and hence his teaching is much more clear and explicit. So striking is the similarity between his words and the terms in which at the present day we are accustomed to prepare children for their first Communion that, at the risk of overstepping the limits set for this section, I cannot refrain from quoting a few extracts : " Since he has said of the bread 'This is my body,' who shall venture to doubt ? Since he has said and asserted 'This is my blood,' who shall ever doubt that it is his blood ? He once changed water into wine, which is akin to blood ; shall we not therefore believe when he changed wine into blood ? When called to a bodily marriage he miraculously wrought that wonderful work ; and on the 'children of the bridechamber' shall he not much more be acknowledged to have bestowed the enjoyment of his body and blood ? . . . Consider therefore the bread and the wine not as bare elements, for according to the Lord's declaration they are the body and blood of Christ ; for even though sense suggest this to thee (*i.e.* that they are merely bread and wine), yet let faith give thee firm certainty. Judge not the matter from the taste, but by faith be fully assured without doubt that the body and blood of Christ have been vouchsafed to thee. . . . The seeming bread is not bread, though sensible to taste, but the body of Christ ; and the seeming wine is not wine, though the taste will have it so, but the blood of Christ." [2]

St John Chrysostom

The need of faith in the Real Presence in order to overcome the apparently contrary suggestion of the senses is emphasised in almost identical terms by St John Chrysostom : " Let us then in everything believe God and gainsay him in nothing, though what is said may seem to be contrary to our thoughts and senses, but let his word be of higher authority than both reasonings and sight. Thus let us do in the Mysteries also, not looking at the things set before us, but keeping in mind his sayings. For his word cannot deceive, but our senses are easily beguiled. That hath never failed, but this in most

[1] *Catech.* xxiii 21, 22.

[2] *Catech.* xxii 1, 2, 6, 9 and *passim*. *Cf.* St Thomas's hymn :

Visus, tactus, gustus in te fallitur,
Sed auditu solo tuto creditur.

things goes astray. Since the Word saith, ' This is my body,' let us both be persuaded and believe, and look at it with the eyes of the mind." [1]

I conclude this brief selection of texts from the Fathers with two more passages from St John Chrysostom: [2] " How many now say, I would wish to see his form, his shape, his clothes, his shoes. Lo! thou seest him, thou touchest him, thou eatest him. And thou indeed desirest to see his clothes, but he gives himself to thee, not to see only, but also to touch and eat and receive within thee. . . . Look therefore, lest thou also thyself become guilty of the body and blood of Christ. They (*i.e.* the Jews who crucified him) slaughtered the all-holy body, but thou receivest it in a filthy soul after so great benefits. For neither was it enough for him to be made man, to be smitten and slaughtered, but he also commingleth himself with us, and not by faith only, but also in deed maketh us his body. . . . There are often mothers that after the travail of birth send out their children to other women to be nursed; but he endures not to do this, but himself feeds us with his own blood, and by all means entwines us with himself." A similar passage occurs in his 46th homily (on St John): " We become one body, and members of his flesh and of his bones. Let the initiated follow what I say. In order then that we may become this not by love only but in very deed, let us be blended into that flesh. This is brought about by the food which he has freely given us, desiring to show the love that he bears us. On this account he has mingled himself with us; he has kneaded his body with ours that we might become one thing, like a body joined to the head. . . . He has given to those who desire him not only to see him, but even to touch and eat him, to fix their teeth in his flesh and to embrace him and satisfy all their love. Parents often entrust their offspring to others to feed; ' But I,' he says, ' do not so. I feed you with my own flesh, desiring that you all be nobly born. . . . For he that gives himself to you here much more will do so hereafter. I have willed to become your brother, for your sake I shared in flesh and blood, and in turn I give to you that same flesh and blood by which I became your kinsman.' "

General considerations on the Fathers

These extracts from the writings of the Fathers of the first four centuries, though representative, are of course far from exhaustive. Moreover, passages have been selected in which the Fathers speak quite clearly of the real presence of the body and blood of Christ in this sacrament. It would be a mistake to suppose that they always speak so plainly; in fact passages may be found in the writings even of those whom we have seen emphasising the Real Presence, which at first sight would seem to favour the view of the Zwinglians, that the Eucharist is merely a figure of the body of Christ. An exhaustive treatment of their teaching would require all these texts to be

[1] Hom. 82 in *Matt.*, n. 4. [2] *Ibid.*

considered individually in their context, so that their complete meaning might be made clear. Obviously such a procedure is out of the question in this short essay. But for those who desire to devote some time—and it would be most profitably spent—to the study of the early Fathers on the Eucharist the following considerations may serve as some guide in the interpretation of their thought. In the first place it should be remembered that the Eucharist is a sacrament, *i.e.* a sacred sign. There is an external element in the Eucharist, the appearances of bread and wine, the proper function of which is to signify; and these are rightly called the sign of the body and blood of Christ. If, therefore, a writer who clearly believes in the Real Presence refers to the Eucharist as the sign of the body and blood of Christ, evidently he must be understood to mean that the appearances of bread and wine are the sign of the body and blood of Christ which are really, though invisibly, present beneath them. This consideration is of particular use in the interpretation of many texts in the works of St. Augustine.[1]

Moreover, the body and blood of Christ, although they are truly, really and substantially present in this sacrament, are nevertheless present with an extraordinary mode of existence, which we can only —for want of a better word—call sacramental. They are present invisibly, intangibly, so that our senses cannot reach them. Hence it need not surprise us to find some of the Fathers referring to a "spiritual eating" of Christ, in order to differentiate the sacramental eating of the flesh of Christ from the gross and materialistic sense in which the people of Capharnaum had understood his words. So St Cyril of Jerusalem, in the very same discourse from which we have selected the striking passages above quoted, laments the unbelief of the people of Capharnaum in that "they, not having heard his saying in a spiritual sense, were offended, and went back, supposing that he was inviting them to eat flesh." And yet in the previous paragraph he had said that "his body and blood are distributed through our members."

Finally, it is well known that the early Fathers delighted in symbolism. This is especially true of the great theologians of Alexandria, and also of St Augustine. Now the doctrine of the Eucharist lends itself in a special way to symbolical treatment. The connection between the mystical body of Christ and his physical body present in the Eucharist, already noticed by St Paul,[2] was a frequent subject of allegorical speculation and caused some of the Fathers to use phrases concerning the Eucharist from which we should carefully abstain at the present day. Not that statements which were true fifteen hundred years ago have now become false. It is not the truth that changes, but the manner of expressing it that varies according to the exigencies of popular devotion and of controversy. In days when

[1] *Cf. e.g.* Ep. 98; *Contr. Adimant.* xii, 3; *Enarr.* in Ps. iii 1.
[2] 1 Cor. x 17.

the Real Presence was not impugned by heretics but was tranquilly believed by all Catholics there was no danger of such symbolical phrases being misunderstood. But since the denial of the Real Presence by the heretics of the Reform we should hesitate to use any expression concerning the Eucharist which might seem, in the changed circumstances, to exclude the reality by excessive emphasis upon the symbolism that surrounds it.

Of the numerous liturgical documents of antiquity and of the frequent references to the Eucharist in Christian epigraphy we have made no mention, nor does space allow us even to outline the evidence of early belief in the Real Presence which may be found in these sources. But even the little that we have seen of patristic teaching suffices to make it abundantly clear that the Church from the beginning has taught that the body and blood of Christ are truly, really and substantially present in this Sacrament.

§ V: TRANSUBSTANTIATION

Transubstantiation and the Real Presence

No less essential to the doctrine of the Eucharist than the dogma of the Real Presence is that of Transubstantiation. The decree of the Council of Trent presents them as logically connected with each other: "And *because* Christ declared that which he offered under the species of bread to be truly his own body, *therefore* has it ever been a firm belief in the Church of God, and this holy Synod doth now declare it anew, that by the consecration of the bread and of the wine a conversion is made of the whole substance of the bread into the substance of the body of Christ our Lord, and of the whole substance of the wine into the substance of his blood; which conversion is by the holy Catholic Church suitably and properly called Transubstantiation."[1] In other words, it is only by such a total conversion of the substance of the bread and wine into the substance of our Lord's body and blood that his words, "This is my body; this is my blood," can be verified. Hence when the Jansenists at the synod of Pistoia laid down that it was sufficient to teach that Christ is truly, really and substantially present in this sacrament, and that the substance of bread and wine ceases, only their appearances remaining, omitting all mention of transubstantiation, Pius VI condemned this view. Transubstantiation, he added, must not be passed over in silence as if it were a mere scholastic question; it has been defined by the Council of Trent as an article of faith, and the word has been consecrated by the Church to defend her faith against heresies.

The doctrine in Scripture and Tradition

The subject may perhaps be best approached by considering the plain signification of the words of our Lord at the Last Supper: "This is my body." He held in his hands something which to all appearances was bread, but in reality was not bread; in consequence of the words he had uttered it was his own body. "The seeming

[1] Session xiii, c. 4.

bread," says St Cyril of Jerusalem, " is not bread, though sensible to taste, but the body of Christ; and the seeming wine is not wine, though the taste will have it so, but the blood of Christ." [1] What, then, had happened? All the indications of sense pointed to the presence of bread as before; all that in the bread which is perceptible to the senses—what we call for the sake of convenience the " appearances " of bread—remained unchanged. Yet something was changed, something which lies deeper than the appearances, the " thing " which normally has those appearances, which through those appearances normally manifests its presence, which is the subject of the qualities and activities, the chemical and physical properties and reactions which we associate with bread, this " thing "—which we call the substance—had been changed into another substance, that of the body of Christ, the appearances alone of the bread remaining. This is what is meant by Transubstantiation. No other conclusion is consonant with the words of Christ. That he did not speak figuratively is abundantly clear from what has been said; nor is the theory of Luther reconcilable with the truth of the words " This is my body." If, as Luther claimed, the effect of the words of consecration is to render the substance of the body of Christ present in the bread (impanation) or side by side with the bread (consubstantiation), it is no longer true that *this* is the body of Christ; rather, in such an hypothesis, Christ should have said " *here* is the body of Christ." Rightly, therefore, does the Council of Trent present Transubstantiation as the logical outcome of the words of Christ at the Last Supper.

The Fathers, likewise, do not conceive of the real presence of the body and blood of Christ in this sacrament apart from the conversion of the bread and the wine into them. The word transubstantiation did not come till much later, when theologians had had the leisure and opportunity to realise all that was involved in the Eucharistic miracle. But the essential truth that the bread, while still appearing to be bread, was changed into the body of Christ was seen by the early Fathers to be formally implied in the truth of the Real Presence. Thus they say that after the words of consecration the bread is no longer bread but the body of Christ; they speak of the bread and wine being changed, converted, transmuted into the body of Christ; they compare this change with creation: " If the word of God," says St John Damascene,[2] " is living and efficacious . . . if the earth, the sea, the fire and the air . . . were made by the word of God . . . why should that word, then, not be able to make wine and water his blood? " They compare the Eucharistic conversion with the substantial change whereby the food a man eats is assimilated and changed into his own substance.[3] We have seen, too, how St Cyril of Jerusalem compares it with the miraculous change of

[1] *Cf.* above, p. 850.
[2] *De fide orthod.* iv, 13.
[3] John Damasc., *loc. cit.*

water into wine at the marriage feast of Cana.[1] Clearly, then, the traditional teaching of the Church is that by virtue of the words of consecration the bread and the wine, although their appearances remain, undergo an intrinsic change, as a result of which they are no longer bread and wine, but become the true body and blood of Christ. Transubstantiation means nothing more than this.

Transubstantiation and philosophy

In considering the dogma of transubstantiation it is well to remember what has been said more than once in the course of these essays, that the Church does not define any philosophical system as being of faith. The objection has been made against the Catholic doctrine of the Eucharist that this is necessarily bound up with the scholastic view concerning substance and accidents, a view which is by no means universally accepted, and that the Council of Trent in defining the doctrine of transubstantiation exceeded its powers by making excursions into the field of philosophy. This, however, is not the case. It is true that the term " transubstantiation " is a philosophical one and is associated with the system of the Schoolmen ; it is true that the scholastic view of the relation between substance and accidents has provided the basis of a wonderful synthesis of Eucharistic theology, brought to its perfection by St Thomas Aquinas. But the revealed doctrine which the term transubstantiation is intended to express is in no way conditioned by the scholastic system of philosophy. It is merely an expression in philosophical terms of the truth enunciated by St Cyril : " The seeming bread is not bread but the body of Christ." The inner reality of a thing, as opposed to what the senses perceive, was called by the scholastics " substance " ; and therefore the change of the substance of the bread into the body of Christ was called transubstantiation.

Substance and accidents

Evidently, therefore, any philosophy may be reconciled with the dogma of transubstantiation which safeguards the distinction between " the appearances " of a thing and the thing in itself ; and this is a distinction which any system of philosophy must safeguard if it is not to run counter to right thinking. It is a commonplace of experience that realities are either " things in themselves " or else modifications or qualities of things that exist in themselves. A man, a tree, copper, zinc, these are substances ; they exist in themselves. On the other hand, thought, extension, colour, physical and chemical actions and reactions, are called in philosophical language accidents, because they require a subject, or a substance, in which to " inhere." Thought does not exist except in a thinking subject ; there is no extension, colour, chemical activity, except in a corporeal substance. Substance and accidents, therefore, form a composite unity which is naturally indissoluble ; yet, in reality as well as in thought, they are distinct from each other as that which exists in itself must be distinct from that which, in order to exist, requires a subject of inherence. Thus a bodily substance is not its size, its shape, its colour, its chemical

[1] See above, p. 854.

or physical properties, nor is it the sum of these ; it is that which possesses these properties, is located, acts and reacts by means of them, and through them manifests itself to the senses. The substance *as such* is impervious to the senses ; if a body had no extension we could not touch it, if it had no colour we could not see it. Hence we commonly give to the accidents of material substances the name of appearances, since it is through these accidents, perceived by the senses, that the mind arrives at the knowledge of the substance.

Unique character of this change

The Eucharistic change, then, is one which transcends sense-perception, because what is changed is not the appearances but the substance. The senses of sight, touch, taste and smell reveal in the consecrated elements those properties which are naturally associated with bread and wine ; subjected to physical or chemical analysis they will present the features of bread and wine ; but the substance which is the natural subject of those properties and activities is no longer there : instead there is present the substance of the body and blood of Christ. We have seen how the Fathers use various analogies to explain the Eucharistic conversion ; but it should be remembered that they are analogies and nothing more. There is no change, whether natural or miraculous, to which transubstantiation can properly be likened ; this conversion, according to the Council of Trent, is not only miraculous (*mirabilis*) but unique (*singularis*). In the substantial changes with which we are familiar in the order of nature there is always a substantial element which remains common to either term ; [1] and this is true even of the miraculous conversion of water into wine which Christ operated at the marriage feast of Cana. Moreover, such changes always issue in a reality which is at any rate partially new ; thus the food which we eat adds new tissue to our bodies, the wine into which Christ changed the water did not exist previously. But in transubstantiation the whole substance of the bread and wine is changed into the whole substance of the body and blood of Christ ; and not into a new body and blood of Christ, but into that same which was born of the Virgin Mary, which suffered and died for us, and which now reigns glorious in heaven. Rightly, then, does the liturgy call this " the mystery of faith," for, more than any other miracle, it calls for the unhesitating belief of the human mind in the omnipotence of the Creator, whose hand, having made all things out of nothing, reaches to the very roots of being, and therefore can change his creatures at will.

" Concomitance "

From this fundamental truth, that by virtue of the words of consecration the substance of the bread and wine is converted into the substance of our Lord's body and blood, the rest of Eucharistic theology follows as a logical consequence. But with two points of that doctrine, since their immediate connection with transubstantiation is most evident, I must deal before concluding this section :

[1] According to the scholastic view, the " prime matter," which is successively determined by different substantial forms.

they are " concomitance," and the permanence of the Eucharistic accidents without a subject. Transubstantiation is the conversion of substance into substance, and therefore the formal effect of the words of consecration pronounced over the bread is to convert the *substance* of the bread into the *substance* of the body of Christ. Now the principle of " concomitance " is that whereas the words by their sacramental virtue render present only the substance of our Lord's body, yet because that body is the real body of Christ therefore the substance (as such) of his body must be accompanied (*concomitari*) by all that is really united with it at the moment in which the words are pronounced. Hence under the appearances of bread by real concomitance together with the substance of our Lord's body are present also its accidents (its extension, colour and other properties), his blood, his soul and the divinity which is hypostatically united with his humanity. Likewise by real concomitance under the appearances of wine are present together with the substance of his blood its accidents, the body of Christ, his soul and his divinity. Two important consequences of this doctrine may be noted here. The first is that the separate consecration of the bread and the wine, although—as is shown in the essay on the Eucharistic sacrifice—it symbolises the death of Christ, does not operate any real separation of Christ's body and blood. The second, and practical, consequence is that, the whole Christ being truly, really and substantially present under the appearances either of bread or of wine, the faithful who communicate only under the appearances of bread truly receive the whole Christ, no less than the priest who also partakes of the chalice.

The appearances that remain

There remains the question of the accidents of the bread and wine, which, in order to distinguish them from the accidents of the body and blood of Christ, we shall call the Eucharistic accidents. Experience testifies that, so far as sense-perception is concerned, the words of consecration have brought about no change : the appearance, the taste, all the properties of bread and wine remain as before. Are we to say that these are nothing more than subjective impressions to which no objective reality corresponds, so that the poetic expression of St Thomas : " *visus, tactus, gustus in te fallitur,*" is to be understood quite literally ? Are our senses deceived when they register the presence of a real quantity, a real taste of bread and wine ? The traditional teaching of theologians—unchallenged until the end of the seventeenth century—leaves no room for doubt. Our senses are not deceived concerning what is within their competence, and the normal reaction of our sense organs is evidence of the presence of an external reality which stimulates them. After the consecration there is no longer present the substance of the bread or the wine, but there remains some objective element belonging to those substances which produces the sensory perception which we associate with bread and wine ; and this sensible element is the sign of the real presence of the body and blood of Christ. That this is the teaching of the Church may be seen in the distinction constantly made by the Fathers, and applied in particular to the Eucharist, between the external or sensible element in the sacrament and the internal element, or the thing signified; in fact, in speaking of the Eucharist they refer explicitly to the earthly or sensible thing (or nature) therein contained, as opposed to the heavenly reality which underlies it.[1] It was only with the philosophical system of Descartes that a school of theologians arose suggesting that "the appearances" of bread and wine were nothing else than subjective impressions produced by God in the senses of the observer, to the exclusion of any objective reality belonging to the bread and wine which should be their cause. In the view of Descartes there is no real distinction between a substance and its quantity; and hence he was constrained by the doctrine of transubstantiation to postulate the total disappearance of the accidents of the bread and wine together with their substance.

This view is rejected by all theologians, who, while they hesitate to stigmatise it as heretical, uniformly maintain as a certain theological conclusion that the accidents of the bread and wine remain really and objectively. But although all theologians are on common ground in admitting the real permanence of these accidents, not all are agreed as to the manner in which this comes about. Without entering into a discussion of the various views held by orthodox theologians on this matter, it will be sufficient for our present purpose to set out the explanation given by St Thomas[2] and now generally accepted. It may be stated quite briefly in these terms: the substances of bread and wine having been converted into the substance of the body and blood of Christ, the accidents of bread and wine, since they no longer have a substance in which they may inhere, remain without a subject, God miraculously giving to the quantity—or mass—of the bread and wine respectively the power of sustaining the other accidents and of acting precisely in the same way as the said substances would have acted were they still present. That these accidents have no subject, St Thomas argues, is the inevitable consequence of transubstantiation. They cannot inhere in the substances of bread and wine, for they are no longer there; nor, clearly, can they belong to the substance of the body and blood of Christ, which is not susceptible of the accidents of another substance, nor, for a similar reason, can they inhere in the surrounding air or in the ether. Since no subject is assignable for them, they have no subject. Nevertheless, he goes on to point out, among the accidents of a corporeal substance quantity stands alone as having peculiar properties. It is in the mass or extension of a body that all its qualities, all its active and passive powers immediately reside. Thus quantity alone, says St Thomas, remains in the Eucharist without a subject, and in the quantity all the other accidents of the bread and wine inhere. After the consecration, therefore, quantity plays the role of substance with regard to the other accidents;

[1] See above, p. 852, n. 2.

[2] *Summa Theol.*, III, Q. lxxvii.

it does not actually become a substance, but God miraculously exerts through quantity the activities which normally would be exercised by the substance. This principle provides the explanation how the Eucharistic accidents can nourish the body of the recipient, can act upon and be acted upon by other bodies, can be substantially changed—thus the host may become corrupt, the accidents of wine may turn to vinegar; this finally is the reason why physical or chemical analysis of the species—were any so blasphemous as to attempt it—would give only the normal reactions of bread and wine.

We must now turn our attention to the mysterious manner in which the body and blood of Christ are present in this sacrament, a subject which, by reason of its special difficulty and complexity, must be treated in a separate section.

§ VI: THE EUCHARISTIC PRESENCE

THE Council of Trent, referring to the manner of Christ's presence in the Eucharist, says that " whereas our Saviour always sits at the right hand of the Father in heaven according to his natural mode of existing, yet he is also in many other places sacramentally present to us in his own substance, by a manner of existing which, though we can scarcely express it in words, yet we can conceive with the understanding illuminated by faith, and ought most firmly to believe to be possible to God." To try to explain how this mysterious mode of presence is to be conceived according to the principles of scholastic theology is the purpose of the present section.[1]

The Thomistic synthesis

The beauty of the Thomistic synthesis of Eucharistic theology is what a French theologian has called its " economy in the miraculous." Not that the Angelic doctor attempts in any way to attenuate the stupendous marvels of the Eucharistic miracle; but according to St Thomas the Eucharistic miracle is one, and one only, namely transubstantiation; all else happens as a necessary consequence of this. The basic principle of his explanation of the manner of Christ's presence in the Eucharist is that, since Christ becomes present in this sacrament by transubstantiation, that is by the conversion of " substance into substance," this same miracle conditions the mode of his Eucharistic presence. Having become present by the conversion of substance into substance, he *is* present after the manner of a substance. Let us see, as far as we are able to conceive it, what is involved in this substantial mode of presence.

Substantial presence

It is essential to the proper understanding of this difficult matter to bear in mind first of all the real distinction between corporeal substance *as such* and the accidents—quantity, qualities and various activities—through which the substance as such manifests itself to our senses, acts upon, and is acted upon by, other substances. The substance as such is not perceptible to the senses; it is only through

[1] St Thomas, *Summa Theol.*, III, Q. lxxvi.

its extension or its quantity that it is tangible and occupies space, only as extended and coloured that it is visible, only through its various chemical and physical properties that it acts and thus manifests its distinctive nature to the observer. Precisely as such the substance is discernible only to the intellect. In this matter the imagination is apt to lead us astray; for, every thought being accompanied by a sense-image, we are inclined to confuse the substance, formally and intellectually considered, with the properties and activities which are the object of our sense-experience. If in addition to this important distinction the reader will also remember the principle of real concomitance which has been explained in the previous section, the following statements, though difficult to conceive, will be seen to be the logical consequence of the miracle of transubstantiation.

Christ whole and entire under every part of either species

In the first place, then, the whole Christ—his body, blood, soul and divinity—is present, not only under either species, but under every part of them. Thus when Christ, having consecrated the wine in the chalice, gave it to his disciples to drink, each of them received the whole Christ truly present under the appearances of wine, although the quantity of wine consecrated had been divided. The same truth may be seen implied in the ancient practice of breaking the host after consecration in order to give communion to the faithful. The reason is that Christ is present under the species after the manner of a substance, that is, in the same manner in which, before consecration, the substances of bread or wine were present under their respective accidents. Now, before consecration the whole substance of bread formally considered was present in the whole of its mass, or quantity, and also under every particle thereof. When bread is divided, it is not the substance as such which is divided, but the substance as modified by the accident of quantity; the substance formally as such is indivisible; it abstracts from dimensions or extension. Hence the body of Christ, into which the substance of the bread has been converted, is indivisible and undivided, notwithstanding the division of the species under which it is present.[1]

The presence of the dimensions of Christ

But it must not be thought, because the body of Christ is present in this sacrament after the manner of a substance, that it is on that account deprived of its own dimensions. It is here that our imagination is likely to play us false. When we are told that the body of Christ is present under the dimensions of a small host we are tempted to think of that sacred body as reduced to infinitesimal proportions or even as devoid of extension altogether. This would be an error. It has been seen that the *whole* Christ is present under the appearances of bread and wine. It is true that only the substance of his body becomes present in virtue of the Eucharistic conversion formally

[1] This truth is defined as of faith by the Council of Trent (Sess. xiii, can. 3) as regards the species after division. Evidently the same is true also before division, for the reason given above.

considered, but by real concomitance there is present also all that is actually and really united with that substance, and therefore the natural dimensions of his body. As St Thomas puts it, the dimensions—and the other accidents—of our Lord's body are present in this sacrament *quasi per accidens*, *i.e.* not as the formal effect of transubstantiation, but by reason of their real union with that which is formally present. They are present, if we may say so, because the substance has brought them with it. And here follows a rather attractive piece of reasoning on the part of St Thomas : because the dimensions of the body of Christ are present in the Eucharist only by reason of their real concomitance with the substance, those dimensions have, so to speak, to accommodate themselves to the manner of existence of the substance as such. One thinks of the courtiers of a prince, forced by their attachment to his royal person to content themselves with any lodging that their master may choose. Thus the dimensions of Christ's body, being present by reason of their real concomitance with the substance, exist in this sacrament, not in their natural manner, but after the manner of the substance which they accompany.

To try to picture to oneself such a mysterious mode of presence is fatal to the understanding of it. We always think of quantity as that by which a substance occupies a particular portion of space ; and this is indeed one of the normal effects of quantity. But actual extension in a place is not of its very essence. The essential effect of quantity in a corporeal substance is to give it parts, to make it intrinsically divisible.[1] Now the body of Christ has all its natural parts and dimensions ; each part of his body is situally distinct and relatively to the other parts has its proper and normal position ; but those dimensions are not extended relatively to the surrounding body, or place ; they are not circumscribed by the place in which they are present. Briefly, in the normal course of events a corporeal substance occupies a place by means of its quantity ; in the Eucharist the contrary is the case : the quantity of the body of Christ is present by means of, and therefore in the manner of, the substance.

An imperfect analogy

Some theologians have found it convenient to explain this very difficult point by saying that the body of Christ is present in this sacrament after the manner of a spirit, as the soul is present in the human body. The analogy is useful inasmuch as it enables one to conceive a presence which is not conditioned by quantitative dimensions ; but I have purposely refrained from using it because it may so easily be misunderstood. The presence of a spirit is not conditioned by quantity precisely because it has no quantity : it is immaterial. But the body of Christ—I repeat at the risk of being wearisome—has its own natural dimensions. It is not present in its normal way ; but this is not because the body of Christ has been dematerialised, spiritualised, but because its dimensions exist in this sacrament after the manner of a substance *as such ;* and a substance

[1] Aristotle, *Metaph.* iv, c. 13.

considered formally as such abstracts from dimensions and extension.[1]

Hence when we say that the body of Christ is present in a particular place, in the ciborium, in the tabernacle, in the mouth of the recipient, we mean that in the place occupied by the dimensions of bread (or wine) there is really and truly present the body of Christ, with its dimensions and other accidents, with his blood, his soul and his divinity, present, however, after the manner of a substance as such. It follows that there is no intrinsic impossibility in the simultaneous presence of Christ in heaven and in many places on earth. The multilocation of a body is shown in philosophy to be impossible only because of the limitations imposed by quantitative dimensions ; these, however, as we have seen, do not condition the presence of Christ in this sacrament. There is no multiplication of the body of Christ, no division, because these again are associated with quantity ; it is one and the same body of Christ, present in heaven according to his natural mode of existence, and present upon innumerable altars throughout the world after the manner of a substance.

Consequences of this mode of presence

It is a further logical consequence of the Eucharistic presence that the body of Christ in this sacrament—apart from a further miracle, of which we have no evidence in revelation—cannot do or undergo any action which requires quantitative contact with external bodies ; hence he cannot be seen, felt or heard. Nor, apparently, apart from a special miracle, has Christ the exercise of his senses in this sacrament, because his body has not that contact with external bodies which is required for it. St Thomas, so far as I know, does not raise the question ; but the strict application of his principles would lead one to deny that any such special miracle takes place. Nevertheless, many theologians maintain as a pious opinion that Christ miraculously assumes a power which the sacramental presence would normally not permit.[2] Moreover, no violence can be done to the body of Christ in this sacrament ; external agencies, be they natural or artificial, wilful or innocent, cannot result in any harm to the sacred humanity of Christ in the Eucharist ; these can reach only the appearances of bread and wine, beneath which the body and blood of Christ, present in the manner of a substance, remain undisturbed and inviolate.

The same principles govern the permanence of the body of Christ beneath the sacramental species. The Real Presence lasts as long as the substance of bread or wine would have remained if transubstantiation had not taken place, that is, as long as the accidents and

[1] A further reason for abstaining from such locutions as " Christ is spiritually present in the Eucharist " is that many non-Catholic writers use similar phrases concerning the Eucharist, without implying any true belief in the Real Presence. They mean by the spiritual presence of Christ merely that Christ is present in the Eucharist by reason of the faith of the recipient.

[2] Evidently Christ has perfect knowledge of all that happens in the Eucharist, at least through his infused and beatific knowledge.

properties of bread or wine remain. As soon as such a change has been brought about—whether quantitatively or qualitatively—in the sacramental species as would normally be evidence of a substantial change, then the body of Christ ceases to be present. The reason may be put quite simply in this way: the Sacrament of the Eucharist is the body and blood of Christ really present under the appearances of bread and wine; if the appearances of bread and wine cease to be present, then the sacrament no longer exists, and so the Real Presence ceases.[1]

Such, in brief outline, is the Thomistic explanation of the Eucharistic presence. More, perhaps, than any other abstract truth of our religion, this requires the resolute banishing of pictures suggested by the imagination and the complete concentration of the mind upon intellectual concepts. If in treating this subject some of the greatest of saints and theologians have failed to attain the ideal, then perhaps we need feel no surprise that our minds are at a loss before the contemplation of this mystery of faith. But if we lament the impotence of our minds, let us also adore the omnipotence of God.

§ VII: THE SACRAMENT AND ITS USE

THE intimate connection of the Sacrament of the Eucharist with the Eucharistic sacrifice has been sufficiently explained in the introductory section; the sacrament which we receive is none other than the all-holy victim which through the priest we have offered to God. We must here consider the essential elements of the sacrament, and also certain important matters relating to its use and administration.

The Eucharist a "permanent" sacrament

That the Eucharist merits the name of sacrament—that it is a sign permanently instituted by Christ and an instrumental cause of man's sanctification—that indeed, by reason of the sacred Body of Christ which it really contains, it is the greatest of all the sacraments, is apparent in all that has hitherto been said. But it is not only in its super-eminent dignity that the Eucharist differs from the other sacraments; it is unique in that it is permanent. The other sacraments exist only in the moment of their performance and administration; in fact, they are performed when they are administered. When the two elements of the sacramental sign—*e.g.* the pouring of

[1] With regard to qualitative and quantitative change in the sacramental species, it may be noted in the first place that the length of time during which the Real Presence lasts after reception will depend upon physiological conditions; as a general rule ten minutes is given as the normal period. At what point of quantitative division in the species does the Real Presence cease? From the point of view of dogmatic theology it must, it seems, be admitted that even the most minute particles of the species of bread or wine, though naturally imperceptible to the senses, if they present the characteristics of bread or wine, truly harbour the sacred Presence. In practice, however, such particles must be treated as non-existent, because Christ, who has deigned to give himself to us in this sacrament, wills to be treated as present only when the sign of his presence is perceptible.

water and the saying of the words—are joined together and applied to the recipient, in that moment the sacrament exists, produces its effect—and ceases. The Eucharist, on the contrary, exists as a sacrament independently of its administration; when the form—the words of consecration—has been pronounced over the matter—bread and wine—the sacrament of the Eucharist exists in its complete perfection, even though none may ever receive it; and it continues to exist as long as the sacramental species remain incorrupt.

In consequence of the peculiar nature of this sacrament it is necessary to proceed somewhat differently when we seek to designate its essential elements. We must distinguish two stages: the sacrament, so to speak, in the making, and the sacrament in its completed state; and it is only in the first of these stages that we are able properly to discern the two parts that constitute the sacramental sign. The matter of the sacrament is bread and wine, the form consists of the words of consecration; but these are present only in the moment of the confection of the sacrament. After the consecration, of the bread and wine there remain only the appearances, while the form remains only virtually, that is to say, in the permanent effect of transubstantiation. An accurate treatment, therefore, of the sacrament requires that we consider it separately under these two aspects, in the moment of its confection and in its state of completion.

The matter Little needs to be said here of the matter and the form of the Eucharist. The matter consists of bread and wine. With regard to the bread, the dispute between East and West as to the use of leavened or unleavened bread is well known. In all probability Christ himself used unleavened bread in instituting the Eucharist;[1] but it cannot be established with any degree of certainty that in apostolic or sub-apostolic times there was uniformity of usage. It was not until the eleventh century that the question was raised by the Eastern dissidents, led by Michael Cerularius, as to the validity of the use of unleavened bread; having raised it they answered it in the negative, thus asserting the invalidity of the consecration in the Roman rite. The attitude which the Catholic Church had maintained since the beginning is embodied in the statement of the Council of Florence —the *Decretum pro Armenis*—that " the body of Christ is truly confected in wheaten bread, whether it be leavened or not, and priests of the Eastern or Western Church are bound to consecrate in either according to the respective custom of each rite." The wine used in the Eucharist must be wine of the grape,[2] though in certain circumstances a little alcohol may be artificially added for purposes of preservation. The ritual of adding a few drops of water to the wine at

[1] Matt. xxvi 17.

[2] The suggestion of Harnack (*Brot und Wasser*, Leipzig, 1891), based on a passage of St Cyprian's letter to Caecilius, that the primitive Church used water in the Eucharist instead of wine, has met with so little encouragement that it deserves to be mentioned only as a curiosity.

the Offertory has probably an historical basis in the act of Christ himself at the Last Supper, and its symbolism is beautifully expressed in the prayer which the priest recites as he adds them: "O God who in creating human nature hast wonderfully dignified it and still more wonderfully formed it again; grant that by the mystery of this water and wine we may be made partakers of the divine nature of him who vouchsafed to become partaker of our humanity, namely, Jesus Christ our Lord, thy Son." [1]

The form

The form of the sacrament consists of the words used by Christ himself in instituting the Eucharist: over the bread, "This is my body"; and over the wine, "This is the chalice of my blood of the new and eternal testament—mystery of faith—which shall be shed for you and for many unto the remission of sins." What words may be omitted without affecting the validity of the consecration is a question discussed by moral theologians, and as not being of general interest may be disregarded here. It is held by the Eastern dissidents that the prayer called the Epiclesis, which in certain liturgies follows the consecration, is essential to the effect of transubstantiation. A more detailed treatment of this matter will be found elsewhere; [2] suffice it to state here that according to Catholic teaching transubstantiation is operated solely by the words of institution.

What constitutes the "sacrament"?

Turning now to consider the sacrament in its completed state we are confronted by the preliminary question of what constitutes the "sacrament" properly so called. Is the sacrament of the Eucharist the body of Christ only, or is it merely the species of bread and wine, or is it both together? Subtle theological discussion as to the precise meaning to be attached to the word "sacrament" has caused various answers to be given to this question. If, however, we abstract from such subtleties, we may reply quite simply that the sacrament of the Eucharist is the body and blood of Christ really present, after the manner of a substance, under the appearances of bread and wine, and destined to be our spiritual and supernatural food. Hence not only the body of Christ really present constitutes the sacrament, not only the consecrated species, but both the body of Christ and the species together; for the former without the latter is not a visible sign, and the species without the body of Christ present under them are not the cause of grace.

Reservation and adoration

The Eucharist, being a sacrament, is destined to be received by the faithful. But, as the fathers of the Council of Trent point out, "it is not the less on this account to be adored by them." [3] The practice of the Church of paying to the Eucharist the worship which is due to God alone is but a logical consequence of her belief that

[1] Evidently this small quantity of water does not change the nature of the wine, but it is absorbed into the water naturally contained therein, and thus at the consecration is changed into the blood of Christ.

[2] *The Eucharistic Sacrifice*, pp. 917–918.

[3] Session xiii, c. 5.

therein is permanently present the living Christ, true God and true man. The Feast of Corpus Christi, processions of the Blessed Sacrament, Benediction, are merely the devotional expression, sanctioned or even commanded by the Church, of this traditional faith in the Real Presence. Likewise connected with that belief, and with the sacramental character of the Eucharist, is the custom of reserving the Blessed Sacrament with a view to its administration to the sick. Hence the Council of Trent anathematises those who " say that it is not allowed to reserve the Eucharist in the tabernacle, but that it must be administered to those present immediately after the consecration, or that it may not be carried with honour to the sick." [1] A providential aspect of the practice of reservation is the opportunity thus afforded to the devout faithful of paying those private visits to the Blessed Sacrament which are so fruitful a source of grace and so edifying a feature of Catholic devotional life.

Conditions of lawful reception—state of grace

For the proper reception of the sacrament two conditions are necessary, the state of grace and the natural fast from the preceding midnight. We have seen how vehemently St Paul insists upon the worthy reception of the Eucharist [2] and throughout Tradition we hear the echo of his words. Suffice it to quote two well-known passages : " This food," writes St Justin,[3] " is called the Eucharist, of which none is allowed to partake unless he believes our teaching to be true and has been washed in the laver which is unto the remission of sins and regeneration, and so lives as Christ has commanded." And the Eucharistic prayer of the Didache (a document of the second half of the first century) concludes with the solemn warning : " If anyone be holy let him approach ; otherwise let him do penance." The reason why the state of grace is necessary in the recipient of this sacrament is to be sought not only in the reverence due to the body and blood of Christ, but in the purpose for which this sacrament was instituted. The Eucharist is the divinely appointed food whereby the supernatural life of grace is to be sustained in our souls ; and food is not given to the dead but to the living. Those who are dead in sin must rise to newness of life in baptism, the sacrament of regeneration, those who have allowed themselves again to become subject to the captivity of Satan must be loosed from their sins in the sacrament of Penance,[4] before they can partake of the food of life.

The natural fast

Of the second disposition required for the reception of the Eucharist—the natural fast—St Augustine gives the following explanation " It is clear," he writes,[5] " that when the disciples first received the

[1] Session xiii, c. 7. [2] 1 Cor. xi 27. [3] *Apol.* I, c. 66.

[4] In this connection the following precept of the Council of Trent is important : " For fear lest so great a sacrament should be received unworthily, and so unto death and condemnation, this holy Synod ordains and declares that sacramental confession, when a confessor may be had, is of necessity to be made beforehand by those whose conscience is burdened with mortal sin, however contrite they may think themselves " (Sess. xiii, c. 11).

[5] Ep. 54, c. 6.

body and blood of the Lord they did not receive fasting. . . . Later, however, it pleased the Holy Spirit that, for the honour due to so great a sacrament, the body of Christ should enter the mouth of a Christian before any other food; and therefore throughout the whole world this custom is observed." An earlier trace of this law is to be found in Tertullian's *Ad uxorem*,[1] where he refers to the custom of receiving the Eucharist privately at home "before taking any food."

Reception under one kind

It was the ordinary rule in the early Church that the faithful, as well as the priest who offered the sacrifice, should receive communion under both species. But that on occasion, when convenience or necessity required it, the faithful partook only of one species is evident from numerous documents of early Christian times. Tertullian, in the passage to which reference has just been made, witnesses to the custom of receiving the Eucharist at home under the species of bread only, and it was fairly common to give communion under one species —either of bread or of wine only—to the sick. Young children, to whom the Eucharist was then generally administered, received under the species of wine only, and an indication of the early belief that one species was sufficient for the proper reception of the sacrament may be seen in the very ancient liturgy of the Mass of the Presanctified, where the priest receives under the species of bread alone. Evidently, therefore, the use of both species by the faithful is not of divine precept or institution, since otherwise the above-mentioned practices could never have been introduced without arousing comment and opposition. It was only in the fifteenth century that the Hussites—followed in this by many of the Reformers of the succeeding century—insisted upon the necessity of communion under both species. The whole matter cannot be better summarised than in the words of the Council of Trent: "Holy Mother Church, knowing her authority in the administration of the sacraments, although the use of both species has from the beginning of the Christian religion not been infrequent, yet, that custom having in the progress of time been widely changed, induced by weighty and just reasons,[2] has approved of this custom of communicating under one species, and decreed that it was to be held as a law. . . . This synod moreover declares that although, as has already been said, our Redeemer at the Last Supper instituted and delivered to the Apostles this sacrament in two species, yet it is to be acknowledged that Christ whole and entire, and a true sacrament, are received under either species alone; and that therefore, as regards the fruit, they who receive one species alone are not defrauded of any grace necessary for salvation."[3]

[1] ii 5.

[2] Among these reasons the following may be enumerated: the difficulty of reserving the species of wine; the danger of spilling and other inconveniences attending distribution; the rarity of wine in certain districts; and finally the practical profession of faith in the presence of Christ whole and entire under either species alone, which such custom involves.

[3] Session xxi, c. 2 and c. 3.

One further question, that of the necessity of the Eucharist for salvation, remains to be treated. But as the elements for its solution are provided by the consideration of the effects of the sacrament it will find place more conveniently in the succeeding section.

§ VIII: THE EFFECTS OF THE SACRAMENT

The Sacrament of the divine life

As the Eucharist is the greatest of all the sacraments, so it is particularly fitting that the words in which Christ himself has described its effects should have been preserved for us in the Scriptures with the greatest completeness and detail. In an earlier section reference has been made to the discourse, related by St. John,[1] in which our Saviour prepared his disciples for their first communion. From the beginning of this discourse to the end it is clear that the effect of the Eucharist is life. The Eucharist is " the bread of God . . . that giveth life to the world " ; it is " the bread of life . . . the living bread that came down from heaven . . . the bread . . . that if any man eat of it he may not die . . . if any man eat of this bread he shall live for ever " ; in fact it is the food which is indispensable for life, for " except you eat the flesh of the son of man and drink his blood you shall not have life in you ; he that eateth my flesh and drinketh my blood hath everlasting life and I will raise him up at the last day. . . . He that eateth my flesh and drinketh my blood abideth in me and I in him. As the living Father hath sent me and I live by the Father, so he that eateth me, the same also shall live by me. . . . He that eateth this bread shall live for ever." St Peter could not have expressed more appropriately his faith in his Master's teaching than by saying : " Thou hast the words of eternal life."

And what is this life which is so evidently the proper effect of the Eucharist ? The words of Christ leave no room for doubt. It is the divine life, the life of God himself ; the life which the Son, the second Person of the Blessed Trinity, lives in common with the Father, and of which he, through this ineffable sacrament, communicates to us a finite participation. It is the same life to which we are " born again of water and the Holy Ghost," in virtue of which, being made partakers of the divine nature and receiving the Spirit of adoption, we become the adopted sons of God. It is this community of the divine life which makes all Christians to be one ; as the Father is in Christ, and he in the Father, so all who partake of this life are one in them ; " I in them," says Christ after the Last Supper, " and thou in me ; that they may be made perfect in one." [2] This is the reason why Christ promises that he who receives the Eucharist will abide in Christ as Christ abides in him. By receiving this sacrament we become members of his mystical body, and thus are vivified by the vital principle of that body, which is none other than the divine life of sanctifying grace, the life to which Christ is referring when he

[1] vi 27 ff.

[2] John xvii 23.

says, at the Last Supper, "I am the vine; you the branches; he that abideth in me and I in him, the same beareth much fruit; for without me you can do nothing."

Union with Christ

"The effect of this sacrament," says St Thomas, "is union with the mystical body of Christ,"[1] union with Christ by sanctifying grace and union with all the members of his mystical body. "We being many," says St Paul, "are one bread, one body, all that partake of one bread."[2] "Just as this bread," prayed the Christians of the first century,[3] "was once dispersed upon the hills and has been gathered into one substance, so may thy Church be gathered together from the ends of the earth into thy Kingdom." None of the Fathers has so clearly expressed this fundamental Eucharistic truth as St Augustine. "The faithful," he writes,[4] "know the body of Christ if they do not neglect to be the body of Christ. Let them become the body of Christ if they wish to live by the Spirit of Christ. Only the body of Christ lives by the Spirit of Christ; and therefore it is that St Paul, explaining to us the nature of this bread, says: 'We being many are one bread, one body.' O sacrament of piety! O symbol of unity! O bond of charity! He who wills to live has here the place to live, has here the source of his life. Let him approach and believe, let him be incorporated, that he may receive life."[5]

In order to understand what is meant by this union with Christ which is the proper effect of the Eucharist it is important to distinguish between the actual reception of the Sacrament and the effect of the reception. The very act of receiving Holy Communion involves a union between the body of Christ and ourselves, inasmuch as that Sacred Body, under the appearances of bread and wine, is truly, really and substantially present within our own bodies until the species have become corrupt. But this is not the union with Christ of which we speak as the effect of the Eucharist. The union which the Eucharist effects is a spiritual, supernatural union with Christ by means of sanctifying grace and charity, a union which may appropriately be described as "vital," since it consists in the communication to our souls of the supernatural life of grace, the life of the mystical body of Christ. Just as during his life on earth the healing touch of his body gave sight to the blind and healed all manner of bodily diseases, so his life-giving humanity, sacramentally received by us, gives to our souls the life which makes us members of him and partakers of the divine nature.

The Eucharist and the other Sacraments

The attentive reader will have observed that this effect—union with Christ by sanctifying grace and charity—which the sources of revelation represent as the proper effect of the Eucharist, is none other than the effect which is common to all the sacraments of the New Law; for all these produce sanctifying grace in our souls. And it is

[1] *Summa Theol.*, Q. lxxiii, art. 3.
[2] 1 Cor. x 17.
[3] Didache, c. 9, § 4.
[4] In *Joan.*, tr. xxvi, 13.
[5] See also the passage of St John Chrysostom quoted on p. 855.

this fact, more than any other, that enables us to understand the unique place which the Eucharist holds among the sacraments. For the Eucharist, says St Thomas, " has of itself the power of giving grace." " This sacrament," says the Catechism of the Council of Trent, " is the source from which the other sacraments derive whatever perfection and goodness they possess."

While it is true, then, that all the sacraments produce sanctifying grace, yet the Eucharist alone produces it as its own proper effect—*ex seipso*, says St Thomas. The other sacraments produce grace only in virtue of their essential relation to the Eucharist. And if we consider each of the sacraments we shall see the truth of the words of St Thomas : " The Eucharist is the end of all the sacraments, for the sanctification given in all the sacraments constitutes a preparation either for the reception or for the consecration of the Eucharist." By Baptism, according to the well-known teaching of St Paul,[1] we die to sin in order that we may live to Christ ; the mystical death that we undergo in this sacrament is but the preparation for the mystical life that we live in Christ through the Eucharist. By Confirmation we are armed against the dangers which threaten the unity of Christ's mystical body, a unity which, as we have seen, is the proper effect of the Eucharist. Penance removes the actual sins committed after baptism, sins which are an obstacle to union with Christ by charity, while Extreme Unction removes those last relics of sin, that spiritual weakness which results from sin and handicaps the soul in its endeavour to live for God alone. The relation of the Sacrament of Order to the Eucharist is too obvious to need explanation ; while Matrimony, as signifying the union of Christ with his spouse the Church, is a type of that intimate union of the faithful with Christ which is the proper effect of the greatest of all the sacraments.

The sacramental grace of the Eucharist

The Catechism of the Council of Trent, in the passage already quoted more than once, compares the Eucharist to the source or fountain-head ; and the similitude may be found useful in order to explain more fully the effect of the sacrament. The water that flows at the source has a characteristically stimulating effect. So too, although all the sacraments produce sanctifying grace, yet the grace which is given in the Eucharist has that especially stimulating and invigorating quality which we associate with water that flows fresh from the source. Each sacrament, as is well known, besides giving sanctifying grace, produces an effect—called sacramental grace—which is peculiar to itself. This sacramental grace, says St Thomas,[2] " adds to grace commonly so called and to the virtues and gifts a certain divine help to attain the end of the sacrament." Now the end of the sacrament of the Eucharist is union with Christ by charity ; the sacramental grace of the Eucharist, therefore, is a special help for the attainment of that union which St Paul calls " the bond of perfection " ; theologians call it " the fervour of charity."

[1] Rom. vi 2-10.

[2] *Summa Theol.*, III, Q. lxii, art. 2.

The fervour of charity

The matter is so important that no apology need be made for devoting some little space to the explanation of this effect of the Eucharist. The virtue of charity is that supernatural habit [1] infused together with sanctifying grace, which enables us to love God for his own sake above all things. One who has the virtue of charity has such a habit of mind that he regards God as the last end to which he must direct all his actions, to which his whole life must be subordinated. It is true that he is not always thinking of God; he does not, as theologians say, always "actually" direct all his actions to God's glory; but he is "habitually" so constituted in regard to God that if any action presented itself to his mind as incompatible with God's friendship he would reject it, because he loves God above all things. Such a state is called "habitual charity." But there are times in our lives when the thought of God is strong within us, when we realise more fully that God is the sovereign Good, that all that we have is ours only because it comes from God, and therefore must be given back to him. In such moments we live "actually" for God; all that is ours we actually refer to him, the source of all good; then we have some small understanding of what St Paul meant when he said: "I live, now not I, but Christ liveth in me," and perhaps we feel "our heart burning within us" as did the disciples on the way to Emmaus, so that to God we cry with the Psalmist: "How sweet are thy words to my palate! more than honey to my mouth." [2]

This actual and conscious referring of our actions to God is called the "fervour of charity." Some of the saints have reached the stage of perfection in which this fervour of devotion is alive constantly within them; but with the majority of mankind such moments are comparatively rare. In time of retreat, perhaps, during prayer and as a result of humble and unremitting effort, in the church, and above all after Holy Communion, we may be filled with that actual realisation of all that God is and of the little that we are in his sight, and we may be fired with that zeal for the service of God, with that fervour of charity that makes us say with St Paul: "The charity of Christ presseth us on." [3]

This, then, is the special fruit of the Eucharist. Just as daily contact with Christ during his life on earth must have aroused in the hearts of his disciples an ardent and enthusiastic love for his divine Person, so he who drinks living waters of the fountains of the Saviour, deriving grace from the intimate touch of his life-giving humanity, breaks into fervent acts of divine love, acts which increase [4] and establish more firmly in him the virtue by which he adheres to God the Sovereign Good. And so it is seen how truly this sacrament is called the food of the soul, and how appropriately the body and blood of

[1] See Essay xviii, *The Supernatural Virtues*, pp. 645 ff.

[2] Ps. cxviii 103.

[3] 2 Cor. v 14.

[4] *I.e.* not effectively but meritoriously. See Essay xviii, *The Supernatural Virtues*, pp. 629–630.

Christ are given to mankind under the outward form of bodily food. For "all those effects which material food and drink produce in regard to bodily life are produced in respect of the spiritual life by this sacrament; it sustains, it gives increase, it repairs (the ravages of disease) and it gives delight." [1]

Other effects of the sacrament

That this sacramental food sustains and invigorates the life of the soul is clear from what has been said. But it does not give that life in the first instance; before the soul may be nourished with the heavenly food of the Eucharist it must first have been born to the supernatural life through the sacrament of regeneration; the life-giving virtue of the Eucharist must first have been applied to the soul through the intermediary of baptism, by which man dies to sin that he "may walk in newness of life"; [2] and if by mortal sin he should have become a dead member of Christ's mystical body, that same life-giving power must be applied to him through the sacrament of reconciliation before he can be nourished again by the sacrament of unity.[3] But, just as bodily food repairs the effects of a disease which is not mortal, although it cannot give life to a dead body, so the Eucharist has the effect of remitting venial sin, inasmuch as it arouses in the soul the fervour of charity, to which alone venial sin is opposed.[4] Indirectly, too, such fervour remits the temporal punishment due to sin.

In strengthening the supernatural life of the soul the Eucharist also preserves it from future sin, because the fervour of charity which is the special fruit of this sacrament renders the soul less susceptible to the attractions of the devil, the world, and the flesh, and more prompt in its obedience to the will of God.

A final analogy between the food of the body and the Eucharist, the spiritual food of the soul, is to be found in the pleasure or delight which accompanies its reception. This effect in the case of the Eucharist takes the form of a certain alacrity and spiritual joy in the fulfilment of the divine will, which is characteristic of the fervour of charity. But it is to be noted that, just as one who, being in indifferent health, approaches his meal listlessly and without appetite, will fail to relish his food, so he who approaches this divine sacrament with his mind distracted, with his will not fully detached from the things of earth, will not perceive that spiritual sweetness to which the Psalmist invites us with the words: "O taste and see that the Lord is sweet." [5] On the other hand this spiritual responsiveness to the will of God, which is the normal effect of Holy Communion received

[1] *Summa Theol.*, III, Q. lxxix, art. 1. [2] Rom. vi 4.

[3] It is commonly held, however, that one who receives Holy Communion being unconscious or oblivious of his mortal sin and implicitly sorry for it (with attrition at least) is not deprived of the grace of the Sacrament, since he does not wilfully obstruct its effect.

[4] It should be noted that venial sin does not diminish the habit of sanctifying grace nor the virtue of charity. See Essay xxvi, *Sin and Repentance*, pp. 948–951; cf. p. 575, n. 1. [5] Ps. xxxiii 9.

with good dispositions, should not be confused with that sensible devotion and feeling of religious exhilaration which God sometimes grants as a special and extraordinary grace, but which is by no means an essential accompaniment to the fervour of charity.

It would be a neglect of the express words of Christ himself, as well as of the constant teaching of the Fathers, to omit all mention of the effect of the Eucharist on our bodies. Christ promises the glorious resurrection as one of the fruits of the Eucharist: "He who eateth my flesh and drinketh my blood hath eternal life, and I will raise him up at the last day." So St Ignatius of Antioch calls the Eucharist the "medicine of immortality,"[1] and St Irenaeus defends the doctrine of the resurrection against the Gnostics on the ground that our bodies have been nourished with the body and blood of Christ: "How can they assert that our flesh will be corrupted and never again be revived, when it has been nourished with the body and blood of Christ? . . . Our bodies having received the Eucharist are no longer corruptible, but have the hope of the resurrection."[2] This is not to be understood as if the Eucharist produced any physical quality in the body by reason of which it will rise in glory,[3] but rather in the sense that it is supremely appropriate that the body, which has been sanctified by contact with this most blessed Sacrament of the body and blood of Christ, should be a partaker of Christ's glorious resurrection. The Eucharist, in the words of St Thomas, is "a pledge of glory to come." Hardly less general among the Fathers is the attribution to the Eucharist of a virtue protective against the attacks of concupiscence. This, likewise, is probably not to be interpreted in any physical sense, except so far as the fervour of charity produced by the sacrament enables the soul more efficaciously to resist the temptations of the flesh.

The necessity of the Eucharist

In the light of what has been said concerning the effects of the Eucharist it may be possible now to answer the question as to how far the Eucharist is necessary for salvation. A proper understanding of the matter requires a preliminary definition of terms. In the first place, a thing may be necessary for salvation either as an indispensable means or merely because it is a precept which must be observed. In the former case even the inculpable omission of it would prejudice salvation, whereas if it is a matter of precept evidently only wilful disobedience is imputable. Moreover, a thing may be necessary for salvation either in actual fact, or it may be that the desire of it only is necessary for salvation. Thus Baptism, at least by desire, is necessary as an indispensable means for salvation. It is asked, then, is the Eucharist necessary for salvation?

Of the divine precept to receive Holy Communion there can be little doubt in view of the words of Christ at the Last Supper: "Do this in commemoration of me," and of his express warning, "except

[1] *Ad Eph.*, n. 20. [2] *Adv. hær.*, lib. iv, c. 18.
[3] Some few theologians have held this view.

you eat the flesh of the Son of Man and drink his blood you shall not have life in you." [1] The command of the Church, rendering more definite the precept of Christ himself, that the faithful shall receive the Eucharist at least once a year at Paschal time [2] is no less indubitable and emphatic. Moreover, it is admitted by all that the divine precept does not oblige those who, being either infants or otherwise ignorant of the precept, are incapable of obeying it, and further that the commandment of the Church binds only those children who have arrived at the age at which they are able to distinguish the Eucharist from ordinary food.

But may one go further, and assert that the Eucharist is necessary, not only because its reception is commanded, but as an indispensable means for salvation ? It is quite certain, in view of the condemnation by the Council of Trent [3] of the contrary opinion, that the *actual reception* of the Eucharist is not necessary for the salvation of infants ; it is certain also that an adult who, through no fault of his own, died without ever receiving the sacrament, would not on that account be lost. Clearly, then, the actual reception of the Eucharist is not necessary as an indispensable means for salvation. Is the *desire* of it necessary ? The majority of theologians at the present day content themselves with asserting the divine and ecclesiastical precept, denying that even the desire of the Eucharist is in any proper sense indispensable for salvation ; the only sacrament, they say, of which at least the desire is indispensable, is Baptism. This position is undoubtedly the simpler and, if the word " desire " is understood in its ordinary sense, unassailable. Nevertheless, the view of St Thomas is that the desire of the Eucharist, in a certain sense at any rate, is indispensable for salvation ; and since his teaching helps much to the understanding of the central position which the Eucharist holds among the sacraments, it deserves to be briefly expounded here.

We must distinguish, says St Thomas,[4] between the sacrament itself and the effect of the sacrament. The effect of the Eucharist is union with the mystical body of Christ, and without such union it is impossible to be saved, because outside the Church there is no salvation. Clearly, then, that which is the proper effect of the Eucharist is indispensable for salvation. Nevertheless, it is possible to have the effect of a sacrament without receiving the sacrament itself, namely, through a desire of the sacrament. Thus one may receive the effect of Baptism through desiring the sacrament of Baptism. In like manner, to receive the proper effect of the Eucharist, namely, union with the mystical body of Christ, it is sufficient to have the desire of the Eucharist. Now the desire of the Eucharist is implicitly contained in Baptism, because " by Baptism a man is destined for the

[1] John vi 54.
[2] IV Lateran Council (1215) and Council of Trent (Sess. 13, c. 9).
[3] Session 21, c. 4.
[4] *Summa Theol.*, III, Q. lxxiii, art. 3.

Eucharist, and therefore by the very fact that children are baptised they are destined by the Church for the reception of the Eucharist; and just as it is by the faith of the Church that they believe, so it is by the intention of the Church that they desire the Eucharist, and consequently receive its effect." The desire of the Eucharist, then, is necessary for salvation inasmuch as Baptism, the sacrament of regeneration, by reason of its essential subordination to the Eucharist—for we die to sin that we may live to Christ—implicitly destines the soul to partake of the body and blood of Christ in the Eucharist.[1]

Frequent Communion

Whatever may be the solution of what is, after all, perhaps, an academic question, it is certainly the desire of the Church that the faithful—as long as they are in the state of grace and have the right intention—should approach Holy Communion frequently and even daily. Hence this section—and the essay—may conveniently conclude with the following extract from the decree of Pope Pius X on the reception of daily Communion:

"The Council of Trent, bearing in mind the immeasurable treasures of divine grace which are obtained by the faithful who receive the most holy Eucharist, says: 'The Sacred Synod desires that the faithful assisting at daily Mass should communicate not only by spiritual affection but also by the sacramental reception of the Eucharist.' These words clearly indicate the desire of the Church that all the faithful should be daily refreshed at this celestial banquet, and draw thereform more abundant fruits of sanctification. This wish is in evident harmony with the desire by which Christ our Lord was moved when he instituted the Divine Sacrament. For not once nor obscurely, but by frequent repetition, he inculcates the necessity of eating his flesh and drinking his blood; particularly in the words: 'This is the bread that came down from heaven. Not as your fathers did eat manna and are dead. He that eateth this bread shall live for ever.'"

G. D. SMITH.

[1] St Thomas is careful, however, in the same article to point out the difference between Baptism and the Eucharist in the matter of necessity. Baptism is the sacrament of initiation into the Christian life, and since there is no preceding sacrament in which the desire of baptism can be involved, infants can be saved only by its actual reception.

XXV

THE EUCHARISTIC SACRIFICE

§ I: INTRODUCTORY

A general notion of Sacrifice.

ALTHOUGH it might not be quite accurate to say that some kind of sacrificial rite forms, or has formed, an element in every one of the great religions without exception, yet it would not be far from the truth. Almost universally man has felt the need of entering into close communication with the divinity, and nearly everywhere he has found that the best way of satisfying this need was by means of sacrifice, whether he wished to appease his god, to offer him the highest kind of worship, to ask him for his protection, or to thank him for his favours.

The offering of sacrifice corresponds with a natural prompting of man's heart under the influence of religion, it satisfies an appetite that is deep and urgent. It would seem strange, therefore, if the perfect religion, the religion that is the fulfilment of the law, the religion that is intrinsically Catholic, that is, universal, and capable of offering the full satisfaction to all man's needs, everywhere and always, were a religion without a sacrifice. Such a deficiency would need a lot of explaining away before it could be looked upon as other than a defect. Even though it be granted that the Founder and High Priest of this religion offered the perfect sacrifice once for all, it would still seem strange, human nature being what it is, if he had left his followers without any means of renewing this sacrifice, or if he had made no provision whatever for its perpetuation or its constant reiteration.

Happily the suggested deficiency is simply hypothetical. We have the Mass, the proper and perfect sacrifice of the New Law, wherein, in every place, from the rising of the sun to the setting thereof is offered a clean oblation to the Lord, the body and blood of Jesus Christ.

The purpose of these pages is to justify this assertion by setting forth, as simply as possible, the dogmatic arguments on which it rests, and that done, to add a few theological considerations which may help to a better understanding and realisation of the meaning of the Mass and of its value as the central act of Catholic worship. Readers must not expect to find here any discussion of the many problems connected with the history of the Mass. Nor is it my intention to enter into any of the controversies that have raged around the Mass, be they controversies between Catholics and those who reject the Mass, or be they domestic disputes between different schools or parties of Catholic theologians. Again, this is not meant to be a devotional essay, though, of course, since all true devotion springs from and rests upon knowledge of the truth, every exposition of Catholic dogma must be fundamentally and potentially devotional. My aim is simply expository, to show that the Mass is a sacrifice, and to set forth what that assertion means and implies.

It might be thought that the first thing necessary in such an essay as this is a rigorous definition of terms; that we ought to determine exactly what constitutes a sacrifice, and then go on to show that the Mass verifies all the conditions required. That is the usual method in any theological treatise, the method consecrated by generations of scholastic theologians. Unfortunately in the present case, if it is a question of an exact definition, it is impossible to find agreement among theologians. To attempt such a definition would be regarded, inevitably and rightly, as begging the question. We must content ourselves, therefore, with a looser notion of sacrifice, for the present, leaving until later a more rigorous determination of the idea, and for our purpose it will be enough to transcribe what the Rev. M. C. D'Arcy, S.J., has written in his essay, *Christ, Priest and Redeemer*: "And so now we can enlarge the idea of sacrifice by saying that it is an act of homage which furthers union with God, one's Maker and Last End; and the way that this is done is through the offering of a gift which symbolises interior oblation, and perhaps repentance as well. The gift is sanctified and made holy with God's holiness, since it passes into his possession, if it is accepted by God. His acceptance passes, so to speak, through the gift to the offerer, and the alliance or friendship is ratified by the eating, not by God, but by the worshipper, of what is holy with God's holiness. Sacrifice has thus shown itself as a mode of mediation between God and man."

§ II: THE SACRIFICE OF THE MASS IN THE SACRED SCRIPTURES

The Last Supper

WHATEVER else the Mass may be, it is the commemoration and the repetition of the Last Supper. It is the perpetual fulfilment of the command given by Jesus Christ to his Apostles, and through them, to all his priests until the end of time: "Do this in commemoration of me." As to this, there is agreement, I think, among practically all who claim to be Christians. Hence, it is with the Last Supper that we must begin, and if it prove that this has a sacrificial character it will at once follow that the Mass also must be looked upon as a sacrifice.

Only one thing needs to be noted by way of introduction, namely that the Catholic doctrine of the Real Presence and all that it implies, must here be taken for granted. All this may be found in the essay on *The Sacrament of the Eucharist*, wherein also it is made clear that the passages from the Scriptures now to be considered must be understood in their obvious, literal, and realistic sense.

In the accounts of the Last Supper left us by the Evangelists and St Paul two or three things stand out clearly.

In the first place we cannot but be struck by the sacrificial nature and connotations of the language used. Jesus and his Apostles were Jews; all the circumstances accompanying the solemn institution of the covenant between God and the Hebrew people were well known to them, the words in which it is recorded were often read by them or heard in their worship in synagogue and temple. In the Book of Exodus it is written: "And Moses wrote all the words of the Lord: and rising in the morning he built an altar at the foot of the mount, and twelve titles according to the twelve tribes of Israel. And he sent young men of the children of Israel, and they offered holocausts, and sacrificed pacific victims of calves to the Lord. Then Moses took half of the blood, and put it into bowls; and the rest he poured upon the altar. And taking the book of the covenant, he read it in the hearing of the people . . . and he took the blood and sprinkled it upon the people, and he said: This is the blood of the covenant which the Lord hath made with you concerning all these words."[1] When, therefore, Jesus, giving his Disciples the chalice, said: "Drink ye all of this, for this is my blood of the new testament"[2] (or "covenant" as the Greek word may equally well be rendered), it is impossible to doubt that the Disciples must have recalled the scene described in Exodus, and realised that Jesus was instituting and sealing the new covenant between God and his people of which the old had been but the type and the promise. And as the old covenant had been sealed in the blood of victims offered in sacrifice, so it is clear that the sealing blood of the new is that of the victim who is the sacrifice of the new covenant. The sacrificial character of this blood is still further emphasised by the added words: "which shall be shed for many unto remission of sins," which proclaim the propitiatory effect of Christ's death. Even if it be granted that Jesus, in these words, was alluding directly and primarily to his approaching death upon the Cross, as to which commentators have disputed endlessly, it still remains true that the Supper itself partook of the nature of a sacrifice since Christ's true body and blood were there really present and really given, and were the immediate subject of his sacrificial words.

Another point to be noticed is the connection or relation set up between the Supper and the Cross. The simplest and most direct way of showing this is to transcribe the texts as they stand. They speak for themselves.

The Body: "This is my body which is given for you. Do this for a commemoration of me."[3] St Paul[4] has, "broken for you."

[1] xxiv 4-8.
[2] Matt. xxvi 27, 28.
[3] Luke xxii 19.
[4] 1 Cor. xi 24.

The Blood: "This is my blood of the new testament which shall be shed for many unto remission of sins."[1] St Mark[2] leaves out the words, "unto remission of sins." St Luke[3] puts the same thing in a slightly different form: "This is the chalice, the new testament in my blood, which shall be shed for you," and St Paul: "This chalice is the new testament in my blood: this do ye, as often as you shall drink, for the commemoration of me,"[4] and he adds his own comment, embracing both body and blood in one sweeping phrase: "For as often as you shall eat this bread and drink the chalice, you shall shew (*i.e.* proclaim or celebrate, as his word really means) the death of the Lord, until he come."[5]

Nothing could be plainer. In a few hours Jesus was to be delivered to death and was to shed his blood for men unto the forgiveness of their sins; and now in this last solemn and loving meal with his Disciples, he wishes, by an act of divinely conceived anticipation, to give them his body and blood, and to make them partakers in the sacrifice so close at hand.

We must not leave this point without noting that, according to the Greek text, the phrase "which shall be shed" would run "which is shed," for the verbal form used is the present participle. This reading, while possibly rendering the allusion to the Cross less direct, would, on the other hand, only emphasise and strengthen the actual and present sacrificial meaning and implication of Christ's words.

Lastly, in the Supper there is found that element which was an integral, if not an essential part of nearly all the ancient sacrifices of Jews and Gentiles alike, to wit, the sacrificial meal, of which, after the oblation was made, all those who had assisted at the sacred rite partook, eating and drinking of the gifts that had been offered. We need not now enquire into the various ideas that lay behind and prompted this custom. It is enough to remark that it existed almost universally, and that it has its place in the Last Supper: "Take ye and eat, this is my body; take ye and drink, this is my blood of the new testament." It is St Paul who gives the clearest expression to this sacrificial element in the Last Supper, or rather, to its repetition in the Eucharistic celebration in the Church: "The chalice of benediction which we bless, is it not the communion of the blood of Christ? And the bread which we break, is it not the partaking of the body of the Lord? . . . Behold Israel according to the flesh; are not they that eat of the sacrifices partakers of the altar? What then? Do I say that what is offered in sacrifice to idols is anything? Or that the idol is anything? But the things which the heathens sacrifice, they sacrifice to devils, and not to God. And I would not that you should be made partakers with devils. You

[1] Matt. xxvi 28. [2] xiv 24. [3] xxii 20.
[4] 1 Cor. xi 25. [5] *Ibid.* 26.

cannot drink the chalice of the Lord, and the chalice of devils ; you cannot be partakers of the table of the Lord, and of the table of devils." [1] His argument is clear, and its implication manifest. The Jews partake of the altar, and the heathens partake with devils, when they eat of the things which have been sacrificed on the altar or sacrificed to devils. Similarly if the Christians are partakers of the blood of Christ and of his body, as St Paul says they are, this can only be so because, in drinking and eating of them, they share in the sacrifice in which they are offered upon the table of the Lord. Exclude this idea of sharing in the sacrificial gifts, and his words have no application to the case under consideration, and his argument, which he puts forward as conclusive, loses all its force.

We have then these three points or elements in the Last Supper as celebrated by Jesus Christ, and in its Eucharistic repetition in the Church ; firstly, it is the setting up of a new covenant with God's people, expressed in terms that are clearly sacrificial ; secondly, it is the commemoration or memorial of Christ's sacrificial death on the Cross ; thirdly, it provides a sacrificial meal wherein we partake of the gifts that have been offered in sacrifice. The conclusion is inevitable that it is a real sacrifice, and, given the truth of the doctrine of the Real Presence, that it is the sacrifice of the Body and Blood of Jesus Christ.

The prophecy of Malachy

Passing over Hebrews xiii, 10, which, if it refers to the Eucharist (which is a disputed point), is decisive as to its sacrificial character, we must not omit some consideration of the well-known prophecy of Malachy, which, from the earliest times, has been understood by Christian writers to be a clear foretelling of the sacrifice of the Mass. A full discussion of this passage must be sought elsewhere ; here only an outline of the argument can be given.

The Prophet begins, after a short exordium, by reproving the priests of Israel for their neglect of God's commands in the matter of divine worship, by offering unclean and defective gifts upon the altar of sacrifice. God, through the Prophet's mouth, declares that he will no longer look with favour upon their sacrifices, and announces that the time is coming when, instead of these defective sacrifices offered at Jerusalem only, a clean oblation will be offered constantly and in every place unto his name. " For from the rising of the sun even to the going down, my name is great among the Gentiles, and in every place there is sacrifice, and there is offered to my name a clean oblation ; for my name is great among the Gentiles, saith the Lord of hosts." [2]

This clean oblation that is to be offered everywhere among the Gentiles is evidently something different from the Jewish sacrifices, which could be offered nowhere but in the Temple at Jerusalem, and which, since this was destroyed, have not been offered anywhere.

[1] I Cor. x 16-21. [2] Mal. i 11.

Nor can it be understood simply of the sacrifices of prayer and praise and thanksgiving which all worshippers of God offer continually to the Lord. This sense is incompatible both with the context, which throughout refers to real, material sacrifices only, and with the meaning of the words used. The Hebrew word *mincha*, which is translated *oblation*, nearly always has in the Old Testament the specific signification of unbloody sacrifice, and, though occasionally meaning any sort of real sacrifice, is never used to signify interior acts of worship or such exterior oblations as are not real sacrifices ; [1] and this may be said also of the other terms employed.

The Prophet announces the coming abrogation of the old rites and the institution of a new and universal sacrifice. His hearers, of course, could not understand the full meaning of his words, but ever since the days of the Apostles, Christian writers have been unanimous in interpreting them as a reference to the sacrifice of the Mass. The Council of Trent authoritatively confirmed this interpretation in its decree upon the sacrifice of the Mass : " And this indeed is that clean oblation which cannot be defiled by any unworthiness or wickedness in those who offer ; the clean oblation which the Lord, speaking by Malachy, foretold would be offered in every place to his name, which would be great among the Gentiles." [2]

The order of Melchisedech

Finally, something must be said of the argument to be drawn from Christ's priesthood " according to the order of Melchisedech." [3] The argument, as repeated in dozens of theological textbooks, may be thus briefly set down. Priesthood and sacrifice are correlative ; priests of the same order must offer sacrifice according to the same rite. Melchisedech offered sacrifice in bread and wine, therefore so did Christ. But the only time he can possibly be said to have done this was at the Last Supper, and therefore the Eucharist is a sacrifice.

Intrinsically and as a purely scriptural argument this may seem to be defective. The Greek word translated " order " refers rather to rank, quality, manner, than to the sacrificial rite. To this no reference seems to be made either in the Psalm or in the Epistle ; in the latter the writer is wholly occupied with the eternity and superiority of Christ's priesthood as compared with that of Aaron. This he illustrates and explains by saying that Christ is " a priest according to the order of Melchisedech." The King of Salem is shown to be Abraham's superior by receiving from him the tribute of tenths ; he is the type of the eternity of Christ's priesthood by his manner of appearing in the pages of Scripture, " without father, without mother, without genealogy, having neither beginning of days nor end of life," and therefore he is " likened unto the Son of God (and) continueth a priest for ever." [4] Hence those who are content with the purely objective and apparently obvious interpretation

[1] *Cf.* Brown, Driver, and Briggs, *Hebrew Lexicon*, s.v.

[2] Session xxii, chap. i.

[3] Ps. cix ; Heb. vii.

[4] Heb. vii 3.

of Scripture may reject this argument. But the Catholic has another criterion; for him the Church is the only authoritative interpreter of Holy Writ, and her voice speaks in the constant tradition of her Fathers and Doctors. Looked at in this light the words under review appear as a convincing proof of the sacrificial character of the Last Supper, for, from the beginning of the second century onwards, hardly a Christian writer quotes them without seeing in them a reference to Christ's institution of the Eucharist and a demonstration of the sacrificial character of the Mass. As Petavius puts it: "On this point the ancient writers agree to such an incredible extent, that there can be no room for legitimate doubt in the mind of any Christian." [1]

§ III: THE SACRIFICE OF THE MASS IN CATHOLIC TRADITION

Just as the religious life of the Jews had its centre in the Temple at Jerusalem, because there alone were offered the sacrifices that commemorated the institution of the Covenant and the deliverance from bondage, so the religious life of Christians revolves about the Mass, because it is the commemoration and the perpetual reiteration of Christ's death on the Cross, their deliverance and redemption. It would, then, be remarkable if the Mass had not left a deep impress on the whole of Christian literature, especially on those parts of it that bear upon the practical life of the Church. It must, however, be borne in mind that we possess to-day but comparatively scanty remains of what must have been the abundant output of Christian writers who lived before the middle of the third century, and much of what we have is of such a character as to make any allusion to the details of worship most improbable. Enough, however, is left to enable us to ascertain with certainty the mind and teaching of the primitive Church. From towards the end of the third century the extant testimony of Christian writers is both abundant and detailed. It would be impossible for us to give a hundredth part of the harvest to be garnered from the patristic writers of the fourth, fifth, and sixth centuries; nor would it serve any useful purpose, for all competent scholars are agreed that from the end of the third century the Catholic theology of the Mass was fixed as regards its substantial elements, and that, on all sides, it was held to be the true and real sacrifice of Christ's body and blood.

St Cyprian

Yet it is maintained by many that this is a perversion of the primitive doctrine, and the principal author of the innovation and of the change in the current of theological tradition is said to be St Cyprian. Until his time, we are told, the eucharistic sacrifice was considered to be simply a spiritual sacrifice of praise and thanksgiving, containing no real and objective offering; or at the most, the

[1] *De Incarnatione*, Bk. 12, Chap. xii.

offering was merely one of bread and wine. He introduced the idea of the sacrifice of Christ's body and blood, and his influence was so powerful that, in a comparatively short time, the old teaching was forgotten and the Church was definitely committed to the new line of eucharistic speculation. We shall begin, therefore, with an examination of St Cyprian's teaching. Then, working backwards, we hope to be able to make it clear that, instead of being an innovator, he was a continuator, that he added nothing to the accepted doctrine and did not change the current of theological teaching, but only stated clearly some things that others had said obscurely, and made some things explicit that had always been implicitly believed.

St Cyprian's writings are full of references to the eucharistic sacrifice, but as a rule they are incidental allusions only or passing references which, though couched in most realistic language, might possibly be interpreted in a metaphorical sense or are not sufficiently clear to enable us to discover with certainty their full significance. We have, however, one of his letters wherein he sets out his teaching in considerable detail.[1] A certain bishop, Caecilius, had informed him that, in some places in Africa, the custom had grown up of using water only in the chalice in the celebration of the Eucharist, and sought his opinion and advice in the matter. From St Cyprian's lengthy answer we extract a few of the more telling passages. "Jesus Christ our Lord and God, who instituted this sacrifice."[2] "Nor can his blood, which is our redemption and our life, be discerned in the chalice, when the chalice lacks wine."[3] "For who is more truly the priest of the most high God than our Lord Jesus Christ, who offered sacrifice to God the Father, and offered the same as Melchisedech had offered, that is bread and wine, to wit his body and blood?"[4] "Whence it appears that the blood of Christ is not offered if there be not wine in the chalice, nor is the Lord's sacrifice celebrated rightly and holily unless our oblation and sacrifice correspond with Christ's passion."[5] "Therefore, dearest brother, let no one think that he ought to follow the custom of those who have thought that water alone should be offered in the chalice of the Lord. The question is, whom have these followed? For if in the sacrifice that Christ offered, Christ alone is to be followed, then indeed we must do what Christ did, and obey his command as to what should be done. . . . And if we are not allowed to depart from the least of the Lord's commands, so much the less is it allowable to infringe his commands in things so high and great, in a matter so closely touching the very sacrament of the Lord's passion and our redemption. . . . For if Jesus . . . himself is the high priest of God the Father, and if he, in the first place, offered himself as a sacrifice to the Father, and then commanded this to be done in commemoration of him, then, in truth, that priest truly acts as Christ's

[1] Epistola LXIII, *Ad Caecilium*; Migne, *Patrologia Latina*, IV, 383 ff.
[2] Chap. i. [3] Chap. ii. [4] Chap. iv. [5] Chap. ix.

minister who imitates what Christ did, and he then offers a true and full sacrifice in the church to God the Father, when he offers according as he sees Christ to have offered." [1] "And since we make mention of his passion whenever we offer sacrifice (for the sacrifice we offer is the Lord's passion), we must do nothing else but what he did." [2]

St Cyprian, then, holds that the Eucharist is a true and real sacrifice, that it was instituted and first offered by Jesus Christ at the Last Supper, and that in it we truly offer to God Christ's body and blood under the appearances of bread and wine, and that it is the passion or the commemoration of the passion of Christ. Such was the doctrine taught in Carthage in the middle of the third century, and no theologian of the present day teaches anything different. But was it new doctrine in St Cyprian's day?

Tertullian

Let us interrogate Tertullian, the fiery Christian apologist who flourished in Carthage forty years or so before St Cyprian, and who, after having been the foremost champion of the Church, drifted into the heresy of Montanism, and died no one knows how or when. In his writings, whether Catholic or Montanist, there is no such formal and direct treatment of the eucharistic sacrifice as is provided by St Cyprian, but allusions both to the sacrament and the sacrifice abound, and are nearly always couched in realistic terms that can leave no doubt in the impartial reader's mind as to the writer's underlying belief.

Here is his approving estimate of the conduct of pious Christian women: "You do not make the round of the temples, or frequent the games, or take part in the festival days of the Gentiles. For it is because of these assemblies and the wish to see and be seen that all kinds of vanities are publicly paraded; . . . but you go abroad only for some serious (or holy, *tetrica*) reason; either because some sick person among the brethren is to be visited, or because sacrifice is offered, or the word of God administered." [3] Here is the word: "sacrifice is offered"; there is no explanation; the Christian woman would understand.

But the modern non-Catholic scholar often does not or will not see what Tertullian means. To show that the African apologist had no notion of an objective and real eucharistic sacrifice, he seizes on the following few words from the treatise *Against Marcion*, III, 22: "In every place a sacrifice is offered to my name, a clean sacrifice [4] that is the proclaiming of his glory and blessings, and praises and hymns." [5] But the conclusion is unwarranted. Tertullian's interpretation of this prophecy is not meant to be either exclusive or comprehensive. He is making a particular point against Marcion and, as is his wont, gathers together all the texts he can find that can

[1] Chap. xiv. [2] Chap. xvii.
[3] *De cultu feminarum*, II, 11 (*Patr. Lat.*, I, 1444-5).
[4] Mal. i 11. [5] *Patr. Lat.*, II, 381.

be brought to bear on it. That the eucharistic sacrifice consisted in something more than the singing of hymns and the praises of God is clear from what he says about the things that women were not allowed to do in church. "Let us see whether those things that ecclesiastical discipline prescribes concerning women are applicable to virgins. It is not allowed to a woman to speak in church, but neither to teach, nor to baptise, nor to offer (*i.e.* sacrifice), nor to claim a part in any man's duty, much less to share the duty of the priestly office." [1] But they were certainly allowed to join in the prayers and hymns. To offer (*offerre*), then, is something more than the giving of thanks and singing of hymns ; it was a function strictly reserved to priests, whose duty it was to preside at the meetings where the Eucharist was celebrated.

We find many allusions to the traditional custom of celebrating the Eucharist for the dead and in honour of the martyrs, on their anniversaries, and always Tertullian's language is most definitely sacrificial. Passing over these, we must consider in some detail an illuminating passage from the *De Pudicitia :* [2] "And so the apostate will recover his former garment, being clothed again in the Holy Ghost, he will receive again the ring, the seal of baptism, and once more Christ will be slain for him." These are the relevant words and, if the allusion is really to the eucharistic sacrifice, they are clear evidence that Tertullian regarded it as, in some way, the re-iteration of Christ's death. This allusion is, however, disputed, it being alleged that the reference is to Hebrews vi, 6, "crucifying again to themselves the Son of God."

This treatise is one of Tertullian's violent Montanist writings, in which he attacks the Pope for having made it known that all sorts of sinners, even those who had apostatised, might be reconciled to the Church after doing penance. Catholics, supporting the Pope, appealed to the parable of the prodigal son as a supreme and unanswerable argument. The question now in dispute is, therefore, the interpretation of the parable, for Tertullian recognises that, if it be understood to refer to the fallen Christian, his own case is hopeless. So he uses all his power as a rhetorical debater to show that it can only be applied to the heathen who, having wandered far from God, and spent his substance in riotous living in the darkness and corruption of paganism, comes back to the Father and is received by him in Baptism. "He remembers God his Father, having made satisfaction he returns, he receives his former garment, namely that state which Adam lost by his transgression ; likewise then he receives the first ring, by which, after being interrogated, he seals the compact of faith,[3] and so finally is feasted with the fatness of the Body of the Lord, namely, the Eucharist."

[1] *De virginibus velandis* (*Patr. Lat.*, II, 950).

[2] Chap. ix, *Patr. Lat.*, II, 1049.

[3] This refers to the questions put to the catechumen at baptism.

Here we have the key to the meaning of the words in dispute. Tertullian understands the welcome given by the prodigal's father to his son as being realised in the two sacraments of Baptism and the Eucharist, but will not allow that the parable can apply to the penitent apostate, for, if it does, the consequences will be absurd, because "not only adulterers and fornicators, but idolaters and blasphemers and deniers of Christ, and every kind of apostate will be able to make satisfaction to the Father if the parable be so interpreted. And in this way the whole substance of religion is really destroyed. For who will fear to waste what he can afterwards get back? Who will take the trouble to keep for ever what he cannot lose for ever? Safety in sinning means to lust after sin. And so the apostate will recover his former garment, being clothed again in the Holy Ghost; he will receive again the ring, the seal of Baptism, and again Christ will be slain for him, and he will once more sit upon that seat from which those who are unworthily garbed, to say nothing of the naked, are taken by the torturers and cast out into darkness."

It is clear that, in this passage also, which runs on the same lines as the former, Tertullian is referring to the same two sacraments, Baptism and the Eucharist, and that he envisages the latter both as a sacrifice and a banquet. He regarded the Eucharist, therefore, as a sacrifice, which was offered upon the altar (*altare*, *ara*) of the Lord, by priests (*sacerdotes*), the victim being Christ, and the faithful partaking of his body.

St Irenaeus

St Irenaeus, who witnesses to the tradition of both East and West, sets forth the same teaching at the end of the second century. He even takes the reality of the eucharistic sacrifice as the starting-point of his argument against the heretics, that is, as common ground between himself and them. As we have not the space to quote him at any length, and any other sort of quotation is unsatisfactory, we may refer the reader to his *Adversus Haereses*, book IV, chapters xvii and xviii, and pass on at once to St Justin.

St Justin

His testimony is interesting chiefly by reason of the account he gives of the way the Christians carried out their liturgical worship at Rome in the middle of the second century. This is the earliest description we have of the Mass, for before this time Christian literature contains nothing but passing, and often obscure references. Though St Justin's account be well known, it will bear quotation here, for in it we can discover many of the elements of the liturgy which have remained substantially the same from his day until now. It is to be found in chapters lxv to lxvii of his first Apology, and runs thus:

"We salute one another with a kiss when we have concluded the prayers. Then is brought to the president of the brethren bread, and a cup of water and wine, which he receives; and offers up praise and glory to the Father of all things, through the name of His Son and of the Holy Ghost; and he returns thanks at length, for our being vouchsafed these things by him. When he has concluded the prayers and thanksgiving, all the people who are present express their assent by saying *Amen.* This word *Amen* in the Aramaic language means 'so be it'; and when the president has celebrated the Eucharist, and all the people have assented, they whom we call deacons give to each of those who are present a portion of the eucharistic bread and wine and water; and carry them to those who are absent. And this food is called by us the Eucharist, of which no one is allowed to partake unless he believes the truth of our doctrines; and unless he has been washed in the laver for the forgiveness of sins, and unto regeneration; and so lives as Christ has directed. For we do not receive them as ordinary food, or ordinary drink; but as by the Word of God Jesus our Saviour was made flesh, and had both flesh and blood for our salvation, so also the food which was blessed by the prayer of the Word which proceeded from him, and from which our flesh and blood, by assimilation, receives nourishment, is, we are taught, both the flesh and blood of that Jesus who was made flesh. For the Apostles in the records which they made, and which are called gospels, have declared that Jesus commanded them to do as follows: 'He took bread and gave thanks, and said, "This do in remembrance of me: this is my body." And in like manner he took the cup, and blessed it, and said, "This is my blood," and gave it to them alone.'"

This is Justin's account of the celebration of the Eucharist on the occasion of the baptism of neophytes. A little further on he speaks in a similar way but more briefly of the ordinary Sunday celebration in town or country. But as this introduces no new element, beyond the mention of the sermon, we need not quote it.

The reader will have noticed that in the passage quoted there is not a word about sacrifice, and may, therefore, wonder why it has been given. Apart from its historical and liturgical interest as the first account of the Mass, it has two points of dogmatic importance. The first is the evident connection between the Christian Eucharist and the Last Supper, since St Justin explains the one by the other and by Christ's command to his Apostles to repeat what he did. The second point is the witness to the Christian belief in the Real Presence. The eucharistic bread and wine were, for St Justin and his fellow-Christians, not common food and drink, but, quite simply, the flesh and blood of Jesus Christ. Even though many have written much to prove that Justin could not possibly have believed in Transubstantiation, his simple, straightforward profession of faith in the Real Presence cannot be gainsaid. We must bear this in mind in reading the following passages from his other work, the *Dialogue with Trypho the Jew.*

The most notable and important is in chapter lxi, where we can clearly discern the theme of the thanksgivings offered by the celebrant, referred to in the Apology, which are now fixed in our present Prefaces. " And the offering of meal which it was prescribed to make for lepers who had been cleansed, was the type of the bread of the Eucharist, which Jesus Christ our Lord taught us to offer in memory of the sufferings he underwent for the cleansing of men's souls from all iniquity ; so that we may give thanks to God for having created the world for us, and all things in it, for having delivered us from the evils that oppressed us, for having completely destroyed the principalities and powers, by him who was made the Suffering One according to his will.

" Also concerning the sacrifices which you were wont to offer to him, God says, as I have mentioned already, by the mouth of Malachy, one of the twelve : ' My will is not in you, saith the Lord, and your sacrifices I shall not accept from your hands. Therefore from the sun's rising unto its going down, my name is glorified among the nations, and in every place incense is offered to my name, a clean sacrifice, for great is my name among the nations, says the Lord, while you profane it.' But of the sacrifices offered to him in every place by us, the nations, the sacrifices, that is to say, of the bread of the Eucharist, and likewise of the cup of the Eucharist, of these he foretells when he says that we glorify his name, but you profane it."

Similar passages occur in chapters lxx and cxvii of the same book, and also elsewhere, which, taken together, make it clear that Justin looked upon the celebration of the Holy Eucharist as a real sacrifice, wherein are offered bread and wine which, however, are not common bread and wine, but the Body and Blood of Christ, of whose sufferings and death this sacrifice is a memorial or commemoration.

Still earlier references

Previous to St Justin we find but brief and, generally, casual allusions to the Eucharist as for example, in St Clement's *Letter to the Corinthians* [1] and the Letters of St. Ignatius to the *Ephesians* [2] and the *Philadelphians*,[3] and finally, in the very early document, of uncertain authorship and date, known as *The Teaching of the Apostles*.[4] Though nothing very definite is to be gathered from these scattered allusions, they yet all point the same way. There is not only no sign of any purely commemorative and non-sacrificial conception of the Eucharist, but there are positive indications that its celebration was always looked upon as a sacrificial act fulfilling the prophecy of Malachy. We know also that, from the first, the Christians believed the consecrated bread and wine to be Christ's real Body and Blood.[5] But we cannot separate these two ideas ; they are the two indivisible elements of the one doctrine that the Mass is the true sacrifice of Jesus Christ's real Body and Blood. We may allow that there has been some development from Clement through Justin to Cyprian,

[1] Chaps. xl and xliv.
[2] Chap. v.
[3] Chap. iv.
[4] Chaps. xiv-xv.
[5] See *The Sacrament of the Eucharist*, pp. 848–857.

but it has been logical and inevitable, and consisting rather in the clearer explication and co-ordination of these two primitive elements than in the addition of anything new, or the introduction of anything from without.

§ IV: THE ATTACK UPON THE MASS

The Protestant attack on the Mass

THERE has never been a time when the Church has been untroubled by heresies. They began to spring up before the Apostles were dead, and, in one place or another, new ones have been constantly arising ever since. And just as heresy has been universal from the point of view of time, so it has been impartial in the doctrines chosen for attack, though it is true that some periods have been specially noteworthy for heresies concerning Christ, others for false teachings about the Trinity, others, again, for attacks upon the Papacy, or the Sacraments, or the nature and attributes of God. We have seen some indications of a eucharistic heresy in St Cyprian's time; the Mass was the object of attack by the Albigenses in the twelfth century and again by some of Wyclif's followers two hundred years later. But the great onslaught upon it was launched by the Protestant sects in the sixteenth century. Although the Mass was not singled out as a thing to be destroyed from the first, it was soon seen that there was no room for it in Protestantism, and that, if the religious revolt were to make headway and have any logical justification at all, the sacrifice of the Mass must be utterly abolished. No heresy can be logical all through, from beginning to end. That is the exclusive privilege of the true faith. But no heresy can be altogether illogical and have any chance of life, especially in an age, such as was the sixteenth century, when the power of clean, straight thinking is still both strong and common. Therefore, when once the Protestant leaders had adopted the doctrine of justification by faith only, and had thrown over the reality of sanctifying grace as the supernatural life of the soul, there was nothing for it except to give up belief in operative and grace-producing sacraments. So the Real Presence and Transubstantiation had to go, and the Eucharist had to lose altogether its sacrificial character and be retained simply as a memorial of the Last Supper whereby the soul is moved to prayer and enabled in some way to enter into communion with and to receive Jesus Christ. There were also other reasons, less respectable than the claims of logical consistency, but into which we need not go, which prompted the Reformers to abolish the Mass. Hence it is not surprising that, to a great extent, belief in the Mass became the touchstone of Catholic orthodoxy and that, all through the subsequent centuries of controversy with Protestantism, Catholic theologians should have used all their powers of argument and all their resources of learning in its defence. It was natural too that the Council of Trent should give to this question the most careful and minute consideration, focusing upon it the attention of the most brilliant gathering of theologians the world has seen, and debating every point with the greatest possible thoroughness and acuteness. The decrees and definitions drawn up as the outcome of the Council's deliberations not only form the Catholic's rule of faith in this matter, but may be taken as the foundation and starting-point of all subsequent theological speculation. They are the test by which any theory must be tried, and they are so important, so full and so carefully drawn that they deserve to be quoted at length.

The Council of Trent

The translation here given is taken from *The Canons and Decrees of the Sacred and Oecumenical Council of Trent, translated by the Rev. J. Waterworth*, published in 1848. If it cannot lay claim to elegance it has the great merit of being faithful to the original, and, indeed, is as near to being a literal rendering as is possible in readable English. These decrees and definitions were approved during the twenty-second session of the Council held in September 1532.

" Chapter I.—On the institution of the most holy Sacrifice of the Mass. Forasmuch as, under the former Testament, according to the testimony of the Apostle Paul, there was no perfection, because of the weakness of the Levitical priesthood ; there was need, God, the Father of mercies, so ordaining, that another priest should rise, according to the order of Melchisedech, our Lord Jesus Christ, who might consummate, and lead to what is perfect as many as were to be sanctified. He, therefore, our God and Lord, though he was about to offer himself once on the altar of the cross unto God the Father, by means of his death, there to operate an eternal redemption ; nevertheless, because that his priesthood was not to be extinguished by his death, in the Last Supper, on the night in which he was betrayed—that he might leave to his own beloved spouse the Church, a visible sacrifice, such as the nature of man requires, whereby that bloody sacrifice, once to be accomplished on the cross, might be represented, and the memory thereof remain even unto the end of the world, and its salutary virtue be applied to the remission of these sins which we daily commit—declaring himself constituted a priest for ever, according to the order of Melchisedech, he offered up to God the Father his own body and blood under the species of bread and wine ; and, under the symbols of those same things, he delivered (his own body and blood) to be received by his Apostles, whom he then constituted priests of the New Testament ; and by those words, ' Do this in commemoration of me,' he commanded them and their successors in the priesthood, to offer (them) ; even as the Catholic Church has always understood and taught. For, having celebrated the ancient Passover, which the multitude of the children of Israel immolated in memory of their going out of Egypt, he instituted the new Passover (to wit), himself to be immolated, under visible signs, by the Church through (the ministry of) priests, in memory of his own passage from this world unto the Father, when by the effusion of his own blood he redeemed us, and delivered us from the power of darkness, and translated us into his kingdom. And this is indeed that clean oblation, which cannot be defiled by any unworthiness, or malice of those that offer (it); which the Lord foretold by Malachias was to be offered in every place, clean to his name, which was to be great among the Gentiles; and which the Apostle Paul, writing to the Corinthians, has not obscurely indicated, when he says, that they who are defiled by the participation of the table of devils, cannot be partakers of the table of the Lord; by the table, meaning in both places the altar. This, in fine, is that oblation which was prefigured by various types of sacrifices, during the period of nature, and of the law; inasmuch as it comprises all the good things signified by those sacrifices, as being the consummation and perfection of them all.

"Chapter II.—That the sacrifice of the Mass is propitiatory both for the living and the dead.

"And forasmuch as, in this divine sacrifice which is celebrated in the Mass, that same Christ is contained and immolated in an unbloody manner, who once offered himself in a bloody manner on the altar of the cross; the holy Synod teaches, that this sacrifice is truly propitiatory and that by means thereof this is effected, that we obtain mercy, and find grace in seasonable aid, if we draw nigh unto God, contrite and penitent, with a sincere heart and upright faith, with fear and reverence. For the Lord, appeased by the oblation thereof, and granting the grace and gift of penitence, forgives even heinous crimes and sins. For the victim is one and the same, the same now offering by the ministry of priests, who then offered himself on the cross, the manner alone of offering being different. The fruits indeed of which oblation, of that bloody one to wit, are received most plentifully through this unbloody one; so far is this (latter) from derogating in any way from that (former oblation). Wherefore, not only for the sins, punishments, satisfactions and other necessities of the faithful who are living, but also for those who are departed in Christ, and who are not as yet fully purified, is it rightly offered, agreeably to a tradition of the Apostles."

Passing over the other chapters as less important to our present purpose, we transcribe the following canons wherein the Protestant errors are condemned.

"Canon i —If any one saith, that in the Mass a true and proper sacrifice is not offered to God; or, that to be offered is nothing else but that Christ is given us to eat; let him be anathema.

"Canon ii.—If any one saith, that by those words, Do this for a commemoration of me, Christ did not institute the Apostles priests; or did not ordain that they and other priests should offer his own body and blood; let him be anathema.

"Canon iii.—If any one saith, that the sacrifice of the Mass is only a sacrifice of praise and of thanksgiving; or that it is a bare commemoration of the sacrifice consummated on the cross, but not a propitiatory sacrifice; or, that it profits him only who receives; and that it ought not to be offered for the living and the dead for sins, pains, satisfactions and other necessities; let him be anathema.

"Canon iv.—If any one saith, that, by the sacrifice of the Mass a blasphemy is cast upon the most holy sacrifice of Christ consummated on the cross; or, that it is thereby derogated from; let him be anathema."

Matters of debate

These decrees and canons contain the whole of the Church's defined, dogmatic teaching on the sacrifice of the Mass. No one can be a Catholic who knowingly denies any of the doctrinal points here made, and in later sections we shall have something to say of each of them. But a careful reading will at once show that they do not answer all the questions that occur to the mind, and that they by no means shut the door upon theological speculation. Indeed, the centuries that have passed since the Council was held have been remarkable for the amount, the variety, the intensity and the liveliness of Catholic theological speculation upon the Mass. From this point of view we may divide the time roughly into two periods. In the first, immediately succeeding the Council, the theologians were moved mainly by defensive and controversial reasons, and had their eyes always fixed upon the necessities of the anti-Protestant campaign; whereas in the second and present period, which has begun only in comparatively recent years, the interest of the theologians has coincided with the wonderful modern revival of Eucharistic devotion, and the mainspring of their speculations is their desire to increase and more solidly to establish that devotion by giving the faithful a better and deeper knowledge of and insight into the mystery of the Mass.

Yet in both periods, the chief matter of debate is the same, in spite of the diversity of motive. For the Council of Trent, while clear and definite in its statement that the Mass is a true and real and propitiatory sacrifice of the body and blood of Christ, makes no attempt to prove it except by arguments drawn directly from authority and revelation. This mode of procedure is traditional with the Councils of the Church which are, as regards their authoritative decrees, teaching bodies and not theological debating societies. The lengthy and minute debates that precede the final casting and conciliar approval of the decrees are in the nature of private discussions, having no authority beyond that of the theologians taking part in them. Hence it is left to the theologians to find a rational justification of the dogmas defined, to give exact definitions of the terms employed and to work out scientific proofs of the doctrines, in so far as these are capable of being thus proved. In the present case the question to be settled is, how exactly is the Mass a sacrifice, in what way and in what particular action does the Mass verify the definition and fulfil all the necessary conditions of a real, propitiatory sacrifice?

In the next section we shall set forth briefly some few of the many ways in which theologians have tried to answer this question.

§V: THEOLOGICAL THEORIES AND SPECULATIONS

It is impossible to give more than a sketch of three or four of the principal theories about the way in which the Mass verifies the definition of a sacrifice, which have at various times found favour with Catholic theologians of repute. Moreover, in a subject of such difficulty, which is the subject of such lively debate, it would not be seemly in such an essay as this, for the writer to put forward any theory as definitely preferable to all others, whatever may be his own opinions or convictions in the matter. He may, however, be allowed to state the objections which seem fatal to some theories, and which, in the course of time, have caused them to be abandoned by practically all theologians to-day.

The essential part of the Mass

The first difference of opinion to be noted refers to the part of the Mass wherein lies the essential element of sacrifice. According to some it is contained wholly within the consecration, others have thought that it consists in the consecration together with the communion, while a few have gone so far as to look upon the communion alone as the sacrificial act. It is hardly necessary to discuss this last point, since it is agreed by practically all theologians to-day that, although the communion belongs to the integrity or completeness of the sacrificial rite, it does not form part of the essential sacrificial act. In other words, although Christ's body and blood are offered in sacrifice, in order that they may be afterwards partaken of by the faithful, or by the priest alone, in a sacrificial banquet of communion with God, and although sacrifice and banquet are two parts of one liturgical rite, yet they are two separate acts, differing from one another, not only by the separation of time, but also by a difference of nature.

Without going further into this, and taking it as settled that, in the Mass, it is the twofold consecration and transubstantiation of the bread and wine which alone constitute the essential act of the sacrifice, we go on to look at some of the theories put forward to show how this is so.

The theory of "destruction"

The line of argument adopted by many theologians runs somewhat in this way. In any real sacrifice the victim or thing offered suffers some kind of destruction. So the animals offered under the Jewish law were killed, the libations of wine were poured out upon the ground, thus being rendered unfit for consumption and undergoing practical destruction, the fruits of the earth were either burned or set aside and not devoted to common use, thus being given over to what may be said to be equivalent to destruction. But in the Mass there is a real sacrifice of Christ's body and blood. Therefore there must be some kind of destruction of Christ's body and blood. It is abundantly clear that Christ cannot suffer any real death or destruction in the Mass, and so the theologians' efforts were wholly given to showing that he undergoes something more or less equivalent to a sort of destruction.

It was pointed out, for example, that transubstantiation puts him upon the altar in the form of food and drink destined for consumption, which almost amounts to destruction. Again, the suggestion was made that, in the consecrated elements, Jesus Christ, though indeed really and wholly present as living man and God, is yet living a special kind of life which is on a lower plane than his glorious life in heaven, and in which he is deprived of the natural exercise of his human, physical faculties ; and this condition of reduced existence may be said to be equivalent to destruction, since it is the utmost limit to which he can go in this direction.

Although these theories are quite orthodox and may be defended, there are few to uphold them to-day. The first great objection against them springs from a common-sense idea of the value of words. It is seen and recognised that the processes or conditions mentioned cannot be said to constitute a destruction or anything equivalent thereto, except by an abuse of terms which robs them of any real value and is dangerous to true thinking.

A second objection goes deeper. These explanations rest upon the presupposition that transubstantiation is an action that, somehow or other, affects Christ, does something to him. But the best theological thought of the Church, the " classical theology " of St Thomas Aquinas, will not allow this, holding, instead, that the process or action of transubstantiation touches and affects only the substances of bread and wine, Christ's body and blood being simply the finishing point of the process, and remaining in themselves wholly unchanged and unaffected.

A subtle variant

Under the force of these objections and others which we need not set down, a more refined and subtle variant of the " destructionist " theory has been worked out. This starts from the fact that a sacrifice, just as a sacrament, comes under the category of signs, and draws much of its strength from the Catholic doctrine of eucharistic natural concomitance, which is fully explained in the essay on the *Sacrament of the Eucharist*.

Here is a brief exposition of the theory. In the consecration of the bread, though Christ is made present in his integrity as man and God, yet, so far as the words of consecration—" This is my body "—are operative of themselves, only his body is made present on the altar. The presence of his blood, soul, and divinity, is the effect, not of the words of consecration, but of natural concomitance, the result, that is, of his being a living Person, no longer subject to death or mutilation. Likewise, in the consecration of the wine, the words used are operative of themselves to the extent of making his blood alone to be present, the presence of the other elements of the living Christ being again due to concomitance. The sacramental effect of the twofold consecration, therefore, that is, its effect in so far as it is a sign seen and heard, is the separation of the body from the blood. This, it must be most carefully noted, is not a real separation. It is only a sacramental or symbolical separation. But, it is contended, in the case of a victim who cannot possibly be really immolated or killed, and who is offered in sacrifice, not under his own human form and appearance, but only under the forms and appearances of bread and wine, such a sacramental separation of body and blood, such a symbolical immolation or killing, is quite enough to constitute a real sacrifice of that victim. It is a real sacramental representation and symbolical re-enactment, in which the same victim is actually present, of the immolation consummated on Calvary, and this fully entitles it to be regarded as a real sacrifice.

There is much to be said for this theory, which has many supporters at the present day. Of all the theories involving some kind of destruction of the victim as a necessary condition, it is certainly the most spiritual in its conception, and the most closely in accord with the theological teaching of St Thomas on Transubstantiation.

The theory that the Supper and Calvary form numerically one Sacrifice

As the reader will have noticed, all these theories look upon the Last Supper, and therefore upon the Mass, as a sacrifice complete in itself, though subordinated and relative to the sacrifice of Calvary. But of recent years another opinion has been put forward, and as warmly supported in some quarters as it has been strongly opposed in others, which considers the Last Supper and Calvary as the two component and complementary parts of but one and the same complete sacrifice. At the Last Supper, so this opinion has it, Christ as Priest made to God the offering of himself as the victim destined for immolation on Calvary. Thus the sacrifice was begun. This act of oblation continued in being, active and operative, throughout his Passion. The shedding of his blood and his death on the cross sealed and crowned this act of his will, and the sacrifice was thus consummated by this actual and physical immolation of the victim. Now, the only difference between the Mass and the Last Supper is that, while the latter was the offering of the victim who was about to be immolated, the former is the offering of the same victim who has already been immolated. The Last Supper was the ritual oblation looking forward to the future real immolation, the Mass is the ritual oblation looking backwards to the real immolation once for all completed. The Last Supper was the consecration to God of the victim about to suffer, the Mass is the continued presentation to God of the victim who has suffered.

This is an attractive explanation which solves many difficulties and has gained many friends. But it has been hotly attacked, mainly on the ground that it does not fully satisfy all the implications of the Tridentine decrees. As, however, we have no intention of entering into these domestic theological controversies, we cannot discuss the pros and cons of this question.

A further theory

In common with the other explanations previously advanced, this one also requires the immolation of the divine victim as a condition for the complete sacrifice, though, differing from them, it does not find any such immolation in the Mass, which it regards as the oblation of the victim already immolated. At the risk of wearying my readers, I must now speak of yet another theory which differs from all these, in that, while recognising the value of the victim's immolation, it does not look upon it as essential to sacrifice. This explanation considers sacrifice to consist essentially in the ceremonial offering of a gift to God, as an expression or symbol of homage, petition, thanksgiving, repentance and so forth. By offering a gift to God is meant handing it over wholly to him, for his possession, use, and service, while the word *ceremonial* implies that the complete handing over of the gift must be outwardly and suitably expressed. Hence arises the common, though not universal, element of destruction or immolation, since ordinarily nothing expresses so suitably as this, the fact that the gift has passed altogether from man's possession and service into God's.

Now, from the first moment of his Incarnation, Jesus Christ consecrated his manhood to God, giving it wholly into his possession, for his use and service, to do his will in all things, by an act of his human will that was perfect from the first and irrevocable. Here was the offering of a gift to God, but not yet a sacrifice because not yet a ceremonial offering. He first gave outward and suitable ritual expression to the offering at the Last Supper, when he took bread and wine and spoke the words, This is my body given for you, This is the chalice of my blood shed for you. And so he then offered sacrifice. Again on Calvary, by delivering himself into his enemies' hands and allowing them to shed his blood and take his life, he gave outward and suitable expression to the continuing act of perfect offering, and therefore offered sacrifice. Not another sacrifice, since it is the same offering differently expressed, and the Last Supper and Calvary have a unity of signification. But when he began his glorious life in heaven he did not give up his priesthood, nor did he retract or alter the act by which he consecrated his manhood wholly to God's service ; his manhood is still offered and given to God to do his will in all things, it is God's possession. And in every Mass he again gives ceremonial expression to this continuing act in the presentation of his body and blood under the forms of bread and wine, and the words of consecration. Thus the Mass fulfils all the conditions and contains all the elements of a true and real sacrifice. There is no intention of discussing the merits of this theory, but it may be pointed out that it seems to escape the inconveniences attaching to the view mentioned in *Christ as Priest and Redeemer*,[1] and to satisfy all that is implied in the decrees of Trent as set out above.

Oneness of faith and difference of view

Some readers may be surprised and even disturbed by the existence of such a wide diversity of conflicting views on a matter of great importance. It may seem to them that the oneness of faith claimed by the Church as her exclusive possession is not the perfect thing it should be. But, in truth, there is no ground for concern. Examination of the various theories shows that all are based upon the same universally accepted truths. When the Church, in her definitions of doctrine, uses such terms as substance, person, sacrifice, and so forth, she does not, as a rule, intend to give them a strictly determined scientific meaning, but only the meaning they have in the current speech of men of good education. The same word may mean something a little more definite and exact to a philosopher than to the educated man who has not made a special study of philosophy, but in a definition of doctrine the philosopher's extra exactness and definiteness is not included.

So in the present instance, not only do all Catholic theologians accept whole-heartedly the Tridentine definitions and decrees, but all understand them in the same way as the Council meant them to be understood. Oneness of faith is thus fully safeguarded. Differences begin to show themselves only when theologians, in a legitimate and, generally, praiseworthy endeavour to probe deeper into the recesses of revealed truth, or with the object of showing how one truth exactly fits in with another, or again, with the laudable motive of defending the faith against attack or making it more attractive to the believer and stronger in its appeal to his mind, embark upon the scientific search after and explanation of the how and why of the doctrine. But these differences do not touch the faith. Moreover, every truly Catholic theologian, as soon as he sets out upon these speculations, fully recognises his constant liability to error ; he speaks under correction and in a spirit of humble diffidence, and though he may defend with ardour his own opinions against those of other theologians, he is always ready to give them up should it be proved that their logical outcome would be inconsistent with revealed truth, or should competent authority decide that it is dangerous or imprudent to hold them.

We have now to examine some further questions of importance contained in the Tridentine decrees or arising therefrom.

§ VI: THOSE WHO OFFER THE SACRIFICE OF THE MASS

Christ offers

The Council of Trent in the second chapter of the decree set out above states that, in the Mass " the victim is one and the same, the same (person) now offering by the ministry of priests, who then

[1] Essay xiv, pp. 486–489.

offered himself on the cross." At every Mass, then, Jesus Christ is the High Priest who offers the sacrifice. This is clear from the fact that, as the Fathers are never tired of pointing out, the priest, when he comes to the consecration, the very act of sacrifice, no longer uses his own words, or a prayer composed by men, or even the words of the Evangelist, but Christ's own words, spoken in the first person, "This is my body, this is the chalice of my blood." He speaks these words in the person and power of Christ, and through him Christ speaks and offers the sacrifice. It is not necessary to postulate that, at every Mass that is offered daily, Jesus Christ makes a fresh act of self-oblation, though this is maintained by some theologians. It is quite enough that he should have made this act once, since, made definitely for once and always, never retracted, it remains for ever operative and effective throughout all time. The practical value and application of this truth will appear later.

The Church and its members offer

But Jesus Christ is not the only one who offers this sacrifice. The Council of Trent says, in the same place, that the Church offers it, through the ministry of priests. Here is a great truth, the consequences of which are often but little understood or realised by the faithful, much to the detriment of their spiritual life. It is the direct outcome of that other great truth that Jesus Christ and all the members of his Church form but one body, of which he is the head. For a full exposition of this teaching readers are referred to *The Mystical Body of Christ.*[1] All that needs now to be said is that the sacrament of Baptism effects a real incorporation with Christ, and in him a real brotherhood with one another; that all thus incorporated, unless separated by mortal sin, are animated and vivified by the same principle of supernatural life, which is his Spirit, the Spirit of charity, the living soul of the Church; and that all, therefore, being in him, and he in them, being branches springing from and attached to the same trunk, share necessarily in the life of the Head, and are united with him in all his priestly work and functions.

Hence when Christ exercises his priestly ministry, and renewing the oblation of his sacrifice, offers it once again in homage to the adorable Trinity, he does not and cannot act alone, but we act with him, all the members of his Church, each according to his own degree of participation in Christ's life and priestly office. Hence the individual priest who celebrates the Mass does not offer the sacrifice as an individual, nor even simply as the minister of Jesus Christ, God and Man, but rather as the minister of Christ, eternal High Priest and inseparable head of his mystical body, the Church, which he wedded to himself through and in the sacrifice of Calvary to be the partner in his eternal priesthood.

The liturgical prayers recited during Mass make it quite clear that it is the whole Church that offers the sacrifice. So, for example just before the consecration the priest says: "We therefore beseech

[1] Essay xix.

thee, O Lord, to be appeased, and to receive this offering which we, thy servants, and thy whole household do make unto thee," and then, " This our offering, do thou, O God, vouchsafe in all things to bless, consecrate, approve, make reasonable and acceptable, that it may become for us the body and blood of thy most beloved Son, our Lord Jesus Christ." And as a last example take the prayer said immediately after the consecration, when Jesus Christ is now present upon the altar: " Wherefore, O Lord, we, thy servants, as also thy holy people, calling to mind the blessed passion of the same Christ, thy Son, our Lord, and also his rising up from hell, and his glorious ascension into heaven, do offer unto thy most excellent majesty of thine own gifts bestowed upon us, a clean victim, a holy victim, a spotless victim, the holy bread of life everlasting, and the chalice of eternal salvation."

In the light of this truth we can understand those words of St Peter: " Be you also as living stones built up, a spiritual house, a holy priesthood, to offer up spiritual sacrifices, acceptable to God by Jesus Christ . . . but you are a chosen generation, a kingly priesthood, a holy nation, a purchased people." [1] The Apostle is not using the language of pious hyperbole, or even of metaphor, but of strict and literal truth; all the members of the Church do form a holy and kingly priesthood because they are a purchased people, purchased with the blood that the royal victim shed and the kingly priest offered, and by baptism raised to membership in his body and participation in his priesthood; and, therefore, taking their part with him in the continual offering of his sacrifice. So also St John speaks of " Jesus Christ who . . . hath washed us from our sins in his own blood, and hath made us a kingdom and priests to God and his Father." [2] Whence also it follows that every Mass is pleasing to God and an acceptable sacrifice, not only because it is offered by the spotless High Priest, Jesus Christ, but also because it is offered by the whole Church, in whom the Spirit of holiness always dwells. The unworthiness, even possibly the rank wickedness of the individual priest who celebrates, can neither pollute the victim he offers, nor sully the pure intention and the holy disposition of the sacrificing Church whose minister he is.

Various degrees of participation

But, although the sacrifice is offered by the whole Church in common, it by no means follows that every individual member of the Church has the same part in the offering, or an equal participation in the ministerial office, with regard to every, or indeed, to any Mass that is celebrated, or, we may add (though of this something must be said later), an equal share in the fruits of the Mass.

The Priest

The priest naturally holds the first place. We are speaking, of course, of the dignity of his office and of his official position, not of his personal character or merit, of his personal holiness or the opposite.

[1] 1 Peter ii 5 and 9. [2] Apoc. i 5-6.

Whether he be far advanced in sanctity, or but a very ordinary good man, or even if his soul be stained with many grievous sins, his official character and dignity are not affected, nor is his official closeness to Christ, as his immediate minister, lessened. It is through his mouth that Christ speaks, through his actions that Christ becomes present on the altar, in his hands that he is lifted up, through him that the sacrifice and offering of Calvary are re-enacted. Moreover, he has been specially chosen, set aside and consecrated to represent the Church, and has been given thereby a very special share in Christ's royal priesthood. Hence many of the prayers at Mass are said by him in the first person, and often he asks God to purify his heart that the offering may be made more worthily. "Brethren," he says, turning to the people, "pray that my sacrifice and yours may be acceptable to God the Father Almighty"; to which the answer comes, "May the Lord receive the sacrifice at thy hands, to the praise and glory of his own name, to our own benefit and to that of all his holy Church." And again at the end he prays, "May my worship and bounden duty be pleasing to thee, O holy Trinity; and grant that the sacrifice which I have offered all unworthy in the sight of thy majesty may be received by thee and win forgiveness from thy mercy for me and for all those for whom I have offered it up."

Those who provide the stipend

Next in order to the priest comes the person (or persons) who by providing the material elements of the sacrifice and making provision for the support of the clergy who offer it, enables it to be offered.

For many centuries it was the custom for the faithful to supply the clergy in kind with all that was necessary for their support and for the exercise of worship. They brought the bread and wine that were used in the sacrifice of the Mass, and other gifts also which were needed by those who, being consecrated to the service of the altar, were forbidden by the Church's law to support themselves by trade and commerce. What was left, after the needs of the clergy were satisfied, was applied to the support of the poor, of whom some were to be found attached to and dependent upon every church. Gradually, as the circumstances of life changed, offerings in money took the place of gifts in kind. Now, in order that Mass may be offered, it is not only necessary that bread and wine should be available, but also that there should be a priest who, as much as anyone else, needs to be fed and clothed and housed. All therefore who contribute to his support and to the upkeep of the church wherein he ministers, and the sacred vessels and vestments which he uses, and which are necessary for the celebration of Mass, or for its splendour and beauty, or at least its decent and reverent celebration, have a special part in the Masses offered by him.

But with regard to any particular Mass the foremost place among all who share in the offering of it is taken by the one who most directly and immediately provides for its celebration by giving the stipend fixed by custom or law, which is to be reckoned as taking the place of the gifts that used formerly to be made. That they who make these gifts or contribute an equivalent sum, are to be considered as having a real part in the offering of the sacrifice, as being truly co-offerers with the priest, is attested from the earliest times. So we find St Cyprian upbraiding a wealthy but mean woman who came to Mass on Sundays, bringing no offering but receiving Communion. "You come to Mass without a sacrifice, when you take part of the sacrifice which a poor man has offered," [1] referring in the final words, not to the priest, but to the poor man who had supplied the necessary elements for the sacrifice; while St Gregory the Great speaks of a man "for whom on certain days his wife was accustomed to offer sacrifice." [2]

The provision of the necessary elements for the sacrifice confers on the giver a right to the disposal of some part of the fruits of the sacrifice, of which, however, we shall speak later on.

Those present at Mass

Little more needs to be said on this point. It is evident that those who are present at a Mass, following its action and prayers and uniting their intention with that of the priest, and that of the person who has given the stipend, enter into its offering more closely and nearly than the absent, while if there be among these latter any who actually advert to a Mass that is being celebrated and, in spirit, take their stand before the altar, they, of course, take a higher place as co-offerers than others who give no thought to it. Those, therefore, who, through illness or some other cause, are prevented from going to Mass on Sundays and holy days, or are excused from attendance, ought to try to be present in spirit, and, if possible, follow the course of the Mass at home so as to have as great a share as possible in its offering and to suffer as little loss as may be from their enforced absence.

Our share in Christ's victimhood

Before going on to speak of the fruits of the Mass and of the ends for which it is offered, we may say something here of another matter which, though not unimportant, is too often neglected, even by devout and instructed Catholics.

This also, just as the foregoing, is a truth that follows directly upon the fact of our incorporation with Jesus Christ, of our being one with him in his mystical body the Church, of which he is the head. As, through this oneness with him, we share in his priesthood and in its exercise, so likewise we are one with him in his rôle of victim, and therefore, in the Mass, when he offers himself and we, sharing his priesthood, offer him, so also he offers us as partners in his victimhood, and we likewise offer ourselves with him. It is well worth while to examine this truth a little more closely and to note some of its consequences and implications.

It is St Paul who, in a phrase as startling as any he ever penned, reveals to us this truth. "Who now rejoice in my sufferings for

[1] *De opere et eleemosyna*, chap. xv. [2] *Dialog.*, bk. IV, chap. lvii.

you, and fill up those things that are wanting of the sufferings of Christ, in my flesh, for his body, which is the Church." [1] Were Christ's sufferings, then, incomplete or insufficient? Is it not the constant teaching of the sacred Scriptures, repeated by all the Fathers and by all theologians, that his sufferings were superabundant, and that the least of them would have been more than enough to make full satisfaction for all the sins of the whole human race? Assuredly, but in saying that we have only touched the fringe of the mystery. To stop here is to leave out of account the great truth underlying St Paul's words, the truth of which he never tires, the oneness of Christ the head, and his body the Church, whereby in all things there must be unity and correspondence between his life and hers.

Hence although he paid in full the debt of satisfaction due to the divine Majesty, his members have still to suffer in order that Christ's body may be in harmony with the Head. The Church must live the life of her Head, sharing in his sufferings in order to share in his glory. He has been offered as a victim, and every day he reiterates the offering so that we, his members, may make it with him, and therefore we must also bear our measure of suffering with him, if we wish to be united with him and collaborate in his sacrifice. To live a true Christian and Catholic life involves necessarily some suffering and mortification, such as prayer, fasting, abstinence, purity, the sanctification of Sunday, the avoidance of occasions of sin, without speaking of such special sufferings as sickness, poverty, bereavements and so forth. They who refuse to accept these mortifications refuse to suffer with Christ, refuse to offer sacrifice with his mystical body, and shirk their participation with him in his rôle as victim. On the other hand, they who accept them gladly and generously, thereby fill up in their flesh "those things that are wanting of the sufferings of Christ." "And if one member suffer anything, all the members suffer with it," [2] so since Christ and the Church are one body, when we his members suffer, he suffers with us. Not of course in the sense that he can experience or feel our sufferings, but in so far as he reckons them as his own, since he lives in his members—"I live, now not I, but Christ liveth in me" [3]—so that it can truly be said that his Passion will continue until the end of time, so long as there is still one suffering member of his mystical body.

Hanging on the Cross, he looked down the ages and embracing in his outstretched arms all who were to be his brethren, he offered them with himself, their sufferings with his own in full and consummated homage to his Father. And as his prophetic vision is fulfilled in the unrolling of the years, we, his members, offering ourselves with him in the Mass, "fill up those things that are wanting in the sufferings of Christ." "As the church is the body of this

[1] Col. i 24. [2] 1 Cor. xii 26. [3] Gal. ii 20.

head " (Christ), says St Augustine, " through him she learns to offer herself." [1] His mystical body forms the " universal sacrifice," to use St Augustine's phrase, which the whole Church offers through the High Priest, therefore St Paul beseeches his readers to offer their bodies " a living sacrifice, holy, pleasing to God." [2] The same truth is enshrined in the prayers of the liturgy, wherein the Secret for St Paul of the Cross (April 28th) runs, " May these mysteries of thy passion and death, O Lord, bring upon us that heavenly fervour with which holy Paul, when he offered them up, presented his body as a living sacrifice, holy and pleasing to thee."

The practical consequences of this truth are clear. We need do no more than point out how important it is that the faithful should join all their sufferings with those of Jesus Christ, in order that, being offered with his, they may become truly sacrifices, being incorporated in and absorbed by the one infinite sacrifice offered by him in praise and satisfaction to God. And so we see again that the Mass is the centre of the Christian life, because in it the whole Church and every individual member share with Christ in the exercise of his two highest human activities and offices, in his royal priesthood, and in his victimhood, whereby he redeemed the world.

§ VII: THE ENDS FOR WHICH THE MASS IS OFFERED

TURNING back once more to the decrees of the Council of Trent, we find it laid down in the third Canon that the Mass is not only a sacrifice of praise and thanksgiving, but also a propitiatory sacrifice, and that it is rightly offered for the living and the dead, for sins, pains, satisfactions and other necessities. And in the second chapter we read that " the holy synod teaches that this sacrifice is truly propitiatory, and that by means thereof this is effected, that we obtain mercy, and find grace in seasonable aid, if we draw nigh unto God, contrite and penitent, with a sincere heart and upright faith, with fear and reverence. For the Lord, appeased by the oblation thereof, and granting the grace and gift of penitence, forgives even heinous crimes and sins. . . . Wherefore, not only for the sins, punishments, satisfactions, and other necessities of the faithful who are living, but also for those who are departed in Christ, and who are not as yet fully purified, it is rightly offered, agreeably to a tradition of the Apostles."

Praise and Thanksgiving

It will be noticed that the Council in its decrees lays but little stress upon the Mass as a sacrifice of praise and thanksgiving, but gives nearly all its attention to its quality and its effects as a sacrifice of propitiation. The reason of this is wholly in the circumstances of the time. The Reformers rejected the Mass but kept a ceremonial

[1] *City of God*, Bk. X, chap. xx ; *cf. ibid.*, chap. vi.
[2] Rom. xii 1.

celebration of the Lord's Supper, which they were quite ready to call a sacrifice of praise and thanksgiving. On this point there was no quarrel between them and the Church, and therefore the Council, concerned almost wholly with dogmas that were denied or disputed, made but passing mention of it.

But we cannot pass it by so lightly. Praise or adoration of God and thanksgiving to him are man's first and fundamental duty, apart from all question of sin and satisfaction. Adam before he fell was bound to adore God and thank him, and the all-holy Jesus Christ was not, in so far as his human nature is concerned, exempt from this duty. It is an essential condition of the relation between the creature and the Creator, a condition that can never fail or be removed. "The heavens and the earth are full of thy glory," and the life of the angels and saints in heaven is one never-ending act of adoration and praise and thanks.

Also it is clear that we are bound to offer God the highest adoration and the best thanksgiving of which we are capable and to express them in the most perfect manner possible. And for this end nothing is so well adapted as the offering of sacrifice. As St Thomas puts it: "Since it is natural to man to attain to knowledge through the medium of his senses, and most difficult for him to rise superior to the things of sense, God has provided him with a way of using these things for the commemoration of the things of God, so that, the human mind being incapable of the immediate contemplation of God, his attention may be the better directed towards divine things. For this reason God instituted visible sacrifices, which man offers to him, not because God has any need of them, but so that it may be made manifest to man that he must direct himself and all that he has to God as to his last end, and the creator and ruler and lord of all things." [1] And again, "Among those things that appertain to worship sacrifice holds a place apart . . . for the outward sacrifice is the manifestation of the true inward sacrifice whereby man offers himself to God, as the first cause of his being, as the principle of his activity, and the object of his beatitude." [2]

But no outward or inward sacrifice that mere man can offer is worthy of God, none can give to him the homage that is his right; even were man sinless, the abyss between the finite and the infinite, the creature and the Creator, is too wide for him to bridge. God, indeed, might condescend to accept man's offering, but that would not increase its intrinsic value, or bring it, by a single span, nearer to the infinite standard, which, alone, is the measure of what is owing to him.

But the Mass bridges the gulf. Just as the Incarnation spans the chasm between the human and the divine by uniting manhood with Godhead in oneness of Person, so Christ, by taking us into fellowship with himself in his mystical body, the Church, through Baptism,

[1] *Cont. Gentes*, iii, 119. [2] *Ibid.*, iii, 120.

and by sharing with us his priesthood, and making us his co-offerers of himself in the Mass, enables us to reach from earth to the highest heavens, to give to God a gift that is worthy of him, and to offer him adoration and thanks that, since they are Christ's and not merely ours, are fully equal to the infinite claims of the divine Majesty. The liturgy gives beautiful expression to this truth when the priest, holding the Blessed Sacrament over the chalice, and making with it a triple sign of the cross, says, " By him, and with him, and in him, is to thee, God the Father almighty, in the unity of the Holy Ghost, all honour and glory." All honour and glory, that is, perfect adoration and praise, because it is his act whose every act, since he is God, is infinite in its moral dignity and worth. Yet it is our act too, for we have our part in his priesthood.

It is for this reason that every Catholic is bound, under pain of mortal sin, unless there be legitimate excuse, to sanctify the Lord's holy day, Sunday, by assisting at Mass. There is no other way in which he can worship God as he should be worshipped, no other way of giving God what is his due, " all honour and glory." Hence wilfully to neglect Mass is not only to fail in duty to God, but is also to rob God, as far as lies in our power, of that perfect homage which is his right.

We have spoken of the Mass mainly as a sacrifice of adoration, but all that has been said applies to it equally in so far as it is a sacrifice of thanksgiving, and there is no need, therefore, to say more on this aspect of it, and we go on to consider it from the point of view of its propitiatory and impetrative character and effects.

Propitiation

Fundamental to the idea of propitiation is the reality of sin, and with this, the realisation of guilt. The sinner realises that he has trespassed upon God's sovereign rights and overturned the due and proper order of things, by refusing submission to God and trying to be his own god ; for the sinner, in reality, tries to put himself in God's place by making himself his own last end. As long as this subversion of the right moral relation of man to God continues, the divine sovereignty can only be maintained by God's exclusion of man from that intimacy of friendship which, in this life, is called the state of grace, and in the next, the state of glory and happiness in the beatific vision.

We express, imperfectly, this state of things by saying that God is offended with the sinner, or even angry, and that he must be placated or propitiated before he will take him back into friendship. That this way of speaking, which is both scriptural and natural, does not express the whole truth is evident when we remember the continual insistence of Jesus Christ upon God's fatherly love for sinners and his unwearying efforts to win them back. But it does, nevertheless, express a reality. Sin is a subversion of the right moral relation of the creature to his Creator ; something real is wrong that must be put right, and until it is put right, the effect upon man, so far as his final destiny is concerned, is the same as if God were really moved by indignation and anger. For there is opposition of man's will to God's, and where there is not oneness of will there cannot be the intimacy of mutual friendship, there cannot be a life lived in common ; and, since God's will must prevail, the effect upon man is exile from him, a life apart and deprivation of the end for which he was made, that is, final failure and consequent eternal misery.

As it is man who, by sin, overthrows the order set up by God, so it is he who must, as far as possible, restore it. By his rebellion he refuses to submit to God, to give himself and all he has and is to God. Therefore, in order to put things right, he must give back what he has withheld, he must make to God the offering of his whole self, mind, will, even life. Being man he feels the need of giving outward expression to this inward act of self-surrender, and this he does by the offering of a gift or victim in sacrifice. God, accepting the penitent sinner's surrender and sacrifice, is said to be thereby propitiated and placated, and receives him again into friendship ; and in truth, the subverted order has been really restored, what was wrong has been put right, union of wills has again taken the place of opposition and discord.

This is the merest outline of what is meant by propitiation. For a more adequate explanation we refer the reader to *Christ as Priest and Redeemer*.[1] Herein also it is set forth how, after man had sinned, it was Christ alone, the God-Man, who could make to God the satisfaction and propitiation necessary for the restitution of the order that had been completely overthrown ; that he did this by the sacrifice of himself which was consummated on Calvary ; and that in virtue of the solidarity that makes of mankind one family in the supernatural order, Christ's personal act is valid for all men, and his merits available for the pardon of all their sins.

But, though available for all, Christ's merits have to be applied to the individual before they can actually profit him, and this application is effected in many ways ; firstly, through God's sheer benevolence and mercy whereby he gives man numberless uncovenanted graces, without any action on man's part, and secondly, as an answer to prayer, through the agency of the sacraments, and through the Mass. The Mass, as we have already seen, is a prayer, the highest possible prayer of adoration and thanksgiving, but we are now looking at it from another point of view, we are considering it as a way of bringing God's grace to man by the process of propitiation. That is, we are looking at it not as the act of the person or persons offering it, but as a thing which, in itself, has the power of moving God to shower his graces upon us. We are looking at it not as something that we do, but as something that we give to God,

[1] Essay xiv, pp. 490 ff.

by way of compensation or satisfaction for our sins, and for which he gives us something in return. And although it is this point of Catholic teaching that the Protestant Reformers and their later followers professed to find so unscriptural and even so shocking, as derogating from the infinite value of the sacrifice of Calvary, it is easy to see that, rightly understood, it contains nothing to offend.

May we, without irreverence, put it thus? Jesus Christ, by his death, opened an account in the bank of heaven into which he poured the infinite riches of his merits, to be used for the relief of all men's needs. Every Mass is a cheque signed by him as Priest and Victim, signed with his own blood, stamped with the Cross, ranking therefore as the presentation anew of his sacrificial death, and therefore entitling the bearer to a share in the riches stored in heaven's treasury. Entitling him, because God, in accepting the High Priest's sacrifice, thereby agreed, and, as it were, bound himself to pay out from the account thus opened whenever it should be presented to him afresh. So far, then, from derogating from the infinite value of Christ's death, the Catholic teaching, in reality, proclaims and emphasises it by insisting on the fact that the propitiatory effect of the Mass lies simply in its power of moving God to dispense to men the treasures laid up for them by Christ.

Impetration

Closely bound up with the propitiatory power of the Mass is its power of impetration or pleading. Here the same principles apply. Jesus Christ "hath an everlasting priesthood, whereby he is able also to save for ever them that come to God by him, always living to make intercession for us," [1] by presenting himself ever as the immolated victim, and letting his glorious wounds plead that the price he paid may be dispensed with divine generosity to help men in their needs. In every Mass that is offered the divine victim thus stands in sacrificial intercession, and quite apart from the prayers that are sent up by those who surround the altar on earth, the divine victim pleads and is "heard for his reverence." [2]

We have now to ask what is the actual effect produced by the Mass as a sacrifice of propitiation and impetration. What fruits does it produce in men, how and in what measure are they distributed among various classes of recipients, and who, if any, are debarred from sharing in them?

§ VIII: THE FRUITS OF THE SACRIFICE

As the Council of Trent puts it, by means of this sacrifice "we obtain mercy, and find grace in seasonable aid . . . for the Lord, appeased by the oblation thereof, and granting the grace and gift of penitence, forgives even heinous crimes and sins . . . wherefore is it rightly offered, not only for the sins, punishments, satisfactions

[1] Heb. vii 24-25. [2] *Ibid.* v 7.

and other necessities of the faithful who are living, but also for those who are departed in Christ, and who are not as yet fully purified."

We shall deal first with the fruits received by the living.

Difference between sacrifice and sacrament

What must be noticed before anything else is that the propitiatory action of the sacrifice is very different from the sanctifying action of a sacrament. This acts upon the soul directly and is an efficient cause producing grace in the soul. It is something that we receive, God's instrument or tool, which he uses to engrave his image upon the soul, or if it be already there, to cut its lines deeper and more clearly. Not so the sacrifice. This is something that we give to God, in exchange for which he gives us a return, grace or the remission of the debt of punishment. Sacrifice acts, not upon the soul, but rather, though the expression be not strictly accurate, upon God ; not as an efficient cause, but by way of moral causation, in so far as God, looking upon the gift, his own Son's self-oblation, is thereupon moved to give in return.

How sins are forgiven through the Mass

What does he give ? To answer this question we must begin by pointing out that he does not give directly or immediately forgiveness of sins. As far as mortal sins are concerned, we do not think that any theologian of repute has ever taught that they can be remitted as the direct result of the propitiatory power of the Mass. This effect is produced by the sacraments of Baptism and Penance, and extra-sacramentally, by an act of perfect contrition ; and, by divine ordinance, cannot be produced otherwise. Yet all are agreed, in accordance with the age-long tradition of the Church, and the teaching of the Tridentine decrees, that the propitiatory power of the Mass is a most efficacious agent for obtaining pardon of sin. The Missal is full of allusions to this. Here are but a few examples. " May these sacrifices, O Lord . . . cleanse away our sins " ; " Grant . . . that the oblation of this sacrifice may ever purify and protect our frailty from all evil " ; " Regard the sacrifices which we offer thee . . . and by this holy intercourse loosen the bonds of our sins " ; " May these offerings . . . unloose the bonds of our wickedness." [1]

These prayers must be understood to mean what they say, and therefore we cannot follow those theologians who restrict the propitiatory efficacy of the Mass to the obtaining of actual graces by which the sinner is led to true penance and sincere conversion. Before the giving of grace for the sinner's conversion, there is something else to be done. However much we may try to avoid anthropomorphic ways of speaking of God, and however much modern sentimentality may dislike the notion of an angry and irritated God, we must realise and recognise that, at least, the effects of what we call God's anger are real, and we must insist that, in his dealings with man, his justice must be given as prominent a place as his love

[1] Secret, 3rd Sunday after Epiph., 4th Sunday after Epiph., Wednesday, 2nd week of Lent, Passion Sunday.

and mercy. For God is justice as truly as he is love. Now sin is an insult to God, an attempt to dethrone him, a refusal to give him what is his, and divine justice demands that, unless compensation be made or satisfaction given, the sinner be left unbefriended and finally cast off for ever. Jesus Christ made the necessary satisfaction; it is offered to God anew in every Mass, and thereby his justice is vindicated, his anger appeased, and instead of punishing the sinner as he deserves, instead of leaving him without help, instead of withholding from him the grace without which return to God is impossible, he looks on him with mercy and showers upon him all those graces which make true penance and conversion not only possible but easy.

A moment's thought will show that the worst punishment that could befall the sinner, in this life, would be God's refusal to give him the grace necessary for repentance. To leave him to himself is tantamount to issuing a sentence of final damnation. But until God's justice be vindicated by some sort of satisfaction offered by that individual sinner, or on his behalf, there can be no positive assurance that the divine mercy will assert itself in his favour and give him the help he so sorely needs. It is here that the propitiatory power of the Mass is exerted; the sacrifice offered for the sinner is the compensation needed, he is brought again within the ambit of God's effective mercy, grace is given to him, repentance becomes possible, and his conversion is now only a matter of his free cooperation with God.

Although we must distinguish in the Mass between propitiation and impetration, we cannot separate these two effects. They run together. As a sacrifice of propitiation the Mass, by making satisfaction for sin, appeases God's outraged majesty, as a sacrifice of impetration it moves his clemency; by propitiation it ranks the sinner among those who are to be helped, by impetration it causes him to become the actual recipient of help. The formal notions are different, the effect is ultimately and actually one and indivisible.

What has been said of mortal sin applies also, as far as the principles are concerned, to venial sins, to our daily faults, infidelities and negligences. The common opinion of theologians is that these also are forgiven only indirectly by the Mass, just as mortal sins. The reasons are the same, for although these sins do not put the soul into a state of enmity with God, yet they do put obstacles in the way of the free flow of his grace. These obstacles must first be removed before divine grace can work unhindered to lead the soul to that state of penitence and devotion necessary for the remission even of venial sins.

Remission of punishment

Besides the power of obtaining in this indirect way the pardon of sins, the Mass, as a sacrifice of propitiation, has also the effect of satisfying for temporal punishments which have to be suffered, either in this world or the next, even after the sins have been forgiven.

Hence the Council of Trent says that it is offered for "punishments and satisfactions." The consideration of this effect brings into our survey not only the living, but also the dead, those who have departed "in Christ but are not yet fully purified." But this effect is produced directly. Here we may usefully call again upon the analogy of Jesus Christ's heavenly deposit of treasure, paid over by him in satisfaction for the penal debts of men. In every Mass he now hands in upon the altar a cheque to draw upon this treasure and to use it for the actual remission of punishment justly merited by sinners.

For the faithful departed

So it is that, from the earliest times, while the Mass has never been offered for martyrs, since it was realised that they were in no need of help, it has always been the custom to offer the holy sacrifice for the rest of the faithful departed, for "it must not be doubted that the departed receive help by the prayers of the Church and the life-giving sacrifice." [1] St Augustine's moving description of his mother Monica's death is well known, and his testimony that her only request to her family was that "everywhere, wherever they might be, they would remember her at the altar," [2] is a witness both to the antiquity of the practice of offering the Mass for the souls of the dead, and to the firm hold it had upon the minds of the faithful.

Here arises a question of considerable interest, of practical importance and of some difficulty. There can be no doubt that, if we consider the Mass in itself, that is, not as our action who offer it, but as Christ's own body and blood, and sufferings and death, offered and presented anew by him to the Father, its value in the way of propitiation for sins and punishments and satisfactions is truly infinite. This point needs no proof; to anyone who realises what the Mass is, it is obvious. On the other hand, it is equally clear that the actual effect produced by any one Mass is limited. Otherwise the Church could not allow hundreds of Masses to be offered for one soul in Purgatory. She could not, indeed, allow more than one Mass to be offered for one soul, or in satisfaction for one sin. Whence, therefore, is the limitation?

Limitation of fruits

On this question theologians are divided. Some attribute it to a positive ordinance of God, holding that, for his own good reasons, among which is his desire to encourage the devotion of the faithful, he definitely restricts the effect produced. Little, if any, real support can be found for this opinion, which seems also to be intrinsically improbable when we consider God's loving desire to give all possible help to men; such an arbitrary limitation would seem to contradict all we know of his mercy and clemency.

Most theologians take another line, with St Thomas, and hold that the propitiatory effect of the Mass is proportioned to the devotion of those who offer it. This seems to be not only good theology, but also sound psychology, not to say common sense. For a sacrifice is a gift, and the acceptability of a gift and the recipient's readiness to

[1] St Augustine, Sermon 172.

[2] *Conf.*, Bk. IX, chap. xi.

give in return, although not independent of the intrinsic value of the gift, are more closely related to the giver's dispositions. The widow's mite stands for proof. So with the Mass. Its intrinsic value is infinite and invariable, but the dispositions of those who offer it, their zeal, love, hope, faith, confidence, are capable of almost infinite variations in degree, from the burning ardour of the saint to the grudging coldness of him who gives from motives of formality, routine or human respect. It is only natural, then, that the effect produced by the Mass, whether by way of propitiation or impetration, should fall far below its own objective worth, and have some proportion to the reality and intensity of the dispositions prompting the gift. This is not to say that the fruit produced is merely on a level with those dispositions; there are good reasons, chief among them the worth of the gift itself, for holding that it far exceeds them, but that there is some true proportion seems to be well established, although it is impossible to say what it is and how exactly it is to be measured. This is God's secret.

When the reader recalls what was said in the previous section about Christ being the first and principal offerer of every Mass, he may urge in objection against this teaching the perfection of his dispositions, and conclude therefrom that the Mass must always produce its maximum effect. It must, however, be borne in mind that a gift or sacrifice offered in propitiation or satisfaction must be offered for a particular person or offence. Its efficacy must be directed by an act of the offerer's will towards the special object for which it is offered. Now, as Jesus Christ has given us this sacrifice for our use and benefit, so he leaves to us the power of directing its propitiatory virtue whithersoever we will. Though, therefore, the Mass is offered by Christ its special application comes from us, and, hence, its actual propitiatory and satisfactory effect is limited and conditioned by the dispositions of him who makes this application, who gives the gift for this or that special object.

It is hardly necessary to add that, as regards this special fruit of satisfaction and propitiation, the privilege of applying the Mass for any particular object belongs to the person who provides for its celebration, that is, nowadays, who gives the priest a stipend with the request to offer the sacrifice for his intention, and therefore, the priest, having accepted the contract, is bound in strict justice to fulfil it by conforming his intention with that of him who gave.

Are they produced infallibly?

On one further point there is but little to be said. It is clear that the effect or fruit of the Mass, either as propitiation or satisfaction, is produced with infallible certainty. But, on the other hand, experience shows that the result wished for, as for example, a sinner's conversion, does not always follow. The reason for the failure is, of course, solely in the sinner's refusal to co-operate with the grace God gives him. Man must do his part, and if he will not, even a million Masses cannot convert him. This lack of dispositions cannot exist in the case of the suffering souls in Purgatory, and with them, therefore, the desired effect, whether it be the alleviation of their sufferings, or the shortening of their time of purgation, must infallibly be produced, limited, however, by the conditions already laid down, and also, perhaps, as many theologians think, by the degree and ardour of charity existing in the soul for whom the Mass is offered. Further speculation on this matter is profitless, for it has no sound foundation in knowledge. All we can do is to rest content with the practice of the Church, and sure that no fraction of the fruits of a Mass offered for a soul in Purgatory can possibly be wasted. God's mercy is our guarantee.

Who are excluded from the fruits of Mass?

When we ask who, if any, are excluded from receiving the fruits of the Mass, we must first of all make a distinction between the living and the dead. To take the former first, it is clear that as Christ died for all men, and wishes all to be saved, so all can be helped by his sacrifice which, whether as impetration or propitiation, can be offered for all. But the application of this general principle is conditioned by the fact that Jesus Christ instituted the Mass for the Church, to whom alone he gave the right and power of regulating and controlling the application of its fruits. She, therefore, has in the course of time made such rules as seemed necessary, both to ensure that the benefits of the Mass should be as widely diffused as possible, and also, on the other hand, to guard it against any risk of profanation or irreverence, and to avoid the danger of throwing her pearls before swine. This is not the place to examine these rules in detail; let it be enough to say that the Church encourages her children to be generous in offering the holy sacrifice for the highest needs of all men, whether or no they belong to Christ's body, the visible Church, that they may be saved from the consequences of their sins, and be converted to the true shepherd of their souls.

As far as regards the dead, the lost in hell are, of course, beyond all help. For the same fundamental reason, the blessed in heaven are beyond the need of help. The blessed have reached their last end, the damned have finally failed to reach it; in neither case is any advance possible, any growth in the happiness of the blessed, any lessening of the misery of the lost. We have, therefore, to consider only the suffering souls in purgatory. All need help, all can be helped. But, here again, the practical question is governed rather by positive ecclesiastical law than by general principles. The only point on which there is nowadays any dispute among theologians and canonists, is as to whether a Mass may be offered for an individual soul, who, during life, was not a member of the visible Church. But even those who maintain that this is still forbidden by the Church's law, yet hold that there is good reason for thinking that God, in his mercy, does not withhold from such a soul any part of the help it would have received if the Mass had been offered for it individually.

Among theologians many other points are disputed concerning

the distribution of the fruits of the Mass, and matters of contract and justice arising from the giving of stipends for Masses ; but these and other things, being hardly suitable for discussion in such an essay as this, intended for the reader unversed in theological niceties, must be passed over.

§ IX: SUPPLEMENTARY

Communion

APART from the few lines given to the matter in the fifth section, nothing has been said about the Communion, although, without a doubt, it is a most important element in the Mass, both in itself, and in its relation to the sacrificial character of the Mass. Nor is it our intention to speak of it at any length now. It is safe to say that the theory advanced, some years ago, by a few theologians, to the effect that the Communion contained the central and essential element of the sacrifice, has met with the fate it deserved, and cannot be seriously entertained. It is now almost universally conceded that the function of the Communion, considered as an integrating element of the sacrifice, is to express man's approach to God and union with him, by becoming a guest at his table, to symbolise the glories and joys of the future life, of which the sacrificial banquet is a figure and anticipation, and to express, likewise, the close union and charity that should unite, as in one family, all who eat of the same table. This symbolism is common to the sacrificial banquets of all religions. When applied to the Eucharistic Communion it becomes, of course, something very much more than mere and empty symbolism because of the Real Presence, but to deal with this would be to consider the sacramental effects of the Eucharist, which are outside our province and are treated in another essay.

One or two other points call for brief mention before we close.

The Epiclesis

In many of the ancient liturgies there is to be found a prayer known as the *epiclesis* or invocation which, on account of its form and its position, has been a difficulty to many and has led some astray. For whereas it is regularly placed after the words of institution, "This is my body," and the rest, it takes the form of a petition to the Holy Trinity, or in many cases, to the Holy Ghost, that by the power of God the bread may become the body of Christ and the wine his blood. Hence arises the question, which are the effective words that act as the instrument of God's power to change the bread into Christ's body, the wine into his blood ? The Catholic Church holds definitely that transubstantiation is effected by Christ's words, the words of institution, as is clear from the fact that in the Roman Mass there is no true *epiclesis*, and from her rubric directing the priest to kneel and adore the consecrated host as soon as the words of consecration, "This is my body," have been said ; and consequently, Catholic theologians teach, as we have already said, that the sacrifice in all essentials is complete as soon as the words of institution have been pronounced over the chalice, that is, as soon as the twofold consecration of the bread and wine has taken place.

Yet it must be added that, although the words of institution alone are operative in effecting transubstantiation and they alone, therefore, contain and embrace the essential elements of the sacrifice, it must not be inferred that the invocation, or indeed any of the prayers that make up the Canon of the Mass are superfluous or unnecessary. The whole of the Canon is the expression in words and actions of various aspects of the one sacrificial act which takes but a moment of time. But, owing to the very nature of words and gestures, dramatic expression must be extended through time, and the proper time relationship of the momentary act to its outward expression must inevitably be obscured, or even seem to be inverted. What has not yet happened must be spoken of as present, what is past must be expressed as still to come.

The foregoing pages contain but little more than an outline of a subject about which there is an immense and ever-growing volume of literature. Saints, fathers, doctors, theologians, spiritual writers, liturgists, historians have all found, and are continually finding, something new to say about the Mass, for in truth the subject is inexhaustible. We have, on the other hand, simply kept to the old, well-worn tracks. After all the highways must be known before the byways can be explored with safety, and indeed, for many, the highways must suffice for all the needs and adventures of life. To those who are still unacquainted with the highways of theology this little essay may be useful; to some others it may appeal as a reminder of the days when they first began to set out upon this journey of labours and delights.

B. V. Miller.

XXVI

SIN AND REPENTANCE

§ I: INTRODUCTION

The purpose of human existence

It is characteristic of our modern civilisation and a result of the ceaseless activity and speed of our lives that men think very little, if at all, about the purpose of their existence. They expect everything else to justify its existence, for the elementary notion of good and bad expresses the attainment or non-attainment of a due measure of perfection ; they call a horse good if it is sound in wind and limb, or the roof of a house bad if the rain enters in. But to the end or purpose of man himself many do not give a passing thought. He is in the universe, not knowing why nor whence, and out of it again " as wind along the waste."

Those who do not base their lives on a principle of religion attempt, perhaps, in a more reflective mood to erect a standard of conduct based on the attainment of some purpose in life : wealth, domestic happiness, scientific discovery, social service, philanthropy, or any other worthy object. It is not the immediate object of this essay to show the essential inadequacy of these things, nor to establish the supreme truth that in the possession of God alone is human happiness and perfection to be found.[1] But it is worth while insisting at the outset that a false idea of the purpose of human existence, by which we understand that which constitutes the final perfection and happiness of man, must inevitably lead to a false idea of the meaning of human evil or sin. It will be conceived by the humanitarian as an offence against humanity, by the materialist as a kind of disease, by the cynic as a breach of established conventions. The very worst thing one might say about it would be that it is inconsistent with the dignity of a rational being. But once granted that God is the end or purpose of human life, the true idea of sin becomes apparent. It is an offence against God.

The Catholic doctrine on sin and repentance has, for this reason, a more immediate and personal application to the individual than any other doctrine. For the sinner does not hurt the immutable God ; he hurts only himself by turning away from his Creator to things created. He introduces into his own being disorder and discord, and, unless he repents, he will remain for ever separated from God. Having failed to attain the only purpose of his existence, he is like a barren tree that is fit for nothing but to be burnt.

[1] *Cf.* Essay ix, *Man and his Destiny*, pp. 303 ff.

Cardinal Newman tells us, in one place, how the doctrine of final perseverance brought home to his mind the existence of two luminously self-evident beings: himself and his Creator. It is uniquely from the point of view of the relation between God and the individual soul that we are going to think about sin, not regarding it as something which brings poverty and misery into the world in general, but as a supreme evil which impoverishes a human soul by averting it from God.

There is a further reason why it is impossible to understand sin except in terms of the destiny of the individual soul. We have been created by God for himself, and in nothing short of the possession of God will the desires of our immortal souls find their ultimate satisfaction. What exactly this union between our souls and God would have been, had we not been raised to the supernatural state, is a matter of pure conjecture. A state of natural beatitude would doubtless have implied some intimate knowledge of God's perfections, mirrored in his creatures, and some corresponding degree of natural felicity, but the unaided powers of our human nature could never possibly see God as he sees himself, face to face. Such knowledge of God is altogether above the capabilities of any created nature, even the nature of the highest angel, for it is the life of God himself. Yet it is to this sublime and supernatural vision of God, not "through a glass in a dark manner, but face to face," [1] that God has destined us. He has adopted us into his family, given us a share in his own life, made us partakers of the divine nature.[2]

The supernatural state

God, being omnipotent, could have effected this plan of his divine goodness in many conceivable ways, but he has revealed to us the way he chose to work this mystery which has been hidden in God from all eternity. The real Son of God by nature became man in order that men might become sons of God by adoption; he deigned to become a sharer in our humanity in order that we might become sharers in his divinity. In the supernatural order Christ our Lord is the link between God and man, the only mediator, the firstborn among many brethren.[3] Through our union with him, branches of one vine, members of one body, our souls are supernaturalised by sanctifying grace, a beginning of the final consummation in the vision of God: "He chose us in him before the foundation of the world, that we should be holy and unspotted in his sight in charity. Who hath predestinated us unto the adoption of children through Jesus Christ." [4]

In the supernatural order in which we are placed sin has this effect: it deprives the soul of sanctifying grace and charity, banishes God who dwells there as in a temple,[5] and leaves the soul empty and desolate, deprived of its supernatural character as an adopted son of

[1] 1 Cor. xiii 12.
[2] 2 Peter i 4.
[3] Rom. viii 29.
[4] Eph. i 4.
[5] 1 Cor. iii 16.

God. "Behold, I stand at the door, and knock."[1] If, in God's infinite mercy, this ruined habitation is once again rebuilt and becomes once more the dwelling-place of God, it will be due to the divine initiative freely holding out the grace of repentance and converting the rebellious sinner again to himself.[2]

The redemption of Christ

To complete an initial understanding of sin and repentance, one more reflection is necessary. We shall attain our last end and happiness as sons of God in being made conformable to the image of his Son,[3] Jesus Christ our Lord, in whose hands the Father has given all things.[4] Whether the Son of God would have become incarnate if sin had not entered the world by the fall of our first parents, is a matter of theological speculation. But the fact of sin is certain, and it is equally certain that no created being could atone for the insult thus offered to the infinite majesty of God. If divine justice required a satisfaction equal to the offence, it was necessary for it to be offered by a divine person. From the first moment of Adam's sin a Redeemer was promised, whose office and dignity became more and more clear throughout the ages waiting his coming. When, in the fulness of time, God appeared in Christ reconciling the world to himself,[5] the prophet and priest, the model and king of all men, he had one supreme work to perform which so predominated in his sacred life on earth that his name was taken from it: "Thou shalt call his name JESUS, for he shall save his people from their sins."[6] We should not even think of sin and its disastrous effects on our own souls without thinking at the same time of Christ, bearing our infirmities, stricken like a leper and afflicted, wounded for our iniquities, bruised for our sins,[7] offering to his Father the fullest possible satisfaction for the sins of the world by dying on the Cross.

And if we should not think of sin apart from Christ's satisfaction, still less can we even conceive the grace of repentance, converting the soul again to God, apart from the merits of Christ, "for there is no other name under heaven given to men whereby we must be saved."[8] When a sinner is turned again to God, every step leading up to the infusion of grace is due to the merits of Christ, "in whom we have redemption, through his blood, the remission of sins."[9]

These essential notions concerning the purpose of life, the supernatural state to which we have been raised by grace, and above all the redeeming office of Christ, are, as it were, the background or setting upon which a more detailed description of sin and repentance can be placed.

The eternal law of God

On these vital premisses we can now proceed a step further. The *Summa Theologica* of St Thomas treats in the first part of God, in the second part of the movement of the rational creature towards God,

[1] Apoc. iii 20.
[2] *Cf.* Essay xvii, *Actual Grace*, pp. 604–605.
[3] Rom. viii 29.
[4] John iii 35.
[5] 2 Cor. v 19.
[6] Matt. i 21.
[7] Isa. liii 4.
[8] Acts iv 12.
[9] Col. i 14.

and in the third part of Christ who is the way by which the rational creature reaches God. Man's movement towards God, his last end and beatitude, is progressive, stretching over the whole journey of his earthly life, and on this journey he is assisted and directed in two ways by his Creator. He is moved internally by divine grace, for, as we have already recalled, his last end being a supernatural one, he is unable to attain to it by his own natural power. He is also directed externally by divine laws which are like signposts on the way. We must examine more closely this notion of law, because sin is intimately connected with it. No human being, not even the greatest sinner, directly and explicitly turns away from God his last end and highest good. He turns from his last end by turning towards something forbidden by the law of God. It is a point which is vital to the proper understanding of mortal sin, and we shall return to it in the next section.

Law is an ordinance of reason made for the common good and promulgated by the person who has care of a community. Whatever category of law we may consider, it is always a reasonable scheme or plan devising means to an end, but the will of the legislator must "ordain" and impose it on his subjects before the plan can be called law: the Budget is merely a scheme before it is passed by Parliament. Law is a plan designed for the good of the whole community, not merely for the benefit of an individual; in fact, laws frequently require the individual interest to be sacrificed to the common good. Moreover, since law gives rise to the obligation of observing it, it must be promulgated by being brought to the notice of the subject, and cannot bind unless it is known.

Now, it will be seen at once that this concept of law refers primarily to God who has care of the whole universe, and the authority of other legislators, no matter what the scope of their "community" may be, is derived ultimately from God. The plan of divine wisdom directing all actions and movements in the whole universe, including physical laws and animal instincts, is called the *eternal law*, and it is the fount and origin of the order in the universe.

The natural law

We are concerned now only with the laws of God governing and directing human beings. How are they promulgated and brought to our notice? We think at once of the Mosaic law, of the law of the Gospel instituted and promulgated by Christ "Rex et Legifer Noster," of the laws of the Church made by Councils and Popes under the guidance of the Holy Spirit, of the just laws of States, of the regulations of religious Orders and other smaller communities.

But, as a matter of fact, there is a law of God governing human beings, which is antecedent to any of those we have mentioned and of far greater obligation, which was binding on the Gentiles, who had never heard of the law of Moses,[1] and to which all men are subject even though they recognise neither the law of the Gospel, nor the

[1] Rom. ii 14.

authority of the Church, nor the ruling of the State. It is called the *natural law*, the participation and reflection in a rational creature of the eternal law of God, and therefore an expression in man of the very essence of God. God was free not to create human nature at all, but having created it he could not but assign to it the moral or natural law. Every created thing has certain well-defined tendencies proper to its nature, and man is no exception to this rule. Unlike the instincts and tendencies of irrational things, the law which governs human nature is law in the strict sense of the word, for the individual is able to obey or disobey, and is not driven along by blind inherent force. The endowment of free will, necessarily accompanying a rational nature, is man's peril as well as his chief glory, for in freely disregarding the laws of his own nature he is responsible for the resulting ruin and disorder.

This law of his being is called the natural law because it can be perceived by the light of reason alone, and because its precepts can be deduced by reason from the data of human nature. To analyse and explain the natural moral law is the purpose of the science of ethics, and we cannot do more than indicate the broad lines of the process. We find from the experience of our own nature that a human being is a complicated organism having many faculties and tendencies and needs. In the interplay of these various parts a certain subordination of the lower to the higher, of the parts to the whole, and of the whole to God, is clearly observed. Let us take a few examples. It is morally wrong to satisfy the desire for food and drink in a way which causes grave harm to the whole body or which obscures the use of reason. Certain faculties, as the power of procreation, having a natural purpose and natural organs for that purpose, it is morally wrong to pervert this purpose by sexual vice. Human nature is social and needs the society of other human beings ; all those things are therefore morally wrong which would make the maintenance of human society impossible ; for example, anarchy or theft. Lastly, human reason can establish the existence of God the Creator and ruler of the universe, a good and beneficent and sapient Being : that blasphemy and hatred of God are morally wrong is a necessary consequence.

In a word, the substance of the Decalogue, with the exception of the third commandment, is nothing more than a written expression of the natural law. If I tell a man to live according to his nature, to develop his faculties harmoniously in accordance with their natural objects, and to live in a manner befitting the dignity of a human being, I am merely telling him to obey the natural law which is a reflection in his nature of the eternal law of God. In telling a man to do good and avoid evil, I am telling him not to break the commandments of God. The two sets of ideas are mutually inclusive.

All this is the natural law. But man is raised to a supernatural state, and in everything which concerns the attainment of his supernatural end, human reason alone is powerless to discover the laws which God has devised for his guidance. He needs to be taught by God. Christ our Lord, who taught the way of God in truth,[1] has brought to our knowledge the necessity of Baptism and of faith and all the other precepts of the Gospel, and the Church continues to teach in his name.

But there is this further important observation to make: even with regard to the natural obligations of the moral law it is necessary for the majority of men to be taught by God; for human reason left to itself will discover the truth, at least in the less obvious precepts of the natural law, only with such labour and difficulty that very few men would come to the knowledge of it. Therefore, the Catholic is taught by the Church his natural duties, and in matters of great moment and difficulty the teaching authority of the Church defines the moral obligations of the faithful; for example, in the use of marriage. That teaching imposed on the whole Church is infallibly true, for it bears the stamp of divine authority.

Definition of sin

Sufficient has been said to show the meaning of divine law, the breach of which is sin. Inasmuch as every species of just law is reduced to the eternal law of God as its fount and origin, the aptness of the classical Augustinian definition of sin is apparent: "Sin is any thought, word, or deed against the eternal law, which is the divine ordinance of reason commanding order to be observed and forbidding its disturbance."[2] It is against this majestic ordinance of God that man dares to act in setting aside the natural law, or the law of the Church, or any other just law. But he cannot evade altogether the eternal law of God "commanding order to be observed," and it is of Catholic faith that the order of divine justice may require the eternal punishment of the sinner.

We may now make a closer examination of mortal sin. In order to avoid confusion and misunderstanding, we must remember that the word "sin" may be employed in various senses: we speak of "original" sin, of "mortal" sin, and of "venial" sin. Confusion will arise if we allow ourselves to think of these three terms as if they denoted three kinds or species of one genus, in rather the same way as we speak of any three sacraments sharing in the generic notion of external signs causing grace. The full nature of sin, in the sense employed throughout this essay, with the exception of the last section, is found only in *personal mortal sin; original sin* and *venial sin* share in that nature only incompletely and analogously. The complete malice and disastrous effects of sin are proper to personal mortal sin and to nothing else. It is the action by which a man knowingly and freely turns from God by fixing his will on creatures. How it is that an offence against the law of God necessarily entails the rejection of God will be explained more fully in the following section.

[1] Matt. xxii 16.
[2] Migne, *P. L.*, xlii 48.

§II: MORTAL SIN

The end of the law

THE eternal law directs rational creatures towards their last end and perfection in God. It is a union which will reach its final consummation in the vision of God face to face, and in this life consists in the mutual love between God and the soul, *charity*, the bond of perfection.[1] The end of the law, therefore, is God, to be loved by the rational creature as his sovereign good, to whom every created good must be subordinated. Hence follows this important consequence : wilfully to disobey that law is to prefer some created finite satisfaction to the infinite uncreated good which is God. To disobey God's law is to show by one's actions that God's will and good pleasure are not the predominant motive of one's life. He who sins grievously implicitly declares : " I know that by this action I am forfeiting God's friendship ; nevertheless I do it." What else is this than to prefer the creature to the Creator, one's own gratification to the express will of God, self-love to the love of God ? " The end of the commandment is charity." [2]

Sin the rejection of God

This might appear, at first sight, an exaggeration. It might be objected that the sinner does not weigh up the relative merits of the Creator and the creature, and decide in favour of the creature. He desires, indeed, to do something which he knows to be forbidden, but he does not regard it as his sovereign good and the sole end of his existence. No sinner directly intends to turn away from God. Such an act would be, in fact, impossible, for the human will necessarily turns towards its highest good and happiness : even a sin like the hatred of God is an aversion not from man's last end, but from God considered under some such aspect as the avenger of evil, and therefore conceived as harmful.

The answer to this objection is that the twofold element in every mortal sin, namely, the rejection of God and adherence to creatures, inevitably coincides in one act of the human will. Self-love and self-gratification in the forbidden enjoyment of creatures is the direct and immediate object of the will. The rejection of God is willed indirectly as involved in the choice of a sinful object. Theoretically the sinner may admit that the self-indulgence which he contemplates is shameful, that it is unworthy of a rational creature's desire, and that God's friendship is the only good infinitely desirable. Yet, in practice, he *acts as though* he regarded that self-indulgence as more desirable than God's friendship, since, in order to enjoy the creature, he is willing to forfeit the love of the Creator. By directly choosing the enjoyment of some created good known to be mortally sinful, the sinner elects to disturb the moral order of God to the extent of losing the divine friendship. He does not want to turn from God, you will say. He does so in turning to a creature, and he does so as deliberately and as inevitably as he who desiring to turn his face

[1] Col. iii 14.

[2] 1 Tim. i 5.

to the east thereby turns his back to the west. " They said, reasoning with themselves : The time of our life is short and tedious . . . and no man hath been known to return from hell. . . . Come therefore, and let us enjoy the good things that are present . . . let us fill ourselves with costly wine . . . let us oppress the poor just man, and not spare the widow . . . let our strength be the law of justice. . . . These things they thought, and were deceived : for their own malice blinded them, and they knew not the secrets of God." [1]

It is because of this double aspect in every mortal sin that its nature can be described in a twofold way. The essential element which makes sin the greatest possible evil in the world is the rejection of God, the love of self carried to the extent of treating God with contempt, the averting of the will from God by a voluntary recourse to creatures. In this respect all mortal sins are alike. But if we desire to discuss the relative gravity of different mortal sins, or to discover some process by which sins may be grouped into different categories or species, we must turn our attention to the positive aspect of sin, and consider the various finite objects for the sake of which God may have been rejected.

Distinction of sins

It is in this sense that the familiar Augustinian definition, given in the previous section, is to be understood. The difference between one mortal sin and another can only turn on the degree and nature of the subversion of the moral order, on the variety of thought, word, or deed against the eternal law of God. In each case the sinful act carries with it the forfeiture of God's friendship, loss of grace, spiritual death. A man is dead whether he has been dead a day, a week, or a year, whether he died by violence or disease, in youth or in old age ; but in each case the cause of death may be differently reckoned and determined. So it is possible for a human being wilfully to forsake God in various ways, according to the manner in which he departs from his law. Theft is an injury done to my neighbour, suicide is an injury done to myself, but each is an offence against God, because each is forbidden, though for different reasons, by the divine law.

We shall see in a later section that the act of repentance reflects this double aspect of sin. Just as sin is the averting of the will from God by a voluntary recourse to creatures, so repentance implies conversion to God accompanied by an act of the will detesting the sin committed. It is because this detestation of sin is an absolutely necessary condition for reconciliation to God's friendship that the Church requires us to confess, in number and species, every mortal sin of which we are conscious.

But are we to suppose that every breach of God's law is so serious as to deprive us of God's friendship ? Not so. We have already insisted that the full nature of sin is verified in mortal sin alone. There is a type of sin which is called " venial," and in a later section

[1] Wisd. ii.

a fuller analysis of its nature will be given. For the present we are speaking only of mortal sin, an act so grievously subversive of the moral order as to destroy the friendship existing between the soul and God, and to frustrate the end of the moral law, which is the due subordination of all created good to God, the infinite and sovereign good.

Grave matter

Before we can say with any degree of certainty that mortal sin has been committed, the action must *objectively* constitute a serious breach of the law of God. Is there any method whereby this may be determined? A Catholic, of course, accepts the authority of the Church in defining the moral law, and the Church, in fact, has frequently settled disputes among the faithful by an authoritative decision: for example, Innocent XI declared that the voluntary omission of Mass on days of obligation was a grave sin. There is also the very clear teaching contained in certain texts of Holy Scripture to the effect that certain evil actions exclude the doer from the kingdom of God,[1] or are worthy of eternal punishment,[2] or cry to heaven for vengeance.[3]

Human reason alone, granted the nature of mortal sin as destructive of the moral order and disruptive of the love of God, can establish that certain disordered actions are of this nature. Charity is the friendship existing between God and man. Even in human intercourse there are actions which merely ruffle the surface of friendship, and there are others which are calculated to destroy it altogether. So also on the plane of divine charity, it is clear that a man cannot remain the friend of God while blaspheming him, or refusing to believe his revelation, or declining to trust in his promises. And because the order of divine charity requires us to love others for God's sake as we love ourselves, it is equally clear that this order of fraternal charity cannot exist among men in the face of certain grave injuries committed by one man against another. On this double precept of charity the whole moral law depends.[4]

Mortal sins will also differ in gravity as compared with one another. Inasmuch as our whole lives are directed by the eternal law in order to bring us to the possession of God, a sin such as blasphemy must be extremely grave, because it is a much greater disturbance of the established order to insult the Creator than to offend his creatures. Similarly, if we consider the moral order imposed on man as a social being, the more precious my neighbour's rights are, the more grievous is their violation; taking an innocent life is a graver injury than stealing property.

It is on this basis of reason applied to the data of revelation that the exponents of moral theology argue that certain actions are to be considered as grave sin, and when there is substantial agreement between them on points which may be a little difficult to determine,

[1] 1 Cor. vi 10.
[2] Matt. xxv 41.
[3] Deut. xxiv 15.
[4] Matt. xxii 40.

the faithful can accept their teaching as certain. For the common theological teaching, owing to its practical influence on the use of the sacrament of Penance, is, in effect, the common teaching of the Church. But even the most careful enquiry often fails to secure certainty, owing to the complexity of the matter and the divergent views tolerated by the Church.

Advertence and consent

So far we have examined the subject, so to speak, objectively. But before any action can be considered as gravely sinful, not merely considered abstractly, but *subjectively* on the part of any particular individual, it is necessary for the individual conscience to appreciate that the action is morally wrong.

Conscience is a judgement of the mind, based on habitual knowledge, that an action is in conformity with the law of God or not. We cannot, in this place, discuss the many important questions concerning judgements of conscience which may be based on erroneous premisses, or be the result of invincible ignorance or scrupulosity. It would take us too far afield, and is not really necessary for a proper understanding of the act of sin. We will assume that the mind has formed a judgement that a proposed action is gravely sinful, in the sense that a serious obligation is involved, and that this decision is not warped by inculpable ignorance or by an abnormal mental condition.

Now, in order that a person may commit a grave sin, that is, an act for which the individual sinner must be held responsible, it is clearly requisite that the will should give consent to the evil, for without free consent there can be no responsibility. It is precisely on this point that doubts and difficulties often arise, especially in sins of thought. The matter is essentially one for the individual to settle for himself, though a prudent confessor can be of great assistance in removing erroneous notions and irrelevant issues, and in helping a person to resolve the doubts which may have arisen on the score of consent, by steering a safe path between scrupulosity and laxity. We can at least see this : the consent of the will is necessarily bound up with, and measured by, the degree of mental awareness or advertence existing at the moment. In a practical issue of such vital importance as mortal sin, the consent must be reckoned insufficient unless it is accompanied by that degree of advertence which is required for any other serious matter in human life. No one could be held bound, at least in conscience, to the terms of a contract which he had signed when half asleep, or when his mind was wandering, or when his judgement was unbalanced by the stress of a strong emotion which he had neither desired nor caused. Similarly no one can commit a mortal sin in these circumstances.

Temptation

We will suppose, then, that the requisite knowledge and advertence are present ; in other words, that a person knows a proposed action to be gravely forbidden by the law of God, even though the reasons for the prohibition are only vaguely perceived ; and, secondly, that he adverts to this knowledge, even though the consequent effects of mortal sin are not fully appreciated at the moment. The human will is now, as we say, being "tempted" to commit sin, and the temptation may arise either from the attractions of the world, or from the desires of our own bodies—the law in our members always fighting against the law of God [1]—or from the instigation of the enemy of mankind.

Faced with the temptation to commit sin, the will may take one of two courses. The evil suggestion may be rejected and repudiated. It may return again and again, even daily, throughout the course of our earthly life, and be rejected again and again. In this there is no sin, but heroic virtue. God allows it, "that it may appear whether you love him with all your heart and all your soul." [2] These temptations are the blows of the hammer and chisel forming in our souls the image of Christ, the measure of our ultimate enjoyment of the vision of God: "Blessed is the man that endureth temptation: for, when he hath been proved, he shall receive the crown of life which God hath promised to them that love him." [3]

Or, on the other hand, with the mind fully adverting to the evil of the suggestion, the will may elect to adopt it. At that moment mortal sin is committed. The cause of this disaster is not God,[4] nor the devil, whom we are able to resist "strong in faith," [5] but the human will, which has freely chosen to transgress the divine law, and by that action has turned away from God its last end and happiness.

The sinful action has been committed and, perhaps, completely forgotten by the sinner. But, until he co-operates with the grace of repentance, the effects of that mortal sin remain in his soul, disfiguring its supernatural beauty and perfection, and making it worthy of eternal punishment. "How is the gold become dim, the finest colour changed, . . . the noble sons of Sion esteemed as earthen vessels." [6] We have now to examine the state of the soul which has so lamentably fallen.

§ III: THE STATE OF SIN

In the present section we shall examine a little more closely the effects caused in the soul by mortal sin, for we can obtain a fuller idea of the nature of any cause by considering its effects. Mortal sin is a free act of the will by which we discard the love of God and cease to be united to him as our sovereign good. Within this idea of freely rejecting the friendship of God is contained everything we can say about the subsequent state of sin. These consequences are, doubtless, not always fully realised by the person who sins, but a little reflection on the data of revelation will bring them more clearly before

[1] Rom. vii 23. [2] Deut. xiii 3. [3] Jas. i 12.
[4] Ps. v 5; Jas. i 13. *Cf.* Essay vii, *Divine Providence*, pp. 240–241.
[5] 1 Peter v 9. [6] Lam. iv 1.

the mind: "Know thou and see that it is an evil and a bitter thing for thee to have left the Lord thy God." [1]

Guilt and stain

The rejection of God, which is sin, is an act performed by a free and responsible agent. The act once committed, the sinner remains in a permanent or habitual state of guilt or responsibility for the evil he has done in offending God, and, inasmuch as sin is a breach of the divine law, he incurs also the liability of being punished in order to repair the moral order violated by sin.

Passing over, for the moment, the question of punishment, we must explain in more detail all that is implied in the state of a soul guilty of mortal sin. For, in the language of Holy Scripture, the word "sinner" is applied to men not only at the moment in which the offence was committed, but afterwards, as a description of their condition of soul, a state which remains until the offence has been forgiven. It is a consequence of sin which is perfectly intelligible, and is evident even in the offences committed by one man against another. The offence and the insult offered to God remain as something imputed to the sinner until reparation has been made. Mortal sin is the turning away from God, and this state must remain until the sinner turns once more to him.

Now, to appreciate what this condition of imputability or guilt entails, we must bear in mind that God has raised us to a supernatural state, endowing our souls with sanctifying grace, making us adopted sons of God, temples of the Holy Spirit, and sharers of the divine nature. Accompanying this free gift of God are the infused virtues and, above all, the virtue of charity, through which we are united to God by supernatural love. Had man not been raised to this supernatural state, grievous sin would not have caused in his soul any kind of privation. But in the present supernatural order the soul is not united to God unless it is in a state of grace and friendship with him, and, therefore, the state of enmity with God means the loss of sanctifying grace and charity.

It is a deprivation often referred to in Holy Scripture as a stain on the soul,[2] filthiness,[3] uncleanness,[4] from which we must be washed by God in clean water [5] and in the blood of Christ.[6] The phrases are used metaphorically, but they convey an accurate idea of the state of a soul in mortal sin. "Corruptio optimi pessima": the better a thing is, the worse is its state of corruption. A corrupted animal is worse than a corrupted plant; a dead human body is more unpleasant to look upon than the body of an animal; a corrupted human soul must be the most ghastly thing in creation except a fallen angel. Uncleanness is a term which applies strictly only to material things, and it is caused by a pure and clean object coming into contact with something that defiles it. The beauty of a human soul

[1] Jer. ii 19.
[2] Jos. xxii 17.
[3] Isa. iv 4.
[4] Zach. iii 3.
[5] Ezech. xxxvi 25.
[6] Apoc. i 5.

consists in the natural light of reason, and, still more, in the supernatural light of divine grace. By mortal sin it is brought into contact with created things forbidden by the law of God, and by this contact becomes stained and defiled. It is a state of soul which can be considered as the darkness or shadow caused by an object, personal guilt, which is obscuring the light; the light of grace is restored to the soul by God's forgiveness of the personal offence which has caused the loss of his friendship. Hence, owing to the intimate connection between the loss of grace and the habitual guilt consequent on personal mortal sin, it is absolutely impossible for one mortal sin to be forgiven unless the guilt of every mortal sin which a sinner may have committed is also removed.

Debt of eternal punishment

Closely allied to the permanent state of guilt consequent on mortal sin is the debt of undergoing punishment for the sin committed. It is a debt, indeed, which the sinner may not be called upon actually to pay, since both sin and punishment may be remitted in this life through the mercy and goodness of God; but every sin infallibly carries with it the liability of paying a penalty proportionate to the offence.

Every law must have a sanction attached to its non-observance, and it is in the nature of things that anyone who acts against an established order is repressed by the principle of the order against which he acts. An offence against the military law is punished by military authority; non-observance of the law of the State is punished by the civil power; a sin against the moral order of God must necessarily by punished by God.[1] The punishment of mortal sin is twofold, thus corresponding to the two elements involved in mortal sin. To the rejection of God corresponds the *pain of loss*, and to the inordinate recourse to creatures corresponds the *pain of sense*. "Depart from me, you cursed, into everlasting fire."[2] The eternity of hell, so clearly taught in Holy Scripture, arises from the fact that the loss of grace is irreparable, as far as the sinner is concerned, and also from the doctrine that there can be no repentance after death.[3] The debt of punishment, therefore, remains as long as the will is turned away from God. The sinner has indulged his own will in seeking a created good, and justice demands that the violated order should be satisfied by his suffering something against his will in punishment. In breaking the eternal law of God he does not, and cannot, escape from it.

[1] The loss of grace being the immediate effect of mortal sin necessarily involves eternal separation from God, should the sinner die unrepentant. In this sense mortal sin is its own punishment. But it is essential to keep well in the foreground the idea of punishment as a penalty exacted and inflicted by God in vindication of the moral order which has been violated. Grace is a free gift of God, and, if a soul is deprived of it, the consequence of that deprival is a punishment inflicted by the author of grace.

[2] Matt. xxv 41.

[3] *Cf.* Essay xxxiii, *Eternal Punishment*.

Temporal punishment

The liability to eternal punishment is an inevitable accompaniment of the act of sin, and the knowledge of it helps the mind to understand, not only the malice of sin, but the mercy of God, who shows his omnipotence in sparing us. Let us for a moment anticipate the doctrine to be explained in the next section, and assume that by repentance the sinner is again converted to God's friendship. The guilt is forgiven and the stain of sin removed from his soul by the infusion of sanctifying grace. As a consequence the liability to *eternal* punishment, contracted by the guilt of sin, is completely removed, but it does not follow that the repentant sinner is freed from the debt of some *temporal* punishment. By mortal sin both justice and friendship have been violated. With the infusion of divine grace and charity the soul is restored to God's love and friendship, but the debt of punishment due to the divine justice remains to be paid, not in eternity—for eternal separation from God is inconsistent with being in a state of friendship with him—but in time. The same is true of human friendship which has been broken off by some act of injustice on the part of one man against another. The offence may be forgiven by the injured person and friendship restored, but there remains the obligation of making adequate reparation for the injustice, by restoring, for example, stolen property.

The sinner may escape the actual infliction of temporal punishment, but the debt is infallibly contracted by the sinner, and it is for this reason that an undertaking to make satisfaction to God is an integral part of the act of repentance. It is important to remember that when we speak of temporal punishment as an obligation infallibly and, as it were, automatically incurred, the statement is strictly true only with reference to punishment, at least, in a future state. The word " temporal " is not to be understood necessarily of this life, for it is a fact of experience that the wicked in this world often live in great happiness : " their houses are secure and peaceable, their children dance and play, they spend their days in wealth " ; [1] so much so that the rest of us who, rightly or wrongly, conceive ourselves as just, may be disturbed at the prosperity of sinners.[2]

The inevitable nature of the penalty exacted for sin arises from a consideration of the divine justice. In his mercy God may accept the vicarious satisfaction of others, and has given to the Church power to remit temporal punishment by applying to individuals the merits of Christ and the saints as satisfaction for their sins.[3] We can be absolutely certain that the obligation of undergoing eternal punishment is entirely remitted when grace is infused into the soul of a repentant sinner, but to what extent our debt of temporal punishment is also remitted we do not, and cannot, know with certainty. As for the sufferings of this life, a Christian tries to bear them patiently as

[1] Job xxi 9-13. [2] Ps. lxxii 3.

[3] *Cf.* Essay xxvii, *The Sacrament of Penance*, pp. 976–980.

making him more conformable to the image of Christ,[1] and he asks God to accept them as part of the satisfaction due to his sins.

These two things, the state of guilt and the liability to punishment, are the chief effects of sin in the sinner. The state of soul we have described would follow upon one mortal sin, and it is called by theologians *habitual sin* in order to distinguish it, as something lasting and permanent, from " actual sin " which is the sinful act. We have not used the term because it is liable to be confused with the " habit of sinning," or the inclination to fall into repeated sins from the force of habit.

Human nature wounded

But we cannot examine the effects of sin without including amongst them the " wounds " suffered by our human nature, primarily as a result of original sin, but also, with due proportion, in consequence of every actual sin committed.[2] The essential principles of our human nature remain intact, but our natural inclination to virtue becomes weakened by sin. That inclination itself will never be entirely uprooted, but we are so constituted that repeated acts of vice form in us an increasing facility or habit in respect of those acts. This is, indeed, an evident and a most lamentable effect of sin upon the sinner, and man knows from experience that after repeated sins the understanding becomes blind to its evil, the will is hardened in malice, resistance is weakened, and passion becomes more unruly. But no matter to what extent the sinner may be " wounded " in this way, whether by his own sins, or by hereditary tendencies due to the sins of his fathers, the essential principles of his nature are not corrupted, and he is able, with God's grace, to surmount these obstacles and lead a life of heroic sanctity.

Other consequences

Such are the effects of sin on the sinner. But in our journey towards God we are not walking alone, we are members of one body of which Christ is the head. We must remember the effect of sin on the passion and death of Christ our Lord, a reflection which can easily lead to perfect contrition. The sins of the world, including our own sins, were the cause of all the sufferings of Christ. One act of God made man would have been sufficient to satisfy the justice of God, but Christ was not content with anything short of a perfect expression of love for men, and there is no more complete sign of love for others than laying down one's life for them. So St Paul speaks of the sin of apostasy as " crucifying again the son of God, making him a mockery." [3]

Closely connected with this aspect of sin, on which every Christian loves to dwell, is the affront which sin offers to the mystical body of Christ, the organic union of all the faithful united to Christ their head by sanctifying grace. For, sin being the deprivation of grace,

[1] Rom. viii 29.
[2] *Cf.* Essay x, *The Fall of Man and Original Sin*, pp. 332–335, 352–353.
[3] Heb. vi 6.

the sinner is a dead and useless member of this body, a withered branch of this vine. It is for this reason, perhaps, that in the *Confiteor* we acknowledge our guilt not only to God, but to our Lady, the Apostles, and all the saints. For the sinner has disfigured the body of Christ, the Church, which God desires to be pure and glorious, " not having in it spot or wrinkle or any such thing, but that it should be holy and without blemish." [1]

Enough has been said about the state of sin and its effects to enable the mind to understand that it is the greatest of all evils in a human being. Just as honour is measured by the dignity of the person who gives honour, so is an insult measured by the dignity of the person insulted. In this sense sin is an infinite offence against the majesty of God.

If the knowledge we possess, from reason and from revelation, concerning the evil of sin, is to be a living force in regulating our own lives, we must, by continual meditation and reflection, bring it home to our minds. It is one thing to understand the meaning of sin, and view it with abhorrence in general, and say with David, " As the Lord liveth, the man that hath done this thing is a child of death." [2] It is another thing to hear the accusing voice of the prophet saying to us individually, " thou art the man," and to see our own sins passing before our eyes, each an object of our own creation and belonging to us more intimately than any other of our possessions. The personal realisation of sin is the first preliminary to repentance. Before the prodigal son in a far country was inspired to rise again and return to his father, he had first to realise his want and hunger, and to discover that his sins had degraded him to the level of swine.[3]

§ IV: REPENTANCE

THE vital element in every movement of man towards God is its supernatural character. Our final perfection and happiness in the vision of God is beyond the capabilities of any created nature, unless raised and assisted by divine grace. A sinful action which averts our souls from God entails the loss of sanctifying grace, and the return to God's friendship implies a reinstatement, a reinfusion of that same grace which makes us sons of God and joint heirs with Christ.

Initial divine movement

It is not our purpose, in this place, to study the Catholic doctrine on grace,[4] but, in order to understand the meaning of repentance, we must at least realise that although the human will is the cause of the loss of grace by mortal sin, yet the human will cannot, of its own power, repair the disaster and restore the intimate friendship with God which sin has forfeited. Such would be contrary to the whole concept of " grace " as something freely bestowed upon us by God.

[1] Eph. v 27.
[2] 2 Kings xii 5-7.
[3] Luke xv 11.
[4] *Cf.* Essays xvi and xvii.

The first movement of repentance comes not from the sinner, but from God: "If anyone says that without the previous inspiration of the Holy Ghost, and without his help, man . . . can repent as he ought, so that the grace of justification may be bestowed upon him, let him be anathema." [1] The mercy of God anticipates our own human action in returning to him: "Convert us, O Lord, to thee, and we shall be converted." [2] Illuminated by this divine action, we make an act of faith in God,[3] even though it be merely an act of faith in the existence of hell. Then, realising that we are sinners and hoping to obtain the divine mercy, we begin to have some initial love of God as the fountain of all justice, and because our sins have offended God we hate and detest them.[4]

The hatred and detestation of sin, the meaning of which is to be explained in this present section, is a necessary disposition in the sinner before he can possibly obtain forgiveness of his sins and be restored to the grace and friendship of God. For, although it is of Catholic faith that the first movement of repentance comes from God, it is equally of Catholic faith that the human will must freely co-operate with the divine action. "If anyone saith that man's free will, moved and excited by God, by assenting to the divine movement and inspiration does not co-operate towards disposing and preparing itself for the grace of justification . . . let him be anathema." [5] The actual grace of God, given to us solely through the merits of Christ our Lord, is necessary for disposing the soul to be received again into the friendship of God as an adopted son; the free movement of the human will hating and detesting sin is also indispensable.

Detestation of sin

In the present section we have to examine all that is involved in this act of detesting sin, which, from whatever motive it may arise, and whether made in sacramental confession or not, is called "repentance." It is an act which disposes the sinner to receive complete forgiveness, and it is simply as a predisposing condition to the infusion of grace that we now consider it. In the next section we shall see how this act of repentance leads to complete forgiveness and the infusion of grace, either through sacramental absolution or as a result of what is known as an act of perfect contrition, carrying with it at least an implicit desire for the sacrament.

If repentance is to have any value as a salutary act, that is to say, as contributing to the restoration of grace in the soul, it must consist of sorrow and detestation for our past sins as offences against the law of God, accompanied by the resolution to amend our lives and make satisfaction. Its chief characteristic, and one upon which all the others turn, is the voluntary detestation of, or aversion from, the sin

[1] Council of Trent, sess. vi, can. 3.

[2] Lam. v 21.

[3] Heb. xi 6.

[4] *Cf.* Catechism of the Council of Trent, Part II, chap. v, q. 8; Council of Trent, sess. vi, chap. 6.

[5] Council of Trent, sess. vi, can. 4.

committed. The doctrine of the early Protestant reformers, which is doubtless held by many non-Catholics at the present day, placed the chief element of repentance, not in the act of the will deliberately detesting sin, but rather in the change of mind by which a sinner, from being in a state of terror and remorse, now believes or trusts that his sins have been remitted through the mediation of Christ.[1] They regarded dwelling on the sins of the past, in order to detest them, and especially reflection on the state of sin with its liability to eternal punishment, as useless sorrow and hypocrisy.[2] Consequently the whole stress in the idea of repentance was placed on leading a new life, to the exclusion of making satisfaction, whether voluntarily undertaken or imposed by the Church, for the sins of the past.[3]

Quite apart from any consideration of the teaching of Holy Scripture, it will be seen that the Catholic doctrine is a logical and necessary deduction from the nature of sin, as we have already explained it, and it is evident also from an analogy with human friendship which has been broken off by a grave and deliberate offence. The sinner, having rejected God to find satisfaction in created things, cannot hope for forgiveness unless he first detests that which has been the cause of his separation from God, or is at least prepared to detest it as soon as it is recalled to his memory. If the evil of sin is understood, detestation of it is accompanied by sorrow when once we recognise either that the evil is actually present, or that it has been present at some time or other in our lives. The resolution to change one's life is excellent, and is necessarily involved in the act of repentance; but how is it possible to elect to change one's life, in the sense of avoiding sin, without at the same time realising that our former life was evil, and, if evil, a matter for detestation and sorrow?

So the great penitents in Holy Scripture are shown to us sorrowing and detesting their sins as a necessary prelude to the resolution of leading a new life and of making satisfaction. "I know my iniquity, and my sin is always before me . . . a contrite and humble heart, O God, thou wilt not despise."[4] "The soul that is sorrowful for the greatness of the evil she hath done . . . giveth glory and justice to thee."[5] "I am confounded and ashamed because I have borne the reproach of my youth."[6] In the New Testament, the tears of Peter[7] and of Magdalen[8] and the grief of the prodigal son,[9] are familiar examples of true repentance.

Purpose of amendment and satisfaction

Into this act of detestation and sorrow for sin there necessarily enters a resolution to amend one's life in the future, and to make whatever satisfaction the justice of God may require. We must not conceive the detestation of sin and the purpose of amendment and of making satisfaction as three entirely separate elements in repentance;

[1] *Cf.* Council of Trent, sess. xiv, can. 4.
[2] *Ibid.*, can. 5.
[3] *Cf.* Council of Trent, sess. vi, can. 13.
[4] Ps. l 5, 19.
[5] Baruch ii 18.
[6] Jer. xxxi 19.
[7] Luke xxii 62.
[8] Luke vii 44.
[9] Luke xv 21.

they are so joined and connected that one is not present unless the others enter, at least implicitly, into the act; that is to say, if a person is truly sorry for his past sins, he necessarily undertakes to amend his life and make satisfaction, even though he does not at the moment directly advert to these obligations. For it is impossible for the sinner really to detest sin unless at the same time he undertakes to avoid it in future. Similarly detestation of sin implies a realisation of responsibility in deliberately breaking the law of God. In sinning against God we are sinning against a legislator who has attached a sanction to his laws, both as a deterrent from future sin, and as part of the order of his eternal justice. In the previous section sufficient has been said about this liability to punishment incurred by the sinner, and there is no need to refer to the subject again. But, concerning the true sorrow and the true purpose of amendment which are involved in repentance, there still remain some necessary observations to make.

Qualities of true repentance and amendment

In the first place, the reason for which sin is detested must be in some way concerned with God against whom sin has been committed. It would be therefore altogether inadequate for a person to detest sin because it results in such consequences as the loss of reputation, or bodily disease; but any salutary motive suffices. Reflections on the disorder of the state of sin, the fear of God's punishment, even on the temporal punishments of this world, provided they are conceived in the light of faith as being inflicted by God in vindication of his justice, are adequate motives. Still more, such considerations as the effect of sin on the passion of Christ, the contempt and ingratitude and rebellion against God, and all the deformity involved in acting against his eternal law, are excellent motives for detesting sin. The supreme motive is to base our repentance on the love of God for his own sake, the act known as perfect contrition, which is the subject of the next section.

It is necessary, in addition, that the sinner should detest sin "above all things," as we say in the act of contrition. This does not mean that we must have *feelings* of sorrow and repulsion regarding sin greater than our feelings with regard to any other evil; for repentance proceeds essentially from the intellect and will, although it generally happens that our emotions share in the sorrow elicited, and there is a prayer in the liturgy asking for the gift of tears to bewail our sins. The phrase "above all things" means that in the judgement of the intellect we estimate sin to be greater than any other evil, and as a consequence of this intellectual judgement the will detests sin more than any other evil. Such a judgement and consequent detestation must necessarily follow from all that has been said about sin and its effects.

It is not only unnecessary, but altogether imprudent and unwise, to attempt to test the sincerity of this judgement by making comparisons between the evil of sin and the evil of undergoing some terrible torture, and asking whether the torture would be chosen rather than the sin. For an imminent sensible evil causes more vehement feelings of fear at the moment, and may interfere with the judgement of the mind. It is sufficient to prefer any evil in general to the evil of sin, without descending to particular comparisons. "The contrite sinner," says St Thomas, "must in general be prepared to suffer any pain rather than commit sin, but he is not bound to make a particular comparison between this pain or that pain. On the contrary, it is foolish to question oneself or other persons on the choice that would be made if confronted with any particular suffering." [1]

The detestation of which we are speaking must extend to each and every mortal sin we have committed. For each of them, taken singly, has grievously offended God; each one is sufficient of itself to cause the loss of grace and divine friendship. We have already seen that it is impossible for one mortal sin to be forgiven without the others, since in the supernatural order the remission of sin is equivalent to the infusion of grace into the soul. If the soul remains unrepentant of one mortal sin, it is not yet disposed for the infusion of grace. One must be careful not to misunderstand the meaning of this doctrine. God does not expect us to do what is morally impossible. Our sorrow is held to extend to all the mortal sins we have committed, even if, after a reasonable examination of conscience, some sins may have escaped our memory. Moreover, as will be explained in the next section, the act of perfect charity, by which the soul loves God above all things and for his own sake, so disposes the soul with regard to its last end, that it would at once detest any sin which is recalled to the memory, even though, when the act of perfect charity was made, the sinner did not explicitly think of any particular past sin. Detestation of sin is implicitly contained in the act of perfect charity.

To turn now to the purpose of amendment, it will be perceived at once that, if sorrow for past sin really has all the fulness which we have attempted to analyse, it must necessarily follow that the will at the same time undertakes to avoid that sin in the future. In very many cases of true repentance the mind does not advert explicitly to the purpose of amendment: it is contained implicitly within the act of sorrow and detestation, and it would be unnecessarily rigorous to require it to be made explicitly in each case. Why, then, must we subject the matter to a still further examination? Because the detestation of past sin and the purpose of amendment are so closely connected that, especially in cases of repeated sin, the purpose of amendment may be an indication of the sincerity of our sorrow.

For this reason it is advisable always to make it explicitly as we find it in the formula of the act of contrition. Moreover, whenever a repentant sinner, looking into the future, foresees the possibility

[1] *Quodlibet.*, I, art. ix; Parma, vol. ix, p. 465.

of repeating the offence, the omission of an explicit resolution to avoid it might argue an insufficient detestation of his sin.

Let us try to see more exactly all that is implied in this resolution. The will must firmly elect to suffer any evil in general rather than offend God again, either by the same offence or in any other way. At the time of repentance it is possible by an act of the will to make this firm resolution, even though the intellect, from past experience, foresees the possibility of sinning again. The knowledge that the same sin has been committed so often in the past need not exclude from the act of repentance a firm purpose for the future, especially when it is united to a strong trust in the mercy of God, who will not suffer us to be tempted more than we are able.[1] It must also be an efficacious resolution ; that is to say, the will must elect to adopt the necessary means for avoiding future sin, especially by keeping away from the occasions which lead to it.

Hence the practical value of a most careful consideration of all that is meant by the purpose of amendment. Repeated falls even into the same sin do not necessarily argue a defective purpose or a defective sorrow ; it may have been a good act of repentance at the time, though subsequent temptation, human infirmity, and the force of habit have induced the will once more to consent to sin. But, in a given instance, the lack of purpose in avoiding an unnecessary occasion of sin, which could easily be put aside, must sooner or later bring the repentant sinner to review his supposed sorrow, and to ask himself whether his alleged detestation of sin is an illusion. It is a momentous question to answer, for repentance, as we have described it, is a condition which is absolutely necessary for salvation in an adult who has committed mortal sin.

Necessity of repentance

Whether God, of his absolute power, could forgive sin and infuse grace into the soul of a person who has not repented, is extremely doubtful. But the question is not what God could do, but what he actually does in the present order of his providence, as revealed to us in Holy Scripture and defined by the Church. For while, on the one hand, it is certain that man could not, of his own power, attain to his supernatural end without the assistance of God's grace, it is equally certain that an adult who has come to the use of reason must reach his last end in a manner which is in accordance with his nature, by freely co-operating with divine grace. He must, that is to say, dispose himself for justification by doing what is possible for a human being to do. For a person who is in a state of mortal sin, the only part of the process of justification that is possible is to detest the sin he has committed. If he were relieved of the necessity of making at least this act of repentance, and so disposing his soul for the reception of grace, he would then perfect his being and realise the purpose of his existence without contributing anything whatever to the process. This would probably be intrinsically impossible, for it would

[1] 1 Cor. x 13.

not be in keeping with the order of things, as we know them, in which everything attains the purpose for which it was created by acting in accordance with its nature. The movement of God, in the order of supernatural grace, anticipates every human action : " No one can come to me except the Father, who hath sent me, draw him " ; [1] but it is a movement perfecting, not destroying, the free will of our nature, which must co-operate with divine grace.

The doctrine is evident in the pages of Holy Scripture, and from the lives of the great penitents. " You have said : The way of the Lord is not right. . . . Is it my way that is not right, and are not rather your ways perverse ? For when the just turneth himself away from his justice, and committeth iniquity, he shall die therein . . . and when the wicked turneth himself away from his wickedness . . . he shall save his soul alive." [2] Therefore Christ warned all sinners that unless they repent they will all perish.[3] The necessity of repentance as a condition for the remission of sin is absolute : " Repentance was at all times necessary, in order to obtain grace and justification, for all men who have defiled themselves by mortal sin. . . ." [4]

But if actual grace is necessary for repentance, it is a grace which is never refused to one who asks. " Converte nos, Deus," is a prayer continually found throughout the Divine Office, and there is a very striking prayer in the Missal which asks God in his mercy to compel our stubborn wills to turn again to him.[5]

Sin is disruptive of divine charity. By repentance the sinner detests the cause of so great a disaster. But of all the various motives which give rise to this detestation there is one which is the highest and noblest that the human mind can conceive. It is the love of God for his own sake.

§ V : PERFECT CONTRITION

Connection with the Sacrament of Penance

A PERSON tied to a post cannot reach another position until he is freed from his bonds. By mortal sin we are bound in a state of slavery until we break those bonds by repentance,[6] and are free to be united again in friendship with God. There is no middle state in which we can rest, as it were, in a condition of neutrality, neither in a state of grace nor in a state of sin. A sinner who has detested his sin and promised amendment and satisfaction has disposed his soul for justification, but he is not yet restored to a state of grace. With the effects of sin still remaining in his soul he still awaits the divine forgiveness which will effect complete reconciliation by the infusion of sanctifying grace. This grace is given solely through the merits of Jesus Christ our Lord, and the channel by which it reaches us is

[1] John vi 44.
[2] Ezech. xviii 25-27.
[3] Luke xiii 3.
[4] Council of Trent, sess. xiv, chap. 4.
[5] Secret, Fourth Sunday after Pentecost.
[6] Rom. vi.

the sacrament of Penance instituted by Christ for the purpose. In this sacrament a priest, authorised by the Church, and acting in the name and person of Christ, absolves the sinner from his sins.

We need not be concerned with discussing all the possible ways in which God could forgive sin ; we know from God's revelation that the sins of the whole world, even before Christ's coming, are forgiven through Christ, " in whom we have redemption through his blood, the remission of sins." [1] Nor need we try to imagine other ways in which the merits of Christ might have been applied to those who have committed mortal sin after Baptism ; we know that Christ, " who did all things well," [2] has left with his Church the power of loosing from sin.[3] By mortal sin grace, which unites us all as one body in Christ, is lost, and the soul becomes a dead and useless member of that mystical body. It was altogether fitting, if one may so speak of the actions of him " in whom are hid all the treasures of wisdom and knowledge," [4] that a sinner should be reunited to the body of Christ through the authority of that body on earth, exercised by men who, in spite of their own sins and unworthiness, are ambassadors of Christ [5] and dispensers of the mysteries of God.[6] And if we reflect more deeply upon all that it means to be a member of the body of Christ, we shall begin to see why it is that our sins will not be forgiven unless we forgive others their trespasses against us. Christ, therefore, has determined that the repentant sinner will find forgiveness in the sacrament of Penance, and unless sorrow for sin has *some* relation to the sacrament it will not issue in the infusion of sanctifying grace. But what this connection and relation is will differ according to a person's knowledge and opportunities.

Every Catholic is aware that perfect contrition remits sin even before the sin has been confessed. But this emphatically does not mean that it is forgiven apart from all connection with the sacrament. A Catholic, who knows of his obligation to submit all mortal sins to the power of the keys, does not make an act of perfect contrition unless he intends to confess his sins at a convenient opportunity. For since the sacrament of Penance is the method instituted by Christ for the remission of sin, no sinner could be called contrite who declined to do what God has laid down as the way to forgiveness : such an attitude would at least argue a lack of the proper undertaking to make satisfaction, which is a necessary condition of repentance. A non-Catholic, whom we will assume to be in good faith and inculpably ignorant of the obligation of confession, nevertheless establishes some implicit connection between his repentance and the sacrament of Penance. For in repenting of his sins, on a motive of perfect contrition, he must necessarily undertake, as part of his satisfaction, to do whatever Christ has determined to be necessary for forgiveness.

[1] Col. i 14.
[2] Mark vii 37.
[3] *Cf.* Essay xxvii.
[4] Col. ii 3.
[5] 2 Cor. v 20.
[6] 1 Cor. iv 1.

Implied in this purpose, did he but know it, is the resolution to confess his sins as soon as his conscience appreciates the obligation.

It would be quite erroneous, therefore, to suppose that there are various ways open to sinners in obtaining forgiveness, of which the sacrament of Penance is one ; for the Church teaches clearly and definitely that although perfect contrition reconciles man to God before the sacrament has been received, yet it does so only by virtue of the desire for the sacrament, which is included, at least implicitly, in the act of contrition itself.[1]

Perfect love of God

Contrition is called perfect when the motive which causes the will to detest sin is the love of God for his own sake : it is called imperfect, or " attrition," when the motive is something quite distinct from this love of God ; for example, the deformity of sin or the fear of hell. Any attempt, therefore, to understand more closely what is meant by perfect contrition, is equivalent to enquiring what is meant by the love of God or charity.

Any love—for example, the love of a son for his parents—can be of a twofold character. As a small child he loves them solely because they are good to him, a comfort in pain, a protection in the troubles of life, a never-failing source from which he draws everything necessary for his life and happiness. But gradually and imperceptibly this selfish kind of love should yield to a love which is more generous and is concerned more with giving than receiving, more with doing them some good than in self-seeking. The love existing between two persons who discover that they are mutually an advantage to each other is an excellent thing, but if the basis of mutual love turns on each person desiring and trying to do the highest amount of good to the other, generously, unselfishly, and constantly, there exists a perfect friendship, than which there is nothing more beautiful in human intercourse. Such love existing between the soul and God is so priceless and dear that we give it the special name of " charity."

Passing over, for the moment, any discussions that might arise, and confining ourselves to what is completely certain, we may say that contrition is perfect when its motive is a love of God, not of the mercenary kind, based on the consideration that he is good to us, but an unselfish love which we conceive for him because he is good and lovable for his own sake, a love whereby we rejoice in his infinite perfections, wishing him well, and desiring him to be known and loved by all men. When we speak of perfect contrition we mean repentance and sorrow for sin based on this motive : the repentance, for example, of the woman to whom many sins were forgiven because she loved much.[2]

In a less strict sense, although identical effects result in the soul, an act of perfect *love* of God in which there is no explicit reference to past sin may also be called an act of perfect contrition ; for it is

[1] Council of Trent, sess. xiv, chap. 4.
[2] Luke vii 47.

impossible for a sinner to elicit this perfect love for God without also repenting of his sins, did he but advert to them.[1]

In both cases, according to Catholic doctrine, the act of perfect contrition results in immediate justification of the sinner, it being presumed that all the requisite qualities of true repentance, as explained in the last section, are at least implicitly present. By the infusion of grace and charity the soul becomes once more a friend of God, a member of Christ's mystical body, and an heir with Christ to life eternal.

It must not be supposed that an act of perfect contrition is in itself the cause of effecting reconciliation with God, for this, since it entails the infusion of grace, is in God's free disposition and beyond the capabilities of any creature. But since God never refuses grace to any man who does all that he is able to do, it is altogether in accordance with his infinite mercy and goodness that grace should not be withheld from one who has made the highest possible endeavour to reach God that any creature can make. Perfect contrition, therefore, though not the cause of justification, is nevertheless so perfect a disposition in the sinner as to call infallibly for the restoration of God's friendship. God's love, it is true, has never faltered, for it is extended to all, even to sinners ;[2] yet friendship does not exist until love is mutual, and charity is nothing else than friendship between God and man. " If any man love me, my Father will love him : and we will come to him and make our abode with him."[3]

The Council of Trent, in expressing the constant teaching and tradition of the Church, takes it for granted that contrition, which is perfect through charity, reconciles man with God before the sacrament of Penance is actually received.[4] The doctrine is certain if by charity is meant the love of God because he is good in himself, not merely because he is good to us. It is only contrition elicited on this motive which is properly called " perfect," and which, in the teaching of the Church, certainly leads to justification.[5]

[1] It is doubtful, however, whether the sorrow for past sin implicitly contained in an act of perfect love of God suffices for the effect of the sacrament of Penance, since, as is explained in Essay xxvii, the sorrow of the penitent is part of the " matter " of this sacrament.

[2] Rom. v 8 ; 1 John iv 10.

[3] John xiv 23.

[4] Sess. xiv, chap. iv.

[5] Some writers, wishing to render an act of perfect contrition as easy as possible, allow the possibility of perfect contrition in the love of God for selfish motives, *i.e.*, because union with him constitutes eternal happiness for us, or because our souls are even now thirsting for the living God like the hart panting after the fountains of water (Ps. xli 1). But this cannot be regarded with certainty as sufficient for an act of perfect contrition, and in a matter of such grave moment we cannot be satisfied with anything less than certainty. Such lesser motives are excellent : they help the sinner to detest sin above all things, and they lead to perfect contrition. But we cannot help seeing on reflection that there is very little difference between love of God, conceived for a selfish motive, and the fear of hell. It is salutary sorrow for sin, but is imperfect, not perfect.

Imperfect love of God

For the word " perfect " implies that nothing is wanting in the action, and that its fulness is complete and entire. But if the motive of contrition is anything short of God's own self, it is evidently not as perfect as it might be.[1] Thus an imperfect motive of contrition might easily be the desire to render to God something due to him, on a title of justice, obedience, or gratitude. It can be understood, from an analogy with purely human relations, that a man might be ready to make reparation to another because he is in his debt or subject to his authority, or because he has received favours from his hands. Yet, while doing this, he might feel wholly unable to regret his offence out of regard for the personal qualities and excellence of the other person.

Still more easily can it be seen that to seek reconciliation with an injured friend, because the loss of his friendship is a grave inconvenience, is a motive which leaves an enormous amount to be desired. Nevertheless, as will be shown more fully in the essay on *The Sacrament of Penance*,[2] the fear of hell, or any other less noble motive leading us to detest sin, suffices, provided the sacrament is not merely desired but actually received. The only point necessary to notice here is that the justification of the sinner, whether in the case of perfect contrition or in the reception of the sacrament of Penance, is brought about in both cases by the infusion of sanctifying grace. But the means by which that grace is given is in one case the reception of a sacrament of the New Law, one of the seven signs instituted by Christ as channels of divine grace, external signs which by virtue of their own action as instruments in the hands of Christ convey grace from the head to the members of his body. In the other case the grace of justification is given to a man who by his own activity, under the divine inspiration, has so disposed his soul by doing all that it is possible for him to do, that God immediately gives the grace of his friendship.

The more perfect our contrition is, in receiving the sacrament, the more pleasing it is to God and the more grace is received. For a soul already justified by perfect contrition, in receiving the sacrament receives still more grace, and becomes more deeply rooted and grounded in charity.

How to make an act of perfect contrition

It should therefore be our constant care to make more and more perfect the motive of our sorrow for sin. It is difficult in the sense that perfect contrition requires complete detachment from our sins, and careful reflection on divine things, which in the modern rush of life is not always easy to secure ; it is difficult, too, because it is not

[1] It is, of course, possible to elicit perfect contrition by a consideration of any one *attribute* of God—his benignity or his mercy, for example—provided it is considered as a divine perfection, and not merely as something very advantageous to ourselves. The reason for this is that the attributes of God, which the human mind regards separately, are not really distinct in God. *Cf*. Essay iii, *The One God*, p. 92.

[2] P. 971.

easy to break away from selfish and excessive preoccupation with our own advantage and happiness, even in matters religious. But, granted a certain degree of generosity towards God, it should be comparatively easy gradually to purify our motives and arrive almost imperceptibly at perfect contrition.

In a matter that concerns so intimately the internal dispositions of each soul it is not possible to suggest any definite rule : each person must follow the line of thought which is most suitable in leading him to perfect contrition. The fear of God is the beginning of all wisdom, and the thought of eternal separation from God would usually be the starting-point. A further step would be to think of the pain of loss as being inflicted by one who loves us with infinite love. Sin is an offence and an insult against God, for whom we should have nothing but gratitude in return for all his favours, both spiritual and temporal, and above all for his unspeakable gift of grace by which we are made his adopted sons in Christ.[1] " How hath he not also with him given us all things ? "[2] Have we made any return for these gifts, or are all our prayers invariably petitions for further favours ? God has been good to us, but why ? Not because there is anything beautiful or lovable about us apart from our union with Christ, for whose sake God loves us.[3] No matter how we look at it, there is nothing in us that we have not received from God,[4] nothing intrinsic to our own deeds to cause God to treat us with such benignity. Why, then, is God good to us ? For no other reason than because he is good in himself.

Nor is this divine goodness something abstract which we can get to know and understand only by a process of philosophic thought. He was made flesh and dwelt amongst us, grew weary in seeking us, shed tears for us, suffered and died for us. Yet this infinite goodness we have insulted and offended by mortal sin. . . . By such gradual and easy steps as these it is possible to develop the motive of contrition from the notion of fear to that of love of God for his own sake. It is only on elevated motives of this kind that we can gradually perfect our lives, not only by avoiding mortal sin, but by gradually eliminating all trace even of deliberate venial sin. Most of all, it is on this motive alone that we shall begin to understand the infinite mercy of God in granting the gift of repentance, from its first stirring in our souls to its completion in the infusion of divine grace. For it is chiefly by sparing and having mercy upon us that God manifests his almighty power.[5]

§ VI: VENIAL SIN

A sin consistent with grace and charity

WE have already recalled the fact that the word " sin " is used only analogously of venial offences.[6] That is to say, there is a certain resemblance between mortal sin and venial sin, inasmuch as each is an

[1] 2 Cor. ix 15. [2] Rom. viii 32. [3] John xvi 27. [4] 1 Cor. iv 7.
[5] Collect, Eleventh Sunday after Pentecost. [6] Above, p. 924.

offence against the law of God. There is, however, a vital difference between them, and that difference it is our object here to explain.

Christ our Lord in his parables often likened the life of our souls to the growth of plants or trees. In the case of these it is often possible to detect some radical defect or disease which will prevent them from ever reaching maturity. Sometimes, on the other hand, one may find minor blemishes—say in a rose-tree, which will not hinder its ultimate blossoming, but which make it less lovely and beautiful in the eyes of an expert. It would be true to say that the law of the plant's growth requires the absence not only of radical disease, but of minor defects also. But it would be much more accurate to regard as, strictly speaking, *against* the law of its nature only those defects which prevent its growth to maturity. No one could refuse to call it a rose-tree simply because the scent and colour of its blossoms were not up to the desired standard.

It is rather similar with the individual soul. It would be true to say that the slightest transgression is against the law of God, but it would be much more accurate to say that only those breaches of the law are to be regarded, in the strict sense of the words, as *against* the law of God which prevent a man from attaining his last end; that is to say, only those sins which are disruptive of divine charity, and which entail the loss of grace and the liability to eternal separation from God.

Like all examples taken to illustrate doctrines, the example of a plant's growth is necessarily imperfect, but it serves to explain the difference between mortal and venial sin. There are many minor offences, forbidden indeed by the law of God, but which do not so radically upset the established moral order as to make the attainment of man's last end impossible. They offend God, but do not offend him to the extent of breaking off the union of charity existing between our souls and him; and since union with God is the end of our existence, they are not strictly against the law of God.

If it is asked why this is so, one can only answer by asking why it is that the germs of certain diseases will utterly prevent a plant from growing to maturity, while other noxious germs are not so destructive. God has so fashioned human nature, and so raised it to a supernatural state, that certain culpable departures from the law which governs man's being have the effect of preventing his end and purpose in life from being realised. "Thy hands have made me and formed me: give me understanding, and I will learn thy commandments." [1]

Man may wilfully transgress the divine law in various ways, but, provided the principle of his supernatural life is not destroyed, he still remains properly disposed towards God, his last end and happiness, and the effects of such actions are not of their nature irreparable,

[1] Ps. cxviii 73.

precisely because the principle of divine grace and charity is not lost. Thus a mathematician engaged in the solution of a difficult problem may make small errors, but, if the principles on which his calculations rest are sound, he can easily retrace his steps and correct the mistakes he has made. Even the healthiest persons suffer some disease or illness at some time or other, but their own strength and vitality suffice to enable them to recover from the ill effects; if, however, the disease is one which has destroyed the life of some vital organ, then nothing short of a miracle will restore them to health.

Those sins, therefore, which do not involve the loss of grace, and whose effects can be repaired by the supernatural principle of grace and charity, which still remain in the soul, are called "venial." The word itself, which is derived from *venia*, "pardon," could equally be used, and was so used by early writers, with reference to repented mortal sin, for there is no sin which God will not forgive. But, inasmuch as the liability to eternal punishment, the necessary effect of mortal sin, is not incurred except by the loss of grace, any sin which does not merit eternal punishment is of its nature worthy of pardon, and the term "venial" is properly applied to it. For no matter how long or how grievous the temporal punishment due to such sins may be, the soul must inevitably reach its last end, as long as it does not suffer the loss of sanctifying grace. He who sins venially is retarded on his journey towards God, but, unlike a person in mortal sin who is averted from his last end, he remains on the way which leads to God and will eventually possess him. "For although, during this mortal life, men, no matter how holy and just they may be, fall daily into small sins, which are called venial, they do not thereby cease to be just."[1]

If, therefore, we compare venial and mortal sin from the point of view of their effects on the soul, the complete difference between the two is apparent. But when we examine venial sin from the angle of the person sinning, it appears, at first sight, that in electing to turn inordinately to creatures in a manner forbidden by the divine law, the sinner shows that, in putting his own will above the will of God, he is choosing some creature instead of God.

If this conclusion were true and necessary it would be difficult to see how venial sin differs from mortal sin. The phrase "the will of God" means, however, in this connection, something which God has forbidden, and we cannot draw any conclusions at all until we have determined whether a thing is forbidden by God under the pain of forfeiting the divine friendship or not. Acts forbidden as venial sins are of such character that they do not forfeit the divine friendship, and it is because the sinner is aware of this that it is possible for him to offend God and at the same time remain united to him.

The same is true of human friendships. A person might easily displease his friend in many minor matters, but would never run

[1] Council of Trent, sess. vi, chap. 9.

the risk of destroying the friendship altogether by doing things which he foresaw would have this result. So also in the case of a person committing venial sin. He is so disposed towards God that if he thought that a breach of the divine law would result in the loss of divine grace and charity, he would not commit it for any reason whatever.

From such considerations as these it will be evident that an erroneous conscience has a most important influence in determining the existence of mortal sin. If a person is so invincibly ignorant that he is in good faith in thinking that an action which is objectively grave is no more than venial sin, then venial sin is actually committed owing to the error. Similarly the persuasion that an action is mortally sinful constitutes mortal sin in the person who commits it, even though his mind was in error in making the judgement.

Also it is most important to recall the necessity of advertence and consent for mortal sin even when there is no sort of error concerning the objective malice of the offence. It can be said with certainty that many offences fall short of the complete malice of mortal sin owing to the consent being, on various counts, defective. We talk of " falling into " mortal sin, but no one can fall into it in the sense of doing it accidentally and unawares. It can be said with equal certainty that the real issue is known to God alone, the searcher of hearts. Unless the venial or mortal nature of a sin is abundantly evident, it is a dangerous procedure for the human mind to attempt to diagnose the guilt, even in one's own sins ; and still more dangerous regarding the sins of other people. There are numerous cases in which the border-line cannot be accurately determined ; for example, in deciding on the consent given to evil thoughts, or in determining the gravity of theft. The only safe rule is expressly to repent of any sin which might conceivably be grave, and to confess it as such.

Effects Let us now examine more closely the effects of venial sin upon the soul. In the first place, sanctifying grace is not lost by any offence short of mortal sin, and, inasmuch as the " stain " of sin is nothing else than the privation of grace, it follows that venial sin does not, strictly speaking, cause a stain, which we have already seen to be the consequence of mortal sin.[1]

Venial sin is opposed to the charity which should exist between the soul and God, not in the sense that it is inconsistent with the habitual state of grace by which we are united to God's love through a vivifying union with Christ, but in the sense that the acts prompted by the virtue of charity are rendered by venial sin less fervent in their expression.

The distinction turns on the difference between habitual grace with the attendant virtue of charity, which every soul well ordered towards its last end possesses, and the fervour of the acts elicited by the soul in that state. The effect of mortal sin is to destroy habitual

[1] Above, pp. 930 ff.

grace and charity, a privation which is called in the Scriptures the stain of sin ; the effect of venial sin is to impede the fervour of the acts of a person, who, while possessing the intrinsic state of friendship with God, nevertheless directs his actions to the attainment of his last end only remissly and tardily.

Just as the word " sin " applies strictly to mortal sin and only analogously to venial sin, so also, if we prefer to use the word " stain " in order to express the effect of venial sin on the soul, it can be used only analogously and imperfectly. There is all the difference in the world between a child who cannot leap and jump owing to a crippled state of limb, and one who is merely suffering from languor and disinclination. In the one case it is due to a permanent and habitual disorder, in the other case the lassitude can be overcome with a little effort. We must therefore remove altogether from our consideration of venial sin and its effects the notion of stain resulting from the privation of grace, and, as a consequence, the liability to eternal punishment incurred by a soul in that state. We can see that from venial sin there results in the sinner the obligation of acknowledging his guilt and the debt of punishment. There is guilt because venial sin is a breach of the divine law and displeases God, though not to the extent of destroying his friendship. There is also the debt of punishment, for the divine order has been disturbed and the sinner must restore that order by undergoing a penalty proportionate to the offence, even though the punishment is of a temporal nature.

These two things, guilt and punishment, are the two immediate effects of venial sin. But before we discuss repentance as applied to these offences we must be aware of certain possibilities arising from deliberate venial sin. It is very necessary to establish a clear and definite division between mortal and venial sin, but in doing so we must beware lest the mind imperceptibly and almost unconsciously should form a judgement that venial sin is a trifling matter of no consequence whatever.

The remarks we have to make apply only to deliberate offences. We have already seen [1] that venial sin may arise from insufficient advertence and consent, fleeting thoughts, sudden access of passion, unthinking and indeliberate movements which are rejected almost as soon as they are experienced. With regard to venial sins of this kind it is the accepted teaching of the Church that not even the holiest person can altogether avoid them. But with deliberate venial sin—a small theft, for example—our judgement must be altogether different.

It follows from the nature of venial sin that no number of such offences will ever be equivalent to one mortal sin. But indirectly, and as a consequence, deliberate venial sin will lead to mortal sin. *Nemo fit repente pessimus*—nobody becomes evil all at once. It is a slow and gradual process which leads the will eventually to commit mortal sin. Deliberate transgression of the law of God in small

[1] Pp. 928–929.

matters causes a habit of mind which grows accustomed to deflections from the moral order, and gradually disposes the sinner to depart from it in a serious matter. Imperceptibly a state of mind is generated which is set on discovering to what extent the law of God can be broken without committing grave sin. It is betrayed by a certain theological dexterity in trying to discover the least obligation consistent with remaining in a state of grace. Is it necessary to point out that a person walking on the edge of a precipice is in danger of falling over ? " He that is faithful in that which is least is faithful also in that which is greater : and he that is unjust in that which is little is unjust also in that which is greater." [1] It is because we are creatures of habit, and because each deliberate sin paves the way to one slightly graver, that spiritual writers often refer to venial sin in terms which to the unthinking appear exaggerated. There is no need of warning from spiritual writers. Everyone knows from his own experience, and from the experience of others, that the commission of mortal sin is the result of a series of deliberate transgressions in smaller matters.

The important thing is to purge the soul from what St Francis de Sales calls the " affection " for venial sin, which he describes as the chief obstacle to that devotion which consists in a ready and willing service of God. " They weaken the strength of the spirit, hinder the divine consolations, open the door to temptations, and, although they do not kill the soul, make it excessively ill." [2]

Remission

Perhaps there is nothing which so completely illustrates the essential difference between mortal and venial sin as an enquiry into the various ways by which venial sin can be remitted. The Catholic doctrine regarding the remission of mortal sin turns, as we have seen, on the sacrament of Penance, which in the present order is the way determined by God for reconciliation with him. If the sinner repents of mortal sin, in the sense explained above, even though it be only through fear of God's punishment, he is in the salutary disposition for justification. By the divine mercy the absolution of a priest authorised by the Church restores the repentant sinner to a state of grace and friendship with God, and if the motive of contrition is the love of God above all things, the soul is immediately justified, even before the sacrament is received, provided it is at least implicitly desired.[3]

Inasmuch as the state of mortal sin is equivalent to the loss of sanctifying grace, and the infusion of grace is identical with the remission of mortal sin, the doctrine concerning the remission of mortal sin can be easily understood and clearly formulated. But it is not possible to state with quite the same directness the method by which the guilt of venial sin is remitted, for venial sin is not accompanied by the loss or diminution of habitual grace and charity ; it causes the

[1] Luke xvi 10.

[2] *Devout Life*, Bk. I, chap. xxii.

[3] See above, pp. 941 ff.

acts elicited by a person in the state of grace to be lessened in fervour; it does not destroy charity, but merely impedes its exercise. It is because the effects of venial sin are of this character that it is difficult to state the doctrine concerning their remission, for the effects must necessarily differ with the individual, and will depend very largely on the degree of virtue and sanctity which has been attained; whereas the effects of mortal sin, as far as the loss of grace is concerned, are identical in all sinners. Nevertheless, on the data already examined, it is possible to outline the ordinary theological teaching.

It is needless to say that venial sin is adequate and sufficient matter for sacramental absolution. This is the simplest and most obvious way of securing forgiveness from God, and is universally practised by the faithful throughout the whole Church. But, inasmuch as venial sins can be remitted in other ways, there exists no obligation to confess them in the tribunal of penance. Furthermore, and as a consequence of this certain doctrine, an act of perfect contrition remits venial sin without any sort of clause or condition referring to the future reception of the sacrament of penance.

We have seen that the sinner, in repenting of mortal sin, is bound to use sufficient diligence to recall the mortal sins that he has committed, in order to repent of each one that he remembers. But, since venial sins need not necessarily be confessed—there being various other ways in which they may be remitted—they need not each be recalled to mind. This does not mean that repentance is unnecessary for venial sin. It means only that the repentance need not be explicit in respect of each venial sin that we have committed. Such explicit repentance is indeed desirable; but it is sufficient that we be prepared explicitly to repent should such venial sins be recalled to mind. A further difference between repentance for mortal sin and repentance for venial sin should be noted: it is possible to repent of one venial sin without repenting of the others, whereas in the case of mortal sin this is not possible.[1] Apart from these differences, repentance for venial sin should include all the essentials of repentance already explained.

It follows, therefore, that various movements of the soul towards God, especially when they are accompanied by the reception of a sacrament or by some public rite of the Church, will have the effect of remitting venial sin, even though there is no formal and explicit repentance. For since we have seen the effect of venial sin to consist in a diminution of the fervour of our actions, it follows that some act of devotion or piety deliberately performed will have the effect of restoring the balance, always provided that an explicit act of repentance would be made did we but advert to the sin. This is especially the case when the act is not merely a private one, such as almsgiving or other works of charity, but is accompanied by some special

[1] See above, pp. 931, 938.

intervention of the Church, as in the use of various sacramentals, blessings, or other sacred rites with which Catholics are familiar.

Most of all is the remission of venial sin obtained by the reception of the sacraments, especially of the Holy Eucharist. It is not only the antidote which preserves us from mortal sin, as the Council of Trent teaches,[1] but it frees us from daily faults. " Just as by bodily food the daily waste and loss is repaired, so also the Holy Eucharist repairs what has been lost through our falls into lesser sins, by remitting them." [2]

In all these ways of securing the remission of venial sin, it must be clearly understood that repentance is necessary, either actually and explicitly, as when venial sins are confessed, or at least implicitly to the extent that the recollection of such sins would be attended by repentance did we but advert to them or recall them to our minds. In this sense all the qualities of true repentance must be present, and in particular the purpose of amendment, if we are to obtain remission of venial sin.

It will be perceived, therefore, that in some ways it is difficult to repent of lesser sins, for it requires very considerable reflection and determination in order to detest a venial sin above all evils. Accordingly, since remission of punishment only follows remission of guilt, we cannot form an exact estimate concerning the extent of our debt of punishment. That debt may be exacted to the last farthing. We may gain plenary indulgences, but the penalty of unrepented venial sin is not included in the remission. A proper appreciation of the nature of venial sin helps us not only to perceive how utterly different it is from mortal sin, but to understand more perfectly the necessity of a cleansing purgation after death, since nothing defiled can enter heaven.[3] Above all, it brings home to our minds something of the meaning of holiness, without which no man can see God.[4]

§ VII: REPARATION

GOD incarnate suffered and died in order to repair the ruin caused by sin, by offering to his eternal Father adequate satisfaction for the affront to God's majesty. The Redeemer of mankind is spoken of in the Holy Scriptures as " bearing our infirmities, bruised for our sins " [5] " made sin for us." [6] But, inasmuch as Christ himself was sinless, he could not make an act of repentance in the sense explained above; hence the Church has strictly forbidden such phrases as " Christ the Penitent " even in a devotional use. He did not repent for the sinners of the world: he offered satisfaction for their sins. The same is true, proportionately, of the many instances in

[1] Sess. xiii, chap. 2.
[2] Catechism of the Council of Trent, Part II, chap. iv, q. 50.
[3] Apoc. xxi 27.
[4] Heb. xii 14.
[5] Isa. liii 4.
[6] 2 Cor. v 21.

the lives of the saints, in which we are told that they undertook penance for the sins of others. Only the sinner can repent in the strict sense of the word; but that part of repentance which is concerned with offering satisfaction to God can be undertaken vicariously by others.

For it has pleased God to redeem all men, who fell corporately in Adam, by incorporating them in Christ the second Adam. From the doctrine of the Mystical Body of Christ [1] many profound truths of deep significance are drawn. In particular the familiar idea of Reparation, included in Catholic devotion towards the Sacred Heart of Jesus, has its doctrinal basis in the fact that all Christians are members of one body whose head is Christ. On this solidarity of the whole human race in Christ rests, not only the justification but the necessity of the Christian practice of offering reparation to God, in various ways, for the sins of the world. For the notion of reparation, while including our own personal offences, is chiefly concerned with satisfaction for the sins of others.

In the plenitude of his desire to expiate for the sins of the world, Christ chose the way of suffering. It is chiefly by suffering, therefore, that the members of his mystical body share in Christ's expiatory sacrifice. Not only do they share in it, but it is the will of Christ that their sufferings should be necessary for the completion of his own. In "filling up those things that are wanting of the sufferings of Christ," [2] St Paul rejoiced in his own sufferings and besought his brethren "to present their bodies a living sacrifice, holy, pleasing unto God." [3]

Deliberately to choose suffering requires an unusual degree of sanctity, as well as a finer appreciation of all that it means to be a follower of Christ. The illustrious examples drawn from the lives of saints, whether in the ranks of the priesthood, or of religious Orders, or of the laity, are imitated in our own times also. But every Christian is expected to suffer with Christ by patience and resignation in adversity, in the pains of illness, in poverty, in subjection to authority, and in performing the duties of his state of life.

The value of our reparation consists, of course, not in suffering as such, but in freely and deliberately offering it to God in union with the passion of Christ. This may be done during times of prayer, but the moment above all others when such reparation should be offered to God is while assisting at the sacrifice of the Mass, which is one with that of Calvary. The priest offers that sacrifice in the name of the whole Church and "of all here present, whose faith and devotion are known unto thee; for whom we offer, or who offer up to thee, this sacrifice . . . this oblation of our service as also of thy whole family." [4] "Even as I willingly offered myself to God for thy

[1] *Cf.* Essay xix.
[2] Col. i 24.
[3] Rom. xii 1.
[4] Canon of the Mass.

sins upon the Cross . . . even so must thou willingly offer thyself daily to me in the Mass." [1] *Per ipsum et cum ipso et in ipso.*

Thus in commending to the faithful the necessity of making reparation to the Sacred Heart of Jesus, Pius XI speaks as follows in the Encyclical *Miserentissimus Redemptor*: "Although the plentiful redemption of Christ abundantly forgives all our offences, yet by that wonderful disposition of the divine Wisdom whereby we have to fill up in our own flesh those things that are wanting of the sufferings of Christ, for his body which is the Church,[2] we can, nay, we must, add our own praise and satisfaction to the praise and satisfaction which Christ gave to God in the name of sinners. It should be remembered, however, that the expiatory value of our acts depends solely upon the bloody sacrifice of Christ, a sacrifice which is renewed unceasingly, in an unbloody manner, on our altars. . . . For this reason, with the august sacrifice of the Eucharist must be united the immolation of the ministers and also of the rest of the faithful, so that they too may offer themselves 'a living sacrifice, holy, pleasing unto God.' [3] Christ, then, as he still suffers in his mystical body, rightly desires to have us as his companions in the work of expiation. In this manner he desires us to be united with him because, since we are 'the body of Christ and members of member,' [4] what the head suffers the members should suffer with it." [5]

E. J. MAHONEY.

[1] *Imitation*, Bk. IV, chap. 8.
[2] Col. i 24.
[3] Rom. xii 1.
[4] 1 Cor. xii 27.
[5] *Ibid.* 26. Pius XI, *Miserentissimus Redemptor*, May 8, 1928, Eng. trans., Burns Oates and Washbourne.

XXVII

THE SACRAMENT OF PENANCE

§ I: INTRODUCTORY—
PENANCE AND THE CHRISTIAN LIFE

" EVEN though, after you have been accepted by him, you should have gone astray, even though you return to him naked, yet God will receive you again as his son, because you have returned to him." [1] In these words the early Christian writer Tertullian expounds the lesson to be learnt from the parable of the Prodigal Son—that God is always ready to forgive the repentant sinner. The same lesson can be drawn from other parables, notably that of the Good Shepherd, and from the general tenor of Christ's teaching and actions. It is impossible to think that God would spurn the sinner who turns to him for pardon.

Since this is so, those who have sinned have surely only to seek for the means of forgiveness. It is with this quest that this essay is concerned. When we consider the effects of sin, and the consequent meaning of forgiveness, we can conjecture at once that sin will be remitted sacramentally. Revelation, coming from God, must be a consistent body of doctrine. Since grace is conferred and strengthened by sacraments, we may well expect that when lost it is by a sacrament that it will be restored.

Moreover, since sanctifying grace is so immensely important, and its loss so great a disaster, it is in keeping with our desires and God's great goodness that some clear sign of forgiveness perceptible to the senses should exist. Otherwise we should be doubtful of pardon, and our very faith, our very repentance, would be sources of misery. The more fully we realised the evil of sin, the more earnestly we lamented our fall, the greater would be our anxiety and fear, the more should we dread the inevitable final judgement.

Thus, even *a priori* reasoning leads us to hope that that final judgement may be anticipated by an earthly judgement, which will give us yet another chance of winning salvation. We should, then, be ready to believe gratefully that such a sacrament has indeed been instituted.

Our knowledge of the sacramental system enables us to make reasonable inferences as to the form such a sacrament would take, and these should guide us in our inquiry. The sacraments are external signs of inward grace ; and, since they are signs, they must accord with the nature of the grace conferred. A sacrament of pardon would confer the grace of remission of sins. But sins are culpable

[1] *De Poenitentia*, viii.

acts—crimes. The natural sign of the remission of a crime is a judicial decision, necessarily preceded by an investigation of the accusation. We should expect to find, then, if Christ did institute a sacrament for the remission of sins, that this sacrament would be a judgement, and would necessitate an inquiry into the sins to be remitted.

Further, sin and its guilt are, at least partially, secret. Hence an inquiry into a sinner's guilt can be made only through his own voluntary admissions—*i.e.*, by means of confession. Such confession must be accompanied by sorrow, for we know from Christian doctrine on grace, that without sorrow sin cannot be forgiven. But our sorrow would be merely fictitious if we were not ready to atone as far as we can for the insult we have offered to God. Therefore, if there be a sacrament by which our sins are forgiven, we should expect it to include confession, contrition, and satisfaction, as the necessary acts of the penitent sinner. And these acts, being part of the sacrament, would have to be expressed externally.

Since the judicial decision that is to follow is also part of the sacrament, this too must be external. It must therefore be uttered by some man. But clearly if a man is to be judge over our souls, then to help him to use that authority rightly, our manifestations of guilt, of sorrow, and of readiness to atone must be made to him. Moreover, mere general avowal of guilt will not help him to judge prudently and justly: our confession then must be a full statement of all that he needs to know before he can give a sound decision.

But if this judicial remission of sin is to be of use, if it is to be sacramental, it must be really effective. The sacraments actually confer grace. Hence this sacramental judgement must be effective, and not a mere declaration of pardon already otherwise secured. The man to whom so immense a power is given must clearly receive it from God, and that such a commission has been given must in some way be evident externally, for we cannot submit to an unknown judge. Hence it is probable that if there be a sacrament of pardon only the officials of the Church, the priests, would be capable of receiving the authority to administer it.

Some sacrament, therefore, whereby sins can be forgiven, is desirable, is in accordance with God's goodness, and is consistent with Christian Revelation. Such a sacrament would be suitably a judgement and would fittingly include confession, contrition, and satisfaction from the penitent, and a sentence from the judge. This judge would probably be one of the priests of the Church, authorised by the Church to pass sentence.

It remains now to see whether Christ did in fact institute such a sacrament.

§ II: THE SACRAMENT IN SCRIPTURE

In our endeavour to ascertain whether Christ instituted a Sacrament of Penance we must distinguish essentials from non-essential details. Many modern customs that surround the administration of the Sacrament are incidental. The one thing that matters is to show that Christ instituted a sacrament which consists essentially in an effective judgement over sinners. If he gave to his Church power to forgive sins or to refuse to forgive them, then he did institute this Sacrament. The ceremonial with which such a power is exercised is not relevant to our inquiry.

The power of the keys

Apart from the general teaching of the Gospels that Christ came to call sinners to repentance, certain texts explicitly declare that he gave to the Church this power to judge sinners effectively in God's name. To St Peter he made the promise first. "And I will give to thee the keys of the Kingdom of Heaven. And whatsoever thou shalt bind upon earth shall be bound also in heaven; and whatsoever thou shalt loose upon earth shall be loosed also in heaven."[1] Using the same words, save for the necessary change in the number of the pronoun, he later gave the same promise to all the Apostles.[2] Finally, after his Resurrection, he carried out his promise and conferred this authority on them. "'As the Father hath sent me, I also send you.' When he had said this he breathed on them, and he said to them, 'Receive ye the Holy Ghost. Whose sins you shall forgive, they are forgiven them: and whose sins you shall retain they are retained.'"[3]

We can summarise the information to be drawn from these texts: Our Lord gave his Church wide discretionary powers, so that she can impose her obligations or remit them, and her action will be ratified by God; in particular, she can forgive sins, or refuse to forgive; her authority in this matter is to be exercised judicially; this involves voluntary avowal of guilt, of sorrow and of readiness to atone, on the part of the penitent; there is no limitation to this power, granted that the penitent is in the requisite condition; it is given not to the Apostles alone, but also to their successors; only the officials of the Church, the priests, are able to exercise it; finally, subjection to the Church's tribunal is necessary for a sinful Christian who desires pardon.

Power of forgiving sin

It is clear from his very words that our Lord gave the Church power to impose burdens or to remove them, and that this includes the power to forgive sins. The metaphor of the keys, the general words used in all three texts, the explicit mention of the forgiveness or retention of sins, can have no other meaning. Isaias uses this same metaphor of the keys, "And I will lay the key of the house of David upon his shoulders; and he shall open and none shall shut;

[1] Matt. xvi 19.
[2] Matt. xviii 18.
[3] John xx 21–23.

and he shall shut and none shall open." [1] This is the obvious meaning of the metaphor, that to St Peter is given supreme power as God's representative to exclude from or admit into heaven. As St John Chrysostom says :

" Those who are living on earth are given the control of heavenly affairs, and have a power which God has given neither to angels nor to archangels ; for it was not said to them, 'Whatsoever,' etc. Earthly rulers have indeed the power of binding but only over the body ; this power of binding, however, concerns the soul itself, and controls heaven ; whatever priests do below, God ratifies above, and the Lord confirms the decision of the servant. For what else did he give them than complete heavenly power ? For he said, 'What sins you shall remit they are remitted, and what sins you shall retain they are retained.' What power could be greater than that ? 'The Father has given all judgement to the Son.' And I see them entrusted with all this by the Son." [2]

This is so clearly a fair summary of the meaning of these texts that we can leave the saint's explanation without further discussion. The Church, then, has power to bind and to loose, and this power includes that of forgiving sin.

A judicial power, requiring confession

This power over sin is judicial, and necessitates confession from the penitent. If the Church's ministers are to forgive or to refuse to forgive, they must be adequately informed about the sinner's state of soul. Otherwise they could not use this power rightly. As St Jerome wrote about the clergy, " Having the power of the keys, in a certain manner they judge before the day of judgement." [3] But no man can judge even earthly offences without a full knowledge of the crime ; still less can we suppose that the Church is to exercise her dread power arbitrarily, with insufficient knowledge. Therefore it is that St Jerome also writes that priests should not bind or loose according to their moods, but only when, having heard the kinds of sin, they know whom to bind and whom to loose.[4] St Gregory the Great sums up this inference from our Lord's words :

" Great is the honour, but terrible the responsibility of the honour. . . . The cases must therefore be considered, and then the power to bind and to loose exercised. The fault that has been committed, the repentance that has followed the fault, must both be known, so that those whom Almighty God has visited with the grace of repentance, the judgement of the pastor may absolve." [5]

Our Lord's words, therefore, give the Church power to absolve judicially from sin, and this power necessitates full confession from the penitent.

It is so obvious that the sinner must be repentant, and must avow

[1] Isa. xxii 22.

[2] St John Chrysostom (344-407), *De Sacerdotio*, iii.

[3] St Jerome (*c.* 342-420), Letter to Heliodorus, Ep. xiv 8.

[4] *Commentary on St Matthew's Gospel*, iii (in chap. xvi, ver. 19).

[5] St Gregory the Great (540-604), *Homilies on the Gospel*, xxvi.

his sorrow, that we need do no more than mention it. Moreover, this repentance must clearly include readiness to atone. These truths follow from the Christian teaching on Sin and on Repentance.[1]

Some have interpreted this power as the commission to baptise and to preach the gospel of Redemption. But this is against the plain meaning of the words; it overlooks the fact that the commission to baptise was given on another occasion; and it limits the Church's power to remitting by baptism the sins of the unbaptised, whereas our Lord said in entirely general terms, "Whose sins," and "Whatsoever you shall bind." A Christian who has sinned may well insist that when our Lord gave the Church power to forgive, he did not withdraw her subjects from her control.

Universal power

Moreover, no sin is excluded, for our Lord's words are as wide as possible in their reference. As St Augustine tersely wrote: "There are some who said that penance was not to be allowed to certain sins; and they were excluded from the Church, being heretics."[2] St Pacian also thus answers the Novatians who attempted to except some sins from the Church's power to forgive:[3] "He excepted nothing at all. He said, 'Whatsoever.'" These quotations are short, but to the point. To deny the universality of the Church's power to forgive is to deny the words of Christ.

Permanent power

St Pacian also proves that this power was not given to the Apostles alone, but was to be passed on to their successors:

"But perhaps this power was only given to the Apostles? Then to them alone was it permitted to baptise, to them alone was it permitted to give the Holy Ghost, and to them alone was it granted to remove the sins of the world. For all these were ordered to no others but to the Apostles. . . . If, therefore, the power to baptise and to confirm has come to the bishops from the Apostles, so too have they the power to bind and to loose."[4]

He states here the principle by which we know that this power was given to the Church permanently: whatever powers are needed for the Church's work, even though the words conferring them were necessarily spoken to the Apostles alone, are also given to their successors. The power of forgiveness is obviously necessary for the salvation of men. Our Lord indeed makes it clear that he gave it to the Church that she might continue his work; he introduces its bestowal by saying, "As the Father has sent me, I also send you."

This power, therefore, is one that the Church must wield for all time, for it is given to her to enable her to accomplish her mission.

Granted only to priests

It is also at least suggested by our Lord's words that only priests can forgive sins. It is, as we have seen, a judicial power. But no judge can exercise his authority without a definite commission, a commission which in any society is given only to qualified officials.

[1] *Cf.* Essay xxvi.

[2] St Augustine (354-430), *Sermons*, ccclii 3.

[3] St Pacian (*c.* 390), *Epistles*, iii 12.

[4] Ep. i 7.

The Church is a perfect society, with her own officials, and normally these alone can exercise authority in matters concerning the purpose of the society; therefore these alone can validly exercise this judicial power.

"This right is granted only to priests." "Christ granted this right to his Apostles, and it was transmitted by the Apostles to the priests."[1] In these two sentences St Ambrose sums up for us Christian tradition and the implication of our Lord's words.

Necessary power

Finally, these words show that if we desire pardon we must submit to this tribunal of the Church. To bestow authority over subjects and not to enforce subjection on the subjects is an inconsistency we dare not attribute to God. If, when the Church refuses forgiveness, pardon can be nevertheless secured, then our Lord was jesting with his Apostles, and has failed to carry out his promise. Thus St Gregory VII asserted boldly his authority over all Christians. "Who, I ask, thinks himself excluded from the jurisdiction of Peter in this universal grant of the power to bind and to loose? Unless, indeed, it be some unhappy man who, refusing to bear the yoke of the Lord, subjects himself to the burden of the devil, and wishes not to be numbered among Christ's sheep."[2]

Though St Gregory is here speaking particularly of the claim that kings were above the power of the Church, his words show us how futile would be the gift of authority if the subjects could with impunity withdraw themselves from its control. We must therefore recognise that, apart from submission to the Church's forgiving power, there is no pardon for grave sins.

This, then, is the plain meaning of our Lord's words, these are the necessary implications. It has been suggested that our Lord did not mean what his words say, but merely authorised his Apostles to declare that sins are pardoned which have been already forgiven apart from their decision. But thus to reduce the power of absolution to a barren declaration is not only to distort Christ's words but also to make them, especially in so solemn a setting, an absurd anticlimax. Our Lord has sent the Apostles to carry on the work of redemption; to help them in this onerous task he has given them the Holy Ghost; it is inconceivable that he should then proceed to tell them in very misleading language that they would be able to declare sins forgiven after they had been forgiven independently of their action. These words, to fit the solemnity of the occasion, must bear their obvious meaning, that the Apostles are empowered by divine commission to judge sinners and to pass on them effective sentence.

Nor may we limit the power of remission to the remission of punishment alone. Eternal punishment cannot be remitted apart from the guilt, for the two are inseparably joined. Punishment is the

[1] St Ambrose (*c.* 333-397), *De Poenitentia*, i 2; ii 2.
[2] St Gregory VII (*c.* 1020-1085), Letter to Heriman of Metz, 1081.

inevitable consequence of guilt. If the punishment is remitted, then the guilt also must be remitted. On the other hand, the temporal punishment due to sin can be lessened or remitted in so many other ways that any Christian can secure this by his own actions. It is unthinkable that our Lord's solemn injunction, and his gift of the Holy Ghost, could issue in so trivial a conclusion as the bestowal of a power already enjoyed by all Christians. It would be unsound exegesis to accept an interpretation of our Lord's words so unsuited to the context, and at the same time so remote from the plain meaning of the words themselves. We must then conclude that Christ gave to the Apostles and to their successors a power so great as to seem almost incredible—the power effectively to forgive the sins of men or, equally effectively, to refuse forgiveness.

"What is impossible for men is possible to God, and God is able to grant pardon for sins. . . . It seemed impossible that sins should be forgiven through penance; yet Christ granted this to his Apostles and by the Apostles it was handed on to the ministry of the priests. Hence what seemed impossible has been made possible." [1]

"But God who promised mercy to all makes no distinction (between forgiving slight and grave sins), and concedes to his priests the power of forgiveness with no exceptions." [2]

"In baptism surely there is remission of all sins; what does it matter whether priests exercise this power granted to them, at baptism or through penance? In both there is the one mystery." [3]

These sayings of St Ambrose sum up the plain meaning of our Lord's words as always understood by the Church. We may therefore conclude with St Leo: "And then did the Apostles receive power to forgive sins, when after his Resurrection the Lord breathed on them and said, 'Receive the Holy Ghost. Whose sins you shall forgive they are forgiven.'" [4]

Other scriptural evidence is in itself not so clear. But if we remember our Lord's words it becomes clearer, and affords at least indications that the Apostolic Church claimed and exercised this power to forgive sins. The Apostles knew well that Christians sinned seriously, and yet did not write of such sinners as though they were finally lost. They even write of them as though they could still enjoy effective membership of the Church.[5] It is true we have no detailed narrative of the actual exercise of the power of absolution; there are at best some possible references.[6] But knowing our Lord's words to the Apostles, knowing, too, the Christian teaching on salvation and on the Church, we can justifiably see in this treatment of sinful Christians evidence that the Church was using the power to forgive that had been conferred upon her.

[1] St Ambrose, *De Poenitentia*, ii 2.
[2] *Ibid.*, i 3. [3] *Ibid.*, i 8.
[4] St Leo, Sermon lxxvi, *De Pœntecoste*, ii 4.
[5] *Cf.* 1 Peter, 2 Corinthians, Titus, Apocalypse, *passim.*
[6] *Cf.* Acts xix 18 *sqq.*; Jas. v 16, and 19-20, etc.

Some objections

Certain difficulties have been raised and must be resolved. The comparative silence concerning the use of the forgiving power is best treated when we encounter the same difficulty in later history. There are also texts which seem at first to suggest either that a sinful Christian had no hope of salvation or that there was a limit to the Church's power to forgive.

In the Epistle to the Hebrews (vi 4-6) St Paul writes: "For it is impossible for those who were once illuminated, have tasted also the heavenly gift and were made partakers of the Holy Ghost, have moreover tasted the good word of God and the powers of the world to come, and are fallen away, to be renewed again to penance, crucifying again to themselves the Son of God, making him a mockery."

Taken out of its context, this passage does seem to imply that if a Christian sinned he was finally lost. But in its context the meaning is clear. The Epistle is written for Jewish Christians to stress the fact that Christ is the Messiah and that they can look for no other; if they desert Christ then they cannot expect salvation, for God's promises have been fulfilled, and to expect another Messiah is to wish to crucify the Son of God again and to make him a mockery. This is therefore no difficulty to the doctrine of Penance; it is, indeed, a part of that doctrine: the sacramental power comes from Christ's sacrifice alone.

Again, both our Lord and St John speak of a sin that shall not be forgiven. Our Lord calls it blasphemy against the Holy Ghost,[1] and St John writes of the sin unto death.[2] The explanation of these statements removes all difficulty. This sin has been identified by some as final impenitence, which manifestly is not forgiven. A fuller explanation is that this sin is the hardening of the heart against grace, which makes a man refuse to seek pardon. Such a sinner certainly is not forgiven, for he will not ask. This is the age-long explanation of the Church's writers, and is consistent with the scriptural statements. Neither our Lord nor St John says that the sin *cannot* be forgiven, but that it *will not* be forgiven.

Scriptural evidence therefore shows us clearly that Christ did indeed institute this Sacrament of Reconciliation which we so deeply need, and that its nature is what we might have anticipated.

§ III: THE SACRAMENT IN TRADITION

In discussing this doctrine we cannot neglect its history; by its development it has become better understood, errors have been averted, and we have learnt to practise it more frequently and with greater profit.

Comparative silence of early centuries

We must first treat of the difficulty we met in Scripture and find again in later history, that references to the Sacrament are so vague

[1] Matt. xii 31. [2] 1 John v 16.

and so comparatively rare that some misguided scholars have even denied its Apostolic origin.

Many reasons account for this comparative silence. Of course, we must not expect modern phrases, such as " going to confession," or " saying one's penance." These phrases are merely our way of describing the practice.

We are somewhat disappointed in the early references to Penance because we too often do what early Christian writers did not: we are apt to concentrate on one belief at a time and to forget the Christian Revelation as one united system. If we remember Christian teaching on the Church, on salvation, and on membership of the Church, much apparently vague language of early writers becomes very definite, teaching that Penance after sin avails for sanctification and procures for us pardon by authoritative reunion with the Church.

Also the first Christians used Penance less than we do. It was used mainly for the pardon of grave sins. Consequently, as it did not figure so frequently in their lives, it did not come into their minds so readily. The majority of them had been converted from the horrors of paganism, and their great act of Penance was their conversion, the passage from vice to virtue. Therefore when they thought of Penance they thought most readily of their baptism, which had meant so great a change in their lives.

Again, as the doctrine was not as yet fully developed, the rites varied considerably from place to place. Consequently the evidence is not only slight but often confusing. Even on doctrinal points there were discussions which authority had to settle before we could hope for uniform evidence.

Two writers at least give us another reason for primitive silence on this doctrine. Tertullian and the author of the *Pastor* both tell us that they were reluctant to mention Penance lest they should thereby lead converts to minimise the change that ought to have taken place at Baptism, lest they should even be encouraging Christians to sin, by showing that after Baptism pardon could still be secured.

We can now turn to the actual evidence. Space forbids a full survey; we must be content to record the most telling testimony.

Clement of Rome

St Clement, Bishop of Rome in the first century, wrote to the Corinthians about a schism. He stresses the duty of submission to lawful authority and exhorts sinners to repent.

" You therefore who are responsible for this sedition, be subject in obedience to the priests, and bending your knees in spirit receive correction unto penance. . . . It is better for you to be insignificant and of good fame in the flock of Christ, then to be rejected for excessive pride from all hope of him." [1]

It is difficult to see in this anything other than a statement that after sin submission to the priests unto penance can secure membership of the Church again, and with it hope of salvation, whereas a

[1] St Clement (Pope 92-101), First Epistle to the Corinthians.

refusal to submit involves the loss of salvation. This is the Catholic teaching on Penance.

Though second-century authors seem at times to imply that there is no hope for the sinful Christian, they are in reality merely repeating St Paul's teaching to the Hebrews. St Irenaeus, moreover, tells of heretics pardoned,[1] and divides Christians into those who persevered from the beginning and those who were restored after a fall by repentance.[2] Finally, these writers stress the Christian doctrine of the connection between membership of the Church and salvation;[3] hence we know that for them a restoration of membership involved pardon of sin.

Pastor *of Hermas*

The two chief witnesses before the controversies of the third century are the author of the book known as *Pastor* of Hermas and Tertullian. The controversies make it certain that the Church of the third century taught our doctrine of to-day; Tertullian and the *Pastor* show the same for the earlier period.

The *Pastor* is difficult, for its allegory obscures its teaching. But the use made of it during the later controversies, and the very meaning of the allegory show that it teaches a belief in sacramental absolution for sin. Written in the middle of the second century at Rome, it is divided into Visions, Commandments, and Parables. The allegories teach that the Church is an organised society, membership of which is necessary for salvation. The book itself is mainly an exhortation to penance, and certain doctrines are plain. Repentance is open to all and can secure forgiveness; but it is only to be used once; however, if a man fall again after this his state is not entirely desperate; Penance is an external rite and results in formal, external reunion with the Church, and therefore in internal freedom from guilt; this last point is made abundantly clear by the close parallel instituted between the unquestionably sacramental baptism and the second Penitence.

That this interesting allegory may relieve the tedium of exposition we give short extracts from it.

When the author is shown in vision a tower built upon water, and the rejection of many stones from the building, he speaks to the lady who is his guide: "'And what, Lady, is the use of my seeing this if I do not understand it?' Replying she said to me, 'You are a cunning man, wanting to know all about the tower.' 'Yes, Lady,' I said, 'that I may tell the brethren, and they may be gladdened.' . . . She, however, said: 'Many indeed will hear, and some will rejoice, but others will mourn. But even they who mourn will rejoice when they have done penance. . . . The tower you saw being built is myself, the Church' . . . I asked her: 'Why is the

[1] St Irenaeus (*c.* 140-200), *Adversus Hæreses*, i and iii.

[2] *Ibid.* i.

[3] *Cf.* St Ignatius (martyred 107), Letter to the Philadelphians; Second Clementine Epistle to Corinthians, *c.* 150; St Irenæus, *Adversus Hæreses*, iv, v. (Note especially the importance of Christ, and the gravity of apostasy.)

tower built upon the water, Lady?' She said: '. . . because your life is saved and will be saved through water. . . . Hear now about the stones. . . . Those square white stones which fitted so well are the Apostles, bishops, doctors and deacons, who have lived holy lives in God. . . . Those which were cast away . . . are those who have sinned and wish to do penance. And therefore they are not thrown far outside the tower, for if they do penance they will be useful in building. . ' So she ended her exposition of the tower. . . . I asked still more, whether all the stones which were rejected were unsuitable for the building, or whether there was yet repentance for them, and they might have a place in the tower. 'They have,' she said, 'an opportunity for penance, but they cannot be put into this tower; they will be put into another and much lesser place, after they have suffered and accomplished the days of their penance.'" [1]

Later in the Commandments:

"'Yet still, Sir,' I said, 'I wish to ask questions.' He replied, 'Speak.' 'I have heard,' I said, '. . . that there is no other penance save that one when we descend into the water and receive remission of our earlier sins.' He answered, 'You have heard rightly . . . for he who receives remission of sins ought not to sin again, but should remain chaste. Since, however, you ask about everything carefully, I shall disclose this also to you—not, indeed, to give temptation thereby to those who . . . have just come to faith in the Lord. . . . But for those who were called before these days the Lord has provided penance . . . and to me the power of this penance has been given. But I say to you that after that great and holy calling (*i.e.*, baptism) if anyone . . . should sin, he has one chance of penance. If, however, he sin again, and does penance, it is useless, for with difficulty he will have life."' [2]

This last sentence needs comment. In the early Church, as we shall see, sins due to malice were treated more severely than those due to weakness. Public penance was, as a rule, imposed on grave, malicious sins, especially if they were public, though there were exceptions; this public penance could be used once only. There was a tendency evidently to feel that sin renewed again and again indicated a lack of sincerity in the repentance, which rendered forgiveness difficult. Sinners who, after once doing public penance, relapsed into sins that normally deserved this public penance, were usually not re-admitted to communion; but they were allowed to assist at worship within the Church, and their case was not considered desperate. Occasionally, perhaps, individual bishops would readmit these sinners privately, or possibly even publicly; our evidence is, after all, imperfect. But certainly they were not considered finally lost, and equally certainly there was no salvation apart from membership of the Church. This severe practice, however, though perfectly lawful, was ill-suited to Christian teaching, which gradually

[1] Vision III. [2] Commandment iv 3.

reacted against it; in doctrine it is certain that the Church never taught that a grave sin after penance was irremissible. This is really the tenor of the *Pastor's* teaching here. He is apt to make a sweeping statement that requires modification, and to add almost at once the modification needed. We have an example of this at the opening of this quotation. Here at the end is another. We must therefore understand the word "useless" in the light of the subsequent phrase, "with difficulty."

In the Parables penance is often mentioned. Thus, the angel of penance shows Hermas a field. "And he showed me a young shepherd. . . . And there were many sheep grazing, enjoying themselves luxuriously and in their joy leaping hither and thither; and the shepherd was joyful with his flock, . . . and he ran about among his sheep. . . . 'This,' he said, 'is the angel of luxury and pleasure. He destroys the souls of the servants of God, turning them from truth, deceiving them with evil desires in which they perish. . . . For these therefore there is no penance leading to life; they have added to their sins and have blasphemed the name of God. Death is the fate of such sinners. The sheep which you saw standing still are those who have given themselves indeed to luxuries and to pleasure, but have not blasphemed against God; . . . for them there is the hope of penance by which they may live. . . .' He showed me a tall shepherd, rough in appearance, with a knapsack on his shoulder and holding a knotted rod and a great whip. His appearance was so savage that I was afraid of him. . . . This shepherd received those sheep who enjoyed themselves in luxury but did not skip about. And he drove them into a steep and thorny place full of thistles, so that they were caught by the thorns and thistles. These . . . being beaten by the shepherd suffered cruel torments. . . . And when I saw them thus flogged and tortured, I was sorry for them and said: '. . . Sir, who is this savage and cruel shepherd so pitiless of his sheep?' 'This,' he said, 'is the angel of punishment. . . . When they have suffered every kind of torture they are handed over to me for admonition, and are confirmed in the faith, and for the rest of their lives they serve God with pure hearts.'"[1]

Tertullian

Tertullian's evidence is similar. Before his fall into heresy he wrote *De Pœnitentia*. In this he treats first of the virtue of repentance, then of that virtue at baptism. He then explicitly declares that there is a second penitence which is also the last. He mentions it reluctantly, "lest by treating of the help of repentance yet left to us, we may seem to afford opportunity of sinning again."[2] However, he does mention it, and compares it with Baptism, thus indicating its sacramental nature. Though he says that penance can be used only once, he suggests that this was not universally held. "Let nobody

[1] Parable VI.

[2] It is difficult to give precise references. The book is comparatively short, and I have summarised long passages with occasional citations.

therefore become worse, because God is so good, renewing his sin as often as he is pardoned. Otherwise he will come to the end of his opportunities for pardon before coming to an end of his sins." This certainly suggests a frequently renewed pardon, and in the context a formal pardon.

He asserts even more clearly the existence of this second repentance. He tells us that having been once saved from shipwreck we should avoid further danger. But lest Christians should fall before the devil's attack God has provided other means of salvation. "God therefore knowing these poisons,[1] although the gate of innocence is closed and bolted by baptism, has yet left somewhere an opening. He has placed in the vestibule a second penance which will open to those who knock. But this is once only, for it is the second time. . . . Let the soul be weary of sinning again, but not of repenting again. . . . Let no one be ashamed; for renewed ill-health there must be renewed medicine."

After this he describes the second penance. "Confession of sin is as much a relief as concealment is an aggravation of the burden." The second penance "commands to lie in sackcloth and ashes, to hide the body in squalor, to abase the mind with sorrow, to accept hard treatment for the sins committed, to abstain from food and drink, . . . to throw yourself before the priests, to kneel to those dear to God, to join the petition of the brethren to his own prayer. All this penance does . . . that it may, I will not say frustrate eternal punishment by temporal sorrow, but that it may wipe it out. When, therefore, it abases a man it raises him up the more; when it accuses him it excuses him; when it condemns him it absolves him."[2]

This is clearly an external ceremony. Indeed, Tertullian continues by expressing regret that some from shame avoid confession. He compares them, as so many other early writers do, to patients ashamed to disclose secret illnesses to doctors. Then he asks why sinners should fear to manifest their sins to the brethren who, united in one Spirit from one Lord and Father, will welcome their sorrow, not mock their shame.

"In each member is the Church, but the Church is Christ. When, therefore, you throw yourself at the brethren's knees, you are touching Christ, you are imploring Christ; and when they shed tears over you it is Christ who suffers, Christ who prays to the Father. . . . Is it better to be damned in secret than to be absolved in public?"

To encourage confession he insists upon its effectiveness.

"If you shrink from confession think of hell, which confession will extinguish for you." "Therefore since you know that after the first protection against hell given by the Lord's baptism, there is still in confession a second help, why do you defer your salvation?"

[1] *I.e.*, the poisons of the devil.

[2] The confusion of pronouns is in the original.

From this we must infer that Tertullian knew of the existence of the power to forgive sins. He doubted, indeed, whether it could be used for one person more than once, but he implies that this doubt was not shared by all Christians. Especially he teaches that second penance, like baptism, is an external ecclesiastical rite, and therefore effective before God. Finally, he expounds the doctrine in its right setting: the Christian is saved by union with Christ in the Church; this union is broken by sin, penance restores it, and that restoration therefore involves absolution, and is indeed effected by it.

Thus Tertullian and the *Pastor* teach the same doctrine. It is clear from their testimony that Christians in the second century believed in the Church's sacramental power to forgive sin. But they also show that this power was used chiefly for grave sins and that there was dispute as to its extent, a dispute as yet not authoritatively settled. In the third century this led to serious controversies, for which Tertullian himself is one of our main authorities.

The Montanist heresy

After being so great a Christian champion he was unhappily misled by the Montanist heresy. This, like so many of the great heresies, was Puritan and Manichæan in its doctrines. The frequency with which this Puritan, Manichæan spirit rises against the Church is in itself an interesting exposition of Catholic belief. Puritanism, which over-stresses human wickedness, distrusts the goodness of God's creation, and is therefore excessively hard on the sinner, and even on innocent worldly pleasures, is inevitably opposed to Christianity. All Catholic doctrine, being God's revelation, is consistent; knowing its basic doctrines of the goodness of God, and the union of Justice and Mercy in the Incarnation and Redemption, we must expect that the Church would reject any doctrine too harsh towards the sinner. She is a forgiving Church, because she is the body of the forgiving Christ, our Saviour.

Consequently the Popes of the third century, notably St Callixtus, rejected the incipient tendency to severity, and asserted that pardon of any sin would be given to all who repented. Tertullian, then a Montanist, attacked him bitterly. He declared that the power to forgive could be wielded only by spiritual men, and that homicide, adultery, and idolatry, could not be forgiven at all.

However, the Montanists in their severity were the innovators, not the Catholics in their lenience. He boasts that he has advanced and has put away the things of a child. "Even in Christ knowledge has different ages." [1] This statement again displays a tendency of most heresies, to think that Christ's Revelation can be altered to suit the times, a tendency to-day called strangely "Modernism."

In his *De Pudicitia* he tries to demolish the arguments whereby he had formerly defended Catholic clemency. His effort shows us the true meaning of those arguments. It becomes clear that the Church claimed to forgive sins by the ministry of her hierarchical

[1] *De Pudicitia*, i.

officials, and that she claimed to forgive all sins. The Catholic tradition and development was in favour of lenience and against excessive severity. Its greatest opponent then proves that the authority of Rome was conservative, ecclesiastical, and clement.

Another attack on St Callixtus, however, implies that he was innovating.[1] This was delivered by that strange St Hippolytus, saint, schismatic, even materially heretic, ultimately martyr, and the first anti-Pope of history. He had been opposed to St Callixtus, and afterwards reviled his memory. But his very bitterness invalidates his testimony. He accuses Callixtus of having encouraged all sins, even concubinage and infanticide, thus making him responsible for the misuse that some made of his gentleness. This is the bitterness of a defeated rival, whose anger has obscured his judgement. He himself mourns that Callixtus had his followers and drew even good men after him; and we know that the papal teaching prevailed, even in conservative Rome. We are forced, then, to conclude, on the evidence of Tertullian, of earlier and of later history, that the supposed innovation was merely the rejection of an excessive Puritanism that misguided zealots were trying to introduce.

Shortly afterwards Novatian, also a schismatic, tried to revive this severity at least against the sin of apostasy. Though before his fall he had written to St Cyprian of Carthage, maintaining the Catholic tradition, he later reacted against the growing lenience. But though he succeeded in establishing a party temporarily, the truth was too strong, and Novatianism failed as had Montanism.

With this defeat the existence of the Church's power to forgive all sins to repentant sinners was clearly established. Whatever discussions were still possible, whatever rites were actually used, the existence of the Sacrament of Penance is beyond doubt from the third century onwards. Gradually lenience increased, the use of the Sacrament became more frequent, venial sins were more often submitted to the tribunal, and forgiveness was accorded more easily, and repeated again and again as often as a sinner repented. But all this development involved no new doctrine. From now to the Protestant rebellion, the fundamental doctrine of Penance was not seriously attacked.

Even before the third century it is clear that the Church's teaching was the same. The very controversies of that century lose all point if the Church were not then making the claim to forgive all sins. Of what use also Tertullian's earlier exhortations, of what use the severity described both in the *Pastor* and by Tertullian, of what use to question lenience, if sinners could secure forgiveness without submission to the Church, or if the Church were not claiming to forgive?

The evidence of the first three centuries shows that heresy doubted or minimised the Church's power to forgive sin; Catholic truth

[1] St Hippolytus (*fl. c.* 200). *Philosophumena* is the work here used.

maintained this power in its fulness. As Lactantius at the opening of the fourth century wrote:

"That is the true Church, in which there is confession and repentance, which cures effectively the sins and wounds to which carnal weakness is subject." [1]

§ IV: THE MATTER OF THE SACRAMENT

The acts of the penitent

In discussing the sacraments it is convenient to follow the usual division into Matter and Form. The Matter of a sacrament is that part of the external sign, which of itself is not fully significant, but is capable, when defined by the Form, of being a constituent of the sign.

Usually the "matter" of a sacrament is actually material. But in Penance this is not so; it is a sacrament that concerns human acts, and there is no tangible thing in its composition. The Council of Trent, therefore, using the language of St Thomas Aquinas, declared that the acts of the penitent—confession, contrition and satisfaction—are the quasi-matter of this Sacrament.

The use of this term, which reflects the fact that Penance has no tangible "matter," has left the way open to dispute. Some theologians say that the essence of the Sacrament, comprising both matter and form, is the Absolution, the acts of the penitent being conditions necessary for validity. The majority, however, hold that the acts of the penitent are the actual matter of the Sacrament. The dispute has little importance, for it is certain that the acts of the penitent are necessary for the validity of the Sacrament.[2]

Before we discuss these acts severally, there are some general considerations to be made which apply to them all.

Though the acts of the penitent are normally taken to be the matter, the very sins confessed are clearly connected materially with the Sacrament, and are essential to it. They are not indeed part of the sign of forgiveness, but they are indispensable to the sign. They are therefore usually called the remote matter.

Essential matter must be distinguished from integral. Essential matter is that without which the Sacrament cannot exist. Integral matter, though necessary for the perfection of the Sacrament, and therefore normally even for its validity, is not essential, and may therefore, provided there are adequate reasons, be lacking without destroying the Sacrament.

Further, since this is a sacrament—*i.e.*, an outward sign—the acts of the penitent must have some external expression. Full external manifestation is integral though not essential. Thus normally there

[1] Lactantius, writing *c.* 305, *Divinae Institutiones*, iv, 30-36.

[2] The chief importance of the dispute in practice is in connection with the absolution given to an unconscious man, unable to give external signs of his penitence.

must be full confession, clear expression of sorrow and of the readiness to atone. Where circumstances render these impossible, there must be such external manifestation as is possible.

These general points concern all the acts of the penitent equally. We must now discuss them severally.

Contrition

Contrition is obviously necessary. It is shown in another essay [1] that without sorrow we cannot expect forgiveness; also that perfect contrition, arising solely from love of God's goodness offended by sin, of itself secures pardon, though it necessarily includes a will to submit to the tribunal of Penance if this be possible. We need not repeat what has been said there concerning the qualities necessary for true sorrow.

It is enough here to observe that the imperfect sorrow called "attrition" is adequate for the purposes of this Sacrament. That this is a good thing in itself and useful for salvation no Catholic can doubt, for it has been defined by the Council of Trent. That attrition is also adequate for Penance is assumed by the Council, and is now universally held by Christians. If it were not adequate we should be forced to conclude that the Sacrament never actually produces the effect—the remission of sin—for which Christ instituted it. For perfect contrition, as soon as it occurs in the soul, cleanses it from sin. Though it includes the desire to submit to the Sacrament, it frees from sin even before that submission. Consequently, if perfect contrition were the only sorrow adequate for Penance, then absolution would always be given to souls already pardoned. Thus some other form of sorrow must be adequate.

Again, the insistence of the Church upon the need for absolution and the traditional Christian horror of dying without it, show that absolution can give pardon which could not otherwise be obtained—*i.e.*, can give pardon even to those who are not capable of perfect contrition. Thus St Celestine, writing of refusal to absolve the dying, says: "What is that practice other than to slay the dying and to kill the soul most cruelly, if it be not absolved?" [2] In the words of Duns Scotus, if attrition be not adequate, "then the Sacrament cannot be the second plank of safety after shipwreck, since it never frees the shipwrecked from the peril of drowning." [3] Attrition, in short, is able to do all that is required for the sacramental effect—to remove the continued attachment to sin which is an obstacle to pardon. Therefore, since the sacraments when administered secure their effect, provided there is no obstacle to the presence of grace in the soul, attrition is adequate for this Sacrament.

Confession

The second act of the penitent is confession. Here we are confronted with certain historical problems, which we have not the

[1] Essay xxvi, *Sin and Repentance.*

[2] St Celestine (Pope 422-432), *Epistle*, iv.

[3] John Duns Scotus (*c.* 1270-1308), *Comm. in Sent.*, in iv dist. 14, q. 4, n. 6.

space to treat fully. They are not, however, of such doctrinal importance as to make this matter for serious regret.

Secret confession in history

The problems can be summarised:

It is sometimes stated that secret confession is seldom explicitly mentioned before the fourth century; that in the early Church public sins were publicly confessed, publicly punished, and publicly pardoned; that gradually the clergy usurped authority over men's souls and instituted private confession; that this is unnecessary and therefore wrong.

Even if the supposed facts behind this false statement were true, they would not be incompatible with Catholic doctrine. Our Lord did, as we have seen, give the Church power to forgive sins by a judicial process. This makes confession in some way necessary. Even if at first this confession had been usually public, this would merely mean that at first the Church used her power in a different manner. Even if secret sins had not been confessed at all, this would mean that secret sinners did not avail themselves of that power. Christian doctrine develops, and the development is sound since it does not destroy what was formerly believed, nor add new dogmas to those revealed by Christ. All that development does is to make the Christian Revelation more fully understood in all its implications, to give to it clearer expression in order to avert error, and finally to introduce new practical applications.

Even if the Church had at first used public confession as a rule, she would be within her rights, as experience showed the value of private confession, to decide in the interests of penitents themselves that cases should be heard *in camera*. Secrecy would secure candour of confession, and make the use of the Sacrament easier for Christians. Such a development would not affect Christian doctrine itself. In fact, it would merely illustrate one Christian belief: that the sacraments are given to men in their own interests.

Thus the Council of Trent anathematises anyone who says "that secret confession to the priest alone, which the Church from the beginning has always observed and observes, is alien from the institution and command of Christ and is a human invention." [1] Christ's words do not indeed mention secrecy, but they involve confession of sins, and therefore suggest secrecy. For, as Christ did not impose public confession, it is manifest that if confession is to be made at all, the Sacrament will be more widely used, Christ's gift will be the more valuable, if secrecy is preserved. Consequently the Council does not question the existence of public confessions, but merely asserts that the Church did make use of private confession, and that this is consistent with Christ's institution, and even arises from it.

But although we could therefore admit the supposed fact of the wide use of public confession in early days, to do so would be

[1] Sess. XIV, Canon 6.

historically unsound. The documents do not show that private confession was rare, and there are even indications that it was the usual practice.

Certain preliminary considerations help us to interpret the documents more accurately than is often done.

The word used by early writers which is translated "confession" usually refers to the whole penitential rite, without specific reference to the actual confession. This rite certainly was public when considered as a whole, but that fact tells us nothing of the actual avowal of sins, which may have been, and probably was, private. To remember this wide connotation of the word translated "confession" will help us to interpret many of the apparent references to public confession more cautiously.

Again, the interest of early writers on Penance is nearly always about the extent of the power to forgive. Hence they rarely give us more than a very vague account of the actual rites. These, moreover, were in their details very varied in the different churches, and it is therefore difficult to acquire precise knowledge of them.

Finally, these very controversies on the extent of the power show us that the Church claimed to forgive all sins. But some sins of their very nature it would be undesirable, and even almost impossible, to confess publicly. Apart from sins the public avowal of which might cause grave social difficulties within the particular Christian community affected, there are, as St Basil pointed out later, sins which could hardly be confessed publicly for fear of the secular law. One of these, be it noted, was a sin which certain heretics declared the Church could not forgive—homicide. The existence of the controversy indicates that the Church did forgive this sin, yet it is difficult to think that it would often be confessed publicly.

When we turn to the documents we find that they do not force us to set aside this reasoning and accept the theory that confession was always or even normally public. Even such a description of the penitential rite as that given by Tertullian and quoted already does not show that confession as such was public, but merely that the penitential rite involved public shame. Public penance, and public absolution, especially in days when penance was normally only used for grave sins, would certainly do this. The other quotations already given are capable of the same interpretation, and this interpretation, as we have seen, is the natural one.

Moreover, there are certain texts that are definitely more consistent with the practice of private confession than with that of public detailed avowal of sins. Thus Origen recommends Christians to consider their choice of confessor carefully, "so that if he should judge your sin to be such that it ought to be declared and pardoned by the whole Church," [1] the penitent should be willing to submit

[1] Origen (185-254), *Homily on Psalm* 37, ii 6.

to his ruling. He also says that "if we have revealed our sins not only to God but also to those who can heal our wounds and our sins, then these are remitted."[1] Both these texts, especially the first, imply a confession, with a view to absolution, made to a priest alone. Certainly they are more consistent with such a secret confession.

St Methodius, commenting on the Jewish precept that lepers should show themselves to the priests, says: "As the ancients showed themselves to the priests, so do we to the priest."[2] This saying also is surely more compatible with private consultation than with public confession.

St Cyprian, when treating of the sin of apostasy, recommends those who have sinned only in thought to confess with sorrow to the priests.[3] The same saint and the Council of Carthage insist, in view of the different degrees of guilt, on the examination of each case.[4] Again, such an investigation and the confession even of thoughts are more suggestive of a private tribunal, especially as the investigation seems to have had for its purpose to settle whether there was need of public penance. This we can see at a later period in a remark of St Augustine's that some are sinners through weakness, others through malice; that the first should not be compelled to endure the grievous and mournful penance, but the others should be made to submit to it.[5] It is clear from this that in the fifth century, certainly some sinners were absolved without any publicity; but it also shows us that there was always private confession first, and then for some people public penance. In the absence of any evidence of change, and in view of Origen's advice, this surely illustrates the practice of the third century, where there was also this preliminary private consultation.

Thus, though the actual documentary evidence is slight, it does not prove that public confession was the rule, but actually suggests that a private confession preceded the penitential rites, and that sometimes, if the judge so decided, a penitent was not subjected to this grave trial. It would be impossible to maintain that there was an optional private tribunal for those penitents who did not like the public shame; it is equally impossible to assert that there was no private element in early penitential discipline. There was certainly a practice of consulting priests secretly about sin. This practice, taken in conjunction with the existence of the power to absolve, and the facts of human nature, forces us to hold, since no evidence contradicts, that there was confession, and that not all confession was public.

That this preliminary avowal was a sacramental confession it seems impossible to deny. The existence of the Sacrament demands

[1] *Homily on St Luke* xvii.

[2] St Methodius (died *c.* 311), *De Lepra*, vi.

[3] St Cyprian (*c.* 200-258), *De Lapsis*, xxviii.

[4] *Epistles*, lv, lvii.

[5] St Augustine; *De Diversis Quaestionibus*, lxxxiii: xxvi, *De differentia peccatorum.*

such an avowal; we have it here and it is connected with the subsequent judgement: absolution or refusal to absolve.

As St Leo said when condemning a local practice of enforcing public confession, that practice was against Apostolic tradition. "It suffices to expose one's guilt to priests alone in secret confession." [1]

The difficulty that if secret confession were normal it would be more frequently mentioned, especially by such preachers as St John Chrysostom, who devoted much eloquence to the praise of penance, is a negative argument. As such it cannot stand against positive evidence, however slight this may be. Moreover, the difficulty is not so great as it appears. When public penance was the rule, that would be the most striking feature of the Sacrament; private confession would be comparatively easy. Consequently, attention was naturally focussed on the severe public discipline. Moreover, Christian writers, to insist upon the sacramental nature of absolution, usually wrote of the confession as made to God, in whose name the priest was acting. That St John is silent is indeed an example of how faulty such negative arguments are. For by this time there can be no doubt that private confession existed. We can only conclude that his silence affords us no evidence at all of the non-existence of private confession.

The nature and extent of the obligation

We must now treat of the nature and extent of the obligation to confess. Obviously, from what has been said, all those in mortal sin, if they desire pardon, must confess their sins to a priest. There is also the positive precept of Easter Duties. This was first issued by the Lateran Council, 1215. Strictly there is no time assigned for the fulfilment of the obligation. But, as Easter is appointed for the obligatory annual communion, the confession is conveniently joined to it. This practice, moreover, the Council of Trent declared, ought to continue. Since only mortal sins must be submitted to the sacramental tribunal, this precept does not bind those who are not in mortal sin. We might add that it is at least more in keeping with Christian duty to confess any mortal sins as soon as possible after they have been committed. Only thus can they be remitted, and it is not consistent with Christian duty voluntarily to remain in mortal sin for any length of time.

Certain characteristics that confession must have should be mentioned. It must normally be vocal, and not in writing nor by signs. This is a positive precept of the Church due to the greater security vocal confession gives. Also confession must be secret. The validity of public confession in earlier days is not questioned. But the practice of the Church, confirmed by experience, has decided against publicity with its dangers and difficulties.

The most important characteristic of confession is the need for integrity. This means that mortal sins are necessary matter for the Sacrament. All must therefore be confessed. In addition, they

[1] St Leo, *Epistle* clxviii 2.

must be so confessed that the priest knows exactly what kind of sin has been committed. Therefore all circumstances which alter the kind of sin must also be told. Finally, the number of times that each sin has been committed must be mentioned as far as possible. Venial sins, though not necessary matter, are sufficient matter. There is therefore no obligation to confess venial sins, but they can be confessed. Some sin must be mentioned if the Sacrament is to be conferred. Hence a penitent who wishes to secure an increase of grace by keeping to his regular confession, but who has committed no sin that he can remember since his last confession, must repeat in general terms some sin of his past already forgiven. Material integrity, however, is not essential ; in some cases this is impossible ; the confession must be as complete as circumstances allow.

Satisfaction

Satisfaction is the last of the penitent's acts. At one time, as is evident from what has been written, the penances imposed were very severe. There has been a practical development toward lenience, and to-day, as all Catholics know, the penances given are very slight. Still, as no act of a creature in itself can atone for an offence against the Creator, the expiatory value of the penance imposed is not wholly judged by its severity. All satisfactory acts depend for their value on their union with Christ's atonement. But whereas ordinary acts depend on the fervour of the agent for the degree of their union with Christ's merits, the penance given in confession has a sacramental value which is independent of the devotion of the penitent. Nevertheless, as modern penances are so slight, it is desirable that penitents should increase their value by earnestness in their accomplishment, by other works, and by gaining indulgences.[1]

§ V: INDULGENCES

It is convenient to append here a treatment of Indulgences, since these concern penance chiefly in that they complement the sacramental satisfaction.

Meaning

As few Catholic doctrines are so misunderstood, sometimes even by Catholics, we must begin with a clear definition. According to the Catechism, " An Indulgence is a remission, granted by the Church, of the temporal punishment which often remains due to sin after its guilt has been forgiven." This, of course, is to be understood as meaning that the remission avails before God.

Thus an indulgence can never be considered a permission to commit sin, nor even an encouragement. Anyone who sinned the more readily because he could so easily get all punishment remitted would be defeating his own ends : he would not gain the indulgence

[1] The actual performance of the penance imposed is not necessary for the validity of the Sacrament ; it is sufficient that at the time of absolution the will to do the penance be present. But the performance of the penance is an integral part of the Sacrament, and therefore any penitent who culpably omitted it would commit a sin.

because of that very presumption. Finally, an indulgence is not a pardon of sin; that can be obtained only by the Sacrament of Penance.

Doctrinal bases

Before discussing Indulgences further, we must expound shortly the doctrinal bases of the system. Three doctrines are involved, the Communion of Saints, the existence of a spiritual treasury, and the power of the keys enjoyed by the Church.

For a full treatment of the first we can refer to the essay on *The Mystical Body of Christ.* Here we must be content with a short summary. The Church is not merely a number of individuals joined by belief in the same truths, by the practice of the same worship, and by submission to the same authority. It is this, indeed, but it is more. It is the Mystical Body of Christ. By his death Christ made it possible for us to gain that supernatural life of sanctifying grace whereby " we are made partakers of the Divine Nature." Those who possess this life are united with each other by their common union with Christ from whom they all receive it. Thus Christ's merits and satisfaction are shared by faithful Christians through their union with Christ in the Church. Further, so close is this bond of union that, as our Lord said, the Christian Church may be likened to a vine and its branches. The whole of this body, then, is benefited by the spiritual health of any one member, as the branches flourish with the vine.

Following on this doctrine of the Communion of Saints is that of the existence of a spiritual treasury. As in this world any act results in an indefinite series of effects, so, too, in the supernatural life any act of virtue once posited must have a value. If it be not immediately productive of its full effect, it remains, as it were, in existence, capable of being used so that its full benefit may be secured. Thus Christ's atonement being infinite is inexhaustible, and all the sins of the world can be expiated by it. Moreover, the saints have often made satisfaction in excess of what they require to atone for their own sins. This satisfactory value of their acts, not being used for themselves, remains in existence and can be used for others. This is that spiritual treasury often called the " Treasury of Merits," from which can be unceasingly drawn satisfaction for the sins of Christians.

Since, as we have seen, the Church has the power of the keys of the Kingdom of Heaven, this treasury is in her control. She can therefore draw from it satisfaction which she can apply to the souls of her members. This is an obvious corollary of the doctrine discussed in an earlier page. If the Church has the power to loose, surely she is able to loose from penalty, especially as she has at her disposal expiatory acts which the solidarity of the Christian Church renders of value to any Christian to whom they are applied.

History

If, therefore, we find that the early Church taught and put into practice these doctrines, then, even though she did not confer indulgences according to modern forms, the system is none the less primitive. It is certain that she taught both the Communion of Saints and her own power to bind and to loose; these points are discussed elsewhere. Did she use this power to bind and to loose so as to remit penalties as well as guilt? And if she did, did she do so by applying to Christians the expiatory merits of Christ and the Saints? If we can answer these two questions in the affirmative, we show at once that the system of indulgences is but the practical application of doctrines contained in Revelation.

We have almost answered our questions by wording them as we have done. Most certainly the whole penitential system of the Church was considered to remit partially at least the temporal punishment due to forgiven sin, and equally certainly it was by the application of Christ's merits to the individual soul that this was effected. This is the clear implication of most of our quotations on this subject. Hence we can conclude that the doctrines that underlie the system of indulgences were always taught and practised by the Church.

But the Council of Trent declared not only that the power to confer indulgences had been bestowed on the Church, but also that she had always made use of this power.[1] Consequently, we might expect to find a clearer use of this power elsewhere than in the Sacrament alone. We must not, however, look for modern forms; it is sufficient if we find that the Church authoritatively remitted penalties in virtue of its control of the treasury of merits. In the second Epistle of St Paul to the Corinthians there is recorded the pardon granted by the Apostle to the incestuous Corinthian. This is often regarded as the prototype of indulgences. St Paul's act does, indeed, show that claim to control sin and its effects which underlies the whole system, even though we must acknowledge that to speak of it as an indulgence is somewhat too sweeping.

But in the first centuries there are examples of relaxations of ecclesiastical penalties with subsequent readmission to union with the Church.[2] As the penalties were considered of effect in the sight of God, and as admission to communion was thought to imply a full restoration to the friendship of God, such concessions are truly of the same kind as indulgences. They were remissions of temporal penalties, valid before God, made by ecclesiastical authority through the application to the soul of the merits of Christ.

Though we should hesitate to describe definitely as indulgences the remissions granted through the intercession of martyrs, yet the "letters of peace," given to a repentant apostate by a martyr about to die, if accepted by the bishop, are formal applications of the doctrines by which indulgences are justified. The bishops, by re-

[1] Session XXV, *Decretum de Indulgentiis*.

[2] The most frequent cases were at the moment of death, the reconciliation of converted heretics, the reconciliation of penitent clerics. See d'Alès, *L'Edit de Calliste*, pp. 443-449.

laxing at the request of a martyr the penalties imposed by the Church, clearly implied that they could relax efficaciously the penalties due to sin, and that they did so because the martyrs, possessed of abundant merits, implored the favour.

To see that these examples justify us in regarding the system of indulgences as primitive, we have only to remember the teaching of the Church on sin, its punishment and its forgiveness. Christians who sinned, and then in repentance submitted to the judgement of the Church, were restored to supernatural life, and their penance was efficacious before God. Hence any dispensation from this penance, which was accompanied by readmission to the Church, assumes the belief that the Church could control the penalty due to sin.

After the days of persecution and of primitive severity rapid development occurred. For various reasons a system of commutation of ecclesiastical penalties grew up. But the substituted work was in the circumstances often of less difficulty than the original penalty. Consequently discussion arose on the propriety of thus easing satisfaction. In the course of this discussion the power of the Church to apply the merits of Christ and the Saints began to be more clearly understood. The Crusades gave impetus to the development. Participation in them was declared authoritatively to free a man from all the temporal punishment due to his forgiven sins. Gradually, after the system was in existence, the doctrinal bases were fully elaborated, and erroneous, misleading, and insufficient wording was removed.

There were still abuses, however. The wide use of indulgences in days when there was no printing, no speedy means of communication, and consequently less efficient central control than to-day, was attended with great difficulties. Undoubtedly some bishops were too lavish, undoubtedly almsgiving was sometimes too prominent among the works imposed as conditions for the reception of an indulgence, thus suggesting simony; undoubtedly also there were too many frauds among the preachers, who often either abused their authority, or having no authority played upon the credulity of the simple.

One phrase in particular was dangerous: *Indulgentia a poena et culpa* ("Indulgence from penalty and from guilt"). To understand this phrase rightly, we must understand jurisdiction.[1] When an indulgence was granted it was often joined to a "confessional letter," which entitled recipients to choose as confessor a priest who had not faculties, or had restricted faculties, and to give him full faculties in the name of the Church. This phrase was invented to describe such concessions. Certainly it is liable to abuse, and was at times abused; but when it occurs officially, as it rarely does, it has always the sense explained.

[1] See below, p. 982.

As a result of the abuses and partly as a result of the attacks occasioned by them, the Council of Trent reformed the practical use of the system, but avoided the Protestant error of condemning the whole system because of the abuses.

Kinds and conditions

In modern times, then, the system is as described at the beginning. The conditions on which an indulgence can be gained are three. The recipient must be in a state of grace, must have the intention of gaining the indulgence, and must perform the prescribed works.

The indulgence, when gained, is gained through the authority of the Church. It is not the reward of the recipient's virtue, but a grant by the competent authority. Hence when a living person gains an indulgence it is by an authoritative act on the part of the Church. But some indulgences may be applied to the souls in Purgatory. Over these the Church has not disciplinary authority. Consequently these indulgences are not applied to the suffering souls by an authoritative decree, but the Church offers to God expiation from her treasury in the interests of the soul to whom the indulgence is applied. As this offering is official and as the expiation offered is from the treasury of merits, on which only the official Church can draw, an indulgence so applied is more certain of its effect than our own personal prayers for the suffering souls.

Finally, there are two kinds of indulgences, plenary and partial. A plenary indulgence remits all the penalty still due to forgiven sin. Partial indulgences, which are still conferred in terms of the former penitential discipline, remit as much of the temporal punishment due to sin as would have been remitted by the penalty mentioned in the concession. It is futile to ask how much of the temporal penalty is therefore remitted: we cannot say definitely. The remissions are as effective as was the former penitential discipline. That is all we know. With special indulgences, such as the Portiuncula, the Jubilee, indulgences *in articulo mortis*, we cannot deal here.

Thus indulgences, so often misunderstood, are merely further examples of God's untiring goodness to his children. It is for us to see to it that we do not, through indifference, fail to secure the full benefits of membership of the Church so richly endowed.

§ VI: THE FORM OF THE SACRAMENT AND ITS MINISTER

The form

THE form is that part of a sacrament which, added to the matter, makes up the whole sign, by defining precisely the significance more generally indicated by the matter.

In penance the form is the absolution uttered by the priest which gives to the penitent's acts their full significance, by making it clear that the Sacrament is a judgement, and not mere humiliation or general petition for forgiveness.

In the Latin Church the full form is:

"May Almighty God have mercy upon thee, and having forgiven thy sins, may he lead thee to eternal life. Amen.

"May the almighty and merciful Lord grant to thee pardon, absolution, and remission of thy sins. Amen.

"May our Lord Jesus Christ absolve thee; and I by his authority absolve thee from every bond of excommunication (of suspension) and of interdict, as far as I can and you need. Therefore I absolve thee from thy sins, in the Name of the Father and of the Son and of the Holy Ghost. Amen.

"May the Passion of our Lord Jesus Christ, the merits of the Blessed Virgin Mary, and of all the saints, whatever good thou hast done, and whatever evil thou hast borne, avail thee for the remission of sins, the increase of grace, and the reward of eternal life. Amen." [1]

However, though this full form is normally obligatory, it contains much that is not strictly necessary to give sacramental significance to the matter. Thus for good reasons the first and last prayers may be omitted, and only the actual absolution uttered. In cases of extreme necessity there is an even shorter form prescribed, since it contains all that is required to make the Sacrament.

"I absolve thee from all censures and sins, in the Name of the Father and of the Son and of the Holy Ghost. Amen." Though even shorter forms, such as "I absolve thee from thy sins," would be probably valid, few occasions would arise to warrant their use.

The form must be spoken by the priest in the presence of the penitent. To avoid difficulties and abuses, a judgement delivered in writing or by signs is not normally permitted.

Moreover, the judgement must be definite; its effect must not be doubtful. Thus conditional absolution is valid only if the condition is one already fulfilled. But it is only when there is no possibility of verifying the fulfilment of the condition that a priest is allowed to use a conditional form.

The form in early times

The form in the Latin rite is indicative. This is necessary for validity in the West. An assertion is the most fitting way in which to pass sentence, and therefore in the West only an indicative form is allowed.

But in the early Church, and still in Oriental rites, deprecative forms were, and are, valid and permissible. The priest gave absolution at one time, and still does in the East, by a supplication to God to forgive the penitent's sins.

Two difficulties arise from this. It seems at first strange that an essential part of the Sacrament should be variable. A sacrament is instituted by our Lord, and its essentials can therefore surely not be altered even by the Church. Actually, however, nothing essential has been altered. Our Lord founded this Sacrament as a judgement,

[1] Actually, of course, the form is in Latin.

but he said nothing as to the actual form of words to be used in passing sentence. Indeed, there is even now no set form for retaining sins by refusing absolution. It is therefore enough that the judgement should be preserved; over the form of words to be used in delivering judgement the Church has authority. If the words prescribed by the Church are compatible with a judicial decision the essence of the Sacrament is untouched.

But this seems to make the deprecative forms invalid. A supplication to God seems hardly consistent with a judicial sentence passed by the priest. Does any judge pass sentence in an optative form expressing his hope that the accused be acquitted or condemned by someone else? No judge in England, for example, ends a trial by saying: "I trust that His Majesty will agree that you are guilty and that you ought to go to prison for ten years."

However, such forms are valid, even in earthly judgements, if they are the recognised mode of judicial decision. It is, for example, conceivable that the tradition of English justice should have imposed such a form as that imagined above. If it came at the end of a trial, after the hearing of evidence, and were the legally admitted form of passing sentence, it would be a true judgement. In short, the form of this Sacrament must be indicative in its true meaning in the circumstances, even though it be deprecative in the apparent meaning according to a dictionary. It is certain that both in the early Church and in the East the deprecative forms used are to be understood as conveying the definitive sentence of the judge. They are therefore valid.

However, the indicative form has this advantage, that it stresses clearly the judicial authority of the priest, which in the other forms is obscured by the customary meaning of the words.

The minister

With the form it is convenient to discuss the minister who utters it. Any priest and only a priest can be minister of this Sacrament. It is true that in earlier days bishops were the usual ministers, but even then priests occasionally dispensed the Sacrament. Any instances of laymen or of deacons administering this Sacrament are isolated. They can be explained, when it is a question of genuine attempts to administer the Sacrament, and not a mere matter of hearing confessions without attempting to absolve, by a mistaken desire to do all that was possible for a penitent in the absence of a priest. At no time has the Church, as such, sanctioned the administration of the Sacrament by any other than a priest.

Jurisdiction

But the priesthood alone does not enable a man to absolve validly. He needs, in addition, jurisdiction from the competent authority—normally from the bishop of a diocese. To explain this a parallel is useful. In creating a judge the Government cannot make an indiscriminate appointment; certain legal qualifications are normally necessary in the man to be appointed. But even when he is created judge a man must be assigned a definite area in which to exercise authority, before he can validly do so. He cannot walk into any court he likes and decide to try cases there. So with Penance. Only a priest can be appointed, but when, by his ordination, he has been given the power to absolve sacramentally, he still needs a further commission before he can exercise this power even validly. He must have subjects definitely assigned to him.

This is usually expressed by saying that a priest must have faculties. If a priest without faculties were to attempt to absolve, he would not remit the sins. The Church, like the State, can decide upon what conditions she will permit her judges to pass effective sentence.

A priest, therefore, must have received, normally from the bishop, faculties to administer Penance in his diocese. Outside that diocese he still indeed has the power, but he cannot exercise it. In a canonically constituted parish, the parish priest has this jurisdiction by the very fact of his appointment. Other priests must receive definite commissions from the bishop. In those houses of religious orders which are exempt from episcopal control, the superior gives faculties for hearing the confessions of those under his authority. Of course, the Pope has full jurisdiction over the whole Church, and can therefore give faculties for the whole Church.

Historically this need for jurisdiction has always been realised. In the early Church the bishop, who by his appointment receives authority, gave the absolutions. As the number of Christians increased, bishops delegated priests to do a work that had become too great for the bishops single-handed. During the Middle Ages the Church was very strict on this matter of jurisdiction ; hence arose the confessional letters which we mentioned in connection with Indulgences. Finally the Council of Trent definitely taught that both orders and jurisdiction were necessary for the valid administration of Penance.

There are certain cases where the Church grants general jurisdiction to any priest. Thus, when circumstances are such that absolution could not otherwise be given, and is strictly necessary, as at the moment of death when there is no possibility of securing a priest with faculties, any priest validly absolves. Also, when there is an unavoidable and widespread error, so that the faithful are generally and inculpably receiving absolution from a priest, who in some way lacks authorisation, the Church supplies the necessary jurisdiction.

Reservation

Connected with the question of jurisdiction is the practice whereby certain sins are reserved. The authority conferring jurisdiction may limit it, and withdraw certain sins from the priest's power. Some of these reservations are made by the general law of the Church, and the sins are reserved either to the Holy See or to the bishops. Moreover, bishops within their own dioceses may reserve other sins to themselves. This means that a priest cannot normally [1] absolve from these sins, without first applying for special faculties from the authority to whom the sins are reserved. Meanwhile the penitent must wait. The practice is in keeping with the traditional severity of the Church towards certain sins. It is intended to have a remedial value, by deterring people from certain very grave sins, especially when there is danger of their frequent commission. But for the ordinary Christians reservation has not much practical importance, as the sins reserved are always very grave and are comparatively few.

Judge, physician, teacher

As minister the priest has certain duties. He must act as judge; he must decide whether the penitent is adequately disposed for absolution; should he, as rarely happens, decide that the penitent is not so disposed, he must refuse absolution. Though he must not try to compel a penitent to confess in greater detail than is necessary, as judge he may ask for necessary information and is entitled to receive it.

He is also doctor. As doctor it is his duty to do what seems to him possible to heal the souls of his penitents by strengthening their wills and helping them to avoid sin. This duty is particularly pressing with penitents who are habitual sinners. The priest must, of course, proceed with prudence, but he would be wrong to neglect this duty altogether.

Finally, he is a teacher. The intimacy of confession may disclose ignorance in his penitents which it is his duty to remove. This is particularly true when the penitents are young or illiterate.

The seal of the confessional

There remains to be discussed the grave obligation of preserving the secrecy of confession; "keeping the seal," as it is usually termed. The priest cannot, without the gravest sin, make any use of confessional knowledge to the detriment of the penitent, however slightly, nor in such a way as to risk discrediting the Sacrament. He should therefore not normally use his knowledge even to the penitent's advantage, as this might be misunderstood and might cause Christians to hesitate to use the Sacrament.

In practice, the observance of the seal has been remarkable. There are few cases recorded of direct breach. Even of indirect breach—*i.e.*, a disclosure of confessional knowledge, not by explicit statement, but through carelessness and by inference—there are not many examples. The observance is indeed strangely easy. Gradually the priest seems to acquire two distinct mental sections, the confessional and the non-confessional, and it becomes easy to keep the two apart. Moreover, even if a priest wished, he would often find it difficult to break the seal. To the penitent his confession is the only one; to the priest it is but one of hundreds heard in the dark, through a grating, and in a whisper. Normally it is difficult

[1] There are certain cases in which reservation loses all force, and any confessor has general faculties; the two most notable are the moment of death, and when to apply for special faculties would endanger the seal.

to remember anything clearly, or to connect anything remembered with any definite person.

The strictness of this secrecy has, of course, developed, but secrecy is of divine imposition, for it arises out of the words of institution. There were indeed difficulties in the early Church. The extent and the strictness of the obligation at first were not always so clearly understood as to-day. Though confession was secret, penance was public; as the Sacrament was used only for grave sins, submission to it involved the public acknowledgement of the commission of a grave sin, even though that were not specifically told.

Still, the manner in which confession was made, injunctions such as those quoted from Origen on the choice of confessor, comparisons of confession to medical consultation, the manner in which early writers such as St John Chrysostom always talk of confession as made to God alone, all point to the recognition of the need of secrecy. St Leo gives us a summary of the traditional teaching:

"I decide also that the breach of apostolic rule which I learn lately some have dared to commit should be entirely suppressed; I mean that in penance, which is demanded by the faithful, the written confession of their sins should not be recited publicly, since it is sufficient that these manifestations of guilt in conscience should be made to priests only in secret confession. . . . For then, indeed, many can be excited to penance, if the conscience of the penitent be not published to the ears of the people." [1]

Thus St Leo gives us not only the existence of the seal, but one reason for it, that without it Christians would be reluctant to use this Sacrament so necessary for their salvation.

During the Middle Ages the duty of secrecy was clearly recognised. But theologians did discuss its extent. The strictness of the obligation, however, was so fully appreciated that Lanfranc—though wrongly—advocated confession to a cleric not a priest, if confession to a priest involved danger of the breach of the seal. [2]

At length in the seventeenth century Innocent XI ended all possible dispute. He condemned the proposition that confessional knowledge could be used to the detriment of the penitent, even though there was no revelation of sin, and though the non-use of confessional knowledge would be more to the detriment of the penitent than its use. Thus to-day the obligation of the seal is as strict as it can be. Even reservation is removed if the priest deems it impossible to apply for faculties without danger of breach of the seal; the Church accords him general faculties in these circumstances. A priest, then, can in no way use his confessional knowledge outside confession to the harm of the penitent or the discredit of the Sacrament.

[1] St Leo, *Epistle*, clxviii 2.

[2] Lanfranc, Archbishop of Canterbury (1070-1089), *De Celanda Confessione.*

The gravity of this obligation does not arise merely from the natural duty of secrecy concerning solemn confidences. Doctors and lawyers are bound to secrecy by ordinary natural law. The priest is bound, in addition, by the positive revealed law of Christ, though the exact basis in revelation is disputed. Here we may add to the reason given by St Leo this further consideration, that the priest in confession has the grave responsibility of acting in God's name. He is there not as man merely, but as God's representative. And he must not betray the secrets of God. Hence this obligation is so strict that nothing can destroy it. No advantage for any man, no law of any state, no command from any superior, even the Pope, no evil to be averted, not death itself, can ever justify a priest breaking the seal of confession.

§ VII: THE EFFECTS AND USE OF THE SACRAMENT

Effects

It is clear from what has been said that the chief effect of this Sacrament is the remission of mortal sin, and the consequent restoration to the soul of sanctifying grace, lost by grave sin. For a treatment of what this means to the soul we must refer to the relevant essays in this work.[1]

As a further consequence of the remission of mortal sin, eternal punishment is necessarily remitted also; for this is closely connected with sin as its inevitable sequel.[2] A soul from which sin has been removed cannot therefore be under sentence of eternal punishment. This, though not expressly defined, is certain Catholic doctrine, and is assumed by the Council of Trent.

Eternal punishment follows from mortal sin inevitably. But even when the sin has been forgiven there remains a debt of temporal punishment which must be paid to restore right order upset by sin. This temporal punishment is not necessarily entirely remitted by the Sacrament. We have incurred it through our own fault, and it is but just, after God's exceeding mercy in remitting our sin and its eternal punishment, that we should in some way atone for our guilt. But the Sacrament does lessen the amount of punishment due to us. It applies Christ's merits to our souls, and therefore the performance of satisfactory acts as part of the Sacrament has a greater effect than the same acts would have independently thereof. But as even these could lessen the temporal punishment due to us, clearly the sacramental satisfaction can lessen this punishment even more effectively.

Since, however, any mortal sin is incompatible with the presence of grace in our souls, one mortal sin cannot be remitted while others

[1] *Cf. Sanctifying Grace, The Supernatural Virtues, Man and his Destiny, Sin and Repentance, Eternal Punishment,* and *Heaven,* in particular.

[2] *Cf.* p. 931.

are retained. Consequently if a man has committed more than one grave sin, he must be sorry for all, before he can be pardoned.

Venial sin also can be forgiven sacramentally, as we have already seen in the course of this essay. But venial sin does not destroy the life of grace. Therefore it is possible for us to be pardoned for our mortal sins, and to be restored to supernatural life even though no venial sin be remitted. Hence this Sacrament forgives those venial sins for which the penitent is sorry, and only those.

With the restoration and strengthening of the life of grace there is restored and strengthened all that accompanies that life. Thus those supernatural virtues [1] which have been lost by sin are restored to us by this Sacrament, and are even strengthened. Also the merits which we formerly possessed and which we forfeited by our sin, are given back to us, at least in some measure, by the sacramental absolution.

These are the necessary sacramental effects. It is possible, however, for subjective dispositions to modify these effects, though, as long as we are not interposing obstacles to grace, mere lack of fervour cannot prevent them altogether. But intensity of devotion can increase them. Hence the extent to which temporal punishment is remitted, grace strengthened in us, our merits restored to us, is determined partly by the earnestness with which we receive the Sacrament.

Practical use of the Sacrament

So important is this Sacrament in the lives of Christians that some practical advice seems desirable as a complement to a doctrinal treatise. We have to use our knowledge to guide our actions.

One grave danger must first be mentioned. The practising Catholic receives this Sacrament so often that he is sometimes apt to forget that it is a Sacrament, a momentous event in his life. For those in mortal sin, confession is like a new baptism, as we have seen the Fathers of the Church insisting. We should therefore remind ourselves of this and strive to make our confessions the notable occurrence they should be. In them we are entering into sacramental union with Christ on the Cross, and if we are receiving pardon for mortal sin, then nothing in our lives save baptism is of equal importance. For those in mortal sin confession is even of greater immediate necessity than the Sacrament of the Eucharist.

Since this is so, and since many of the effects of the Sacrament are increased by fervour, we should try to be as fervent in its reception as possible. It not merely forgives our sins, it also gives strength to resist sin in future. Penitents, however, who are struggling against some habit of sin, often fail to secure the full benefit of their confessions, because they do not make effort enough when they receive the Sacrament.

[1] *Cf.* Essay xviii, *The Supernatural Virtues*, pp. 640–641.

To secure this fervour we should remember that this is a Sacrament of sorrow. Our preparation should largely consist in an effort to arouse in ourselves deep and true sorrow. In our examination of conscience we should avoid excessive introspection; if we are frequenting the Sacraments regularly, serious sin will come to our minds easily, and if we have to search with notable diligence, it is reasonably certain that the deliberation in our acts was so slight as to deprive them of all gravity. But having found our sins we should dwell almost fiercely on the motives for sorrow: on the goodness of God, on the vileness of even the slightest venial sin, on its ingratitude to God, who gave us the very powers we use in sinning and who keeps us in existence while we sin, and above all on the Passion of our Lord, endured because of sin. This should be the chief part of our preparation if we are to receive the full benefit of this Sacrament. Our very resolution against sin is rendered far stronger, if we have, though only for a time, felt real sorrow for our sins and a genuine detestation of them.

In confession, again, we should be humble, inspired thereto by our sorrow, anxious to disclose fully and truthfully our shame as a punishment for the foul guilt we so deeply regret.

Our thanksgiving and our satisfaction, too, ought to be quickened by this same contrition. We should feel intense gratitude to God for his goodness in thus enabling us to be free from the shame of sin. We should say our penance with real earnestness, only sorry that it is so slight, and that of ourselves we can do nothing to atone for the sins for which we are now so repentant.

A confession so made will have permanent effect, especially if we frequent the Sacrament regularly as we should do. It is a good practice to go to confession once a week, for thus we receive regularly an increase of grace to strengthen us against sin, and form gradually a habit of resistance to sin, by frequently renewing our sorrow for it, and our detestation of it. Even, therefore, if we should be so fortunate as not to have fallen since our last confession, yet we should go at the usual time and renew the confession of past sins, and sorrow for them.

To secure more fully the benefits of the Sacrament, Origen's advice is important: to choose our confessor carefully. Regular guidance is useful to the soul. A doctor, for complete efficiency, needs to know the medical history of his patient, and the circumstances of his life that may affect his health; so, too, the priest can help us better the more he knows of our spiritual history and of the circumstances of our life that may affect our spiritual well-being.

In choosing this confessor we should be guided by spiritual motives. He should be a man we find sympathetic and spiritually helpful. Normally one who knows us outside confession is able to be of more use to us than a stranger. He knows our lives, our circumstances, our difficulties, very fully, has no need to ask many questions, and is less likely to be ignorant of some fact, perhaps important, that we overlook through a failure to realise its importance. Of course, if our regular confessor be not available and we have urgent need of absolution we should go to any priest who is at hand; it would be foolish, because of the absence of any one man, to remain longer in mortal sin than is necessary.

Having chosen a confessor, we should help him by asking for guidance if we need it. Otherwise he may be hampered by fear of intruding on a soul, and perhaps doing harm by offending his penitent.

We must remember, above all, that this is a Sacrament, and an astounding proof of God's great goodness. If it did not exist, we should earnestly desire it. God in his goodness has given it to us. To fail to use this gift, then, or to use it carelessly, is to add to our other sins the crime of black ingratitude to God for the immense favour he has bestowed upon us.

H. Harrington.

XXVIII
EXTREME UNCTION

§ I: INTRODUCTORY

God in his infinite mercy has encompassed the life of man on earth by the gracious net of his life-giving sacraments. Supernatural life is first opened to him by baptism. The sacrament of the new birth removes the stain of original and of any subsequent sin and constitutes him the adopted son of God, his heir through the Beatific Vision and co-heir of Christ. In the first years of adolescence, when the struggle with sin begins, God sends him the Holy Ghost in Confirmation to strengthen his soul for the combat which continues all the years of his life. As no life is ever maintained unless sustained by appropriate food, God with gracious bounty supplies a celestial food for the support of the supernatural life of man ; he gives him the Manna that comes from heaven in the Holy Eucharist.

During man's sojourn on earth there occurs in the natural order no greater or more important change than marriage. A new world of duties and responsibilities as well as trials then begins to surround him and God created the mighty sacrament of Matrimony to support him in his task.

As God knows the clay of which we are made and the frailty of our human nature, he foresaw the shipwreck many would make of their supernatural life. In the sacrament of Penance he gave man a plank of safety by which even those who sinned mortally after baptism might be rescued from being engulfed in eternal damnation.

And finally with divine ingenuity God created the sacrament of Extreme Unction to be the complement and consummation of Penance. By this Unction at the end of life sin itself and the remnants of sin can be totally undone and man prepared for immediate entrance into everlasting glory.

In itself Extreme Unction is a sacrament of the living. It is meant for those whose souls are in the state of sanctifying grace, but who need support in the stress and strain of grave illness that leads to bodily death. But by an excess of long-suffering pity God made it avail even for those whose souls are in grievous sin but who have begun to return to him by imperfect repentance and who are so overcome by their illness that they can think and act no more. Extreme Unction may therefore be regarded as a final triumph of God's tenderness towards men, saving them to the uttermost, and almost in spite of their own weakness and the wiles of the evil one.

§ II: THE INSTITUTION OF THE SACRAMENT

A. Scripture

Unction as practised by the Apostles

The Council of Trent teaches us [1] that the unction of the sick was instituted by Christ our Lord, as truly and properly a sacrament of the New Law, insinuated indeed in the Gospel of St Mark, but recommended and promulgated to the faithful by St James.

The words in St Mark vi 12-13 are these: "Going forth they preached that men should do penance: and they cast out many devils and anointed with oil many that were sick and healed them." Some have seen in these words an account of the use of the sacrament of Extreme Unction during our Lord's life on earth, but the Council of Trent with great caution uses the term "insinuated in Mark," making the healing unction performed by the Apostles rather a foretelling and prefiguring of this sacrament than the sacrament itself. It is indeed most likely that the unctions and healings performed then by the Apostles were not sacramental in character. Their anointings and prayers over the sick did not constitute an outward sign instituted by Christ signifying and effecting divine grace in the souls of the recipients in virtue of the very sign performed. We need not doubt that the Apostles used unction in the healing of the sick at our Lord's own command. Our Lord used his own spittle mixed with earth to anoint the eyes of the man he cured; he may well have commanded his Apostles to use unction in their healings, but such unction had as direct meaning and purpose the bodily health of the recipients and only indirectly the bestowal of divine grace on their souls. If divine grace was given, it was an uncovenanted mercy in accordance with the faith and repentance of the sick or their friends, not the outcome of a sacrament.

What the Apostles had practised during their missionary journeys when our Lord was on earth, was transformed and raised to the dignity of a sacrament when they went forth into all the world and preached Christ and his resurrection.

The text of St James' Epistle

We have no record when and how precisely our Lord thus instituted this Sacrament of the New Law, but we learn from St James, the Brother of the Lord, in his Epistle to the Jewish Christians, that if anyone were sick amongst them, he was exhorted to receive this sacramental rite.

"Is any man sick among you? Let him send for the priests of the Church and let them pray over him, anointing him with oil in the name of the Lord. And the prayer of faith shall save the sick man and the Lord shall raise him up, and if he be in sins, they shall be forgiven him; confess therefore your sins one to another and pray one for another that you may be healed, for the fervent prayer of a just man availeth much." [2]

[1] xiv 9, 1.

[2] v 14-16.

If we consider these words in detail we gather that the first condition for this sacrament is a state of bodily sickness, and that of a serious nature, for the Greek word used indicates some grave ailment. The sick man is evidently in such a state of weakness that he cannot go to the church or the dwelling-place of the priests, but has to beg them to come to him. The English phrase " send for the priests " well renders the Greek expression, which implies not a mere asking of a favour as one might desire a pious and kind friend to come and pray, but an authoritative demand that these priests should come in their official capacity to do something for the sick man which he could not do for himself. It is to be noted that the word " priests " is in the plural. This fact is undoubtedly the reason why both in East and West, in many places and during many centuries, this sacrament was administered not by one, but by several priests, sometimes seven, or at least as many as were conveniently available. But though the text suggests, yet it does not absolutely demand, a plurality of priests. The priests are thought of as a group of men within the reach of the sick person ; to send for them can mean to bid them send any one, or several from their number to perform their required functions. For many centuries in the West the custom has prevailed that the sacrament be administered by one priest alone, and this is now the only one sanctioned by authority. This therefore constitutes an infallible interpretation of the meaning of the text.

It is natural to ask whether the words " let him send " constitute a strict command, or merely a wholesome advice, which might be disregarded without serious sin. The words immediately preceding : " Is any of you sad ? Let him pray ! Is he cheerful in mind ? Let him sing ! " suggest a counsel rather than a command, but the following words containing a promise of forgiveness of sin for the sick man point to something more than a mere counsel. For a more definite interpretation of the passage we must go beyond the text itself to the interpretation of the Church.

It is obvious that the expression " the priests of the Church " cannot mean " the elders " in the sense of people of more advanced age, but must designate some special officials of the Church, who even in St James' day were designated by the term " presbyteroi," a word of which " priest " is but an abbreviation.[1]

These priests should pray over the sick man. Note that the expression is not " pray *for* " the sick man, which might be done by anyone anywhere, but *over* him, as if they were to recite some powerful formula of impetration, while standing over him recumbent on his bed of sickness. This is in keeping with the words which follow : " anointing him with oil in the name of the Lord." The praying and the anointing go together and constitute one combined action. Now this anointing is done " in the name of the Lord." It

[1] For information regarding the functions of the priesthood see Essay xxix.

is not merely some expression of the personal faith either of the sick man, or the priests or the bystanders, some symbolic action indicative of their personal desires or some natural medicinal practice, but an actual use of the power of Christ and an exercise of his authority committed to the priests. They act in the name of their Master. It is their Master's power which is brought into play and they are but the functionaries or officials, instruments in the hands of the Lord of the Church.

The effect of this use of divine power is thus indicated: " The prayer of faith shall save the sick man and the Lord shall raise him up." The prayer is said to be " of the faith "; it is not the mere informal expression of individual supplication by anyone, Jew, pagan, or Christian, who might be asking a favour of the Almighty, but it is the official exercise of the Christian Faith. It is an appeal to the power of Christ, sanctioned by him and carried out by his representatives. It is most emphatically an act of believers, unmeaning and useless to those not of the faith. The sending for the priests, the acceptance of the Christian rite by the sick man, the administration of it by the functionaries of the Church are typical manifestations of the faith, provoked by the extreme need of the ill person in danger of death. This prayer shall save the sick man.

The word " saving " is quite a general term, as also the expression " the Lord shall raise him up," and considered in itself might refer to bodily healing as well as to spiritual, and to both. The Greek word rendered " raising up " implies awakening, resuscitation, stirring up, bringing to life from torpor or dullness. We must note that in the last verse another word is used, " that you may be healed or cured "; this is normally used of bodily healing alone. If, then, St James here uses a wider term it is natural to conclude that it stands for a wider idea. In the first place the Epistle is throughout concerned with supernatural ideas: a merciful judgement, a happy coming of the Lord, saving the soul from death, the crown of life, the possession of the kingdom, the gift of patience and so on; hence to interpret the word " save " exclusively as meaning the recovery of bodily health would be out of harmony with the mind of St James. Moreover, a spiritual but conditional effect is next mentioned, and it is in the highest degree improbable that forgiveness of sins would be thus casually attached to bodily healing; and, finally, the verbs " to save " and " to raise " here indicate an unconditional result of the rite performed. Now St James cannot have spoken of the rite as an unconditional means of bodily healing, for it would mean an automatic escape from death, which is an absurdity.

" And if he be in sins, they shall be forgiven him." St James here clearly suggests that the proper state of the sick man when receiving the sacrament should be such that there be no guilt of grave or venial sin upon his soul; but so great is the efficacy of the sacrament that should there be still some stains of sin they will be deleted.

The text continues : " Confess therefore your sins one to another and pray one for another that you may be healed, for the fervent prayer of a just man availeth much." These words have led many to believe that St James had in his mind the combination of the two sacraments : Penance and Extreme Unction.

The priests of the Church administered the last rites to the sick man ; but no technical distinction of the two sacraments of Penance and Extreme Unction seems to have been in St James' mind, especially as the early form of absolution was in deprecative form, not in that of a judicial verdict. Should there have been any grave matter to confess and the sick man still capable of confessing it, the priests would remit this by a specific prayer for its forgiveness and thus reconcile the sinner to God before the anointing ; but if the patient were speechless, if the priests knew of no grave fault which needed reconciliation, or if the sick man could recall no serious sin, then the prayer with unction would remit whatever sin there might be on the man's soul, which would prevent or retard his entrance into heaven.

" Confess one to another " is an expression like " obey one another, instruct one another, help one another," with the obvious implication that some are superiors, others inferiors, some teachers, some taught, some in need of help, others able to give it. As St James has mentioned presbyters in the plural, the expression is a natural one ; in the Christian community people have to confess one to another, some to make and others to accept the confession. But as St James is not writing a technical treatise on the sacraments but giving homely advice about well-known matters, the mention of forgiveness of sin brings him to urge open avowal of them in the Christian community, but in the proper way and to the proper persons. Then again the prayer of the priests suggests to him the universal power of prayer and its suitability in days of illness : " pray one for another that you may be healed." This cure may not always be infallibly obtained, but the prayer of just men is of great power.

Some interpreters detach the words " Confess therefore . . ." from the preceding and suggest that St James therewith begins a new train of thought unconnected with Extreme Unction. There can be little doubt, however, that the particle *therefore*, though lacking in some manuscripts, is part of the true text, and in consequence we must postulate some connection with what goes before. Nor is this difficult if we keep in mind St James' unstudied flow of thoughts and expressions, so different from the elaborate treatises of later centuries. The attempts of non-Catholics to utilise the last sentence to rob the previous ones of their sacramental meaning, and on the other hand the endeavour of some Catholics to prove sacramental confession from the last sentence apart from its context or the interpretation of the Church, are alike fruitless.

B. Tradition

Rare early references

The existence of this sacrament, which is thus so clearly indicated in Holy Scripture, is also taught by Christian tradition. Scarcity of direct references to Extreme Unction in the extant literature of the early Church is only what we might expect. The Epistle of St James is not a New Testament writing to which early commentators would first turn their exegetical or homiletic efforts. Didymus the Blind, born in A.D. 313 at Alexandria, is the only early Father who is known to have written a commentary on St James, and this, with the exception of a few fragments in a Latin translation, is lost. We have to wait four hundred years for the next commentator, St Bede. In apologetic literature the defence of the Christian faith against paganism would not naturally call for a reference to Extreme Unction. Great sermons that are handed down to posterity usually deal either with great historical occasions or with topics which need lengthy and repeated exposition to the faithful. They deal with public functions, feast days, or such parts of the life of the faithful as need considerable preparation. Hence reference to Baptism, Confirmation, Eucharist and the penitential discipline are not infrequent.

Extreme Unction is in some sense a private matter withdrawn from the public life of the Church; though the sick were sometimes brought to the Church, this was of necessity a very rare occurrence. Moreover, Christians of the first four centuries, living in overwhelmingly pagan surroundings and at a great distance from priests, would very often be unable to call them to their sick-bed for the purpose of anointing. In our own day public references to Extreme Unction, whether in the pulpit or in print, are not frequent, and we cannot expect them to have been more frequent in the early days. The bulk of the faithful now have easy access to their priests and there are not many obstacles to the reception of this sacrament. Most of our present-day references consist in exhortations to call the priest to the sick in good time and the Last Sacraments are referred to generally without separate and express mention of the Unction.

In early days the technical term, Extreme Unction, had not yet been invented; the rite was often called the "imposition of hands." But as the same name was also given to Reconciliation, or Penance, as we now call it, it is not always possible to prove that Extreme Unction is meant; the more so as the imposition of hands for the Unction was regarded as supplementary to the Reconciliation and as constituting one whole with it, just as Confirmation was attached to Baptism as the complete initiatory rite. Thus the distinctness of the sacrament is often not directly emphasised.

If we take all this into consideration it is rather surprising that allusions to Extreme Unction should be so frequent as they are. A number of early Latin, Greek, and Syrian Fathers refer to the unction of the sick, though only incidentally. These indications are indeed clear enough, especially in their cumulative force, for Catholics who already believe that Christ instituted this sacrament, but hardly strong enough to convince a gainsayer.

Tertullian

Tertullian rebukes heretics for abolishing the distinction between priests and laity, and says that they even permit women " to teach, to dispute, to perform exorcisms, to undertake cures, perhaps even to baptise." This is evidently a series of specifically clerical functions. There was therefore a function of healing the sick which was exclusive to the clergy. This cannot be miraculous or charismatic healing, which Tertullian, even if oil were used for the purpose, did not limit to the priests. He can therefore only be alluding to sacramental healing according to the prescription of St James: " let them send for the priests." [1]

Origen

A direct reference to the texts dealing with Extreme Unction occurs in Origen's second homily on Leviticus (*c.* A.D. 240) and, remarkably enough, in a list of means of the forgiveness of sins after baptism.

Aphraates

Aphraates, born in Persia in A.D. 336, extolling the power of oil in the Christian religion, writes of it as the token " of the sacrament of life by which Christians (in baptism), priests (in ordination), kings, and prophets are made perfect, it (oil) illuminates darkness (in confirmation [2]), anoints the sick, and by its secret sacrament restores penitents." [3]

Non-sacramental anointings are here included, but in any case they are an enumeration of spiritual effects of the use of Holy Oil among Christians, and the natural implication of the words is the existence of a grace-giving rite administered by unction to the sick for a spiritual purpose and not merely for bodily healing.

Chrysostom

St John Chrysostom (about A.D. 380), in the third book of his famous treatise on the Priesthood, has a passage the significance of which can hardly be overlooked. He wishes to show that we owe to priests even more than to our parents ; the latter gave us natural birth, but the former a supernatural one. " There is between the former and the latter as much difference as there is between the present life and the life to come. For our parents cannot shield their children against bodily death, or drive away oncoming illness ; but priests have often saved the soul that is sick and about to die.

" For some souls they have lightened the punishment, others they did not allow to fall at all, and this not only by their teaching and their advice, but by the help of their prayers. Nor is this only so when they regenerate us (by baptism), but afterwards also they have the power to forgive sins, for indeed, ' Is any one sick amongst you, let him send. . . .' " [4]

[1] *De Praescr.*, c. 41, compared with *Ad Scap.*, c. 4.
[2] This initiatory rite is called in the East *photismos* : illumination.
[3] *Dem.* xxiii 3.
[4] In Greek " saved " and " sick " are the identical terms of St James.

St Bede

The attestations increase in number and clearness as the centuries pass on, and by about A.D. 700 it is historically demonstrable that amongst Christians there existed a sacramental, grace-giving rite conferred upon the sick to purify their soul and restore their bodily health, if God sees fit. Our own St Bede is a conspicuous witness, attesting the faith of Celts and Saxons, less than a century after the arrival of St Augustine from Rome and the death of St Columba in Iona. It is worth while to quote his commentary on St James: "As he (St James) had given his counsel to the man who is sad, so he gives it also to the man who is sick, how he has to guard against the folly of murmuring, and he accommodates the kind of medicine to the kind of wound. . . . If anyone is sick in body or in faith he commands that he who received the greater injury should remember to cure himself with the help of many, and indeed of priests . . . and let them pray over him. We read in the Gospel,[1] that the Apostles did this also, and now the custom of the Church holds that the sick should be anointed with consecrated oil by the priests and that by the added prayer they should be healed."

So normal in those days was the administration to the sick of the three sacraments, Penance, Viaticum, and Extreme Unction, that in a capitulary of Charlemagne of 769, amongst the ordinary duties of the clergy this threefold administration is inculcated. Nor was this custom limited to the West, it existed also in the East, and even sects separated from the Church since the fifth century retained it, and referred its origin to Apostolic times. It is inconceivable that this universal practice should not be what it claims to be: part of the grace-giving system of outward signs derived from Christ himself.

Extra-sacramental use of blessed oil

Sometimes indeed there may be doubt in an individual case whether the sacrament of Extreme Unction is meant, or merely some sacramental, a pious rite instituted by the Church for the restoration of bodily health. It is certain that at least for some five hundred years the use of blessed oil as a sacramental, apart altogether from the sacrament, was common in many places.

This is parallel to the use of holy water or even of baptismal water, consecrated on Holy Saturday, as a sacramental, independently of Baptism itself. It was customary for the faithful during the Mass to offer and for the priests to bless oil, which the faithful then took home with them and used either as a drink or a liniment in case of illness, with pious trust in the prayers of the Church for those who used it in faith and reverence. It seems also that locally and for a time even oil consecrated for Extreme Unction was allowed so to be used by the faithful, obviously on the understanding that, unless it were used officially by the priests of the Church with the proper prayers for the administration of the sacrament referred to by St James, it was no sacrament, but only a sacramental for private use. Such at least is the almost unavoidable implication of the famous

[1] Mark vi 13.

letter of Pope Innocent I (A.D. 416) to the Bishop of Eugubium in which he speaks of "the holy oil, which, blessed by the bishop, not only priests but all Christians may use for anointing themselves and theirs when in need." The oil here spoken of is certainly that blessed for Extreme Unction, which, according to this Pope, bishops and priests use in carrying out St James' behest, and which may be used only for the faithful, not for those who are excluded from the sacraments.

Distinct from sacramental use

There are instances on record in the lives of the saints which show that in practice sacramental use of Holy Oil for the sick was clearly distinguished from charismatic use. A telling example is that of St Hypatius, who died about the year 446 in the East. This saint, before he was ordained, used to perform miracles of healing by anointing the sick with consecrated oil, though he was not in Orders. Yet he was fully aware of another kind of anointing which only priests could perform. We read in his life story, written by a contemporary: "When there was need of anointing the sick man, he informed the abbot, for he was a priest, and had the unction with the consecrated oil performed by him. And it often occurred that through God's co-operation with his efforts, he sent the man home restored to health." [1] Clearly the priest-abbot could do something which the lay-monk could not do.

No doubt sometimes amongst the uneducated or superstitious charismatic unction conferred by some reputedly holy lay-monk may have been preferred to sacramental anointing, or the two may have been confused in the minds of a few, but never by Church authorities or by the well-informed laity. Isaac of Antioch, a bishop who died in A.D. 460, in great old age, thus rebukes foolish women who for the unction prefer a wandering unknown monk to the proper priest of the circuit: "Woman, give thy alms to the recluse, but receive the unction from thy priest; support the monk, but let thy oil be that of the Apostles, the oil of the Crucified One, receive the unction from the priest. They neglect the oil of the Apostles and martyrs who have suffered for the truth, and the oil of fraud glistens on the face of perverted women. Christ's servants, the right-believing, have indeed the custom of bringing their sick to the altar but dare not administer the oil lest they should seem to contemn the home of expiation. Where there is a priest to lead the people, they observe the true laws." The very condemnation of these abuses by this famous poet-bishop indicates the correct ecclesiastical usage.

That a clear distinction was drawn between the official, public sacramental use of oil by the priest and its private use by the faithful is plain from the occurrence of distinct formulas of blessing for the two purposes. A remarkable instance is found in the prayer over the oil of the sick in the Sacramentary of Serapion, the Bishop of Thmuis, a friend of St Athanasius (about A.D. 350).

[1] See his Life in the Bollandists, June 17.

"We invoke thee, thou who hast all authority and power, Saviour of all men, Father of our Lord and Saviour Jesus Christ, and we pray thee to send healing power from heaven from the only-begotten Son on this oil in order that from all those who are anointed or who partake in thy creatures here present it may drive away all sickness and all infirmity, that it may serve them as an antidote against every demon, that it expel from them every unclean spirit and banish every evil spirit, chase away every fever and chill and every sickness, that it may grant them good grace and remission of sin, that it may be unto them a remedy of life and salvation, that it may bring them health and integrity of soul, of body, of spirit, a perfect constitution. O Lord, may every satanic power, every demon, every snare of the adversary, every blow and torment, every sorrow, pain, or shock or disturbance or evil shade fear thy holy name which we invoke at this moment, and the name of thy only-begotten Son. May they vanish from within and without thy servants, that glory be unto the name of him who was crucified for us and rose, who bore our ills and our weaknesses, even Jesus Christ who shall come to judge the living and the dead. Through him be unto thee the glory and the power in the Holy Ghost now and for ever. Amen."

On the other hand, the prayer to be said over the oil during the Mass is much shorter and of much more general import. The blessing of oil for the sick, intended for devout but not sacramental use, now only survives in the beautiful blessing of the oil of St Serapion, but formerly it was very widespread and for a time almost universal. Such use of oil in illness was so common that St Chrysostom, preaching at Antioch, could appeal to the experience of his congregation to acknowledge that many were cured by being anointed with the oil of the holy lamps in church.

In legends of the early saints, whether priests or layfolk, miraculous cures are ascribed to unction with oil. Here there is no question of the ordinary administration of a sacrament, but the cure is attributed to the intercession of a saint in fulfilment of Christ's last promise recorded in St Mark xvi 17, 18. "These signs shall follow them that believe: In my name they shall cast out devils . . . they shall lay their hands upon the sick and they shall recover." This use of oil as a sacramental in the early Church, with its consequent employment by the saints as an instrument for the exercise of miraculous powers, has led some non-Catholics to the erroneous supposition that Unction as a grace-giving rite for the sick and a true sacrament emerged only later in the Catholic Church. Of such gradual development, however, history knows nothing. The only rational interpretation of the facts is that sacrament and sacramental existed side by side from the beginning, but that the almost total discontinuance of the devout private use of blessed oil made the grace-giving character of the Jacobean rite stand out more clearly in the eyes of the children of the Church.

Faith of the Church in this sacrament

When in the twelfth century theological precision singled out from all sacred ceremonies in use in the Catholic Church seven, and seven only, that were outward signs of inward grace, instituted by Jesus Christ, bestowing *ex opere operato* the grace they signify, Extreme Unction was always mentioned among them. But already much earlier, the Penitential attributed to Egbert of York (766), but containing also matter of a century after his death, refers to the unction prescribed by St James for the sick and says : " Every one of the faithful must, if possible, obtain for himself this unction and whatever is ordered concerning it, for it is written that if anyone submits to this discipline his soul after death will be as pure as that of a child dying forthwith after baptism." The phrase *scriptum est*, " it is written," though it does not refer directly to a text of Scripture, shows that the writer was not giving some private opinion of his own, but merely echoing the long-established teaching of the Church. No writer at any time shows any indication that he is innovating ; rather he stresses the traditional character of the usage. In many ordinances of those days priests are told to instruct the faithful in this sacrament and to deter them from foolish superstitions then so rife in time of sickness. Priests are to carry the Holy Oils on their person when on a journey in order always to be able to anoint the sick. It is one of the normal functions of their ministry. They are gravely responsible if, through their fault, the faithful should die without this sacrament, to which they have a strict right. Some writers go even so far as to speak of it as necessary. All connect the practice with the text of St James, but none says that it was instituted by him, but only recommended or commanded. Its origin goes back to Christ himself, and the apostolic anointings at the command of Christ during his earthly lifetime are a foreshadowing of it. In fact, the faith of the Church on this point in the eighth century is demonstrably identical with that of the twentieth, and from the eighth century backwards whatever evidence exists—and it is considerable—points in the same direction ; while there exists no cogent evidence to the contrary at all.

The absence from the four Gospels of explicit mention of the institution of this sacrament should not cause surprise. In Christ's final address to his Apostles he told them to teach all nations " to observe all things whatsoever I have commanded you." One of those many observances which he had commanded may well have been a grace-giving rite of anointing the sick. He may have spoken of this during the forty days he spoke to them after the resurrection about the Kingdom of God ; he may have taught them before the resurrection, or again he may have revealed it to them by direct revelation after Pentecost. One thing is certain, he alone can attach a spiritual grace, the forgiveness of sins, to any outward sign ; he alone can institute a sacrament. Christ alone, therefore, instituted Extreme Unction, and even had St James never recommended its use, it would still be what it is, a sacrament which Christ gave to his Church.

No definite heresy is known to have existed with regard to this sacrament before the Reformation. The Albigensians seem to have had a contempt for the use of it, but their tenets, being dualistic and Manichean, can hardly be regarded as a heresy from Christianity, since they are a fundamental denial of it. Their special hatred and contempt may have been aroused by the undoubted abuses in its administration, which were apparently widespread. The clergy—for several priests were then often engaged in conferring it, either together or on consecutive days—insisted on payment for their services and made the reception of it a burden on the poor. The law that the sacrament be administered by one priest alone in the West was made chiefly to deal with this difficulty, and also in consequence of the ostentation of some of the rich, who made vain display of their wealth by calling in a number of priests to administer it.

The Reformers were unanimous in rejecting this sacrament though they differed amongst themselves as to the grounds of the rejection. In England the Reformers at first retained it, but it was omitted in the Second Prayer Book of Edward VI. Recent attempts to reintroduce the Unction of the sick among English Protestants are not intended to restore this ceremony as a grace-giving rite, or as a true sacrament in the Catholic sense, but have in view a charismatic gift of bodily healing, such as they think it to have been in the early Church. Their practice therefore, even if it were not invalid for lack of priests and for lack of consecration of the oil, has nothing in common with Extreme Unction in the Catholic Church.

§ III: THE ADMINISTRATION OF THE SACRAMENT

Ordinary minister

THIS sacrament can be validly administered only by a priest. The ordinary minister according to strict Church law is the parish priest of the place where the patient lies sick, and the administration of this sacrament by another priest against the will of the parish priest would be illicit. Religious institutes, however, are usually exempt by Pope or bishop, and the normal minister would be the superior or the chaplain. In case of necessity, or with the permission of parish priest or bishop, whether actually given or reasonably presumed, any priest may administer it. The parish priest is bound in justice to do so, or at least see that it is done. His curates obviously possess a permanent delegation in this matter. Strictly speaking, therefore, the sick person has no absolute right to demand any priest of his choice for the administration of Extreme Unction, although he can choose any confessor he likes; but the sick person's expressed wish, unless quite unreasonable, will rarely be refused. In case of necessity any priest is bound by the law of charity to administer this sacrament.

Eastern practice

The law in the West requires the sacrament to be administered by one priest only, but in the Greek Catholic Church it is administered when possible by several priests, though the sufficiency of one priest is of course acknowledged. Where several priests are employed the procedure has varied considerably; sometimes they anoint and pray successively, either on the same or consecutive days, sometimes they anoint and pray altogether, each anointing a separate member of the body, or each anointing the same member. Pope Benedict XIV denounced the practice in which some anointed silently and the others prayed without anointing, and declared that at least one priest should both pray and anoint at the same time.

The anointings

There has likewise been considerable variation with regard to the parts of the body anointed in this sacrament. At present the eyes, the ears, the nostrils, the lips, the hands, and the feet are anointed. The anointing of the feet may for any reasonable cause be omitted, and when there is danger in delay or any other sufficient reason a single anointing of one organ of sense, or better, of the forehead, suffices for the validity of the sacrament. But the priest is strictly bound, as soon as the necessity ceases, to continue with—or, if possible, later on, to supply—the anointings and the prayers for each of the five senses. It is held by some that in such cases the supplementary anointings become merely ceremonial, strictly obligatory indeed, but not part of the sacrament itself. The obligation to supply the five anointings would be similar to that of supplying the ceremonies of baptism, grave both for the priest and for those in charge of the child; yet such ceremonies are not part of the sacrament. Most theologians, however, hold that in the case of Extreme Unction these anointings belong to the integrity of the sacrament itself, and that they have sacramental efficacy in destroying the consequences of sin committed by the respective senses.

If the sole reason for the short form of anointing be the immediate danger of death of the one patient, the priest would forthwith continue with the five prayers and anointings after the first prayer and anointing on the forehead. If, however, the necessity arises from another source, the needs of others in a hospital, on a battlefield, an accident in which many are injured, the danger to the priest himself in pestilence or war, then the five anointings must be supplied later, if possible within about an hour, otherwise the moral unity of the administration of the sacrament is broken. These anointings may be supplied either by the priest who anointed the patient's forehead, or by any other priest; the parish priest of the place would have the obligation of doing so.

The laity are anointed in the same way as bishops and priests, with the exception that the latter are anointed on the back of the hands, whereas the laity are anointed on the palm. This distinction is at least as old as the twelfth century and the reason given is that the palm of the hands of the priest is anointed at his ordination; it is thus expressive of the reverence due to the sacredness of those hands which have been in constant contact with the Body of Christ and were instruments in administering the other sacraments; it also reminds the priest who is anointed that sins done by consecrated hands are invested with a greater malice and quasi-sacrilegious character, needing the special mercy of God.

The form

The sacramental form or the words used in Extreme Unction in the Latin Church are: "By this holy anointing and by his most tender mercy may the Lord forgive thee whatever thou hast done amiss by thy sight, hearing, smell, speech, taste, touch, and walk." This essential form is preceded and followed by prayers and imposition of hands, the omission of which, however, would not invalidate the sacrament.

In the Greek Church Prayer-Unction (*Euchelaion*) is given in these words: "Holy Father, physician of bodies and souls, heal this thy servant from the infirmity of body and soul that holds him." This form is pronounced only once while the forehead, chin, cheeks, hands, nostrils, and breast are anointed.

The anointing is done in the form of a cross by the thumb of the priest, unless in case of infectious disease it be advisable to use some intermediary matter, as wool or cloth. The Oil used is olive oil blessed by a bishop, or by a priest who has received authority from the Pope to do so.

In the Greek Church by a permanent delegation from the Pope the priests bless the Holy Oil each time before administration. In the Latin Church the blessing of the Holy Oils for Baptism, Confirmation, and Extreme Unction takes place once a year on Maundy Thursday, during the Sacrifice of the Mass, with great solemnity. The Oil for the sick is first exorcised and then blessed in this way:

Exorcism. "I exorcise thee, most foul spirit and every invading devil and ghost, in the name of the Father and of the Son and of the Holy Ghost, that thou depart from this Oil so that it may become a spiritual unction to strengthen the temple of the living God: that the Holy Spirit may dwell therein through the name of God the Father Almighty, and through the name of his most beloved Son our Lord Jesus Christ who is to judge the living and the dead and the world by fire. Amen.

"Let us pray: Send down, we beseech thee, O Lord, thy Holy Spirit from heaven on this olive oil, which thou hast deigned to produce from the green wood unto the health of mind and body, and may it be through thy holy blessing unto everyone who is anointed by the unction of this heavenly medicine a safeguard of mind and body to drive away all pains, all infirmities and every sickness of mind and body. Since thou hast anointed kings, priests, prophets, and martyrs, let thy ointment be perfect, O Lord, blessed for us by thee and remaining within our inmost selves. In the name of our Lord Jesus Christ."

The consecrated oil

Administration with unconsecrated Oil would certainly be invalid. If by mistake the Oil for Baptism or Confirmation were used, it would be doubtfully valid. If in the West the Oil for the sick were blessed by a priest without a special Apostolic faculty to do so, this would not only be illicit, but Extreme Unction, conferred with such Oil, would be invalid. Different explanations of this fact have been given. The best seems to be this : that the power and dignity required for the blessing of the Oil is by Christ's will inherent in the Episcopate alone, but through delegation the power and dignity of the simple priesthood can be so enhanced that priests can be the instruments to convey this episcopal blessing. Whether this is merely a matter of jurisdiction, or also of the sacrament of Order, cannot be decided. Nor can it be determined with certainty whether the power of the priests in the East comes to them directly from the Pope, or from their bishops with consent of the Pope.

The Holy Oils, thus consecrated once a year, each parish priest is bound forthwith to obtain from his own bishop, and he is not allowed, except in case of necessity, to use those consecrated in the previous year. He is bound to keep the Holy Oils in a locked cupboard in the church. They are usually kept in the aumbry in the wall of the sanctuary on the Gospel side. He is not allowed to keep them in the presbytery except for some good reason, approved by the bishop. In England, where frequent and sudden sick calls in large parishes make it desirable that the priests should have the Oil for the sick always immediately at hand, this is often permitted, especially if the presbytery is at some distance from the church. This, of course, applies only to the Oil for the sick ; the Chrism for Confirmation and the Oil for Baptism must always be kept in the church. If during the year the Oil for the sick should give out, it is permissible to add unblessed olive oil to the Consecrated Oil, but always in minor quantity. The Oil of the previous year is poured into the sanctuary lamp and thus or otherwise burnt.

Circumstances of administration

The sacrament can only be administered to the faithful who after having reached the age of reason are in danger of death through illness or old age. Hence it must not be administered to non-Catholics, though they have been baptised and though they may be in good faith. Since for baptised persons, who are in mortal sin, but who have the implicit wish to receive this sacrament, it may be the only way to remission of sin and eternal salvation, some theologians argue that it might be given to well-disposed non-Catholics who are unconscious and in grave danger of death, if this could be done without scandal. Be this as it may, no priest could administer it to a non-Catholic, even though he asked for it in good faith, as long as he refused to be received into the Church.

The age of discretion required cannot be precisely determined.

The child must be able to distinguish between good and evil, and this it normally begins to do about the age of seven. The subject must be in danger of death through infirmity, *i.e.* either some specified disease or at least old age. Hence it cannot be given to soldiers before battle, or criminals before execution. It is essentially a sacrament for the sick. But the danger of death here referred to does not need to be immediate. Any grave illness, any illness the final issue of which is seriously doubtful, justifies the administration of this sacrament. Hence it may be given in illness requiring a major operation or any disease of which a considerable percentage normally die. It is most emphatically not a sacrament of the dying, but a sacrament of the sick.

Delay in administration.

The delay in asking for the sacrament till death is near or almost inevitable is a lamentable abuse, unfortunately all too frequent. It arises from lack of faith, foolish superstition, or false kindness, or from all these causes combined.

Lack of faith is shown by failing to realise on the one hand the great spiritual needs of the sick, when the soul is enfeebled by bodily pains and sickness, and, on the other, the great might of this sacrament to comfort the soul in its distress. Lack of faith appears likewise in not trusting to the divine power of this sacrament for the healing of the body but confiding merely in human medicine, to the exclusion of that supernaturally provided by God. Foolish superstition not infrequently makes either the sick or their neighbours fancy that the coming of the priest to administer the last rites is a bad omen, almost inevitably foreboding death. This superstition is dishonouring to God and degrading to common sense, as well as to the religion which these people nominally profess.

The third reason, false kindness, is perhaps the most frequent reason for delay. It is imagined to be cruel to let the sick man know of his danger. "Humanitarian" doctors, relatives, and friends often vie one with another in the attempt to hide from the unfortunate patient his real state of health; they try to buoy him up with the promise of speedy recovery until the last hour of his life. No one around the sick-bed dares to tell the truth, they fear that the knowledge of the gravity of the disease will have an adverse psychological effect on the patient, robbing him of that calm and strength of mind which are so powerful a factor in restoring health. Often, however, this is only a pretence or a self-deception. The real reason is moral cowardice, no one having the courage to perform the unpleasant duty and face "a scene." As to the plea that it is better for the patient not to know, those who argue in this way forget that the sick person is often worried more by uncertainty than by knowing the worst. The patient may often think it a fine thing to show a brave exterior, while inwardly he is tormented by doubts as to his real state, and it often comes to him as an immense relief to be told the facts and to throw off the mask of forced gaiety. He can then calmly begin to set aright his troubles of conscience, which disturb him more than any bodily pains.

The fear also of exhausting the patient's ebbing forces by the exertion of receiving the sacraments is usually idle. Priests are hardly ever fussy men, their calling makes them accustomed to the needs of the sick-room. When one considers the quiet and matter-of-fact way in which the sacraments are administered, the few short minutes it takes to go through the Church's ritual, the soothing effect of a few murmured prayers, the last sacraments, even from a purely psychological standpoint, are more likely to further than to hinder the patient's progress. An excited and nervous visitor may easily harm the sick man ; the priest, who with a still and steady voice speaks of God's infinite might and mercy, is not likely to do so. This is borne out by the experience of non-Catholic as well as Catholic nurses and doctors in hospitals. No loud and impassioned appeal as at revival meetings is made by priests in a sick-room. Nineteen centuries of experience have made Catholic priests experts in dealing with the sick so as not to hamper the work of the physician of the body. The effect of the reception of Extreme Unction is almost invariably to increase the resistance of the sick person to the power of the disease if the sacrament is received in time. Hence it is cruelty to postpone the suggestion of its reception till nothing but a miracle can save the patient from death.

Catholic doctors in this matter have an important duty, since, owing to their scientific training, they are usually the first to gauge correctly the state of the patient. Direct deception as to his true state, which would lead to the loss of the last sacraments, would be grievously sinful. On the contrary, they are bound under pain of grave sin to tell the patient of his immediate danger and in default of other informants to warn the priest ; this, however, only in the case of Catholics who have been notoriously slack in their religious duties and are probably in mortal sin. The last sacraments, and especially Unction, in the case of the unconscious may be the only available means of eternal salvation, and the law of charity binds every man to aid his neighbour in extreme spiritual need when this is reasonably feasible. In the case of pious Catholics the duty of telling the patient or the bystanders of the danger, and of informing the priest if no one else is available, lies with the doctor at least under pain of venial sin. A Catholic doctor who habitually neglected this duty of charity, treating all his patients indiscriminately, whether Catholic or non-Catholic, whether pious or notoriously slack, without ever troubling to warn them of their danger, or to see that the priest is informed of their need of the last sacraments, would certainly be committing a grave sin against the law of charity. In like manner any visitor, neighbour, or friend is bound to do what he can to ensure that one who is seriously ill should not be deprived of the last rites of the Church.

The obligation of receiving the sacrament

This brings us to the question of the obligation of receiving Extreme Unction. The Church teaches that, though this sacrament is not of itself necessary for salvation, yet no one is allowed to neglect it; hence every effort and diligence must be used to see that the sick receive it when they still have the full use of their senses. Only in one set of circumstances would this sacrament be absolutely necessary for salvation, namely, if a baptised person, being in the state of mortal sin and unabsolved, became unconscious after having made only an act of imperfect contrition. If such a sinner becomes unconscious and thus incapable of making any internal act of mind and will, he can only be saved by this sacrament; if he remains unconscious till death, it is his only and last means of salvation. Even should he up to the very moment of unconsciousness have elicited no act of sorrow whatever for his sin, but later on, though bereft of speech or other means of communication, internally regain consciousness and ask God's forgiveness without attaining perfect contrition, his sins would be forgiven him and his ultimate salvation secure. This presupposes that he had at least the habitual desire of dying with the last rites of the Church, for should even this desire have been lacking, Extreme Unction would be of no avail.

But if a man is not conscious of any grave sin or at least has confessed it and been absolved, is he still bound under grave obligation to receive Extreme Unction? The existence of divine positive precept in the matter cannot be proved either from Scripture or tradition. The existence of an ecclesiastical precept of such grave obligation that the omission would in itself be mortal sin and thus entail eternal damnation is also very difficult to prove. The transgression of the canon law [1] probably does not by itself involve mortal sin. On the other hand, in the Catechism of the Council of Trent, which for centuries has been the most generally used handbook of instruction in Christian doctrine and thus well represents the mind of the Church, we read: "It is a very grievous sin to defer the Holy Unction until, all hope of recovery now being lost, life begins to ebb and the sick person is fast verging into a state of insensibility."

It may be argued from the context that this probably refers to the priest's obligation to administer, and not to the sick man's obligation to receive, though it seems hard to understand that it should be a deadly sin to delay the administration of a sacrament until a person is less fit to receive it, if there is no grave obligation to receive it at all. Be this as it may, if the refusal of this sacrament arose from contempt, or if it gave scandal, this would involve grave sin. If, however, a person refused Extreme Unction merely because he superstitiously regarded it as an augury of death, or for some foolish reason which excluded contempt or scandal, the priest could give him the benefit of the doubt, administering only Penance and Viaticum, urging him to allow the Unction at least when unconscious, or some time before

[1] Canon 944.

death. If even this were refused, the priest would have a right to doubt the patient's sanity or to suspect contempt.

Repetition of the sacrament

Extreme Unction cannot be repeated in the same illness, unless the sick person after Unction recovers and falls into a fresh danger of death. The reason for this is plain: the right to actual graces which this sacrament bestows continues as long as the illness which caused the danger of death continues. Hence where there is simply a gradual decline towards death without any perceptible sign of recovery, the sacrament cannot be repeated however long this slow decline may last. In this matter, however, one must judge by common estimation rather than by the scientific laws of medicine. Medical science may regard the slow wasting of strength in tuberculosis or cancer as one long uninterrupted process, which may continue for two or even more years; but after the first onslaught of the disease there may be at least an apparent recovery of relative health and the danger of death removed at least for some months. In such cases where there has been at least a seeming amelioration and the person has been somewhat active and able to move about, no priest would scruple to administer the sacrament again when there is a marked relapse and a recurrence of immediate danger of death. The same may be said of the danger of death through sheer old age, when the aged have shown many months of rejuvenescence.

The sacrament should not be repeated when it is ascertained that it was received in a state of unrepented mortal sin or even sacrilegiously, but only if a person who had at first no intention of receiving it (as might be the case with apostates or heretics) later on changed his mind, and became willing to receive it.

Intention of recipient

It is not permissible to administer it to the impenitent who contumaciously persevere in mortal sin, and if this is doubtful it must be given conditionally.[1] The reason is that such contumacious perseverance in sin would normally imply unwillingness to receive the rites of the Church, and the absence of intention to receive the sacrament would render the sacrament invalid. Hence the need of the administration under condition: "if thou art capable."

Naturally the sick who are unconscious or bereft of speech should be given every benefit of the doubt; in some cases, unfortunately, no reasonable doubt is possible of deliberate, defiant, and prolonged continuance in sin and overt refusal of repentance till the last. In such cases nothing can be done. When the patient becomes unconscious or incapable of further intercourse he must be left to the mercy of God. The priest who, under pressure from sorrowing relatives, administered the sacraments to a manifestly evil liver of whose defiant perseverance in evil there could be no reasonable doubt, would sin against his sacred profession and duty. Freemasons who refuse to abandon the craft, those who persist in ordering cremation of their bodies, or who refuse to comply with a grave

[1] Canon 942.

precept of the Church must be classed amongst contumacious and impenitent sinners and should not be anointed.

If the sick man has expressed a wish for the visit of the priest and the priest on arrival finds him already unconscious the mere wish for the presence of the priest will normally be taken as indicating goodwill however evil the previous life of the penitent may have been, and Extreme Unction will be given. It is usually preceded by conditional absolution, but the validity and efficacy of Extreme Unction under these circumstances is more certain than that of the sacrament of Penance. It is doubtful whether Penance is valid without some outward manifestation of guilt and sorrow, whereas by God's infinite mercy Extreme Unction is certainly valid even when given to those who are incapable of any outward or inward acts at the time of reception. The unction bestows divine grace on the soul as long as the sick man has turned from his sin and has the general intention of dying with the last rites of the Church.

Conditional administration

Modern science has taught us that after the last breath life may often remain for a short time in those who are apparently dead, and thus the actual severance of soul from body may take place considerably after the reputed moment of death. Extreme Unction is therefore sometimes given to those who have seemingly passed away. If apparent death occurs after a long illness or old age, life may sometimes remain for about half an hour ; if apparent death is sudden, or due to an accident and especially to drowning, life may remain for two hours and even longer. Those in charge of the dying should therefore send for the priest even though he may only arrive after death has apparently occurred. In such cases the priest will anoint the person conditionally in case life should not be completely extinct and the soul not yet have appeared before the judgement-seat of God. This condition, "if thou livest," and the condition, "If thou art capable of receiving it," are the only conditions which the priest is ever allowed to make in administering this sacrament. The latter condition might be required in the case of doubtful baptism, or doubtful willingness of the patient to receive it, for no sacrament is valid when administered against a person's will. But the condition, "if thou hast repented," or, "if thou art worthy," must never be added, for the person, though unrepentant at the very moment of administration, may repent afterwards and so obtain the grace of the valid sacrament received, as long as he was not directly unwilling to receive it.

Danger of death

There is sometimes a reluctance to ask for Extreme Unction for those who are indeed in danger of death by sickness but who are still capable of sitting up and moving about, and that for the sole reason that they are not actually in bed. This reluctance is entirely unreasonable and blameworthy. There is no need to be in bed for the administration of this sacrament. Some persons are mortally ill, yet do not take to bed till a few days or hours before death ; some, in fact, do not take to bed at all; the long-expected death carries them off in a moment. It would be a cruel folly to deprive such persons of the great graces of this sacrament received in time. Moreover, as the anointing of the feet may for any reasonable cause be omitted, there is no difficulty in anointing someone sitting in a chair, nor is there anything unseemly or improper for a person, who has received Extreme Unction, to be up again and moving about soon afterwards. This Unction is most emphatically not a sacrament of the dying, but a sacrament of the sick; anyone seriously ill should receive it.

Operations

A doubt has been raised whether a person who would be in danger of death if he did not undergo an operation, but who is in no danger if he does, would be a fit subject for this sacrament. The doubt is more theoretical than practical. A person who, according to the ordinary laws of nature, is certain not to die if he takes the proper medicine, undergoes the proper treatment or submits to a minor operation, properly speaking is not in danger of death at all. Many diseases were formerly fatal which have ceased to be so because the proper treatment has been found. A minor operation may be defined as one of which experience teaches that it has normally no fatal issue, so that the person who undergoes it is not appreciably in greater danger of death than he normally is. On the other hand, a state of body necessitating an operation which considerably enhances the chances of death is obviously a serious illness, making the patient a fit subject for Extreme Unction; hence it should be administered before the operation and not after, even if a high percentage of those undergoing it regain consciousness and completely recover.

It is quite certain that this sacrament, if conferred upon persons in perfect health, would be invalid, and such attempted administration would constitute a sacrilege. Unfortunately a custom of this kind exists among the schismatic Greeks, but has been definitely reprobated by the Catholics.

The validity of repeated administration

Another question is whether the sacrament could be validly repeated in the same illness. Such repetition, as we have seen, is at present against Church law if the patient remains in exactly the same danger of death. But would it be invalid if it were done? For instance, it is not a rare occurrence in great hospitals or busy parishes for a priest mistakenly to anoint a person who has already been anointed before by another priest. We possess no absolute certainty in this matter, but everything seems to point to its being valid, though according to present legislation illicit. For many generations in many districts Unction used to be given to the sick on seven, or at least on several, consecutive days. Now it is hard to believe that only one of these administrations was a valid sacrament, or that altogether they constituted only one sacrament, which became valid only on the seventh day after the last administration. The same practically applies when several priests anoint consecutively on the same day, all performing the Unction and pronouncing the words. Such repeated administration might be compared to the repeated administration of the sacrament of Penance, which is at present in use, when a penitent after a lapse of a few days or even only hours begs for absolution, submitting to the keys in confession only sins formerly confessed and already sacramentally absolved. Extreme Unction is the complement of Penance, normally intended, if not for the removal of mortal sin, then for the removal of venial sin, and of all consequences of sin. Such repeated remission, whether by Penance or by Extreme Unction, is valid, because at each administration there is a further infusion of sanctifying grace for the undoing of sin. On the other hand, the title to actual graces of comfort and strength throughout the whole of his illness is valid and sound at the first administration of the Unction, and there is no further strict need for its repetition in the same sickness.

Though the Church allows the repetition of Absolution and urges repeated reception of the Viaticum for the sick man, at present for wise reasons she does not allow the repetition of the Unction for the sake of mere devotion as long as the same danger of death lasts. Her practice, however, is very lenient in this matter, and no priest need have any scruple of exposing the sacrament to invalidity in a case of doubt, whether in a protracted illness the same danger of death has continued or not. There is certainly no need for him to add a condition "if thou art anew in danger of death," when in common estimation the patient has had a recovery and a relapse.

As Extreme Unction is instituted as a sacrament of the living, for the increase of sanctifying grace, not for its first bestowal, the patient is bound, if conscious, to place himself in the state of grace before reception. This he can do either by an act of perfect contrition or by attrition with the sacrament of Penance. Only in the case of Holy Communion does the Church command previous actual confession and absolution for those in mortal sin. The case is different with regard to Extreme Unction. It is sufficient that the sick man be in the state of grace acquired whether by perfect contrition or by the sacrament of Penance. Naturally, if confession could be made, it would be hazardous for anyone in grievous sin to trust to an act of perfect contrition; and it would be foolish, for the grave obligation would remain to confess before death, even after reception of Extreme Unction.

§ IV: THE EFFECTS OF EXTREME UNCTION

Remission of guilt

THE effects of this sacrament are best stated in the words of the Council of Trent: "This effect is the grace of the Holy Ghost, whose Unction blots out sins, if any remain to be expiated, and the consequences of sin, and alleviates and strengthens the soul of the sick person, by exciting in him a great confidence in the divine mercy, sustained by which he bears more lightly the troubles and sufferings of disease and more easily resists the temptations of the demon lying in wait for his heel and sometimes, when it is expedient for the soul's salvation, recovers health."

If we analyse this statement we see that it includes four distinct results of the sacrament:

(1) Remission of the guilt of sins, if the sick man has any.
(2) Remission of the "reliquiæ," remnants or consequences of past sin.
(3) Strengthening of the soul by exciting confidence in God, thus giving patience and vigour against temptation.
(4) Restoration of bodily health, if expedient.

The remission of the guilt of sin is mentioned first because of its supreme importance, although it is an effect which is not always produced, because the sick man may happily not have the guilt of any sins on his soul. The word "sins" refers to sins quite generally, whether mortal or venial. If it be thought that surely everyone has some sins on his soul, at least venial sins, and that therefore the very condition "if he be in sin" has no meaning unless mortal sin be meant, this thought does not correspond with facts. The sick man may have made a good confession even of his venial sins immediately previous to reception of Extreme Unction, or he may by an act of perfect contrition or by acts of intense love of God have had all his venial sins forgiven. In such a case, which we need not restrict to the saints only, Extreme Unction does not remove any stain of guilt.

"Habitual" sorrow necessary

It will at once be asked what must be the state of soul of the recipient in order to allow this sacrament to remit the guilt of his sins. In the case of mortal sins the person must be at least in a state of "habitual" repentance, *i.e.* after his last mortal sin he must at least once have elicited an act of contrition and never have revoked the same. If in such a state unconsciousness and the danger of death should overtake him, Extreme Unction would remit his sin and open to him the gate of heaven. Should he previously to death regain consciousness and have the opportunity of confession, he is still bound to confess his sin, for such is the will of Christ; but his soul, having been cleansed from mortal stain, is safe for eternity and has escaped the doom of eternal loss. It is this wonderful efficacy of Last Anointing which creates its unique importance in the eyes of priests and faithful, especially in the case of careless Catholics, who may be suddenly overtaken by unconsciousness and the danger of death. In such cases it is of greater importance than priestly absolution, for the validity of absolution pronounced over those who are totally unconscious and thus unable to give any outward sign of acknowledgement of sin and repentance is a matter of doubt. Conditional absolution is indeed always given in such cases, but whether such absolution, in the absence of any outward token of repentance whatever on the part of the recipient, is a valid sacrament is not certain. The sacrament of Extreme Unction needs no such outward sign on the part of the recipient; a mere inward willingness, once conceived and never retracted, suffices for its validity, and a mere inward state of attrition, if never retracted, suffices for its efficacy in remitting sin.

The efficacy of this sacrament is so great that it might produce its effect even should it have been received in a state of unconsciousness by a sinner, who had not yet repented of his sins, but who had the general wish to die as a Catholic and make his peace with God before he died. If such a sinner regained a moment's consciousness and in that moment conceived a horror for his sin and asked God's pardon by some inward act, however imperfect, his sin would be forgiven him in virtue of this sacrament and he would be certain of eternal salvation. God only can tell how many owe their escape from everlasting loss to Extreme Unction alone. It is the last haven of refuge provided by the infinite divine mercy for those who were about to make the final shipwreck of their lives. "And if he be in sins, they shall be forgiven him," wrote St James, thereby manifesting the almost incredible lengths to which the loving-kindness of a merciful God can go.

Venial sin

So much for the forgiveness of mortal sin, should the sick man have it on his soul. But what of venial sin? The sick man is strictly bound to be in the state of grace either by confession or contrition previous to reception of Extreme Unction. There is no such strict obligation to be free from venial sin. No doubt every good Catholic normally would confess all the venial sins he remembered in the confession preceding Extreme Unction, and thus obtain forgiveness of them in the sacrament of Penance. Yet we must not forget, first, that in strict obligation he is not bound to do so, and secondly, that a valid absolution of one or more venial sins does not necessarily involve the remission of all of them. In consequence the existence of the guilt of venial sins in a person's soul previous to Extreme Unction is surely not a rare occurrence, even in the case of those who have led good lives and are accounted practising and devout Catholics.

Does Extreme Unction remit such venial sins or does it not? We may answer with almost absolute certainty in the affirmative. There has indeed been no explicit declaration on this question by Pope or Council. "If he be in sins, they shall be forgiven him," said St James. No valid reason can be shown why in this text we should limit the meaning of "sins" to mortal sins, and such limitation seems irreconcilable with the nature of Extreme Unction. This sacrament has eminently a medicinal character, it is a sacrament of Healing, and a complement of the sacrament of Penance in the case of the sick. The forgiveness of mortal sin is rather of the nature of a resurrection than a healing, hence such forgiveness is not the primary purpose of the sacrament. It is rather the forgiveness of venial sins that would seem to be characteristic of the sacrament of Healing. Venial sins are in fact the great cause of spiritual sickness and their removal the very essence of the healing of the soul and restoration to spiritual health.

May we then hold that Extreme Unction always remits all venial sins in the recipient ?

Although in a sense the answer is in the affirmative, yet we must explain and limit our affirmation. No sin is ever forgiven without repentance, and this applies to venial sins as well as to mortal ; hence the guilt of venial sins to which the penitent is still attached, and for which he has no real purpose of amendment, remains upon the soul, and this no sacrament can remove without a real change of mind. Deliberate feelings and acts of uncharity, deliberate refusal to rectify small matters of dishonesty or to unsay words against the character of one's neighbour, deliberate murmurings at the hardness of one's lot, and a great number of other small faults may still mar the soul even of those who are stretched on a sick-bed and who would shrink from any grievous sin or from venial sins of the more serious kind. The human heart is so strange and intricate a labyrinth of motives and affections that it is possible to show genuine fervour in prayer and almost at the same time to manifest glaring faults of character continued with unmistakable deliberation and full consent. So long as these thus continue, Extreme Unction cannot directly remove their guilt, for without repentance there is no forgiveness. It is quite true that the guilt of venial sins can be removed indirectly by the intensity of the love of God without these faults being individually remembered and repudiated. Venial sins are a retardation in our journey towards God, not a complete deviation or aversion from our last end ; hence greater fervour in our tending towards God undoes the harm venial sin has done. Yet as long as the complacency of the will in evil continues, so long does the inhibition remain, and the soul is hampered and hindered by affection to sin, be it only venial. Extreme Unction, then, removes the guilt of all those venial sins from which the heart has turned with at least implicit sorrow.

The forgiveness of sin, whether mortal or venial, by Extreme Unction remains, however, a purely conditional effect : " if he be in sins." Scripture and tradition presuppose that the sacrament is often received when no guilt of sin, whether mortal or venial, stains the soul of the recipient. In such happy circumstances has this sacrament then nothing to do with the removal of the effects of sin ?

The " remnants " of sin

When we consider that the Council of Trent calls Extreme Unction " the complement of Penance," and, moreover, that St James plainly connects the two sacraments of Penance and Unction by adding " Confess therefore your sins one to another," it becomes clear that even when no guilt actually stains the soul of the recipient, Extreme Unction extends its power in some way to the consequences of sin. The sacrament being essentially one of spiritual healing must affect every spiritual infirmity which is the outcome of sin. This is implied in the very form employed in the Church: "May God pardon whatever thou hast done amiss," "Indulgeat quidquid deliquisti." If, then, there be no actual guilt, only the consequences of sin can be meant, and this is expressly stated by the Council of Trent. What, then, precisely does the Council mean by *reliquias peccati*, "remnants of sin"? Every sin committed enfeebles the soul and makes it more prone to sin. The wound of sin, even though it be healed, leaves a scar. The healing of sin is a complicated progress. It is the complete restoration to full health of mind and will after these have been debilitated by the sinful embracing of evil. All sin engenders a certain obscurity of mind and frailty of will, a lack of vigour in resistance to further evil. These things may remain even though the total aversion from God in mortal sin, or the clinging to temporal good to the detriment of our love of God in venial sin, has actually ceased and the guilt of past sin has been forgiven by the application of Christ's atonement to the repentant sinner.

The memory of past sin, moreover, is constantly with the sinner, even though he has been sacramentally absolved, and the cry "*amplius lava me ab iniquitate mea*" naturally rises to his lips. Confidence in God is harder for the man who has to look back on a life of sin, or a life of innumerable venial faults, than for the saint who has served his God for many years and who can say with St Antony: "I have served my Lord for eighty years, why should I fear to meet him now?" It is this complete healing from all spiritual sickness induced by past sin which Extreme Unction is intended to achieve.

In the numberless touching representations of the death of our Blessed Lady which mediæval sculpture or painting has left to us, St Peter and the Apostles surround her death-bed, according to legend, but the artist with truly Catholic instinct has never attempted to represent the administration of Extreme Unction. The sinless Mother of God had no need of this sacrament, which is in its nature a complement of Penance and is intended to remove, if not always directly the guilt of sin, at least the consequences of it. Her soul needed no healing of any kind to render it strong and vigorous in the hour of death. St John is indeed often represented as giving Holy Communion to the Mother of God, for she could receive this great sacrament of spiritual life to increase her love for her divine Son; but a sacrament which suggests at least the memory of past sin was not for her.

Be all this said to make clear what is meant by "the remnants of sin" counteracted by the grace of Extreme Unction.

Temporal punishment

There remains the further question whether Extreme Unction also remits the temporal punishment due to forgiven sin, and this question also has to be answered in the affirmative. It has been the constant teaching of theologians that this sacrament constitutes the final consummation of all spiritual cure, by which man is made ready for participation in heavenly glory. The purpose of Extreme Unction is that at the moment of death nothing should remain which might be a hindrance to the soul's immediate entrance into its eternal reward.

It may well be asked: if this sacrament is intended to remove even the temporal punishment of sin, what then remains of purgatory for those who receive it? Why further blessings and the gaining of indulgences? The answer is that all sacraments do indeed give the grace which they signify, but the measure of the grace bestowed depends on the disposition of the recipient. Millions receive Holy Communion day by day, all receive the same kind of grace, but amongst them all there are perhaps not two who receive exactly the same amount. So likewise of those who receive Extreme Unction in the same hospital, or on the same battlefield, hundreds may receive the same sacred anointing, which signifies and effects the healing of nature wounded by sin, and is meant to render the soul sound and fit for immediate entrance into glory, yet perhaps not two receive exactly the same measure of grace.

If they are conscious, the measure of grace received will depend upon the actual devotion at the moment of reception and the state of their soul previous to it; if they are unconscious but in a state of repentance—habitually attrite as theologians would say—it will depend upon the state of their soul when the sacrament is administered. Certainly the guilt of mortal sins will infallibly be forgiven, likewise the guilt of some venial sins. But it may well be that the guilt of many venial sins will remain, owing to lack of repentance for them, therefore also the debt of punishment due to them. Extreme Unction is not an automatic means of escape from Purgatory, though the purpose of the sacrament is undoubtedly to remit the debt of temporal punishment, and it does indeed remit it entirely, if received with perfect dispositions.

The case of Extreme Unction is not unlike that of a Plenary Indulgence. A Plenary Indulgence is intended to remit the whole of the temporal punishment due, and if received in perfect dispositions and without any attachment to sin it will always achieve its object. But it would be rash to assert that all who perform correctly the outward works prescribed are thereby acquitted of all debt of purgatory. Indulgences are not sacraments, of course, but they at least resemble them in this that when applied to the living they are an exercise of spiritual power to which some spiritual result is infallibly attached, if the work prescribed is performed in proper dispositions.

Spiritual strength

We now come to the most characteristic grace bestowed by Last Anointing, the grace of "raising up" the sick man. "The Lord shall raise him up." The Greek word used might almost be translated "stir up," "wake up." It means the bestowal of unwonted strength and vigour on those who are prostrate through sickness.

By lowering vitality and introducing disorder into the sensitive life grievous illness is apt to interfere with the workings of the soul in mind and will. Sickness means lethargy, exhaustion, inability to concentrate, stupor, and even illusions, and hence extreme difficulty in prayer when prayer is the great necessity. Sickness means fever, unnatural excitement, physical irritation, inward annoyance, and perhaps intense pain; all these make the continuance of spiritual activities most difficult. Sickness may mean horror of approaching death, an almost complete enfeeblement of natural powers, a conjuring up of phantasms which lay the soul open to suggestions of despair, or at least to lack of trust in God; and to these may be added the paralysing dread of appearing before the Great Judge. It has been and still is the constant conviction of all those who are versed in spiritual matters, that the devil takes advantage of the enfeeblement of disease in men for his own purpose and that he uses his utmost endeavours for the perdition of a soul before that soul passes out of the sphere of his power by a holy death. It is not in vain that myriads of Catholic lips for centuries have prayed: " Pray for us sinners now and at the hour of our death." If after the daily Sacrifice we pray to St Michael to defend us in the day of battle, we stand in utmost need of every defence on the day when the final issue hangs in the balance.

The mercy of God has invented this sacrament to assist us in our utmost need: a medicine, a healing unction to counteract supernaturally the danger to the soul arising from the impending dissolution of the body; a strengthening and invigoration of the soul to overcome the languor and the confusion of mind connected with serious illness, and the menace of death.

It is remarkable that the two sacraments which have the special purpose of imparting strength of soul and vigour in combat have the anointing with oil as outward sign of their inward grace: Confirmation and Extreme Unction. They have this in common, that by anointing the body they signify the preparation for battle. But Confirmation, which is the complement of Baptism and imparted at the beginning of life's struggle, views man as a child of God regenerated and fresh from God in the integrity of his new spiritual life. It anoints the body of the young warrior who goes out to battle. In Extreme Unction the same warrior is regarded as in many ways worsted and defeated and overcome by sin. The Church again anoints him and the essential meaning is the same. The gift is called a " confortatio animæ," even as Confirmation was called a *confirmatio*, a strengthening for combat. If the words used in administration are different, it is because the circumstances are different. After a long fight with sin the warrior needs that his wounds be healed; and so God is asked to deal kindly with all things in which the weary warrior has failed in the past. The aim of this sacrament is to restore the sick man to that complete health and vigour of soul in which

Baptism and Confirmation had placed him at the beginning of life's combat.

A theological discussion

There has been and to a certain extent still is a discussion amongst theologians which is the principal effect of these many spiritual effects just enumerated: (1) the remission of grievous sin, (2) the remission of venial sins, (3) the remission of the remnants of sin, (4) the remission of the temporal punishment of forgiven sin, and (5) the strengthening of the soul in its hard and perhaps final struggle. Which, it is asked, is the essential grace of which the sacrament is the efficient sign, the grace which it must always of necessity produce if worthily received and from which the other effects follow?

Some have held that the essential grace is the undoing of past sin, if not in its guilt, at least in its consequences. These theologians appeal to the meaning of the sacramental form as now used in the Latin Church: "May God pardon whatever thou hast done amiss."

Others have placed the essential grace in the strengthening of the soul, so necessary in the time of sickness. They have argued that if we regard the sacrament as essentially remissive of sin, it could not be validly received by a person who by confession or perfect contrition had been freed from the guilt of all his sins, by a Plenary Indulgence had paid the whole debt of punishment due, and by a life of great holiness had undone all the scars and wounds of sin. A sacrament, they urge, that cannot give its essential grace is no valid sacrament. These authors plead that some of the very greatest saints have been anointed, and it might well be supposed that on their death-bed they had undone all their sins by their intense love of God. Moreover, St James seems to stress the raising up of the soul of the sick man, rather than the conditional forgiveness of sin, if the sick man have any. These reasons would at first sight seem decisive, but for the strong and insurmountable argument to the contrary derived from the Latin sacramental form, which is indicative of pardon of sin. A sacrament must always give the grace it signifies, and the form of words used in administration must needs indicate this grace.

The solution of the problem lies no doubt in the fact that no person on earth can be completely free from all consequences of past sin. He may be free from any guilt of sin, he may be free from all temporal punishment due to sin, the justice of God may be completely satisfied, yet some consequences may still remain. Our Lady excepted, no one has ever led a life without all sin, however slight, but all sin leaves some enfeebling result on the soul. It impairs a man's spiritual strength, it lowers his strength. In a state of illness and approaching death a person needs all the strength and full supernatural health of soul to face his dangers, and it is this complete health of soul which the sacrament intends to give. The sacrament deals not with abstractions but with realities, and in reality, Mary excepted, no saint can claim that he never knew sin. Hence all can profit by a sacrament which restores divine grace that was in some degree impaired by a past fault. The bestowal of spiritual vigour on a sinner in bodily illness is therefore at the same time an undoing of sin; and therefore the form of this sacrament indicates the undoing of sin: "Indulgeat . . . quidquid deliquisti."

Moreover, the great need in illness is the divine assurance of a merciful judgement to come. Dread of the holiness of God and the rigour of his justice may disturb the soul, however slight the sins committed and however great the repentance of the sinner. It is this distressing and agonising fear which the sacrament intends to counteract. It is intended to fill the sick man with a Christian courage that through God's loving-kindness and infinite mercy the victory over evil will lie with him.

We conclude therefore that in reality the *confortatio animæ* and undoing of sin coincide; they are but the negative and positive aspect of identically the same grace. It is essentially a sacrament of healing, but healing is undoing of disease and that by an inpouring of strength. Logically, no doubt, the *confortatio animæ* precedes, but in fact the two coincide. We must carefully note that the Latin form does not directly mention the forgiveness of the guilt of sin, but uses deliberately the general expressions: *indulgeat tibi Dominus*, "may God deal mercifully with thee"; *quidquid deliquisti*, "with regard to anything there is still amiss," in consequence of any sins committed.

The restoration of bodily health

Finally, we have to deal with the last result of this sacrament: the restoration of bodily health if God sees it to be expedient. Is there any rule or principle on which God acts in this matter and which we can know?

Some have suggested that God always restores to health if this is for the ultimate spiritual good of the patient. In consequence, if he foresees that, if now restored to health the patient would finally die in sin and be lost or at least would make a less good death than now, God would not arrest the course of the disease. This suggestion is, however, hardly tenable, for it would practically be equivalent to a private revelation to all those who recovered after Extreme Unction in the hour of death, that they could be certain of final salvation.

How then is this temporal effect connected with the sacrament? Is it a miracle? Does God suspend the laws of nature and on the occasion of Extreme Unction use his omnipotence apart from natural laws? It would seem not, because we are repeatedly warned not to postpone the reception of Extreme Unction precisely because this would be to force God's hand to work a miracle by raising up a man actually in the throes of death.

If, then, the restoration is not necessarily miraculous, but some utilisation of nature's forces by God, how have we to conceive this? "The Lord will raise him up." This raising up is by actual graces bestowed upon the soul; for the soul reacts upon the body, as well as the body on the soul. Medical science will tell us that cheerfulness, mental happiness, and the encouragement of bystanders, normally make a great difference to the patient for betterment. Despondency is most deleterious to those in sickness, courage and brightness of character are of immense importance. Many a person recovers by the sheer will to live and struggles against the physical laws of sickness by an indomitable character.

If science tells us this in the purely natural sphere, how much morc is this true when God by supernatural actual graces affects the soul for its strengthening and comfort ? Beyond all doubt God can and sometimes does directly act on the bodily frame of man, thus curing him in a directly miraculous way, either by increasing natural recuperative power, or by directly creating new forces which make for health. For all we know he does so sometimes on account of the sacrament received. But there seems no absolute divine rule always connecting such miracles with Extreme Unction. Miracles must always be rare ; they are the exception, not a matter of steady regularity. The sacrament bestowed on unconscious persons in the very throes of death does but exceedingly rarely restore bodily health. If it always did, death would be abolished. Hence it is presumptuous folly to postpone its reception till the last moment and expect escape from death. But even when received in the early stages of illness and received with great piety and devotion there seems to us no apparent rule by which God acts.

We are bound to believe that God will do so if it is expedient. Expedient to whom ? To all men ? To some men, amongst the relatives and household ? To the sick man himself ? It is certainly expedient to the sick man that he die at some time, for death is the gateway to heaven. If he be well-disposed, it may be expedient that he die now. The expediency, however, will be judged by God, whose Providence attains all men and takes every circumstance into account. Now the Council of Trent says : " if it be expedient to the soul's salvation," and thus evidently includes in the reasons for recovery the spiritual profit of the man's soul. On the other hand, the Council distinctly adds the word *interdum*, " sometimes," thus suggesting that, even if there is some foreordained plan and rule whereby these things are regulated, we do not know it. No doubt priests, doctors, and nurses have repeatedly noticed the most amazing changes for the better in sick persons after Anointing, and it is no wonder that people have often cried " miracle " after such a surprising recovery. God thus vindicates the dignity and the power of his sacraments, and the early devout reception of Extreme Unction is certainly a powerful appeal to the omnipotent mercy of God for the recovery of bodily health.

The " revival " of the sacrament

The revival of this sacrament, although briefly alluded to previously, needs a few words of explanation. Baptism, Confirmation, and Order may be received without due disposition. In such a case these sacraments are valid and cannot be repeated, but the grace of them is not bestowed until the recipient repents and puts himself in the necessary state of soul. Such subsequent resurrection of sacramental energy goes by the name of reviviscence. This is universally accepted in the case of the three sacraments just mentioned, because they imprint an indelible mark on the soul and can be received only once in a lifetime. It is practically certain that the same is true of Matrimony. Though it leaves no indelible mark on the soul, yet it is normally received only once in life, and it is hard to believe that a married person should for ever be deprived of the graces needed for the married state owing to his sinful state at the moment of his wedding. There is probably no reviviscence of Penance, because being itself the sacrament of Penitence, it is utterly invalid when penitence is absent; and the reviviscence of Holy Communion, if received in mortal sin, is usually considered impossible.

In the case of Extreme Unction there exists no absolute certainty of its reviviscence; yet this can hardly be doubted. Theologians are practically unanimous that when received in the state of unrepented mortal sin it revives if the sick man later repents. Such reviviscence of the grace of Unction is, however, strictly limited to the period of the illness and would not occur if the patient only repented after the recovery of health. During the same danger of death through illness Extreme Unction, once validly received, remains an efficacious title to grace, though its effect is suspended as long as the patient remains in unrepentant mortal sin. Let him remove the obstacle by repentance and the grace will be bestowed. Should, however, a fresh mortal sin be committed after the reception of Extreme Unction, the guilt of this could only be removed either by perfect contrition or attrition with the actual reception of the sacrament of Penance. Extreme Unction can remit the guilt of sin incurred before and in its reception, but not that of sins committed afterwards. The priest then, should he learn that the patient was in unrepented mortal sin during the reception of Extreme Unction, should not repeat the administration, for according to Church law it must be given only once in the same illness. The only possible reason for repeating the rite would be if the priest ascertained that the patient had been unwilling to receive it, for no sacrament is valid if bestowed on an unwilling subject.

However great the divine ingenuity in contriving means of grace for the children of men, God's benign purposes can be foiled by the malice of man, but as far as the indulgence of the divine Father in heaven can go without destroying human liberty, so far does his tender mercy reach in this most Holy Unction.

J. P. Arendzen.

XXIX

THE SACRAMENT OF ORDER

§I: THE PRIESTHOOD OF CHRIST AND THE CHRISTIAN PRIESTHOOD

A. The Priesthood of Christ

" EVERY high priest taken from among men is ordained for men in the things that appertain to God, that he may offer up gifts and sacrifices for sins." [1] St Thomas Aquinas [2] teaches that the proper office of a priest is to be a mediator between God and men, inasmuch as he is the representative of the people with God, offering to him their sacrifices and prayers, and the representative of God with the people, bringing to them in return for their " gifts and sacrifices," both pardon for sin, and those " most great and precious promises " by which they are " made partakers of the divine nature." [3] Who then is so fitted for the sacred office of Priesthood as the God-man, Jesus Christ, who, because he is the Son of God, is the natural representative of God with man ; and, because he is the Son of Man and the Head of the human race, knowing our infirmities, and " one tempted in all things as we are, without sin," [4] is also the acceptable representative of sinful man with God ? By virtue of the hypostatic union, then, Jesus Christ was anointed High Priest, and remains " a Priest for ever," [5] and the " one Mediator of God and men, the man Christ Jesus." [6]

Priesthood and sacrifice are therefore correlative.[7] The essential act of priesthood is the offering of sacrifice, both as the supreme act of man's worship of God (latreutic), and in expiation for the sins of men (propitiatory) ; and our High Priest and Mediator, Jesus Christ, performed this supreme act of his Priesthood when he offered himself in sacrifice to his Heavenly Father on the Cross both as the perfect and supreme act of divine worship, and as the efficacious expiation of the sins of the world.[8]

[1] Heb. v 1.
[2] *Summa Theologica*, III, Q. xxii and Q. xxvi.
[3] 2 Peter i 4.
[4] Heb. iv 15.
[5] Heb. v 5-6.
[6] 1 Tim. ii 5.
[7] Council of Trent, sess. 23, c. 1.
[8] See Essay xiv, *Christ, Priest and Redeemer.*

B. *The Christian Priesthood*

Another act of Our Lord as High Priest and Redeemer was to establish his Church for the salvation of the world through the merits of his Sacrifice on Calvary. He, the eternal Priest, would be its Head and High Priest. But since he was about to withdraw his corporal presence from his Church, it was necessary that his Priesthood should be exercised visibly and externally by a body of ministers appointed by himself and acting in his name.

Our Lord, therefore, on the day before he suffered, having for the last time celebrated with his Apostles the legal feast of the Paschal Lamb, instituted the Eucharistic Sacrifice of the New Testament, first, as the perennial commemoration of the Sacrifice of Redemption on Calvary, and secondly, in order that the merits of the Sacrifice of the Cross might be applied to individual souls for the remission of their sins. Further, in order that this memorial Sacrifice might be offered in the Church till the end of time, and " shew forth the death of the Lord *until he come*," [1] by the words, " Do this for a commemoration of me," he ordained his Apostles priests and gave them power to ordain others in their turn, and thus established in his Church a permanent and perpetual Order of Christian Priesthood. All this we are taught by the Council of Trent in sess. 22, c. 1. Consequently, " If anyone shall say that by the words: ' Do this for a commemoration of me,' Christ did not ordain the Apostles priests, or did not enjoin that they and other priests should offer his body and blood, let him be anathema." [2] Moreover, to the power of consecrating and offering his Body and Blood, Our Lord on Easter Day added the power over his mystical body, the power, namely, of forgiving and retaining sins. " If," therefore, " anyone shall say that there is not a visible and external priesthood in the New Testament, or that there is no power of consecrating and offering the true body and blood of the Lord, and of remitting and retaining sins . . . let him be anathema." [3] Other Sacraments also were instituted by Our Lord as the channels or vehicles of the grace of the Redemption, and committed by him to his Apostles, and through them to the Church, so that St Paul was able to speak of himself and his colleagues as " the ministers of Christ and the dispensers of the mysteries of God." [4]

In all this we see the realisation of that greater wonder which Our divine Lord promised to Nathanael: " Greater things than this shalt thou see. And he saith to him: Amen, Amen, I say to you, you shall see heaven opened and the angels of God ascending and

[1] 1 Cor. xi 26.
[2] Council of Trent, sess. 22, can. 2.
[3] *Ibid.*, sess. 23, can. 1.
[4] 1 Cor. iv 1.

descending upon the Son of Man." [1] What was this greater thing that they should see ?

It was, first of all, this, that whereas heaven had hitherto, on account of unexpiated sin, remained closed to mankind, they should see heaven opened, or, more correctly according to the Greek, open, standing open, as a result of the accomplishment of the Redemption ; and secondly, that they should see the Cross, upon which was hanging the Son of Man, the Redeemer and Mediator, like Jacob's ladder, " standing upon the earth, and the top thereof touching heaven, the angels also of God ascending and descending by it." [2] In other words, in the New Dispensation the Cross of Christ unites earth with heaven, and the ministers of Christ, the priests of the Church, ascend " upon the Son of Man," that is, by the ladder of the Cross of Christ, to heaven, bearing with them " the gifts and sacrifices " for the sins of the people, and descend from heaven by the same means, bringing as the gift of God for the people the sacramental and other graces of which they stand in need. The word " upon " (ἐπί) in the phrase " upon the Son of man " is to be understood in its literal sense of stepping upon the Son of Man as upon a ladder ; for the Cross of Christ is the only means of passage from earth to heaven and heaven to earth. Moreover, there is abundance of Biblical authority for interpreting " the angels of God " as the priests of the Church ; for are not the angels " ministering spirits sent to minister for them who shall receive the inheritance of salvation ? " [3] Hence the episcopal heads of the seven Churches are called Angels by St John in the Apocalypse ; and St Paul directs women to veil their heads in church " because of the angels." [4] " The lips of the priest," says the Prophet Malachy, " shall keep knowledge, and they shall seek the law at his mouth, because he is the angel of the Lord of hosts." [5]

It is noteworthy also that the Angels of God are here said first to *ascend* and then to *descend* upon the Son of Man. If the allusion was literally to the Angels of heaven, we should naturally expect them to *de*scend before *as*cending. But the priest, the angel of earth, first *as*cends to heaven with the gifts of men to God, and then *de*scends from heaven bearing God's gifts to men. So also Jacob, in his dream at Bethel, the House of God, the place of sacrifice of the Patriarchs and Judges, saw the angels first ascending and then descending by the ladder that joined earth with heaven.

The wonderful thing, then, that Nathanael and the others were to see was precisely this. The Redemption of the world was to be actually accomplished in their lifetime, and as the result of it they would see heaven once again lying open to men, and the Ministers

[1] John i 50-51. It is curious and significant that Our Lord, though apparently addressing Nathanael alone : " Greater things shalt *thou* see. And he saith to *him*," suddenly changes to the plural : " Amen, I say to *you*, *you* shall see, etc."

[2] Gen. xxviii 12. [3] Heb. i 14. [4] i Cor. xi 10. [5] ii 7.

of Christ representing man with God and on man's behalf offering to God the Eucharistic Sacrifice, and in turn representing God with man, and as such administering the grace-giving Sacraments for the sanctification and salvation of the world.[1]

Such in brief outline is the Christian Priesthood.

§ II: THE THREEFOLD POWER OF THE CHURCH. THE POWER AND CHARACTER OF ORDER

A. The Threefold Power of the Church

Jurisdiction in general

THE purpose and object of the existence of any society is the pursuit and attainment by its members of some common end by the use of some common means. Experience, however, has proved over and over again—so much so, indeed, that it has long been a first principle of practical life—that no society, from the sovereign State to the smallest cricket club, is successful, unless it is governed by some competent authority, whether it be a king or a president, a chairman or a committee, a cabinet, a board of management, a managing director, etc. There must be some ruling power, whether individual or collective, whose office it is to govern, direct, legislate, judge, and even coerce and punish, all with the one object of securing the success of the society in the achievement of the purpose of its existence, which is the good, happiness, pleasure, in some way or other, of its members. Without some such governing authority any society is doomed to confusion, chaos, failure, and extinction. This ruling authority or power of government is called *Jurisdiction*.

Now most of the societies of which we have experience in ordinary life are societies whose aim it is to procure some natural good or pleasure or profit for the members ; and we find that they have at their disposal, or they are able to obtain, the means which are necessary in order to enable them to attain their object. These societies are natural societies, the end that they have in view is natural, the means of attaining it are natural. All that is necessary is that the ruling authority in such a society should direct, guide, and control its members in the use of the means at their disposal to the best advantage for the common good.

Spiritual and supernatural jurisdiction

But there is one Society within our experience which is a supernatural society, a society among men indeed, and for men, but having a supernatural origin and a supernatural end and purpose. This Society is the Catholic Church, founded by Jesus Christ for the sanctification and salvation of the human race. This Church is the supernatural, spiritual kingdom of Christ, existing in the world, but

[1] St Catherine of Siena likens the hypostatic union to a bridge built by God, and stretching from heaven to earth. This beautiful idea is, of course, analogous to Our Lord's own comparison of himself hanging on the Cross to a ladder uniting earth with heaven, etc., as explained in the text above.

not of the world. Being a kingdom, it is a perfect society; and as such, it must have a government, and one which has received from its founder a power and authority that is proportioned to the spiritual nature of the society, and competent to direct its members to its supernatural end. Jesus Christ, therefore, provided for this power of government, *i.e.* the spiritual Jurisdiction of the Church, when he said to Peter: "To thee I will give the keys of the kingdom of heaven"; [1] and to the whole body of the Apostles: "Whatsoever you shall bind upon earth shall be bound also in heaven: and whatsoever you shall loose upon earth shall be loosed also in heaven." [2]

Teaching authority and power of Order

But since the end for which the Church was founded is a supernatural one, it follows that the means which it has at its disposal for the attainment of that end, are supernatural also; for the means must be proportioned to the end. In this then the Church is not like natural societies, which find at hand the means they require for their purposes. If the means which the Church needs are supernatural, they must be provided for her by Jesus Christ, her Founder. Now what are the means which the Church requires? They are two, divine truth and supernatural grace. We need divine truth, *i.e.* the truths of supernatural revelation, that we may know the mysteries of God himself, that we may know ourselves as we are before God, that we may know what God has done for us, and what he would have us do. They teach us the divine standards of human conduct, and show us what are the means that God has placed at our disposal to enable us to maintain those standards. This is the first means. The other is supernatural grace, sanctifying grace, by which we receive the adoption of sons,[3] and are "made partakers of the divine nature," [4] and by which also (together with actual grace) the operations of the soul are raised to the supernatural plane and directed to the end and purpose of life eternal. Both these means have been placed by Our Lord in the hands of the governing authority of his Church, as we are taught by St John: [5] "The Word was made flesh, and dwelt among us full of grace and truth, and of his fulness we have all received, and grace for grace. For the law was given to Moses: grace and truth came by Jesus Christ." Thus, besides the power of Jurisdiction (alluded to above), which Christ had conferred on the Apostolic Hierarchy, he committed to them two further powers, one to propose, expound, and define the truths of revelation (which involves the corresponding obligation of the assent of faith on the part of those who are taught), and this is called the Magisterium, or teaching authority, which Christ bestowed on the Apostles when he said to them: "Going therefore teach all nations: . . . teaching them to observe all things whatsoever I have commanded you." [6] The other is the power to dispense divine grace to the faithful through the

[1] Matt. xvi 19.
[2] *Ibid.*, xviii 18.
[3] Rom. viii 15; Gal. iv 5.
[4] 2 Peter i 4.
[5] i 14-17.
[6] Matt. xxviii 19-20.

Sacraments, and this power is the power of Order, which is signified in the same commission of Our Lord to the Apostles: "Going therefore . . . baptising them in the name of the Father and of the Son and of the Holy Ghost"; [1] and when he said to them: "Do this for a commemoration of me." Hence St Paul desires that the Apostles be regarded as the "dispensers of the mysteries of God"; by which term we understand both the supernatural truths of God which are concealed from human reason, and the sacred, symbolic, sacramental rites, which contain hidden within them the supernatural grace of God.

B. The Sacrament of Order

Having thus established the existence of the power of Order in the Church, we have now to show that it is conferred and transmitted by means of a symbolic and ritual consecration, which in theological language is called a Sacrament; and we cannot do this better than in the words of St Thomas Aquinas: [2]

"It is clear that, in all the sacraments of which we have spoken hitherto, spiritual grace is bestowed under the sacred sign of visible things. Now every action should be proportionate to the agent. Hence these same sacraments should be dispensed by visible men having spiritual powers. For angels are not competent to dispense sacraments: but men clothed in visible flesh, according to the saying of the Apostle,[3] 'Every high priest taken from among men is ordained for men in the things that appertain to God.'

"This may be proved in another way. Sacraments derive their institution and efficacy from Christ; of whom the Apostle says: [4] 'Christ loved the Church, and delivered himself up for it, that he might sanctify it, cleansing it by the laver of water in the word of life.' It is also clear that at the Supper he gave the Sacrament of his body and blood, and instituted it for our frequent use: and this is the greatest of all the sacraments. Seeing then that he was about to withdraw his bodily presence from the Church, it was necessary that he should institute others as his ministers, who should dispense the sacraments to the faithful, according to the Apostle's words: [5] 'Let a man so account of us as of the ministers of Christ, and the dispensers of the mysteries of God.' For this reason he entrusted his disciples with the consecration of his body and blood, saying: [6] 'Do this for a commemoration of me': to them he gave the power to forgive sins: [7] 'Whose sins you shall forgive, they are forgiven them': and on them he conferred the office of teaching and baptising, saying: [8] 'Going, teach ye all nations, baptising them.' Now the minister is compared to his master as an instrument to the principal agent:

[1] Matt. xxviii 19. [2] *Contra Gentiles*, iv, cap. 74.
[3] Heb. v 1. [4] Eph. v 25-26. [5] 1 Cor. iv 1.
[6] Luke xxii 19. [7] John xx 23. [8] Matt. xxviii 19.

for, just as the instrument is moved by the agent in order to produce an effect, so a minister is moved by his master to execute his will. Again, the instrument should be proportionate to the agent. Therefore Christ's ministers should be conformed to him. Now Christ wrought our salvation, as master, by his own authority and power, in as much as he is God and man: in that, as man, he suffered for our redemption, and, because he was God, his sufferings were made efficacious for our salvation. Consequently Christ's ministers must be men, and also have some share in his Godhead by a kind of spiritual power: since the instrument shares in the power of the principal agent. Of this power the Apostle says [1] that 'the Lord gave him power unto edification and not unto destruction.'

"Now it cannot be said that this power was given to Christ's disciples in such manner that it would not be transmitted by them to others: for it was given to them unto the edification of the Church, according to the Apostle's words. Therefore this power must last as long as the Church needs to be edified: that is to say, from after the death of Christ's disciples until the end of the world. Consequently, spiritual power was given to Christ's disciples in such wise that others were to receive it from them. Hence Our Lord spoke to his disciples as representatives of the rest of the faithful, as we may see from his words,[2] 'What I say to you, I say to all.' Again he said to his disciples: [3] 'Behold I am with you all days, even to the consummation of the world.'

"Accordingly, this spiritual power flows from Christ to the ministers of the Church, and the spiritual effects (whether of spiritual power or of grace) accruing to us from Christ are conferred under certain sensible signs; [4] and consequently it was proper that this spiritual power also should be conferred on men by means of sensible symbols. These are certain forms of words, certain actions, as for instance the imposition of hands, anointing, delivery of book or chalice or some such thing that pertains to the exercise of a spiritual power. Now, whenever something spiritual is bestowed under a bodily symbol, this is called a sacrament. It is clear, therefore, that in the bestowal of spiritual power a sacrament is enacted: and this is known as the Sacrament of Order. Now it is a part of the divine liberality that whosoever receives power to perform a certain work, receives also whatsoever is required for the suitable execution of that work. Since then the sacraments that are the purpose of this spiritual power, cannot be becomingly administered without the assistance of divine grace, it follows that grace is conferred in this sacrament, even as in the others.

"But since the power of Order is directed to the dispensing of the sacraments, and since of all the sacraments the Eucharist is the most sublime and perfect, it follows that we must consider the power of

[1] 2 Cor. xiii 10. [2] Mark xiii 37. [3] Matt. xxviii 20.
[4] Cf. Essay xxi, *The Sacramental System.*

Order chiefly in its relation to that sacrament: for a thing takes its name from its end.[1] Now it appears that the same power bestows a perfection, and prepares the matter to receive that perfection: thus fire has the power to communicate its form to a thing, and to prepare the material for the reception of its form. Since then the power of Order extends to the effecting of the sacrament of Christ's body and the distribution thereof to the faithful, it follows that the same power should extend to the preparation of the faithful, that they be made fit and worthy to receive this sacrament. Now the faithful are made fit and worthy to receive this sacrament by being freed from sin: otherwise spiritual union with Christ is impossible in one who is united with him sacramentally by receiving this sacrament. Consequently the power of Order must extend to the forgiveness of sins by the dispensation of those sacraments that are directed to the remission of sin, such as Baptism and Penance. Wherefore, Our Lord, having entrusted to his disciples the consecration of his body, gave them also the power to forgive sins, which power is indicated by the keys, of which he said to Peter:[2] 'To thee will I give the keys of the kingdom of heaven.' For heaven is closed and opened to a man according as he is shackled with or freed from sin: and for this reason the use of these keys is expressed as binding and loosing, namely from sins."[3]

The Council of Trent therefore defines: "If anyone shall say that Order or sacred ordination is not truly and really a sacrament instituted by Christ the Lord, or is only a man-made fiction, invented by men unskilled in ecclesiastical affairs; or that it is only the ceremony of choosing ministers of the word of God and of the sacraments, let him be anathema."[4]

The power of Order, then, is conferred and transmitted by means of a sacramental consecration, which we call the Sacrament of Order. On the other hand, the power of Jurisdiction and the teaching authority, since their direct object is not the production of the spiritual effects of power and grace in the soul, are not bestowed by a sacramental rite, but by a commission received either from Christ himself (as in the case of the newly elected Pope) or from the lawfully constituted ecclesiastical governing authority.

It remains only to point out that there exists a close connection and mutual interdependence between the power of Order and the power of Jurisdiction. For on the one hand, the power of Order

[1] This phrase and the equivalent Latin reading *nominatur*, appears to make no sense here. There is, however, another reading *dominatur*—*unumquodque dominatur a fine*, "everything is governed or controlled by its end and purpose"—which has logical sequence.

[2] Matt. xvi 19.

[3] We have used the translation of the Dominican Fathers for the above quotation; but we have substituted other words where they seemed to express the original better.

[4] Sess. 23, can. 3.

cannot be legitimately exercised except in accordance with the ordinances and regulations prescribed by the supreme ecclesiastical authority; and on the other hand, the power of Jurisdiction regularly, ordinarily, and con-naturally resides in the highest rank of the hierarchy of Order, *i.e.* in the Episcopate, as the very name itself implies.

C. The Character of Order

Order is not only one of the seven Sacraments, but it is also one of the three Sacraments that imprint a character on the soul. "If anyone shall say that by means of ordination a character is not imprinted on the soul . . . let him be anathema." [1] A character, in the theological sense, is a spiritual seal or stamp impressed on the soul by God to indicate the consecration of that soul to him in some official capacity. Character receives its name from the stamp or brand imprinted upon the bodies of those who were enrolled in the imperial armies in ancient times, to show that they had the right and duty of fighting their country's battles. It expresses the idea of service of a master in some public ministerial office. The sacramental character therefore denotes some special ministerial relation to Christ in his Church; *e.g.* the character of Baptism carries with it the office and rights of a *follower* of Christ; the character of Confirmation those of a *soldier* of Christ; the character of Order those of a *minister* of Christ. To put it in another way, the sacramental seal or character imports a spiritual power or capacity in regard to the sacred and divine things possessed by the Church. Baptism gives the capacity to *receive* these divine gifts; Confirmation confers the power and office of *defending* them against hostile assaults; Order bestows the power and office of *dispensing* and *ministering* them to the faithful. In each case there is a sacramental consecration of the soul to Christ and to his service. It follows that the sacramental character is indelible; for it is the spiritual seal of the eternal Prince stamped on the immortal soul; nor is it possible for the servant of Christ, having once accepted and been dedicated to his service, to repudiate that service and divest himself of his ministerial power and office. Consequently, to confine our further remarks to the Sacrament of Order, this Sacrament once received cannot be repeated. The recipient of the Sacrament remains for good or ill "a priest for ever," though he be so unfortunate as subsequently to fall from grace, or even to apostatise from the faith of Christ. The ministers of Christ must necessarily form a class apart, a body of men distinguished from the general mass of the laity in the eyes both of God and men. "Since in the Sacrament of Order, as in Baptism and in Confirmation, a character is imprinted which can never be effaced or removed, the holy Synod rightly condemns the opinion of those who assert that the priests of the New Testament possess only a temporary power,

[1] Council of Trent, sess. 23, can. 4; cf. sess. 7, can. 9.

and that those who are once duly ordained can become laymen again, if they do not exercise the ministry of the divine word." [1]

The term " Sacrament of Order " may be used both of the external ceremonial rite, and of the power or character which is conferred by that rite. But, as St Thomas teaches : [2] " The interior character is essentially and principally the Sacrament of Order." The external sacramental rite is more properly termed Ordination.

§ III: THE APOSTOLIC ORDINATIONS AND THE ECCLESIASTICAL HIERARCHY

A. The Apostolic Ordinations

WE have seen that Our divine Lord at the Last Supper bestowed the Priesthood on his Apostles by the words, " Do this for a commemoration of me " ; that he gave them the power to forgive sins, when on Easter Day he breathed on them and said, " Receive ye the Holy Ghost. Whose sins you shall forgive they are forgiven them : and whose sins you shall retain they are retained " ; [3] and that in them he established the Christian Priesthood as a permanent and perpetual institution, to be handed on by them to others in continuous succession to the end of time. We have seen, too, that the handing on of the priesthood was to be carried out by means of an external, sacramental rite. But the rite that the Apostles were to employ in passing on the priesthood to others was not that which Our Lord had used in ordaining them. He, as the High Priest and Redeemer and the Institutor of the Sacraments, was above the Sacraments, not subordinated to them ; and he did not need any sacramental rite in order to confer the effects of the Sacraments.[4] Consequently, though Our Lord in ordaining the Apostles did make use of an external ceremony and pronounce certain words, they were not intended to be the means by which the sacerdotal powers were to be handed on in the Church. They were super-sacramental.

The Acts of the Apostles

When, therefore, we examine the records of the Apostolic Church, particularly in the Acts of the Apostles and in the Epistles of St Paul, we find that there is one rite of sacramental ordination and one only uniformly in use at that time.[5] That rite was the imposition of hands accompanied by prayer, the imposition of hands, of course, constituting the sacramental matter, and the prayer the sacramental form. Thus in the Acts of the Apostles,[6] when the people, directed by the Apostles, had chosen seven candidates for the office of " the

[1] Council of Trent, sess. 23, can. 4.
[2] *Sum. Theol.*, *Suppl.*, Q. xxxiv, art. 2, ad 1.
[3] John xx 22-23.
[4] St Thomas, *Sum. Theol.*, III, Q. lxiv, art. 3.
[5] We prescind for the present from the distinction of the various Orders, and confine our examination to Ordination in general. [6] vi 6.

daily ministration," "these they set before the Apostles: and they praying, imposed hands upon them."—Later on, when the time appointed by divine Providence for the evangelisation of the Gentile nations had come, "there were in the church which was at Antioch prophets and doctors. . . . And as they were ministering to the Lord and fasting, the Holy Ghost said to them: Separate me Saul and Barnabas for the work whereunto I have taken them. Then they, fasting and praying and imposing their hands upon them, sent them away."[1] This most probably refers to the episcopal ordination of St Paul and St Barnabas; though all commentators are not agreed on the point. At any rate, we see them, immediately after, going forth on their mission, and appointing presbyters in the Christian communities which they established in the various cities which they evangelised.—"When they had ordained to them priests in every church and had prayed with fasting, they commended them to the Lord, etc."[2]

Pauline Epistles

We turn now to St Paul's Epistles to his disciples Timothy and Titus. These three Epistles were addressed to them to explain the duties of the pastoral office, and to guide them in the discharge of those duties; and in the course of his instructions and exhortations he refers to the ceremony of ordination. He gives to Timothy this admonition: "neglect not the grace that is in thee: which was given thee by prophecy, with the imposition of the hands of the priesthood," or college of presbyters.[3] Similarly in 2 Timothy i 6: "I admonish thee that thou stir up the grace of God that is in thee by the imposition of my hands." In these words are indicated an external rite, the

[1] Acts, xiii 1-3.

[2] *Ibid.*, xiv 22. The Greek word here used, which is translated in our version "ordained," is χειροτονήσαντες. This word, which certainly later on in the ecclesiastical writings had the definite meaning of imposing hands, did not originally express this idea. The literal or classical meaning of the verb χειροτονεῖν was "to extend the hand," especially in the act of voting; just as nowadays a vote is taken in public meetings by a show of hands: whence it came to mean to elect, to appoint, to establish. So in this passage the Vulgate has the Latin word "constituissent," "had appointed." The Greek term for the imposition of hands originally was χειροθεσία (ἐπίθεσις τῶν χειρῶν), and χειροθετεῖν; but in course of time the word χειροτονία acquired a more precise signification, and from a more generic and indeterminate term became even more specific than χειροθεσία, which was used of "imposition of hands" for any purpose whatever, while χειροτονία was reserved exclusively for the episcopal imposition of hands in the Sacrament of Order. As regards the ceremonial by which St Paul and St Barnabas appointed priests in the local churches founded by them, there can be no doubt that it consisted essentially in the imposition of the hands and prayer; for though the word χειροτονήσαντες does not of itself and etymologically express the idea of the laying on of hands, nevertheless the very fact that in the second century we find this very idea to be the fully developed and universally accepted signification of the term, becoming gradually more explicit as it descended in direct line from the Apostles, proves that the imposition of hands was implied in the term from the very beginning.

[3] 1 Tim. iv 14.

imposition of hands, and an effect of grace produced by the rite. Guided by God through the prophets, St Paul himself had chosen Timothy for the sacred ministry, and he, together with the presbyteral college, had laid hands upon him and thus made him a pastor of the Church. The imposition of the Apostle's hands was the direct instrumental cause [1] of the sacramental effect; but the essential action of the minister of the sacrament was accompanied by the imposition of the hands of the assembled presbyters as accessories or co-operators.[2] The sacramental effect of grace was something permanently abiding in the soul ("the grace that is in thee"), which could be revived or made active, brought into operation at will. It was a grace which gave a supernatural fitness for the exercise of the pastoral office, and was described by St Paul in the next verse: "For God hath not given us the spirit of fear, but of power and of love and of sobriety."[3] These were the special graces received by the Christian pastor or bishop to fit him to discharge worthily the arduous duties of his office—fortitude, to profess and teach the faith and to govern the Church amid all the difficulties and dangers which a bishop must necessarily encounter from a hostile world, love of God and of the brethren, and moderation or self-discipline.

In this ceremony, therefore, we find all the elements necessary for a sacrament—the outward sign, the imposition of hands, which of course was always accompanied by appropriate prayer; the competent minister, St Paul himself; and the internal grace which Timothy was admonished to rekindle within himself. Finally, the institution of Christ is implicit through it all, for it was undoubtedly in pursuance of the command of Christ: "Do this for a commemoration of me," that the symbolical imposition of hands was introduced and handed down as an established rite in the Church for the ordination of her ministers; and without the institution of Christ the ceremonial rite could have had no effect of grace.

Another reference by St Paul to the ceremony of ordination is found in the injunction: "Impose not hands lightly upon any man,"[4] which shows that Timothy had the power to impose hands on others, and so possessed the plenitude of the pastoral or episcopal office.

The only allusion to ordination in the Epistle to Titus is in i 5: "For this cause I left thee in Crete: that thou . . . shouldst ordain priests in every city, as I also appointed thee." In this passage the original word for "ordain" has only the general sense of appointing, constituting, and does not express the laying on of hands. But it is to be noted that the references to the imposition of hands that occur in the Epistles to Timothy are in a sense casual and accidental. St Paul is not instructing his episcopal delegate *how* to ordain. It is clear that he assumes Timothy's perfect familiarity with the manner of

[1] διά, 2 Tim. i 6.
[2] μετά, 1 Tim. iv 14.
[3] 2 Tim. i 7.
[4] 1 Tim. v 22.

ordaining priests, and that in doing so he will perform the ceremony as he has learnt it from his Apostolic chief. And so it is with Titus. He was just as familiar with the ordination ceremony as was Timothy, and needed no instructions from St Paul how to ordain. Hence, when he is told by the Apostle to "ordain priests in every city," it is taken for granted that he will do this in the usual way, as he was ordained himself and had seen others ordained, *i.e.* by the imposition of hands. Indeed, he had already received his instructions in the matter by word of mouth from the Apostle: "as I also appointed thee." This text therefore does furnish good evidence that the Pauline practice and manner of ordination was carried out throughout the whole of the region that was evangelised by the Apostle. In other words, the imposition of hands was the Apostolic tradition.

The Council of Trent therefore teaches: "Since it is clear from the testimony of Scripture, from Apostolic tradition, and from the unanimous consent of the Fathers, that grace is conferred by sacred ordination, which is performed by words and external symbols, no one may doubt that Order is truly and really one of the seven Sacraments of Holy Church. For the Apostle saith: I admonish thee that thou stir up the grace of God which is in thee by the imposition of my hands. For God hath not given us the spirit of fear: but of power and of love and of sobriety." [1]

B. The Ecclesiastical Hierarchy

Hierarchy of jurisdiction

Hitherto we have treated of Ordination in general and as a whole; but now we must consider it in its various grades or degrees, which constitute the ecclesiastical hierarchy. The term *Hierarchy*, meaning sacred rule or government, may be used in several senses. It may denote the whole body of those men in whom is vested the power, authority, and control in sacred things; and as this power or authority is given to various members of the ruling class in various degrees or grades, the Hierarchy is the whole class of those possessing sacred power or authority, organised in their successive grades and ranks. And since the ecclesiastical power is of two kinds, the power of order and the power of jurisdiction,[2] the term Hierarchy may be used of both these powers. Thus the hierarchy of jurisdiction is

[1] Sess. 23, cap. 3.

[2] It is true that the power of jurisdiction and the teaching authority are two distinct powers if considered in their essential natures and in the abstract, and so the correct scientific division of ecclesiastical power is into the three powers of jurisdiction, teaching authority, and Order; but when taken in the concrete and in their actual exercise, the teaching authority and the power of jurisdiction are closely connected, and the former implies the latter in respect of the members of the Church. It is usual therefore in practice to divide the ecclesiastical power into two, Order and jurisdiction, instead of into three kinds.

generally understood to consist of the highest class of ecclesiastical rulers, the diocesan bishops, who possess by virtue of their office authority to rule their dioceses as true princes of the Church. It is in this sense that we use the term when we speak of the restoration of the English Hierarchy.

Hierarchy of Order

There is also, however, the Hierarchy of Order, which is constituted by the various degrees or ranks of those who have received the power to effect or to minister those sacred things which are the vehicles of grace to the members of the Church. We have seen earlier how the hierarchy of jurisdiction and the hierarchy of Order largely coincide in the same body of men, *i.e.* the hierarchy of jurisdiction is practically identified with the highest rank in the hierarchy of Order ; but the two hierarchies differ in their essential characters and in their powers, as is evident. Of the hierarchy of Order, then, the Council of Trent teaches as follows : " Since the ministry of so holy a priesthood is something that is divine, it is fitting that, in order that it may be more worthily and more reverently exercised, there should be several different Orders of ministers, whose office it is to serve the priesthood." [1]—" The holy Council declares that besides the other ecclesiastical grades, the bishops, who have succeeded to the place of the Apostles, constitute the chief rank in this hierarchical Order ; that they have been placed, as the Apostle says,[2] by the Holy Ghost to rule the Church of God ; and that they are higher than the priests or presbyters." [3] Consequently, " If anyone shall say that there is not in the Catholic Church a hierarchy instituted by divine ordinance, and consisting of bishops, priests, and ministers, let him be anathema " : and " If anyone shall say that the bishops are not higher than the priests ; or that they have not the power to confirm and ordain ; or that they hold this power in common with the priests (presbyters) . . . let him be anathema." [4]

The ecclesiastical hierarchy, then, consisting of bishops, priests, and deacons (at least), is an institution not merely of Apostolic, but of divine origin ; *i.e.* it was not established by the Apostles on their own authority and by their own initiative, in pursuance of their general commission to found the Church ; but it was received by them from Our Lord himself. Nevertheless we must not expect to find the hierarchy fully constituted and everywhere functioning normally in the Apostolic times. The first age of the Church was the age of infancy, of the first beginnings, of growth and development. The Church was in the making ; and it would be unreasonable to look for the completed organisation, although that organisation already existed in principle and in its original model.

Twofold mission of Apostolic Office

But, in order that we may understand how the hierarchy of Order, and especially the monarchical Episcopate, came to be firmly established throughout the early Church, we must have a clear conception

[1] Sess. 23, cap. 2.
[2] Acts xx 28.
[3] Sess. 23, cap. 4.
[4] Sess. 23, cap. 6, 7.

of the nature of the Apostolic office.—After Our divine Saviour had bestowed the fulness of the priesthood on the Apostles at the Last Supper and on Easter Day (as regards the power of forgiving sins), and after he had conferred the Headship of the Apostolic College and of the whole Church upon St Peter,[1] he gave to them their final commission, saying: "All power is given to me in heaven and in earth. Going therefore, teach ye all nations: baptising them in the name of the Father and of the Son and of the Holy Ghost: teaching them to observe whatsoever I have commanded you. And behold I am with you all days, even to the consummation of the world": [2] and, "You shall be witnesses unto me in Jerusalem, and in all Judea and Samaria, and even to the uttermost part of the earth." [3] Here then we see the teaching and ruling Church constituted in the Apostolic College presided over by Christ's Vicar, St Peter. Moreover, the Apostolate comprised a twofold mission, one to found the Church, and the other to conserve, extend, and govern the Church once founded, and to minister to it unto the consummation of the world. The first mission was extraordinary, temporary, given to the Apostles personally and alone. It was not to be handed on to successors, but was to cease with them. It consisted in two things. The Apostles were first of all constituted promulgators of the whole Christian revelation. They had to form the deposit of the Christian faith, so that the whole body of revealed truth was handed on from them, and no new public revelation was to be expected after they had passed away. Secondly, it was the work of the Apostles to build up the Church according to the design which Christ had drawn for them, and to build it in such manner that it would remain to the end essentially or constitutionally the same as it was in its first foundation. —Now, as this mission was personal to the Apostles themselves and they had no successors in it, so also there was complete equality among them in its possession. I do not say that there was complete equality in the *execution* of their mission; for St Paul, as he himself testifies, "laboured more abundantly than all" the rest.[4] But all the Apostles possessed equally and without limitation or restriction the prerogative of infallibility in carrying out the divine plan of the Church as Christ had designed it for them, and in contributing to the deposit of the Christian revelation. What each Apostle did in the formation of the deposit and the constitution of the Church possessed identical authority and identical stability. Consequently, when an Apostle in the course of his missionary labours founded a local Church, the very gift of infallibility which he possessed for this work required that he should make it a part of the one ecclesiastical fabric that was being built on the foundation of Peter. In other words, each local Church, as it was founded by an Apostle, was placed by him under the supreme government of St Peter.

[1] John xxi 15-17.
[2] Matt. xxviii 18-20.
[3] Acts i 8.
[4] 1 Cor. xv 10.

Establishment of Monarchical Episcopate

This brings us to the second part of the Apostolic office, or the second mission contained in it, the Apostles' permanent and ordinary mission, which was to conserve and rule the Church thus established, and to minister in it to the end of time. Since each Apostle in his work of foundation built upon the Rock of Peter, since every part of the Church, as it came to be established, fell automatically under the supreme dominion of the Prince of the Apostles, it follows immediately that in the second part of their mission, viz., in maintaining, ruling, and ministering to the Churches, the Apostles were not all equal, but were subject to their supreme Head. Their jurisdiction or governing authority as individual Apostles was not supreme and independent, as was that of Peter, but subordinate and dependent; nor was it universal, but limited to the particular local Churches which they themselves had founded. "Certainly," says St Gregory the Great in his letter to John, Patriarch of Constantinople, who had roused the indignation of the Pontiff by claiming the title of "Universal Bishop," "Peter, the first of the Apostles, is a member of the holy and universal Church. Paul, Andrew, John, what are they but the heads of particular peoples? and yet they are all members under one head." [1] The Apostles remained bishops of these local Churches until they appointed successors to themselves in those particular sees. Each was at liberty to follow his own methods and frame his own policy in the organisation of the Churches he had established. One Apostle might immediately constitute the monarchical bishop at the head of each local Church, and leave him to govern his flock with full jurisdiction. Another might regard it as necessary or opportune to keep the supreme government of his Churches in his own hands, and rule either through episcopal delegates or through each resident body of presbyters. But, as a matter of history, we know little or nothing of the missionary methods and policy of the Apostles except those of St Peter, St Paul, and St John. We gather from tradition that St Peter ordained St Evodius as his successor in the bishopric of Antioch; and that he sent St Mark to be Bishop of Alexandria, and St Apollinaris Bishop of Ravenna; and it would appear natural that St Peter, since he was the supreme Head of the whole Church, should at once establish the monarchical episcopate, subject to his own supreme jurisdiction, in the Churches founded by himself.

St John

As regards St John, the writers of the second century unanimously attribute to him the establishment of the resident episcopate in Asia Minor. The Churches of that country, after the death of St Paul, became subject to the Apostolic authority of St John; and he, with his headquarters at Ephesus, traversed the neighbouring districts both to appoint bishops and to organise the Churches. We learn from the Apocalypse,[2] that there were resident bishops at seven at least of the principal cities of Asia Minor; and there is no reason to suppose that the other local Churches had not each a bishop of its

[1] Ed. Maur., 1, 5, ep. 18. [2] c. 2.

own. We know too that St John appointed St Polycarp Bishop of Smyrna.

St Paul

We derive a certain amount of information about St Paul's methods of organisation and government, at least in their chief characteristics, if not in their details, from the Acts of the Apostles and from his Epistles; though the indications leave us in some uncertainty on various points. It is clear, first of all, that he kept in his own hands the government of the Churches which he had evangelised. In 2 Corinthians xi 28, he speaks of "my daily instance, the solicitude for all the Churches." As we have already seen, Paul and Barnabas appointed "priests (Presbyters) in every church"; [1] just as they already existed in the Church of Jerusalem.[2] But it seems certain that St Paul never, as long as he lived, appointed resident bishops for the local Churches. Timothy and Titus were undoubtedly bishops, but they were itinerants, acting as St Paul's delegates and coadjutors wherever he might send them.[3] It is true that the term "episcopus," "bishop," is used by St Paul both in the Acts and in the Epistles; but there can be no doubt that the term "episcopus" and the term "presbyter" are used synonymously in the New Testament. Moreover, it is most probable that when they are so used, they are intended to signify not the bishop in our sense of the term, but the second rank in the ecclesiastical hierarchy, the simple priest. The fact was that in the first initiation of Christianity, Greek and Latin were the languages of pagan nations, and their words expressed ideas belonging to the ordinary natural human life, or ideas distinctively pagan; so that their terminology had to be adapted to the new and supernatural conceptions which called for expression in the Christian Religion. The selection and adaptation

[1] Acts xiv 22. [2] Acts, *passim*; Jas. v 14.

[3] Some authorities consider that St Paul definitely appointed St Timothy Bishop of Ephesus, and St Titus Bishop of Crete. If that is so, then we have evidence of an earlier establishment of the monarchical episcopate in two at least of St Paul's Churches. But the evidence is not conclusive. On the contrary, there are good reasons for thinking that St Timothy and St Titus were to the end of St Paul's Apostolate his episcopal delegates and coadjutors. The entire tenor and tone of the Pastoral Epistles suggest very strongly that St Paul was still as much the head as he had ever been, and that the chief pastor was writing to his subordinates. Besides, both had previously been sent by the Apostle on temporary missionary delegations; and it seems clear that these latest appointments of both bishops were meant by St Paul to be equally temporary; for he recalled them both, and sent Tychicus and Artemas to replace them.—"Make haste to come to me quickly. . . . Only Luke is with me. Take Mark and bring him with thee, for he is profitable to me for the ministry. But Tychicus I have sent to Ephesus" (2 Tim. iv 8-12).—And to Titus: "When I shall send to thee Artemas or Tychicus, make haste to come unto me to Nicopolis. For there I have determined to winter" (Titus iii 12). Titus obeyed the summons and accompanied St Paul to Rome; but was sent thence into Dalmatia (2 Tim. iv 10). St Timothy also seems to have gone to Rome to be with St Paul in his last days; but was himself imprisoned, and afterwards released (Heb. xiii 23). He appears to have returned later to Ephesus as its diocesan bishop.

of the most appropriate terms for these Christian ideas naturally required time. Hence during the Apostolic age the terminology was in great measure in a fluid state, and only gradually settled down and became crystallised. What we therefore do find in St Paul's organisation of the Churches, is that he constituted everywhere a body of presbyters to the charge of the local congregation, and also appointed deacons to serve the Church. His episcopal delegates Timothy and Titus were also instructed to ordain priests and deacons. But over them all St Paul himself was the one bishop and pastor.

Clement of Rome and Ignatius of Antioch

By the end of the first century, *i.e.* the end of the Apostolic age, both the hierarchical terminology and the offices themselves were everywhere definitely determined and established. This very rapid development throughout the Church shows that it took place by virtue of Apostolic ordinances, the Apostles having made provision, according to the essential constitution of the Church delivered to them by Christ himself, for the monarchical bishops to rule the Churches in succession to themselves. St Clement of Rome in his first epistle to the Corinthians (about A.D. 95) writes: "Our Apostles knew through Our Lord Jesus Christ that strife would arise about the name of the episcopate. Wherefore, endowed with perfect foreknowledge, they appointed the aforesaid, and then issued an ordinance that when they had passed away, other well-tried men should succeed to the sacerdotal office (λειτουργίαν)." [1] Some years later, the letters of St Ignatius, Bishop of Antioch, who was martyred in A.D. 107, reveal the hierarchy of bishops, priests, and deacons in full working order. St Ignatius is so important and valuable a witness to Apostolic tradition in this matter that his testimony must be quoted here.—"That, perfect in one obedience, subject to the bishop and the presbyterate, you may be in all things sanctified." [2]—"Your commendable presbyterate, worthy of God, is united with the bishop as the strings with the lyre." [3]—"Since then I have been deemed worthy to see you through your bishop, Damas, worthy of God, and your worthy priests Bassus and Apollonius, and my fellow-servant, Zotion, in whom I would fain have joy, because he is subject to the bishop as to the benignity of God, and to the presbyterate as to the law of Jesus Christ." [4]—"I exhort you to strive to perform all things, the bishop presiding in the place of God, and the priests in the place of the Apostolic College, and the deacons most dear to me, to whom is committed the ministry of Jesus Christ." [5]—"It is necessary, as in fact you do, to do nothing without the bishop, and to be subject to the presbyterate as to the Apostles of Jesus Christ. The deacons also, who are the ministers of the mysteries of Jesus Christ, should do all they can to please all. For they are not the ministers of food and drink, but ministers of the Church of God. . . . Let all likewise reverence the deacons as they would Jesus Christ; the

[1] n. xliv. [2] Ep. to the Ephesians ii. [3] *Ibid.* iv.
[4] To the Magnesians ii. [5] *Ibid.* vi.

bishop also, who is the figure of the Father, and the priests as the senate of God and the council of the Apostles. Without these there is no Church. I am convinced that these are your sentiments in these matters."[1]—" I salute the Church of Philadelphia . . . especially if they are united with the bishop and his priests and deacons who have been appointed according to the will of Christ."[2]—" Strive to use one Eucharist: for there is one flesh of our Lord Jesus Christ, and one chalice in the unity of his blood, one altar, as there is one bishop with the presbyterate and deacons."[3]—" I cried with a loud voice, the voice of God: Obey the bishop, the presbyterate, and the deacons."[4]—" Obey the bishop as Jesus Christ did the Father, and the presbyterate as the Apostles, reverence the deacons as the command of God."[5]—" I salute the bishop, the presbyterate, and the deacons."[6]—" I am ready to lay down my life for those who are obedient to the bishop, presbyterate, the deacons."[7]

Bishops succeed Apostles in ordinary mission

The bishops are the successors of the Apostles, as we are taught by the Fathers of the Church and by the Council of Trent.[8] They do not, however, succeed the Apostles in their mission of *founding* the Church, but in their office of ruling and governing the Church as its ordinary pastors. Our divine Lord did not give two constitutions to his Church, one for the Apostolic age only, and the other to come into force only when the Apostles had passed away. He gave it one constitution, which was embodied first in his Apostles, and after them in their successors. This was certainly the view of St Thomas Aquinas, who wrote in the *Summa Contra Gentiles*:[9] " To Peter alone he made the promise:[10] To thee will I give the keys of the kingdom of heaven, in order to show that the power of the keys was to be received by others from him, so as to safeguard the unity of the Church. It cannot be said that, although he conferred this dignity on Peter, it does not pass from him to others. For it is evident that Christ so instituted his Church, that it would endure to the end of the world. . . . Hence it is evident that those who were then in the ministry (*i.e.* the Apostles), he appointed in such wise that their power was, for the good of the Church, to be transmitted to their successors until the end of time."

Divine Constitution of the Church

When, therefore, Our Lord ascended into heaven, he had already instituted his Church and given to it its constitution, the most important element of which was the Apostolic College with Peter at its Head. This, with the divine ordinance to constitute priests and deacons as the lower orders of the hierarchy, was the divine model of the Hierarchy of the Church for all time. The supreme power, whether of Order or government or teaching, resided in the Head,

[1] To the Trallians ii, iii.
[2] To the Philadelphians i.
[3] *Ibid.* iv.
[4] *Ibid.* vii.
[5] To the Smyrnians viii.
[6] *Ibid.* xii.
[7] To Polycarp vi.
[8] Sess. 23, c. 4; see above, p. 1035.
[9] I, iv, c. 76.
[10] Matt. xvi 19.

St Peter, and in the Apostolic College as such with their Head; and to this succeeded and succeeds the Pope, and the Pope with the whole body of the bishops, the successors of the Apostles, whether assembled in General Council, or dispersed throughout the world. On the other hand, the individual Apostles (other than Peter) governed those local sees which they founded, with a limited jurisdiction,[1] which they handed on to the local resident bishops who succeeded them in those sees. They also ordained priests and deacons to serve the Churches; and thus was established the hierarchy of bishops, priests, and deacons, which the Council of Trent has defined to belong to the essential constitution of the Church as instituted by Jesus Christ. Thus also was preserved in the Church for all time the office of the Apostolate, viz., in the Apostolic See of Peter and in the whole body of the Catholic bishops subject to that See. Hence Cardinal Baronius in his *Annales Ecclesiastici* (for the year 58) thus comments on the assertion of St Jerome and the other Fathers that the bishops are the successors of the Apostles:[2] "If the bishops have succeeded to the place of the Apostles (as all Catholics are agreed), the origin and dignity of the Episcopate are the same as of the Apostolate."

[1] The difference of St Paul's tone in his Epistle to the Romans from that of the Epistles to the Corinthians and Galatians, for example, is remarkable. In the latter he speaks as a true episcopal ruler and superior, teaching, legislating, commanding, rebuking, threatening, punishing. But he makes no claim of jurisdiction over the Romans. He rather "takes good care, throughout the whole Letter, to treat with respectful reserve this Christian body, upon which he had no claims either as their Founder or their Evangelist, excusing himself for his boldness in writing to them, limiting his projected ministry in their city to 'visiting them on the way' when he shall start out on his journey Spainward, in order to enjoy the consolations of their society. One humble wish sums up all his ambition so far as they are concerned: 'God is my witness how unceasingly I remember you, evermore beseeching him in my prayers that, if it be his will, he would now at length afford me some favourable opportunity to come unto you, for I feel a great need of seeing you, to make you partakers of some spiritual gift' (i 9-11)." (Fouard, *St Paul and His Missions*, pp. 329-30). He informs them that his Apostolic labours have been devoted only to those regions which had not been evangelised and where Christ was unknown; and he disclaims any intention of trespassing on the mission-field of another Apostle, "lest I should build upon another man's foundation" (xv 20).

[2] It is true that the Apostles exercised, even in Churches already well established, certain powers of jurisdiction which far surpassed the powers of an ordinary diocesan bishop. For instance, they appointed bishops to dioceses, or laid down the method of choosing future bishops; and they also exercised a pastoral superintendence over whole provinces and countries. Thus St Jerome relates that St John, when residing at Ephesus, ruled all the Churches of Asia. These, however, were extraordinary powers possessed by the Apostles in their capacity as *founders* of the Church, and as Apostolic vicars of St Peter. A similar power was exercised later by the Patriarchs of Antioch and Alexandria (both Patriarchates having originated from St Peter), who also appointed the bishops of their provinces, and possessed super-episcopal rights of jurisdiction over them and their dioceses. These powers the Patriarchs certainly held as delegates of the Supreme Pontiff.

§ IV: THE ONE PRIESTHOOD (SACERDOTIUM): THE EPISCOPATE AND THE PRESBYTERATE

A. The One Priesthood

THE Hierarchy of Order, then, is constituted of "bishops, priests, and ministers." Now we must take a step farther. The Council of Trent also teaches as follows: "Since the ministry of so holy a priesthood is something divine, it was fitting, in order that it might be exercised more worthily and with greater reverence, that in the most orderly organisation of the Church there should be several orders of ministers, whose office it is to serve the priesthood; these orders being so distributed that those who had received the clerical tonsure, should pass through the minor orders to the major orders. For the sacred Scriptures mention expressly not only *priests*, but *deacons* also; and teach in most grave terms those things which have to be especially observed in their ordination. And from the very beginning of the Church the names of the following Orders, with the ministerial functions proper to each, are known to have been in use, viz., of the Subdeacon, Acolyte, Exorcist, Lector, and Porter. But these are not equal in degree, for the Subdeacon is classed by the Fathers and Councils among the major Orders." [1]

Here then we have on the one hand the Hierarchy of "bishops, priests, and ministers," and, on the other hand, the Priesthood, with six attendant Orders of ministers from the Diaconate downwards. We shall treat directly of the six Orders of the Ministry in the next section. The point now is that while there are the two degrees of bishops and priests or presbyters in the Hierarchy of Order, yet the Council mentions only one Order of Priesthood. In this, as we shall see, there is no contradiction or inconsistency. What concerns us at the moment is this, that the Christian Priesthood, like the Priesthood of Christ himself, is one and only one. For "Sacrifice and Priesthood are so intimately related to each other by divine ordinance, that both exist under every law. Since therefore in the New Testament the Catholic Church received from the institution of Christ the holy visible Sacrifice of the Eucharist, it necessarily follows that she possesses also a new visible and external Priesthood, into which the priesthood of the Old Law was translated." [2] Hence St Thomas Aquinas lays down the principle that the Sacrament of Order exists for the Sacrament and Sacrifice of the Holy Eucharist, and that the primary and essential act of the Christian Priesthood is the consecration and oblation of the Body and Blood of Christ. The power of consecrating the Holy Eucharist and of offering the Eucharistic Sacrifice, therefore, is the essential power of the Priesthood; and since this power is one and indivisible, the Christian Priesthood also

[1] Sess. 23, cap. 2.

[2] Council of Trent, sess. 23, cap. 1.

is one and indivisible, so that all who have received sacerdotal ordination equally possess the order and power of the Priesthood in its substantial essence. Consequently the Council of Trent presents the Priesthood (sacerdotium) to us as the supreme Order, to which all the others, major and minor Orders, lead up as so many steps, and for which they all exist.[1] St Thomas therefore draws from his principle the conclusion that the Episcopate is not, strictly speaking, an Order distinct from the Presbyterate, because the bishop has not a higher power than the simple priest to consecrate and to offer the Holy Eucharist. In other words, there is one Order of the Christian Priesthood, the Sacerdotium.

B. The Episcopate and the Presbyterate

Pre-eminence of the Episcopate in power of Order

It is nevertheless equally true that there are two divinely instituted degrees in the Sacerdotium, the Episcopate and the Presbyterate, the bishops and the simple priests ; and it is of faith that the bishops hold in the ecclesiastical hierarchy a superior rank to that of the simple priests.[2] This has been made sufficiently clear already in the previous section, when treating of the ecclesiastical hierarchy, at any rate as regards the power of jurisdiction. But the Episcopate holds a pre-eminence above the simple priesthood in the power of Order also. It is true that the essential act of the Priesthood is to consecrate and to offer the Eucharistic Sacrifice, and that in this the Episcopate possesses no superiority. But the continuance and permanence of this essential priestly power is exceedingly important, and even vital, for the Church, and this permanence is secured according to Christ's institution in the Episcopate alone. Only the bishop can transmit to others the power to consecrate the Holy Eucharist. The bishop, as the successor of the Apostles, has the power to generate sons like unto himself in the priesthood, so that he holds to the simple priest the relation of Father in God, and, in the words of St Jerome, " What Aaron and his sons were in the temple, that are the bishops and the priests in the Church."[3] The bishop, too, as the prince of the Church, has the power to enrol soldiers in the army of Christ as the ordinary minister of the Sacrament of Confirmation, and he alone can consecrate churches and other sacred things. The bishop, therefore, for all these reasons, but chiefly of course because he possesses the power of handing on the priesthood, is superior to the simple priest in the sacramental power of Order.

Distinctive power of Episcopate

His distinctive power, though of the greatest importance, is not the essential power to consecrate the Holy Eucharist, but is subsidiary to it. It is an extension and complement of the Presbyterate, and so it does not constitute a distinct Order. But it is a power essentially connected with the Sacrament of the Holy Eucharist, for it

[1] Sess. 23, can. 2.

[2] Council of Trent, sess. 23, can. 7.

[3] Ep. 146 to Evangelus.

is the power to hand on the power to consecrate, and consequently it forms a superior rank within the Order of the Priesthood. St Robert Bellarmine says in this connection: "The Episcopate is one Order with the Presbyterate; but they are different grades. For Orders are reckoned according to their relation to the Eucharist; and because the highest power with regard to the Eucharist is the power of consecrating it, the first Order is the Priesthood, *i.e.* the Order of those who have the power to consecrate the Eucharist; nor can any other Order greater than or superior to this be conceived. But because this power is shared by bishops and priests in different ways, there are therefore two grades of priests. The simple priests (presbyters) are dependent on the bishops in the consecration of the Eucharist, at least as regards the exercise of the power; for the bishops can forbid them to consecrate, or suspend them temporarily, or command them to celebrate at such a time and place, and in such a way. Besides, simple priests do not so possess this power that they can transmit it to others; but bishops both possess the power and can transmit it to others." [1]

Two ranks in one Order

The Catechism of the Council of Trent teaches the same doctrine: "These are the chief functions of the Sacerdotal Order, which, *although it is one*, has different degrees of dignity and power. The first degree is that of the simple priests. . . . The second is that of the bishops, etc." [2]

There are indeed theologians who would prefer to call the Episcopate a distinct Order from the Presbyterate; who nevertheless understand the matter precisely as we have explained it above. To dispute about mere terms would be futile. But it certainly seems more correct to speak of two degrees or ranks in the same Order of the Sacerdotium, than of two Orders which are not adequately distinct from each other.

So far we have described the relations of the Episcopate and the Presbyterate according to the common view of the Scholastics and the practice of the Church. For it is a fact that in actual practice no one is consecrated to the Episcopate who has not already been ordained priest, and consequently that the Episcopate does not actually confer the essential power of the priesthood, but only those additional and complementary powers which have already been enumerated as proper to the Episcopate. Those who hold this view maintain further that previous ordination to the Presbyterate is essential to the Episcopate, so that the episcopal consecration of one who was not already a priest would be null and void; for the conferment of the extension or complement of a spiritual power is not conceivable, if that power does not already exist in the recipient. This is certainly the general view of theologians; and, as we have said, it is confirmed by the universal practice of the Church. There are some, however, especially among the canonists, who regard the Episcopate as an Order

[1] *De Ordine*, cap. v.

[2] *The Sacrament of Order*, No. 26.

entirely distinct from the Presbyterate; so distinct indeed, that it does not even presuppose, of its own nature, ordination to the priesthood. In other words, the Episcopate, in this view, is the *whole* priesthood, and of itself confers the whole priestly power, or would confer it if it happened (quite unlawfully, to say the least) that someone were consecrated bishop without previous ordination to the priesthood: the Episcopate is the whole, and the Presbyterate is a part contained in it. The ground on which this opinion is based is the supposed historical fact of episcopal consecrations in the early ages which were not preceded by ordination to the priesthood, *i.e.* there exists no record of such ordination. They instance the Apostles themselves; but the Apostles did not receive their episcopal power by means of the Sacrament of Order. They received it supersacramentally from Our Lord himself. The only other argument used is that from silence, which is inconclusive and treacherous. We have therefore deemed it unnecessary and undesirable to depart from the common view and the common practice, which enumerates seven Orders, culminating in the Priesthood or Sacerdotium.

Sacramental nature of Episcopate and Presbyterate

Whichever of these views be accepted of the distinction of the Episcopate and Presbyterate from the point of view of Order, there can be no dispute as to their sacramental nature.[1] Let us take the Presbyterate first. The Priesthood or Presbyterate, which consists in the essential power of the Sacrament of Order, viz., the power to consecrate the Holy Eucharist and to absolve from sins, is, beyond all controversy, a Sacrament. It is the very heart of the Sacrament of Order. It is for this power that all the other powers of Order exist, even the power of the Episcopate, for that in its essence is the power to hand on and perpetuate the power of consecration.—Moreover, the Presbyterate possesses the three elements that are required to constitute a sacrament—outward sign, institution by Christ, and the power to produce sanctifying grace in the soul of the recipient. The outward sign exists, *i.e.* the external ceremonial rite by which the priesthood is conferred;[2] the institution by Christ has already been proved from Scripture, from Apostolic Tradition, and from the definition of the Council of Trent;[3] and finally, the ordination rite confers sanctifying grace, because, as St Thomas argues, "The works of God are perfect;[4] and consequently whoever receives power from above receives also those things that render him competent to exercise that power. This is also the case in natural things, since animals are provided with members, by which their soul's powers are enabled to proceed to their respective actions unless there be some defect on the part of matter. Now just as sanctifying grace

[1] Some theologians, by a certain confusion of thought, have identified the terms "Order" and "Sacrament" in reference to the Episcopate, arguing that if the Episcopate were not a separate Order, it would not be a Sacrament. This is not so, as will be made clear.

[2] Cf. below, pp. 1053 ff.

[3] Sess. 23, can. 1 and 6.

[4] Deut. xxxii 4.

is necessary in order that man may receive the sacraments worthily, so is it that he may dispense them worthily. Wherefore as in Baptism, whereby a man is adapted to receive the other sacraments, sanctifying grace is given, so is it in the sacrament of Order whereby man is ordained to the dispensation of the other sacraments." [1]

Moreover, the Council of Trent defines that "by sacred ordination the Holy Ghost is given; and therefore the bishops do not say in vain *Receive the Holy Ghost.*" [2] The Presbyterate is therefore a Sacrament.

The Episcopate too, though it is not a distinct Order from the Presbyterate, is also a Sacrament. For it is the complement, the fulness, the consummation of the Sacerdotium, conferring a distinct power in reference to the Holy Eucharist, viz., that of transmitting the power of consecration (as well as the power to perform other hierarchical functions), by means of an external rite, which also confers grace. All this has already been proved above.

One Sacrament

The Presbyterate and the Episcopate, however, are not two distinct Sacraments, nor (to express the same thing in other words) do they produce in the soul two distinct sacramental characters. The Presbyterate gives the essential character of the Sacerdotium; but it is an incomplete, imperfect, immature character, because it is incapable of reproducing and perpetuating itself. The Episcopate amplifies and perfects the character of the Presbyterate, giving to it that further power which was lacking to its fulness and completeness. Hence the Sacrament of Order is one, and the character of Order is one; and they exist in their ultimate perfection in the bishop, who possesses the plenitude of the Sacerdotium.

In the view of those who would prefer to hold that the Episcopate does not presuppose the Presbyterate, and contains in itself the whole Sacerdotium, the rite of episcopal consecration would be in itself the complete and perfect Sacrament of Order, and would produce the complete and perfect character of the Sacerdotium; while the Presbyterate would be only an imperfect participation of the Sacrament and of the character of the Episcopate.

But whichever view we may elect to take, the Sacrament of Order is one, and the character of Order is one; and the Episcopate in the concrete is the plenitude of the Christian Priesthood. The canonists and theologians who maintain that the Episcopate, though it necessarily presupposes the Presbyterate, which it completes and perfects, is a distinct Order, hold as a consequence that it confers a new and distinct character. This is probably, as we have already suggested,

[1] *Suppl.*, Q. xxxv, art. 1.

[2] Sess. 23, can. 4. This does not mean that the words "Receive the Holy Ghost" constitute the *form* of the Sacrament of Order; but that the ordination rite which contains those words does actually have the effect of giving the Holy Ghost and sanctifying grace. Since the words "Receive the Holy Ghost" occur in the ordination rites of bishop, priest, and deacon, this argument applies equally to all these three ordinations.

merely a difference of opinion about the more correct form of expression, as certainly appears to be the case with St Robert Bellarmine,[1] who prefers to say that the Episcopate confers a new character.—But if the dispute is about realities, and if it is contended that two distinct and disparate characters are necessary for the fulness of the Sacerdotium, it may perhaps be difficult to defend the unity of the Sacrament of Order.

§ V: THE INFERIOR OR MINISTERIAL ORDERS

We have now to consider the various Orders of the Ministry. The term " Ministry " (and " Ministers ") is now used not in the sense in which even priests and bishops are ministers—" Ministers of Christ and dispensers of the mysteries of God," like St Paul.[2] It is the Ministry as distinguished from the Sacerdotium, the Ministers whose official duty it is to serve the priest or bishop in the discharge of their sacerdotal functions. The teaching of the Council of Trent on the subject of the Ministry has already been quoted :—first, that the divinely instituted hierarchy of Order consists of bishops, priests, and *ministers*,[3] and secondly, that the Orders of Ministers are the Deacons, Subdeacons, Acolytes, Exorcists, Lectors, and Porters.[4]

A. The Diaconate

In the New Testament

The word " Deacon " means " minister," and the Diaconate may be described as the plenitude of the ministry (in the sense of the word explained above).—It is narrated in Acts vi that " In those days, the number of the disciples increasing, there arose a murmuring of the Greeks against the Hebrews, for that their widows were neglected in the daily ministration. Then the twelve, calling together the multitude of the disciples, said : It is not reason that we should leave the word of God and serve tables. Wherefore, brethren, look ye out among you seven men of good reputation, full of the Holy Ghost and wisdom, whom we may appoint over this business. But we will give ourselves continually to prayer and to the ministry of the word. And the saying was liked by all the multitude. And they chose Stephen, a man full of faith and of the Holy Ghost, and Philip and Prochorus and Nicanor, and Timon and Parmenas and Nicholas, a proselyte of Antioch. These they set before the Apostles : and they praying, imposed hands upon them." [5]

This is the first recorded ordination of Deacons. We learn, first of all, what was the *occasion* of this ordination. It was to take charge of the temporal administration of the goods of the Church. The first Christians of Jerusalem were living a common life. " As many

[1] *Loc. cit.* [2] 1 Cor. iv 1. [3] Sess. 23, can. 6.
[4] *Ibid.*, cap. 2 and can. 2. [5] 1-6.

as were owners of lands or houses sold them and brought the price of the things they sold, and laid it down before the feet of the Apostles. And distribution was made to every one according as he had need." [1] In order therefore that the Apostles themselves might not be distracted by temporal cares from their much more important spiritual duties, men were chosen to administer the common goods, and to see that none went in need. These men constituted a class of sacred ministers, subject to the Apostles; and it was only fitting that the temporalities of the Church should be administered by a special class of officers of the Church.

But this material ministry was not their only, or their highest office. Had it been so, the Apostles would hardly have made it a condition that they should be "full of the Holy Ghost and wisdom"; nor would they have dignified their appointment with a solemn religious ceremony. Moreover, the Christian tables were closely associated with the "agape," and through the "agape" with the celebration of the Holy Eucharist.[2] Furthermore, we find the Deacons Stephen and Philip (the others receive no further mention) immediately engaged in the work of preaching the Gospel, instructing converts, and baptising. The Deacons, then, formed a class of sacred ministers instituted to serve the Apostles not only in material affairs, but also in their spiritual functions. St Paul associates them with the Bishops as a class distinct from the general body of the faithful;[3] and describes the virtues and qualities that are to be required of them.[4]

In the Apostolic Fathers

The writings of the Apostolic Fathers confirm and clarify the indications which are given in the New Testament. We read in the *Didache* or *Doctrine of the Twelve Apostles*:[5] "Meeting on Sunday, break bread and give thanks, after you have confessed your sins, that your sacrifice may be pure. Let no one who is in disagreement with his friend join you until he is reconciled, lest your sacrifice be sullied. For the Lord has said: 'In every place and time let there be offered to me a clean sacrifice, for I am a great King, saith the Lord, and my name is wonderful among the Gentiles.'[6] Appoint *therefore* among you bishops and deacons worthy of the Lord, men of meekness, unselfish, truthful, honourable: for they minister to you the ministry of the prophets and doctors. Do not, then, despise them: for they have been honoured among you together with the prophets and doctors."[7]—In this passage we have a testimony from the Apostolic age both to the Sacrifice of the Holy Eucharist, and to the active ministry which was assigned to the deacons in that Sacrifice.

St Clement of Rome[8] declares: "The Apostles were made preachers of the Gospel to us by the Lord Jesus Christ; Jesus Christ was sent from God, and the Apostles from Christ; and both these

[1] Acts iv 34-35.
[2] See 1 Cor. xi 20 ff.
[3] Phil. i 1.
[4] 1 Tim. iii 8-13.
[5] A.D. 80-100.
[6] Malachy i 11.
[7] xiv-xv.
[8] 1st Ep. to the Corinthians, about A.D. 93-95.

things were done in order according to the will of God. Having therefore received their commands, and being fully convinced through the resurrection of the Lord Jesus Christ, and trusting in the word of God, with sure confidence in the Holy Ghost, they went forth announcing the coming of the kingdom of God. Preaching the word, therefore, through the countries and cities, they appointed their first converts, having proved them in the spirit, the bishops and deacons of the future believers. Nor was this a new institution; for many centuries before it was written of bishops and deacons. For thus says the Scripture in a certain place: 'I will appoint their bishops in justice and their deacons in faith.'" This clearly shows that Pope Clement attributed the episcopate and the diaconate equally to divine institution.

We have already seen [1] that St Ignatius of Antioch places the Deacons in the third rank of the ecclesiastical hierarchy; and teaches that to them "is committed the ministry of Jesus Christ"; that they "are the ministers of the mysteries of Jesus Christ; for they are not ministers of food and drink, but ministers of the Church of God"; and that without the deacons, the bishops, and the priests, "there is no Church," *i.e.* they belong to the essential constitution of the Church, and are therefore of divine institution; as appears also from his exhortation to reverence the deacons because they are the "command of God," and "have been appointed according to the will of Christ."—Similarly, St Polycarp, Bishop of Smyrna († 166), writes that "the deacons must be faultless before the justice of God, as the ministers of God and Christ, and not of men." [2]

In this connection one can hardly omit the testimony of the great Martyr Deacon, St Laurence († 258), as recorded by St Ambrose († 397). Laurence, the Archdeacon of Rome, meets Pope Sixtus on the way to martyrdom, and thus addresses him: "Whither are you going, my father, without your son? Whither do you hasten without your deacon? You were never accustomed to offer the Sacrifice without your minister."

A favourite name of the ancient Fathers for the Deacon was that of "levite"; and they compared the ecclesiastical hierarchy of the New Testament with that of the Old. Thus St Clement of Rome in the first century: "The high priest has his proper functions; to the priests their place is assigned; and the levites discharge their ministry." [3] And St Jerome in the fifth century in his letter to Evangelus: "That we may know the Apostolic traditions taken from the Old Testament: what Aaron and his sons and the levites were in the temple, that the bishops and priests and deacons are in the Church."

Office and divine institution of Diaconate

Apostolic tradition therefore presents to us the Diaconate as a sacred ministry, whose principal functions are attendance on the bishop in the offering of the holy Sacrifice, the distribution of the

[1] pp. 1039-1040. [2] To the Philippians v.
[3] 1st Ep. to the Corinthians xl 5.

Holy Eucharist, the administration of baptism, and the reading and preaching of the Gospel; and further, it attests that the Diaconate is a divine institution.

An interesting suggestion

An interesting suggestion has been made that the seven Deacons whose ordination is narrated in the sixth chapter of the Acts of the Apostles, were not the first to be appointed to that office. It is to be noted that the occasion of the election of these seven deacons was the dissatisfaction of the Greek or Hellenist converts with the treatment which their widows received in the daily ministration. Their complaint was that the Hebrews received more favourable consideration. Already, in c. 4, v. 4, the number of men alone in the Christian community had reached 5000; and they were constantly receiving additions to their ranks. Among these the Hebrews would naturally be in the majority. Moreover, the disciples had everything in common, so that the daily ministration was necessarily an official service. It seems reasonable then to conclude that even if the Twelve had performed this duty themselves, they would have been compelled to call in others to their assistance. But we are further told that when the Hellenists complained of unfair treatment, the Apostles replied that it was not fitting that they should leave the word of God and serve tables. Their work was a spiritual one, prayer and the ministry of the word.[1] So, obviously, they had not themselves been engaged hitherto in this work of food distribution, but had entrusted it to subordinate officers. These officers would naturally have been chosen from the Hebrews; and it was their alleged favouritism of which complaint was made by the Hellenists. Confirmation of this is found in the fact that the seven Deacons chosen in c. vi, were themselves all Hellenists, as is proved by their very names, which are all Greek. The appointment of seven Hellenist deacons for the whole community, the majority of whose members were Hebrews, could scarcely be justified, and would undoubtedly have been a fruitful source of further discontent and dissension, this time on the part of the Hebrews. These considerations are singularly strengthened by a variant reading, or probably a gloss, of the Codex Bezae (sixth century), which in c. vi, 1, has "in the daily ministration (diaconia) *of the Hebrews*"; and the Palimpsest of Fleury (fifth or sixth century) reads as follows: "that the widows of the Hellenists were neglected in the daily ministration *by the deacons of the Hebrews.*" We may then reasonably conclude that the suggestion that other deacons already existed when the seven were appointed for the Greeks, is neither new nor unsupported by evidence.

B. The Subdiaconate and the Minor Orders

We pass on now to the Subdiaconate and the Minor Orders. The position with regard to these is not quite the same as that of the Diaconate. It is of faith that the Diaconate belongs by divine

[1] vi 2, 4; cf. v 42.

institution to the ecclesiastical hierarchy; and the proposition that the Diaconate belongs also by divine institution to the Sacrament of Order, if not a doctrine of faith, is only one step removed from it; in other words, it is certain theologically. But it is freely disputed among theologians whether the Subdiaconate and the Minor Orders are or are not parts of the Sacrament of Order. St Thomas Aquinas and most of the early Scholastics, as well as many of the more modern theologians, hold that they do form part of the Sacrament. Others with the great majority of modern theologians teach that the Subdiaconate and the Minor Orders are only ceremonies instituted by the Church, and have not the nature of a Sacrament. We will give the arguments of both sides in the discussion, and will leave the reader to form his own considered opinion on the point.

It is common ground that these Orders do not appear in ecclesiastical history till about the middle of the third century; and it is certain that in the Apostolic and sub-Apostolic times bishops, priests, and deacons were the only ministers of the Church. As an immediate consequence, those who hold the negative view infer that the Subdiaconate and the Minor Orders are not Sacraments, on the principle that the Church has not the power to institute Sacraments. The reply to this argument is that there is no question of the institution of Sacraments by the Church. St Thomas explains the matter thus: "In the early Church, on account of the fewness of the ministers, all the lower ministries were entrusted to the deacons. . . . Nevertheless all the said powers existed, but implicitly in the one power of the deacon. But afterwards divine worship developed; and the Church transmitted explicitly in several Orders that which had hitherto existed implicitly in one Order. This is what the Master (Peter Lombard) means when he says in the text that the Church instituted other Orders." [1] The full ministry of the Diaconate comprises all the various services, both remote and proximate, that may be required for the Holy Sacrifice of the Mass; and as these various services are of their nature distinct and separable, the Church, when the exigencies of public worship called for it, separated them and committed them to distinct persons, who thus constituted the lower Orders of the Ministry, the plenitude of which remained in the Diaconate. This, it is contended, is not to institute a Sacrament; and, in this view, it is not necessary that the Minor Orders should be of the same character and number at all times and in all parts of the Church.

But, further, it is denied that the Church possesses this power of separating the various ministries, because she would have to institute the ceremonial rites by which these various Orders are conferred; and the Church cannot determine the matter and form of a Sacrament. —On this point the exponents of the affirmative view have much to say; but as we shall meet it again in the next section on the matter

[1] *Suppl.*, Q. xxxvii, art. 2, ad. 2.

and form of the Sacrament of Order, we may now postpone its consideration.

It remains now only to mention the arguments from authority. Thus, the Decree for the Armenians, published in the Council of Florence by Pope Eugenius IV (A.D. 1439), which, though probably not an *ex cathedra* definition, is a practical instruction on doctrine emanating from the highest teaching authority of the Church, and as such is a theological document of the first rank,[1] has the following on the Sacrament of Order: "The sixth Sacrament is Order, whose matter is that thing by the handing of which the Order is conferred; as the priesthood is given by the handing of the chalice with wine, and the paten with bread; the diaconate by the giving of the book of the Gospels; the subdiaconate by the handing of the empty chalice with the empty paten upon it; and *in like manner the other Orders* (*i.e.* the Minor Orders), by the presentation of the things that appertain to their respective ministries."

Furthermore, the Council of Trent, while admitting it had no intention of authoritatively deciding the theological controversy in question, appears to use language which favours the affirmative opinion. Thus in sess. 23, c. 2, the Council enumerates the seven Orders, including the Subdiaconate and the Minor Orders; in canon 2 it defines that besides the priesthood there are in the Church other Orders, both major and minor; in canon 3 that Order or sacred ordination is truly and literally a Sacrament instituted by Christ; in canon 6 that there exists in the Church the divinely instituted hierarchy, consisting of bishops, priests, and *ministers* (the word *deacons* is not used, when it might just as easily, and with even more propriety, have been used, if deacons only were meant); and finally in chap. 2 it teaches that there are "several different *orders of ministers*."

Nevertheless, the question is an open one, and we leave it so. But whichever view is preferred, it remains true that the inferior ministries represented by the Subdiaconate and the Minor Orders are all contained supereminently in the Diaconate; and consequently that, even if those Orders are admitted to possess and confer each a sacramental character, those characters are not something extrinsic to the Diaconate, but are implicitly contained in it, and when the Diaconate is actually received, are absorbed into the sacramental character of the plenitude of the ministry.

Moreover, the Diaconate itself, the plenitude of the ministry, is not a power independent of the priesthood (sacerdotium). Indeed, the Diaconate does not confer a *power* in the strict sense of the term. It commits to the recipient a *ministry* to be exercised *ex officio*. All therefore that is conferred by the Diaconate is contained supereminently in the Priesthood; for if the priest can *offer* the holy Sacrifice, he can *a fortiori* minister to another who is offering it. Hence the character of the Diaconate is contained in, incorporated

[1] This question also will recur below, p. 1058.

into, the character of the Priesthood. And since we have shown the sacramental unity of the Priesthood and the Episcopate, it follows that the unity of the Sacrament of Order is established, no matter how many and diverse may be the Orders which it includes.

§ VI: THE MATTER AND FORM OF ORDER

Common ground in the controversy

It may be thought that this question has already been decided in section III, *A*, when the Apostolic Ordinations were discussed; for there we saw that bishops, priests, and deacons were all ordained by the imposition of hands with prayer. It seems reasonable therefore to conclude that we have here the matter and form of the Sacrament of Order. But the question is not to be settled quite so simply. There is indeed a certain amount of common ground in this controversy. It is admitted on both sides (1) that the imposition of hands was the original and sole matter of the priesthood, etc., dating back to the time of the Apostles; (2) that the ceremony of the imposition of hands has always and everywhere been retained in the sacramental rite throughout the universal Church down to the present day; (3) that the Oriental Rites have retained the imposition of hands as the *only* matter of the Sacrament down to the present time, with the sole exception of the Armenian Rite, which borrowed the tradition of the instruments from the Latin Rite about or after the middle of the twelfth century;[1] (4) that the Latin Rite itself did not possess the ceremony of the tradition of the instruments until certainly the tenth century; and until that time the imposition of hands was the only matter of the Sacrament in the Western as well as in the Eastern Church.

The tradition of the instruments

But from that date in the Latin Church the ordination rites gradually expanded and developed by the addition of other significant ceremonies, which both enhanced the solemnity of the occasion, and especially brought out more clearly the sacramental symbolism. One ceremony in particular was introduced into the ordination rites of the priesthood and the diaconate, which vividly expressed the power to be conferred; and this ceremony was the tradition or handing to the candidate of the things used in the exercise of the Order in question—the chalice with wine and the paten with bread for the priesthood, and the book of the Gospels for the diaconate, together with a form of words signifying the power conferred by the ordination. By the thirteenth century the tradition of the instruments had been universally adopted throughout the Latin Church; so much so that the Scholastics began to teach that this tradition of the instruments with the respective form of words belonged to the sacramental matter and form.

The Church and the "substance" of the sacraments

The question then arises: Was the imposition of hands in the Latin Church deposed from its status as the matter of the Sacrament

[1] Cardinal Van Rossum, *De Essentia Sacramenti Ordinis*, nn. 242 ff.

by the tradition of the instruments? *Could* it have been so deposed? —These questions can be answered with certainty only when we have settled the controverted point whether the Church has the power to interfere with the matter and form of the Sacraments. That the Church *has* power over the Sacraments is undoubted, and was taught by the Council of Trent. But the difficulty is to define the precise extent of that power. "The Council declares that the Church has always possessed the power in the *dispensation* (*or administration*) of the Sacraments, *saving their substance*, to determine or to change those things which it judges to be more expedient for the utility of the recipients or for the reverence due to the Sacraments themselves, according to the diversity of the circumstances of time, place, etc."[1] "*Saving their substance.*"

What does this mean or involve?—First of all, since Christ Our Lord alone could institute Sacraments, and what he did is inviolate and immutable, if he determined the matter and the form of the Sacraments specifically and definitely, the Church has no power to change them. It is admitted on all hands that this is true of Baptism and the Holy Eucharist. Our Lord chose water for the matter of Baptism, bread for the matter of the Holy Eucharist; and nothing else can ever be admitted. Similarly, he made the legitimate marriage contract the outward sign of Matrimony. But in the cases of Confirmation, Order, and Extreme Unction, it is contended that they were instituted only with a generic determination of their outward sign. The effect, whether of power or of grace, which they were designed to produce in the soul was indicated; and it was left to the Apostles and to the supreme authority of the Church to determine "according to the diversity of the circumstances," as the Council of Trent says, the particular thing or sign which should be chosen to signify and produce the sacramental effect in the soul.

Now the Sacraments are essentially signs, practical signs of an inward spiritual effect. "The Sacraments cause what they signify, and inasmuch as they signify." In other words, it is its significance which constitutes the metaphysical essence of the sacramental sign. If there are two material things which signify the same spiritual effect, then that which is important and vital and substantial in the sign is the identity of the signification, not the physical constitution of the material thing, which is of no account and negligible. Hence, of two signs that are of equal value in signifying, the Church can, according to Trent as above, select this one or that one, this one for that time and the other for another time, this one for one place and the other for another place, or she can use both together, as may seem to her expedient—where the matter has not been precisely determined by Christ himself. In other words such action on the part of the Church pertains to the administration, not to the substance of the Sacrament. If two or more distinct forms of words having the

[1] Sess. 21, c. 2.

same meaning, whether in the same language or in different languages, can be and are admitted as the equally valid forms of the same Sacrament, it is difficult to see why two or more material things which express the same idea, cannot be adopted by the Church according to circumstances to symbolise the effect of a Sacrament. If, then, Christ did not determine the matter of the priesthood specifically, the Church had to do so, and can change it within the limits described. —This is the argument of the one side.

Another view

But those theologians who hold that the imposition of the hands alone is the complete matter of the priesthood base their view precisely on their conviction that the Church has no power at all of this kind over the Sacrament of Order. They hold that Our Lord definitely fixed the imposition of hands as the matter.—Let us test the strength of their position. Cardinal Van Rossum [1] writes: "Sacred Scripture so clearly and frequently records the matter of the Sacrament of Order that it is impossible to say that it was not specifically determined by Our Lord."—We have seen earlier what the New Testament does say. It makes no statement of any such specific determination of the matter by Our Lord himself. The Apostles were ordained priests and bishops not by the imposition of hands or by any Sacrament, but by the words, "Do this for a commemoration of me." The Apostles, of course, had to ordain bishops, priests, and deacons; but we have no record of any instruction given to them by Our Lord how they were to do it. Moreover, the sacramental matter would be just as clearly and frequently indicated in the New Testament, if it had been determined by the Apostles themselves and not by Our Lord. There is therefore certainly some plausibility in the theory that Our Lord left the choice to the Apostles.

Sacramental efficacy of imposition of hands

But even though we may accept the view that the Church possesses this power, if we are to be persuaded that she, some time after the tenth century, deprived the imposition of hands of its sacramental efficacy, and transferred it to the tradition of the instrument, we shall require very conclusive and rigorous proof. Of course, if it could be shown that the Church suppressed the imposition of hands entirely in the ordination rite and substituted the tradition of the instruments for it, there could be no question. But the Church has not done this. The imposition of hands has kept its place in the ordination of bishops, priests, and deacons, from the time of the Apostles to the present day. What has been done in the Latin Church is to *add* the tradition of the instruments to the Ordinal. What then has to be shown is that the Church, while leaving the imposition of hands to hold its place in the rite of ordination, has nevertheless deprived it of its importance and efficacy, and reduced it to a mere ceremony. This, we venture to say, has not yet been proved; nor, in our belief, can it be proved. The Church, like Our Lord himself, came not to destroy but to fulfil. She has ever been jealous and

[1] *Op. cit.* n. 470.

tenacious of her venerable traditions and institutions, especially those that are traced right back to the Apostles themselves, as is this tradition and institution of the laying-on of hands for the sacramental transmission of the Christian Priesthood. In such vital matters as this, the Church's instinct and practice is not destruction but preservation and perpetuation. If she were to take away from the imposition of hands its sacramental efficacy (assuming that she had the power to do so) she would be depriving the Sacrament of Order of its Scriptural testimony, and the Apostolic Succession of its Scriptural guarantee. So, throughout the history of the development of the sacramental liturgy, the tendency has always been towards growth—additions and accretions, the effort to obtain a fuller, more perfect, more clearly significant symbolism. Thus many beautiful and highly appropriate ceremonies have from time to time been added to the Ordinals in use in various parts of the Church, but nothing has been discarded ; [1] and notably, the imposition of hands holds in every one of them the same position, and has the same significance and import that it has ever held and possessed.

If then the Church has deprived this ceremony of its sacramental causality, we shall require a compelling proof, which can be found only in a positive act of the supreme magisterium of the supreme authority. No such decree is forthcoming. No attempt has ever been made to allege any act of the supreme authority of the Church which could be construed to decree the reduction of the imposition of hands in the rite of ordination to the condition of a mere empty ceremony. On the contrary. If such a thing has ever happened to the imposition of hands, it must have been between the eleventh and the thirteenth centuries ; so that at the time of the Council of Trent the ordination ceremony was precisely as it is now ; and if the imposition of hands ever lost its efficacy, it had lost it then. Yet the Council teaches that the ministers of Extreme Unction are bishops and priests who have been ordained by the imposition of hands ; [2] and in sess. 23, c. 2, 3, it proves the sacramental nature of the ordination rite *then actually in use* from the famous text of 2 Timothy i 6-7 on the imposition of hands. It seems clear that the Council had no knowledge of any essential change ; for how could they appeal to this text, if the imposition of hands had been shorn of all its sacramental significance ?

Anglican Orders

There is still another significant indication of the attitude of the supreme authority of the Church in this matter. In the Bull *Apostolicæ curæ*, by which Leo XIII declared Anglican Orders to be null and void, the Pope argues thus : " In the examination of any rite for the effecting and administering of the Sacraments, distinction is

[1] This, however, is precisely what was done in England at the Reformation. The Ordinal was mutilated and essential parts suppressed with an heretical intention ; and the whole rite of ordination was thereby invalidated.

[2] Sess. 14, c. 3.

rightly made between the part which is *ceremonial* and that which is *essential*, which is usually called the *matter and form*. All know that the Sacraments of the New Law as sensible and efficient signs of invisible grace, must both signify the grace which they produce, and produce the grace which they signify. And this signification, although it should exist in the whole essential rite, that is, in the matter and form, nevertheless pertains chiefly to the form ; since the matter is the part which is not determined of itself, but which is determined by the form. And this appears more clearly in the Sacrament of Order, *the matter of which, in so far as we have to consider it in this case, is the imposition of hands* ; which indeed of itself signifies nothing definite, and is used equally for several Orders and for Confirmation. But the words which until recently were commonly held by Anglicans to constitute the proper form of priestly ordination—namely, 'Receive the Holy Ghost,' certainly do not in the least express definitely the sacred Order of Priesthood, or its grace and power, which is chiefly the power 'of consecrating and offering the true body and blood of the Lord,' [1] in that sacrifice which is no 'nude commemoration of the sacrifice offered on the Cross.' [2] . . . Let this argument suffice for all. From the prayers of the Ordinal there has been deliberately removed whatever sets forth the dignity and office of the priesthood in the Catholic rite. That form therefore cannot be considered valid and sufficient for the Sacrament which omits what it ought essentially to signify."

Leo's argument therefore is that the matter of the Sacrament of Order, " in so far as we have to consider it in this case," is the imposition of hands with a form of words expressing the order or its power and grace ; and since the Anglican Ordinal had excluded any such form, its ordinations were invalid. Now Leo XIII knew quite well that the Anglican Ordinal had also suppressed the tradition of the instruments. If then he had also known that the Church had substituted the tradition of the instruments and its form for the imposition of hands and the invocation of the Holy Ghost as the matter and form of the Sacrament of Order, he would have had his argument ready to hand :—You have suppressed the true matter and form, viz., the tradition of the instruments with the accompanying words, and you have substituted the handing of a Bible and another form, which are not sacramental at all. But Leo apparently knew nothing of the substitution of the instruments for the imposition of hands. In fact, he had already earlier in the Bull shown that he regarded the tradition of the instruments as at best doubtful matter—in this following the uniform practice of the Church. But he has no such doubt about the imposition of hands and its form. That these belong to the outward sign of the Sacrament of Order is absolute with Leo XIII, and affords a *certain* proof of the invalidity of Anglican Orders. We are therefore entitled to conclude from all this that the Church has no

[1] Council of Trent, sess. 23, can. 1. [2] *Ibid.* sess. 22, can. 3.

knowledge of this alleged substitution of the tradition of the instruments for the imposition of hands, and that, in point of fact, no such substitution was ever made. Consequently, the imposition of hands still remains the matter of the Sacrament of Order ; and this is the practically unanimous view of the modern theologians, and may be regarded as certain.

Sacramental efficacy of tradition of instruments

But the further question now arises : Is the imposition of hands the complete matter ; or has the tradition of the instruments been conjoined with it to constitute one composite sacramental matter ?

While it is not conceivable that the Scriptural imposition of hands has lost its sacramental status, it can readily be imagined that, assuming that the Church has the power, there has been development along the line of more explicit signification and more vivid representation of the power of the priesthood. That there have been such accretions to the Ordinal is an incontestable fact : there we actually do find the tradition of the instruments, with the appropriate form expressing the conferring of the power of the priesthood. The only question is whether it is a mere accessory ceremony, or an integral part of the sacramental matter.

We have already mentioned the famous Decree for the Armenians, published by Eugenius IV in the Council of Florence. This Decree teaches that " The sixth Sacrament is Order, whose matter is that thing by the tradition of which the order is conferred."—We do not propose to enter into the merits of the controversy about this Decree, whether it is an infallible document, as one side claims, or theologically erroneous, which is the opposite extreme view. It suffices for us that it is an official document of the highest authority of the Church, recognising the sacramental status of the tradition of the instruments. Nor is the imposition of hands thereby deposed from its place ; first, because the Council of Florence itself, just as the Church before and since has always done, acknowledged the validity of the Oriental rites having the imposition of hands alone. But the case was not the same for the Armenians. They had always preserved the imposition of hands ; but they alone, of all the Oriental Rites, had recently adopted into their rite from the Roman Church the tradition of the instruments.[1] Hence, Eugenius IV, pre-supposing, not rejecting, the imposition of hands, instructs the Armenians about the tradition of the instruments, in the exact words of St Thomas Aquinas. Yet, St Thomas, although he most emphatically attributes the impression of the character of Order to the tradition of the instruments as the instrumental cause, does not thereby exclude the imposition of hands from the matter of the Sacrament. On the contrary, both in his Commentary on the Sentences [2] and in almost the last question of the *Summa Theologica* written by him before his death,[3] he attributes

[1] Theologians seem almost entirely to have overlooked this significant historical fact.

[2] IV, D. 24, Q. ii, art. 3.

[3] III, Q. lxxxiv, art. 4.

the grace of the Sacrament of Order to the imposition of hands. "By the imposition of hands is given the plenitude of grace by which they are fitted for their high offices." Now if St Thomas could write this, and yet teach that the matter of the Sacrament is the tradition of the instruments, why could not Pope Eugenius copy these words into his decree in the same sense, viz., assuming that the imposition of hands has preceded the tradition of the instruments as the sacramental preparation for the completion of the rite ?

Reference to the Roman Pontifical must not be omitted. In the preliminary instructions the bishop is directed to "warn those to be ordained to touch the instruments, *by which the character is imprinted.*" And in the ceremony itself the candidates are called "Ordinandi" as far as the anointing of the hands. Then immediately follows the tradition of the instruments with its form, and they become at once "Ordinati."

My final conclusion, then, is that the imposition of hands with the invocation of the Holy Ghost are certainly the sacramental matter and form of the Episcopate, Priesthood, and Diaconate ; and that probably the tradition of the instruments with its form also belongs to the sacramental outward sign of the Priesthood and Diaconate. Of the Subdiaconate and the Minor Orders the tradition of the instruments and the accompanying words alone constitute the matter and form, whether sacramental or otherwise.

§ VII: THE MINISTER AND THE RECIPIENT OF ORDER

1. *The Minister.*—Only a consecrated bishop can confer those Orders which certainly belong to the Sacrament, viz., the episcopate, the priesthood, and the diaconate. It is said that Innocent VIII gave to the Cistercian Abbots the power to ordain deacons ; but this concession is of very doubtful authenticity, and may certainly be ignored by the theologian.

The Pope can authorise a simple priest to confer the Subdiaconate and the Minor Orders ; and the common law of the Church grants to Cardinals who have not received episcopal consecration, the right to confer the Tonsure and the Minor Orders. Also Vicars Apostolic, Prefects Apostolic, and Abbots and Prelates who have territorial jurisdiction, can in their own territory and while they hold office, give the Tonsure and the Minor Orders to their own subjects and to any others who are furnished with the necessary documents from their bishops ; and also monastic Abbots, provided that they are in priest's orders and have received the Abbatial blessing, can confer the Tonsure and the Minor Orders on their own subjects by religious profession, and on these only.[1]

For the consecration of a bishop three bishops are required. But

[1] See Code of Canon Law, Canons 239, 957, 964.

this is most probably only a matter of custom and ecclesiastical precept, and is not necessary for the validity of the consecration.[1]

2. *The Recipient.*—Two conditions are required for valid ordination, the male sex and baptism. That women cannot be validly ordained is clear from St Paul's Epistles, 1 Corinthians xiv 34-35, and 1 Timothy ii 11-12, from Apostolic tradition and from the constant practice of the Church. St Epiphanius remarks that if it were lawful for women to be priests, Mary, the Mother of God, would certainly have been the first.

That baptism should be an absolute condition of ordination is obvious ; for baptism is the door to the other Sacraments ; and one must be a member of the Church before he can be an officer, a leader and teacher in it.

The simple priesthood is a pre-requisite of the episcopate, at least according to the actual practice of the Church. We have already dealt sufficiently with the theoretical question whether the episcopate is the whole sacerdotium independently of the presbyterate, or whether it essentially presupposes the latter, of which it is the complement and ultimate perfection.

One might write at great length of the spiritual qualities required of the recipient of the Sacrament of Order ; but that would be outside the scope of this small dogmatic treatise, and it has already been well done by many eminent writers. This therefore brings to a close our study of the theology of the Sacrament of Order.

NOTE ON CLERICAL CELIBACY

The practice of Christian Celibacy is based on the words of Our Lord by which he proclaimed the virtue of chastity to be a Christian ideal and one of the evangelical counsels : " Not all take in this saying, but they to whom it hath been given. For there are eunuchs who were born so from their mother's womb, and eunuchs who were made such by men ; and there are eunuchs who have made themselves such for the sake of the kingdom of heaven. He that can take this in, let him take it in." [2] Hence St Paul teaches : " To the unmarried and to widows I say, it is good for them if they remain even as I. . . . He that is unmarried hath a care for the things of the Lord, how he may please the Lord ; but he that is married hath a care for the things of the world, how he may please his wife, and he is drawn different ways. . . . Now this I say for your own profit, not that I may cast a snare upon you, but for the sake of seemly and devoted and undistracted service of the Lord." [3] This being so, to whom can the words of the Apostle be so appropriately applied as to the " ministers of Christ and dispensers of the mysteries of God ? " By

[1] This doctrine is described by Pope Pius XII as being " beyond all doubt ". Constitution *Episcopalis Consecrationis*, 30 Nov., 1944 (*A.A.S.*, 1945, p. 131).—*Editor's Note.*

[2] Matt. xix 11, 12 ; Westm. Vers.

[3] 1 Cor. vii 8, 32, 33, 35 ; Westm. Vers.

their very vocation their whole life is dedicated to "the service of the Lord" and of the souls placed in their charge. They are the spiritual fathers of the faithful, and the pattern to them of all virtue. It is fitting then that they should be free from the cares and ties, the distractions and hindrances of the natural family life. Celibacy therefore has from Apostolic times been regarded as the appropriate state for the ministers of the Church.

St Paul does indeed say that the bishop, the priest, and the deacon must be the "husband of one wife"; [1] but he certainly does not intend to stultify his own life and his words, as well as the words of Christ himself, by making marriage obligatory on the clergy. He is merely stating what is really only a negative qualification for the ministry, viz., that no one may be admitted to it who has been married *more than once.*[2]

It is certain that there is no *divine* law of celibacy binding upon the clergy; but it is disputed among theologians whether they were bound to it by *Apostolic* precept or not. It appears impossible, however, to prove the affirmative. What is certain is that celibacy was recommended to the clergy from Apostolic times, and also that large numbers did actually practise it. The writers of the third and fourth centuries (*e.g.* Tertullian, Origen, Eusebius, St Cyril of Jerusalem, St Jerome, St Epiphanius) show indeed that the practice was held in honour by the great body of the clergy throughout the Church from the earliest times.

The written law of clerical celibacy appears for the first time in the Latin Church in the epistle of Pope Siricius (an. 385) in which he states that "all priests and deacons are bound by an indispensable law" to observe chastity from the day of their ordination; and he implies that this is no new obligation, but one of long standing. Later subdeacons also were included under the law. Finally, the 1st Lateran Council (an. 1123), can. 3, and 2nd Lateran Council (an. 1139), can. 7, not only re-enacted the general law, but also declared the marriages of clerics in sacred orders to be invalid.[3]

The law is not the same in the Oriental Church. Married men (*i.e.* married only once) may be ordained to sacred orders (but not to the episcopate) and still live the married life; but if the wife should die, they may not marry again. Indeed all marriages of clerics in sacred orders are null and void just as much in the Oriental as in the Latin Church.[4]

C. CRONIN.

[1] 1 Tim. iii 2, 12; Titus i 6.

[2] Compare with 1 Tim. v 9.—The consequence of the Apostle's prohibition is that bigamy in the canonical sense, *i.e.* two successive valid marriages, has always constituted an irregularity, or impediment to sacred orders. Cp. Codex, can. 984.

[3] Cf. Conc. Trid., sess. 24, can. 9; Codex, can. 132, 1072.

[4] Second Trullan Synod, an. 692; Pope Benedict XIV, Const. *Etsi Pastoralis*, etc.

XXX

CHRISTIAN MARRIAGE

§ I: THE SACRAMENT OF MATRIMONY

THE following description of Christian marriage is designed chiefly for the Catholic laity. It is a part of Christian doctrine which cannot be taught adequately to children, with the result that many Catholics remain uninformed about it, and receive the sacrament with no accurate perception of all that it implies. Because the marriage contract is the *sign* of this sacrament, it becomes necessary to expound, in its broad lines, the law by which the Church regulates everything concerned with it. Canonical legislation must of necessity be more in evidence in this part of Christian doctrine than in any other. But a word of warning is necessary. The reader, even though the contents of this account have been understood, must beware of passing any judgement on the validity of the marriage contract in any given case. This is the province of professional theologians and canonists, and requires a degree of technical knowledge and experience which few laymen possess. With this reservation, and it is an important one, a simple statement of Catholic principles, which avoids obscure issues and controversial details, may help the recipients of this sacrament to understand it better, and understanding it to appreciate more fully the sacrament which signifies the union between Christ and the Church.

* * * * * * * * * *

A type of Christ and the Church

The first blessing given by God to man, as he stood in original beauty and innocence fresh from the hand of God, was a human companion. " It is not good for man to be alone ; let us make him a help like unto himself." [1] That first marriage, hallowed by God in order that the human race should increase and multiply upon the earth, would have achieved its purpose and peopled the earth with a holy and sinless race, if our first parents had not fallen and involved us all in their ruin.

The second blessing from God was the promise of a Redeemer, who was to be the seed of a woman, a promise repeatedly made throughout the ages waiting his coming. From the time when that promise was centred in the chosen family of Abraham, the marriage of his children became invested with a fresh meaning, and it was a sorrow and a reproach to the daughters of Israel to be childless. When at last the fulness of time was come, and, as Isaias foretold, a virgin conceived and bore a son, it was under the protection of

[1] Gen. ii 18.

marriage between Mary and Joseph that our divine Lord and Saviour Jesus Christ came into the world; the first miracle that he wrought took place in Cana of Galilee, during the marriage blessed by his presence.

The eternal Son of God, coming into this world, wedded his divinity to our humanity. He shared in our humanity, in order that we might have some share in his divinity. From Christ our head divine grace flows into all the members of his body; from the stem of the vine the sap of life invigorates all the branches. This complete and supernatural union between Christ and the Church is called his Mystical Body. It is through this union that we are regenerated into the family of God and share in his inheritance. This is the mystery hidden in God from all eternity, and there is no other way to salvation except this.

Even though the inspired words of St Paul had not taught us explicitly, we could hardly fail to see how closely earthly marriage is the type and symbol of this union between our souls and God, through Christ our Lord. The eternal Son of God so loved men that he took unto himself our nature and, by the Incarnation, the divine and human natures became united inseparably and indissolubly in one divine person. In the holy state of matrimony, man and woman are also united as one principle, a union that no human power can break asunder. The two become so joined that the joys of the one are the joys of the other, the sorrows of the one the sorrows of the other, "for better for worse, for richer for poorer." So also the Son of God took on our infirmities and bore our griefs; being rich he became poor for our sakes in order that by his poverty we might become rich.[1] And if, in the design of God, the natural purpose of marriage is the generation of the children of men, it is also the design of God that these children of men should be raised up by grace to be sons of God, "fellow citizens with the saints and the domestics of God."[2] This is a supernatural end which is brought within our reach by Christ's Redemption and the sacrament of regeneration. But in this lofty and sublime purpose the Christian parent co-operates. Through the holy state of marriage the Church increases and multiplies, and the number of the elect is brought to completion. When St John saw in vision the end of the world and the whole Church coming forth in glory to meet its Redeemer, he could think of no human symbol to describe that scene more fittingly than the espousals of a bride: "And I, John, saw the Holy City, the new Jerusalem, coming down out of heaven from God, prepared as a bride adorned for her husband."[3]

Earthly marriage is a sign, a type, a symbol of the union between Christ and the Church; the points of resemblance are from their nature ethereal and mysterious. But, in an age like the present, when current views on matrimony are often the reverse of ethereal,

[1] 2 Cor. viii 9. [2] Eph. ii 19. [3] Apoc. xxi 2.

it is all the more necessary that a Catholic who is married, or contemplating marriage, should bear in mind the mysteries it typifies. Irregular unions, adulterous remarriage, and birth prevention can be demonstrated as wrong, on principles of natural ethics. But for a Christian, the abuse of marriage can almost be called sacrilegious, since it violates the heavenly signification of the union between Christ and the Church. "Husbands, love your wives, as Christ also loved the Church and delivered himself up for it. . . . So also ought men to love their wives as their own bodies. . . . For no man ever hated his own flesh, but nourisheth and cherisheth it, as also Christ doth the Church. . . . This is a great sacrament: but I speak in Christ and in the church."[1]

Because of its mysterious significance, the Church surrounds earthly nuptials with sacred rites, reserves for its recipients the most solemn blessings, and mingles the marriage rite with the holy sacrifice of the Mass. The sacrament of Matrimony, like all the sacraments, is subordinated to the Holy Eucharist and derives grace therefrom, as from a common fountain or source. The effects and purpose of the one are intimately connected with the effects and purpose of the other. By the sacrament of Matrimony a remedy is offered for the concupiscence of the flesh, lest bodily sin should prevent the reception of the body of Christ. By receiving the body of Christ we are incorporated into his Mystical Body, and of this ineffable union between humanity and Christ the sacrament of Matrimony is the type and the sign.

A sacrament

Profound, beautiful, and mysterious as this doctrine of St Paul is, yet, in saying that Matrimony is a sacrament, we mean something even more definite and explicit. We mean that it is an outward sign, ordained by Jesus Christ, not only *signifying* but *effectively causing* grace in our souls. The seven religious rites, known as sacraments, have been regarded from the earliest Christian times as conferring grace. Many writers before the thirteenth century did not use, of course, the technical terms that have been introduced in the course of centuries for the purpose of refuting heresies, and explaining more clearly the doctrine of the Church. But the sacramental teaching in its substance was always there. In the case of some of the sacraments, there is explicit reference in the New Testament establishing their institution by Christ. Others, like Matrimony, are not so explicitly mentioned, but the doctrine with regard to them is contained in tradition and rests ultimately on the infallible authority of the Church. The Fathers, ritual books, and the universal faith of the Church, both East and West, are witnesses to this living tradition which every Catholic holds so dear. "If anyone says that Matrimony is not truly and properly one of the seven sacraments of the New Law, instituted by Christ our Lord, but was invented by men in the Church and does not confer grace, let him be anathema."[2]

[1] Eph. v 25-32.

[2] Council of Trent, Sess. xxiv, can. 1.

This doctrine, as the Council of Trent says, is *inferred* from the New Testament. The explicit teaching of Christ is concerned primarily with the " indissolubility " of marriage, reasserting this essential property of marriage " as it was from the beginning," and abrogating the Mosaic permission of divorce.[1] We infer, from the amazement of the disciples at the difficulty of this doctrine, that special grace is necessary for preserving the marriage union intact, and that Christ would not have taught a doctrine so difficult to observe, unless he had instituted marriage as a sacrament of the New Law.

A similar inference is drawn from the text of St Paul already quoted. It would not, indeed, be correct to take the phrase " this is a great sacrament " as bearing a direct reference to " sacrament " in the strict dogmatic sense with which we are familiar ; the word bears rather the meaning of a secret, sacred or mysterious thing. But from the beautiful way in which St Paul regards marriage, as symbolising the union existing between Christ and the Church, we infer that it is a sacrament causing grace. From the fact that, in speaking of marriage, he uses an analogy with the headship of Christ, from whom all grace flows to us as branches of the vine, we infer that this grace-bestowing power belongs to marriage. For, if the sacraments are instruments in the hands of Christ, and the means by which our union with him is effected, then the sacramental nature of marriage is fully proclaimed in this text of St Paul.

The living voice and teaching of the Church is paramount in declaring the Christian revelation ; without this voice, even the New Testament cannot be accepted as the inspired word of God. It is in the unanimous and constant faith of the Church that we find the surest argument, if any were needed, that Matrimony is a sacrament. It would be beyond the scope of this account to develop the argument fully by means of quotations from patristic sources. The Fathers speak of Christian marriage as a holy thing, carrying with it special blessings from God, and therefore to be contracted religiously under the guidance of the Church. Such phrases we find in abundance, especially in the commentaries on the marriage feast at Cana. With the progress of centuries, owing to the suppression of various heresies and the solutions given in cases where the sacraments were administered doubtfully, sacramental theology gradually determined more explicitly their nature.[2] In the light of this gradual analysis, we can determine more closely and exactly the sacramental *sign* in Matrimony.

It is of the essence of a sacrament to be an external sign, instituted by Christ and causing grace. Human nature is so constituted that the spiritual part of our nature cannot operate except through the channel of the bodily senses. The external ceremonies and worship of the Catholic Church rest on this fact. The Incarnation of the

[1] Matt. xix 8 ; Mark x 11 ; Luke xvi 18.
[2] Cf. *The Sacramental System*, above, pp. 758–766.

invisible God is itself an accommodation to our weakness, dependent as we are on material and bodily things: "That knowing God in visible form, we may by him be drawn to the love of things invisible." [1] God has accommodated his power still further to our weakness and needs in instituting external visible signs, by means of which invisible grace may be conferred upon our souls. Thus, the sacramental sign of Baptism is the pouring of water with its accompanying words; the sign of Extreme Unction is anointing with oil accompanied by prayer.

The contract is the sacramental sign

What is the external sign which constitutes the sacrament of Matrimony? It is simply the contract validly made by a man and woman to live together as husband and wife, a contract which existed as a holy thing from the beginning of the human race. Christ our Lord, who made all things new and brought to the world a fuller outpouring of divine grace under the New Law, has taken this contract and elevated it to the dignity of a sacrament. Whenever a contract or agreement to live as husband and wife is made by two Christians validly, it is a sacrament and causes grace. *This fact is the very core and centre-point of all matrimonial doctrine and legislation.* The marriage contract of two Christians is a sacrament, and if there is no valid contract there is no sacrament. In order to have even a superficial understanding of the subject, this fact must be constantly borne in mind whilst reading the following pages.

It will be seen on examination that, because the sacraments are external signs, there is in all of them an element which is undetermined—generally some material thing like oil or water; and there is an element which crystallises, completes, and determines the signification—generally the accompanying words. The medieval theologians, familiar as they were with the terminology of Aristotle, found that the sacramental sign could be analysed by its aid. They therefore styled the indeterminate element *matter* and the determining element *form*. These terms have the greatest value in establishing with accuracy the external sacramental sign, and they have been universally adopted by the Church. For, without them, it would be difficult to decide in some cases whether the rite has been validly performed. For example, the sign of Extreme Unction is anointing with oil accompanied by priestly prayer.[2] But what kind of oil, what kind of prayer? The sacramental signification is indicated in the New Testament, but it needs a more precise determining by the Church, to whose care the mysteries of God are committed.

These common terms are therefore a convenient analysis of the sacramental sign, but their use improperly understood might cause confusion instead of elucidation. Thus, if we were to make it a rigid rule that the *matter* is always a material thing, and the *form* always words, we should find some difficulty in analysing the sign of matrimony. But taking the terms in their proper meaning, the matter as

[1] *Preface* for Christmas Day. [2] James v 14.

the indeterminate element and the form as the determining element, their application becomes clear. For in every contract there is an offer and an acceptance, and the offer is not determined as a contract until it has been accepted. The matrimonial contract is concerned with the mutual agreement to live as husband and wife, and, since it is a mutual transfer of the same rights, it follows that the external consent, usually expressed in words, is both the matter and form of this sacrament.

The ministers

It may appear, at first sight, that this accepted use of the terms *matter* and *form* has no particular importance, but its value is seen if we proceed to a further point. A sacrament requires a minister. Christ is the author and principal minister of them all, and he has deputed men to act in his name. It is not clear from the Gospel record at what precise time our Lord instituted this sacrament. It may have been at the marriage in Cana of Galilee, or it may have been when Christ declared the indissolubility of the Christian union. The one thing quite certain is that Christ instituted all the sacraments, which are as instruments in his hands, conferring grace from him to the members of his Mystical Body. Apart from this intimate union with Christ they cannot confer grace. The person who administers a sacrament contributes to its effect as a secondary cause or agent, but the primary cause is Christ, in whose person the minister acts.

Now, for quite a long period the view was held by many that the minister of matrimony is the officiating priest. This idea arose partly from a mistaken view about the matter and form, the contract of the parties being considered the matter and the blessing of the priest the form. Another circumstance probably served to strengthen the misconception. The Council of Trent had framed a decree known as *Tametsi*, which required the assistance of the parish priest, as well as witnesses, for the validity of a marriage contract. At a time when the efforts of ecclesiastical authority turned towards abolishing secret or clandestine marriages, it was obviously an advantage to hold that the priest's presence was necessary as the minister.

But a moment's reflection will show that this view cannot be the true one, nor is it now defended by any theological authority. For it is universally admitted that the contract is the sacrament, and that in every sacrament it is the minister who uses the matter and form, thus effecting the sacramental sign. Now, it is clear that no one is able to make a contract except the contracting parties, and in this sacrament the contract is the sacramental sign, *i.e.* the matter and form. Therefore, the contracting parties, not the officiating priest, are the ministers of the sacrament.

Moreover, it has always been recognised by the Church that in certain cases, provided for by Canon Law, marriage may be contracted and the sacrament received without the presence of a priest.[1] It is almost impossible to explain how this can be true, if the priest

[1] See p. 1077.

is the minister. The presence of a priest is absolutely necessary for the marriage of Catholics, in normal circumstances, and without a priest there is no sacrament and no valid contract, as we shall establish more fully later on. But the priest is not the minister of the sacrament.

If we now regard the contracting parties from the point of view of recipients of sacramental grace, it may be stated as a general principle that all baptised persons, not affected by a diriment impediment,[1] are capable of receiving this sacrament validly. Baptism is the door to all the other sacraments, which, because of their intimate connection with Christ, cannot be received unless the recipient is first incorporated into the Mystical Body of Christ by the sacrament of regeneration. Non-Catholics, therefore, provided they are validly baptised and have no diriment impediments, normally make this sacramental contract validly; for they are definitely excluded from the ecclesiastical law requiring the presence of the parish priest, and their unions are in all essential respects identical with those of Catholics, except that they do not receive the nuptial blessing.

Sacramental grace

It is the chief effect of the sacraments to cause or increase grace in the soul, *i.e.* habitual sanctifying grace, making us sons of God and sharers of the divine nature.[2] It is that quality, infused into our souls, which is the very kernel of the supernatural life, which increases with our growth in holiness, and by mortal sin is lost altogether. God, who has bestowed this supreme gift upon us in baptism, can increase its growth in any way he pleases, but the normal channel of sanctifying grace is through the sacraments.

How, then, do the seven sacraments differ from each other, since each of them causes grace? They differ in this respect, that the grace bestowed by each of them carries with it a title to divine assistance, strengthening the Christian soul in its journey through this world, and enabling it to fulfil all its duties. Every condition and state of life is attended by certain difficulties and obligations. The grace of the sacrament of Matrimony entitles the recipient to God's help, in perfecting earthly love and fidelity, and in surmounting triumphantly the cares and difficulties of married life. The primary end and purpose of marriage is the generation and education of children, a task which often entails very considerable sacrifice and self-denial. In some cases the burden may be so great as to be, humanly speaking, unbearable. "Come to me, all you that labour and are burdened: and I will refresh you."[3] The grace of God will assist human weakness and make what is hard and difficult easy to bear. Again, if two people are living together in a permanent indissoluble union, some friction and discord may perhaps arise; the grace of this sacrament will preserve mutual love and affection in spite of everything. Even though in some cases the wine of earthly

[1] Cf. pp. 1080 ff. [2] 2 Pet. i 4. [3] Matt. xi 28.

love has begun to fail, then it is that at the word of Christ the new wine of spiritual love and charity will appear at the nuptials, overflowing to the brim and surpassing in sweetness the old. " Husbands, love your wives, as Christ loved the Church."

These are the needs our Lord referred to when he said, " Ask and you shall receive." If people live their married life with no reference whatever to God, not seeking his grace, but rather putting an obstacle to its operation, the divine help to which they have a sacramental title is not obtained. One cannot help thinking that many excellent Catholics forget all about the sacramental grace once the sacrament has been received. We are perfectly familiar with the idea that the grace of Holy Order supports a priest in the difficulties of his life, and the same is every bit as true in the married state. Like the Ordination rite, a proper Catholic marriage is mingled with the sacrifice of the Mass, which is interrupted at the Pater Noster in order that the solemn nuptial blessing may be given. Christ is present on the altar as he was at Cana in Galilee, and blesses a union without which the number of the elect cannot be brought to completion. " This is a great sacrament : but I speak in Christ and in the Church."

The power of Church and State

A vital consequence follows from the fact that the marriage of Christians is a sacrament—namely, that everything pertaining to it must be regulated by the Church. It is a right that has always been claimed and used by ecclesiastical authority, which continues as in the past to enforce a legislation which is often completely at variance with civil laws. Our Lord's teaching on divorce, and the " privilege of the faith " referred to by St Paul,[1] were contrary to Roman Law. At the Council of Trent the doctrine was reasserted : " If anyone saith that the Church could not establish impediments invalidating marriage, let him be anathema. . . . If anyone saith that matrimonial causes do not pertain to ecclesiastical judges, let him be anathema." [2] Leo XIII, in one of his famous encyclicals, has dealt authoritatively and fully with this point : " Since marriage is holy by its own power, in its own nature, and of itself, it ought not to be regulated and administered by the will of civil rulers, but by the divine authority of the Church. . . . To decree and ordain concerning the sacrament is, by the will of Christ himself, so much a part of the power and duty of the Church, that it is plainly absurd to maintain that even the smallest fraction of such power has been transferred to the civil ruler. . . . Among Christians every true marriage is, in itself and by itself, a sacrament, and nothing can be further from the truth than to say that the sacrament is a certain added ornament, or outward endowment, which can be separated and torn away from the contract at the caprice of man." [3] Civil enactments, therefore, which

[1] 1 Cor. vii 12 ; cf. p. 1097. [2] Sess. xxiv, can. 4 and 12.
[3] *Arcanum*, Eng. trans., C.T.S., pp. 189, 193. Cf. also *Casti Connubii*, C.T.S., Do. 113, §§ 37-43.

interfere with the substance and essential properties of marriage—as, for example, divorce laws—are regarded by the Church not only as evil and unjust, but also as an unwarranted interference with the rights of the Church.

This central truth once understood, we must acknowledge in the State quite a considerable power with regard to the purely civil effects of Christian marriage—for example, everything relating to the property of husband and wife and questions of intestacy. In order to deal adequately with these civil questions, the State rightly insists that certain formalities must be observed before a civil registrar.[1] There is, secondly, the question of the marriages of unbaptised people, which are not sacraments. These unions are, nevertheless, good and holy, and must be regulated by the natural law of God. But this natural law often requires an official interpretation, and the usual view is that the marriages of these persons are to be regulated by the civil authority, provided nothing is enacted which is contrary to the natural law.

The big conclusion to be drawn, and one which dominates the whole subject, is the cardinal fact that the matrimonial contract of Christians is a sacrament. Everything which invalidates the contract invalidates also the sacrament. In the following section we must make a closer examination of the contract as such, since many essential features of Catholic doctrine turn upon a proper understanding of all that it implies.

§ II: THE MARRIAGE CONTRACT

Object and essential properties

THE first thing to examine in any contract is its object, and it will usually be found that there are certain qualities or properties bound up with it. Thus, the contract of sale has for its object the transfer of goods in exchange for money; as a quality or property of this object, it follows that the price paid must be a just price. A further element in any contract, and one of vital importance, is the consent of the contracting parties. In the contract of sale, for example, the agreement might be vitiated by fraud. The sacramental contract of marriage must be examined under this twofold aspect.

In marriage, two persons become united as one principle for the purpose of the procreation of children. This is the primary object of the contract. The union, it is true, encourages mutual love and affection; it is a remedy for concupiscence; it issues in good and lawful actions causing physical pleasure of the highest kind. But in none of these things does the *primary* object of marriage consist, for they all presuppose and take for granted certain actions which are of their nature fitted for the generation of children. This contract and its essential object have their origin in the law of nature[2]—that is to

[1] Cf. *Arcanum*, Eng. trans., C.T.S., p. 201. *Casti Connubii*, C.T.S., Do. 113, §§ 129-134.

[2] Cf. below, pp. 1089 ff., for a fuller explanation of the natural law.

say, the purpose of the union is founded in the nature of the human species—it is natural for the human race to be propagated in this way. The natural law itself, in this as in other human activities, is a participation in the rational creature of the eternal law of God, who created our first parents and blessed them, saying: "Increase and multiply and fill the earth."[1] Marriage, even in its purely natural aspect, is a holy thing, established at the dawn of the human race by the command of God. It is an institution recognised by the common consent of men. But when we consider that man has been raised to a supernatural state, and will share, as an adopted son of God, "spiritual blessings in heavenly places,"[2] then we see a new beauty and radiance in the fecundity of the marriage contract. For this reason, St Paul regarded marriage as a type and symbol of the union between Christ and the Church, for it is only by Christ, "through him, with him, and in him," that we attain this supernatural end.

Children born of this union are unable, for many years, to preserve their existence alone and unaided. Therefore, united inseparably to the procreation of children is their physical and moral education or rearing. It is the right and duty of the parents to supervise everything pertaining to the education of their children; to bring infants into the world and take no further care of them is patently unnatural, and is, in fact, at variance with the mere instincts of most animals.

We have to stress the child-rearing aspect of marriage as its primary object, for it is from this fact that the two essential *properties* of marriage are deduced—namely, its UNITY and INDISSOLUBILITY. That a Christian marriage, validly contracted and consummated, cannot be dissolved except by death, is a doctrine of such importance that a special section will be devoted to its discussion. It may be noticed now that the chief natural reason why divorce is wrong is the fact that the children's good requires that their parents remain permanently united.

Unity of marriage

Facilities for divorce are increasing in many modern states, but our Western civilisation has not yet, at least overtly, discarded the principle "one man, one wife"—*i.e.* the principle of the UNITY of marriage. This essential property of marriage is a necessary deduction, as we have said, from its primary object, which is the procreation of children. The simultaneous possession by one woman of more than one husband is clearly and directly opposed to the natural law; it would be impossible to say who was responsible for the rearing of the children, for the parentage would be completely uncertain. The practice would be separated only by a very thin line from a general promiscuity of the sexes; the comparatively few examples of customs tolerating such promiscuity are a sign of decadence among the communities in which they exist, and offer no proof whatever that the unity of marriage was unknown in primitive times.

[1] Gen. i 28. [2] Eph. i 3.

Polygamy

Polygamy, in the strict meaning of the word, is the possession by one husband of more than one wife, and is also opposed to the natural law, but much less clearly and directly. It is not opposed to the generation of children—on the contrary—nor is it opposed to their proper care and education, granted certain conditions of human society. But law has to consider the effects of actions in the generality of cases. Polygamy is generally harmful to the proper rearing of children, since the presence of more than one wife is calculated to lead to domestic disturbance, and threatens that peaceful cohabitation which is essential for the proper upbringing of children. The practice is forbidden by the natural law.

We are faced with the objection that polygamy was practised by the patriarchs and tolerated by the Mosaic Law.[1] To appreciate the solution, both of this difficulty and of the similar objection drawn from the Mosaic permission of divorce, we should bear in mind the common analysis of the natural law into *primary* and *secondary* precepts. A given practice may be of such a kind that the end or purpose of nature is thereby rendered nugatory and completely frustrated : promiscuity of the sexes and unrestricted divorce are of this kind. Another practice may be adverse to the natural order, in the sense that the purpose of nature is thereby made more difficult of attainment, but not defeated altogether : polygamy and divorce, restricted to specific cases by legitimate authority, are of this nature. The former set of practices is said to be against the *primary* precepts, the latter against the *secondary* precepts of the natural law. Now, whereas it is altogether repugnant that God should dispense the natural law in its primary precepts, there is no reason why the secondary precepts should not be so dispensed for a time and for adequate reasons. Polygamy was allowed by God for the Jews under the Old Dispensation, although monogamy was the primitive law of nature. But now, under the New Law of the Gospel, this dispensation or toleration has been abolished, as well as the limited toleration of divorce, and marriage is restored to its pristine dignity. The Councils of the Church have always insisted that polygamous unions are no longer valid or lawful, even for non-Christians, for the natural law is binding upon all, whether baptised or not. The reason for this abrogation is not far to seek, if we recall the doctrine that Christian marriage typifies the union between Christ and the Church, one head and one body. One head and several bodies, one body and several heads, is a monster. "Christ brought matrimony back to the nobility of its primeval origin, by condemning the custom of the Jews in their abuse of the plurality of wives, and of their power in giving Bills of Divorce. . . . He raised marriage to the dignity of a sacrament ; to husband and wife, guarded and strengthened by the heavenly grace which his merits gained for them, he gave power to attain holiness in the married state ; making marriage in a wondrous

[1] Cf. Deut. xxi 15, xxv 5 ; Matt. xxii 24.

way a type of the mystical union between himself and his Church, he not only perfected that love which is according to nature, but also made the natural union of one man with one woman far more perfect through the bond of heavenly love." [1]

Second marriages

It is because of this mystical signification, and because second marriages may sometimes be injurious to the children of the first union, that the Church has looked less kindly on a second marriage even after the death of the first partner, and some of the Fathers condemned the practice severely. There is still a prohibition known as "irregularity" which forbids sacred orders to a man after the death of his second wife. But one cannot insist too strongly that there exists no sort of ecclesiastical law against second marriages as such: "A woman is bound by the law as long as her husband liveth; but if her husband die she is at liberty; let her marry to whom she will, only in the Lord. But more blessed shall she be if she so remain according to my counsel." [2] Not only is such a marriage not forbidden; it is recommended by the Church, if there is any danger of incontinence, or if it is desirable for the welfare of existing children.

Consent

Having examined the nature of the matrimonial contract, we can now turn to the CONSENT by which the union is effected. It is an act of the will, by which each party gives and accepts the perpetual and exclusive right to actions which are in themselves fitted for the generation of children. It is the manifestation of consent which constitutes the contract and the sacrament, and if the proper consent is lacking nothing can supply the defect—the marriage is invalid.

From the fact that a sacrament is an external sign, it is clear that the consent must be *manifested externally*, and normally it is given in words. It must be *mutual and simultaneous*, since it is the union of the two acts of the will which effects the contract. Most important of all, it must be *free and deliberate*, since it is a personal individual act which no one can make except the contracting parties. It will be recognised on reflection that, chiefly on the score of insufficient *freedom*, consent may sometimes be defective.

Ignorance

Consent is an act of the will, but it presupposes some knowledge in the understanding. A person signing a document in ignorance of its terms, or labouring under a fundamental error about the responsibilities assumed, may be drawn into litigation on the strength of his signature, but he would feel no obligation in conscience with regard to it. *Ignorance or error* concerning the meaning of the marriage contract may be of such a vital kind as to make true consent impossible. The parties must at least be aware that the primary object of marriage is the procreation of children. An accurate perception of all that the act of generation entails is not necessary, but

[1] *Arcanum*, p. 181. *Casti Connubii*, C.T.S., Do. 113, § 35.
[2] 1 Cor. vii 39.

some knowledge—at least, of a general and confused character—that begetting children results from this union is clearly requisite.

Error

Moreover, in these days, unfortunately, there are current many erroneous views concerning the nature of the contract, *e.g.*, some marry with the intention of preventing the birth of children or of getting divorced should the necessity arise ; others completely reject the sacramental character of marriage. Errors of this kind, if they enter expressly into the contract or if they are made a condition of consent, *may* sometimes invalidate the contract. We can only say the marriage *may* be invalid. It is the province of ecclesiastical authority to decide on the evidence whether the intention to contract marriage is predominant, or whether the consent is vitiated by an immoral condition or positive act of the will, levelled against the primary object of marriage or one of its essential properties. There may exist, in a similar manner, *errors concerning the individual* with whom the contract is made. The normal rule of guidance is that a person's qualifications (*e.g.*, health or social status) cannot usually be regarded as a substantial element affecting valid consent. There is an exception to this rule in what is, in effect, a very ancient ecclesiastical impediment, namely, the error made by a free person in marrying a slave.

Fear or violence

If a marriage is defective on the score of insufficient consent, it is more usually due to *fear or violence*. A person, forced into making a contract unjustly and unwillingly, might give a purely external and fictitious consent to its terms, in which case—at least in conscience—there would be no valid agreement. Even if some consent were given to a contract made under duress, grave fear unjustly inflicted would rightly be considered sufficient reason for rescinding the terms of an agreement made in these circumstances. This is perfectly true of human contracts in general, which can be revoked by mutual consent. But a ratified and consummated marriage, as we shall see more fully in a later section, cannot be rescinded ; it is of its nature indissoluble. Yet, on the other hand, it would be intolerable if matrimonial consent, extorted by fear, were allowed to stand. Abuses of this sort have existed from the earliest times, and grave penalties were inflicted by the Church upon those who forced women into marriage. This legislation gradually took the form of constituting *fear and violence* a diriment impediment.[1] Grave fear, unjustly inflicted in order to extort consent, invalidates the contract. It must be grave and imminent—at least, in the estimation of the person concerned—though other people might consider it very slight ; filial fear of a child for its parents might easily be of this nature.

The reader, who reflects on the matter, will easily perceive that it is precisely because the marriage contract cannot be dissolved that it is necessary to secure, by all means open to canonical legislation, a sufficiently perfect consent on the part of those who contract, and

[1] See p. 1081.

to penalise the non-observance of these laws by declaring the contract to be null and void.

In all cases of defective consent arising from ignorance, fear, or any other cause, the defect is remedied by the parties renewing and making good their consent by a fresh act of the will. The possible flaws in matrimonial consent are usually very difficult to detect and establish. Any priest could say whether there are sufficient grounds for suspecting their presence, but an authoritative decision must be left to the competent ecclesiastical authority.

A proper appreciation of the importance of *consent* in this contract, and some knowledge of the possible obstacles existing, must not blind our judgement to the fact that in nine hundred and ninety-nine cases out of a thousand there is never the remotest danger of any defect. In the one case where the defect exists, and where the parties refuse to renew their consent, the marriage *may* be declared invalid.[1] But in cases of such complexity it would be idle for anyone, except professional canonists, to pass a judgement on the validity or invalidity of the contract.

It is because of the paramount importance of consent, as the very core and centre of the sacrament, that the Church requires it to be given publicly and with legal formalities, under pain of nullity. This aspect of the subject will now be explained.

§ III: MARRIAGE LAWS

Tridentine form

It is known to everyone that the marriages of Catholics which take place in register offices, or in Protestant churches, are not valid. The opinion is no doubt fairly widespread that the reason for this invalidity is the fact that Matrimony is a sacrament, and therefore requires a priest to administer it. But we have already seen that the priest does not administer the sacrament; the contract is the matter and form, and the ministers are the two contracting parties.

Why, then, does the Church require, under pain of nullity, the presence of an authorised priest at the marriages of Catholics? The reason is that it is the office of the Church to legislate for everything connected with the sacraments. The State regulates civil contracts in a similar manner, *e.g.*, conveyancing of land requires legal formalities; marriage has many civil effects, and unless certain formalities are observed before a registrar or other authorised person, the union is not regarded as valid in civil law. What the State does for the contract in its civil effects, *a fortiori* the Church should do for the very substance and essence of the union. These laws are not merely formalities, but necessary safeguards for securing the validity of marriage.

Although the Church has always required the contract to be blessed by a priest, yet, up to the time of the Council of Trent, it

[1] See pp. 1098–1099.

was commonly recognised that marriages without the presence of a priest were valid sacraments, since the contract was the sacramental sign.

But though these marriages, which were called "clandestine," were valid, they were attended with many evils and abuses. It was comparatively easy for a man to repudiate his obligations, and desert his wife and children ; it was difficult to establish with certainty the validity of these contracts, since there was no competent person present to make enquiries regarding the freedom of the parties to marry and the absence of diriment impediments. In a word, a most solemn and sacred contract, which should be certain and beyond all suspicion, was rendered doubtful and uncertain. The Church had always regarded clandestinity with the utmost disfavour. It was one of the great reforms of the Council of Trent to remedy these abuses by the famous decree *Tametsi :* "Those who shall attempt to contract marriage otherwise than in the presence of the parish priest, or of some other priest by permission of the parish priest, or of the Ordinary, and in the presence of two or three witnesses ; the Holy Synod renders such wholly incapable of thus contracting, and declares such contracts invalid and null." [1]

"Ne Temere"

Largely because of the disturbances of the Reformation, England and a few other places were excepted from the terms of this law, and marriages in these places were governed by the pre-Tridentine law. This in itself was a considerable source of difficulty ; there was also much confusion arising from the fact that the parish priest mentioned in *Tametsi* was the priest in whose territory the contracting parties were domiciled, and if people moved about frequently it was not easy to decide who was really their parish priest. Therefore, Pius X stabilised and simplified the legislation of the Council of Trent by the decree *Ne Temere*, which came into force at Easter, 1908 (April 19). From that date the law is to be observed throughout the whole Church, and the parish priest is made competent for the validity of all marriages within his territory, whether the parties are actually domiciled there or not.

Priest and witnesses

The law now applies throughout the whole world. Catholics of Oriental rites and all non-Catholics, when contracting marriage amongst themselves, are exempt from its provisions ; so also are the children of non-Catholics who happen to have been baptised in the Catholic Church, but afterwards have been educated from infancy in heresy or schism. These exceptions are very important, for all baptised people are subject to ecclesiastical law, whether they acknowledge the authority of the Church or not, and the Church legislates for them. With regard to the *form* of marriage, however, baptised non-Catholics, when contracting marriage with each other, are exempted from the law requiring the presence of the parish priest or his delegate. It follows that, granted they have been validly

[1] Sess. xxiv, cap. 1.

baptised, and are on other grounds free from diriment impediments, their unions are most certainly to be regarded as valid sacramental contracts. It must be clearly understood that the exemption of one party is not shared by the other. Non-Catholics are exempted only when they contract amongst themselves, but if they marry Catholics the *Ne Temere* form must be observed.

The witnesses should, of course, be Catholics, but any persons of sound mind and of the age of puberty are capable of exercising the office validly.

In addition to two witnesses, it is necessary for *validity* that the matrimonial consent should be asked and received by the parish priest or Ordinary of the place where the marriage is taking place, or by their delegate. By " Ordinary " is meant the bishop or anyone taking the place of the bishop, *e.g.*, a Vicar-Apostolic in missionary countries. All kinds of technical offices are, for the purpose of matrimony, included in the term " parish priest " ; it means, in effect, the senior priest in charge of a parish. It may happen that large and important churches, belonging to religious Orders, are free from parochial cares and responsibilities ; in their case the regular clergy have no competence for marriages. The parish priest or Ordinary has power to delegate any other priest to perform the office. If the curates or junior clergy assist at a marriage, they do so in virtue of delegation either from the Ordinary or from the senior priest. When, therefore, it is desired that a priest friend or relative from another place should assist at a marriage, it is absolutely necessary for him to obtain the requisite delegation.

For the priest's function to be exercised not only validly but *lawfully*,[1] the parties should be attached in some way to his territory either by being domiciled in it, or by actual residence for thirty days, and it is the rule that the marriage should be performed by the parish priest of the bride.

Cases of necessity

In urgent necessity, when the competent priest cannot be had, an exception is made to the law in two cases, and the sacramental contract is valid if entered into before two witnesses only. The case of necessity occurring at once to the mind is the danger of death. It might seem at first sight that no one would want to get married at this time, but what the law has in mind is the revalidation of an irregular union, *e.g.*, a civil marriage which has not been recognised by the Church. It is supposed that, as a matter of conscience, one of the parties wishes to make good this defect before dying, and that the competent priest cannot be had.

Outside the danger of death, marriage may be contracted in a similar manner before witnesses only, whenever there is grave inconvenience in delay, and it is foreseen that a competent priest cannot be had within a month. Circumstances of this kind might easily arise in missionary countries, and it is said that during the persecutions

[1] See p. 1080 for the distinction between *valid* and *lawful*.

in Mexico marriages have been contracted by this method, owing to the laws directed against the Church and the priesthood in that country.

Civil formalities

It is not the purpose of this essay to discuss the civil formalities attendant on marriage. In all modern States these laws are usually just and necessary, and, although the Church claims the right to legislate in everything pertaining to the marriage contract, it is fully recognised that the civil effects of the contract make it necessary for the State to intervene, and officially to register the fact that the contract has been made. Granted, as usually is the case, that the civil requirements do no violence to conscience, it is most imperative that the law should be obeyed, and that no sacramental contracts should be made, unless the civil effects are secured by observing the civil formalities. Otherwise there would arise a quite unnecessary conflict between the two authorities, and a given marriage would be valid in the eyes of God yet denied its civil status as such. Usually, however, when any conflict arises between the two authorities, it is due to the non-observance of the canonical form, although the civil formalities have been observed. It is the duty of every Catholic, who has any influence with friends and relatives living in this unhappy condition, to try to induce them to regularise the union. One can do so with tact and with respect for their feelings, but it must be definitely understood that these persons are not married in the eyes of God, and cannot live together as married people until the defect has been remedied.

Engagement

We may usefully consider, at this point, a somewhat similar legal formality attendant on the *engagement* of two parties. From the earliest times the promise of future marriage has been regarded as a sacred compact, but no legal form was attached to it until recently. The purpose of the legislation is to abolish certain abuses and inconveniences arising from private engagement. It is, of course, a promise of a very solemn character, exaggerated by some and minimised by others. One person might become engaged impetuously and without reflection, and though realising later that the union was altogether disastrous, might feel bound to keep the promise made. Another person might break it lightly and, in the absence of any record, even deny that it was made. A written and witnessed document would go a long way towards preventing these abuses. The present law is that a promise of future marriage, whether unilateral or bilateral, is null and void unless made in writing, signed by both parties and either by the parish priest or Ordinary of that place or by two witnesses. There is no strict obligation on people contemplating marriage to become formally engaged in this way, but its advantages are manifest.

Banns

The observance of the matrimonial legislation is largely assured by the publication of *Banns*. Impediments may be discovered by this means, secret unions may be avoided, and parents or other interested persons have the opportunity of intervening, if necessary. They must be published in the parish church of each place in which the parties dwell and, should there be a serious suspicion of some unrevealed impediment, it may be necessary to publish them in other places as well. The names are usually read out in the church on three successive Sundays or holidays of obligation, during Mass, or any other service attended by a large concourse of people ; or they may be affixed to the notice-board at the church door. If, as a result of this publication, any impediment is detected, the person who is aware of it is bound to make it known to the clergy of the church.

A priest must not administer the sacraments to the unworthy. Although he is not the minister of this sacrament, his assistance is normally required for its validity, and it is his duty to make all necessary enquiries before doing so. The faithful should understand this point, and, especially if they are strangers in the parish, should gladly supply all the relevant information. They certainly should not regard the priest's enquiries as unduly inquisitive, for he is bound by his office to put certain questions in the interests of the parties themselves. He should be told of a proposed marriage at least a month before the time fixed for its celebration. For exceptional reasons the formalities may be arranged in a day or two, but such short notice is a source of considerable trouble and expense to all concerned. Sufficient knowledge of the Catholic religion and of the sacrament of Matrimony may generally be presumed in Catholics, but the priest may occasionally have to satisfy his conscience on the point. A certificate of baptism must be obtained. The priest must also be assured that there are no impediments to the union, and, if either of the parties has been married before, the death of the previous partner must be certified.

Every Catholic should, of course, go to confession before being married. The full Catholic rite presupposes it, since Holy Communion is received at the nuptial Mass. But quite apart from this fact, Matrimony is a sacrament of the living, and sacrilege is committed by receiving it in mortal sin.

Closed times

The marriage rite must be celebrated in a church, unless the bishop authorises its celebration elsewhere. It may take place at any time of the year, but the accompanying solemnities of nuptial Mass and Blessing are forbidden from the First Sunday of Advent till Christmas Day, and from Ash Wednesday till Easter Sunday inclusively. For proper reasons the bishop may permit these solemnities during the *closed times*, but no unnecessary festivities should accompany the marriage.

A large part of the matrimonial legislation finds expression in the form of *impediments.* These will be explained in the following pages.

§ IV: THE IMPEDIMENTS

THE limits of this short description of Matrimony do not allow space for more than a brief enumeration of the impediments. They are obstacles arising from the natural law, or from the positive legislation of the Church, which render a marriage either unlawful or invalid.

The distinction between *lawfulness* and *validity* has a very important bearing on all the theology of the sacraments. A sacrament is valid when the sign determined by Christ has its effect, *e.g.*, the pouring of water accompanied by the prescribed words in baptism. But the Church surrounds this initiation into the Mystical Body of Christ with fitting rites and ceremonial. If baptism is administered without these rites, except in cases of necessity, it is a valid sacrament, but its administration is unlawful and may be gravely sinful.

The same doctrine applies to the contract which is the sacramental sign of Matrimony. There are some impediments, called *diriment*, which make the contract invalid; there are others, called *prohibiting* impediments, which forbid the union and make it altogether unlawful, but which in no way affect its validity. If persons go through the rites of marriage in a Catholic church with a diriment impediment, there is no valid contract—therefore no sacrament at all; it is as though baptism were administered with all the ceremonies but without the pouring of water.

There is a further vital division of impediments into those of the *divine or natural law* and those of *ecclesiastical law*. For example, a previous existing marriage is a diriment impediment of the natural law; Holy Order is also a diriment impediment invalidating marriage, but it does so by the ecclesiastical law operating only in the Latin Church. The value of this distinction is that impediments of the divine or natural law are not subject to change, and cannot be dispensed even for the gravest reasons. On the other hand, the ecclesiastical impediments have often varied and can obviously be dispensed by the authority which instituted them. It is sometimes difficult to determine with exactness where the natural law ends and ecclesiastical law begins. In cases of doubt the Church is not accustomed to dispense. Moreover, certain ecclesiastical impediments, owing to their extreme gravity (*e.g.*, the priesthood), are never dispensed for the private good of any individual. There is a further implication arising from this distinction between natural and ecclesiastical law; unbaptised persons are not subjects of the Church, and are therefore not bound by her marriage laws, except when contracting with Christians. On the other hand, all baptised persons, including heretics and schismatics, are bound by the laws of the Church unless expressly exempted.

Abduction

§ 1. THE DIRIMENT IMPEDIMENTS can be examined, first of all, from the point of view of obstacles liable to affect *consent*. The lack of the legal formalities which surround the consent is often referred to as the impediment of CLANDESTINITY; we have already discussed these requirements in some detail.[1] ERROR, VIOLENCE, and FEAR are also called impediments, but it has been found more convenient to explain these radical ideas in an earlier section.[2] Closely connected with fear and violence is the impediment of ABDUCTION, which invalidates marriage between a man and a woman whom he has abducted or violently detained against her will, as long as she remains in his power.

Age

By the natural law, a person of any age is capable of marrying, provided there is sufficient understanding about the nature of the contract. But marriages of children are so clearly undesirable that the Church has instituted the impediment of AGE, by which a youth before the completion of his sixteenth year, or a girl before the completion of her fourteenth year, is prevented from validly contracting marriage.

Impotence

IMPOTENCE, which is antecedent to marriage and permanent, whether in the man or in the woman, whether known to the other party or not, whether absolute or relative, invalidates marriage by the law of nature. By impotence is meant not sterility, but incapability of rendering the marriage debt. This impediment is closely connected with true consent, since no person can validly undertake obligations which he is incapable of performing.

Relationship

There are various impediments which arise from some sort of relationship, and many of them existed under the Old Law. In the case of *Consanguinity*, the reason for the impediment is partly physical: conditions are more favourable to the bodily and mental health of a child if its parents are not closely related. But, quite apart from this fact, there is a certain piety and reverence due towards parents, and consequently towards other relatives, which is inconsistent with carnal intercourse. The kind of relationship which now invalidates marriage is that arising, within certain degrees, from consanguinity, affinity, spiritual relationship and adoption.

CONSANGUINITY is the bond uniting persons of the same blood. In the direct line it invalidates marriage, by the natural law, between all ascendants and descendants; in the collateral line it extends to the third degree inclusively. There are as many degrees as persons in one line, excluding the common stock—*e.g.*, the children of cousins are in the third degree, collateral line.

AFFINITY is the bond which unites a person to the blood relations of his or her partner in a valid marriage. In the direct line it invalidates marriage in all degrees, in the collateral line to the second degree inclusively. Degrees are computed in much the same way as in consanguinity. The blood relations of one partner having been determined, it follows at once that the other partner is related to them

[1] Pp. 1075 ff.

[2] Pp. 1074 ff.

by affinity in exactly the same degree. Thus, A marries B; B is related to his cousin C in the second degree of consanguinity, collateral line; it follows that A is related to C in the second degree of affinity, collateral line. The pivot on which this ecclesiastical impediment turns, in the present legislation, is valid marriage. If two parties are living together, but not validly married, the similar relationship which arises constitutes the impediment of PUBLIC DECENCY. It has its origin either from an invalid marriage or from public and notorious concubinage, and, by ecclesiastical law, it invalidates the contract between one party and the blood relations of the other, to the second degree in the direct line only.

The very ancient impediment of SPIRITUAL RELATIONSHIP, which arises from the sacrament of regeneration, invalidates marriage between the minister of baptism and the person baptised; also between the godparent and the person baptised.

Those who are prevented from validly contracting marriage by the civil law, owing to the relationship arising from ADOPTION, are also prevented by Canon Law.

Previous marriage

The remaining diriment impediments cannot be placed in any group or class. A person held by the existing bond of a PREVIOUS MARRIAGE cannot validly remarry. For a proper understanding of this impediment, the whole of Section VI on "Divorce" should be read. Somewhat similar is the bond arising from HOLY ORDER and SOLEMN VOWS. A marriage attempted by a cleric in sacred orders (Subdiaconate, Diaconate, and Priesthood), or by a religious with solemn vows, is invalid.

Order

Difference of worship

An impediment, known as DIFFERENCE OF WORSHIP, invalidates marriage contracted between a non-baptised person and one baptised in the Catholic Church, or converted to it from heresy or schism. Under the present legislation, it no longer exists between a baptised non-Catholic and an unbaptised person. Before a dispensation is granted, guarantees similar to those required in *mixed religion* [1] must be given.

Crime

Lastly, marriage cannot be contracted validly between persons who, with a promise of marriage, have committed adultery; nor between two persons who have committed adultery, of whom one has also caused the death of his or her lawful partner; nor between two persons who have conspired in causing such death, even though no adultery has taken place.[2] This rather intricate impediment, known as CRIME, is of ecclesiastical origin, though based on a very natural repugnance that an adulterer or conjugicide should marry his accomplice in sin.

[1] Cf. *infra*, p. 1083.

[2] Adultery in this connection must be understood not in the loose sense of a grave sin against the sixth commandment, but in the strict legal sense of an act, fitted in itself for generation, performed by two persons, of whom one at least is already validly married to a third party.

§ 2. The PROHIBITING IMPEDIMENTS are fewer in number. BETROTHAL, CLOSED TIMES, and PARENTAL PROHIBITION are practically equivalent to impediments. If two people are betrothed,[1] it is clearly unlawful for either of them to marry someone else, until their engagement is formally broken off. The meaning of CLOSED TIMES and the extent to which PARENTAL CONSENT is required, are explained elsewhere.[2] Marriage is also unlawful in the face of a PROHIBITION OF THE CHURCH.

Vow

It has already been said that *Solemn Vow* is a diriment impediment. The following SIMPLE VOWS constitute prohibiting impediments to marriage: the vow of virginity, of perfect chastity, of not marrying, of receiving Holy Orders, and of embracing the religious state.

Adoption

Wherever the civil law prohibits marriage because of the relationship of ADOPTION, it is equally forbidden by Canon Law.

Mixed religion

The Church forbids most severely, and in all places, marriages between Catholics and baptised non-Catholics. This impediment of MIXED RELIGION must be carefully distinguished from *Difference of Worship*, which is diriment of marriage. The reason why the Church is so severe regarding mixed marriages is that there always exists in these unions some danger to the faith of the Catholic party. If this danger is effectively removed, or made more remote by guarantees, the impediment may be dispensed for proper reasons. The guarantees required, before a dispensation is granted, are written promises to the effect that the religion of the Catholic will not be menaced, and that all the children born of the marriage shall be brought up Catholics. There is a further obligation on the Catholic party to secure, if possible, the conversion of the non-Catholic. These regulations might appear to many non-Catholics unfair and one-sided, but in reality they are perfectly just and logical. The Church is merely exercising the right of any society to protect its members. Mixed marriages are viewed with such concern because they are a menace to the faith, and, even when a dispensation is granted, the Church does not smile on the union. The beautiful Catholic rite of nuptial Mass and Blessing, so reminiscent of Christ's presence at the marriage feast, is forbidden, and the ceremony is reduced to a minimum.

Unworthiness

For similar reasons the faithful are not allowed to contract marriage with apostates, members of forbidden societies, public sinners, and those censured by the Church. As a rule, one rarely finds a lapsed Catholic, or one of notoriously evil life, joining some heretical sect. Yet, it is evident that the Church must regard with disfavour the marriages of her children with people of UNWORTHY LIFE, and it may often happen that the surest way of averting danger to the Catholic party, in cases where grave reasons exist for

[1] Cf. above, p. 1078.
[2] P. 1079; p. 1086.

permitting the union, is by securing written guarantees as in mixed marriages.

Dispensations

§ 3. The presence of any impediment should be sufficient reason for abandoning a proposed marriage. Nevertheless, a dispensation may sometimes be obtained, for proportionately grave reasons, and under certain conditions. If it is an impediment of the natural law, it cannot be dispensed and the marriage cannot possibly take place. If it is one of ecclesiastical origin which the Church is not accustomed to dispense (*e.g.*, affinity in the direct line), it would be almost futile to seek a dispensation. The rest can be dispensed for urgent reasons, but the proper attitude for a Catholic, if no grave harm be feared, is to break off the proposed union. Laws are not made for the purpose of being dispensed, and, in particular, the impediments are constituted because marriages affected by them are altogether undesirable.

One practical point should be remembered. The grant of a dispensation entails expense, on the part of ecclesiastical offices, in examining the petition. Except in the case of poor persons, who can pay nothing at all, it is just and reasonable that this expense should be borne by the parties who profit by the dispensation. The faithful who apply for dispensations should make enquiries from the parish priest on this matter, for it often happens that the clergy or bishops have to bear the expense themselves, when this very obvious duty has been neglected.

§ V: MATRIMONIAL OBLIGATIONS

Preparation

If the dignity and holiness of marriage is understood, as a sacrament signifying the union between Christ and the Church, it will necessarily follow that the way to it must be prepared by a life which is at least not in flat contradiction to the holiness of this state. It is true, of course, that the grace of God is powerful and can effect anything. Cases are known, for example, of youths who from leaving school have led irreligious and even dissolute lives, and yet after receiving this sacrament have been exemplary husbands and fathers. "The unbelieving husband is sanctified by the believing wife." [1] It is equally true that the grace of repentance may be given at the moment of death, but in neither of these cases do we detect the ordinary workings of Providence.

No Catholic, unless he denies the principles of his faith, can give even an implicit approval to the process known as "sowing wild oats," if by that phrase is meant that healthy young people are under some sort of necessity of breaking the moral law for a certain period. What we are saying applies to all sin, but it has a special application to sins against the virtue of chastity. Violent temptations often assail the young in this matter, but like any other inclination to sin

[1] 1 Cor. vii 14.

they can be overcome with God's grace. It is when a soul is not in a state of grace that resistance becomes most difficult. An exhortation to a holy life is not the immediate purpose of this essay, but we must insist on this : the ordinary channels of grace are the sacraments, and it is the neglect of them that leads almost inevitably to ruin. The virtue of chastity is best safeguarded by a regular and frequent reception of the sacraments.

The subject is mentioned here because of its close connection with the matrimonial contract. Popular judgement usually expects a woman to be pure and undefiled on the day of her nuptials, but it does not always expect the same qualities in the man. This view, though rarely expressed in words, is fundamentally wrong, and is utterly opposed to Catholic principles. It is true that the effects of sexual sin may be graver in the woman than in the man, but looked at from the point of view of moral guilt, the sin is equal. A young man who is tempted to indulge in sexual excess should be restrained chiefly because it is a grave sin against God. He should also remember that the day may come when he will desire to be united for life to a pure and good woman, and it will be difficult for him to do this with a clear conscience if he is himself seared with vice.

The sacred obligations assumed in marriage, its sacramental character, and the indissoluble bond arising from it, all point to the necessity of a careful and *reasonable* judgement on the part of persons who are contemplating the married state. It may be objected that marriage is entirely an affair of the heart, not of the head. Certainly, the union must be based on mutual affection, and, if this is lacking, a marriage which is on other counts most suitable, can hardly be anything else but a failure. But while the decision must depend very largely on the affections, these must not be allowed to run loose until prudent reflection has shown the proposed union to be suitable. For in no other serious affair of human life are we accustomed to undertake grave and serious obligations of a permanent character without serious thought. A person who is thinking of joining a religious Order is wrapped up in his desire, yet no one takes the first steps toward this vocation except after receiving advice from competent people, and the Church requires a long period of noviciate before even simple vows of a temporary nature are taken. Marriage is equally a vocation, and the bond which results is more binding than the vows of any religious Order, for these can be dispensed for grave reasons. In the name of common sense, we must repudiate the romantic notion that there is some sort of sacred love urging marriage imperatively between two people from the first moment of their meeting each other. Such attractions exist, but there is nothing particularly ethereal about them. Granted the union is not undesirable on other grounds, this deep natural tendency will flower into the perfect love between husband and wife of which St Paul speaks. But if this " love at first sight " is going to violate the most elementary rules of prudence, how can it survive? If it were any other contract the parties could learn from experience and be more careful the next time; but, seeing that the bond of marriage cannot be untied, a Catholic is bound to resist a sudden attraction of this kind until he has formed a reasonable judgement on the suitability of the union.

What are the obvious points to be examined? The first thing is to see whether there are any impediments which either prohibit or invalidate marriage. Although some of these impediments may be dispensed for grave reasons, the proper course is to obey the laws of the Church and not contemplate a marriage which for any reason is forbidden. Every just law is a friend, not an enemy to be circumvented and defeated. This applies especially to the impediments of "difference of worship" and "mixed religion."

From the purely material and temporal point of view, a marriage is usually more suitable if both parties belong to the same status in society; their habits, tastes, and general outlook on life are more likely to be in agreement.

Parental consent

One would readily admit that many happy unions have been contracted in spite of these and other possible obstacles, but the question can only be discussed as it appears in the generality of cases. Whether a proposed union is advisable can only be judged with some degree of certainty by a person of experience who knows all the circumstances. It is precisely for this reason that marriage should not normally be contracted without parental consent. No priest may assist at the marriage of minors, in the face of opposition on the part of their parents, without previously consulting the bishop. But it would be wrong to conclude that children who have reached their majority are free to flout the reasonable wishes of parents in this matter. Quite apart from the fact that they are commanded by God to honour their parents, no one on earth could be more fit to give advice and guidance. There are doubtless parents who treat their grown-up children as though they were still infants, and there are exceptional cases where children are entitled flatly to contradict the wishes of their parents in this matter; but, speaking for the generality of cases, their consent should most emphatically be obtained before engagement.

On the other hand, undue parental influence might easily interfere with the complete freedom of matrimonial consent. Only the contracting parties are capable of making a pact, whose object is concerned with intimate rights that the parties alone can give. We must make a closer examination of these rights and corresponding obligations.

The marriage debt

Since matrimony is a bilateral contract, the primary purpose of which is the procreation of children, each of the contracting persons has equal rights in everything relating to this object. There is, accordingly, the gravest obligation not to violate these rights in any way. The malice of adultery and infidelity consists in their infringement. The headship of the family must reside in the father, to whom all the members of the family owe obedience in everything pertaining to its government, and the wife is not excepted from this rule: "Let women be subject to their husbands as to the Lord, because the husband is the head of the wife, as Christ is the head of the Church." [1] But, in the use of marriage itself, the husband has no greater authority than the wife; the two parties are absolutely equal in this respect, and the equality of rights must be respected: "Let the husband render the debt to his wife, and the wife also in like manner to the husband. The wife hath not power over her own body, but the husband. And in like manner the husband hath not power over his own body, but the wife. Defraud not one another, except perhaps by consent for a time, that you may give yourselves to prayer; and return again together lest Satan tempt you for your incontinency." [2] It is a general and universal principle, obvious from the nature of the contract, that if one party desires the debt to be paid, the other must render it in justice. The principle, however, does admit of a few exceptions.

If husband and wife, by *mutual consent*, agree not to exercise their rights, they are perfectly entitled to do so. It is even a counsel and a deep Christian instinct to refrain at sacred times from motives of Christian temperance, and it is in many ways a matter of regret that the holy practice of Tobias is not more universally observed: "For they who in such manner receive matrimony, as to shut out God from themselves, and from their mind, and to give themselves to their lust, as the horse and the mule which have not understanding: over these the devil hath power. But when thou shalt take her, go into the chamber, and for three days keep thyself continent from her, and give thyself to nothing else but to prayers with her . . . and when the third night is past, thou shalt take the virgin with the fear of the Lord, moved rather for love of children than for lust, that in the seed of Abraham thou mayest obtain a blessing in children. . . . Then Tobias exhorted the virgin, and said to her: Sara, arise and let us pray to God to-day and to-morrow and the next day, because for three nights we are joined to God, and when the third night is over, we will be in our own wedlock. For we are the children of the saints, and we must not be joined together like heathens that know not God. So they both arose and prayed earnestly that health might be given them. . . . Have mercy on us, O Lord, have mercy on us, and let us both grow old together in health." [3]

It is good, therefore, to abstain in this way, and at other holy times, not because rendering the marriage debt has the slightest element of wrong in it—on the contrary, it is holy and good, and symbolises the union of Christ and the Church—but because it is easier to raise the mind to spiritual things if earthly pleasures are for

[1] Eph. v 22. [2] 1 Cor. vii 3. [3] Tobias vi, vii.

a time restrained. But whilst all this is profoundly true, and is one of the signs of conjugal chastity, we must insist that all abstention, even on spiritual grounds, must be mutual; if ever a rendering of the debt appears necessary, in order to forestall the danger of incontinence, it is not only lawful but obligatory to pay it, even at the most sacred times.

The debt may sometimes be refused, without any violation of justice, even though there is no mutual agreement. No general rule can be formulated, but the individual conscience must be formed in view of the particular circumstances of each case. Thus, everything which justifies *separation*,[1] justifies also the refusal of the marriage debt; the right to it is forfeited by a well-grounded fear of bodily harm or disease resulting; it may easily be a grave obligation of charity, if not of justice, for the husband not to ask the debt to be rendered at certain times. In all these and similar cases, where some doubt may exist, the proper course is to seek advice in order to avoid the possibility of causing grave injustice. But if the object sought in marital intercourse is some vicious and unnatural act, subversive of the primary object of the contract, it may be obligatory to refuse. The matrimonial contract is concerned with everything leading directly or indirectly to the generation of children, and, provided this purpose is not frustrated, married intercourse is good and holy; at the most there might be some venial sin of excess. On the other hand, if married relations are so exercised that the primary object of the act is defeated, by being performed in an unnatural manner, there is undoubtedly mortal sin.

Birth prevention

The subject of birth prevention is engaging the earnest attention of all thinking men, and the most widely divergent views are held and disseminated amongst the masses of the people. The teaching of the Church on this matter, as on most matters, is clear and definite, and most people of any education at all are quite aware that the practice is forbidden by the Catholic Church. But what it is exactly that the Church forbids, and the reasons of the prohibition, are not always understood. When people, for example, appeal to the Church to change or modify her judgement on this practice, they betray a complete misunderstanding of the Catholic standpoint; they would appear to think that birth prevention is forbidden in much the same way that eating meat on Fridays is forbidden; that the law can be traced to some Council or other, which imposed it on the faithful; that an infringement of the law merely implies disobedience to the sacred legislation of the Church, and that the authority which made the law can dispense it. The truth is, of course, that the practice is forbidden by the Church, because it is already wrong with an initial fundamental wrongness. The obligations of married people in this matter are antecedent to all ecclesiastical law—they are clearly derived from the *natural law*.

[1] Cf. pp. 1096–1097.

The statement that an action is forbidden by the natural law requires a little explanation. It takes us out of the realm of detailed discussion of minutiæ, and engages our attention on a matter of vast importance, namely, the distinction between moral good and evil. Speaking in quite general terms, we call a thing "good" when nothing is wanting to the perfection of its nature: good coal or a good racehorse. A human action is good when it makes for the ultimate perfection of human nature, but inasmuch as only those actions capable of being controlled by reason and will are specifically human, we use the qualifying word "moral" for describing this particular type of goodness. But how am I to know whether a given human action of mine is perfecting my nature or not? A growing plant will develop into a good one, provided its needs for water, air, and sunlight are supplied. But the needs, appetites, and activities of a human being are so varied and complex, he enjoys the use of so many faculties, that it is occasionally difficult to determine exactly whether a given action is good or not. We can at least, without any difficulty, understand this: in a complex organism, the perfection of the whole will be achieved by employing each separate individual faculty in accordance with its natural object. The most universal and most elementary test in distinguishing between moral good and evil consists in determining whether a human faculty is being used in a natural manner, and in subordination to its natural object. For it is the immediate object of an action which primarily gives it a moral goodness or badness. No amount of good intention, no wealth of pressing circumstances, can ever justify an action which is bad from its object. This is a proposition to which most people would assent; the Church insists on sustaining it rigorously and logically.

Now the natural law, of which we are speaking, presupposes a law-giver. Granted that God exists, the creator and ruler of the universe, his plan of divine wisdom, which directs all created things, is law in the fullest sense. It is called "eternal" because it is the fount and origin of all law. Physical laws and animal instincts are all reflections of the eternal law of God, but it is only a creature endowed with reason and will who can be said, in a strict sense, to *obey* law. For this reason the term "natural law" is restricted in its use to signify the participation of the eternal law of God in a rational creature. It is called "natural," because its chief precepts can be perceived by unaided reason, and because it is deduced from human nature. When, therefore, a person employs a human faculty in an unnatural manner, perverting its natural object, he is disobeying the natural law, which is nothing else than the law of God.

With this brief outline of the principles governing moral conduct, we can proceed to see why it is that the Church, in declaring and explaining the natural law, has always maintained that birth prevention is forbidden by the law of God, and cannot be dispensed by any human authority. In showing that a certain line of conduct is immoral and opposed to the natural law, there are two lines of procedure. One may approach the subject *directly*, examining the act itself, and demonstrating its wrongness from the unnatural use made of a human faculty; or one may approach it *indirectly*, showing that the effects of such conduct are detrimental to the individual or to the race.

Of these two methods, the second is the more popular and attractive because easier to understand, but it is by the first method that the most fundamental and exact conclusions can be reached. For, with regard to the nature and purpose of the faculty of generation, there cannot be two opinions. A man eats food for the purpose of supporting the individual; he uses the faculty of generation for the purpose of supporting the race. It requires no great acumen to see that eating must be regulated according to the purpose of the act; the use of emetics solely for the pleasure of eating repeatedly is clearly immoral. Similarly, the frustration of the natural purpose of the act of generation is immoral; the immorality consists in gratifying sexual pleasure while frustrating the object of the act. Grossly unnatural sexual vice is punished by every civil code, and between actions of this kind punishable by law, and actions which frustrate the purpose of normal sexual relations, there is only a difference of degree; in both cases an unnatural use is made of the human body.

We may examine the practice from the more popular angle of the consequences which follow from it, but the fundamental position turns on what has already been said. Even though it could be shown that no harmful consequences follow from using emetics in order to enjoy three dinners in one evening, such conduct would still be immoral. The exponents of Catholic morality fully recognise the difficult economic conditions of modern life. They recognise that, in most cases, the advocates of birth prevention promulgate their views with the good intention of alleviating human misery and want. But the Catholic standpoint is absolutely committed to the doctrine, that an action which is objectively wrong cannot become right, no matter what the circumstances or intentions of the agent may be.

The first thing which occurs to one is an enquiry into the purely physical effects of this malpractice on the health of the individual. From the lay point of view, it is a little disconcerting to find that medical opinion is not in complete agreement about the effects of anti-conceptional practices. A few writers advocate methods ranging from mutilation to mechanical devices, and maintain that, if physical injury results, it is due to their unskilful and unhygienic use. It is difficult, of course, to make any general statement with regard to medical opinion on the whole, as distinguished from that of a few extremists, but it can certainly be said, without any prejudice, that the best and most representative opinion of medical authority has been adverse to the practice. There is fairly substantial agreement that the persons who use anti-conceptional methods at least run the risk of physical injury to their own bodies. Even this modest conclusion supports the ethical contention that the unnatural use of the faculty of generation is morally wrong.

There are various ills of a nervous character resulting very easily from the practice. To many people the fear of bearing children makes a strong appeal in restraining sexual desire; take away the possibility of conception, and one of the strongest human impulses is left to satisfy itself without any check. The knowledge of birth-preventive methods leads inevitably to other immoral actions, for it removes the natural sanction deterring people from illicit intercourse. Of the social effects we need not speak. The subject has been fully discussed and statistics are available. Nearly every European country is threatened by a continual decline in the birth-rate, and in many cases the civil government is taking more or less futile steps to avert the evil. On the face of it, it seems unlikely that people will refrain from immoral conduct on motives of patriotism, when they are not deterred by the fear of God.

For there is one last supremely evil effect far outweighing all the rest, which experience proves to be the chief reason refraining people from this unlawful practice. It is the fact that their conduct is an offence against a personal God, the fear of whom is the beginning of wisdom; for when we say that an action is forbidden by the natural law, we mean that it is forbidden by the law of God. "Any use of matrimony whatsoever in the exercise of which the act is deprived, by human interference, of its natural power to procreate life, is an offence against the law of God and of nature, and those who commit it are guilty of grave sin."[1] The human legislator, affixing a sanction to the non-observance of his laws, is only reflecting the government of God. No matter how curious it may seem to certain modern exponents of Christianity, a Catholic must believe that his sins may be punished by God for all eternity.

It is sometimes alleged that the Church has failed to impose this doctrine on birth-prevention upon the faithful as a whole. If by this is meant that the ruling is not accepted by people who are nominally Catholics, but who from indolence and indifference do not practise their religion, the statement may be true. But if it means that a Catholic can practise his religion, frequent the sacraments regularly, and yet defend this malpractice, the statement is completely false. People who do not set foot in a Catholic church, except perhaps for the purpose of getting married, are Catholics only in the sense that they owe no allegiance to another religion, but one can hardly be surprised if they refuse to be guided by the Church in this arduous matter.

It may be asked to what extent a Catholic who is true to his religion may limit his family without committing sin. It is a popular

[1] *Casti Connubii*, C.T.S., Do. 113, § 56.

misconception that the Church requires Catholic parents, under pain of sin, to have large families ; the only thing insisted upon is that they should not exercise the marriage act in a sinful manner. If, for any reason whatever, married people agree to live in mutual continence, they commit no sin and their restraint may even be virtuous. It is also the considered judgement of the Church that married persons may be prudently allowed to use their marriage rights at those times when conception is less likely, although it must be admitted that competent medical opinion is by no means agreed that conception is, as a matter of fact, less likely at these times. The most obvious method of restricting birth, and the only sure way that is not sinful, is to refrain from exercising marriage rights.

This is all that can be usefully said here on this important topic. The doctrine is not the opinion of a few rigorous theologians, but the considered and universal teaching of an authority which every Catholic knows cannot err in matters affecting Christian morals. It may seem hard and severe, but it is based on a logical application of principles which lie at the very roots of moral conduct. The inherent difficulty of observing the law is lessened from the fact that the marriage contract is a sacrament, conferring divine grace on the recipients, and enabling them to fulfil all the obligations of their state of life.

§ VI : DIVORCE

PERHAPS there is no teaching of the Church so well known to the whole world as the Catholic doctrine of the indissolubility of marriage. It rests on the supreme fact, so often recalled in these pages, that the marriages of Christians signify the indissoluble union between Christ and the Church, but it is also a doctrine intimately connected with the natural law. Because of its importance, it is all the more necessary to have an accurate appreciation of the very definite limits, within which no human authority whatever can dissolve the marriage bond. It can be expressed quite briefly by saying that those marriages are absolutely indissoluble which have been *ratified and consummated.* A *ratified* marriage is the contract validly made between two baptised persons, *i.e.*, it is the sacrament. It is *consummated* when the physical act which the contract has in view is performed, the act by which the parties are made one flesh. Accordingly, if a marriage falls short of its complete fulness, either because it is not ratified or because it is not consummated, it is possible for the union in certain cases to be dissolved ; but if it is ratified and consummated, a divorce is impossible.

While bearing in mind this necessary qualification, it must be our first care to establish the substance of the teaching that marriage is indissoluble. We shall then be able to appreciate more clearly the cases in which the doctrine cannot be strictly applied. We are sometimes accustomed to regard the indissolubility of marriage as something specifically imposed on the Christian Church by the positive will of Christ. Our Lord did indeed restore marriage to its primitive state, and by his divine authority abolished divorce, which was permitted for certain reasons under the law of Moses. But it would sadly weaken the doctrine if we regarded it solely as a matter of positive law, for it rests ultimately on the natural law, which is and must be binding on the whole of humanity.

Natural law

The institution of marriage being ordained by nature for the procreation of children and their education, everything tending to frustrate this purpose is forbidden by the natural law. It is chiefly from the aspect of the children's good that the natural reasons against divorce are deduced. It will be conceded at once that, if by divorce is meant that married persons may separate at will or caprice and contract fresh unions, the situation would differ very slightly from a general promiscuity of the sexes, which is clearly adverse to the nurture of children. But no one, except the wildest fanatic, advocates divorce in this sense ; public opinion requires grave reasons and the intervention of authority before the marriage bond may be severed. Here precisely is the snare and illusion. Everyone knows that the introduction of divorce laws in modern states has caused a gradual and inevitable increase in the number of divorces, the laws have become less rigorous, the grounds of petition more fictitious, and the elimination of collusion more difficult. What is this but a gradual destruction of the institution of marriage altogether ?

Even though the principle be restricted to its narrowest limits, divorce would still be forbidden by the natural law, for all law must regard the common good and the generality of cases. Divorce, even in the most restricted sense, tends to make the end and purpose of marriage more difficult of attainment.[1] The possibility of having a new partner and a new family would deflect parental care from the present offspring. Even if there were no children from the first marriage, the possibility of divorce being contingent on this fact would be an added inducement to birth prevention, and would act still further against the purpose of matrimony.

If we regard the matter not only from the angle of the children's good, but from the point of view of the two parties who make the contract, we shall find similar natural reasons operating The possibility of divorce must weaken the mutual love and fidelity between husband and wife, which is the most beautiful thing on earth. Little differences of character and outlook would gradually assume enormous proportions, if it were possible to break off the union ; on the other hand, granted the firm persuasion that whatever happens divorce is impossible, differences will be minimised and mutual forbearance encouraged. If facilities for divorce are to be granted even for exceptional cases, the number of hasty and ill-considered marriages

[1] See p. 1072, on the primary and secondary precepts of the natural law.

would be increased. If allowed for misconduct, it would be almost an encouragement to commit adultery. It was for such reasons as these that the Syllabus of Pius IX reasserted the doctrine that marriage is indissoluble by the law of nature. Christ abolished whatever toleration was extended to the Jews in this matter, and restored marriage to its primitive state: "Moses, by reason of the hardness of your hearts, permitted you to put away your wives, but from the beginning it was not so." [1]

St Matthew xix

A closer examination of this and parallel texts must now be made, since in one place our Lord appears to allow an exception to an otherwise universal law. For a Catholic, the meaning of Christ's teaching is known, not by wrangling over texts, but by the infallible authority of the Church. But this particular difficulty is so important, and so many people are persuaded that Christ sanctioned divorce subsequent to the sin of adultery, that we must show that Christ's words are best interpreted in the orthodox Catholic sense. The passages of the New Testament are as follows in the Douay version:

St Matthew

"And it hath been said, Whosoever shall put away his wife, let him give her a bill of divorce. But I say to you, that whosoever shall put away his wife, excepting for the cause of fornication, maketh her to commit adultery; and he that shall marry her that is put away, committeth adultery" (v 31, 32).

"Moses, by reason of the hardness of your hearts, permitted you to put away your wives, but from the beginning it was not so. And I say to you that whosoever shall put away his wife, except it be for fornication, and shall marry another, committeth adultery: and he that shall marry her that is put away committeth adultery. His disciples say unto him: If the case of a man with his wife be so, it is not expedient to marry" (xix 8-10).

St Mark

"Whosoever shall put away his wife and marry another committeth adultery against her. And if the wife shall put away her husband, and be married to another, she committeth adultery" (x 11).

St Luke

"Everyone that putteth away his wife and marrieth another committeth adultery; and he that marrieth her that is put away from her husband committeth adultery" (xvi 18).

St Paul

"Therefore, whilst her husband liveth, she shall be called an adulteress if she be with another man: but if her husband be dead, she is delivered from the law of her husband" (Rom. vii 3).

"But to them that are married, not I but the Lord commandeth that the wife depart not from her husband. And if she depart, that she remain unmarried, or be reconciled to her husband. And let not the husband put away his wife" (1 Cor. vii 10).

[1] Matt. xix 8.

In the Gospel texts, the Pharisees had hoped to set Christ at variance with the law of Moses which sanctioned divorce. Christ's answer was that Moses *permitted* it because of the hardness of their hearts, and he quoted Genesis ii 24 in support of his words that from the beginning marriage was indissoluble. St Paul's teaching, especially in 1 Cor. vii 10, is absolute, and, like the texts from St Luke and St Mark, makes no exception. This is all the more striking in view of the fact that, in the succeeding verses, he mentions the exception to the indissolubility of marriage known as the Pauline privilege,[1] thus bringing into stronger relief the absolute indissolubility of Christian marriage. The phrase "if she depart, that she remain unmarried" means what we now understand by separation. It is, of course, the Catholic interpretation also of St Matthew's text, that the exception refers merely to the right of separation. There is less difficulty in the words of chapter v of St Matthew. They can be taken in the sense that a man who puts away his wife "maketh her to commit adultery"—*i.e.*, he is responsible for her sin in remarrying, except only in the case where she is put away justly owing to her fornication, when the responsibility is entirely her own. In any case, "he that shall marry her that is put away committeth adultery."

It is in chapter xix that the chief difficulty occurs. For it appears to say that a man who puts away his wife and marries another is not committing adultery, provided his first wife was put away for fornication. Many solutions have been suggested in order to evade this unorthodox meaning. There is considerable obscurity caused by the word "fornication," for the word usually refers to sin which is committed by unmarried people. Some therefore understand it to refer to pre-matrimonial sin not discovered until after marriage, and suppose that the exception mentioned is tolerated because the first marriage is invalid, owing to the matrimonial consent being conditional on the woman being a virgin.

Other explanations turn on the Greek used in the exceptive clause, which is certainly capable of being translated: "He that shall put away his wife, which is not allowed even for fornication." Again, a whole class of interpretation is concerned with reconstructing the text of St Matthew, for many scholars have come to the conclusion that St Mark's Gospel is the earliest, and where discrepancies occur his rendering is to be preferred to the others. St Matthew's exception is regarded as an insertion by a later hand, in order to make the Gospel law tally with the Jewish practice and the laws of the Roman Empire. But this method of reconstructing the text is foreign to Catholic principles. For us the Vulgate is the authentic version for doctrinal purposes, and the Vulgate contains the difficult reading which has to be explained.

Leaving the minutiæ of interpretation, and regarding the passage in the broad lines of its context, we are forced to conclude that Christ

[1] Cf. p. 1097.

did not contemplate any exception to the indissolubility of a Christian consummated marriage; that the traditional Catholic interpretation is the correct one, and that the "putting away for fornication" refers to separation and not to divorce. We are on the strongest possible ground, if we approach the difficulty of this passage by insisting that the exception cannot refer to divorce without doing violence to the whole context, especially as the Catholic interpretation is fully supported by the texts from St Mark, St Luke, and St Paul. For the whole passage is concerned with explaining the difference between the Old Law and the New. Marriage is to be restored to its primitive purity as it was "from the beginning." Divorce, tolerated of old "for the hardness of their hearts," is to be tolerated no longer. If, having taught this, Christ allowed that it was nevertheless lawful in the case of adultery, his teaching would not be vastly different from the Old Law; there would be no need for him to speak with all the solemnity of making a startling change; the astonishment of the disciples would be inexplicable.

In the text itself, the exception must be restricted to "putting away," and must not be extended to "marrying another." For a Catholic, Christ's meaning in this and other texts of the Gospel is to be found in the constant and infallible teaching of the Church. Although certain local Synods, as well as the schismatic Oriental Churches, have admitted adultery as a cause for divorce, on the strength of this text, yet the Church Universal has never admitted it: "If anyone saith that the Church has erred in that she hath taught, and doth teach, that the bond of matrimony cannot be dissolved on account of the adultery of one of the parties . . . let him be anathema." [1]

Separation

Although divorce is forbidden, it is taught by the Church, with equal insistence, that there are many causes which justify separation between husband and wife.[2] The sin of adultery, as Christ teaches, gives the innocent party the right to complete and permanent separation. The right cannot be claimed if misconduct is mutual, nor if the offence has been tacitly condoned. Condonation need not necessarily mean forgiveness, but it means that a person cannot exercise married rights while at the same time intending to secure a separation.

There are other reasons which justify separation for a time, *e.g.*, public apostasy, grave spiritual or bodily danger, or cruelty; but when the cause of rupture has been removed, the offending partner must be received back again, unless the Church decides otherwise in exceptional cases. For we must always remember that the matrimonial causes of Christians are subject to the ruling of the Church; before a Catholic can have recourse to the civil power, valid grounds in conscience must exist. In many cases the justifying reason is quite apparent, but often it is extremely doubtful. The matter should

[1] Council of Trent, Sess. xxiv, can. 7. [2] *Ibid.* Sess. xxiv, can. 8.

be put before the parish priest, who, if it is necessary to do so, will have recourse to the diocesan authorities.

When we say that a person has a right to separation, the question is regarded solely from the point of view of justice: in using the right, there is no violation of the marriage contract. But, on a principle of Christian charity and forgiveness, it will be equally evident that the innocent party should often not use this right. Occasions may arise when a prudent survey of all the circumstances points to the extreme course of securing perpetual separation. But the grace of the sacrament, its sacred character and its mystical significance, should always inspire the parties of a Christian marriage to complete forgiveness and forbearance.

Pauline privilege

We can now examine shortly the exceptional cases in which marriage can be dissolved, owing to the fact that it just falls short of being *ratified and consummated.* A ratified marriage implies the valid and sacramental union between two baptised persons, for the Church is immediately concerned only with people brought under her authority by baptism. Therefore, the marriages of unbaptised persons amongst themselves remain outside the care of the Church, until one of the parties becomes a Christian by baptism. In these cases of conversion, it may happen that the unbaptised party is opposed to Christianity; in fact, the fear of possible disturbance might even prevent a person from becoming a Christian. In these circumstances, and under certain conditions, the marriage contracted in infidelity may be dissolved, even though it has been consummated. The procedure is known as the "Pauline privilege,"[1] since it was first promulgated by St Paul. In every case in which the privilege is used, it is not baptism, but subsequent marriage which dissolves the previous bond.

Non-consummated marriage

It remains to examine two instances of the possible dissolution of a ratified sacramental contract among Christians, which has fallen short of its full completion by remaining unconsummated. The valid contract alone is without any doubt the sacrament of Matrimony; but, until conjugal rights have been exercised, the two persons are not yet one flesh, and we should expect to find that their marriage is not regarded in quite the same light as those which have been consummated. The bond of a non-consummated marriage may be dissolved, for adequate reasons and under certain conditions, by a papal dispensation or by solemn vows in a religious Order. The fact of non-consummation must be completely established, for once the union is consummated no power on earth can dissolve it.

The papal prerogative, in this matter, has been used for centuries; from this fact alone we are forced to conclude that the Papacy has exercised this power because such is the will of Christ, who is with his Church until the consummation of the world.

[1] 1 Cor. vii 12-17.

In the second method of dissolving these marriages, it is the solemn profession which causes the dissolution of the previous non-consummated marriage. This power has also been recognised in the Church from very ancient times, and is beautifully analysed by St Thomas: "Before bodily union, there exists between married people a spiritual tie, but after the marriage has been consummated there exists also a bodily tie. After bodily union a marriage is dissolved only by bodily death; but before bodily union it is dissolved by religious profession, which is a kind of spiritual death whereby a person dies to the world in order to live to God." [1]

Nullity decrees

Lastly, a word must be said about *decrees of nullity*, for these are sometimes, in the popular mind, confused with divorce. From the doctrine explained in the previous pages, it will be evident that occasionally some flaw may exist which renders a marriage invalid, *e.g.*, a defective consent or a diriment impediment. The care which surrounds the celebration of marriage will usually result in the obstacle being detected; if it is not detected until after the ceremony has taken place, the invalid union can usually be revalidated. But supposing the defect in question cannot be removed (*e.g.*, the bond of an existing marriage), or supposing it is an impediment which the Church refuses to dispense (*e.g.*, affinity in the direct line), or supposing that the parties themselves, after discovering the invalidity of their attempted marriage, refuse to have it revalidated? In all these cases the invalid marriage must remain invalid, and it is often necessary and advisable to secure an official ecclesiastical declaration, to the effect that the bond of marriage has in this case never existed. This is what is known as a *decree of nullity*.

It is sufficiently rare to be quite outside the experience of ordinary people, but perhaps one may hear of some prominent person obtaining a decree and marrying again; the news is spread abroad, and very often the impression is wilfully created that a divorce has been obtained. Nothing could be more ridiculous than an error of this kind. *Divorce* is a declaration which pretends to dissolve the bond of a ratified and consummated marriage; a *decree of nullity* is a declaration, following upon a most careful and repeated survey of the evidence, that the bond of marriage has never existed.

The misconception is occasionally of a more offensive character. It is sometimes alleged that the machinery of nullity decrees is merely a legal expedient for divorce, and that impediments and obstacles are multiplied for this purpose. Well, in the first place, the impediments have been gradually reduced, and in the present legislation are more restricted than they have ever been before. Moreover, voiding laws are not peculiar to ecclesiastical legislation; for example, previous marriage and lack of legal formalities invalidate the contract in the eyes of the civil law also. Any suspicion that the Church grants these decrees easily, and without sufficient reason, is dispelled

[1] *Summa, Suppl.* lxi, art. 2.

if the procedure is examined. The case is twice tried by separate judges, and each diocesan tribunal has a "defender of the bond," whose business it may be to appeal to Rome for a final confirmation of a verdict of nullity. The more important and interesting cases are printed in full in the *Acta Apostolicæ Sedis*, and any competent person may study the evidence on which a judgement is given. A mere comparison between the small number of nullity decrees granted in the Catholic Church, and the appalling number of divorces granted in France or America is more than sufficient to show that any suspicion that these decrees are merely evasions of the law is due either to prejudice or ignorance.

* * * * * * * * * *

Conclusion

It has not been possible to explain accurately the sacrament of Matrimony without drawing attention to the obstacles which may arise in the contract, the sins which married people are liable to commit, and the obligations which accompany this as any other state of life. But "how can we describe the happiness of that marriage which the Church unites, the oblation confirms, and the blessing seals"?[1] We can describe it best, as we have done so often, by saying that it typifies the eternal love with which Christ has loved us. Strengthened by his divine grace, the recipients of this sacrament will easily surmount the difficulties of life, fulfil the obligations of their state, and experience to the full that happiness which the Church has invoked upon them.

We cannot close this account of Christian marriage more fittingly than by recalling some of the phrases used in the prayer of the nuptial blessing, which, like all liturgical prayers of the Church, is a precious synthesis of doctrine. After the Pater Noster, the priest celebrating the nuptial Mass turns to the bride and bridegroom, kneeling in the sanctuary, and says over them the following prayers:

"Be propitious, O Lord, to our supplications, and deign to assist what thou hast instituted and ordained for the propagation of mankind, and preserve by thy assistance what thou hast joined together by thy authority. Through Jesus Christ our Lord."

"O God, who by the might of thy power didst create all things out of nothing, who, when the beginnings of the Universe were set in order, and man was made to the image of God, didst ordain the indissoluble assistance of woman, in such wise that thou gavest beginning to her body out of the flesh of man, teaching thereby that what thou didst please to form of one could never lawfully be put asunder: O God, who hast consecrated the marriage bond by such exceeding mystery, that in the covenant of matrimony is signified the sacrament of the union between Christ and his Church. . . . Look mercifully upon this thy handmaiden, who, entering upon wedlock, earnestly desires to be strengthened by thy protection:

[1] Tertullian, *Ad Uxorem*, lib. ii, c. 9.

may it be to her a yoke of love and peace, may she marry in Christ faithful and chaste, and remain a follower of holy women ; may she be amiable to her husband like Rachel, wise like Rebecca, long-lived and faithful like Sara. . . . May she be fruitful in offspring, approved and innocent, and attain with the rest of the blessed to the kingdom of heaven ; that they both may see their children's children unto the third and fourth generation, and arrive at a desired old age. Through the same Jesus Christ our Lord. Amen."

E. J. Mahoney.

XXXI

DEATH AND JUDGEMENT

§I: THE CAUSE OF DEATH

Physiological aspect of death

DEATH has with man far-reaching philosophical and theological implications. We may grant to the physiologist all he wants and all he claims; he is no enemy of the Christian faith so long as he remains within his own province of physiological and material happenings. We may leave it to him to explain to us how death occurs. No doubt scientists find it as hard to define death in terms of biology as theologians and philosophers find it difficult to give an answer to all the queries that are raised by the materialist and the unbeliever. As an instance of such an attempt on the part of science to state the causes of death in terms which have some meaning, I may quote from the *Encyclopædia Britannica*, under the word Biology: "Recent investigations point to the conclusion that the immediate cause of the arrest of vitality, in the first place, and of its destruction, in the second, is the coagulation of certain substances in the protoplasm, and that the latter contains various coagulable matters, which solidify at different temperatures. And it remains to be seen, how far the death of any form of living matter, at a given temperature, depends on the destruction of its fundamental substance at that heat, and how far death is brought about by the coagulation of merely accessory compounds." From this passage we see the hesitation of even the most recent investigators when they try to define death otherwise than by the accidental signs which show that it has occurred. Catholic theologians and philosophers will welcome further elucidation of the causes of this terrible phenomenon.

Death natural but penal

As Christians we have our own problems on the matter of death, one of which may be assigned to the theologian and one to the philosopher. The theologian inquires why it is that mankind in general regards death as a penal arrangement. The philosopher's question is different: he asks how the phenomenon can take place in spite of the spiritual soul.

Catholic faith, which is the proper province of the theologian, teaches that the death of man is a punishment: "By one man sin entered into this world and by sin death; and so death passed upon all men." [1] Catholic faith does not consider the death of animals to be in any way or in any sense penal, but of man's death it deliberately says that it is the result of sin. How did such a reading of the phenomenon of death originate? Why is it considered to be a

[1] Rom. v 12.

punitive measure, when to all appearances it has the inevitableness of a similar law of nature to that which governs the death of animals? How can an event in the natural order be turned into a castigation? The answer is found in the potency of a presupposition. Faith presupposes something of which it alone can have knowledge: it presupposes that God made the bodily frame of man immortal by means of a special gift, a gift added to human nature, even detachable from it. God intended all mankind to possess this extra gift—the gift of immortality. Man lost it through his sin, through his own guilty act. So—always in the presupposition of this additional gift—it is perfectly accurate to say that death is a punishment, not a normal occurrence. Theologians commonly admit that without that gift man is not, indeed could not be, immortal in his body. We do not pretend to know or say that it would not be possible for the Creator to make a living bodily organism which could endure for ever in virtue of its own intrinsic natural constituents. Perhaps it is not beyond the power of the Creator to produce such an organism; theology is not concerned with such an hypothesis. Our speculations must be confined to that organism of which we have experience and of which it is said in the Book of Genesis that it was formed from the slime of the earth. Of such an organism theology says that, though left to itself it must sooner or later decay, such decay was not according to God's first intentions, but that he planned to prevent that decay by an additional gift of an entirely preternatural character. The forfeiture of this gift through the act of sin may be truly considered as the cause of death in this relative sense of a presupposition. Some would not deny to God the power to make a bodily organism which should be *naturally* immortal. Had he so made man, sin would not have had death for its penalty, since God never destroys that which is according to nature. Such, however, were not the ways of God in the creation of man. He made him naturally mortal, but he added to mortality the gift of preternatural immortality. Now that which is beyond nature—except, of course, the state of Beatific Vision—can always be lost or forfeited. That terrific insistence of God on man's fundamental mortality is the key to the chapter of the Fall in Genesis: "In the sweat of thy face shalt thou eat bread till thou return to the earth, out of which thou wast taken: for dust thou art, and into dust thou shalt return." [1] The gift of immortality conferred by God on man was entirely gratuitous and preternatural in quality. In what it really consisted it is impossible for us to say or even to imagine. It was more than an external watchfulness, guarding man from all possible forces that might have caused death; it was an inherent and intrinsic quality,[2] though one that could be lost, as grace also could be lost. It was in man's power to live, but it was also in his power to die, if he chose to prove

[1] Gen. iii 19.
[2] For a different view see p. 327.

faithless to God's pact with him: "Of the tree of knowledge of good and evil, thou shalt not eat. For in what day soever thou shalt eat of it, thou shalt die the death." [1]

Death, then, was known to man as a possible contingency even in the days of his innocence. Adam did not know evil; he did not know that he was naked; but he did know, even then when he was in that state of blissful ignorance, that he could die; the meaning of the word death was clear to him: "Of the fruit of the tree which is in the midst of paradise, God hath commanded us that we should not touch it, lest perhaps we die. And the serpent said to the woman: No, you shall not die the death." [2]

This clear appreciation of the meaning of death by man, when as yet he knew no evil, brings out most strongly the gratuitous, one might almost say the precarious, nature of the gift of possible immortality which had been bestowed on him.

It is therefore evident that the Catholic tradition which considers death as a penal arrangement in no wise interferes with the investigations of the physiologist into the causes of death. Is it not the very essence of Catholic thought in this matter to assume that man's punishment lies in this particular thing, that his body should be left to its congenital weakness, to its natural decay, when the arresting or healing preternatural quality of immortality is gone? Let us sum up these considerations in the concise words of St Thomas: "Death is natural on account of the conditions of matter, but it is penal on account of the loss of the divine gift which has power to preserve from death." [3]

Death and the immortal soul

But the theologian is not the only authority to be assailed by the exclusively secular explanation of death. The Catholic philosopher, and especially the scholastic philosopher, is called upon to explain how, with the doctrine which he holds concerning the human soul, he can pretend to leave death to merely physiological causalities. If a spiritual essence, an immortal soul, animates the body, if it is, in scholastic terminology, the *forma* of the body, is it not to be assumed that death occurs then only—can occur then only—when that soul departs from the body? For, since the soul is supposed to be the very principle and source of life to the body, so long as it is in the body the physical organism must be alive. Now, says the physiologist, the phenomenon of death belongs entirely to the material realm of things; at no time, at no stage of bodily decadence is anything either arrested or modified by some mystical agency called the "soul." It has not been found necessary to define death as the departure of the soul; death is sufficiently explained and amply described, says not only the materialist but even the vitalist, through causes which do not transcend the order of observable data. The physiologist is, of course, quite right in his contention as to the

[1] Gen. ii 17. [2] Gen. iii 3, 4.
[3] *Summa* II-II, Q. clxiv, art. 1.

physical nature of the factors that bring about death in man ; but he is wrong in supposing, as he constantly does, at least by implication, that if there really were an immortal soul in man things would take a different course. The innuendo is, obviously, that there is no soul at all ; with a soul man could not die, such is the unspoken conclusion of the adversary of spiritualistic philosophy. It is, however, the very nature of the soul's abiding presence in man to be of such a kind that the phenomenon of death is not meant to be arrested by the soul at any time or under any circumstances, nor to be interfered with by it ; Catholic philosophy has never regarded the soul as having any such office or function. We may say that the presence of an immortal soul in man may be viewed either loosely or strictly, according to the school to which Christian thinkers belong. The looser view is more imaginative, more phenomenalist ; it looks upon the spiritual soul as upon an extramundane substance dwelling in a material body. To those thinkers or rather philosophical poets who hold such views death would be the destruction of the house of the soul, a destruction brought about by quite material agencies. The house being destroyed, the soul takes to its wings, goes forth into the world of pure spirits, either good or bad. Such poetry would be sufficient to visualise death as being a fact entirely of this earth.

The task of the strict scholastic, who is also the more exact Catholic thinker, will, however, be more difficult. For him the spiritual soul in man is the " form " of the body, the principle of oneness in man's life and personality. The soul, in orthodox Catholic philosophy, is much more than a dweller in the body ; it is to the body the cause of much that makes of it what it is. Can the scholastic, who is also a Catholic, serenely ignore the soul in the phenomenon of death, when his whole philosophy makes him hold that the union between soul and body in man is the greatest and most intimate of all partnerships ? The answer is that the schoolmen, like the modern physiologists, look to entirely material agencies as the causes of death in man. And this is in conformity with that special mode of function which our philosophy attributes to the soul. The soul is to the body a formal cause, not an efficient cause : this distinction is the root of that important piece of created reality. A spirit like the soul can only be the " form " of a body if certain material dispositions and predispositions are provided for its reception. These all-important predispositions are produced by efficient causes, the generating parent, and many other factors. Now, other efficient causes may undermine those indispensable dispositions, nay, even destroy them completely. This is the action we call death. The dispositions gone, the soul can no more be " form " to the body : the very definition of " form " would be against any such continuance. We are not here concerned with the survival of the soul after death nor the soul's fate and future when it ceases to " inform " the body ; these are points to be treated fully by and by. Our task now is to make clear that, according to the very tenets of our spiritualistic philosophy, our belief in the presence of a soul in man does not compel us to explain death otherwise than by a chain of causes which are exclusively of the material order.

§ II: DEATH AND THE SUPERNATURAL ORDER

Death and predestination

If in the first section we have conceded all that is needful to the modern views concerning the natural and material explanation of the phenomenon of death in man, we do not on this account deprive death of all supernatural and spiritual significance. Though it be the result of forces that are not by any manner of means mystical, death is a most mystical factor in the economy of man's ultimate sanctification and salvation. According to Catholic theology, death has a threefold action on the whole scheme of final election: its occurrence is part of man's predestination; its universality is part of man's satisfaction to divine justice; its wholesale destructiveness puts an end to man's power of meriting, and places him in the *status termini*, the condition of finality, with regard to his spiritual state. God has kept this instrument of severity in his own hands, and uses it for the purposes of his mercy and justice, not only in a general way, but in relation to individual human beings.

We need not enter into all the profundities of the Catholic doctrine of predestination. It is orthodox to confess that all those who are saved are brought into the harbour of eternal life through a direct act of God, whilst it is heresy to say that those who are lost are predestinated by God to so terrible a fate. Catholic theology upholds most energetically the necessity of predestination, but it knows of no predestination that is not for heaven. To bring about this end God multiplies graces and shapes the external settings of the individual human lives of the elect. The *opportunitas mortis*, the propitious moment of death, is the principal of those outward arrangements of the predestinating Providence, man being taken away from this earth, which is the place of temptation and of crisis, at a time when he is in the friendship of God, when he is fit for heaven. It is possible for God to bestow on a human being the gift of impeccability. Our Lady possessed it; so also did the Apostles, in the sense that after the descent of the Holy Ghost they could never more sin grievously. The predestined are said to be confirmed in grace, not through an inherent gift, but through the fact that, through the providence of God, death overtakes them in a state of grace. Such an opportuneness of death is a part of the positive ordinance of God to secure the ultimate salvation of the soul: "But the just man, if he be prevented with death, shall be in rest. For venerable old age is not that of long time, nor counted by the number of years: but the understanding of a man is grey hairs. And a spotless life is old age." [1]

[1] Wis. iv 7-9.

Unless a man be endowed with the supreme gift of confirmation in grace, at no time of his life is his virtue such that it could not fail under the stress of temptation ; it is always an act of God's merciful disposition if he sends death at the time when a man is in a state of grace. Quite technically, the great Spanish theologian, Joannes a S. Thoma, puts the matter thus : " If we consider death as the indispensable condition for acquiring fixity in the state of grace and for being admitted to heavenly glory, death thus viewed is a gift of God's especial providence. . . . The special gift of death may be called an exceptional favour of an external nature because it means a very particular protection on the part of God against temptation and against those obstacles which stand in the way of eternal glory, lest they arise or lest they overcome man if they do arise." [1]

Satisfaction of divine justice—Martyrdom

The second supernatural aspect of death, the satisfaction of divine justice, opens out a vast theological field. We can only lay down here the fundamental principle of satisfaction by human death in its widest outlines. We must make clear distinction between death and those ills, more or less consciously felt by men, which in most cases precedes death and are its forerunners. What we say on death in this essay is to be understood to bear exclusively on the cessation of life ; whether that cessation be painful or not does not affect our speculation. The laying down of life, the return of man to the dust from which he was taken, this is death, with all its theological implications. Now this is, in God's supernatural providence, a complete atonement for all sin, provided we include in the cycle of human death the death of the God-Man Jesus Christ, as it should be included. It is a universal proposition, which for Christians is unassailable, that death has satisfied for man's sin. No other human happening has this effect to the same extent. The relationship which exists between the death of ordinary human beings in their countless millions and the death of the Son of God will be seen in another place ; but we may consider at once the extent to which the death of every individual man is a power of satisfaction for sin. That it is the normal, the most efficacious mode of paying to God what is technically called the " debt of temporal punishment " is evident from the very words in which God announced to Adam the results of his sin. Above all we must consider the death of the Christian who willingly and consciously accepts the chastisement in union with Christ's death, to be the most potent cleansing of man's soul. There is, of course, more ; there is in death a possibility of justice and sanctification which goes beyond its penal character. Man may die for justice' sake, as a martyr for Christ, as a witness to the Faith of Christ. Now martyrdom must include death : *Mors est de ratione martyrii.*[2]

In martyrdom death as death is the glory, quite apart from the many virtues that may have preceded it while the martyr languished

[1] *De Gratia*, Disp. xxi, art. 2. [2] II-II, Q. cxxiv, art. 4.

in his torments. To have died for the Faith of Christ is the supreme ennobling of human death, is its highest supernatural role in the merely human sphere.

Death the end of spiritual progress

The third connection which death has with supernatural life is of a less positive character than the two preceding ones, though its theological importance is truly unfathomable. Through death there comes a sudden and permanent standstill to that mighty forward movement of man's soul which had been produced by the grace of God. The period of spiritual change, of merit, of progress, is for ever at an end. Henceforth there can be manifestation of the life that is in man through grace, but there can be no further advance on the road of sanctity; death destroys in man the very capacity to change, to progress, to rise higher. This "power of meriting," as it is technically called, vanishes at death as completely as life itself. We do not consider at this stage that state of fixity of purpose in which the soul of man finds itself through its separation from the body at death; that is a separate factor, and will be dealt with in this essay in due course. At death man's soul becomes unchangeable. But this is not the reason of that tremendous halt in his spiritual life which Catholic faith associates with death. Man ceases to merit, to gain fresh rewards, because death destroys in him all his true human working powers. All the supernatural store of merit must be acquired by deeds done in the body; we know of no virtue that is not a deed done in the body, however sublime and mystical that virtue may be. "You have not chosen me: but I have chosen you; and have appointed you, that you should go and bring forth fruit; and your fruit should remain: that whatsoever you shall ask of the Father in my name, he may give it you." [1] The fruitfulness referred to in the text is to take place on this earth; there will be no fruitfulness hereafter, only the gathering of the fruits. This cessation of merit at death is an essential doctrine in the Catholic view of man's justification and salvation. Innumerable authorities could be quoted to show the persevering conviction of the Church that the present life is man's only chance for doing the works that will be rewarded with increased heavenly bliss: "I must work the works of him that sent me, whilst it is day: the night cometh, when no man can work." [2] In these words Christ undoubtedly states that very far-reaching truth. Christianity would indeed be quite incomprehensible if we did not take the bodily death of man for an absolute and final limit of his spiritual possibilities. The great systematiser of practical spiritual life in the sixth century, St Benedict, voices the mind of the Church in his own period, a period of great maturity in the Christian conscience: "If we would arrive at eternal life, escaping the pains of hell, then—while there is yet time, while we are still in the flesh, and are able to fulfil all these things by the light which is now given us—we must hasten to do what will profit us for all eternity." [3]

[1] John xv 16. [2] John ix 4. [3] Prologue, Holy Rule.

It would be difficult to give the ultimate reason why, in the dispensation of God's grace, death has become this impassable limit. Is it a positive ordinance or is it in the very nature of things ? It is certain that at death man ceases to be truly man ; though his spirit survives, he cannot do the deeds of man any more, so it would seem that it becomes inevitable for merit and progress to be then brought to a standstill. The glories that come to a soul when it enters heaven, the splendours of the risen body on the day of the general Resurrection, will not be new things, they will merely be the manifestation of the perfections that were in us when we lived and died in the supernatural state : " Dearly beloved, we are now the sons of God : and it hath not yet appeared what we shall be. We know that when he shall appear we shall be like to him : because we shall see him as he is." [1]

§ III : THE PROVISIONAL NATURE OF DEATH

Destruction of death by Christ—the Resurrection

NOTHING is more certain in Christian faith than the provisional nature of death. However dimly the saints of the Old Law may have apprehended this truth, with the Resurrection of Christ from the dead the idea that death is not final but only provisional established itself with unconquerable splendour of certainty. In the words of St Paul, Jesus Christ " hath destroyed death and hath brought to light life and incorruption." [2] Death, in the phraseology of the New Testament, is considered as an enemy to be conquered by God. Death is personified, not only in the Apocalypse of St John but also in the writings of the Apostles, very much as it was represented in all medieval literature and art. Now this grim tyrant must be overcome completely if the work of God is to be a success at all.

We may here make a distinction between the doctrine of the Resurrection and that other truth, the destruction of death and its ultimate defeat. It may be said that the Christian belief in God's final victory over death is a larger and more comprehensive faith than the belief in the Resurrection, because the raising up of the dead might be followed, at least hypothetically, by another death, whilst that triumph over death of which the New Testament speaks is a complete abolition of death for all times, under all circumstances, both for the good and for the wicked. That such is Christian doctrine is beyond all question, and it is important in our days to lay stress on this ancient dogma of the Church. To-day more than ever men preach a restoration of things in Christ which does not contain the destruction of death ; they even speak of Resurrection in the Person of Christ and also for the human race, in terms which are not truly expressive of a victory of God over death. Man, they say, is given a new life. Out of death new existences are born ; the spirit triumphs over death in the sense that it survives death, it mocks

[1] 1 John iii 2. [2] 2 Tim. i 10.

death, it eludes death in a mystical triumph, but death, as death, is not overcome. Now, this is not Christianity. Unless we profess that God will one day abolish that very order of things which he established when he said to man: "Thou shalt die the death," we have not grasped the full power of Christ's Redemption. Catholic thought is all in favour of the blissful state of the souls of the elect during that period of expectation which precedes the resurrection of the flesh; in fact, we are so used to the spiritual intercourse with the saints as they are now in the state of disembodiment that it is one of the tasks of the accurate theologian to remind the Christian people that the present state of the elect, however blissful, is by no means that state of glorious consummation towards which all things are working in the great dispensation of the mystery of Christ. We are inclined, more or less consciously, to endow the spirits of the saints with that condition of complete human personality which will only be real and actual after the Resurrection. But, even if the spiritual prerogatives of the elect in their disembodied existence were greater than they are, it is certain that such bliss is by no means and in no sense that victory over death which is Christ's own particular triumph and glory. By way of a bold hypothesis, let us suppose that those elect were given a bodily frame by God's omnipotence, entirely disconnected with anything they ever possessed in their mortal days, such a completion of their personalities would not be that triumph over death which is Christ's supreme act and the final evidence of his possession of all power. The words of our Scriptures are so telling that nothing but a complete reversal of those conditions which exist since man's fall will do them justice. Death is cancelled by Christ. Death is swallowed up by Christ: "Who is on the right hand of God, swallowing down death that we might be made heirs of life everlasting."[1] Death is wiped out, as sin is wiped out, by Christ. The human race, through the power of Christ as its Redeemer, will be a race of beings that were dead and live again for ever and ever, even as Christ was dead and lives for ever and ever, as if death had never touched them, so complete is Christ's mastery over death.

Immortality even for the reprobate

It is Christian faith to admit that not the elect only will rise from the dead but the whole human race, good and bad: "The hour cometh, wherein all that are in the graves shall hear the voice of the Son of God."[2] The resurrection of the elect and their immortality presents no special difficulties, as we can readily grant to Christ the power of pouring out gifts of life of the supernatural kind on those blessed ones who share his life. But how shall we explain the immortality of the reprobate? Here, of course, we cannot give as an explanation the bestowal upon them of supernatural vitalities, as, by very definition, they are excluded from all such vitalities. At this point we see the necessity of a dogma vaster than the dogma of

[1] 1 Pet. iii 22. [2] John v 28.

the supernatural resurrection in Christ; we need the dogma of Christ's universal victory over death, not only in the supernatural but even in the natural order. How mankind, universally speaking, prescinding from the supernatural and the natural order, will be rendered inaccessible for ever to death, need not be explained here. The new world which God will make out of the old will have properties and qualities, even on the material side, not known to this present order of things.

§ IV: THE DEATH OF THE SON OF GOD

The death of Christ exemplary

It would be a grave omission in our speculations on death if we did not pay a good deal of attention to the mystery of the death of Jesus Christ, the Son of God. The fact that the God Incarnate died so deeply affects the Christian theology on death that one might almost say that to the Christian death has an entirely different meaning from its significance in exclusively pagan thought. It is, of course, evident that the event of Christ's death on the Cross can be studied, and indeed, must be studied, from many different angles. Above all, that great death is the supreme ritual sacrifice of the New Covenant, but nothing is more certain in Catholic theology than the reaction of all the happenings of Christ's career on similar happenings in the careers of ordinary human beings. Thus all the virtuous deeds of the God-Man whilst here on earth have a direct influence on our own acts of virtue, and we must take it for granted that the death of man is immediately affected, in some very true though mysterious fashion, by the death of the Son of God. If God himself died, if God at one time was amongst the dead, death cannot any longer be an unmitigated evil: to be dead cannot be a desperate and hopeless condition: to die cannot be any more a matter of real terror: "Therefore because the children are partakers of flesh and blood, he also himself in like manner hath been partaker of the same: that, through death, he might destroy him who had the empire of death, that is to say, the devil: And might deliver them who through the fear of death were all their lifetime subject to servitude." [1] There is, as we know, in the death of Christ that supreme value of satisfaction to the justice of God through which we have confidence in God at all times, in life and in death; but there is also in the death of Christ the aspect of exemplariness in a high degree: Christ died in order to share that universal human condition, and to give that condition the supporting splendour of his personality. So it is an ever-recurring thought in New Testament theology that between life and death there is no longer any real chasm, because Christ, having tasted of both conditions, life and death, has bridged the abyss between the two. "For none of us liveth to himself: and no man dieth to himself. For whether we live, we live unto the Lord: or whether we die,

[1] Heb. ii 14, 15.

we die unto the Lord. Therefore, whether we live or whether we die, we are the Lord's. For to this end Christ died and rose again: that he might be Lord both of the dead and of the living."[1] Life and death are equally profitable to the Christian: "For all things are yours . . . the world, or life, or death, or things present, or things to come."[2]

Devotion to the death of Christ

The devotion of the Christian people to Christ in his death is one of the soundest and deepest manifestations of the genius of our spirit: to glory in the death of Christ is the source of Christian joyfulness: "Together, death and life in a strange conflict strove. The Prince of life, who died, now lives and reigns."[3] The Church in her liturgy never grows tired of those ideas that through death we have life, that in death we are vivified, that the death of God is man's birth. Death is no longer something catastrophic, but, through Christ, has become one of the functions of our supernatural life in the Son of God; it is good for us to die, even as Christ has died: "For God hath not appointed us unto wrath: but unto the purchasing of salvation by our Lord Jesus Christ, who died for us: that, whether we watch or sleep, we may live together with him. For which cause comfort one another and edify one another, as you also do."[4]

Difference of his death from ours

We ought not to omit here certain considerations which belong more directly to a treatise on the Incarnation, but whose connection with the present matter is evident. Though Catholic theology upholds the exemplariness of Christ's death and considers it as a pivotal thought in Christian mentality, it is also the concern of that same Catholic theology to bring out the differences between the death of Christ and the decease of all other human beings. That there are profound differences is evident. The one thing certain in Christ's death is this, that his Spirit, his Soul, left the Body: "Being put to death indeed in the flesh, but enlivened in the spirit."[5] Perhaps we may say that Christ's is the only death which consists precisely in this, that the soul was separated from the body. We know for certain that the divine Nature was not separated from Christ's Body at death. The Body which Joseph of Arimathea and Nicodemus laid in the tomb remained as much the temple of the Godhead, remained as completely and as immediately united hypostatically with the Second Person of the Trinity as it had been during life. Moreover, we know that this most holy Body never saw corruption, the process of organic disintegration is no part of the death of Christ. For this reason and others the doctors of the Church have always looked upon Christ's death as one of the marvels of the Incarnation; they have never fallen victim to the temptation of heaping up indignities in order to make the stupendous sacrifice even more impressive to the imagination.

[1] Rom. xiv 7-9. [2] 1 Cor. iii 22. [3] Easter Sequence.
[4] 1 Thess. v 9-11. [5] 1 Pet. iii 18.

§ V: MAN'S SOUL AT DEATH

Christian immortality embraces the whole man

It has become the ineradicable fashion of philosophical writers to apply the term immortality, not to man's bodily organism, but to his soul. Of the soul it is asked whether it be mortal or immortal, and in modern phraseology the whole question of man's immortality centres round the hotly debated point whether the human soul survives the disintegration of the body, or if there be no such survival. That the paramount doctrine of immortality in Christian thought is primarily concerned with the whole man, with man in his bodily frame as well as in his spiritual elements, seems to be an idea which has been dislodged from the contemporary intellect for ever. The revelations in the New Testament concerning immortality are, as we have seen, invariably expressions of the vaster faith, man's total restoration in Christ; the soul's survival is hinted at, but St Paul's inspired enthusiasms about our future state reveal without exception the sense of victory over bodily death through the resurrection of the flesh.

Spirituality of the soul

With this overwhelming mode of expression in modern philosophical and theological literature, it becomes inevitable that the great problem of the survival of man's soul should be described as the problem of the soul's immortality; but it would be sufficient, and vastly more logical, to speak of the soul's spirituality. If it be admitted that man's soul is a truly spiritual substance, with no material elements in its composition, then its imperviousness to death, its so-called immortality, is for ever established. No man in his senses would for one moment hesitate to admit such a conclusion. Death makes no difference to the soul's real status, it becomes neither more spiritual nor more imperishable than it is during man's lifetime; it remains what it has always been—an unmixed spiritual substance. So the problem of the soul's immortality and survival should not be deferred to the moment of death; the consideration should be formulated and discussed at every stage of man's career, at his birth, at the maturity of his conscious powers, at the period of his decadence. Is there or is there not in man a spiritual substance called "soul" which is superior to all sense-life? If this mighty query be answered in the affirmative, then we have the soul's immortality, even were we to take a child's conscious life as the field of our philosophical investigations. The only new problem which death would present is the mystery of the soul's abode, as we might call it, when the bodily habitation which it enjoyed has become the howling wilderness of disintegration. Although the great problem of the soul's immortality is not first raised on account of death, but is only rendered more acute thereby, it is natural for man, when he sees human personality thus brought to nought, to ask himself with increased insistence and anxiety whether there is anything in man that does endure for ever, whether he may in truth say of himself *non omnis moriar*. Thus from this point of view the soul's survival becomes more particularly associated with death, though the reasons on which Christian doctrine bases the possibility of such survival are reasons which hold good through every period and condition of man's life. The only ground on which we can establish the principle that the soul cannot die is this, that it is spiritual and that it has always been spiritual ; it is not death-proof through some hidden, extrinsic quality which only asserts itself at the demolition of the body.

The evidences which establish the doctrine that in man there is a truly spiritual substance, united with the body though independent of it, are, in the last analysis, easily classed under three headings. There is first the whole attitude of the Christian Church, which assumes a spiritual soul in man. Secondly, there is the natural, historic tradition of mankind. Then, in the third place, we have the findings and conclusions of spiritualistic philosophy, from the Greeks down to our own days.

The testimony of the Church

I call the Church's testimony in this matter an attitude. The fact is that Catholicism, in its whole presentment of spiritual life as the outpouring of the Holy Ghost, postulates in man a spirit that is the fit recipient of the graces of the Paraclete, of the regenerative power of the Sacraments, of the mystical union with Christ. The practical view which the Church takes of man, the whole man, is such that unless there be in him a higher thing than flesh and blood the Church's ministry would be meaningless.

Little is said, either in the Old or the New Testament, of the soul of man in sharp contra-distinction to the body, as is so largely done in the non-inspired and more modern religious literature. As already said, Christianity has founded its own hopes of immortality on Christ's victory over death, and it has never thought it necessary to explain the soul's immortality with a kind of feverish insistence, in order to strengthen the belief of Christians in an eternal life. But life in Christ as propounded by Christianity is such that it demands at all times in man that image and likeness of God which is the spiritual soul.

Of the human race

Mankind has always believed in a spirit in man, a spirit that could withdraw from the body at death. But since it is of less interest to men to know that there is in them a spiritual soul while they enjoy the good things of life than it is to be assured that at death all their chances of existence have not come to an end, this unreasoned faith has certainly been more pronounced with regard to the dead than with regard to the living. Thus on most men this great philosophical and religious matter presses more urgently in connection with death rather than during life. All this implies that the immense majority of human beings always have held the conviction that in man there was a spirit which would go forth from him at the moment of his bodily decease.

The findings of rational psychology are varied in mode of approach, but they are at one in the centre. The activities of man during life are of a kind that presupposes in him a principle which transcends matter, sense, space and time. Whatever we may call this tremendous force, whether a sense of duty, a desire of immortality, a love of beauty or universality of thought, it is always one and the same mysterious reality: an activity in man which is not limited by sense-life. Therefore the principle of such activity, the soul, is ultimately beyond the senses. But I must not pursue this line of thought further; if fully followed up volumes might be written upon it.

Immortality in the Old Testament

Wonder has been expressed very often that throughout the Old Testament there is almost complete silence on the subject of man's soul and on the fate of that soul at death. Critics have gone so far as to accuse the writers of the Old Testament of materialism, of lack of faith in a Hereafter. But the same reproach might be formulated against the New Testament also; special and express mention of the soul is not easy to find either in the Gospels or the Epistles; man himself is always the theme of the inspired writers.

Now there is nothing clearer than the view which the two Testaments take of man. Either individually or as a nation, man is essentially a being with definite moral responsibilities, and those responsibilities are of the highest kind, at all times. God enters into judgement with man, has clear relationships with him, both in his social and individual status. Herein may lie a difference between the Old and the New Testaments, that the ancient writers and prophets were more concerned with mankind as a nation, while in the New Testament greater allowance is made for man, individually. But even this distinction must not be pressed, as the corporate life of the Christians is not less pronounced than the corporate life of the Jewish race, that perennial bride of God. Should we not see in this very uniformity of thought in the inspired writers a mark of their supreme grasp of man's true nature and mission? It would certainly be an immense loss to our religious literature if the prophets and the Apostles had abandoned their vast style of visualising mankind and had sunk to mere solicitude concerning individual souls. Let us always remember that the inspired writers are what they are because they express, not the thoughts of man, but the thoughts of God.

§ VI: THE STATE OF THE HUMAN SOUL AFTER DEATH

The disembodied soul

THE survival of man's soul after the disintegration of death once granted, there arises the entrancing but also perplexing subject of the conditions under which that soul exists when thus separated from the body. This grave question, in spite of its obscurity, has always possessed a kind of allurement for the human mind. From the cult of the saints down to necromancy, the powers of the discarnate human spirits have always played a great rôle in the religious history of mankind. The data of Catholic revelation are clear but few, and they are concerned only with the souls of the elect, the saved. At death, says the Catholic Church, the human soul, if it be in a state of perfect charity, will enter into heavenly bliss, without any retardation. It will enjoy the Vision of God in an entirely intellectual way in a degree that will correspond with the supernatural merits acquired by it during life. The soul will not be in a state of unconsciousness, but will be fully aware of its own existence, its election, its final escape from evil. To a great extent it will be in a state of expectation, awaiting reunion with the body ; without which man's life, even his glorified life, cannot be full and entire. In that condition of disembodied happiness the souls of the saved constitute a portion of Christ's Church ; they are the Church Triumphant ; they are in communion with the Church here on earth, they receive our prayers, they intercede for us before the Throne of God.

If the soul of the Christian, though in a state of grace at death, yet be not perfect in charity, then admission to heavenly bliss is retarded ; the soul is perfected through a mysterious process called purgatory. Discarnate spirits in that state are also part of the Church ; they are the Suffering Church ; they are in communion with the rest of the Church passively, receiving the benefit of the intercession of all other Christians.

All these things will be said excellently in other essays of these volumes ; my task is to make clear the more intimate conditions of the disembodied human soul, conditions which will apply to all souls, irrespective of the supernatural state, irrespective even of happiness and misery.

The question to be settled here, as far as it is possible to do so, is the special psychological state of those spirits of the dead. What is a disembodied human soul ? What powers, what consciousness, what knowledge does it possess ? In other words, we are trying to find out the natural results of death on the soul itself. In this investigation we have only rational philosophy to guide us ; all our conclusions come from the true understanding of the difference between matter and spirit, sense and intellect.

Now such a study has been made with very great care and assiduity by Catholic thinkers, chiefly by the scholastic philosophers ; they have left us a body of sound speculation on this abstruse subject which is the last word in the matter, so far, indeed, as man can speak a last word on so high a plane of thought. St Thomas has quite a preference for the subject and his reasonings on the *Anima separata* —the separated soul—are a great contribution to Catholic speculation. The Scriptures cannot help us in this sphere of abstract consideration ; they take for granted the survival of the soul, principally the elect soul ; when they speak of it they necessarily give it all the attributes of a complete human personality, ascribing to it a behaviour that belongs to the risen state, when body and soul will be reunited: "And when he had opened the fifth seal, I saw under the altar the souls of them that were slain for the word of God and for the testimony which they held. And they cried with a loud voice, saying: How long, O Lord (Holy and True), dost thou not judge and revenge our blood on them that dwell on the earth? And white robes were given to every one of them one. And it was said to them that they should rest for a little time till their fellow servants and their brethren, who are to be slain even as they, should be filled up."[1]

In our liturgical life we do the same thing. We address the saints in heaven, not as discarnate spirits, but as fully constituted human personalities. We could not, under any circumstances, render them present to our thoughts in a disembodied state.

Only the immaterial remains

The philosophical principles which have enabled Catholic thinkers to establish the spirituality of the human soul on rational grounds are also the principles which have guided them in laying down clear data concerning the disembodied human spirits. We say that man's soul is entirely spiritual because during life it has entirely spiritual operations. From this St Thomas concludes, with all other scholastics, that only such portions or powers of man's soul are found in the discarnate state as are entirely spiritual; for the whole scholastic case with regard to the soul's survival turns on that one fact, the complete immateriality of certain acts of man in lifetime. So they arrive at this very rational conclusion that only those things remain after death which are entirely immaterial, without any admixture of matter and sense-life. If the discarnate spirit were supposed still to possess material elements or sense-life, even of the most refined description, there would be no reason, says St Thomas, why we should not grant immortality also to the souls of animals. If sense-life of any kind could survive death, then the animal soul could survive death; but this hypothesis is an absurdity to Catholic thinkers. So all our philosophical premisses postulate this, that only an entirely immaterial substance, with immaterial powers and immaterial operations, can survive death. Consequently the discarnate soul of man is, in the eyes of Catholic philosophers, an exclusively spiritual being; in fact, it is a spirit.

From this we see that Catholic philosophy, whilst upholding the soul's survival, admits that the havoc of death is much greater than less logical thinkers would make it. All that part of the human mind which is concerned with sense-life, even of the highest type, perishes at death. There is in man, truly, the perishable mind as Aristotle already saw it, but there is also in man the imperishable mind, also as Aristotle saw it, I mean the exclusively intellectual mind; that mind remains. Only let us remember that when we speak of the perishable and the imperishable mind we are not speaking of two

[1] Apoc. vi 9-11.

souls, but of two different powers in the one soul, whose root or substance is entirely spiritual. So the discarnate spirit of man is credited by scholastic philosophy with two powers only, the power of intellection and the power of volition; all other operations, however wonderful, however æsthetic, have been left behind at death, they perish with the body. So our dead are truly for us mysterious beings; we can only think of them by clothing them in our imagination with a humanity which is not theirs any more, but which will be theirs again when death will be overcome by Christ.

Intellect and will

The question to ask now is this: what is the extent of that intellectual and volitive life which Catholic philosophy grants to the separated human soul? To begin with the intellect. St Thomas is willing to concede to the discarnate soul a measure of knowledge which is truly astonishing. The guiding principle which Aquinas follows is this: through death the soul of man becomes a spirit in the truest sense of the word, though it be the lowest degree of spirit; accordingly, let it be endowed with spirit activities, let it receive all that a spirit ought to possess. As insinuated already, this has nothing to do with the soul's sanctity or lack of sanctity; such intellectual enlargement would not even mean happiness unless other factors of the supernatural order come into play. The soul is naturally a spirit after death, be it for weal or woe. We cannot, of course, enter into details; St Thomas is wise enough not to do so. We cannot give a description of that new intellectual life of the discarnate soul; all we can say is that it is a spirit, the lowest spirit, yet a spirit, and that it knows all those things which naturally belong to its sphere.

Volition of the disembodied human soul is a matter which is not without its terrors, for happiness and sanctity, as well as their opposites, ultimately depend on the state of man's will. Now though it is admitted by all theologians that the spirit, of whatever degree it be, has an unchangeable and an unchanging will, even scholastics are not united over the explanation of that unchangeableness, while they all admit it as a certain fact. Some say that it comes from God's withholding further graces; some think that the root of the unchangeableness lies in the very essence of the spirit-nature. A fact, however, which is certain and, as I said, terrifying, admits of no doubt: the discarnate human soul, like all other spirits, has its will fixed unalterably: it remains in the same loyalty which it had embraced at the end of life, whether this means God or self.

Executive powers

A point raised by Catholic thinkers has a further interest: are the discarnate human souls endowed with certain executive powers of acting, of doing, nay, even of moving, in the spirit-sense of moving? Those spirits whom we call angels or demons have certainly such powers. Some scholastics, like the Scotists, have no hesitation in admitting that the souls of the dead can do things as other spirits can do them. St Thomas seems to hesitate, yet, even with him the matter admits of no doubt; a careful study of his works reveals the fact that he, too, grants powers of acting to the dead ; he falls back on the universal principle that the human souls have become pure spirits and must possess spirit-life, however exiguous that spirit-life may be.

An incomplete substance

The disembodied human soul could hardly be called a human person, it is an imperfect person, as it is an incomplete substance ; it has an innate fitness, which is called a natural desire, to be reunited with the body, for it is only in that dual state of sense and spirit that the human personality is entire and has its full range of activities. These considerations, which are the best which Catholic philosophy can offer, do not present a cheerful view of the world of the dead. Even independently of the possibility of actual reprobation, man's soul, separated from the body, outside the supernatural sphere, must be regarded as a maimed being, one that is deprived of the splendours of human life and human personality, for though our theologians grant spirit-activities, such powers are no real enjoyment to the souls that possess them. We are not surprised, therefore, to find that human tradition, outside the influences of the Christian revelation, has taken a gloomy view of the realm of the dead.

§ VII : THE INTERCOURSE OF THE LIVING WITH THE DEAD

Necromancy in the Old Testament

It is one of the oldest beliefs of mankind that the living may, under certain circumstances, get into touch with the dead. This superstition, if we must give such a name to this belief, is at least an indirect evidence that men have always admitted in practice some kind of survival of the human personality after death. It would be difficult to describe with any accuracy the kind of existence that men have attributed to their dead, yet they have endowed them with substance and reality sufficient to make them agents of good and evil in practical life. In the oldest portions of the Scriptures, in Deuteronomy, we find this practice of holding intercourse with the dead condemned as one of the great sins among the doomed races of Canaan : " Neither let there be found among you any one that shall expiate his son or daughter, making them to pass through the fire : or that consulteth soothsayers, or observeth dreams or omens. Neither let there be any wizard, nor charmer, nor any one that consulteth pythonic spirits, or fortune-tellers : or that seeketh the truth from the dead. For the Lord abhorreth all these things : and for these abominations he will destroy them at thy coming." [1] The earliest instance of necromancy recorded in the Bible is an attempt to consult one who was among the dead, as to the future ; Saul the king went to the woman that had a divining spirit at Endor : " And he said to her : Divine to me by thy divining spirit, and bring me up whom I shall tell thee." And the rest of the story may be told in

[1] Deut. xviii 10-12.

the full text, for the methods of necromancy have not altered in the course of the centuries. "And the woman said to him: Whom shall I bring up to thee? And he said, Bring me up Samuel. And when the woman saw Samuel, she cried out with a loud voice, and said to Saul: Why hast thou deceived me? for thou art Saul. And the king said to her: Fear not. What hast thou seen? And the woman said to Saul: I saw gods ascending out of the earth. And he said to her: What form is he of? And she said: An old man cometh up; and he is covered with a mantle. And Saul understood that it was Samuel, and he bowed himself with his face to the ground, and adored. And Samuel said to Saul: Why hast thou disturbed my rest that I should be brought up? And Saul said: I am in great distress; for the Philistines fight against me; and God is departed from me; and would not hear me, neither by the hand of prophets nor by dreams. Therefore have I called thee, that thou mayest shew me what I shall do. And Samuel said: Why askest thou me, seeing the Lord has departed from thee, and is gone over to thy rival? . . . And forthwith Saul fell all along on the ground, for he was frightened with the words of Samuel." [1]

From this long narrative taken from the Book of Kings, we can gather what is meant by the expression in the older Biblical document, Deuteronomy, "to seek the truth from the dead." It is not merely some form of vain observance by which definite meanings would be attached to happenings concerned with the bodies of the dead; by the dead are meant the spirits who are not seen, but who are credited with knowledge, and who may, under given circumstances, impart that knowledge to the living. Shall we say *a priori* that this ancient belief of mankind is a complete deception, and that the dead are powerless to do anything either for or against man? Here, of course, I must remind the reader that I am concerned with this problem in its natural aspect only; the intercourse which the living may have with the holy dead, with the elect, the spirits of the just, is a different matter altogether, belonging to that great mystery, the Communion of Saints; in that blessed sphere anything may happen in God's providence, the saints may appear to the living and teach and guide and help them on to eternal salvation. Our subject demands no such exceptional state; we are simply asking whether the spirits of the dead—in other words, the dead—have it in their power to influence the living. This question may be approached from three different points of view. Firstly, we may ask in an abstract manner whether any spirit can manifest himself to man. Secondly, we may inquire if that special class of spirit, the discarnate human soul, has it in his power so to do. The third point to be settled is of a general order; granted that spirits have such power, is it within God's providence to allow them to exercise the power? And here we must recognise the difference between the *absolute* and the *conditional* in

[1] 1 Kings xxviii 11-16, 20.

the divine ordinances. In his omnipotence God may prevent spirits of every class from the exercise of such power, or he may permit them to exert it, even though its exercise would be against his commands, and would, in fact, be a sin on the part of the spirits.

Natural power of spirits to communicate with man

There is such a bulk of tradition that spirits not only may exert influence over man but may actually manifest themselves to him, speaking with him in his own language, that it would be temerarious to refuse to the spirit-world this privilege of communicating with humanity. We take it for granted here that a spirit when he enters into converse with man does so under definite human forms which it is in his power to assume ; it matters little to our purpose whether these forms are merely subjective impressions on man's senses or have some objective consistency. The saints of heaven have come and talked to their friends and clients here on earth, angels have appeared, and demons have been allowed to tempt Christ's disciples as they tempted the Master himself in the desert.

Discarnate spirits

Must we make an exception for the discarnate human soul in its natural state ? There seems to be no *a priori* reason why we should do so ; the separate human soul possesses spirit-qualities and it ought to be granted those powers which spirits ordinarily possess. We may, indeed, limit those powers to the least possible range compatible with a spirit-nature—after all, the discarnate soul is the lowest and weakest form of spirit—but to refuse it spirit-activities, spirit-motions, would be illogical. So I should not advise any antagonist of necromancy and spiritism to base his denunciations of that black craft on the powerlessness of spirits to do anything ; it is just possible that such spirits might be able, and even might be allowed, to do much. Thus this question is really one of divine ordinance. Does God allow such intercourse, in the sense that he does not inhibit, through some act of his providence, the activities of the discarnate, human spirits ? We know, of course, that he does not prohibit the activities of demons absolutely, though he may limit and confine them, lest we perish. This is the intention of our daily prayer after Mass : " Holy Michael, Archangel, defend us in the day of battle ; be our safeguard against the wickedness and snares of the devil. May God rebuke him, we most humbly pray ; and do thou, Prince of the heavenly host, by the power of God, thrust down to hell Satan and all wicked spirits, who wander through the world for the ruin of souls." It is our constant cry to God to defend us against our spiritual enemies ; we are given the armour of the Spirit that we may be able to withstand them. Does God restrict the evil human soul in its discarnate state in the same manner ? I use the term " evil " here in connection with the souls of the dead, because in this matter we are concerned only with such spirits as are neither in purgatory nor dwelling with Christ in heaven. On general theological and psychological principles it would be safe to assume that God deals with human spirits in the same way as with all other spirits; thus we may base on these foundations the same attitude which mankind has instinctively held for so many ages and ascribe to the dead real powers, we may give them initiative, we may without hesitation accept it as a possibility that certain human spirits may make their presence felt among the living, especially in those places which were the scenes of their human activities.[1]

The divine ordinance

Thus our considerations are brought down to this very simple issue: whether or not it is lawful for man here on earth to attempt to enter into communication with the dead and, in the words of Deuteronomy, to seek truth from them. Now it is evident that the Catholic Church has never hesitated in her condemnation of every kind of spiritism; for her, spiritism is merely necromancy. I need not enter here into the phases of modern spiritism; the "seeking of truth from the dead" is one of the most serious wounds in our modern society. That strange things do happen at séances is a matter beyond doubt; it would be rash to treat it all as delusion or imposture. Orthodox writers differ in their interpretation of the origin of these alarming occurrences. Some say that the evil spirits, the demons, the fallen angels, are the dark powers that manifest themselves; they seem to take it for granted that human souls could not in any way show such activities. But, as we have already said, there is not the least reason why discarnate human souls should not behave in the same way as demons. The principal conclusion at which we should arrive is this: that to whichever grade those spirits may belong which are responsible for the communications of the medium, they are not good spirits but bad spirits; whether they be human or demoniac matters but little in the ultimate outcome.

Modern spiritism

This conclusion is, obviously, supremely abhorrent to the bulk of modern spiritists. They deny on principle that it is an evil thing to seek truth from the dead, and maintain, therefore, that if the dead answer, such behaviour, far from being blameworthy, shows love and interest on the other side. When the spiritist is reproached with the apparent futility, nay, even the nauseousness of many of the spirit-communications, his answer is that, if not all intercourse with the dead is above suspicion, there may be a kind of communication that has all the quality of a highly ethical act. If spirits are consulted by men of science and virtue concerning good and holy things, even with respect to religious issues, and if the spirits give reply worthy of a wise man, is not spiritism justified through the very decorum of its behaviour? I readily admit that a type of spiritism might be developed which would deceive even the very elect, and from which all coarse and vulgar elements could be eliminated, though it would not seem that hitherto spiritism has been anything but a degrading necromancy. I do not think that there is any other answer against spiritism when considered in all its possible aspects than this: God has proscribed it for man as he forbade man to partake of the tree of

[1] For another view see Essay xxxiii, pp. 1209–1210.

the knowledge of good and evil. This is the standpoint of the Catholic Church; and unless people are ready to accept this divine prohibition they are not unlikely to fall into the snares of the spiritists.

The following typical case, under the pseudonym of Titius, was propounded to the Holy See: Titius, banishing from his mind every intention of holding intercourse with evil spirits, is in the habit of calling up the spirits of the dead. He behaves as follows: finding himself alone, without any preliminary, he prays to the chief of the heavenly army that from him he may obtain power to enter into touch with the spirit of a given person. He waits a little, holding his hand ready to write, and all at once he feels that his hand is moved; thus he knows that the spirit is present. He asks what he wants to know and his hand writes the answers to his queries; these replies invariably squaring with the Catholic faith and the Church's doctrine concerning eternal life. As a rule they have to do with the state in which the soul of some dead person finds itself; they speak of the necessity of prayers for the dead and also complain of the ingratitude of relatives and so on. Is this manner of acting lawful on the part of Titius?

The answer of the Holy See was clear. Such behaviour is not lawful.

Again in 1917, with equal definiteness the Holy Office gave a complete denial as to the legitimacy of the practices described thus: Whether it be lawful to be present at any kind of spiritistic locutions or manifestations, questioning souls or spirits, listening to their answers, or even looking on, although there might be a tacit or express stipulation that there was no intention whatever to enter into any sort of co-operation with evil spirits. From the nature of the case such transgressions would be grievously culpable, as they would be sins against a grave precept of religion. So far the Church has not attached any kind of censure or excommunication to spiritistic practices, but she considers them to be mortal sin.

§ VIII: THE JUDGE OF THE LIVING AND THE DEAD

God's judicial power

No attribute is more constantly predicated of God than judgement. With the boldness of a friend, Abraham appeals to God and reminds him of this supreme quality when interceding for the men of Sodom: "Far be it from thee to do this thing, and to slay the just with the wicked, and for the just to be in like case as the wicked. This is not beseeming thee: thou who judgest all the earth, wilt not make this judgement." [1]

It would be a big volume that would be written were all the utterances of the canonical writers concerning God in his capacity as Judge to be gathered together. By God's judicial power we mean

[1] Gen. xviii 25.

something very definite and clearly discernible from other divine operations; we mean a constant intervention of God in the affairs of the created universe, arranging and rearranging both spiritual and material issues on account of the free actions of his rational creatures. Though judgement is more obviously associated with God's punitive interference it is not, of course, confined to the divine severities; the most adorable portions of his judgements are those providential mutations in the course of the universe which are the rewards of the virtuous actions of the children of God.

Present as well as future

There is, however, one important fact to be borne in mind, that right through the Old Testament God is represented as exercising the supreme function of Judge, not in the distant future only, but in the immediate present, with men, with nations living now on this earth. The prophets who announced the great Judgement were not speaking of an event to take place in a future world, but of severities and rigours to be shown by God towards the living generations of men. God's function of Judge is, in scriptural thought, essentially a continuous function, an unceasing function, not one that is reserved exclusively for a special date hereafter. I do not say that there are not very clear allusions by the prophets to a judgement at the end of times, but the bulk of their vaticination is of judgements to be executed within a short space of time. Thus Isaias uses language which goes far beyond the threats against Egypt or Babylon or Tyre: "With breaking shall the earth be broken . . . with shaking shall the earth be shaken as a drunken man, and shall be removed as the tent of one night. And the iniquity thereof shall be heavy upon it: and it shall fall and not rise again." [1]

If we come to the New Testament, to the Person of the Incarnate God, we find that he likewise is endowed with the power of judging, with the power of separating good and evil, of awarding to men their due, according to their deserts, long before the hour of final judgement. It is in the New Testament that the expression occurs "Judge of the living and the dead." This name for God is not found in the Old Testament, and in the New Testament it is given invariably to the Person of Christ: "He commanded us to preach to the people and to testify that it is he who was appointed by God, to be a judge of the living and the dead." [2] How are we to understand this extension of God's judicial power to the dead? Does it mean that God has not judged men in their lifetime to the full extent, so that he completes after death the judgement of men? Or shall we see in this formula only a drastic expression of the all-embracing power of divine justice, from which nothing can escape? It is indeed not easy to see the full meaning of this inspired phrase. As every generation of living men will soon belong to the world of the dead, it is not apparent who are the living in contradistinction to the dead whom God is said to judge. Doubtless, the simplest

[1] Is. xxiv 19, 20. [2] Acts x 42.

interpretation is this: that as God deals with men and nations on this earth according to the dictates of his justice, so he will dispose of them in that other state, the state of death, giving to each man his due. By the formula "Judge of the living and the dead" is meant, I think, not always a twofold classification of human beings, but the complete career of the same beings, their conditions of life and death, whose happenings, whose details, are equally in the scales of divine justice. This phrase, used by St Peter and St Paul, has also been inserted in the oldest symbols of the faith: "He shall come again with glory to judge the living and the dead." As the Creed identifies Christ's judgement of the living and the dead with his second Coming, it may be said that, in this instance at least, by the living are meant those human beings who shall be found alive on this earth at his advent, while the dead are those who will come forth from their tombs. But as we have seen in a former section, it is New Testament language to give Christ a general dominion over the living and the dead in a kind of universal visualising of the whole human race: "For to this end Christ died and rose again: that he might be Lord both of the dead and of the living." [1]

We may now come to the interesting point how the various judgements which are attributed to the supreme Judge of the living and the dead are to be distinguished from each other and yet correlated; for Christ, even as is the Father, is always seated on the throne of judgement.

Temporal and eternal judgements

The distinction I submit in order to proceed clearly in this vast subject is as follows: we must recognise God's *temporal* judgements and also his *eternal* judgements. The discrimination between the temporal and eternal judgements is a most far-reaching doctrine in this matter: the decrees of the temporal judgement have a concluding point, while those of the eternal judgement are endless in effect. Again, each of these distinctions contains a sub-distinction: God's temporal judgements are concerned with men either in their bodily state on earth or in their disembodied state; his eternal judgements deal either with individual men or with the whole race. So we have four aspects of the great doctrine of God, the Judge of the living and the dead. Men, either individually or as races or nations, as families or even as religious bodies, receive rewards or punishments while they are on earth. Or again, if the divine justice in its temporal equalisation of conditions is not satisfied, there is that other adjustment which goes by the comprehensive name of purgatory, and which all theologians agree in describing as a portion of the temporal punishment for sin. At death the soul of man is definitely fixed either in election or reprobation, its eternal fate is sealed, it is said to be condemned by God's justice or to be admitted into the society of the elect, also by God's justice, though theologians, with edifying humility, generally prefer to say that the soul is granted entrance to

[1] Rom. xiv 9.

everlasting life through the mercy of God. This portion of the eternal judgement is hidden and affects, so to speak, the very substance of man's individual personality. To it is given by all theologians the name of particular or private judgement. This denomination we may keep here, provided we remember that even in the first class of judgements—the temporal judgements—there is also something very particular and private to the individual, such, for instance, as the punishment due to each soul in purgatory for its own sin. The judgement of a man who dies in mortal sin ought to be called the particular eternal judgement, in contradistinction to the particular temporal judgement which is the lot of one dying in a state of grace, who yet has to undergo temporal punishment.

Then there is finally the Last Judgement, the results of which will also be eternal, but which will be concerned essentially with the whole human race, in soul and body, with the greatest possible manifestation of all hidden things. It is pre-eminently the Day of Judgement, the one great act of God as the supreme Judge of the living and the dead. In the following pages we shall give a fuller account of these four divisions of God's judicial activities; at present I am trying to make clear to the reader the connection of the different spheres of the divine justice; for it is evident that, radically speaking, there is only one judgement, and the four acts constitute one mighty drama of God's sanctity. Theologians constantly warn us that there are never new judgements, but that the one judgement is progressive till it reaches consummation on the Last Day.

This, then, is that divine march of him who, in the words of Abraham, "judges all the earth." The temporal administration of divine justice has this one great object, to vindicate God's sanctity even in the case of those who will ultimately be saved, because they, too, have offended much against his justice; even the saints are punished here on earth lest the anger of God destroy their chances of salvation; the elect are punished after death in the avenging flames of the purgatorial state because, though they be saved, they are saved out of many sins "as through fire." The grave judgements of God here on earth have, moreover, a power of grace for man, that man by them should be converted and live, that he should be warned and frightened when he hears the blows of the divine judgements. The writings of the Fathers are full of that *leit-motif*; they seem to have understood the judgements of God in their temporal aspect more clearly than we do. So we may say that God's temporal judgements in this life and after death have an essentially providential character in the sense that they are meant as chances of ultimate salvation; they are temporal, because the punitive arrangements of which they consist will end sooner or later. The human being to whom the judgements of God have been, to the very end of his life, a useless lesson will be judged finally at death as one incapable of eternal life, because he did not want to understand the judgements of divine justice. It may be said, with full theological accuracy, that man is judged and condemned eternally because he despised God's temporal judgements.

The relation of the Last Judgement—the fourth act—to these preceding ones has been a favourite theme with the Fathers and theologians of all ages. Why will there be that great, that universal Assize, when it is apparent that the justice of God has never been idle, in fact, seems to have had its full scope; when all those who are unworthy of eternal life are already condemned, when God has punished man, has brought things back to the golden rule of justice with his unceasing severities towards men in their days of life and even after death, in purgatory? The most satisfying view and the one that seems to have the support of reiterated scriptural language is this: that the Last Judgement is truly the manifestation of all the judicial acts of God that have gone before; there is no new judgement, but there is the proclamation to all flesh of the complete justice of God in all previous judgements. For the three previous judgements are mostly hidden, are incomprehensible to man, they cannot be followed by the eye of man, they are too complex to be understood by man. Now it is the special function of the Last Judgement to make clear before all creation that not one evil thing has remained unvisited, not one good thing has passed unrewarded, in all the vast history of the human race: "Every man's work shall be manifest. For the day of the Lord shall declare it, because it shall be revealed in fire. And the fire shall try every man's work, of what sort it is." [1]

St Thomas gives expression to this thought in a very lucid fashion: there are two operations in God; the first, the creation of all things; the second, the government of all things. Both these operations have as their complement a judgement. To the operation of creation corresponds the Last Judgement, while the other set of judgements are congruous to the operation of government; and this for very clear reasons: "Through the judgement which corresponds to the government of the world—which could not be carried out without judgement—everyone is judged individually for his works, not only as far as it concerns himself, but also as far as it concerns the government of the world. For this reason the reward of one man is delayed for the benefit of other people, and the punishment of one becomes the benefit of another. For this reason it is necessary that there should be another universal judgement which is the direct counterpart of the first creation of all things; so that, in the same way as all things then came forth from God without an intermediary, so there will be a final finishing off of the world, everyone receiving ultimately what is due to him according to his own personality. Therefore in that judgement divine justice will show itself manifestly in all those things which are now hidden, for this very reason

[1] 1 Cor. iii 13.

that one man is sometimes so treated as to be of utility to other men, a treatment contrary to that which his well-known works seem to merit. For this reason, too, there will then be the most extensive separation between the good and the bad, for there will be no longer room for that arrangement by which evil men are helped by good men and good men are helped by bad men; for as long as the present state of life is under the government of divine providence there is this mixing together of the good and the evil for their mutual benefit." [1]

§ IX: THE TEMPORAL JUDGEMENT

Christ the present judge

WE may now consider the various judgements in themselves, and we may watch Christ at his great work as Judge of the living and the dead. As all judgement has been given to him, we shall use indiscriminately the name of God and the name of Christ in connection with judgement for the remainder of our essay.

The temporal judgements are indeed a most important province of Christ's activities in his judicial capacity; if we left them out of our theology the whole matter of God's judgements would become distorted and even incomprehensible. As already insinuated, by temporal judgements we mean those ordinances of Christ, be they punitive, be they remunerative, which take place in time, outside eternity. We do not say, of course, that their results will not go beyond time, will have no eternal repercussions; everything God does is meant in some way to have effects that modify man's everlasting destinies. The distinction between eternal judgements and temporal judgements is to be found in the arrangements of divine providence, of which some are transient, some are permanent. Thus, for instance, if through a just judgement of God a Christian prince were to lose his temporal powers, for, say, not being loyal to the Church, this would be a temporal judgement, since the loss of power would not necessarily affect the eternal fate of the prince's soul; the punitive arrangement is not, in such a case, an immutable state, affecting eternity itself.

Christ, since he ascended to heaven and took up his position at the right hand of the Father, is most certainly acting as the Judge of mankind. Judgement is more than providence, or better still, it is the moral side of providence. The free deeds of men and above all of Christians, their prayers, their virtues, their sins, are matters which the divine Judge contemplates unceasingly, and he orders all things in perfect equity. This is the meaning of St Paul's splendid words to the Corinthians: "For he must reign, until he hath put all his enemies under his feet. . . . And when all things shall be subdued unto him, then the Son also himself shall be subject unto him that put all things under him, that God may be all in all." [2]

[1] *Suppl.* xlvii, art. 1.

[2] 1 Cor. xv 25-28.

The coming of Christ is itself described as a judgement. That separation between good and evil which is the purpose of all judgement, begins with the Incarnation : " And Simeon blessed them and said to Mary his mother : Behold, this child is set for the fall and for the resurrection of many in Israel and for a sign which shall be contradicted." [1] But the separation was not then manifest, it only began to become visible, at least relatively, after the Ascension, when there took place in such terrible and evident fashion the casting away of that people who had rejected the Son of God. Christ's Redemption on the Cross is the greatest act of divine judgement. He was then struggling beneath the burden of all the injustice committed by man against the Father, he was judged by God as though he bore the guilt of all sins, and by his acceptance of that suffering and that death in his own flesh he made complete payment of the debts of his brethren to divine Majesty : " Blotting out the handwriting of the decree that was against us, which was contrary to us. And he hath taken the same out of the way, fastening it to the cross." [2] So we hear Christ saying confidently a few days before his Passion : " Now is the judgement of the world : now shall the prince of this world be cast out." [3] And again Christ says that the Spirit will convince the world of judgement " because the prince of this world is already judged." [4] The Baptist had made the same announcement in a metaphor of unmatched power : " He shall baptise you with the Holy Ghost and with fire : Whose fan is in his hand : and he will purge his floor and will gather the wheat into his barn : but the chaff he will burn with unquenchable fire." [5]

The temporal judgement of Christ is concerned with spiritual punitions and rewards as well as with temporal ones ; for let us bear in mind that divine judgements are exercised over that most important possession of man, his graces, as well as over his external goods : " And Jesus said : For judgement I am come into this world : that they who see not may see ; and they who see may become blind." [6] The temporal severities are announced when Christ speaks of what is manifestly the end of the Jewish people as his " day," for by " day " is here meant judgement : " Even thus shall it be in the day when the Son of man shall be revealed. In that hour, he that shall be on the housetop, and his goods in the house, let him not go down to take them away : and he that shall be in the field, in like manner, let him not turn back. Remember Lot's wife." [7]

It is true that several times our Lord says that he came, not to judge the world but to save it : " God sent not his Son into the world to judge the world : but that the world may be saved by him." [8] How are we to reconcile these apparently contradictory utterances ? The explanation seems to be a simple one, namely that during the

[1] Luke ii 34.
[2] Col. ii 14.
[3] John xii 31.
[4] John xvi 11.
[5] Luke iii 16, 17.
[6] John ix 39.
[7] Luke xvii 30-32.
[8] John iii 17.

days of his mortality, before his exaltation, Christ did not, as Man, exert his judicial power, at least in the external government of the world. Thus it is in the same sense that he says he was only sent to the lost sheep of the house of Israel, though we know he was sent to the whole human race. But after Christ's Ascension Christians never hesitated to attribute to him the vastest activities as Judge of the world; they looked to him for the redress of their grievances when they suffered at the hands of persecutors; they confidently believed that the pagan world, above all, pagan Rome, would soon feel the heavy arm of the divine Judge: "Therefore shall her plagues come in one day, death and mourning and famine. And she shall be burnt with the fire: because God is strong, who shall judge her. . . . Rejoice over her, thou heaven and ye holy apostles and prophets. For God hath judged your judgement upon her."[1] "True and just are his judgements, who hath judged the great harlot which corrupted the earth with her fornication and hath revenged the blood of his servants at her hands."[2]

Christ himself is seen coming out of heaven by the prophet of Patmos at a period of human history which does not appear to correspond with the end of the world: "And I saw heaven opened: and behold a white horse. And he that sat upon him was called faithful and true: and with justice doth he judge and fight."[3] This is the true view of Christ; this makes him into a living power. Genuine Christian sentiment has ever been deeply impregnated with this trait of Christ as the just Judge, and Christians have always found it possible to love him with the tenderest love because they know him to be such; they speak to Christ with all the familiarity with which Abraham spoke to the Lord his friend, when he praised his justice as they overlooked the cities of Sodom and Gomorrha. Our Jesus would be less amiable if he were less true and less powerful in his judgements.

The doctrine of the divine judgements is stated very often in other terms, such as the doctrine of temporal punishment for sin; but it is in truth one and the same thing. Christ punishes man with temporal punishments because he executes judgement over man. The doctrine of temporal punishment says that man owes the divine justice satisfaction, and even great satisfaction, after the stain of sin has been taken away from his soul by the grace of God. The punishment is meted out by God's providence, either in this life or in purgatory.

Purgatory

In no province of sacred theology are we so much in need of the fundamental doctrine of Christ's judicial power, for the sake of clearness, as in the case of the Church's teaching on purgatory. It seems difficult to give any other explanation why so many amongst the saved must pass through the purgatorial state than the truth so simply expressed in the old Catholic phrase that the souls of men

[1] Apoc. xviii 8 and 20. [2] Apoc. xix 2. [3] Apoc. xix 11.

have to pay a debt to divine justice. A more superficial view of purgatory would be this: that the souls of men pass into the other life ignorant, with the stains upon them of many venial sins and the impediments of innumerable imperfections.[1] We exclude, of course, the state of mortal sin, as such a state is tantamount to eternal reprobation. We might call this view of purgatory the psychological view, as it implies that the process of purgatorial purification would be a gradual transition of man's disembodied spirit from a lower to a higher grade of power. But such a view seems excluded by another very important consideration: the souls in purgatory are pure spirits. Now spirits operate at all times with the entirety of their being. So theologians have to admit that the moment the saved soul enters into the spirit-state it turns to God with a completeness of surrender which is not comprehensible to man here on earth, and which establishes it in perfect charity. So the purgatorial process ought to be taken in an exclusively juridical sense. The word *purgare* in Latin law means "to pay the full amount of the punishment due." So our best theologians in speaking of purgatory use the language of the law courts; the divine Judge decides, assesses, the amount of penalty to be undergone for offences and neglects not fully repaired during mortal life. What those pains and penalties are, we need not investigate here; they belong to another portion of theology. But it seems evident that nothing can account for the burdens thus put on those holy spirits except the direct act of the divine Judge; nor could a finite authority settle how much or how little of penalty each such spirit must undergo. "Be at agreement with thy adversary betimes, whilst thou art in the way with him: lest perhaps the adversary deliver thee to the judge, and the judge deliver thee to the officer, and thou be cast into prison. Amen I say to thee, thou shalt not go out from thence till thou repay the last farthing."[2] The purgatorial adjustment of the divine claims might almost be called an afterthought in God's providence, because the general plan of salvation which God has produced for man is such that if man were faithful he would reach the hour of death in a state of perfect justice, having done his day's work, and having produced for his Master that amount of profit which his Lord has a right to expect from him.

The Church's liturgy is full of invocations to God and his Christ that man may find mercy with his Judge. These prayers, which are so profoundly Christian, refer, of course, to the temporal judgement, for the eternal judgement is unalterable. When we hope to be judged leniently we expect Christ to relinquish in our favour some of his rights as Judge, either in this life or in purgatory. It is in connection with this judgement also that we have those solemn promises of Christ that according to the mercifulness of our own judgements, judgement shall be shown to us: "Be ye therefore merciful, as your Father also is merciful. Judge not: and you shall

[1] Cf. Essay xxxii, pp. 1143 ff.

[2] Matt. v 25, 26.

not be judged. Condemn not: and you shall not be condemned. Forgive: and you shall be forgiven. Give: and it shall be given to you: good measure and pressed down and shaken together and running over shall they give into your bosom. For with the same measure that you shall mete withal, it shall be measured to you again." [1]

§X: THE ETERNAL JUDGEMENT OF INDIVIDUAL SOULS

Particular judgement

THE designation of "particular judgement" has been applied for a long time now as a kind of technical term to that act of God by which the soul of man at death is either received into the society of the elect or is rejected and cast away for ever. The main features of the particular judgement thus understood are its peremptoriness and its complete secrecy. Of no human being do we know with certainty that he has been rejected by God, though, on the other hand, we do know of definite human beings having been admitted into the society of the elect, as, for instance, all the canonised saints. But no eye has seen what really happens between God and the human soul at that first moment when the soul finds itself in eternity. Though this name "particular judgement" more commonly brings home to us the idea of possible reprobation of individual souls, such a one-sided aspect of this act of God would leave in obscurity the most marvellous manifestation of the divine sanctity and justice. For the elect, for those who are saved, that moment which constitutes the soul in eternity is an overwhelming revelation of God's fidelity; not only does it become immensely clear to the soul that it is saved, that it is in a state of grace, that it belongs to God for ever and ever, but all the works done in the supernatural order during the mortal life are remembered by God, are brought to the knowledge of the fortunate soul, are seen in their full setting; and God rewards as only God can reward. "For I know whom I have believed and I am certain that he is able to keep that which I have committed unto him, against that day." [2] Or again: "I have fought a good fight: I have finished my course: I have kept the faith. As to the rest, there is laid up for me a crown of justice which the Lord the just judge will render to me in that day: and not only to me, but to them also that love his coming." [3]

Of the elect

In the case of the elect there is this double marvel of divine justice and truth: they are given, firstly, that eternal life which they have always sought, and secondly they are also granted that additional glory which comes from every fresh merit. The inspired writers seem to have been particularly struck by God's fidelity in remembering all the works of the elect. It is divine judgement in its most glorious and most consoling form; it is justice superabounding, because not

[1] Luke vi 36-38. [2] 2 Tim. i 12. [3] 2 Tim. iv 7, 8.

a cup of cold water given in the name of Christ will be without its reward. The good works of the elect follow their entry into eternity like a cortège of angels: "And I heard a voice from heaven, saying to me: Write: Blessed are the dead who die in the Lord. From henceforth now, saith the Spirit, that they may rest from their labours. For their works follow them." [1] Though for many of the elect the bestowal of that reward may perhaps be delayed through the captivity of purgatory, still their immense treasure of merits is for ever secure, the justice of God will not allow him to let anything go unremunerated. Merit and reward belong to another part of theology, here we look upon them as the pronouncement of a judgement. In their essential quality they will be bestowed on the discarnate human soul when it is admitted into heaven; when it will be granted not only the blessed Vision of God but various degrees in that Vision. May we not say, speaking now naïvely, that the greatest surprise of the elect at that blessed moment will be to find how God has remembered even the least of their deeds; how their works, long forgotten by themselves, are truly recorded in the Book of Life.

Theologians have gone deeply into the matter of that "finding" of all the merits of a long life at the first moment of eternity. They would love to construct theories which would account for the presence of all that past merit in the soul; they say, for instance, that grace has never ceased growing as merit grew, so that the soul at death has already the full wealth of spiritual beauty, though in a hidden way. However, with the ups and downs of human life, and very often with long interruptions of mortal sin, it seems difficult to explain completely how all the works of the elect revive when they enter heaven, unless we admit God's own power of restoring to man all his past merits.

The term "to judge" has, in New Testament language, generally the unfavourable sense of judgement for condemnation, though the word "judge" as substantive stands for God in his office, both as rewarder of merit and avenger of sin. So our Lord says: "He that believeth in him (Christ) is not judged. But he that doth not believe is already judged: because he believeth not in the name of the only begotten Son of God. And this is the judgement: Because the light is come into the world and men loved darkness rather than the light. For their works were evil." [2]

Of the reprobate

With this divine utterance we approach the dreadful subject of man's condemnation to eternal reprobation after death. In reprobation, as in election, there are two elements which must be kept apart in our consideration of the subject: man is admitted into the society of the elect because he dies in the state of grace, but he also receives a higher or lower degree of eternal life according as his merits are great or small. So, on the other hand, man is cast into eternal death because temporal death found him in a state of mortal sin, but

[1] Apoc. xiv 13. [2] John iii 18, 19.

his degree of punishment will depend on the amount of evil which he did in life and which had not been forgiven. In very exact theology we should say that man is admitted to eternal life or is cast away, not by a judgement that takes place over him after the separation of the soul from the body, but by that judgement through which God decided that death should overtake the holy one in a state of grace, whilst, through the permissive will of the divine justice, death was allowed to come to the sinner when he was in the state of mortal sin. Theologians would not be unwilling to say that there is no real pronouncement of sentence, either of eternal life or of eternal death, these great issues following naturally, as it were, from the state of the soul at the moment of death. In this matter we have our Lord's own words in the verse quoted above: "He that believeth in him is not judged. But he that doth not believe is already judged: because he believeth not in the name of the Son of God. And this is the judgement. . . ."[1] But we may, of course, take the less technical view and say that souls are condemned or are exalted by a just judgement of God when they enter eternity. We certainly cannot get away from a definite act of God which settles for ever man's fate by putting an end to the period of mutability and change.

Degrees of punishment

There is, however, in the case of the reprobate as well as in the case of the elect, the great question how God deals with individual guilt, because he cannot treat alike, even in reprobation, the great criminal and the ordinary sinner. The fact of reprobation itself, of being cast for ever into exterior darkness, is a necessary result of final unrepentance, of the state of mortal sin at death. Between reprobation thus considered as a deprivation of eternal life, and the just punishment to be inflicted for the great human sins, there must, of course, be a very grave difference. How this difference makes itself felt in the lost spirits of all degrees of guilt it is not possible for us to say. We have no clear guidance on this subject. We know definitely what constitutes the higher or the lower degree of reward among the saved: it is always a deeper comprehension of God in his Essence. More or less of divine life is added unto the soul. With the lost we have no such provision. So we may content ourselves with the general principle that sin is visited in eternity according to its gravity. The Inferno of Dante is the poetical presentment of a very grave truth. Yet it is good Christian feeling to hold that the vindictive justice of God is not as comprehensive as is his remunerative justice; even the reprobate is punished less severely than he deserves. One theological principle whose validity is beyond doubt could be invoked here to bring out this difference in remuneration and punishment. Whatever supernatural merits man had during lifetime, those merits are counted unto him as an increase of glory, though it may have happened very often that by the act of mortal sin the merits were, so to speak, killed. If the sin is repented of, if the Christian

[1] John iii 18, 19.

die in a state of grace, all his merits are revived for him. Now there is no such bringing back of past sin. So, if a man has sinned much but has repented, even if afterwards he sin again and die in his sin, those sins are not brought back to him of which he had repented.

The profoundest thing said by any theologian in this matter of eternal reprobation is the utterance of St Thomas Aquinas: "Eternity of pain does not correspond to the gravity of the guilt but it corresponds to the irreparable nature of the guilt." [1]

It may seem strange at first sight that a less guilty man should be lost everlastingly as much as one who may be a million times more guilty. Now according to St Thomas the real punishment inflicted by divine justice does not lie in the fact that it is everlasting, for such everlastingness is the condition of everything spiritual, but that the special burden lain on the reprobate spirit corresponding to his guilt is indeed the direct act of the divine judgement. What this punishment is we have no means of knowing. But as Catholic theology has always maintained that reprobation is entirely the result of divine justice, this doctrine has its mitigations in its very definition. We do not say of any man that he is eternally subject to this or to that torment; in such a case we should find it difficult to give an explanation that would be satisfying. But we say that God visits justly all sins for which there is not due repentance before death. So to speak, we approach the whole subject from God's point of view, and we leave it with God; we know he could do nothing unjust without denying himself.

§ XI: THE LAST JUDGEMENT

Its catastrophic nature

THE phraseology of the Scriptures does not always make it very apparent whether certain happenings which are prophesied are to be catastrophic events of short duration or long periods of God's visitation. Thus, in the various utterances of Christ concerning the end of the world it is not easy to distinguish lengthy times of tribulation from sudden manifestations of God's anger, appearing with the rapidity of lightning. Many of God's judgements are long drawn-out punitions and the catastrophic chastisements are, on the whole, rare. A thought frequently expressed in a certain class of modern literature is this, that the World's History is the World's Judgement. There is much truth in such a view. There is, however, no doubt whatever concerning the nature of the Last Judgement; it is described as an event of terrifying suddenness and as something entirely outside the historic development of mankind. Its date is so mysterious that no one knows it, not even the angels of God: "But of that day and hour no one knoweth: no, not the angels of heaven, but the Father alone." [2] Even the signs which are to be the precursors of that day will be no clear indication of its exact hour: "For yourselves

[1] *Summa*, I-II, Q. lxxxvii, art. 5.

[2] Matt. xxiv 36.

know perfectly that the day of the Lord shall so come as a thief in the night. For when they shall say: Peace and security; then shall sudden destruction come upon them, as the pains upon her that is with child. And they shall not escape."[1] The Last Judgement, therefore, ought to be regarded by us as a great mystery, as to its date, as to its nature, and as to its purpose. We can, in a way, understand the meaning of those temporal judgements of which we have spoken above; we can even grasp the doctrine of God's dealings with the soul at death; but when we come to the Last Judgement we are in presence of a dogma which is entirely outside all experience and for which we have no terms of comparison. Very wisely, in a passage quoted in an earlier page, St Thomas considers the Last Judgement as the counterpart of the creation of all things out of nothing. No finite measure can be applied to that greatest of all events, it is an act on an infinite scale. It is true that several very precious hints are dropped by the inspired writers as to its tremendous import, but the few suggestions which are given are in themselves allusions to possibilities quite beyond our grasp. The most constantly recurring idea is this, that God will reveal all things on that day; but it is easy to see that such revelation is a mystery, great beyond all words. So we must exert our faith and believe that God will make all things manifest, as we believe that at the beginning he created light. How this revelation will take place no finite mind can know, because it is truly the revelation of an infinite thing—the whole economy of God's grace on the one hand, and the whole range of the created free will on the other; so that not only facts but even possibilities will be disclosed, in order to discover to every eye God's providence in all its perfection.

A unique event

Nor would it be in keeping with Catholic thought to say that the Last Judgement is nothing else than the beginning of eternity or the state of eternity. It is to be an event, a passing act of finite duration, not an everlasting condition. There will be a moment when that great judgement will begin and there will be a moment when it will end, though its results will be interminable. In other words, it will be an act of God such as he never did before and such as he will not again repeat. Never again will the human race be gathered in all its entirety as at that supreme hour, but that such an assemblage of all the human beings that ever existed will take place is one of the very few clear indications concerning that act of God that has been made known, though the race, thus brought together, will be separated again, and this for all eternity: "And when the Son of man shall come in his majesty, and all the angels with him, then shall he sit on the seat of his majesty. And all nations shall be gathered together before him: and he shall separate them one from another, as the shepherd separateth the sheep from the goats: And he shall set the sheep on his right hand, but the goats on his left."[2] A revelation

[1] 1 Thess. v 2, 3.

[2] Matt. xxv 31-33.

will then be made which will be truly miraculous in its effects, but transient as a divine act. This revelation will be given to the wicked as much as to the elect. It is a manifestation of God's justice and sanctity, different in kind from that Vision of God which the elect in their souls enjoy even now before the great day. Nothing but an act of divine omnipotence can explain that manifestation of God's justice to all flesh. This great event is invariably called the "day of the Lord" as if it were an event so particularly different from all other historic happenings as to be the one day outside eternity worthy of the Son of God. Its importance will be commensurate with the Person of the God Incarnate.

Four manifestations

The day of the Lord consists in four manifestations of God's omnipotence whose literal reality cannot be doubted by any Catholic: there will be the destruction of the physical world through fire; there will be the raising up of all the dead; there will be the revelation of all the hidden things of man's conscience and God's providence; and then, ultimately, there will be the separation of the good and the wicked. The day of the Lord will contain all that, and the term "Last Judgement" may be applied to this whole complex of divine operation. It is certain that the Resurrection of the dead will precede the judgement, properly so-called; there is more room for doubting the sequence of happenings with regard to the universal conflagration, but it would seem that the fire in which all men then living will find their death will be the first act in this tremendous drama. Out of the ruins of the world that was till then, a new world will be created which will be truly part of the Resurrection. It will be in that new world that the judgement will take place; it will be in that new world that Christ will appear in glory and majesty. St Thomas adopts this order for these great mysteries. The world will be purified in that searching fire and the reprobate will be cast out of it, because they will be unworthy of it in its new perfection.

It is evident that no pictorial presentment can be attempted of so vast a change of all things. The great ideas of the Scriptures are still the most potent and most satisfying expressions. To try to depict the Last Judgement will always be a miserable failure, even if the artist be a Michelangelo. Just let us take in their literal meaning words like the following, in which the four great facts are described, and we shall be as near visualising that solemn truth as it is possible for man to be.

"The Lord delayeth not his promise, as some imagine, but dealeth patiently for your sake, not willing that any should perish, but that all should return to penance. But the day of the Lord shall come as a thief, in which the heavens shall pass away with great violence and the elements shall be melted with heat and the earth and the works which are in it shall be burnt up. Seeing then that all these things are to be dissolved, what manner of people ought you to be in holy conversation and godliness? Looking for and hasting unto the coming of the day of the Lord, by which the heavens being on fire shall be dissolved and the elements shall melt with the burning heat. But we look for new heavens and a new earth according to his promises, in which justice dwelleth."[1]

"Wonder not at this: for the hour cometh, wherein all that are in the graves shall hear the voice of the Son of God. And they that have done good things shall come forth unto the resurrection of life; but they that have done evil, unto the resurrection of judgement."[2]

"Their conscience bearing witness to them: and their thoughts between themselves accusing or also defending one another, in the day when God shall judge the secrets of men by Jesus Christ."[3]

"Then shall the king say to them that shall be on his right hand: Come, ye blessed of my Father, possess you the kingdom prepared for you from the foundation of the world. . . . Then shall he say to them also that shall be on his left hand: Depart from me, you cursed, into everlasting fire, which was prepared for the devil and his angels."[4]

Christ judges

Christ will do the judgement in Person, he will appear as the God-Man, in full glory. Whether his coming will be before or after the conflagration and the Resurrection it is not possible to say; but that he will execute judgement is in the very essence of our Creed: *Qui venturus est judicare vivos et mortuos.* Much more, indeed, could be said concerning the many speculations of theologians about things of such magnitude; but there is just one article of St Thomas which, through its very dignity, is not out of place here: "Whether the judgement be done by word of mouth." "It is difficult to say with any certainty what is true in this matter; however, it seems more probable that all that judgement from the point of view of the discussion, from the point of view of the accusation of the wicked, and of the praise of the good, and from the point of view of the sentence pronounced over both classes, will be carried out only mentally. For if the deeds of every one were spoken orally, a length of time would be necessary, great beyond all concept."[5]

The elect judge

There are in the Gospels and in the Epistles words of great solemnity which compel us to stop one moment more in our considerations on the Last Judgement. Christ and his Apostles declare, with the greatest emphasis possible, that the elect will also judge, that they will be seated in majesty as judges on that day: "And Jesus said to them: Amen, I say to you that you, who have followed me, in the regeneration when the Son of man shall sit on the seat of his majesty, you also shall sit on twelve seats judging the twelve tribes of Israel."[6] St Paul makes use of this great Christian hope in order to pour contempt on the quarrelsomeness of some of the Corinthians who went to law before the unbelievers: "Know you not that the saints shall judge this world? And if the world shall be judged by

[1] 2 Pet. iii 9-13.
[2] John v 28, 29.
[3] Rom. ii 15, 16.
[4] Matt. xxv 34 and 41.
[5] *Suppl.* lxxxviii, art. 2.
[6] Matt. xix 28.

you, are you unworthy to judge the smallest matters? Know you not that we shall judge angels? How much more things of this world?"[1] Such words are too clear to admit of any other interpretation than a literal one. There will evidently be an active participation of the elect, or at least some of the elect, in that final condemnation of the world. The Fathers freely use a term which no doubt recalled a familiar scene in the Roman law courts, they speak of assessors, men who sat by the side of the judge, by their very presence giving support and approval to his verdict; it was natural for them to say that the saints will be Christ's assessors on that day. The practice of religious poverty in life or the merit of martyrdom would single out a person to be specially fit to be Christ's assessor when he will speak his terrific anathema over sinful mankind. But even without metaphors it ought to be easy for us in a way to understand that the very contrast between the high sanctity of so many of the elect and the darkness of the reprobate will be a judgement severe beyond words.

Christ's alleged eschatological obsession

We could not conclude this section without reference to a matter which is one of the undying controversies of both friend and foe. The enemies of Christ's Godhead have often said—and they are still saying it—that Jesus had what might be called an eschatological obsession; he was under the impression that the world would soon come to an end, and he announced his appearance as Judge of the living and the dead as an event not far distant, in fact to take place in the lifetime of the men who were his foes. And as such a catastrophe has evidently not taken place, Christ's claim to be God is an untenable ambition. On this subject volumes have been written. It is certain that our Lord warned the men with whom he lived, and especially the Apostles, always to watch lest their Lord and Master, coming at an unexpected moment, find them asleep. But, on the other hand, it is just as evident that Christ leaves the hour of that advent in great uncertainty and that no one could conclude from his words that he taught a coming in the immediate future. There is in all those passages which either inculcate vigilance or else leave the date of the Master's return in such uncertainty, a blending of the near future and the mysteriously remote future which is truly unparalleled. Thus, speaking of the near future, Christ says: "Take ye heed, watch and pray. For ye know not when the time is. Even as a man who, going into a far country, left his house and gave authority to his servants over every work and commanded the porter to watch. Watch ye therefore (for you know not when the lord of the house cometh, at even, or at midnight, or at the cock-crowing, or in the morning): Lest coming on a sudden, he find you sleeping. And what I say to you I say to all: Watch."[2] All this sounds as if Christ meant his Apostles to expect the possibility of the judgement at any time, and yet in the verse before: "But of that day or hour

[1] I Cor. vi 2–3.

[2] Mark xiii 33-37.

no man knoweth, neither the angels in heaven, nor the Son, but the Father," [1] we have his most emphatic utterance as to the unknowable character of the great event.

So we have again a description on the part of our Lord of the kingdom of God which is anything but catastrophic : " And he said : So is the kingdom of God, as if a man should cast seed into the earth, and should sleep and rise, night and day, and the seed should spring and grow up whilst he knoweth not. For the earth of itself bringeth forth fruit, first the blade, then the ear, afterwards the full corn in the ear. And when the fruit is brought forth, immediately he putteth in the sickle, because the harvest is come." [2] Here we see the world's history described in the metaphor of a ripening field : the Sower himself, who is evidently Christ, is as one who leaves the seed to itself to do its work, as one who has gone away. So we might multiply instances of that mysterious blending of the two ideas, the necessity of watchfulness and the remoteness of the final harvesting. But if we bear in mind what has been said in an earlier page, how Christ's judicial operations are unceasing, we can readily understand how there is need for every man to be always on the watch. The coming of Christ to each one at death is a complete judgement, and he who is not prepared for that coming is truly a foolish man. Thus those well-known parables on the necessity of watchfulness have been applied by the Christian doctors both to the individual human being, always in danger of death, and also to the whole human race, always in danger of the catastrophic advent of Christ. This is truly a divine grasp of the situation ; what is true of man in his universality is also true of man individually. If we take it for granted that Christ at no moment ceases to be Judge, then we shall easily comprehend the complete actuality of all his parables and utterances with regard to the imprudence of being unprepared for his coming. It is a terrible thing to fall into the hands of the living God. Even without waiting for that new world we serve him now with " fear and reverence. For our God is a consuming fire." [3]

Whatever may have been the thoughts of the Apostles before Pentecost concerning the establishment of a triumphant kingdom of their Master during their own lifetime, it is certain that when once they had begun their great ministry the catastrophic coming of Christ was as much part of their preaching as it had been in that of their Lord. It was a certainty ; the date of it mattered but little for practical behaviour, Christians had always to be ready : " But the heavens and the earth which are now, by the same word are kept in store, reserved unto fire against the day of judgement and perdition of the ungodly men. But of this one thing be not ignorant, my beloved, that one day with the Lord is as a thousand years, and a thousand years as one day. The Lord delayeth not his promise, as some imagine, but dealeth patiently for your sake, not willing that

[1] Mark xiii 32. [2] Mark iv 26-29. [3] Heb. xii 28, 29.

any should perish, but that all should return to penance. But the day of the Lord shall come as a thief, in which the heavens shall pass away with great violence and the elements shall be melted with heat and the earth and the works which are in it shall be burnt up." [1]

Millenarism

Another form of illusion in this great matter of Christ's second advent has been much more universal, much more persistent, and is, in a way, more easily forgivable. This form of religious dreaming is even older than the Gospels; it is man's hope of the millennium. It has always been the faith of certain pious people, whom the iniquities of the world have afflicted in their souls, that there would be on this earth some day a very magnificent kingdom of God. With the advent of Christianity it was, of course, Christ who would be the King of that happy era of human sanctity. It is not easy to contradict people and prove them to be wrong if they profess a hope in some mighty triumph of Christ here on earth before the final consummation of all things. Such an occurrence is not excluded, is not impossible, it is not at all certain that there may not be a prolonged period of triumphant Christianity before the end. The point of division between the legitimate aspirations of devout souls and the aberrations of false millenarism is this: the Chiliasts—as believers in the millennium are called, from the Greek word for thousand—seem to expect a coming of Christ and a presence of him in glory and majesty on this earth which would not be the consummation of all things but would still be a portion of the history of mankind. This is not consonant with Catholic dogma. The coming of Christ in the second Advent—the Parousia, as it is called technically—in orthodox Christianity is the consummation of all things, the end of human history. If before that final end there is to be a period, more or less prolonged, of triumphant sanctity, such a result will be brought about, not by the apparition of the Person of Christ in Majesty but by the operation of those powers of sanctification which are now at work, the Holy Ghost and the Sacraments of the Church. The Chiliasts of all times and shades of opinion, and there are many to be found even to-day, seem to despair, not only of the world, but even of that dispensation of grace which was inaugurated at Pentecost; they expect from the visible presence of Christ a complete conversion of the world, as if such a happy result could not be otherwise brought about. They have still to learn the meaning of Christ's words to the Apostles: "It is expedient to you that I go. For if I go not, the Paraclete will not come to you: but if I go, I will send him to you." [2]

The Catholic Church has full confidence in the present order of supernatural life, and if she sighs for the return of her Christ it is not because she despairs of the work he has done, but because she desires to see that work made manifest to all men, that it may appear what wondrous things Christ accomplished for man before his Ascension into heaven.

ANSCAR VONIER, O.S.B.

[1] 2 Peter iii 7-10.
[2] John xvi 7.

XXXII

PURGATORY, OR THE CHURCH SUFFERING

§ I: PARDON AND PENANCE

Penance follows pardon

IN purgatory, souls suffer for a time after death on account of their sins: either for venial sins that are not repented nor forgiven before death; or for sins whose guilt was forgiven in this life, but whose due of punishment is to be completed after death.

Healthy-minded children feel it quite natural that after forgiveness of a fault they have still penance to do for it. The child is forgiven as soon as he is brought to see that he has done wrong and to be sorry. He is forgiven in a moment; the father takes him back into friendship again. But it is a serious, chastened friendship. He sees his father's love shown now in trying to make him a better boy, teaching him to realise the wrongness of what he has done, and the seriousness of wilfully choosing such wrong-doing. He feels that his fault calls for punishment; he accepts the punishment and takes it understandingly, not welcoming it, but seeing that, just because he does not like it, it is what he needs to set right his sin. In such a child, the actual bearing of the punishment when it comes does not lead to any rebellion or sulkiness. It may be that for a week, night after night, he has to be sent to bed early, while the other children are not. Each time it is a hard and bitter reminder of his fault and repentance; but he knows it is the thing that ought to be, and he feels no soreness about it. In the daily life of a Catholic school, one of the most beautiful things is to see this acceptance of punishment going on constantly: the boy doing his penance at the appointed times, and in the intervals exchanging thoughts with the teacher in the most frank and friendly way. On the other hand, a child who knows he ought to be punished and is not, feels at first that in some way right is not being done and wrong is to be let go free. Soon, no doubt, he loses his sense of right and wrong about his own doings. But, as manhood approaches, often he blames his parents that they did not correct him when he had no sense to correct himself.

A healthy-minded child sees this truth, that after repenting and obtaining forgiveness, we should then take our punishment. But many parents do not see it. If their temper is roused, they punish the child; if not, they do nothing to check his fault; and so the child is spoiled. Their only notion of forgiveness is forgiving punishment. Yet even they in many cases feel the need of making atonement when they have offended a neighbour and been forgiven.

Anyone who wants to understand the existence of purgatory must ponder this point till he feels the need for punishment as well as forgiveness.

The Catechism speaks often of bearing punishment for our sins after God has forgiven our guilt. The guilt is the badness in the will, the badness which consented to do this wrong. Repentance is changing our mind, judging sin as God judges it. Not merely " I know it was wrong and ought never to have been done," but " I wish, as God wishes, that I had never done it." That change of mind God himself enables us to make, in contrition and in confession ; and thereby he forgives us and makes friends with us. What punishment shall we now suffer, to atone to him ? The priest appoints us penance, by God's authority. Not always is this enough ; perhaps not often. There will be other penances appointed by the Church, fasting and abstaining, to satisfy for our sins. And yet others, the best penances of all, sent by God himself—crosses, sicknesses, pains ; and we should say " Lord, I take these for my sins." Again, we ourselves should devise further atonements ; either by doing good works to satisfy for our bad works, or by punishments self-inflicted. Here the Church helps us. She suggests good works and penances for us to choose from, when we seek something to offer to God in atonement. By her power of loosing on earth what shall be loosed also in heaven, she makes these good works and penances take the place of much longer and greater punishment, if our sorrow and desire to atone be such as to fit us in God's sight to receive this indulgence. And after all this, when we depart this life, we expect to find that we have not fully paid our due punishment for our sins. We set the littleness of our penances and good works beside the majesty of God and his outraged love ; we see how unsteady and incomplete are our highest efforts, and how our daily weaknesses and unmastered habits stain us anew after all our repentings and atonings ; and we look for the days of purgation, when there shall be no distraction nor weakness nor power to sin, and the soul can give its whole being to suffer in an agony of longing to be clean.

Suffering needed for atonement and cleansing

Why is suffering needed to cleanse us ? Some have thought of God as a hard creditor, fixing the tax of pain for every sin or every sinner. But we must not think that right and wrong are fixed arbitrarily by God ; for they rest on his very nature. Not, It is right that we should suffer for sin, since God so commands ; rather, He commands it because it is right. And in his goodness he has made us like himself ; giving us light not only to see what is his will, but also to see to some extent what he sees. Therefore let us try to see why it is right that after repenting our sins we must suffer for them.

Consider a spirit, angel or man, that defies God and disobeys his will. Imagine that God consents to this ; treats the rebellious spirit as a welcome friend, as a fitting companion for the sinless angels and for God himself. Imagine that God creates spirits such that they can find eternal and untroubled happiness in defying their Maker, and can bask unrebuked in his love. Do we not feel at once that this is not God that we are picturing ? that in some way eternal justice would be violated if these things were possible, and the holiness of God would be profaned ? If God be God, such defyings and rebellion and all unholiness must be hateful to him. His very nature requires that all sin shall bring its own punishment on the sinner.

Again, consider the sinner who discovers and realises what he has done in defying his Maker. He sees at once that punishment unthinkable is his due. Only two alternatives seem possible to him : the despair of devils and of Judas, if he has lost all love for God ; or, if he keeps any root of love, then the wish to suffer to the limits of his nature, that in some way he may acknowledge the majesty and the holiness that he has outraged. To him comes the gift of hope ; the seemingly unbelievable yet certain knowledge that God's all-mastering power can so change him from his sin that he shall be as if he had never sinned. The Magdalen shall dwell unabashed with the spotless Mother of God ; yea, and with God himself. With this hope to enlighten him, the sinner sees he is to make an atonement far ampler than he had thought. He will suffer now, and by his sufferings not only atone to the Majesty he had insulted, but also restore to God the servant and friend who seemed lost, rendering up his own soul new-made in the fires of God's love.

There are, therefore, two reasons for suffering for sin : first, atonement to God ; and second, the re-making of our souls. And we can see that suffering for these purposes may well last long. If we look at the suffering endured to atone to God, there is no reason why it should ever end, except his mercy. And the remaking of our souls is slow. A wound or sprain is received in an instant, but very slowly is it healed. A sin is committed in an instant by an act of will, and forgiven in an instant when the will submits in love to God ; but the mischief wrought by the sin in our nature is deep, and slow to mend.

A drunkard can repent in an instant ; he may struggle for years before he is a sober man again. By his sin, his bodily appetite for drink has grown unnaturally strong ; as do all bodily appetites that are sinfully indulged. The bodily appetite has to be brought back to its natural state by painful self-denial. His will has lost the habit of controlling the body. Probably it has even made itself the servant of the body, using its reason to find ways of gratifying the body's desires. Slowly the soul must regain its natural mastery over all its servants—the appetites, passions, habits, imagination, and other powers. And in the very soul itself, evil habits have formed—habits of pride ; of self-will and stubbornness ; the all-pervading habit of untruth, that seeks excuses for telling itself that the sin is not sinful, that the danger is not dangerous, that the voice of God is not his voice. And it may easily be that the soul has grown fond of being ruled by its servants and of indulging their desires.

With God's grace and man's faithful labour, all these mischiefs can be undone in the end. But we cannot wonder if it takes a very long time, and is still uncompleted when death comes. "With the Lord, one day is as a thousand years," in this as in all else. To our seeing, the new making of our souls is a task for a thousand years. But the power and the mercy of God can do it in an instant. The Church sings of the martyrs fitted for heaven *Mortis sacrae compendio*, by the crowded action of their holy death. For what God does slowly through our years of prayer and self-denial and suffering is still God's work, not ours. He it is that gives to these exercises the power to rebuild the soul. But when he chooses to do this himself, he has no need of the long delays and the painful processes ; his word, his will, does its work in an instant.

How suffering cleanses

We have said that to repair the ills that sin has wrought in our nature, suffering is ordinarily necessary and is the means appointed by God. Let us now consider how suffering does its work of healing. There are three points to consider : the bodily appetites, overgrown and unhealthy, have to be brought back to their natural limits ; the soul's control over the body is to be restored ; and the soul itself is to be freed from all wrong habits and desires.

Common experience teaches us that in sickness or in great pain all the bodily appetites are numbed and silenced for the time being. The body has no pleasure in its work nor in its resting. And the same effect on the body can come from mental anguish ; from worry or great grief, when a man can neither eat nor sleep. But these are only temporary effects, lasting while the suffering lasts. Carried on long enough, such pain or grief might reduce to natural strength a drunkard's craving for drink, or a passion for gambling, and other such overgrown appetites. But, meantime, temper may be growing to unnatural strength ; or melancholy, or nervous fear, or some other passion. For there is a natural balance in the body, and a reaction and resistance against repression. So that when the suffering is over, old cravings may reassert themselves, and new cravings may have developed during the pain. It is clear, therefore, that suffering does not of itself set right the bodily nature. It is an instrument that can help to set it right, but only if the soul uses it for that purpose. If the soul is firmly resolved to master the craving for drink or other vices, it can do so by subjecting the body to regular work, by denial of ease and of many gratifications and comforts ; and by inflicting positive sufferings with prudence and moderation, at times when it is necessary to distract the body from a sudden awakening of its craving. By such self-denial and wilful suffering a man can reduce his unnaturally strong cravings for a time to something like their natural force ; and so he at the same time regains to some extent his soul's control over the body. Some saints, by continuing this discipline wisely, gently, but unrelentingly, have reduced their bodily passions to far below their natural activity, and so acquired a more than natural control over the whole body.

For the sake of his business career, a man might resolve once for all to master his craving for drink, and therefore undertake to discipline and deny his body and finally succeed and be free from the craving. Or an athlete may discipline his body for the sake of his sports. The healthy state of the body so acquired, and the soul's control over the body, are both good as far as they go. But they only go as far as the purpose which inspired them. In things that do not endanger the business career or the athlete's success, he will allow the body its own way. Or worse, the soul, the will, may make itself the servant of the body's delights in other ways, to compensate for its hardships and discipline. In such case it is evident that the sufferings inflicted on the body are only making it healthy in part and subjecting it to the soul in part. Meanwhile there may be other cravings and passions in the body growing to unnatural proportions and enslaving the soul.

There is another danger, of forming bad habits and vices in the soul itself. The Pharisee fasted twice in the week, and the only effect on his soul was to make him proud that he was not as the rest of men. A defiant schoolboy may seek punishments simply to show that he will not be mastered by them. In times of famine or distress, parents may bear double hunger for the sake of their children, and at the same time embitter their own souls against God who allows such things. In all these cases the suffering that is borne undoes no sin nor effect of sin, but is misused by the soul to bind itself deeper in sin. There is another more spiritual sin. A man, for instance, who has prided himself on a perfectly honourable life, falls once into dishonesty when faced with sudden strong temptation. He will not move among honourable men any more. He says he cannot look an honourable man in the face, being himself a thief. He is told to repent, to atone, to begin a new life. " If I did so," he says, " I should still be a thief. Nothing can undo the fact that I am a thief, nor make me an honest man." He is told that God's power and God's love will make him into an honest man again, and will forgive him. He answers, " I could never forgive myself." This is sin, in the very depths of his spirit. All that God offers him does not satisfy him. For it will not give him the one thing that he wants. He wants to regain his pride in himself, as one who was always honourable. He knows that God cannot give him this, and therefore he rejects God. For God is not offering him pride in himself, but on the contrary humility. His sin is not to be undone as a thing that never was. All its evil effects are to be undone, and the memory of it is to live with him for ever, embodied in his humility. God is all and I am nothing. I did nothing but sin ; he has taken me, the thief, from the dunghill and changed me till I am fit to sit with the princes of his people in his kingdom.

It is to this humility and perfect truth that God calls us ; and the path by which we are to reach it is the path of suffering. We must chastise the body and bring it into subjection ; the soul too must suffer in its own way. But these chastisings and wilful sufferings must never be separated from the consciousness that it is I that ought to suffer, because it was I that consented to the sin. With that thought, we can safely punish and mortify the body, and accept humiliations and wrongs from our neighbours, and crosses and sufferings from the hand of God. These will do the work that God means them to do in our souls. By making our nature and giving us free will, God has made us unable to receive any spiritual good to our souls unless we consent. We give him the consent he wants when we say, I ought to suffer to atone for wronging the majesty of God ; gladly I give myself into his hands to suffer, and by suffering to be cleansed and rebuilt.

Penance after death

At death a soul may be in one of three states. Thinking of sin, we say that a person dies in mortal sin, or in venial sin, or dies free from all sin. We can see more clearly by thinking of the love of God ; that charity of God which is poured forth in our hearts by the Holy Ghost, who is given to us in baptism.[1] A soul may be entirely without this love of God—either because it has never received it and is still in the state of original sin ; or because after receiving the gift of love in baptism, it has rejected God's love for the sake of self or of creatures, and thereby has fallen into mortal sin. If death finds a person in this state, the lack of divine charity shuts him out of heaven for ever. Another soul may have the love of God still living in it, and be determined to love him, but hampered and hindered by attractions to creatures, by bad habits that have been formed by small sins and have not been uprooted. A soul dying in this state goes to purgatory—not to hell, for its love for God is that sanctifying grace that is the beginning of his eternal friendship in heaven. But not yet can it enter heaven, till all unworthiness is burned out of it by suffering wilfully accepted.

A third soul at death may be filled with the love of God and free from all stain of sin, and therefore pass straight to behold God in heaven. Such was our Lady's soul ; such also are the souls of babes baptised who die before they can sin. In such a soul, the whole nature is prompt at the service of God. The soul in man's nature holds a position like to that of the commander of a ship or of a regiment in the king's service. To do his duty perfectly, the commander must on one hand have his men completely under his control, and so trained that he can be sure of instant and thorough obedience to all his orders. And on the other side he must himself be at all moments at his king's call ; his will firm to carry out the king's

[1] Rom. v 5.

commands perfectly; his mind habitually devoted to studying his business, so that he may promptly understand the commands he receives and how to carry them out. So in the glorious Mother of God, her soul's will was unshakably set to do the divine will in all things. Her whole study was to understand and rejoice in his love. And the whole of her nature was prompt to do the biddings of her soul, as she moved her servants to do her Lord's will. In a new-baptised babe, the soul has not begun to take charge of its servants in the lower nature; nor is there yet any power to actually think of God or to actually love him. So that the inpouring of love in baptism is seen most clearly to be a pure grace, an utterly unearned gift from God's love; and the bringing the babe to heaven at death is simply due to his divine joy in giving happiness.

We who have sinned know too well how disordered is our whole nature. We do not get from our servants, the powers and passions of the body, the obedience they should give, instant, tranquil, joyous. When we want them to obey God's commands, we have to fight to make them do it. And in our souls there is little power to understand promptly the will of God. We are deaf to his whisperings, and awake to the clamour of the world. What little we understand of his bidding, we water down by blending it with the folly of human knowledge and maxims and prudence. As to our very will to serve him, we can, it is true, by his grace resolve in an instant that he must be obeyed always, in all things, completely; but the will does not last. And the Church has to warn us to pray that he will steady it and force it to keep right; *nutantia corda tu dirigas*; *nostras etiam rebelles compelle voluntates.* And since we find ourselves always or nearly always in this state, it is reasonable to think that most of us will still be in this state when death comes. And we shall still be looking forward to the day when all our powers and our whole nature will move in complete accord with the soul, and the soul will unceasingly move, as do the angels in heaven, in complete and loving accord with the will of God. That day will come when our purgatory is over. There our inconstancy and our many backslidings will bring their own punishment, when through much pain we acquire that freedom and mastery which here we threw away, and clear the soul from all hindrances till its love for God can burn steady and untroubled.

False religions, such as Buddhism and Spiritualism, have recognised this fact, that at death most men are not yet fitted for eternal rest. All false religions are built of fragments of truth, built up into a nightmare of falsehood. Here the question they face is a real question. All our lives we see before us a high standard calling us to live up to it, and at death we have not reached it; how are we to reach it after death? They invent wild and sometimes ghastly answers. But the true answer is: by the power of God, through the purifying power of suffering; and this we name purgatory.

These false religions think only of the perfecting of man's soul, not of giving God his due. And thereby they leave out the highest part of man's perfection. Certainly man should grieve that he has lowered and degraded himself by sin, and should rejoice to rise to better things. This grief is a necessary part of the whole agony entailed by sins; but if it stand alone it is merely pride, part of a great rejection of truth. For the chief cause of agony ought to be the knowledge that he has ill-treated God, despised his majesty, outraged his holiness, rejected his love. The soul in purgatory, realising what is due to God, loving him with its whole being, will wish above all things to atone for its sin by suffering worthy punishment. If it could be content to leave in the smallest degree unrepaired the wrongs it has done to God, it would be far from the perfection that is possible to saints even in this life. In purgatory the soul longs to suffer in order to be clean, to suffer in order to reach God; but above all these is its longing to suffer in order to make amends to the Divine Majesty, Holiness, Love. For its love of God is everything to it now; its desire for its own purification and happiness is part of its love for God.

Those who are entangled in these false religions are likely to lose all sense of what is due to God. They may talk of man rising through sphere after sphere to perfection; but the perfection they talk of is simply their fancy of the moment; for they have lost sight of man's true perfection. And often they seem to fall into a further blindness. In thinking of man's future perfection as compared with his state in this life, they see his present faults and falls as merely an earlier stage of development; as imperfections to be grown out of, not as sins to be lamented and atoned for. They lose first the sense of God, and then the sense of sin.

§ II: THE PAINS OF PURGATORY

The love in purgatory

WE must keep in mind the main facts.

The suffering souls are still on the way to heaven; but they have arrived at the stage when their salvation is sure; there is no further doubt or danger of not reaching heaven. Death found them loving God, each with his own degree of love. That love can never now grow to greater heights nor fall lower; for their time of trial is over.

That love has earned them the right to go to heaven; and therefore the right to be freed from all that delays their entering heaven.

The hindrances that keep them back are their unrepented venial sins; and the attachments to creatures that through sin have taken root in their souls; and the atonement they must make for their now forgiven sins.

Since their time of trial is over, they themselves can do nothing now to fit themselves for heaven. Therefore the removing of these hindrances must be done by God. The means by which he removes them is suffering.

Their love for God makes them long to atone to him and to be wholly pleasing to him. Consequently they long to suffer all that is needed to atone and to make them pleasing to God.

In trying to picture the state of a soul in purgatory, we must put first its intense love for God. This love it had in this world, where those who are to be saved acquire each in their own degree a love of God above all else ; some thirty-fold, some sixty-fold, some a hundred-fold. The level of love they have reached at death is the level of what they will be capable of for all eternity. Immediately after death, this love is released from all the distractions and darknesses that sin has wrought in the body, and is drawn towards God by the sight of his love for the soul he has made and saved. From that moment, this love for God is the one overmastering activity of the soul. Whatever other activities it may have, we must think of them as included in this love, springing from this love, and giving effect to it. Looking at his majesty as Creator of all, this love sees that it is worth dying even the death of the cross to give him his due reverence, and atone to him for sin. Looking at his holiness, love sees that it is worth dying the death of the cross to purify souls from all that is unworthy to God. Looking at his love, the soul sees and feels the overwhelming truth : he loves even me, and is drawing me to a complete union of love with himself.

This love for God gives to the soul happiness unspeakable. But at the same time it finds itself hindered by its past sins from flying freely to the love of its God ; and this hindrance is an agony to it, becoming the cause of its grief and its longings. At seeing that it has insulted the majesty of God and outraged his love, it is in anguish. A fire like hell springs up within it, says St Catherine of Genoa. Its love is tortured at being held back from God, at knowing itself stained by sin, and therefore unfit for him. We must remember always that these pains and griefs are not a distraction from its love for God, but are the fruit of the working of that love. It is precisely because the love is working so vehemently that it produces these agonies of grief. The love itself is such a joy that the hindrances become unspeakable pain.

From this love also spring all the longings of the soul ; the longing to atone to God for sin ; the longing to be clean from all stain, for God's sake, that his servant may be what he wishes ; the longing to be with God ; the longing to suffer all that he wills, which is also a joy in suffering and being cleansed as he wills, when he wills, how he wills. For this joy in his will being done is the highest part of the soul's love for him. So it rejoices in knowing that he is purifying it in his own way, and that he will in the end bring it to himself, purified through and through.

Our Blessed Lord has shown us in himself the pattern and model which the soul imitates in purgatory. It was his love for his Father's glory, and his love for souls and for their purity, that brought him on earth to die. We know how intense were the sufferings he took on him, by his agony, when he prayed, "If it be possible, let this chalice pass from me."[1] But he showed how these sufferings were part of his love for his Father and his hatred of sin, when he said, "I have a baptism wherewith I am to be baptised: and how am I straitened till it be accomplished."[2] His love for his Father gave him always the very happiness and joy of the blessed in heaven; and this very love called for and embraced the sufferings that would give effect to his love's desire.

After this pattern, the love which a soul in purgatory has for God produces, and calls for, and embraces the sufferings of purgatory. It would not for anything be without these sufferings, since they are the necessary and just and holy means appointed by God to satisfy its love for God, by atoning to him and fitting the soul for him. And in this sense it suffers willingly, and with its whole being chooses to suffer, as did our Lord. But, at the same time, the very essence of the suffering is that the soul is hindered from what it most desires and chooses—to be wholly pleasing and spotless in God's sight, to be united with him in a love complete and untroubled.

Pain of deferment

There is in us a power to love the best, and a longing to be partakers of it. The best that we know is God's joy in all that is holy, all that is noble; secondarily, in the created holiness and nobility of men and angels; but first, and wholly, in his own uncreated holiness and generous love. This holiness and love is himself, and his joy in it is infinite. And his very self is that uncreated joy in his infinite holiness and love. Into that joy we long to enter. Even now on earth we have this longing, and we look forward to death as the gate whereby we shall enter into that joy. At death, released from the distractions and attractions bred by sin in the body, we shall see far more clearly the loveliness of the joy of God, and our longing for it will be the only longing left in us, possessing therefore the whole strength of the soul. But if we are still stained with sin unrepented or unatoned for, we shall know instantly that we are unworthy to enter into that joy; and this knowledge is agony to the soul. Our very love for that infinite holiness of God makes it a horror to think of intruding upon it unclean. Our agony at being shut out from it is blent with the deeper agony at our having outraged it.

In making intelligent beings, us and the angels, Almighty God has inseparably bound up our happiness with his own glory. He made us for happiness; he made us for his glory. It is part of his glory, a very tiny part, that he gives eternal happiness to one of us. But the whole of our happiness lies in giving him the glory that is

[1] Matt. xxvi 39. [2] Luke xii 50.

his due, such glory as can come from us. We desire our own happiness; deepest in our hearts is the undying longing for eternal rest. But our folly and our sin is that we put asunder what God has joined; we would have happiness without giving him glory. At death the soul awakes to a new knowledge: to see the beauty of God's holiness, the majesty of his glory that fills heaven and earth with his kingship; to feel with its whole being the drawing of his love, infinite, special and individual to this one soul. At once the soul sees where its true bliss lies—to dwell with purest joy in uncreated holiness, to bathe with delight in the fire of everlasting love.[1]

From this bliss the soul was shut out when on earth by a barrier that God had made to try it, the veil of its unglorified body. And now after death it finds itself again shut out by its sins, a barrier of its own making.

We must not picture it as like a struggling soul still in this life, weary of battling with sin and longing blindly for God and rest. The soul in purgatory sees what it longs for, sees more clearly as its cleansing progresses. It longs to be with God, and sees itself unfit. It longs that God should have his will, enfolding it in that love for which he made it; and it hates the stains that hold it from him. It sees how it has stabbed him whom it loves supremely, and it longs to make amends. Helpless now to do anything, it seeks for sufferings and pains to endure, for atonement and for cleansing. If in this life we realised these truths we should turn to fastings, scourgings, and other bodily punishment for this purpose. In our purgatory, therefore, we expect positive pains and punishments to the soul, as well as the anguish of being still unfit for heaven.

Positive punishments

The root of these positive punishments we can see by considering the way that sin takes hold of us. In all sin we are unduly seeking something that is not God. There is often a positive delighting in the creature, called inordinate delight, because it is against reason and against the will of God. This delight calls for positive suffering, to atone for it. Again, when we consider the will that seeks or consents to this delight, it is evident that there may be in the will an habitual readiness to accept this delight; a readiness more or less strong in different souls. "Some venial sins cling to the soul more than others; inasmuch as our affection is more drawn to them and more strongly fixed on them," says St Thomas Aquinas.[2] And in this he finds the reason why some souls suffer longer in purgatory than others, though not necessarily more severely. For the keenness of pain corresponds to the quantity of the sin—that is, of delighting in creatures inordinately. But the length of purgation depends on the rootedness of the sins in the soul; for what clings deeper in the soul takes longer to cleanse. St Paul helps us to understand this deep-rooted clinging of the sin in the soul. In the seventh chapter of the Epistle to the Romans he describes the agony of the soul even

[1] Is. xxxiii 14. [2] *S. Theol.*, *Suppl.*, Append., Q. ii, art. 6.

in this life in its conflict with the attraction of sin. "To will is present with me, but to accomplish that which is good, I find not. . . . For I am delighted with the law of God, according to the inward man; but I see another law in my members, fighting against the law of my mind, and captivating me in the law of sin." [1] This division of our nature against itself causes the agonising conflicts of temptation which are an agony even when the soul faithfully fights through and refuses all consent to wrong. But by weakening and consenting even to small sins, the soul gives the law of sin a hold on its very will, the will which has so often chosen to yield to sin. The soul remains divided against itself. Looking to God, it is delighted with his law. Yet, turning again to think of the creatures that have captivated it, it finds that it cannot tranquilly govern its thoughts of them to rejoice simply in doing God's law in their regard. For it finds it has an affection for them, drawing it to delight in them in disregard of God's law. Thus the very soul is divided against itself, and has no peace. "That which I work, I understand not. For I do not that good which I will, but the evil which I hate, that I do. . . . Unhappy man that I am, who shall deliver me from the body of this death?" [2] The body which was created in innocence to be the soul's partner in glory, the flesh which, as David [3] says, "thirsts for God, oh how many ways;" this body sin has corrupted, making it for a time the body of death. At death soul and body are parted, and the soul has no longer to battle with the body's inclinations, humours, passions. But the habits of thought and will are in the soul itself, and their corruptions are not shed by merely shedding the body. Such as they were at the moment of death, the soul carries them to judgement and to purgatory. The soul will not be fit for heaven till this division has ceased in it; till the all-pervading love of God has replaced all other attractions; till the soul can think of all creatures alike and have no slightest desire about any of them except the desire that God may be glorified in them. The almighty power of God could make this change in the soul in one moment. The soul's love for him could be raised to such intensity as to burn out instantly all other loves, desires, attractions. This we believe God does in the souls of his martyrs, who lay down their lives for him with a love than which no man hath greater. But in other souls there is no reason to suppose such a miracle of grace. It is fitting that they should go through the long agony of painfully detaching their souls from the wrong affections to creatures which they have wilfully and persistently encouraged to take root in their souls. Moreover, a soul so divided against itself, unless roused by the spur and challenge of martyrdom, is not likely to consent to such a fiery act of love for God as would consume at once all its habitual affections for creatures.

[1] Rom. vii 18, 22, 23.
[2] Rom. vii 15, 24.
[3] Ps. lxii 2.

The keenness of the pains in purgatory depends on two things.

The soul, burning with love for God, is faced with its own sins, and with the evil affections these sins have left in the soul to hold it back from God.[1] One thing that increases the soul's anguish is the quantity of its sins. For the greater the quantity, the more keenly will it feel the wrong it has done to God. And the second thing is its own love for God, acquired before death. The more intense its love is, the more will it feel the anguish of having wronged and being separated from him whom it loves.

The keenness of the soul's pain is a different thing from the length of time it must suffer. This depends not on the quantity of sin, but on the rootedness in the soul of those wrong affections which sin has implanted. The deeper their roots, the longer will it take to be freed from them.

As the purifying of the soul goes on, and it is more and more cleansed from its wrong affections, it is more and more open to the inflowing of the love and joy of God ; for these wrong affections were the only hindrance to complete union with him. Consequently the soul's happiness increases as time goes on. But the agony of being still hindered from him and unfit for his complete love will not be lessened ; rather we should expect it to be more unendurable when the soul is nearer its heaven and still delayed.

When the soul's purifying is complete, no purgatory nor hell itself could cause it any suffering. For since there is now in the soul nothing displeasing to God, there is likewise nothing displeasing to the soul itself, whose whole being is given to loving God and his will. And therefore there is nothing in the soul that any grief, sorrow, or pain can lay hold on.

The early Fathers spoke of the purifying fire. The word fire is used in the Scriptures sometimes literally and sometimes figuratively —*e.g.*, " We have passed through fire and water ; "[2] " gold and silver are tried in the fire, but acceptable men in the furnace of humiliation."[3] And the Fathers may have understood the word literally in some cases and figuratively in others. But the Church has made no pronouncement concerning the existence of a real fire in purgatory. The point was raised by the Greeks, when an attempt was made to bring back the Greek Orthodox Church into the fold of Christ, at the Council of Florence (1439), and they were told that the Church had given no dogmatic decision that there is real fire. St Catherine of Genoa says, " This sense of the grievousness of being kept from beholding the Divine Light, coupled with that instinctive longing which would fain be without hindrance to follow the enticing look of God—these things I say make up the pains of the souls in purgatory." This seems to mean that the pains of purgatory are entirely the spiritual pains resulting from seeing God's love and

[1] For another view see Essay xxxi, p. 1130.

[2] Ps. lxv 12. [3] Ecclus. ii 5.

its own sin. St Catherine's teaching was examined and approved before she was canonised.

On the other hand, St Thomas Aquinas, after pointing out that Scripture reveals nothing on this question and that no decisive argument can be brought forward to settle it, considers it more probable and more in accordance with private revelations to hold that, as a rule, souls suffer their purgation in the fire of hell itself. And he applies an illustration of St Augustine's, " In one same fire, gold glows and straw smokes," to show how the fire which endlessly torments the devils can purify a soul that dies in the charity of God.[1]

§ III: THE STATE OF THE SUFFERING SOULS

The souls suffer willingly

We sometimes meet the suggestion that the souls in purgatory murmur at their pains, are restless under them, and turn to human intercessors in the hope that their prayers may win God to grant them mercy rather than strict justice. The mistake is to imagine that the holy souls lose sight of their love for God, and weigh their sufferings in the darkness of their own thoughts, as we do on earth. In our moments of love we resolve to bear gladly whatever pains he sends us. But when disappointment comes, or ill-treatment, or injustice, it is easy to weigh these things in a merely human way, judging them as between ourselves and our wrongers, or wondering what we have done to deserve such suffering. In our darkness this seems an innocent thing to do, for we are only trying to see the rights and wrongs of the case. But when we get back to the light of God, we see that we have been separating his treatment of us from the love that guided that treatment, and so have missed seeing the essential truth about it. And we see that this losing sight of his love, and studying his work without it, was an imperfection at least, and a flagging in our love for him. No such imperfection or flagging is possible to the soul in purgatory in its activity towards God. For with the laying aside of the body, it has laid aside all other activities except the active loving of God ; and now all its thoughts about itself and its sufferings are merely part of its love for God. Since its sufferings are appointed by him, since they are the means to remove all hindrances to loving him perfectly, it would not for anything be without those sufferings. As our blessed Lord would not be without his Passion, nor would his martyrs be without the torments of their death.

In the same way, apart from God's love the soul has no thought of gaining relief through the intercessions of others. But so far as it is his will that it should be thus aided by others' prayers, the soul desires this to be done, with the same intensity that it desires his will to be done in all other ways. In many ways we can see a fittingness in God's appointing that the soul's relief shall come through

[1] *S. Theol., Suppl.*, Append., Q. i, art. 2.

others. His work is to spread in us his love; love for him who is all, and joy in our own nothingness. The suffering soul knows that it can do nothing to end the mischief it has wrought in itself, to cleanse itself from the stains of its sins. It is a cause of joyful humility to see that God will cleanse us for the sake of the loving prayers of others. Again, thinking of those others who pray for us, we see God doing in their souls God's own work, when he moves them to pray for the cleansing of souls; for this means that they love both the holiness of God and the souls that God has made.

They do not merit

This life is the time to win our place in heaven. After death all that is to happen is what we earned in this life, whether joy or punishment or both. If no prize were offered, no one could win a prize. God has offered and promised a prize of eternal life, to be won by all who strive aright. So the soul that dies in the love of God has won a strict right to heaven. And likewise it has won a definite place in heaven. For it has reached a definite height or strength of love for God, and it is too late to win any higher, as it is also too late to fall any lower. Purgatory will not raise its love of God to a higher level, but will only let that love act continuously and remove all hindrances to its action. Its sufferings win no reward; they only free it to enter into the reward already won.

At death we had won the right to enter heaven. That must include the right to have removed everything that hinders us from entering heaven. By dying in the love of God, we won the right to have forgiven those venial sins that we had never repented in this life, and the right to be freed from those affections to sin that have taken root in our souls. As to the venial sins, we have indeed won the right to have them forgiven; but none the less they can only be forgiven when the will rejects them. Our right, therefore, is to have from God the help to reject these sins by the act of the will, and this help he gives us when the soul at death sees his love and puts itself into his hands to be cleansed by suffering. This act of the will is the means appointed by God to win forgiveness of the venial sins that were unrepented at death; therefore St Thomas sees no difficulty in saying that by this act the soul merits their forgiveness. For the soul is still on its way to heaven; and though it cannot now earn a higher place in heaven, it must earn freedom from the hindrances that keep it out.

As to the sufferings that are to free the soul from the rust of its sins, from those affections that remain while the soul is quite resolved never to yield to them again, only God knows when and how far these sufferings can be replaced by the intercessions of the Church on earth for the soul. But this also was a thing earned by the soul in its lifetime on earth; either to be helped by the love of friends on earth, or to pay the last farthing of its debt ere it may depart. So St Augustine says that the prayers and Masses offered on earth benefit only those who on earth earned that they should be benefited by them.

They do not sin

The Church had to condemn an error of Luther's, that the souls in purgatory sin ceaselessly, by desiring rest and shrinking from their sufferings. This error comes from not understanding that all sin is in the will, and in the act of the will; the act whereby we choose definitely to do this and not that. Besides this act of choosing, there are many other desires in our nature; and these may be the cause of sin, or the material of sin, or the effect of sin; but they are not sin. Consider a man who has a long-standing dislike of another, which has often led him to follow trains of thought hostile to that man, and ending in finding further reasons for disliking him. Sin was committed in the act of consenting to follow these thoughts. Suppose some day he recognises that his dislike is unjust, and from that time resolutely shows outward kindness to the man, and turns away instantly from all thoughts against him. His will is acting rightly, but against the grain; for the old habit of dislike is still in him, ready to break out into action at any moment if he would allow it. It is true that this dislike is a wrong one. And precisely because he sees that it is wrong, the man is constantly repressing it, doing all he can to wear it down and hoping some day to find that it is dead. The existence of the desire is therefore wrong, a result of sin, but not sinful. And it is no longer the cause of sins, but is now the material of virtuous acts every time that the will resists it and acts against it. Such as this are the habitual desires, attractions, and repulsions that the soul may carry with it to purgatory, because they have not yet been worked out of its being in this life. In purgatory they must be removed from the soul; not now by work, nor by the soul's resisting them and acting against them, but merely by suffering.

In purgatory such a dislike could never lead to sin. For in this world it leads to sin because the soul is still in the body. Through the senses, through the humours and state of the body, the will is provoked or drawn to indulge these desires or dislikes; and at the same time and for the same reasons, it easily loses sight of God and his love. In purgatory all the distractions of the body are gone; and the soul's love for God absorbs it continuously and prevents it attending to any other desire. The bad desire or repulsion is latent in the soul, as it is in this life at the times when it does not trouble a man. But in purgatory there is no possibility of its ever breaking out into action. It is simply burning out slowly in the fire of suffering.

Luther did not suggest that the suffering soul could sin in this way, but in the very fact of finding its sufferings painful. We have seen that to the soul it is intensely painful to be held away from God, to know that it has insulted him and is unfit to approach him. Plainly it is right that these things should be painful to the soul; it would be wrong if the soul could be satisfied with them. And the soul's act of will is to accept this pain because it is right. This act of will is completely pleasing to God, but wins the soul no higher place in heaven. For its place in heaven was won during its life on earth.

Forgiveness of venial sin

When a soul departs this life in venial sin, it has two reasons to suffer for that sin: one because it has never repented the sin; the other because, after repenting and being forgiven, the soul will still owe a debt of punishment to atone for the sin. The meaning of saying that the soul is in sin, whether mortal or venial, is that the soul has consented to that sin and has never withdrawn its consent. The guilt of the sin therefore remains on the soul; for the soul's attitude to that sin is still just what it was when it committed the sin. If the sin was mortal, the soul in committing it rejected God and his love; and as long as it does not repent, it continues to reject God. If the sin was venial, the soul committing it did not in any way reject God or withdraw from his love; but it yielded unduly to the attraction of a creature. This undue yielding has the effect of hardening the will against God and making it slow to follow his guidance. As long as the soul does not repent the venial sin and withdraw its consent to it, this hardness and slowness of the will remains.

It is very evident that a soul in this state cannot enter heaven. For in heaven its whole nature must be prompt and instant at the service of God, whereas now its very will is hard and slow to obey. The change of will must be made in purgatory, by means of suffering. To trace out how this is done will require us to keep steadily in mind all the facts about the soul's state and about repentance.

We are speaking of a soul that at death was in the love of God. This love of God, more or less intense, is the sanctifying grace which makes it certain that this soul will ultimately be in heaven; and in heaven its nearness to God will be determined by the degree of love for him which it had reached in this world at the hour of death. With this love for God, there can and does coexist guilt, the guilt of venial sin, incurred by yielding to undue attraction to some creature. The sin was not in the attraction, but in yielding to the attraction. The attraction may have been there for years, or for a lifetime; the result of original sin, or of sins actually committed by the soul. This attraction, more or less deeply rooted in the soul by the soul's own acts of sin, will have to be slowly burned out of it in purgatory. But at present we are thinking of the actual sins whereby the soul consented to yield to that attraction. This wrong consent must be repented and withdrawn before the sin can be forgiven, even if the sin be one of the smallest. Now in this life this repenting and withdrawal is done in two ways—one, just as mortal sins are repented, by considering the individual sin and its offensiveness to God, and for his sake wishing we had not done it and resolving to atone for it. The other way that venial sins are forgiven is that our love of God is for some reason strongly moved—perhaps by Holy Communion or meditation or thankfulness. And this love, in action in the soul, so stirs the will, that every remembered sin and everything offensive to God that could possibly come to mind would be hateful to the soul and rejected by it. In this way the soul, without counting over its venial sins, does yet truly reject them all and hate them all, and so is forgiven them. In either repentance, we see that the soul's love for God becomes active and destroys its previous consent to the venial sin.

When a soul comes to its death in the state of venial sin, it is easy to see that before it can enter heaven its consent to the venial sins must be undone and destroyed by its love for God. And it is easy to see that, once it is parted from the body and all its desires and needs, the soul's love for God will be ceaselessly active, longing for his glory, hating its own sins, desiring to be with him. In this way the soul will withdraw and hate all its consents to sin.

There have been discussions as to when this takes place. It seems unlikely that there should be any delay, that the soul should only gradually arrive at the stage of repenting its venial sins. If, then, there be no delay after death in repenting, and if too the repentance was not made before death (for we are speaking of souls that die with venial sins unrepented), there remains only the moment of death for repenting. The moment of death has two sides. On this side it is the ending of life, the surrendering of the soul into the hands of its Maker. On the other side it is the moment of judgement, when the soul in the light of God suddenly sees all things as God sees them; sees his love and its own sins, and judges of them as God judges. Some have said that in the act of dying men repent their venial sins. And certainly such a thing can happen, when a soul consciously and lovingly gives itself into the hands of God, as did the martyrs and some other saints. But St Thomas calls it frivolous to suggest that all men thus make their death a willing act: " Someone, after venial sin, might give no thought to it, either to reject it or to hold to it; he might think of the three angles of a triangle equalling two right angles, and with this thought fall asleep and so die." Moreover, such a repenting of venial sins, when it does take place, is made in this life; the soul does not die in them.

There remains the moment of judgement, which is the beginning of purgatory. At this time surely all the soul's love for God is stirred into action, and such strong action as to detest once for all its wilful disobediences to him. St Thomas, without defining the time, contents himself with concluding that " Venial guilt, in one who dies in the grace of God, is remitted after this life through the fire of purgatory; for by the virtue of grace, that punishment, which is in one way willing, will have power to atone for every guilt that can coexist with grace."

Duration of purgatory

It is the constant teaching of the Church that all purgation will be completed when the general judgement comes at the end of the world. All the souls that are to go to heaven will at that judgement be reunited to their bodies and enter into their everlasting reward. But as to the duration of the purgation of individual souls we know nothing from our Lord's teaching. He tells us in a parable, " thou shalt not depart thence till thou repay the last farthing." [1] This shows the need of perfect purity before we can enter heaven ; but reveals nothing about the length of time of imprisonment. The Church allows perpetual Masses to be arranged for one soul. This is because she does not know how long that soul may be suffering, nor how much atonement God will accept on its behalf from men. We have to remember that all times are alike present to God. There is nothing unlikely in supposing that prayers and Masses now being offered for one who died before the Reformation were the means of that soul entering into heaven many hundreds of years ago, as our Lord's Passion was the means of saving Adam's soul. The visions God has allowed of souls begging for prayers many years after their death are evidence that these souls have been in suffering all that time. And if there are authentic visions where souls have also told that their purgatory was to last many years yet, these also may be believed without fear of contradicting Catholic teaching.

Those who are alive at the end of the world, and whose souls are stained with venial sin or owe a debt of punishment, must have their purgation like other such souls before they can enter heaven. About these, people have wondered over two questions, of which God has not taught us the answers. First, as to their bodies. Are they to pass alive into heaven or hell, or are they to die and rise again at once ? And as to their souls, when are they to suffer their purgatory, since they are not judged till the general judgement, and after that judgement there is no purgatory ? This is asking Almighty God how his doings are to be fitted into the tiny measures of time and space that he has made for our bodily life. He gives us glimpses to let us know how narrow is our vision, and that we must be content to know that he is infinitely above our understanding. We must not attempt to limit what he can do in what we call the " moment " of judgement. " Of this one thing be not ignorant, my beloved, that one day with the Lord is as a thousand years, and a thousand years as one day." [2] And on our side we know that a moment of intense anxiety, waiting to know will a falling stone crush a child, seems like an age. The work of purgation to be done in these souls is the same as in the souls of the martyrs. In the martyrs it is done in their sometimes brief dying. As easily can God do it at the last day.

§ IV: PURGATORY IN TRADITION AND SCRIPTURE

Tradition

THE belief in purgatory is an excellent example of what is meant by tradition in the Church. When the belief is challenged, when we are asked to cease praying for the dead, it is sufficient to answer,

[1] Matt. v 26. [2] 2 Pet. iii 8.

" But we have been praying for them since the time of the Apostles." The mere fact of praying for them implies the belief that these souls are not yet in heaven, nor hopelessly lost in hell; that they will reach heaven in the end; that our prayers may help them. And this, duly weighed, is seen to imply further that the bond which holds together God's spiritual family or communion is not mere justice, but love. Once we realise that the work of his kingdom is to spread in our hearts love for God and love for each other, it seems quite natural that those who have offended him should be helped by each other's prayers. All this belief is embodied in the most effectual way in the practice of praying for the dead; for by learning that practice and the meaning of it, and by doing it, we learn it not simply as a thing to believe, but as a fact to be dealt with, and calling for action. In the Church from the beginning there has been the practice of praying for the dead and offering the Mass for them. Very early we find recorded the custom of offering special prayers and Masses on the thirtieth day and on the anniversary of death. The writers speak of these things simply as the established traditional practice of the Church. This traditional practice of the Church is a running stream of witness to her belief. And when we find the earliest written references to it speak of it as the traditional and unquestioned practice of the Church, we have an argument to show that the doctrine has been believed and acted on from the time of the Apostles. When Popes and Councils are called on to define a doctrine that heretics are challenging or perverting, they demonstrate what the Church has always believed by examining the practices which the Church has followed or encouraged, and pointing out what truths are implied in these practices. The infallible declaration of Popes and General Councils is argument enough for a Catholic; for the living voice of the Church teaching even in St Peter's time was no surer nor holier than is the living voice of the Pope to-day, seeing that always it is the voice of the Holy Spirit, leading Christ's Church into all truth, and bringing back to her mind whatever Christ taught her.[1] But it is sometimes an encouragement, and always a joy, to find St Gregory the Great or St Augustine talking of the prayers and Masses offered for this soul and for that, and the hope of benefiting such souls, in the same matter-of-fact and simple way as a school-child talks of them to-day.

Since the truth of God's teaching can never vary, though it may become plainer and more fully known to men as time goes on, let us try to see the oneness of his teaching about purgatory, whether through his Church, or through his Scriptures, or through the visions and revelations of his saints. We will look first at the Church's practice to-day, which embodies her teaching, brings it before her faithful, and enables them to carry it into effect. Next we shall see the same doctrine taught and acted on in the beginning of the Church.

[1] John xvi 13.

Then we shall consider passages in the sacred Scriptures, which either spring from the same teaching or give the grounds for it. And lastly there are private revelations which God may have made to saints and other holy souls. We must see how these stand to the Church's teaching: sometimes condemned by it, sometimes confirming it and throwing light on it.

First, the Church's practice to-day.

The Church's practice to-day

It would not be easy to make a list of the intercessions for the dead that make part of the Church's daily work. The moment a soul leaves the body the priest and the others who may be there begin praying for it. Before the funeral the body can be brought to the church, and the Office for the Dead, consisting of Vespers, Matins, and Lauds, can be sung or said for the soul. This Office is called in English a dirge, *dirige* being the first word of the Matins. At the funeral all the prayers are intercessions for the departed soul. Besides this praying for the soul of one lately dead, there are habitual prayers for all the faithful departed. The laity are taught to make these a part of their daily prayers morning and night, and even of their thanksgiving after meals. The clergy, in reciting their daily Office, recall at Prime the dead they specially wish to pray for that day, and pray for all the faithful departed at the end of most of the canonical hours through the day. In every Mass after the consecration the priest stops a moment to recall to mind the souls that he or others wish to be remembered, and then begs "a place of refreshment, light and peace" for them and for all that fall asleep in Christ. Above all this, the Church has drawn up the Masses for the dead, in which prayers for the dead occupy those places which on another day might be devoted to commemorating our Lord's birth or resurrection or for the feast of a saint. Of these Masses, there is one that can be said on the day of death or of burial; one for the third or seventh or thirtieth day after death; and one for the anniversary day. Further, there is an "everyday Mass" for use whenever the priest or the faithful desire to offer Mass for the dead on a day that is open for such Masses. Not every day is open, for the Church has provided Masses for the greater feasts and for Ember days and Lenten days, and these are not to be lightly set aside. One day in the year, November 2nd, is set aside as All Souls' Day. A full Office of the Dead—Vespers, Compline, Matins, Lauds, Prime, Terce, Sext, None—is recited or sung by the clergy; every Mass that day is a black Mass, offered for all the faithful departed. On that day, too, every priest is privileged to say three Masses, as on Christmas Day. Later in the month, the religious orders of monks and nuns repeat this intercession for the dead of their own order.

All this is the official practice of the Church. It is her highest authority that arranges and regulates it all. No departure from this practice nor innovation may be made without her sanction. If, therefore, anyone asks what is the belief of the Church at this moment about intercession for the dead, here is his answer: it is the belief that is embodied and implied in these practices. Some points may be noticed. First, how this fact that the dead must be prayed for is always with us, through the day, through the year. In our soul's life it is as common and familiar a fact as that prayer is heard or that Christ is God. It is bound up with the most practical problem we have to deal with—that our daily sinning does not cease, and that it will all have to be undone and wiped out ere we can enter heaven. *Peccantem me quotidie, et non me poenitentem, timor mortis conturbat me.* Praying for the dead, we foresee ourselves dead and needing to be prayed for.

We notice also that the Church's public prayers are made for the faithful only. Only a Catholic can have Catholic burial, or Masses publicly offered for his soul's repose. For living non-Catholics, the Church's one prayer is that they may be brought to know the Church that Christ sent to teach them. For till they know his will they cannot do it. Once they by faith accept his Church, she can give them all the other gifts he has put in her hands for his brethren. But it would be a breach of trust to give these gifts alike to those who accept and to those who refuse his first gift of faith, which is the foundation of all the rest. So she cannot pray publicly for those without, as if they were brethren. But God in binding his Church to her appointed work did not bind up his own mercy; and knowing this, we pray in secret for those dead for whom we cannot pray in public.

Again, we notice that the Church continues offering prayers and Masses for a soul indefinitely. One reason for allowing priests to say three Masses on All Souls' Day is that Masses may thus be offered for those who in past ages endowed monasteries, in the hope that Masses would be said for them till the end of the world. Again, the Church encourages us to intercede specially for those who are near to us, members of our own family, of our own religious order. For the charity of Christ, which extends our love to all whom he loves, does not wipe out but deepens the natural love he has given us for our near ones. Besides her own official intercessions, the Church approves and encourages practices that arise from the devotion of the faithful: confraternities that meet to pray for the dead, Purgatorial Societies whose members have Masses said jointly for themselves as they die.

Witness of the early Church

Next, to get an idea of the belief and practice of the early Church, we will begin with St Gregory the Great, who was Pope from A.D. 590 to 604 and sent our St Augustine to convert the English. From him we will work backwards. Two hundred years earlier, St Augustine, Bishop of Hippo, the great doctor of the Church, was writing and preaching in Africa, and he shall be our next witness. Again, we will go two hundred years earlier to Tertullian. He is not a quiet witness like the others. He argues, where they simply mention how they earnestly carried out the belief and practice of the Church in their day.

Tertullian was a convert to Catholicism, and later fell away into the heresy of the Montanists; and he writes to defend and justify the religion he holds. In his writings as a Montanist, he may be defending the parts of Catholic truth that he still holds, or he may be attacking the parts which he has rejected; but in either case he bears witness to what was the teaching of the Catholic Church in his day. And we find him justifying the belief in purgatory. Before him and after him there are the inscriptions on tombs in the catacombs and elsewhere, which show in the simplest and surest way the thoughts of the Catholic faithful about the dead.

As a specimen of St Gregory the Great's writing on purgatory, we will take the following passage from the fourth book of his Dialogues. The incident here related would seem to be the origin of the custom of saying Masses for a dead person on thirty successive days, which are sometimes called Gregorian Masses.

> Here also I can not but tell you that which happened three yeares since in myne owne Monastery. A certaine monke there was called Justus, one very cunninge in physicke, and whiles I remayned in the Abbey, served me very diligentlye, attending upon me in my often infirmities and sickenes. This man him selfe at lengthe fell sore sicke, so that in very dede he was broughte to the last cast. A brother he had called Copiosus that had care of him, who yet liveth. Justus perceiving him self past all hoope of life, tolde this brother of his, where he had secretly laid up three crownes of golde. . . . Which thing so sone as I understoode, very much grieved I was, and could not quietly disgest so great a synne at his handes, that lived with us in communitye, because the rule of my Monastery was, that all the monkes thereof should so live in common, that none in particular mighte possesse any thinge proper to him selfe. Being therefore much troubled and grieved at that which had happened . . . at lengthe I sent for Pretiosus Prior of the Monasterye, and gave him this charge: Se (quoth I) that none of our monkes do so muche as visit Justus in this his extremitye, neither let any give him any comfort at all: and when his last houre draweth nighe, and he doth desire the presence of his spirituall brethren, let his carnall brother tell him, that they do all detest him, for the three crownes which he had hidden; that at least before his death, sorrow may wounde his hart and purge it from the synne committed: and when he is deade, let not his body be buried amongest the rest of the monkes, but make a grave for him in some one dunghill or other, and there cast it

in, together with the three crownes which he left behinde him, crying out all with jointe voice: thy money be with the into perdition, and so put earth upon him. In either of which thinges my minde and desire was, both to helpe him that was leaving the worlde, and also to edifye the monkes yet remayninge behinde, that both griefe of death mighte make him pardonable for his sinne, and such a severe sentence against avarice, might terrifye and preserve them from the like offence: both which by Gods goodenes fell out accordinglye: For when the foresaide monke came to dye, and carefullye desired to be commended to the devotions of his brethren, and yet none of them did either visit him, or so much as speake to him: his brother Copiosus tolde him, for what cause they had all given him over: at which wordes he straightwaies sighthed for his synne, and in that sorrowe gave up the ghost. . . . Thirty daies after his departure, I began to take compassion upon him, and with great grief to thincke of his punnishment, and what meanes there was to helpe him; whereupon I called againe for Pretiosus Prior of my Monasterye, and with an heavy heart spake thus unto him. It is nowe a goode while since that our brother which is departed, remayneth in the tormentes of fire, and therfore we must shewe him some charity, and labour what we maye to procure his deliverye; wherefore go your waye and see that for thirty daies following sacrifice be offered for him, so that no one day passe in which for his absolution and discharge, the healthfull sacrifice be not offred: who forthwith departed, and put my commandement in execution. In the meane tyme, my mynde being busied about other affaires, so that I tooke no heede to the daies how they passed: upon a certaine night the same monke that was deade, appeared to his brother Copiosus who seing him enquired of his state in this manner: what is the matter brother? and how is it with you? to whom he answered thus: Hitherto have I bene in badd case, but nowe I am well, for this day have I received the communion: with which newes Copiosus straightwaies comming to the Monasterye tolde the monkes: and they diligentlye counting the daies, founde it to be that, in which the thirtith sacrifice was offred for his soule: and so thoughe neither Copiosus knewe what the monkes had done for him, nor they what he had seene concerning the state of his brother, yet at one and the same tyme both he knewe what they had done, and they what he had seene, and so the sacrifice and vision agreing together, apparant it was, that the deade monke was by the holy sacrifice delivered from his paines.[1]

Writing two hundred years before St Gregory, St Augustine in his moving story of the death of his mother St Monica says: "During

[1] From a translation by P.W. printed at Paris, 1608.

her illness one day a faintness came on her, and for a little she was unconscious. We ran to her; but soon she came back to consciousness, and looked at me and my brother standing there. And she said to us, as if questioning, 'Where was I?' Then, gazing at us who were stunned with grief, she said, 'You will lay your mother here?' I was silent, holding back my tears. But my brother said something, that he hoped she would die not abroad, but more happily in her own country. Hearing this, her face grew anxious and her eyes smote him for wishing such a thing. And then she looked at me and said, 'See what he is saying.' And presently she said to us both, 'Lay this body anywhere at all; the care of it must not trouble you. This only I ask of you, that you remember me at the altar of the Lord wherever you are. . . .' And when now her body was buried, we went and returned without tears. For not even in those prayers that were poured forth to thee while the sacrifice of our redemption was being offered for her, with the body standing at the graveside before burial as is the custom there, not even in those prayers did I weep." [1]

Two hundred years again before St Augustine, Tertullian argues that it is right that the soul be punished alone before the body rises again, because even bodily sins are conceived and consented to by the soul alone before the body does them; and he concludes: "No one will doubt that the soul pays some penalty in hell, while sure of full resurrection, resurrection in the flesh too." [2]

About the same time, Abercius asks for prayers after his death from those who should read the epitaph he composed for himself, and had graven on a stone before his eyes. "These things I Abercius, standing by, dictated to be written here: I was actually in my seventy-second year. Let everyone who understands these things and sympathises pray for Abercius." And in the Roman catacombs are many inscriptions like St Philomena's *Pax tecum filumena* (Peace be with thee, Philomena), which in shorter words is exactly the same prayer as our *Requiescat in pace* (May she rest in peace).

The man who carved "Peace be with thee" on the tomb of the dead maid would be conscious only of his love for her and his trust in God. But he had in him all that the Catholic Church teaches about the souls of the dead, and a questioner would draw it from him by asking, "Do you think her soul still lives? Do you think some souls are in peace and others not? Do you love her so much that you care what happens to her now? Why should you hope she is to have peace? Do you think God will heed your wishing her peace?"

Now let us turn to the Holy Scriptures.

Holy Scripture

In considering the passages of Scripture that bear on purgatory, we must not imagine that the Church at some time noticed these passages, concluded from them that there must be a purgatory, and

[1] St Aug., *Conf.*, IX, chap. xi. [2] *De anima*, n. 58.

thereafter began a new teaching and a new practice of praying for the souls there. For the Church had the Catholic faith and the Catholic religion complete from the beginning in all its substance. The doctrine of purgatory was not learned from the texts in the Scriptures. But these texts were written by men who, in the Jewish Church or in the Catholic Church, already knew this doctrine. That the dead are to be judged according to their works; that their sins make it a terrible thing to be judged by God; that the souls need his mercy if they are to enter heaven; that we, their brethren in the family of God, ought to pray him to show them this mercy—these are the essential facts, known to the Jews before our Lord's time, and familiar to the New Testament writers. Judas Machabeus found concealed on the bodies of his men who had fallen in battle the offerings they had looted from a pagan temple. "And making a gathering, he sent twelve thousand drachms of silver to Jerusalem for sacrifice to be offered for the sins of the dead;" which leads the inspired writer to say that it is a holy and wholesome thought to pray for the dead, that they may be loosed from their sins.[1] Our Lord's disciples were familiar with this knowledge about sin and judgement; and hearing his teachings, they would understand them just as we do, who are familiar with the same truths. They heard him saying that he will render to every man according to his works;[2] that some sins are to be punished with many stripes and some with few;[3] that some people have many sins to be forgiven, and some but few;[4] that for every idle word we shall render an account in the day of judgement;[5] that some sins shall not be forgiven in this world nor in the next.[6] All this would lead them to pray the more for their dead; for while it deepened their sense of the holiness of God before which the dead are judged, it also kindled their hopes of his merciful forgiveness. He told them, indeed, the stern truths of death and judgement and hell; that in this life must heaven be won: "Are there not twelve hours of the day?[7] Walk while you have the light;[8] the night cometh in which no man can work;[9] this night do they require thy soul of thee;[10] the rich man died and was buried in hell;[11] there shall be weeping and gnashing of teeth."[12] But there was nothing to suggest that only the spotlessly pure can escape hell. On the contrary, the judgement, instant and strict, is also just. Each shall receive according to his works; some shall be beaten with many stripes, some with few.

The Apostles have written some things which to us are mysterious, though they seem to have expected their readers to understand them. St Peter says that Christ preached to those spirits that were in prison, which had waited for the patience of God in the days of Noah. And

[1] 2 Mach. xii 40-46. [2] Matt. xvi 27. [3] Luke xii 47, 48.
[4] Luke vii 47. [5] Matt. xii 36. [6] Matt. xii 32.
[7] John xi 9. [8] John xii 35. [9] John ix 4.
[10] Luke xii 20. [11] Luke xvi 22. [12] Matt. viii 12.

for this cause was the gospel preached to the dead, that they might be judged indeed according to men in the flesh, but may live according to God in the spirit.[1] And St Paul says that some are baptised for the dead.[2] Though we do not see their full meaning, this much of it at least is plain—that there were souls of the dead waiting to be brought to heaven, and that Christians on earth were trying to help them. Our Lord speaks of the same mystery: "The hour cometh and now is, when the dead shall hear the voice of the Son of God, and they that hear shall live. . . . All that are in the graves shall hear the voice of the Son of God."[3]

St Paul, looking at the ministers of God working to spread his kingdom among men, sees them building their own mistakes and weaknesses over the foundation Christ had made. He sees this cockle growing with the good seed till the harvest time, in which our Lord had said that every planting that the Father has not planted shall be rooted up.[4]

And St Paul speaks of it under a parable of his own:[5] "Now if any man build upon this foundation, gold, silver, precious stones, wood, hay, stubble, every man's work shall be manifest; for the day of the Lord shall declare it, because it shall be revealed in fire; and the fire shall try every man's work, of what sort it is." St Paul has in his mind the contrast between our working in blindness and judging as men judge in the dark, and the sudden blaze of God's light searching like a flame through all our deeds, when he shall make his judgement known to each of us. By itself, this could apply either to the judgement after death, or to God's bringing home to a man's conscience in this life the true worth or worthlessness of his work. But as he proceeds with his argument, St Paul later says: "Therefore judge not before the time: until the Lord come, who both will bring to light the hidden things of darkness, and will make manifest the counsels of the hearts: and then shall every man have praise from God." It seems clear that he is speaking here of the judgement after death, especially as he contrasts it with being judged by "man's day." So that it is reasonable to think that throughout he is speaking of the judgement in the next world. Continuing his parable, he says: "If any man's work abide, which he hath built thereupon, he shall receive a reward. If any man's work burn, he shall suffer loss: but he himself shall be saved, yet so as by fire."[6] In the last words the thought seems to be of gold purified by fire from its dross, and the soul similarly purified from its rust of sins after death and judgement by God. This purifying is purgatory.

Private revelations

In the Lives of the Saints we constantly read of apparitions of souls from purgatory, or of revelations about them, especially about the pains they suffer. We must distinguish two kinds of these

[1] 1 Pet. iii 19, 20; iv 6.
[2] 1 Cor. xv 29.
[3] John v 25, 28.
[4] Matt. xv 13.
[5] 1 Cor. iii 12-13.
[6] 1 Cor. iii 14-iv 5.

writings. Saints like St Thomas Aquinas and St Catherine of Genoa received in prayer a supernatural light or clearness of understanding, enabling them to see clearly and explain lucidly what ordinary minds find too deep to disentangle. Their conclusions are recognised by the Church as setting forth in a beautiful and convincing light the teachings which she received from God in the beginning. In the other kind of writing, men record the visions they have seen, of individual facts and particular persons. If these visions in any way conflict with the Church's dogmatic teaching, that there is a purgatory of suffering which purifies souls for heaven, the Church condemns them, and knows that they proceed either from evil spirits or from the seer's imagination. On the other hand, the Church recognises that God can, if he will, allow or command such apparitions and visions, and can make the seer know for certain that the vision is real. If he does so, it is right that the seer should believe the vision; and likewise that any others who are convinced by the evidence should believe it. But however many may believe it and be convinced, even if the whole Church does so, as in the case of the apparitions of Lourdes, the fact remains that this is not part of the teaching God gave his Church when he made it. Consequently, these private revelations never become part of the Catholic faith. For the faith is that portion of truth which God committed to his Church to be taught to all mankind. If we receive any truth through these private revelations, we do not receive it from the Church, but from the individual witness whose word we accept. Consequently no one is bound to believe any of these revelations, unless because he is personally convinced that God has manifested some truth to the seer.[1]

In practice, many of the saints and doctors of the Church have believed some of these visions. St Gregory the Great used them to confirm the Church's teaching that prayers and Masses help the suffering souls. St Thomas Aquinas, on the strength of these visions, is ready to believe that some souls are commanded by God to spend their purgatory in some limited spot on earth. And on the question whether the souls in purgatory suffer against their will, he introduces the argument drawn from the fact that they so often ask men to pray for their release.

When these visions show a bodily form, whether amid flames or any other bodily surroundings, we must remember that these forms are purely visionary. For the soul in purgatory is of course separate from its body, a spirit only. And if it take a bodily appearance, it is merely as the angels do when sent to show themselves to men. Whatever effects they produce on the eyes, ears, and other senses, all is mere appearance; for there is no body there. So that the vision of souls in flames calling for our prayers is no more than a parable, a truth shown in figure to the eyes, as when we say in

[1] See Essay i, *Faith and Revealed Truth*, p. 33.

ordinary talk that a soul burns with love, or that the mind seems on fire with its distress, using the bodily figures to suggest spiritual facts that exist in the soul.

§ V: INTERCESSION FOR THE SOULS IN PURGATORY

We share God's love for others

BETWEEN God and man, love is the only standard to judge by. There can be no asking what are the limits of our strict duty to God, nor any claiming from God of our just rights. For he owes us nothing, and we owe him all, even our very being. And the only weighing and measuring between us is, do we give him love in our measure, as he gives us love in his measure ? Now, love calls in its own way for justice. Love will give to the beloved all that is his due, and think it but a small beginning of love's gifts. God's love for us can content itself in nothing less than making us as perfect as our nature allows—perfect in holiness, perfect in love. And our love for God requires that we pay to him every smallest and every greatest duty that a creature can render to his Maker. In setting right our sins, therefore, God's method is to bring us to act, as he acts, for love. In this love we intercede for the suffering souls. He has taught us to forgive our enemies, to pray for them, to try to win them to God when they sin. That is, we must learn to look with God's eyes of love on all who, through sin or through sorrow, need his help. We must wish as he wishes that they be delivered from the bonds of their sin and brought home to his love. In this way it is a holy and wholesome thought to pray for the dead that they may be loosed from their sins.

From the other side, the wish to be prayed for in this way is also part of the spreading of God's love in souls. When we look at our own nothingness and our sins, we see that neither we nor all mankind can do anything to atone, and that there is no hope for us but in that love which God is spreading among men. " If thou, O Lord, shalt mark iniquities, Lord, who shall abide it ? "[1] And just as, when he has forgiven us, the Scripture says, " All ye that fear God, come and hear, and I will tell you what great things he hath done for my soul,"[2] so when we want forgiveness, it is natural to call to all those who love God to pray him to have mercy on us : " I beseech all the saints, and you, brethren, to pray to the Lord our God for me." Thus we are forced into truth and humility by our knowledge of God's ways ; we must flee from all thoughts of justifying or excusing ourselves or setting ourselves right, and take refuge in the world of love that God has made, to redeem the world of sin. The suffering souls in purgatory too will call in the same way for prayers from their brothers on earth, if it be God's will that this particular soul shall be aided by those prayers. For these souls are more

[1] Ps. cxxix 3. [2] Ps. lxv 16.

helpless than we; they can do nothing whatever for their sins but suffer; and their whole activity is concerned with God's love.

Mutual intercession

Many Catholics ask the prayers of the suffering souls in purgatory, and believe that often they obtain favours from God through these prayers. But sometimes a doubt is raised whether this can be; and this for two reasons. One, do these souls know anything that passes on earth? For if not, then they do not even know that we are wanting them to pray for us. And secondly, since they cannot pray for themselves nor do anything to purify themselves but suffer, is it likely that they can pray for us?

As to their knowledge. In this world the soul does not learn what is happening except by hearing, seeing, and the other bodily senses. Consequently when the soul leaves the body it has no natural means of learning anything that happens on earth. This is true alike of the souls in hell, in purgatory, in heaven. It is not difficult to believe that the saints in heaven, who like the angels "always see the face of my Father who is in heaven," in seeing God see all the happenings on earth that he wishes them to see; which is also all that they wish to see, since they now wish only what God wishes. But we cannot say this of the suffering souls, for they do not see God. All these difficulties only amount to saying that we do not know any means by which the dead can see or learn what passes on earth. But if God wills that they should learn it, the difficulties are no difficulty at all. Our reason for expecting God to will it is the bond of love which he has set up between all the members of the Communion of Saints, which is his Church. We are praying for these souls because he loves them, and because for his sake we love them. It seems natural to expect that they will know of our prayers. As to their not being able to pray even for themselves, it is true, as we have seen, that their whole activity is a burning love for God, and the root of their suffering is that they are hindered in this love by the stains of their sins. That intense love will find food and cause of joy in seeing the bond of love that he had made between us and the suffering soul, in seeing how he has moved us to pray for it, in wishing that he will return good to us for the good we have done. And that wish, if God allows it to exist in the soul, is in effect a prayer for us. For all depends on the will of God. We only know that it seems, as far as we can see, worthy of God's holiness and goodness to allow these suffering souls to help us; and therefore we know that if he will allow it, all the difficulties that we see in the way of doing it are due simply to the littleness of our understanding.

Indulgences for the dead

The Church encourages us to gain indulgences and offer them for the suffering souls. But in doing so, she calls our attention to the essential difference between these and the indulgences she offers to ourselves. Over us she has the power of binding and loosing; and she offers to loose us from some or all of the punishment due to our forgiven sins, on condition that we do the good works, prayer, fasting and alms-deeds, which she prescribes. Not that she can guarantee that we shall do these works well enough to gain the offered remission, any more than she can guarantee that we shall make a good confession and be forgiven the guilt of our sins. But in either case, if we do our part rightly, she has power from God to loose us [1]—first in confession from the guilt of sins, and then by indulgence from the punishment still due for those sins. But she has no such power of binding and loosing the dead. They have passed from the shepherding of Peter to the Good Shepherd himself, " God, to whom alone it belongs to give healing after death." All that the Church can now do for them is to entreat him; to offer him prayers, sacrifices, penances, which may be accepted for some of these souls, in the same spirit of brotherhood in which his sacrifice was accepted for the souls of us all.

The Church's prayers for the dead

Many of the Church's prayers for the dead refer not to purgatory but to the judgement—either to the general judgement at the last day or the particular judgement of the soul at death. These prayers never take for granted that the soul is sure of heaven, but they ask for its salvation; that the soul be delivered from the gates of hell; that at the rising from the dead it may breathe freely among the saints. In these prayers our own judgement is brought before our eyes, both to put us on our guard for ourselves and to make us realise the case of those we are praying for. " When thou comest to judge, where shall I hide myself? Woe is me, Lord, for in my life I have sinned exceedingly. Whither shall I flee, except to thee, my God?"

These prayers show the pleas on which we appeal to Almighty God—chiefly his own mercy; for he is a God of mercies, *indulgentiarum Domine*. His cleansing the suffering souls is pure mercy, *remissionis tuae misericordia*. Though he has promised it, and the soul has earned it according to his promise, yet what he has promised is to be merciful. And the promise itself was mercy. To restore the soul from sin to holiness, we appeal to the same love and almighty power that " raised Lazarus when rotting in the tomb." Another plea is that our own praying is done in love, *piis supplicationibus*, and so far is the work of his own Holy Spirit. Again, we plead the gifts he had given to these souls in life—the true faith, the desire to do his will, the apostolic office of the priesthood—not daring to say that the soul made good use of these, but knowing that he gave these gifts in order to bring the souls to the glory of heaven. But most of all we plead the sacrifice of the Holy Mass, which daily is offered for all the faithful departed, as well as for those in this world. The souls suffer for two reasons, to atone to God and to cleanse themselves; and the Mass is both a sacrifice of praise to God and of purification for men.

Our prayers ask that the souls may be cleansed, and may reach

[1] Matt. xviii 18.

their reward. For the cleansing of the souls, the Church asks God's indulgence: that they may have forgiveness of all sins, be made pure and disentangled from sins; that any stains clinging to them from contact with earth may be wiped away, God pouring on them the unfailing dew of his mercy. For their reward in heaven, we ask eternal rest, light perpetual, the company of the saints, a home of refreshment, of blissful calm, clear light. And all is summed up in "May they repose in thy love."

Some have thought that no prayer is made for the suffering souls by the saints in heaven. But the Church is against them. For she appeals for the help of the saints in her prayers for the dead as in all her other prayers: "That they may come to share eternal bliss through the intercession of Blessed Mary ever Virgin and of all the saints." Even in offering the Mass itself, we offer it in partnership with the saints in heaven, and we beg that our offering may be presented before God by his angel.

It is right to dwell on the power of the saints' prayers with God and compare it with our own unworthiness to be heard, as, again, it is right to dwell on the infinite value of the Mass, whereby, as the Church says, "thou hast loosed the sins of the whole world." But we must not pass on to imagine that the offering of the Mass for a soul, or the united prayers of the saints, ought to bring the soul to heaven far sooner than God intends. When we think of the sun, and the seed that under its rays grows to be a tree, it would be foolish to say that those enormous stores of heat and power in the sun ought surely to do all the work of developing the plant in an instant instead of taking years over it. The miracle of the distant sun for millions of years giving life to millions of living things on this earth is indeed great; but it does not blind us to the fact that each of these living things must be brought to perfection gradually, and in accordance with its own nature. So in thinking of purgatory: God is bringing each soul to perfection according to its nature. In this work his almighty power uses the virtue of the Mass and the prayers of the saints in heaven and of men on earth. It is folly for us to think we can know how the work should be done, and to wonder why it is not done in another way.

Masses for the dead

Why are many Masses said for one soul, when the power of a single Mass is infinite? We can only see why this is when we have brought before our mind the full meaning of sin and redemption and atonement.

In every Mass our Lord himself is the chief offerer. There he continues to offer what he offered on the cross—his death, the sacrifice of his life, his body and blood delivered up and shed—for atonement to God and for the redemption of man. By making this offering, he wins for men all the grace and forgiveness and reward that will ever be received by each soul he has created. For each soul in purgatory, therefore, our Lord's own offering wins purification from the stains of its sins and final entrance to heaven. The question therefore is, what difference will be made to this soul by my joining my mind and will on a particular morning with our Lord's as he makes his offering of himself? Clearly we must not think that his offering made by himself alone would leave the soul to suffer for years, but my joining with him will end the soul's suffering at once. We must remember that, had our Lord not offered his life for us, neither the soul's own sufferings nor the prayers of its friends would be of any avail towards purifying it from sin. Whatever these sufferings and prayers do for the soul, all is due to the Mass, in which our Lord offers his sacrifice. Again, we must remember that the spiritual good done to us by God's grace is limited by our willingness to receive it, and likewise by the state and needs of our soul. When we need purification, we cannot yet receive the graces that saints get. God is willing to give grace without limit, but we are not willing or able to receive it because we are attached to unworthy things. Consequently, some souls during their life on earth earned that they should be helped by the prayers of their friends after death; and others did not. For the former class, Almighty God has willed that their purification in sufferings should be aided by the prayers offered for them by the Church on earth. When we pray for them and offer Masses for them, we are not winning him to change his appointed plan for bringing those souls to heaven; we are simply carrying it out.

We feel instinctively and rightly that it is better to offer the Mass than any other good work, prayer, or penance; because these others are merely our own unworthy and faulty efforts, whereas the Mass is the immaculate sacrifice of the Lamb of God. We still want to know, then, what difference it makes to the fruits of the Mass when I join in offering it. It would be blasphemous to think that the Mass earns any more fruit from my joining in it. But our Lord does mean that our asking and our offering his sacrifice shall make some difference, not in the winning of grace, but in the receiving of the grace into souls. And first into our own souls. The whole reason he made Mass was in order that we might take into our souls his own high love, that longs to offer worthy worship to God, not only from his own heart, but from all hearts; and that having conceived this love, we might have a worthy offering to make to God. By this love we become his partners in sanctifying not only our own souls but the souls of others also. In this world he uses those who have his love to spread it to those who have not; to win our brother to God,[1] to preach his gospel to all nations.[2] But in making us partners in his love, he does not make us partners in his knowledge. "It is not for you to know."[3] When we pray for souls in this world or in purgatory, we must not expect to know the results of our prayers, much less tell him what ought to be their results. He wants our

[1] Matt. xviii 15. [2] Matt. xxviii 19.
[3] Acts i 7.

prayers to help in his work : that is our sufficient guarantee that our prayers are not wasted. But to know the results we must wait for the day of the Lord. Meantime, he bids us keep asking, knocking; pray without ceasing, and faint not. So we never cease praying and offering Masses for a departed soul till we have surety that it is among the blessed in heaven, through the Church proclaiming that person Blessed or Saint.

Therefore, when the Mass is offered for a suffering soul, the question is not what this most holy and spotless sacrifice will win, but what my offering of it will win for that soul. And this depends first on how far I am filled with divine love, our Lord's love for God and for men and for holiness. When this love entirely possesses a saint and moves him to pray, he is truly asking in our Lord's name, and his prayer will be granted.[1] Sometimes the saints have found they could not pray, when they were going to ask something that God did not mean to grant. We who are not saints know how poor are our prayers and from what an unloving heart they come, and therefore we ask again and again. He bade us continue knocking and asking; and by constant trying to ask well, we hope some day to ask worthily. And, secondly, the fruit of my prayers for a particular soul depends on the fitness of that soul to receive grace or mercy. For it may be that some souls have on earth deserved to suffer the whole of their penance themselves and receive no relief through others' prayers, like the servant in the parable, who refused mercy to others and asked it for himself.[2]

We call them the Holy Souls because they are in the grace and love of God; they have won heaven, are only waiting to enter. Their active life now consists wholly in that love between God and the soul which we call the supernatural life of the soul. God's love for them keeps their answering love on fire, ceaselessly yearning towards him; and by the agony of that burning love " the almighty and merciful Lord looses them from the bonds of their sins."

Suffering for sins is twofold. First there is the sinless suffering of the Lamb of God, " who his own self bore our sins in his body on the tree, that we being dead to sins should live to justice; by whose stripes we were healed."[3] This suffering is shared by his sinless Mother and by many of his innocent saints. Because they are near to him, they are privileged to drink of the chalice of suffering that he drank of, and to be baptised in his baptism of blood for the sins of the world.[4] Secondly, there is the sinner's suffering in this world or the next to atone for his own sins, a suffering we take up with shame as men who in the sight of heaven have wrought mischief against God and disfigured his image in their own souls. By this suffering we painfully restore our lost likeness to God. But, even in our misery, Jesus invites us in this world to join with

[1] John xvi 23.
[2] Matt. xviii 32-34.
[3] 1 Pet. ii 24.
[4] Mark x 39.

him in working and suffering for the souls of other sinners, and so to have some part with his holy Apostles and martyrs. This we can do by offering prayers and penances for the suffering souls in purgatory.

J. B. McLaughlin, O.S.B.

XXXIII

ETERNAL PUNISHMENT

§ I: INTRODUCTORY

Punishment

PUNISHMENT is pain justly inflicted in consequence of evil done. It is purely medicinal if its sole purpose is to bring the evil-doer to repentance and to enable him to undo the evil wrought. It is purely retributive or avenging if its purpose is to vindicate and restore the glory and honour of one who has been offended by the evil deed, and thus to restore the balance of justice by placing the evil-doer in an evil plight on account of the evil done.

Retributive punishment

Punishments on earth are, or ought to be, chiefly of a mixed character, partly curative, partly retributive. The punishment of hell is purely retributive. It has no medicinal purpose for the sinner undergoing it, though it has also a preventative purpose, by being a deterrent to others.

The righteousness of retributive justice is almost instinctively admitted by every reasonable person. When misdeeds entail no suffering for the offender, when crimes pass unpunished—the wicked prosper and the good succumb—there arises in every human soul the irresistible conviction that something is lacking, something wrong in the arrangement of the universe ; also that such wrong cannot last for ever, and that in the end it must go well with the just and ill with the evil-doer.

This profound conviction is based on the idea that sin and suffering are correlatives ; I mean that every sin committed necessarily entails the liability to a corresponding punishment, so that the balance of justice may be maintained. It is true that repentance obtains forgiveness. But repentance itself contains the will to make satisfaction, and satisfaction is a punishment which the sinner voluntarily inflicts upon himself in consequence of his sin, in order that the great Orderer of the universe may not inflict punishment, which has already been voluntarily endured.

Were, however, no evil consequence to follow the disobedience of an unrepentant sinner, man might rightly accuse the Supreme Guardian of the world of failing to vindicate the law of holiness, and might conclude that no holy intelligence was directing and controlling the order of created things. In strictly technical language, God wills the order of this universe, and must necessarily continue to will it, as long as it exists, for to maintain its existence is to will its order. Now the sinner rebels against this order. He cannot indeed disturb it objectively, for God's will is sovereign and omnipotent, but he can pervert his own will and commit an act contrary to his final end, by adhering inordinately to an object of desire and enjoyment. If the order of the universe is to be maintained, the sinner's will must of necessity be contravened and thwarted in the same measure as he himself has contravened and thwarted the due order by God established. Now all thwarting of the will is sorrow, and if in consequence of sin, such sorrow is punishment.

Its connection with sin

Punishment, therefore, must follow sin as its shadow. Punishment is the counterpoise of sin, demanded by intrinsic necessity to restore the balance of righteousness. As water seeks its own level, so punishment succeeds sin. Sufferings may be self-inflicted, as when we do penance ; or inflicted by God, and then they are called punishment.

Retributive justice, therefore, is in itself the maintenance of order. It is properly called avenging or retributive justice in the case of divine punishments, because God, who maintains the order of the universe, is a personal God, not an abstract force, and all the laws of the universe are enacted by his personal will. The sinner, therefore, not only attempts to break the objective order of the universe in which he lives, but he offends the personal God who created him. The sinner by his deed—as far as in him lies—deprives God of the honour due to him in the obedience of all created wills and their gratitude for the benefit of their own existence. Divine punishments, therefore, vindicate God's glory and in themselves are a manifestation of God's holiness.

When thinking of an avenging God we must eliminate from our mind any idea that God desires or thirsts to be satiated with the sight of suffering. God desires or thirsts for nothing. No sin, however great, can lessen God's happiness. No sinner can hurt God. God is not injured as we are injured on earth, smarting under the pain of the insult. Hence it is not a question of God paying the sinner back in his own coin—for every hurt received a hurt inflicted. God in punishing can have only one motive : his own infinite holiness and nothing else whatever.

Eternal punishment is the everlasting separation of God from the sinner, because the sinner continues to reject him ; it is the allowing creatures to torment the sinner, because he has turned to creatures instead of to God as his ultimate end. This punishment is everlasting, not because God can never be satiated with the sight of the sinner's pain, but because the sinner abides by his final choice, preferring a created good to God, and can no longer change his mind. He is eternally punished because he is eternally in the state of sin.

§ II: THE NATURE OF ETERNAL PUNISHMENT

A. The Pain of Loss

Loss of the Beatific Vision

As in many minds the word hell stands merely for some confused idea of endless horror and misery, without any precise conception of its nature and what the Catholic Church teaches concerning it, we must needs begin with a simple exposition of what the Church means by hell.

What, then, is hell ?

It is primarily the permanent deprivation of the Beatific Vision, inflicted on those who die in mortal sin.

Unbaptised children and unbaptised adults who were so mentally defective as to be incapable of choosing between good and evil will after life also lack the Beatific Vision. Such privation of Beatific Vision, when merely the consequence of original sin, is, however, seldom designated in English by the word " hell," though in Latin the technical term " infernum " is sometimes used for it. In this essay we are not discussing the state of unbaptised infants [1] or mental defectives, we are dealing exclusively with the punishment of those who die guilty of personal mortal sin, a punishment which primarily consists in the penal deprivation of the Beatific Vision.

The Beatific Vision is the sight of God face to face. This supernatural state of final bliss is studied in the essay on *Heaven*,[2] the reading of which will contribute much to a fuller understanding of what is here written on hell.

Here we can consider the Beatific Vision only negatively, because its punitive absence constitutes the very essence of eternal damnation.

The natural end of man would have been to know God indirectly through his creatures, and to love him with a love corresponding to such knowledge. For such natural end man, as a matter of fact, was never destined. God gave him only a supernatural end, which is the direct sight of God without any intermediary, the vision which the Scriptures aptly describe as " face to face."

The chief punishment of hell

To have lost this end through one's own fault constitutes the very nature of hell. It is called damnation, from the Latin word *damnum*, which means simply " loss." It is the Great Loss. It is a loss which nothing can replace. The supernatural end of man having been lost by actual sin, no other end or purpose of a lower or natural kind can be attained. The sinner who loses the Beatific Vision loses his all, for his soul, though endowed with never-ending existence, will never attain the end or purpose to which none the less it must by the force of his nature eternally tend. It is the final and never-ceasing frustration of the craving of an immortal being.

In one sense one might speak of it as an infinite loss. For the object lost is God himself—God as the object of human knowledge

[1] See pp. 355 ff., 779.

[2] Essay xxxv.

and love. On the other hand, the loss is subjectively and strictly speaking not infinite. The pain of loss depends on the realisation of the value of the thing lost. Even on earth two people may lose an object of intrinsically the same value and feel the loss unequally. All the damned lose God, yet the punishment of all, however great, will not be equal, for the loss of God will mean more to one than to another.

It is sometimes said that the damned at the judgement will for a moment see God and then be deprived of his sight for ever. This is, however, an incorrect way of speaking. Once God is seen face to face, the soul will love him eternally; once the Beatific Vision is granted, it will never be withdrawn. Though this particular expression, therefore, is incorrect, still it is prompted by a true idea. Unless the soul were granted a deeper and greater realisation of what God is than it had possessed on earth, the loss of the immediate vision of God would mean but little to it. Some flash of light must pierce the darkened mind, revealing to it the awful greatness and beauty of God at least in some indirect way in order that it may realise what it has lost. For us on earth God always remains something unseen and, as it were, abstract. He is the Great Unknown, at the back of the universe, he is its maker and its maintainer, therefore all creation proclaims him indeed, but at the same time hides him from our sight. His very existence is only an inference, a valid inference, a spontaneous inference of reason, but still only a conclusion. He is not in himself an object of mental sight. We understand that he must contain within himself all perfections of the universe, but in a higher, more eminent way. We know God indeed also by revelation, he stands revealed in Jesus Christ, but even this revelation is not direct sight. The Apostles saw Christ's manhood, not his Godhead, and what they have told us reveals the divinity indirectly but not in itself. Moreover, on earth even this indirect knowledge remains only a dim realisation, because of the thousand attractions of sense which interfere with our religious meditation. In consequence, to lose God does not in this life mean to us that unspeakable calamity which it in reality is.

The loss definitive

The loss of the Beatific Vision is the great failure. On earth no failure is complete, because it is always retrievable, if not in itself, at least in some other way. Hell means total failure, failure of the whole of one's being, failure without any hope of retrieving what is lost.

The impulse to re-start after failure is almost instinctive during this life. There will be no re-starting life after this final disaster. All is over, the soul is forced to face utter ruin, beyond repair. All that is left is blank despair.

Its grievous nature

In the life beyond the grave where all illusions about earthly goods have completely gone, where the turmoil of this material world has ceased, where the soul has outgrown the limitations of this mortal life, and realises with a mental keenness unknown on earth the inner truth of things, the loss of God is a disaster exceeding in extent all that we can now conceive. We now know that we are made for God, and that the possession of God is our final end, but we realise it in a faint, obscure way only. Few people have felt an intense hunger for God. Some saints, indeed, have done so; they have at moments been driven almost beside themselves with a desire to see God, they have felt an agonising pain in the delay, and some have welcomed death, which would give them the object of their desire. Those instances, however, are rare.

The kaleidoscopic variation of earthly affairs distracts us, and the good things of the world satisfy us at least in part; bodily necessities interrupt our higher mental life continually. None of this happens in eternity. Man has come to his final state in which with all his mental power and the whole energy of his will he either possesses God or, losing him, is aware of the complete and everlasting failure of his existence. Every fibre of his being tends toward God by inward necessity; God draws him as a magnet draws iron, his innermost self thrills with longing for God, who is infinite goodness, beauty, and truth, yet he is intimately conscious that his nature is so warped, disfigured, and deformed that it can never be united to God. Between himself and God there is a gulf fixed which no bridge will ever span. Nor is God a distant object, which he might manage to forget. God is intimately present to him, but this presence is a torment, not a joy, for holiness is both an object of horror and of desire to those that are in sin. Every instant of his never-ending life he wants God and he knows that he wants him, yet every instant he feels an irresistible recoil, a disgust, a loathing and a hatred, which turns him from that which he wants.

To speak in a parable, he is like a shipwrecked mariner in a little craft on the open sea. He raves with maddening thirst, though surrounded by water. He lifts the sea water to his lips and then vomits it out, for it is salt. The salt is his sin. His sin has turned even the sweet waters of God's goodness brackish; it is a venom which he always tastes and makes him hate even God as poison, though at the same time he is mad with thirst for God.

If, perhaps, a reader in perusing the following pages feels inclined to think that this is all rhetoric, and not a sober and objective treatment of the problem, he must remember that hell is a matter of revelation, and that the source of our knowledge is what Christ and the Apostles have revealed. If they spoke in figures, our way to truth is by analysing and probing the full truth of what they said.

Christ speaks of hell as the losing of one's soul: "What doth it profit a man if he gain the whole world, and suffer the loss of his own soul? Or what exchange shall a man give for his soul?"[1] This expression, "losing one's soul," does not mean cessation of

[1] Matt. xvi 26.

existence, for we know that the soul is immortal; but it does mean the complete cessation of that supernatural life of grace, which God intended for it, and without which man has utterly failed of the purpose of his being. If a man—an adult, who has had the choice between good and evil and with complete deliberation has chosen evil and died persisting in his choice—fails to obtain the Beatific Vision, there is no substitute for it as the aim of his life. He has lost his soul in the fullest sense of the word. All that remains to him is eternal existence without purpose, or rather with a purpose that can never be achieved, never even be approached throughout eternity. It is the complete aimlessness of a never-ending life which is the appalling state of the lost soul. It is an asking never to receive, a seeking never to find, a knocking at a gate eternally closed, to hear for ever: "Amen, amen, I know you not."

In hell nothing of the supernatural remains except the marks of baptism, confirmation, and the priesthood, nothing except the bitter memory of graces once received, and these things remain to enhance eternal sorrow, the sense of the greatness of what is lost.

In contrast to "the saved," the damned are called "the lost." No word could express more precisely and almost technically their real state. They are lost. By creating us, God sent us on a journey, a journey towards himself, a journey which was meant to end in a home-coming. The home intended is a nestling in the very bosom of God, the complete possession, the closest embrace by mind and will of God himself. For the damned the journey will never end, home and rest will never be; they are lost. For them is eternal restlessness without progression. They are wanderers, idly, foolishly, hopelessly wandering hither and thither, never making headway toward God. Although no belated traveller ever had a fiercer desire than they to be able to say: "Home at last," they will never say it; it is for ever dying on their lips.

St Jude in his epistle has an inspired description of the wicked which because of its very divine inspiration is of the greatest value in understanding the state of the damned. He calls them: "Clouds without water, carried about by the winds; trees of autumn, unfruitful, twice dead, plucked up by the roots; raging waves of the sea, foaming out their own confusion; wandering stars, to whom the storm of darkness is reserved for ever." [1]

A cloud pregnant with beneficent rain is a source of blessing, a steady cloud that is a shield to the glare of the sun is a cause of joy, but clouds without water, swept across the sky by a hurricane, are flimsy things of nothing, the symbol of the utterly useless, the utterly wasted, the thing that was and is gone, and has left no trace.

The wicked are like trees that had chance of bearing fruit, but have not done so. Their summer is over, and no second summer will be given them. They are dead in their innermost being, dug up by

[1] Verses 12, 13.

the roots, severed from all that lives by the Spirit of God, rotting alone in eternal corruption.

The wicked are as the raging waves of the sea, foaming out their own confusion. On the shores of eternity they are breaking the surging waves of their furious passions, but the roar of their turbulent yearnings will never cease and their utmost endeavour will for ever end in idle spray.

The wicked are wandering stars to whom the storm of darkness is reserved for ever. Some comets with a long trail of splendour approach the sun with incredible speed, but they swing round the centre light without touching it, and then start their path back into space and their parabola ends in infinity. Thus out of nothing did God create human souls, endowed them with a trail of glory, and sent them forward towards himself. But some abusing their free will, miss the divine Sun that is the centre and heart of all creation, then to start back into infinity, into a darkness whence they will never return. They are the " sidera errantia," the wandering stars driven into the empty void by the storm-blast of God's wrath.

Let no one set these things aside as mere metaphors, unfit for a scientific exposition ; they are the word of God, and when God himself uses analogy and figure of speech, the study of God's metaphors is the most scientific treatment which the subject can bear.

Christ describes the state of the damned as one of outer darkness. Obviously physical darkness is not the only thing meant ; it is also mental, spiritual darkness. As the eye is destined for the light, so is man's mind destined for the truth, but the truth is God. The inner desire to know is natural to every human being. Promise a man to tell him something new, and you will draw him from afar ; he will submit to every hardship, if only he can come and listen. From the far-off days when Babylonian astronomers searched with naked eye the starry heavens till this day when a man bends over a microscope, the search for the truth is the dominant passion of humanity. Some degraded men may sink their being in sensual, sexual pleasures, but they are few, and even in them some desire for truth can never die. Satan well understood human nature when in Paradise he beguiled the first man with the lying promise : " If you eat from the fruit of the tree, ye shall *know*." God promised man as his supreme reward : " Ye shall know ! " " This is everlasting life : that they may know thee, the only true God, and Jesus Christ, whom thou hast sent." The reward is the clear unclouded sight of God in his own divine nature. This will completely satiate the human mind, which will rest in ecstasy on the object of its knowledge. The supreme Mystery will lie unveiled. But the damned are in darkness, and a cloud of ignorance clings to their intelligence. They know that they might have known, but they do not.

The raving madman is on earth an object of pity and horror to the sane-minded, but the damned are madmen of their own making ;

deliberately they have drugged their own minds with the poison of sin and their delirium is always upon them. Though God is so close to them and the natural forces of their intellect so keen in the world beyond, yet God is the maddening mystery to them, the tormenting problem that will never be solved. The man in a foul, dark fog which stings his eyes and blinds them, feels his gloom the more, if he recalls to himself that somewhere the sun shines and the sky is blue. So the damned grope and stumble along in a mental mist that will never be lifted, though they know that somewhere the majesty and clarity of truth sheds its splendour and entrances beholders with its divine beauty.

The mind is darkened and the will perverted. Those whose work brings them to study the psychology of sin come across many cases of such incipient perversion even on earth. Final perversion is only an intensification, a fixing of a state by no means unknown here. The drunkard drinks, and inwardly curses himself for drinking. The debauchee wallows in sin, and detests himself for his loathsome cravings. The angry man smites in the moment of his anger, yet his own nature cries out while he strikes his friend. His cravings, his passions, his furies are upon him, they cling to him. Their grasp is more than an outward grip, they hold his will by inward compulsion. Sometimes in impotent remorse he cries out: " My tastes are foul, my desires are loathsome ; I am a cruel beast, I know it, but I cannot, I will not change ; I am what I am." When a friend or a priest comes and puts the horror of his conduct before him, he fiercely faces them: " You can tell me nothing I do not know. Preach to me ? Man, I preach to myself every hour of the day, and then laugh in despair at my own eloquence ! Matters have gone too far, I am what I am, better leave me alone ! "

For a long time some vague desire for good remains, a tear sometimes wells up for the virtue that is gone, the innocence that is lost. Then even that state passes away, at least in some rare cases. There is a delight in evil, a wish to spread evil, a hatred for what is good. The victim of lust hates all that is chaste and wants to destroy it. The victim of anger detests what is patient and meek and wants to crush it. The proud man repels the humble and wants to trample upon him. The sight of moral beauty rouses inner antagonism. He wants a recasting of all values. Good must be evil ; evil must be good. Someone recently wrote his impressions of Bolshevik Russia. He was no minister of religion, he was no Catholic, I doubt even whether he was much of a believing Christian, but he wrote that what struck him most in his contact with Bolshevik circles was the existence of an almost demoniacal hate of chastity. An English novelist, who must be nameless, writes for the purpose of destroying the sacredness of marriage, to tear the heart out of the sanctities of wedded life. His purpose is avowed. He glories in it. A Nietzsche writes, or rather screams, that meekness, humility, purity are detestable evils, a morality only fit for slaves ; that all vice is really virtue, all hitherto esteemed virtue is the true vice.

If such things are possible on earth, is it not possible that such things happen in the world beyond ? Is it not possible that at last such state of mind is irremediable, that a man's heart becomes vitiated beyond all cure, that he abides by his choice and will never change ?

The Catholic Church teaches that the human soul remains in that state in which death finds it ; if averted from God it will remain so for ever. Two parallel lines do not meet, even in infinity. The lost soul has definitely chosen another end and purpose than God, an end which is incompatible with God. Because its self-chosen end lies outside God, it will not only never reach God, but will run its life in everlasting opposition to him.

It is difficult for us to understand that anyone should hate God. The perversity seems too monstrous ; no one can hate the Infinite Good. The answer to this difficulty, however, is not far to seek. If the Infinite Good were directly perceived by the damned soul, he could not, of course, hate it. The fact is that the mind of the damned is darkened ; though they are in eternity, they do not see God as he is. However vivid their imagination, however keen the realisation of his presence, it is indirect. It is still by reason and not by an act of intuitive intelligence that they perceive him. As such he becomes an object of their hatred and detestation because he stands in the way of what they want, what they have chosen by a final act of personal choice. He is their supreme antagonist. Of a friend they have made a foe. Not that God has changed, but they have changed. They have perverted themselves.

Now it must not be thought that the drunkard for all eternity will want drink, or the sexual sinner debauch, or the angry man eternal strife. In the changed conditions of the hereafter the precise objects of their choice will, indeed, differ. Alcohol has no attraction certainly for a disembodied soul, nor women nor vulgar brawling. But what underlies these vices is the inordinate desire of self, self-gratification, self-exaltation, of whatever kind it may be. All sin is self-seeking as opposed to God-seeking. Any particular vice indulged in on earth is only a manifestation of the preference of self before God. This self-seeking remains in the damned, and it is the very core of their damnation. The true centre of all things is God, but they are self-centred. The supreme happiness we know is love, but love means to love someone else. To love God is the supreme act of altruism which is rewarded by true happiness, because the Divine Other-One is infinitely good, and to possess infinite good is infinite happiness. The damned can love no more and therefore they are damned. Hell is the home of incurables. The disease that is beyond cure is their egoism. It is incurable because they everlastingly reject the only remedy that could heal them : the love of Some One Else instead of themselves.

B. The Pain of Sense

Positive torment

Although the punitive deprivation of the Beatific Vision constitutes the chief pain of hell, the Catholic Church teaches that, in addition to this negative punishment, there is also a positive pain afflicting the damned. This is commonly referred to as hell-fire. Strictly speaking, however, " hell-fire " is but an aspect of what is called the pain of sense as distinguished from the pain of loss.

For it must be well borne in mind that it does not suffice to say that the pain of sense afflicts the body, whereas the pain of loss afflicts the soul. According to Scripture, hell-fire was prepared for the devil and his angels, but angels have no bodies and therefore cannot be afflicted in them. Nor have lost human souls a body till the last day, yet they will be tormented by fire forthwith after the Particular Judgement. When speaking, therefore, of hell-fire we must keep in mind that we are not necessarily referring to bodily pain in contrast to mental pain, but to a pain which primarily affects the spirit or the soul, though after the General Judgement it will also affect the body. The difference between the pain of loss and that of sense consists in the fact that the former is caused by the absence of something, the latter by the presence of something. The former is negative, the latter positive. This hell-fire is something real, and it is something external to the sufferer who undergoes its tormenting energies. The malice of every sin has two aspects : it is a turning away from God, and it is a turning towards creatures instead of God. The everlasting loss of God is the natural punishment for the rejection of God. What is called the pain of sense is the natural punishment for the abuse of created things, involved in turning to them, embracing them, endeavouring to possess them rather than God. It is, as it were, poetic justice, if such a phrase may pass, that he who refuses God and embraces a created thing, should lose God and have a created thing to torment him for ever.

Real fire, not metaphorical

The reality of this " hell-fire," as the instrument of the pain of sense, has never been defined by a solemn decision of Pope or Council, making the denial of it formal heresy and punishing it by exclusion from the Church, but it is certainly contained in Holy Scripture, in the Fathers, and it is the practically unanimous teaching of theologians. It could no doubt be solemnly defined if occasion demanded, and had the Council of the Vatican not been interrupted, might possibly have been defined. Meanwhile no Catholic can deny it without grievous sin against the faith, though this sin could not as yet be described as one of formal heresy, but only one of wilful error and temerity. In consequence the Sacred Penitentiary at Rome, being asked whether a penitent who declared to his confessor that in his opinion the term " hell-fire " is only a metaphor in order to express the intense pains of the demons, might be allowed to persist in this opinion and be absolved, answered as follows : " Such penitents must be diligently instructed and, if pertinacious, they must not be absolved" (April 30, 1890). This, of course, is a disciplinary, not a doctrinal decree, and obviously is not an infallible definition, but it certainly adds weight to what must be regarded as the traditional view.

Hell-fire, therefore, is not a metaphor for the intensity of mere spiritual or mental sufferings; it is a reality, objectively present outside the sufferer, and the objective cause of his sufferings. We may further ask: Are we bound to believe that God created this instrument of torture, as a new thing, called out of nothing by his omnipotence in addition to the other things he made, so that even if no devil or damned soul ever entered this fire, still it would go on burning, as if it were feeding on itself, though empty of spirits to torture?

Various views concerning its nature

No, not necessarily. Fire, as we have it on earth, is produced by oxygen fed by carbon, and through the vibration of the atoms brings about the disintegration of the body that burns. Such fire hell-fire cannot be, for the bodies of the damned do not disintegrate, and we are not bound to believe that there will be an everlasting supply of oxygen and carbon. Moreover, "hell-fire" affects even the demons, who are pure spirits, and the damned, who until the General Resurrection are without their terrestrial bodies. In consequence, though hell-fire is a reality causing the pain of sense as distinct from the loss of God, and is some external agent whose action the demons and the damned undergo, yet this fire is only analogous to the fire we experience on earth. The instrument of this suffering is referred to in the New Testament no less than thirty times by the word fire, which word must therefore be the nearest analogy in our earthly experience to that which torments the damned.

Many theologians hold that the fire which torments the damned, though of course not an earthly fire like the fire in our grates, is yet some special creation of God, some external agent, specially called into being by God as the instrument of his avenging justice. It is, indeed, prepared for the devil and his angels, something, in fact, which would not have been but for the fact of Satan's sin; something which not only has nothing subjective about it, but is plainly merely an objective reality with which the demons and the damned come in contact and through which they suffer; something which would remain in existence, even though no devil or damned soul came within its power. They urge in support of this view the language of Holy Scripture in which hell is described as a lake of fire into which the damned are cast, described as a definite locality somewhere in the universe, a place which can be entered and left. They urge, moreover, with force that tradition has ever seen in hell, not only some external agent tormenting the damned, but something as it were designed by the justice and holiness of God for the specific purpose of inflicting punishment on those that deserve it. In consequence, it must be something altogether distinct from the rest of God's creation, an awful reality distinct from all the other works of God. It cannot be denied that the reasons brought forward are weighty and appear to many grave theologians conclusive. We must, indeed, always keep in view that the fire of hell is certainly not a mere metaphor for the pain of the loss of God, but some additional reality which will accompany it for all eternity. It is a pain inflicted from without, inflicted by some external material agent doing the behest of God.

Scripture, however, nowhere says that God "created" this fire, but only that he "prepared" it. It would, therefore, not be against Holy Writ to hold that without creating any new substances God so utilised existing creatures as to form them into a fire for the devils and the damned. The lost have turned to creatures instead of God; God in consequence makes creatures the instrument of their punishment. St Thomas in discussing this matter most aptly uses the text: "The whole world will fight with God against the perverse,"[1] and he says: "Not the whole world would fight against the perverse if they were punished only with a spiritual punishment and not with a corporeal one. Therefore they will be punished with a corporeal fire."[2] As St Thomas, following the imperfect physiology of his day, regarded fire as an element, his explanation, however valuable, must be reinterpreted in the light of present-day knowledge, which does not accept fire as an all-pervading constituent element of all things in the universe. The essence of St Thomas's teaching seems to lie in this: that God has armed the whole universe to fight on his side against the devils and the damned. God may have made this visible universe itself a fire tormenting the devils and the damned.

Moreover, there may be a bond of intrinsic necessity between the rejection of God by the damned and their being tormented by fire. Hell-fire is, perhaps, not a punishment separately invented by the ingenuity of divine vengeance, a fierce after-thought as it were of God's wrath, to render the loss of himself more horrible, but the necessary outcome of man's nature in a state of sin, the inevitable result of the opposition between a perverted created will and the will of God, expressed in material creation.

In any case God is not merely the passive spectator of hell by simply allowing nature to take its course. God is no more a passive spectator of hell than he is of heaven. Nature has no being apart from God. God is active in all nature. It must ever be remembered that God is not an impersonal force, but a personal intelligence, and that the demons and the damned are in opposition to a personal Being, and that from this personal antagonism all their evil flows. It is therefore quite correct to speak of God inflicting punishment on his foes, though it is wrong to think of this in human fashion as if God sought the satisfaction of a desire for vengeance.

Whether, then, the fuel of this fire be specially created for the

[1] Wisdom v 21. [2] *S. Theol., Suppl.*, xcvii 5.

purpose or whether it be the very nature of this universe, it is a fire which in its effects and mode of action differs greatly from earthly fire. Earthly fire can only burn bodies, hell-fire burns spirits. Earthly fire disintegrates and destroys what it burns, hell-fire does not dissolve what it burns, but is compatible with never-ending existence. Earthly fire needs a continual supply of new material fuel, hell-fire is everlastingly maintained by the will and the anger of God. Earthly fire is joined to some degree of light, hell-fire is compatible with outer darkness. Earthly fire is limited to some locality, hell-fire accompanies the damned wheresoever they are. Earthly fire burns equally all that is thrown into its furnace, hell-fire burns unequally the souls of the damned according to the greatness of their sin. When we thus multiply the points of difference between the action of earthly fire and the fire tormenting the damned, we realise that we are face to face with a mystery which is beyond all our experience in this world.

How a material fire can torment a purely spiritual being we cannot fully explain. St Thomas explains it by the spirit being hampered, hindered and tied to this fire, which thus limits its freedom of action. This very imprisonment and enchainment is suggested as the cause of the soul's torment. This explanation to some may appear inadequate. However that may be, all that we can, all that we *need* say with regard to the action of hell-fire upon spirits, is that by God's omnipotence fire will directly act upon a pure intelligence so as to cause it to suffer a pain to which the only parallel we possess on earth is the sensation of burning.

Hell a place

Hell is doubtless a place as well as a state. Such, at least, is the most natural inference from the texts of Scripture and was always taken for granted within the Church, though one could not say that it was held as a part of divine revelation. Where in the whole universe hell is, no one can say. Until the development of modern science, hell was spoken of as in the centre of the earth, and this mode of speech, referring to the realms below, or the lowest abyss, will no doubt remain for ever customary, but it does not mean that the speaker has any conviction of faith that hell is somewhere below the earth's surface. The place of hell is simply unknown to us, for it has not pleased God to reveal it.

From what has been said it will be clear that the pain of loss, the chief punishment of hell, is far more grievous than the pain of sense. Nevertheless, it is these latter torments of hell that have most forcibly struck the imagination of men, and our Lord, by speaking in the Gospels of "hell-fire," deliberately stressed this side of eternal punishment, for he knew human nature and knew that sensible imagination would be the strongest incentive to a horror of the dreadful fate awaiting the unrepentant sinner.

Warning against imaginative descriptions

It is true that sometimes both in pictures or in carvings, in sermons or in books, the torments of hell have been described with a crude realism which revolts a decent mind. Adversaries of Christianity have of recent years collected together many medieval prints and sculptures relating to hell, they have collected a number of descriptions of infernal tortures from patristic, medieval, and even more recent writers, and thus pilloried the ghastly ingenuity with which fantastic scenes of agony and cruelty were invented.

But the Christian, who peruses these tendentious works, must always call to mind that it is easy to collect from a vast literature extending over two thousand years quotations which in their accumulation give the impression that Christianity was a religion of terror and despair. It is only a deeper student with a more balanced mind who realises that such fantastic literature forms only an infinitesimally small part of the output of Christian letters ; that as a matter of fact the predominant character of Christianity is one of joy, confidence, and hope ; that the bulk of Christian literature expresses loving amazement at the goodness of God. The devout Christian sometimes pictures hell to himself, but he also has the tender sweetness of the crib of Bethlehem, the bright joy of Easter day, and he pictures the adoration of the Lamb and the saints in glory. Medieval architecture sometimes contains a carving of a devil, as a gargoyle tormenting a damned soul, but the whole creates the impression of majesty, might, and exaltation, not of dread and doom. No doubt in some very few instances the representations of hell may be excessively gruesome and in still fewer even betray an unhealthy spirit. For such morbidities one need offer no defence. Christian writers and artists may have been at fault, but in the main both their purpose and their execution have been wholesome and noble.

The pains of hell exceed in horror all that men can imagine ; it is therefore right and just that even the imagination should be called in to warn men against the supreme and last danger that besets all men. Passion and temptation to sin can be so blinding that nothing but an almost physical recoil from the punishment threatened can succeed in drawing the mind and will away from the false enchantment of evil. One might grant that the psychology of the twentieth century is not quite the same as that of the tenth, that what would be an effective dissuasion from sin in the Middle Ages may not be so effective now, but the human soul remains throughout the centuries substantially the same. The motive of fear will always be potent for good as well as for evil, and with many the threat of bodily pain will be a stronger bridle on such bodily passions as anger and lust than anything else. If all that were ever written or painted or carved expressive of the tortures of hell could be brought before us at a glance, it would certainly fall immeasurably short of the truth. Though the precise agonies dreamt of by a vivid imagination may not be the exact counterpart of the sufferings of the lost, they symbolise a reality exceeding the power of pen, brush, or chisel ; they exceed all earthly imagination.

Degrees of punishment

As in heaven there are different degrees of happiness, so in hell there are different degrees of punishment. The least degree of punishment will exceed in horror all we can imagine on earth, but even in hell there are depths below depths. The soul is alienated from God in the very measure of its deformity. The deformity caused by one sin can be greater than that caused by another, and according to the number of sins the deformity increases. There are therefore degrees even in the loss of God ; the deeper the deformity the farther from God. The greater self-abhorrence in the damned brings about the deeper aversion from God, whose infinite holiness holds up the mirror to the monstrosity of the damned soul. In the pain of sense likewise there must be degrees. The fiercer the sinful grip on creatures which the sinner had in this life, the more fiercely will the vengeful fire torment him in the house of his eternity.

Therefore Dante's play of imagination, when in his *Inferno* he describes all kinds and degrees of punishment, is not idle and useless, if it keeps before our mind that for the lost in some unique way the punishment will always fit their crime.

§ III : ETERNAL PUNISHMENT IN SCRIPTURE

The Old Testament

As the Old Testament was a progressive revelation, the doctrine of everlasting punishment for the wicked gradually gained in clearness as the time went on and approached the fulness of revelation in Christ. The Jews began with an exceedingly vague idea of the world beyond the grave. Considering that the Jews stayed for many generations in Egypt, where the ideas about reward and punishment hereafter were worked out in such minute detail and with such terrible crudity, this mentality must be due to a deliberate refusal to entertain the thoughts of their fellow-countrymen and contemporaries, and it was no doubt the way of Providence to guard them from the fearful superstitions of the heathen world.

Moreover, as the gates of heaven were closed until Ascension Day, no immediate bright future could be promised even to the saints of the Old Testament. It would have been cold comfort to Abraham to promise him two thousand years of waiting in a realm of twilight before the dawn of day. God mercifully shrouded the details of the immediate future in after-life from the Jews of the Old Covenant. As the Patriarchal and Mosaic covenant was a tribal or national one, and had only indirectly to do with the individual, the prophets delivered their message usually to the nation as such ; they promised and threatened national welfare or national disaster as the immediate sanction of national obedience.

The existence of retribution beyond the grave was no doubt implied in the realisation of their responsibility before Jehovah, but no attempt was made to think out its details, and ultimate retribution after this life as a stimulus to well-doing was left to the individual.

Jehovah's rewards and punishments were terrestrial; they were bestowed or inflicted here, whatever happened hereafter. The Hebrew Sheol was apparently very much like the Greek Hades, just the Netherworld. That the good fared well, the wicked ill, in that abode was of course taken for granted, but seemingly one knew too little about it to give it special mention. The prophets predict a great day of judgement and final retribution. This great day of Jehovah, though often conceived as national rather than individual, does involve a final and irreversible settlement of human affairs some time in the future. Some prophets, especially Ezechiel and Daniel, clearly assert the eternal punishment of the wicked in a life beyond this earthly life.

The latter prophet writes: "At that time shall thy people be saved, every one that shall be found written in the book, and many of those that sleep in the dust of the earth shall awake, some unto life everlasting, and others unto reproach, to see it always."[1] In the great Machabean struggle, the certainty of everlasting retribution steeled the wills of the martyrs: "It is better," so they said to the tyrant king, "being put to death by men, to look for hope from God, to be raised up again by him: for, as to thee, thou shalt have no resurrection unto life."[2]

Job certainly asserts the reward of the just after death, and this naturally implies the retribution of the unjust. In some Psalms, especially Psalm xlviii, the doctrine of eternal retribution after life is distinctly asserted. The shade of the wicked will be consumed in hell and have no other dwelling, but God will redeem the soul of the just from hell and take it with him. The Book of Wisdom deals with the lot of the just and the unjust in the world beyond. The first five chapters are directly devoted to the doctrine of everlasting retribution, and it is set out with unmistakable clearness. The lost, reflecting on their earthly life, groan in anguish of spirit: "Being born forthwith we ceased to be, and have been able to show no mark of virtue, but are consumed in our wickedness. Such things said the sinners in hell, for the hope of the sinners is as dust that is blown away by the wind, but the just shall live for evermore and their reward is with the Lord."[3]

There can be no doubt that a century before our Lord's coming the Jews, as a whole, were convinced believers in an eternal sanction after death. Even the Sadducees, who did not believe in angel or spirit or in the resurrection, will hardly have extended their denial to a survival after death and a consequent retribution. In any case, they stood outside the religious development of the vast majority of the Jewish people. The reader of the Old Testament must, however, be warned that the mere use of the word "hell" in an English translation of the Old Testament cannot be taken as a proof of a belief in hell, in the Christian sense of everlasting punishment.

[1] xii 1, 2. [2] 2 Mach. vii 14. [3] v 13-16.

In most cases it represents Sheol, which is the Hebrew term for the world beyond, the pit, the tomb, or the Netherworld.

The New Testament

The New Testament opens with the teaching of St John the Baptist. " Every tree that bringeth not forth good fruit shall be cut down and cast into the fire." Of Christ the Baptist prophesies : " His fan is in his hand, and he will purge his floor and will gather the wheat into his barn : but the chaff he will burn with unquenchable fire." " He that believeth in the Son hath life everlasting, but he that believeth not the Son shall not see life : but the wrath of God abideth on him." [1]

This teaching of the Forerunner is in a most striking way continued by Christ himself. It is almost as if he takes the very words from St John's lips and endorses them. Christ comes to men to place them before an absolute alternative, either to accept his message or take the eternal consequence. " He that shall speak against the Holy Ghost, it shall not be forgiven him, neither in this world, nor in the world to come. Either make the tree good and its fruit good, or make the tree evil and its fruit evil, for by the fruit the tree is known." [2] " He that shall blaspheme against the Holy Ghost shall never have forgiveness, but shall be guilty of an everlasting sin." [3] " I go, and you shall seek me. And you shall die in your sin. Whither I go you cannot come. If you believe not that I am he, you shall die in your sin. Amen, amen, I say unto you that whosoever committeth sin is the servant of sin. Now the servant abideth not in the house for ever." [4] Christ closes the Sermon on the Mount, which is a summary of the moral precepts of the New Covenant, with exactly the same eternal unchangeable alternative. " Every tree that bringeth not forth good fruit shall be cut down and shall be cast into the fire. Wherefore by their fruits you shall know them. Not every one that saith to me, Lord, Lord, shall enter into the kingdom of heaven : but he that doth the will of my Father, who is in heaven, he shall enter into the kingdom of heaven. Many will say to me in that day : Lord, Lord, have we not prophesied in thy name and cast out devils in thy name, and done many miracles in thy name ? And then will I profess unto them : I never knew you. Depart from me, ye that work iniquity." Evil-doers, therefore, will meet a final doom " in that day." These words are graphically brought home to Christ's hearers by the comparison between the wise builder, whose house stands because it is built on a rock, and the foolish builder, whose house perishes because it is built on sand. " It fell, and great was the fall thereof." It is utter ruin ; suggestion of rebuilding there is none ; it is an irretrievable calamity.

The rejection of Christ by many Jews, the acceptance of Christ by many Gentiles, involves for them a definite exclusion or a definite inclusion in heaven without mention of a possible reversal of this

[1] Matt. iii 10, 12 ; Luke iii 9, 17 ; John iii 36.
[2] Matt. xii 32-33. [3] Mark iii 29. [4] John viii 21, 24, 34, 35.

state. " Many shall come from the east and the west and shall sit down with Abraham, Isaac, and Jacob in the kingdom of heaven: but the children of the kingdom shall be cast out into the exterior darkness. There shall be weeping and gnashing of teeth." [1]

When Christ sent out the Apostles to preach, he said: " That which I tell you in the dark, speak ye in the light: and that which you hear in the ear, preach ye on the housetops, and fear ye not them that kill the body and are not able to kill the soul: but rather fear him that can cause both soul and body to perish in hell." [2] Perdition in hell, therefore, is the death of the soul, and obviously a final verdict of damnation.

The Gospel of St Mark gives us the most explicit and fearsome warning from Christ's lips against hell-fire. " If thy hand scandalise thee, cut it off: it is better for thee to enter into life, maimed, than having two hands to go into hell, into unquenchable fire: where their worm dieth not, and the fire is not extinguished. And if thy foot scandalise thee, cut it off: it is better for thee to enter lame into life everlasting than having two feet to be cast into hell of unquenchable fire: where their worm dieth not, and the fire is not extinguished. And if thy eye scandalise thee, pluck it out: it is better for thee with one eye to enter into the kingdom of God than having two eyes to be cast into hell-fire, where their worm dieth not, and the fire is not extinguished, for every one shall be salted with fire." [3]

On the one hand, therefore, is " life," " the kingdom of God," " life everlasting," on the other hand never-ending torment; any hazard whatever on earth must be taken to avoid the latter and secure the former.

The word " hell " comes spontaneously to Christ's lips when speaking of the utmost penalty and the last stage of depravity. The greatest threat against the man who insults his brother is that he is in danger of hell-fire. The greatest crime of the Pharisees is that they make a proselyte twofold more the child of hell than they are themselves, and Christ's threat against them is: " How will you flee from the judgement of hell ? " In all these cases our Lord calls hell by the Jewish term Gehenna, which means literally " valley of Hinnom," and refers to a gorge outside Jerusalem, where rubbish was shot and burnt and where unclean animals fed on garbage. For about two centuries before our era, if not longer, this term had been used for the place of the reprobate, in contrast to Paradise, the place of the blessed. Our Lord used an expression, commonly used and understood even by the most simple, to express an idea of irretrievable final rejection and damnation. In the quotation from St Mark just given the term Gehenna is explained by Christ himself as " the unquenchable fire," and as the place " where their worm dieth not and the fire is not quenched." These last words are a quotation of the final verse of Isaias the Prophet. In this passage God promises

[1] Matt. viii 11, 12. [2] Matt. x 27, 28. [3] Mark ix 42-48.

Israel that " their seed and their name shall stand before him as the new heavens and the new earth, which he will make," " and all flesh shall come to adore before my face, saith the Lord, and they shall go out (of the holy city Jerusalem) and see the carcasses of the men that have transgressed against me: their worm shall not die, and their fire shall not be quenched, and they shall be a loathsome sight unto all flesh."

This closing verse of Isaias describing the final consummation of Messianic times, the final triumph of the just and the punishment of the wicked, seems to have gripped the Jewish mind, for we find it twice quoted in later Jewish scriptures in Ecclus. vii 19 and Judith xvi 21. In the latter book it is said: " In the day of judgement he will visit them, and he will give fire and worms into their flesh that they may burn and suffer for ever."

Christ taught mainly by parables. Now five great parables end with the proclamation of eternal punishment for the wicked. Christ thus explains the parable of the tares and the wheat: " The field is the world, and the good seed are the children of the kingdom, and the cockle are the children of the wicked one. And the enemy that sowed them is the devil. But the harvest is the end of the world, and the reapers are the angels. Even as the cockle, therefore, is gathered up and burnt with fire: so shall it be at the end of the world. The Son of Man shall send his angels, and they shall gather out of the kingdom all scandals and them that work iniquity, and shall cast them into the furnace of fire; there shall be weeping and gnashing of teeth. Then shall the just shine as the sun in the kingdom of their Father."

The parable of the net catching good fishes and bad ends almost in the same words: " So shall it be at the end of the world. The angels shall go out and shall separate the wicked from among the just, and shall cast them into the furnace of fire: there shall be weeping and gnashing of teeth." The parable of Dives and Lazarus also ends in this way. Dives in the Netherworld, being in torments, lifted up his eyes. " He saw Abraham afar off and Lazarus in his bosom: and he cried out and said: Father Abraham, have mercy on me and send Lazarus that he may dip the tip of his finger in water and cool my tongue, for I am tormented in this flame. And Abraham said to him: Son, remember that thou didst receive good things in thy lifetime and likewise Lazarus evil things, but now he is comforted and thou art tormented. And besides all this, between us and you is a great gulf fixed: so that they who would pass from hence to you cannot, nor from thence come hither." [1]

The parable of the wedding feast ends [2] with the word of the king to the waiters concerning the man without the wedding garment: " Bind his hands and his feet and cast him into exterior darkness, there shall be weeping and gnashing of teeth."

[1] Luke xvi 19 ff. [2] Matt. xxii 14.

In the parable of the talents the servant who hid the one talent received the same punishment. The parable of the foolish virgins ends with a final exclusion from the feast by the bridegroom, who peremptorily answers the virgins who knock: " Amen, I say to you, I know you not."

The parable of the servant beating his fellow servants because his master delayed, tells us that the master " shall separate him and appoint his portion with the hypocrites. There shall be weeping and gnashing of teeth." The Greek word " hypocrites," in this text as in several others, doubtless stands for the Aramaic and Talmudic term for the reprobate, the *haniphin*. Such servant is a final outcast, permanently separated from the good.

This ultimate separation of the reprobate from the good is graphically portrayed by our Saviour in his description of the last judgement. " All nations shall be gathered together before him: and he shall separate them one from another, as the shepherd separateth the sheep from the goats, and he shall set the sheep on his right hand, but the goats on his left. Those on the right shall receive eternal bliss in the kingdom of the Father, those on the left shall hear: Depart from me, you cursed, into everlasting fire, which was prepared for the devil and his angels. And these shall go into everlasting punishment, but the just into life everlasting." [1] This is evidently a sentence without appeal, a definite verdict without possibility of reversal.

Although the Fourth Gospel represents a phase of Christ's teaching so deeply distinct from that of the three previous Gospels, yet on this point St John's Gospel is as emphatic, if not in fact more so, than the others. It is the everlasting alternative which is emphasised throughout. " Unless a man be born again, he cannot see the kingdom of God." " As Moses lifted up the serpent in the desert, so must the Son of Man be lifted up: that whosoever believeth in him may not perish, but may have life everlasting. For God so loved the world, as to give his only begotten Son: that whosoever believeth in him may not perish, but may have life everlasting." [2] " My sheep hear my voice, and I know them and they follow me, and I give them life everlasting, and they shall not perish for ever." [3] " Unless the grain of wheat falling into the ground die, itself remaineth alone; but if it die, it bringeth forth much fruit. He that loveth his life shall lose it, and he that hateth his life in this world keepeth it unto life eternal." " He that . . . receiveth not my words hath one that judgeth him. The word that I have spoken, the same shall judge him in the last day. The Father who sent me gave me commandment what I should say, . . . and I know that his commandment is life everlasting." [4] " Father, glorify thy Son . . . as thou hast given him power over all flesh that he may give eternal life

[1] Matt. xxv 32, 33, 41, 46.
[2] iii 5, 14-16.
[3] x 27, 28.
[4] xii 24, 25, 48-50.

to all whom thou hast given him." "Those whom thou gavest me I have kept: and none of them is lost, but the son of perdition."[1] The whole Gospel of St John becomes unintelligible unless the whole of mankind stands before the irrevocable choice between death or life, light or darkness, everlasting life or everlasting perdition. If the acceptance or the rejection of Christ does not involve eternal, but only temporary consequences, if Christ came to save only from a limited punishment, not from a final doom, the words of Christ in the Fourth Gospel are a shameless deception or palpable nonsense. Then the closing command of Christ on earth is much ado about nothing: "Go ye into the whole world and preach the gospel to every creature. He that believeth and is baptised shall be saved: but he that believeth not shall be condemned." If ultimate salvation is secure for everyone, and if no ultimate condemnation exists, these words are unworthy, I do not say of Christ, but of any truthful man.

Christ's teaching is echoed by his Apostles. St John's teaching is easily gathered from the Apocalypse. A few words must suffice. "The devil was cast into the pool of fire and brimstone, where both the beast and the false prophet shall be tormented day and night for ever and ever. I saw the dead standing in the presence of the throne. The books were opened . . . and whosoever was not found written in the book of life was cast into the pool of fire. This is the second death."[2] St Peter writes: "Lying teachers shall bring in sects of perdition . . . whose judgement now a long time lingereth not, and their perdition slumbereth not. These men, as irrational beasts, naturally tending to the snare and to destruction, blaspheming those things which they know not, shall perish in their corruption."[3] St Paul re-echoes his Master's teaching in these words: "Jesus shall be revealed from heaven with the angels of his power in a flame of fire, giving vengeance to them who know not God and who obey not the gospel of our Lord Jesus Christ, who shall suffer as punishment eternal ruin from the face of the Lord, and from the glory of his power."[4]

It is indeed difficult to read the New Testament and maintain that it does not teach the eternal punishment of the wicked. An attempt has indeed been made to maintain that the Greek word translated eternal or everlasting really means only "agelong," designating, indeed, a long period, but not strictly an unending one. This, however, is untenable.

Our Lord, describing the last judgement, ends by saying of the wicked: "These shall go into everlasting punishment: but the just, into life everlasting." In both instances the same Greek word is used, and as no one holds that the reward of the just will come to an end, it is against all reason to suppose that Christ meant the punishment of the wicked to be only agelong, but not unending. Moreover,

[1] xvii 1, 2, 12. [2] Apoc. xx 9-15.
[3] 2 Pet. ii 1, 3, 12. [4] 2 Thess. i 7-9.

the word occurs in the New Testament no less than seventy-one times, of which forty times refer to life everlasting, some ten times to our heavenly reward, such as everlasting kingdom, salvation, redemption, glory, inheritance, dwellings, etc., once in the phrase "everlasting God"; if then we also read "everlasting perdition," it is in the highest degree arbitrary to translate it by "agelong but not unending."

§IV: ETERNAL PUNISHMENT IN TRADITION

Continuous and clear testimony as to existence and eternity of hell

THIS Scriptural teaching has been continuously, unhesitatingly, and emphatically proclaimed by the Church throughout all ages. It would be difficult to find a Christian dogma which, historically speaking, is more undoubtedly an integral part of the Christian revelation than the eternity of punishment for the reprobate. The supreme alternative between final salvation and final reprobation constitutes, and has always constituted, the very warp and woof of the Christian ethical system. The work of Christ in atonement and redemption has always been taken as that of a rescue from eternal damnation, never merely from a temporary punishment. The rejection of Christ has never been regarded as something which involved, indeed, a terminable period of distress, but not a final condemnation by God. The awfulness of the Christian appeal has always lain in the final choice between life and death, not in a reversible choice of a more or less lengthy period of happiness or sorrow. The whole of its moral system, the whole of its soteriology or its scheme of salvation, is essentially, intrinsically bound up with the conviction that this life is a period of trial deciding an eternal issue.

Question of postponement till final judgement

One point, however, may be noted in reading the Fathers: that several, both Greeks and Latins, believed in a postponement of hell till the day of final judgement. Hell in the full sense of the word would begin, both for demons and damned, only after the sentence of Christ on the last day. Meanwhile the devils and the wicked would, indeed, undergo some punishment, but a punishment not complete, unchangeable, and final. In fact, some Fathers were confused in mind how to reconcile four points of divine revelation: first, the existence of purgatory, or the temporary punishment for some; secondly, the absence of the bodies of the damned till the final resurrection, and therefore the incompletion of their damnation; thirdly, the freedom of the devils to roam about the world for the ruin of souls, and their subsequent inclusion in the pit of hell afterwards; finally, the exact bearing and purpose of Christ's sentence at the General Judgement and its relation to the fixing of a man's destiny at death.

In consequence, a few passages may be found which on first reading seem to involve a hesitancy or ambiguity about the eternity and immutability of a sinner's state after death. On second reading, however, it becomes clear that there is no denial of the existence and eternity of hell as a final, unchangeable state for demons and damned.

Question of its possible cessation

There are but few names amongst those of the Fathers which can be quoted as in some sense supporting the possible cessation of hell. Clement of Alexandria seems sometimes to dally with the thought, but the matter must remain obscure. On the one hand he states in a great number of passages the eternity of hell for the wicked, on the other hand he speaks of the medicinal punishments of God, and it is not quite certain that in all these passages he refers only to punishments during this life or at least previous to the last judgement. Scholars are divided on this question. Tixeront holds that Clement was probably unorthodox, Atzberger holds that most certainly he was not.

Origen

Origen was undoubtedly in grave error, and in consequence his doctrine roused the most vehement opposition throughout the Church. Origen was not consistent in his teaching. On the one hand he held that there would be "a restoration (*apokatastasis*) of all things," a final triumph of Christ by the conversion of the wicked; on the other hand he held the permanent freedom of the will in its choice between good and evil, so that neither heaven nor hell were essentially eternal, but were subject to cycles. The restoration and completion of all was again followed by a fall, a trial, and a restoration, a conception which savours more of Buddhism than of Christianity. It must be marked, however, that even Origen does not give this as the teaching of the Church, but tentatively as his opinion on a question, discussion of which was still permissible. He gives it as a matter of possible speculation, and it seems that even he exempted some evil spirits from this general restoration or conversion.

About the year A.D. 300 Arnobius, a layman, in fact only a catechumen, wrote a defence of Christianity against the Pagans, in which he asserts the final annihilation of the wicked after long torments. His zeal made him rush into publicity before his knowledge of Christianity was very perfect. He founds his assertion not on any teaching of the Church, but on a philosophic theory that what is subject to fire must be composite, but that nothing composite can be eternal.

Origenism, which contained many errors besides that of the non-eternity of hell, caused the most violent disturbances everywhere. The great genius and the obvious sincerity of Origen, who had died in the bosom of holy Church, raised him many friends and defenders. Condemnation of an author after death seemed a graceless and unworthy thing to many. It could, however, not be doubted that the seductive talent of so great a writer was a danger to the integrity of the faith. Finally, the Emperor Justinian, at the request of Pelagius, the Papal nuncio, and Menas, the patriarch of Constantinople, published a condemnation of Origen, which they had submitted to him. The Edict ended with ten anathemas, the last of which reads: "If anyone says or thinks that the punishment of the demons and the wicked will not be eternal, that it will have an end, and that then shall take place a restoration (*apokatastasin*) of the demons and of the wicked, let him be anathema." This was signed by Pope Vigilius, by the Synod of Constantinople of 543, and by the whole East, and in fact by the whole Christian world, at least within the dominions of Justinian. Ten years later Origen was condemned in the Fifth General Council, and the condemnation was renewed in the subsequent General Councils.

The doctrine of eternal reprobation is therefore one of those which has been held explicitly from the very beginning, and the unanimous assent to which was only disturbed during a short period when a few, led astray by the great name of Origen, dreamt of a possible cessation of punishment at least for some of the lost.

Teaching of the Church on nature of pains of hell

We must bear in mind that the solemn definitions and the unanimous consent hitherto mentioned refer to the existence and the eternity of hell. With regard to the precise character of the pains of hell, there exists no solemn definition of Pope or Council, but the teaching of the ordinary magisterium of the Church cannot be in doubt. The Athanasian Creed, which dates probably from the fifth century, and which within a few generations afterwards received universal recognition by its practically universal use throughout the Church, ends with the words: "Those who do evil, shall go into eternal fire. This is the Catholic Faith, which unless a man faithfully and firmly believes, he cannot be saved." There can be no doubt that the fire here mentioned was ever understood as some objective reality. The great Pope Innocent III, in his letter of A.D. 1201 to Humbert, the Archbishop of Arles, states that "the punishment of original sin is the lack of the vision of God, but the punishment of actual sin is the torment of everlasting hell." Although this letter was not issued with such formality as to make it formally an utterance of Papal infallibility, yet it was inserted in the *Decretals*, and by this fact became an authentic declaration of the ordinary teaching of the Church. This statement of Innocent III necessarily implies that the punishment of the damned does not exclusively consist in the mere lack of the Beatific Vision, but in something which is described as "perpetuae gehennae cruciatus." This same truth was implied in the approval which the General Council of Lyons (A.D. 1274), gave to the profession of faith of Michael Paleologus, which said that the souls of those who departed in mortal sin or in original sin only, forthwith after death go down to hell, to be punished, however, with dissimilar pains (*paenis disparibus*). And again Pope Pius VI in 1794 condemned the Synod of Pistoia for rejecting the doctrine concerning "the Netherworld, in which the souls of those who depart in original sin alone are being punished with the pain of loss to the exclusion of the pain of fire."

It is therefore of Catholic Faith, though not as yet solemnly defined, that the damned suffer something else besides the mere loss of the vision of God.

Finally, the decree of the Roman Penitentiary ordering refusal of absolution to those who pertinaciously assert that the fire of hell is only metaphor for the mental sorrows of the damned, confirms the existence of a real punishment besides that of loss.

Beyond the assertion that hell-fire is a reality, distinct from the pain of loss, the official and authoritative teaching of the Church does not go. Of the views held by theologians concerning the precise nature of this fire, something has already been said in an earlier page.

§ V: ETERNAL PUNISHMENT AND REASON

Eternal sanction reasonable

COULD human reason, unaided by divine revelation, in all rigour of logic, prove the existence of eternal punishment? Possibly not. In a discussion which involves the appreciation of moral values, it is always difficult to construct an argument so compelling as to leave no loophole for doubt in those who are strongly averse to a particular conclusion.

In the case of all revealed doctrines, human reason can at least always show that they contain nothing contrary to right reason. In the case of the doctrine of hell, human reason can undoubtedly go much further. The human mind distinctly suggests, if perhaps it does not irresistibly prove, the necessity of an eternal sanction for good and evil. All weight of argument is really on one side, and the objections raised against the eternity of hell can be shown not to be the dictates of reason, but rather a darkening of the reason by feeling and sentiment. Human imagination is indeed appalled by the thought of endless suffering, there is an instinctive recoil in the whole sensitive part of man from the picture of ceaseless sorrow, but these spontaneous emotions of our nature are a very unsatisfactory guide to follow in matters of reason.

Though both infinite mercy and infinite justice are found in God, it is beyond the power of our mind to see how they are reconciled. In the hearts of men, mercy and justice are accompanied by contrary affections, which seem to exclude one another. The former is apparently a softening, the latter a hardening of the fibre of our being. In human experience, therefore, mercy often expels justice and justice mercy. We are apt to transfer such emotions to God, and to imagine that infinite mercy cannot co-exist with infinite justice. All this is a play of imagination, not of sound intelligence. We are influenced by it, because we realise that we stand in need of God's mercy for our eternal happiness and stand in dread of God's justice, since no man can think that he never did something amiss. It is therefore difficult in this matter to keep a clear head and let the intellect decide, and not the emotions.

God's mercy and the eternity of hell

Sometimes people express their difficulty in this way: How can we suppose that God will do what no earthly father would do? No earthly father would punish his son for ever. His anger would at least relent, however much that anger was provoked, and at last he would forgive.

A scoffer has said: Christ spoke the parable of the prodigal son, whom his father forgave, and for whom he slew the fatted calf, though that son had lived riotously and wasted his inheritance. Let God himself first forgive man, and then command us to follow his example.

There seems at first something plausible in this bitter remark, but on deeper reflection it is seen to be more sharp than true.

The father in the parable forgave his son because he repented. God forgives all those that repent and forgives them with a loving kindness that far exceeds that of any earthly father. The parable does not say that the father threw open his house to his son as long as he lived with harlots and wasted his goods. Had he given his son entrance to his house while unrepentant, it would have been an outrage on justice and a criminal condoning of vice, instead of a manifestation of paternal love.

God forgives all those that repent. There is a hell because there are some who do not repent for all eternity.

It is wrong to seek the explanation of hell in the divine desire or thirst for vengeance on the sinner, who has outraged the divine Majesty. God desires nothing. God thirsts for nothing. He is in the calm and full possession of his divine happiness.

No doubt there is a sense in which one can speak of the wrath of God wreaking vengeance on the sinner, and the Sacred Scriptures often thus express the punishment of evil-doers. When, however, we speak of God's actions in the language of men, we should never forget that God is not man, and that we can use human terms of him only analogously.

Hell and the sanctity of God

Let us suppose for a moment that there were no hell. What would this involve? It would involve that God is indifferent to sin. God is the author and creator of nature. If, then, our nature were such that whatsoever evil we did and for however long a time we did it, it could make no difference to our ultimate state; if for all eternity God would love us equally well whether we sinned or whether we did not, it would follow that God's nature is essentially indifferent to the morality of human actions. Let it not be said that God could punish the sinner for a time only, and so manifest his sanctity and abhorrence of sin. For there is no proportion between a limited space of time, however long, and eternity. No number of years, however extensive, can express a section or division, or part of an existence that never ends. Eternity cannot be divided by time. Hence a punishment which only lasts for a while is by intrinsic necessity no adequate consequence of a deed whereby the creature rejects his God.

If one being can transgress the will of another being to any degree of intensity and during an indefinite length of time without thereby altering the relation between both, there can be no ethical bond between them. No law can exist without sanction. If the creature knows that notwithstanding his refusal to obey God's law he will be in the loving embrace of God eternally, then he must conclude that God is essentially indifferent whether we conform to his law or not. If God himself is fundamentally indifferent, why should the creature care ? How can an action be evil, if the Supreme Intelligence and the Supreme Good is indifferent whether the action is done ?

If it be retorted that in any case God is unchangeable in himself and therefore cannot be distressed by our sins, we quite agree, in the sense that no sin can rob God of his infinite happiness. But God expresses his will by the very order of nature, and if no sin can leave a permanent result on the human soul, then God, as author of nature, would thereby imply that nothing could permanently alter the relation of an intelligent being to his creator ; in other words, that human actions had for him no ethical value whatever.

Again, to suppose that there is no hell and could be no hell would mean a denial of God's omnipotence. It would mean that God could not create man and put him on trial for an eternal prize. In other words, man's nature would be the measure of God's omnipotence. Once created, man could demand everlasting happiness, and that without being tested and tried, for trial without the possibility of failure is no trial at all.

But could not God have created a world without sin ? Indeed he could, but he has not. Why he has not, is not ours to settle now. He has not, that is the truth that stares us in the face. Given then the fact that sin is, given the fact that men are on trial and some fail, it is a denial of divine omnipotence to assert the impossibility of an eternal sanction. It would make God the helpless tool of his own creation. The creature, once having been created, could make sport of his Creator, safe in the knowledge that whatever befell, the end was secure ; even God could not change it.

Annihilation no sanction

It may be suggested that instead of eternal punishment, God might have decreed annihilation. But annihilation is in itself no sanction at all. It is mere cessation of being ; the non-existent cannot undergo any requital for past deeds. Such annihilation would presumably take place when the sinner was at the height of his sin, when he would suddenly pass away without any retribution whatever into nothingness. Perhaps the suggestion may be carried further that a period of punishment should precede the moment of annihilation. But this suggestion leaves the problem as it was before. Such period of punishment would either improve the sinner or make him worse, or leave him as it found him. If it had improved him, it is strange that it should be followed by annihilation ; if it left him as it found him, or made him worse, annihilation is delayed without rhyme or reason, for his state immediately previous to annihilation would demand retribution as much as, or more than the state in which he was before the first retribution took place. Moreover, annihilation of a being by nature immortal means a reversal of God's own plan ; it is a kind of stultification of his own work and a frustration of energy unworthy of the wisdom of God ; it would be, as it were, a confession of impotence. The root of the difficulty against eternal punishment lies in this, that people picture it to themselves as a satiating of a lust of vengeance in God ; they picture to themselves the damned begging eternally for mercy and God eternally refusing it in spite of their unceasing supplication.

Common objections answered

Now this whole conception is faulty. The devils and the damned never ask for mercy. One moment's repentance would empty hell. But that moment never comes. The damned have made their choice and abide by it ; that is why their abode is hell. Hell is an appalling mystery, but let us at least place the mystery where it really lies. It lies not in any supposed cruelty of God, it lies in the wickedness of man. It lies in the power of self-determination, which man can abuse finally and irrevocably. No one suggests that the damned want hell because they enjoy its torments ; the damned want hell because they have once for all decided that they do not want God, and there is no heaven without God. They need God eternally, but eternally they do not want him.

But this is madness, may be retorted. Indeed it is, but all sin is madness, all sin is unreason, yet men commit it, and freely commit it. The mystery lies in the abuse of the power of self-determination, not in the necessary sanction subsequent to its abuse. If we fully understood what sin is, there would be no difficulty in understanding hell, for hell is only sin continued. A man can fix himself in evil as well as in good. Human nature gradually sets and, if the word be permitted, solidifies. A humble comparison with plaster or cement or molten metal that sets and hardens may not be out of place. In fact, hell is an application of the true law of evolution. Man is a being in progress. He is for a time in a state of transition, in process of development towards his final state, whatever it be. He passes through a period of possible change, but this period is not indefinite ; there is a moment when he has reached the terminus of his possible evolution, and is in a final stationary condition.

In this matter man takes his place in the general evolution of all life. If man had no final state, he would be a contrast to the whole of nature. All life passes through the stages of birth, development, to its final state. Every flower is a germ, a bud, a complete flower. Every tree a seed, a young plant, a full tree. Every animal passes from the embryo stage, to youth, and ends in its final condition. Now injuries done to the plant in its stage of development have permanency of some kind. A tree injured or thwarted grows to final deformity, a deformity which is never reversed by nature till the tree ceases to be. A gnarled oak is what it is through a number of causes during its agelong existence, but its process of evolution is to our knowledge never reversed or altered. In the end it will die, because it is material, and no matter can resist decomposition, but its life cannot be undone and its development rolled backward. If an animal's eye or ear, or hand or leg be destroyed, this destruction is final ; it will be for ever blind or deaf or maimed or lame, as long as it is. Nature does not reverse her process. She does not give it another eye or ear or hand or leg, she does not undo the loss. In every life there are occurrences which are irrevocable as long as that life lasts.

Now the soul-life of man is no exception. Man by his actions can permanently and definitely affect his own innermost being, he can make or mar himself for good, and since his soul has a never-ending existence, he can do what can never be undone, even for all eternity.

What human reason itself suggests is made certain for us by Revelation, which teaches that the relation in which man stands to God at the moment of death is final, definitive.

If man had no final state, he would be an anomaly in God's universe. No act of his could influence his ultimate state, or produce an absolute and permanent result. If his will-acts are indefinitely reversible, then he flounders through an endless existence in helpless impotence. There is no ideal in the ultimate attainment of which he may find repose, no perfect achievement which renders his manhood complete. Buddhists seem at first to accept this strange and sad illusion. Their highest deities can still leave their heaven and sink back to earth in a new re-incarnation, after which they can rise again to some heaven and fall away again. But even Buddhists, though they delight in adding up innumerable *kalpas* of myriads of years each, still finally after billions and trillions of years let a man achieve arhatship and nirvana, that is, permanency of some kind.

Granted an immortal being with free will, surely heaven and hell, eternal conformity or opposition to God, eternal happiness or sorrow seem necessary deductions, unless free will be robbed of its only dignity, of that which alone constitutes its connatural purpose and value.

There may arise in the reader's mind the thought that one earthly life is not long enough to decide an eternal issue. It should be remembered, however, that eternity is not a multiple of time. A life of threescore years and ten stands to eternity in no more distant relation than an existence of a thousand years. The shortness of the time of trial may be regarded as a blessing as well as a hardship. Surely a saint on his deathbed would feel keen disappointment if told that one earthly life was not long enough to purchase a happy eternity. Even the sinner may gain by the fact that the trial is short ; a lengthier trial might have ended in greater disaster.

Sometimes an all too imaginative preacher may picture how, after a long life of virtue, one mortal sin brings a man to hell. To such flights of rhetoric we may reply that there is no certainty that such a thing has ever happened. Of this we may be sure, that God takes no delight in taking the sinner unawares, that he may hurl him into hell after his only mortal sin. God so loved the world that he gave his only begotten Son unto death, yea, unto the death of the Cross. If we want to guess in any way who or how many go to hell, we must never forget that the lake of eternal fire is at the foot of the hill of Calvary, and that no one can go to hell without crossing the path that goes over that hill. As Catholics, we do indeed believe in an eternal hell, and our reason itself almost demands an eternal sanction for good and evil, but it is perversity of mind to forestall the judgements of God, as if we knew that the majority of men go to hell. Bethlehem and Nazareth, Gethsemane and Golgotha, do not tend to show that the bulk of mankind will be lost. To most men now it would seem a poor triumph for the Man of Galilee if at the consummation of the world Satan swept the majority of the children of men away with him into everlasting darkness.

On the other hand, it is equally foolish to indulge in the facile jest: " I believe in an eternal hell, eternally empty." Such words make a mockery of the Gospels, and especially of Christ's words to the wicked on the day of judgement: " Depart from me, ye cursed, into everlasting fire, which was prepared for the devil and his angels from the beginning of the world." God has left us no revelation concerning the number of the lost, and no guess of ours can take its place. If a man dies in mortal sin, if a man dies without sanctifying grace, he is eternally lost, so much we know; but who dies in mortal sin we do not know. Mortal sin requires full knowledge and full deliberation. It is not like some ghastly blunder which a man might commit before quite knowing what he was about. No one goes to hell except he march into it with his eyes open. Not, of course, that he must beforehand realise the awfulness of its pains, but he must fully realise that he chose evil and not good, and he must have persevered in his choice until death.

We know little of the secrets of the individual amount of personal guilt, we know little of the possibilities of repentance. Catholics have always felt it to be a kind of sacrilegious usurpation of God's prerogative to say of any person: " He has gone to hell." Leaving these things alone, our only concern is so to live and so to warn others, that neither we nor they be amongst those who receive Christ's curse on the last day.

§ VI: SPECIAL QUESTIONS RELATING TO ETERNAL PUNISHMENT

THE Scriptural word " fire," as we have seen, may not be taken as a mere metaphor. It has been asked whether we are also to understand literally " the worm that dieth not "; what, in any case, the meaning of the expression may be.

" The undying worm "

The two expressions, " the unquenchable fire " and " the undying worm," are clearly not on the same level. The latter is used in the New Testament only on one occasion, when our Lord, according to St Mark,[1] thrice makes the obvious reference to Isaias lxvi 24, whereas the fire is nearly always mentioned in conjunction with everlasting punishment. Christ, in using a well-known expression of the ancient prophet on this one occasion, does not indicate precisely what is metaphorical and what is not, but both he and the Apostles by their constant and almost exclusive use of " fire " for hell give clearly to understand that this latter word indicates some physical reality. We are therefore free to interpret " the worm that dieth not " metaphorically. As a matter of fact, this is usually done. Some take it as a metaphor for the loathsome and foul state of the damned, which resembles the stench and corruption of the grave. Others have seen in it a symbol for the biting pain of everlasting remorse.

The devils and the damned

A question may be asked regarding the instrumentality of the devils in increasing the torments of the damned. From the earliest even to the most modern pictorial representations of hell it has been customary to portray the damned as undergoing the most excruciating tortures by demons. What have we to believe of all this ? First of all let us remember that the devils are pure spirits, however evil they are. The use of chains, pitchforks, and pincers and of all material instruments of cruelty is obviously a mere play of the imagination. Moreover, it is rather a childish supposition that at the end of all things God should eternally maintain a store of such things for the purpose. Yet beyond doubt the power of the devils to be a source of affliction to the damned is real. This affliction will arise from the twofold source of their companionship and their dominion. Demons and damned are enclosed in the same hell, and the imagery of Holy Scripture leads us to believe that the perpetual and intolerable nearness of innumerable beings will be an added horror to the damned. Moreover, the devils, as angels, are mightier than the damned, who ever remain but men. These men, however, by sin have yielded to the temptation of evil spirits, and therefore chosen them as masters rather than God. They have surrendered to their dominion, and in consequence remain under their tyranny for evermore. How this tyranny is exercised we have no conception. Somehow, overwhelmed and mastered by giants in evil, the souls of the damned will be cowed and terrorised into everlasting submission.

Time in hell

A further question must refer to the existence of time in hell. Eloquent and ingenious preachers have thought of many similes in order to bring home the endless duration of hell, but it must be remembered that according to the Scriptures time then shall be no more. Time is the measure of change. But both the blessed and the lost have come to their final state, and are no longer beings in a

[1] ix 42-47.

state of progress. They have entered a changeless world. They are not, indeed, in eternity as God is, who possesses the whole of his infinite being at once, but they have entered upon a state to which there is no parallel on earth. To count hours and days and years is possible only where material things tend to corruption. What an immutable life implies we cannot imagine, and it is idle to conjecture. At the moment of the death of the damned the clock struck, and the hands will move no more.

Diminution of punishment?

The question has sometimes been raised whether everlasting punishment is a matter completely excluded from the mercy of God and abandoned only to the rigour of divine justice. Although we have not sufficient data in Revelation to answer this question satisfactorily, it has been almost universally assumed by theologians that the punishment of the damned is less than they deserve and less than in strict justice might have been inflicted, so that every sentence of the Great Judge is, in fact, a merciful one. It has further been asked whether some respite or some lessening of punishment could be admitted, at least sometimes, in hell, so that even after the sentence there still remained some play for God's mercy.

There have been some ancient writers who held that there would be some lessening of punishment, as, for instance, the hymn-writer Prudentius. This Spanish Christian poet, born in A.D. 348, imagined that perhaps on Easter night some relief was granted to the lost. St Augustine, in a rather ambiguous though disapproving sentence, seems to allow prayer for the lost previous to the last judgement, though he most strenuously combats those who think that the punishment of the damned is not eternal, or that their state can be in any way changed after the judgement. In a medieval manuscript there was found a prayer for one about whose soul one is in doubt. This prayer asks that the Mass may obtain for him, "if unworthy to rise again to glory, at least that his torments may be more bearable." These slight indications of a hope to lessen the pains of the lost show by their exceeding insignificance and rarity that the spirit of the Church and the common feeling of the faithful are strongly against the practice of praying for the lost. Hence we may well endorse the words of St Thomas Aquinas: "The above opinion is presumptuous; inasmuch as it is contrary to the statements of the saints, it is worthless and resting on no authority. It is not in accordance with reason, first because the damned in hell are outside the bond of charity, by which the works of the living extend to the dead; secondly, because the damned have utterly come to the terminus of their life, receiving the ultimate requital for what they deserve even as the saints, who are in their final home."[1]

A further question has exercised the minds of theologians, viz., whether the life of the lost is one of undiluted sorrow and pain, or is still capable of some natural satisfaction, the joy of attaining some

[1] *Summa*, Supplement, Q. 71, art. 5.

object of desire. The devils, so it is argued, must enjoy at least some malignant satisfaction in tempting men to sin and in succeeding in their endeavour. If, then, they are capable of such gratification, however wicked, it would seem that some joys are still left to them. It is difficult by merely philosophical arguments to disprove the suggestion; but, on the other hand, the scriptural description of hell in no way implies joy or satisfaction of any kind in the place of the damned. "I am tormented in this flame," cried Dives, and the petition that a finger dipped in water should be laid on his tongue was not granted.

So likewise it has been suggested that while the pain of loss is indeed never-ending, because it corresponds to that element in sin which gives it a certain infinity, namely, the soul's aversion from God, yet the pain of sense will sometime come to an end, because it corresponds to the turning of the sinner towards creatures, an abuse of creatures that can have only a finite malice and therefore a finite punishment. This suggestion cannot, perhaps, be proven *a priori* to be unfounded, but scriptural language gives no countenance whatever to the idea. The word "everlasting" is most often attached precisely to the word "fire," and it seems altogether contrary to the tenor of Holy Scripture to maintain that the fire should end but the punishment continue. It is therefore an idle guess, which is difficult to reconcile with the inspired Word of God, a guess which is prompted only by the mistaken feeling that the positive pain of the fire is greater than the pain of loss. It is a guess which finds no support whatever in tradition, and which even on the grounds of reason is very difficult to defend. It must therefore be definitely rejected.

The case of those raised from the dead

A few stories, of a legendary rather than of an historical character, have been current in bygone ages of people having died in mortal sin, who through the prayer of some saint have been raised to life and given another chance of earning heaven. This is not the place to discuss the foundation of fact which may possibly underlie some of these stories. Sober historians would say that it is very little. Be this as it may, were they even true, they cannot be alleged as exceptions to the eternity of hell; they would rather be instances of the suspension of the Particular Judgement normally succeeding death. The instances told in the Gospel of Christ raising the dead, the daughter of Jairus, the son of the widow of Naim, and Lazarus, are such exceptions. Moreover, some dead have been raised to life since Gospel days.

Whether all consciousness ceased between the moment of death and the moment of resurrection we cannot say. In all probability it did. In any case, by a special ordinance of God the divine judgement on these souls did not take place at the instant of their bodily death, as their allotted time of trial was not yet completed. We may rest quite certain that if any return of unrepentant sinners to earthly life has ever taken place, these sinners were not yet in hell. Both revelation and reason make this obvious.

The relation of the damned to those on earth

The question may be asked what is the relation of the inmates of hell to those who still dwell on earth? Of the devils we know that they roam through the world for the ruin of souls. Until the last day in the providence of God the demons are allowed to tempt and to harm men. The fall in Paradise was caused by a devil from hell; no doubt many of the last sins committed before the final doom will still be the outcome of temptations from hell. The abyss will be closed only at the end of time. Do the damned similarly roam through the world for the ruin of their fellow men?

Spiritism

No, the case of the devils is different from that of the damned. The devils, by virtue of their higher nature as pure spirits, can come into contact with us and with the material world, and they can use this power to tempt and harm us. Such power is indeed completely under the control of God's supernatural providence, but it is natural to an angelic being. It is not so with the discarnate souls of men. These souls are by nature the life-principle of a human body, and through this body they come in contact with the material world. In their discarnate state they are incomplete beings. It is not natural to them to act on matter in this incomplete state. They can be active within themselves by thought and will, as they can subsist in themselves even without the body, but there is no connatural means of communication between them and the outer world. Whatever they know of earthly happenings is conveyed to them by some special ordinance of God, whatever influence they possess on the material world is bestowed on them by some preternatural means. We do not know the details of God's dealings with them; we could only know them by revelation. Now revelation tends to show that no such communication, no such influence is normally granted to them. We pray, certainly, to be protected against the devils, we do not normally pray for protection against the damned. If some apparitions of the damned have taken place, they are so exceedingly rare that they must be classed as distinctly miraculous, and not the outcome of their normal powers. The power to manifest themselves and to influence the living is perhaps not infrequently granted to the blessed in heaven and also to the souls in purgatory, but it is apparently seldom, if ever, given to the damned. The few stories told about the damned appearing, speaking, or acting after death contain fearsome warnings to the living. Such apparitions seem to have been allowed by God as an act of mercy to those on earth rather than as a permission to those in hell to hurt the faithful. The claim, therefore, of spiritists that "beyond the veil," as they say, all the dead, whether good or bad, have on occasion the power to communicate with the living is not to be admitted.[1] Whatever power to manifest themselves to the living the departed may possess is a special gift of

[1] For another view see Essay xxxi, pp. 1120-1.

God, not a natural outcome of their state. If then at a spiritistic séance an evil spirit—an earthbound spirit as they would call it—really manifests itself, the presumption is that this spirit is a devil, not a damned soul, though God in his omnipotence could grant such power to the damned. Of this Catholics are quite certain, that if such manifestations really take place—a supposition not readily to be admitted—they are not those of souls in heaven or in purgatory.

Hell and the divine wisdom

A final difficulty is sometimes urged against the doctrine of hell in this wise: surely God would not do what is eternally useless, surely God would not concur in the maintenance of an eternal evil, thereby admitting the eternal failure of his own plans for man!

Hell is not useless. The fear of hell as a motive of sorrow for sin has been, and is, instrumental in making saints. Many a soul has been helped to heaven by a salutary fear of hell. Hell is not useless. The blessed in heaven do not rejoice in the pains of the damned as such, yet they do eternally rejoice that they are saved from so great an evil, and the very greatness of the evil avoided adds to the enjoyment of the happiness secured.

Hell is not an eternal evil. That the damned should be in heaven, the blessed in hell, would indeed be evil, but that every one should receive according to his works is not evil, but good. That man should have free will and decide his own eternity is no evil. Hell is indeed evil to the damned, but not evil to God, not evil in itself. Infinite goodness still remains infinite goodness, though some freely reject it.

Hell is no divine failure. If God willed that all men, whether they freely chose him or not, should go to heaven, then God would indeed have failed if any went to hell. God wills men to go to heaven if they love him, and this divine will is eternally triumphant. If a soul which did not love God above all things were in heaven, this would not be triumph, but defeat. Moreover, God wanted multitudes in heaven, not to increase his own happiness, but to bestow his infinite bounty on them. He carried out his plan to the full; the damned have deprived themselves of happiness, not him. He communicated his divine life of glory to as many as he would. Those that refused the proffered gift still glorify his justice, which withdraws his bounty from all that refuse it. Their very existence is still in obedience to his power and wisdom; they obey him not with their free will, but as irrational and inanimate creation obeys him, by continuing to be in that state which he has adjudged to them.

No one would deny that the doctrine of hell baffles the human mind, but it is a lesser mystery than the mystery of Bethlehem or Calvary. The human mind can understand more easily that God should punish everlastingly those that die in sin, than that God himself should die upon the Cross to save them from everlasting punishment.

J. P. Arendzen.

XXXIV

THE RESURRECTION OF THE BODY

§ I: INTRODUCTORY

"*I believe in . . . the resurrection of the body, and life everlasting.*"—The Apostles' Creed.

The doctrine of the resurrection of the body is an integral part of Catholic belief concerning the Last Things—that is, concerning death and the life after death. It is so intimate a part of this belief that to reject it is to reject a doctrine which was taught from the very beginning of Christianity, and which has been unalterably affirmed by the Church throughout the centuries. While other elements in Catholic belief concerning the Last Things have emerged only gradually into full clearness and obtained precise definition relatively late—as, for instance, the doctrine of purgatory—this element, the doctrine of the resurrection of the body, is explicit from the outset, and has not been subject to the Catholic process of development. By this assertion it is not meant that the doctrine has not been contested and contradicted, for it became at an early date a subject of acute controversy within the Christian body. But notwithstanding such controversy, the faith of the Church has been plain throughout, and that faith has been a simple acceptance of the doctrine in its obvious sense.

The assertion that has just been made may easily be misunderstood. It may seem, that is, to be in conflict with the theological history of the doctrine, and to be belied by the fact that the theologians are not in perfect agreement in their exposition of it. The solution is to be found in a necessary distinction. In every doctrine we may distinguish between the doctrine itself, so to say the substance or core of the dogma, and the many subsidiary questions which may arise concerning its mode of realisation and application. Catholic theology, for example, is explicit in its general statement of the truths which concern the life after death; but it is not dogmatic beyond the warrant of the faith once given to the saints, and it refrains from much detailed assertion. So is it in particular with the doctrine of the resurrection of the body. About the fact of that resurrection, and that a bodily resurrection, Catholic theology has no doubts and there is no controversy; but about subsidiary questions which arise from the doctrine—as, for instance, the question of the nature of the identity which obtains between the earthly and the risen body—about such questions Catholic theology is not dogmatic, and there is room for a legitimate variety of view. In rough and summary antithesis the matter may be stated thus, that there are these two distinct things, the *fact* of the resurrection of the body and the *manner* of this resurrection. Now about the fact of the resurrection there is no question : it is a revealed doctrine, set forth in unmistakable fashion in Scripture and tradition, and taught by the divine authority of the Church. But about the manner of the resurrection, on the other hand, there has always been, and there will probably always be, some variety of theological speculation. In the course of these pages some account will be given of this speculation, and an effort will be made to set forth the state of theological opinion in the matter. But it is important that the reader should not mistake the situation and conclude from this variety of opinion that the doctrine itself is indeterminate and uncertain. In the Apostles' Creed we say : " I believe in . . . the resurrection of the body, and life everlasting." In the Nicene Creed that is used in the Mass : " And I look for the resurrection of the dead and the life of the world to come." There is the substance of our faith, the fact of the bodily resurrection ; the further question regarding the manner of the resurrection—How shall this thing be ?—is subsidiary and relatively unimportant.

This distinction having been made, it is necessary now to explain the character and scope of the argument which this essay will set forth. The doctrine of the resurrection of the body is a revealed doctrine, and in its acceptance we exercise faith. Although a reasonable doctrine, it is not a deduction from reasoning ; it cannot be established by reason, nor can it be disproved by reason. The fact which the doctrine asserts is a miraculous fact, and as such beyond the scope of natural reason. The doctrine is simply part of the deposit of the faith. When, therefore, we profess our belief in it, we are professing our belief in a revealed doctrine, we are accepting the testimony of God and making an act of divine faith. That point is primary, and from that point our argument must start. In the course of these pages we shall adduce the testimony of Holy Scripture and of tradition to show that it is part of revelation ; we shall also consider presently what natural reason may urge in support of the doctrine ; but throughout, in the end as in the beginning, we have before us an unmistakable revealed doctrine, and our effort is in fact confined to exposition and explanation ; no attempt is made to prove that which is in effect unprovable.

The subject of these sections falls naturally into three main divisions, corresponding to three principal questions. First there is the fact of the bodily resurrection, secondly there is the question of the identity of the risen body with the earthly body, and thirdly there is the question of the character of the risen body. In dealing with the first question we are in the region of dogma : the bodily resurrection is an article of faith. In dealing with the other two we are largely in the region of theological deduction and speculation. Much of this deduction will appear necessary and inevitable, if we are to hold the doctrine at all; while some of it has no such necessity. The matter is obscure and defies exploration. Let the judicious reader understand, therefore, that he is not asked to give the assent of faith to any such deduction or speculation, but solely to the doctrine itself.

§ II: THE POSITION AND MEANING OF THE DOCTRINE

THE doctrine of the resurrection of the body holds an important position in the Christian scheme of the life after death, and it will be well, before proceeding further, to determine its exact position in that scheme. The Catechism, in the familiar summary, speaks of Four Last Things: death, judgement, hell and heaven. There is in this summary no explicit mention of the resurrection of the body, although it is implied. Where, then, it may be asked, does the resurrection of the body come in, and what is its relation to the other members of this summary? A brief outline of the whole matter will serve to make this clear.

The soul before the general judgement

When a man dies his body is laid in the grave and goes to corruption; but his soul, the spiritual part of him, is not buried with his body. It is immortal—death can have no power over it—and it enters at once, or rather continues in, its everlasting life. What happens to it when it is separated from the body and becomes a disembodied spirit? It goes immediately, in the instant of its release, before the judgement seat of God for the particular judgement. There it is judged, and there, according to its merits, it receives its judgement and is assigned to its eternal lot. If the man has died in a state of grace, without any stain of sin upon him or any debt of punishment unpaid, then the soul hears the happy summons, "Come, ye blessed of my Father, possess you the kingdom prepared for you from the foundation of the world," [1] and enters into the joy of its Lord in that vision of the intellect and fruition of the will which is the supreme happiness of the rational creature. If the man has died in mortal sin, then the soul hears the terrible words, "Depart from me, you cursed, into everlasting fire which was prepared for the devil and his angels," [2] and is banished at once to the pains of hell. But if the man has died in yet a third condition, so that he is indeed in a state of grace, but has still to atone for venial sin and to expiate forgiven sin, then the soul is dismissed to purgatory and there remains until its purification is accomplished and it is ready to be admitted to the Vision of God.

The Last Day

Now, so far, it will be noticed, we have been writing the history of the disembodied soul; we have not yet encountered the resurrection. It may be that many, as they think vaguely and indistinctly about death and the particular judgement, suppose in some loose

[1] Matt. xxv 34. [2] Matt. xxv 41.

fashion that this process of the soul could be termed " resurrection." But plainly it cannot be so denominated. The soul does not die, the soul therefore cannot rise again ; and if there were no more than this to the matter, then we could not use the term resurrection, and the doctrine would be without meaning. But there is more than this to the matter ; the history of man's last end is not yet complete. Hitherto we have considered only the history of an individual man and the fact of the particular judgement ; to this we have to add the history of the last end of the human race and the fact of the general judgement. For when the last day comes, at a time that is known only to God and fixed in his eternal decree, the whole of mankind is summoned to the judgement seat for the Great Assize of the general judgement.[1]

But before the general judgement there comes the miracle of the general resurrection. It is here, therefore, at this precise point in man's secular history, that our doctrine applies. Here is the exact position of the resurrection of the body. At that last day all the dead will rise again to stand before the judgement seat. The souls of men will be reunited to their bodies. The particular judgement will be reaffirmed and ratified. Henceforth the complete man—soul and body—in full and perfect unity of nature, will undergo his lot of eternal bliss or eternal pain.

Man a compound of body and soul

Such, then, if we may so term it, is the historical setting of the doctrine of the bodily resurrection. Such is the hope which the doctrine enshrines. It is a doctrine which implies that simple and elementary philosophy whereby we regard ourselves as creatures composed of body and soul : of a material body and a spiritual substance which is the vital principle of the body. It is a doctrine which supposes that man remains finally, in the after-life as in the present life, a being of body and soul ; and it implies that such an immortality, not of soul only, but of body and soul, is the proper and normal immortality for man. Pagan philosophers and heretics in all times, emphasising the spiritual part of man and despising and rejecting the body, have formulated another sort of immortality, which men should enjoy as disembodied spirits, released from the " prison-house " or " tomb " of the body and set free from its supposed degrading company. Ancient mythology conceived an after-life in which man became a frail and ineffective wraith ; and something of the sort seems to be indicated by the highly dubious communications of modern spiritualism. But Christianity, taking a more complete and saner view, considers both body and soul as necessary to the full and perfect man, and therefore believes in an after-life wherein body and soul are once again united.

Their reunion after death

They are so united again after the painful separation which is death. The body is laid in the grave and dissolves by natural process

[1] See above, pp. 1134 ff.

so as to be indistinguishable from the earth around it. But such physical dissolution presents no obstacle to the omnipotence of God. No physical law or natural process can be invoked to explain the act of his omnipotence. His *fiat* goes forth, and the body that was dissolved into its elements is reproduced, endowed again with physical life and reunited with its soul. What manner of physical continuity, of identity of matter, obtains between the earthly and the risen body is a question that shall be touched on later. For the present it is enough to set forth the meaning and reality of the bodily rising, and to emphasise its single cause, the omnipotence of the Creator.

§ III: THE BODILY RESURRECTION REASONABLE

Essential union of body and soul

CHRISTIAN theology professes a larger and more complete view of the nature of man than that held by pagan or heretic. Nor is the Church disposed to abandon that theology because certain modern philosophers would revive the views of Plato or the Manicheans. The Christian theology holds that man was created a complete unity of body and soul, and that no mere accidental connection, but a close substantial union. In this creation, furthermore, by the grace of God, he enjoyed a perfect balance of his powers and faculties, the body being the perfect partner and docile instrument of the soul, and endowed with immortality. And so would man have remained, in an everlasting life uninterrupted by death, had not sin intervened. But sin came, the balance of man's nature was upset, and there came also the penalty of death to dissolve the union of soul and body. Yet not finally and for ever. Sin was expiated by the death of the Redeemer, and our resurrection achieved in his Resurrection. So the separation of death was not final. Body and soul were to be united once more, and that for eternity.

To such a theology, therefore, the body is not a prison-house or tomb, in which the soul is confined for a time, and from which it gladly makes its escape ; but it is a real part of the man, united with the soul to form one perfect being. This union of the soul and body, says St Thomas Aquinas, is a natural union, and so close is the union of the two that human nature dreads and shrinks from their separation. " The loss of the bodily life is naturally horrible to human nature."[1] They are wrenched asunder violently in the agony of death. But, says St Thomas again, " It is contrary to the nature of the soul to be without the body ; and, since nothing that is contrary to nature can endure, therefore the soul will not be for ever without the body. Now the soul lasts for ever, and so it must be conjoined again with the body. That is the resurrection. Therefore the immortality of the soul would appear to demand the resurrection of the body."[2]

[1] *Summa*, III, Q. xliv, art. 6.
[2] *Contra Gentiles*, iv 79.

The Incarnation

Such is the spirit of the Christian philosophy. The liberal theologian may alter the natural meaning of the doctrine and maintain that the resurrection which Christians are bound to believe is no more than an immortality of soul. He may declare, for example, that " the form which the doctrine of the resurrection assumes in my mind is the survival of death by a personality which has shed its physical integument for ever." [1] It appears to him that that is a simplification, and that the doctrine is thus made easy to the modern mind. But such a simplification not only empties the doctrine of its meaning—for such a persistence of the personal life in a purely spiritual mode of existence has no just right to the name of resurrection—it is also out of accord with the spirit of Christianity. The central doctrine of the Christian faith is that the Second Person of the Blessed Trinity, not despising the Virgin's womb, became man and took a human body—*et Verbum caro factum est*. And that faith is only consistent with itself when it refuses to despise and reject the body, and claims for it a share in the eternal hope. If God so honoured our humanity, what right have we to despise it ? What philosophy can excuse us for attempting to improve upon the nature which has been given to us ?

Christian theology incarnational

And the Christian theology, which has the Incarnation for its central dogma, is incarnational throughout its whole extent. Hence the liturgy and ritual of the Church, hence, above all, the sacraments. Man is not regarded as a pure spirit, but regarded always and treated as a unity of spirit and body. By visible and tangible means does God work his benefits towards him, and he uses always the visible and tangible body. The body is consecrated and sanctified by prayer and sacrament, and the Apostle bids us remember that our bodies are the temples of the Holy Spirit. Obviously the doctrine of the resurrection of the body is necessary and inevitable to such a philosophy.

The ultimate felicity of man

St Thomas Aquinas argues further that the reunion of body and soul is necessary for ultimate felicity. Without the body the soul lacks something, and to that extent its felicity is imperfect. Just as any part dissociated from the whole to which it belongs is incomplete and imperfect, so the disembodied soul is incomplete by itself and requires the restoration of the integral human nature. And this restoration, this ultimate reintegration, is very suitable on other grounds. For body and soul have lived and worked together ; whatever the man has done or suffered, he has done or suffered as a whole ; body and soul have shared indissolubly and indiscriminately in all the passages of his mortal life. It is right, therefore, and fitting that body and soul should share the eternal issue of that life, whether this be everlasting joy or everlasting pain.

" Ah, wretched body," cries the preacher, " too often have I had to complain of thy burden and of thy exigencies. But, if I have used

[1] H. D. A. Major, *A Resurrection of Relics* (1922), p. 90.

thee to dishonour my life in the eyes of God and of men, I have used thee also to rehabilitate myself. I have used thy knees to prostrate myself before the sacred Majesty which I have offended, thy ears to hear the merciful words that have given me back hope again, thy eyes to weep for my faults, thy breast to sigh and groan in my repentance, thy mouth to utter the lamentations and thanksgivings of my wretchedness, and all thy senses and all thy powers to acquire that knowledge and virtue and to perform those good works which have brought me near to God and made me worthy of him. And must I then bid thee goodbye for ever ?

" O soul and body ! Was the love which united you two, spirit and matter, in a single life and a single activity, nothing but a deceit and a lie ? Must that divine marriage, which set you to share so intimately in all actions and in all merits, be dishonoured by an eternal divorce ?—No, no, that cannot be ! That community of actions and of merits demands a community of reward and punishment. And since there is not in this world either pleasure or pain which suffices for the reward of the just or the chastisement of the wicked, I must believe in the restoration and reconstitution of that human unity which is broken by death, I must believe in the resurrection of the body." [1]

The preacher in these words gives utterance to the natural instinct of our humanity, which everywhere and always has desired this complete immortality. And natural desire and instinctive feeling are not things to be despised and rejected. Although they do not establish the doctrine, yet they persuade it and confirm it. For our human nature is from God, and at its purest and best prepares us for the teachings of its divine Creator.

We therefore regard that philosophy as inadequate and that spiritualism as one-sided and false which despise the body and would allow it no lot or share in the eternal life. There is a delusive simplicity about the theory of those who would have an immortality of spirit alone ; but simplicity is no guarantee of truth, and it often means a partial and incomplete synthesis. St Thomas had to answer those who maintained that were we to become pure spirits without any admixture of body, we should become more like to God and better imitate his perfection. His answer is that there may be thus a closer superficial likeness, but that substantially and really a being is more conformable to the perfection of God when it eternally expresses the divine idea according to which it was created, and when there is nothing lacking to the completeness of its nature, just as there is nothing lacking to the nature of God.[2]

[1] Monsabré, *La Résurrection* (Carême, 1889).
[2] Suppl., Q. lxxv, art. 1, ad 4.

§ IV: THE BODILY RESURRECTION MIRACULOUS

Not self-contradictory, but beyond the powers of nature

But although the resurrection of the body be a reasonable doctrine, and although it would seem to be demanded by our human nature and by any complete philosophy of that human nature, yet the resurrection is in the fullest sense a miraculous event. Many objections have been raised against the doctrine, and are still being raised against it. It is not an easy doctrine. But we both admit this difficulty and supply its adequate solution, when we set it down that the resurrection is miraculous. For a miracle is an event which transcends the power of natural causes and is due to the direct action of the omnipotence of God. It is not an event which is in conflict with natural law, as involving in itself a philosophical contradiction, but an event which passes beyond natural causality and requires omnipotence. If the bodily resurrection involved any contradiction, then it could not take place, even by the power of God. But if it involves no such contradiction, and is in no way contrary to natural law, but only beyond the scope of our experience, then the bodily resurrection cannot be declared scientifically impossible. With God all things are possible.

Scientific objections

If it be said, for instance, that the discoveries of science regarding the constitution of matter and its behaviour make a resurrection of body inconceivable, it may be answered, first, that science has not yet made up its mind about the constitution of matter, and secondly, that the conclusions of science, whatever they may ultimately be, cannot really affect the case. For, if the bodily resurrection be a dogmatic truth, guaranteed by the authority of God, here is a piece of knowledge which science could never reach and which it is not in a position to criticise. So that the scientific difficulties commonly alleged against the doctrine are seen to be, when we realise its miraculous character, irrelevant and ineffective.

Some of the difficulties raised against the resurrection of the body are really concerned rather with the mode than with the fact of this resurrection: they are pertinent especially when we seek to determine the identity that obtains between the earthly and the risen body,[1] but they do not touch the core of the doctrine—*i.e.*, the revitalising of dead matter and its reunion to the soul. Physical science may fairly say that this is a phenomenon which lies outside its experience, but it cannot say that it is impossible or incredible. So that the essence of the doctrine—*i.e.*, the teaching that men will rise again with true bodies—this is independent of any scientific theory regarding the constitution or behaviour of matter, or any physiological hypothesis, and cannot be affected by such. It is difficult, of course, to imagine the reconstitution of the body after the dissolution of death, for no such process does or can come within our experience, or can possibly become a phenomenon which physical

[1] See below, pp. 1232-1242.

science may study. But the doctrine does not stand or fall by the limitations of our experience, nor does it imply that the resurrection is in any respect a physical process. On the contrary, the fact is removed beyond the range of our experience, it is regarded as definitely miraculous, it is attributed to the omnipotence of God as to its only and sufficient cause.

The cause of the resurrection is the divine omnipotence

Such is the fundamental attitude of Catholic theology. That theology teaches quite simply and plainly that the resurrection of the body is a wholly miraculous fact, not to be explained by the operation of natural causes. There is nothing which can be called a causal continuity between the earthly body and the risen body. There is not, as Origen suggested, a reproductive germ in the dead body out of which the risen body develops. The resurrection is to be conceived, therefore, not as a process of generation under natural causes, but as a direct reproduction of the body by the power of God. The resurrection is therefore in the strictest sense miraculous.

St Thomas Aquinas sets forth this teaching in plain terms. Asking whether the Resurrection of Christ is the cause of our resurrection,[1] he answers that the direct cause of our resurrection is the power of God, which effected also our Lord's Resurrection. But inasmuch as all divine gifts come to us through the merits of Christ, so may we say that Christ's Resurrection is the cause of our resurrection. His Resurrection, further, is the exemplar and model of ours. Proceeding, in the second and third articles of the same question, he discusses the efficacy of other alleged causes, only to insist that nothing but the power of God is the direct and adequate cause of the resurrection.

Moreover, much as St Thomas holds that soul and body belong naturally together, and that their reunion in the resurrection restores the integrity of human nature, yet he will not allow that that reunion is " natural "—*i.e.*, the effect of natural process—for there is no natural process from death to life. So that although the body may be said to have a certain passive inclination towards reunion with the soul, there is in nature no active principle which can cause the resurrection, and therefore the resurrection must be preternatural—*i.e.*, miraculous.[2]

Holding, then, that the resurrection of the body is a miraculous event, an effective exercise of the omnipotence of God, we shall not be disposed to set any limits of human imagination to God's power, or to confine it within the bounds of natural causality. As St Paul asked : " Why should it be thought a thing incredible that God should raise the dead ? "[3] And the Fathers, on their part, are content thus to refer the objector to the infinite power of the Creator. Here, for example, is the argument of St Augustine :

" Therefore, brother, confirm yourself in the name and help of him in whom you believe, so as to withstand the tongues of those

[1] Suppl., Q. lxxvi, art. 1. [2] Suppl., Q. lxxv, art. 3. [3] Acts xxvi 8.

who mock at our faith, out of whose mouths the devil speaks seductive words, desiring especially to ridicule the belief in the resurrection. But from your own experience, perceiving that you now exist although you once were not, believe that you will exist hereafter. For where was this mass of your body, and where was this form and structure of your members a few years ago, before you were born? Did it not come forth to light, out of the secret places of creation, under the invisible formative power of God? Is it then in any way a difficult thing for God to restore this quantity of your body as it was, seeing that he was able to make it formerly when it was not?" [1]

This general answer to the objections raised against any resurrection of body will appear comprehensive enough, and, if its assumptions be granted, quite complete and decisive. It is the general answer of Catholic theology, basing itself upon the nature of God and upon his revelation. It may seem, indeed, that when we have so stated the matter, there remains no more to be said. But that is not so. It has yet to be seen that we are justified in regarding this doctrine as a revealed truth, and as such contained in the double source of Scripture and tradition. And, moreover, the doctrine has yet to be explained and defended in one very important particular, namely, the identity of the risen body with the body which we now bear. But this is matter for later consideration.

§ V: THE TESTIMONY OF HOLY SCRIPTURE IN GENERAL

THE doctrine of the resurrection of the body is set before us by the Church as an article of our faith, and that is sufficient for us so that we may give it full credence. Nevertheless, we are doing the will of the Church if we examine and consider the testimonies to her teaching which are contained in the sources of revelation. What are these sources? They are Holy Scripture and Tradition. By Scripture we mean the canonical books of the Old and New Testaments; by Tradition we mean that body of doctrine which is contained in the Creeds of the Church, in the definitions of the Councils, in the writings of the Fathers and in the constant teaching of the living Church. In the present section let us consider the general testimony of Holy Scripture to the doctrine of the resurrection of the body.

Indications in the Old Testament

And first the testimony of the Old Testament. It may be said at the outset—and it is only natural—that we should be unreasonable to expect an absolutely explicit testimony to the doctrine in the books of the Old Testament. The revelation of the Old Testament was to be completed by the New, and in no one point did it need completion so much as in the doctrine of the life after death. For Jewish belief on this point was largely vague and indeterminate.

[1] *De catechizandis rudibus*, c. 25 abbreviated.

Yet there are testimonies scattered throughout the Bible which imply the belief in the resurrection, and these we shall now set out.

The texts which are usually adduced are four in number. First comes the text of Isaias:[1] "Thy dead men shall live, my slain shall rise again . . . the earth shall disclose her blood and shall cover her slain no more." Then there are the words of the Book of Job:[2] "I know that my redeemer liveth and in the last day I shall rise out of the earth. And I shall be clothed again with my skin: and in my flesh I shall see God. Whom I myself shall see and my eyes shall behold, and not another." Next are the words of the Book of Daniel:[3] "And many of those that sleep in the dust of the earth shall awake: some unto life everlasting and others unto reproach, to see it always." And finally there is the text of 2 Machabees:[4] "After him the third was made a mocking-stock, and when he was required he quickly put forth his tongue and courageously stretched out his hands, and said with confidence: These I have from heaven, but for the laws of God I now despise them: because I hope to receive them again from him."

Of these four testimonies it is well to say that only the last is quite explicit and satisfactory. The passage from Job loses some of its force when the version which we have given is compared with the original Hebrew, and the texts of Isaias and Daniel do not clearly prove a general resurrection. This is to take the texts just as they stand and without making any allowance for subsequent Catholic interpretation. But considering their subsequent history in Christian use, we find that these Old Testament testimonies, and especially the text of Job, were used by the earliest Christian writers as direct proof of the doctrine of the resurrection of the body. The words of Job are thus used by St Clement of Rome in his First Epistle to the Corinthians[5] and by a long sequence of Fathers. In virtue of this passage Job figures in early Christian art as a prophet of the resurrection. His words found a place in the ancient liturgies, and they are still embodied in the Office for the Dead. So if we believe—as we must—that the Spirit of God watches over the Church, guiding her teaching, and that she is the authoritative exponent of the Word of God, we naturally find in these texts a real, though obscure, enunciation of the doctrine.

Clearly taught in the Gospels

Turning now from the Old Testament to the New, we pass from comparative obscurity to clear day. During the last century B.C. Jewish thought was much occupied with the question of the life after death, and a considerable quantity of apocryphal writing has come down to us which endeavours to solve the problems of the after-life. In our Lord's time also, as is clear from the Gospels, the Jews were deeply interested in this question, and it was even a chief subject of controversy among them. So when our Lord, from his divine

[1] Isa. xxvi 19-21. [2] Job xix 25-27. [3] Dan. xii 2.
[4] 2 Mach. vii 10-11. [5] xxvi 3.

knowledge, propounded a clear doctrine concerning the after-life, his audiences heard him eagerly and debated his teaching warmly. The Sadducees, that party among the Jews who refused to believe in a resurrection, naturally contested his teaching, and it is especially in answer to their objections that he made his doctrine plain.

We read in St Matthew's Gospel how the Sadducees, "who say there is no resurrection," came to our Lord and put before him the case of a woman who was married successively to seven men. "At the resurrection, therefore, whose wife of the seven shall she be? for they all had her. And Jesus answering said to them: You err, not knowing the Scriptures nor the power of God. For in the resurrection they shall neither marry nor be married: but shall be as the angels of God in heaven. And concerning the resurrection of the dead, have you not read that which was spoken by God saying to you: I am the God of Abraham, and the God of Isaac, and the God of Jacob? He is not the God of the dead, but of the living." [1]

In the Gospel of St John we find several explicit texts. After our Lord had healed the infirm man at the pool of Bethsaida, he speaks to the Jews in defence and explanation of his work and teaching. They marvelled at his healing the infirm man, but he says to them: "Wonder not at this, for the hour cometh wherein all that are in the graves shall hear the voice of the Son of God. And they that have done good things shall come forth unto the resurrection of life; but they that have done evil unto the resurrection of judgement." [2] After the miracle of the Feeding of the Five Thousand, when he discourses upon the bread of life, we have this further testimony: "Now this is the will of the Father who sent me: that of all that he hath given me I should lose nothing, but should raise it up again in the last day. And this is the will of my Father that sent me: that everyone who seeth the Son, and believeth in him, may have life everlasting, and I will raise him up in the last day." [3] And finally, from St John, we have our Lord's words at the raising of Lazarus. When Martha came to him and expostulated with him for his absence, Jesus replied: "Thy brother shall rise again." To this Martha answers: "I know that he shall rise again in the resurrection at the last day." But Martha wanted a present resurrection and not the remote resurrection of the last day. Before granting her prayer, our Lord, to purify her faith, speaks these words: "I am the resurrection and the life: he that believeth in me although he be dead shall live: and everyone that liveth and believeth in me, shall not die for ever." [4]

Not a mere "spiritual" resurrection

From these passages of the Gospels, taken in their obvious sense and with proper appreciation of their context, it is clear that our Lord taught the resurrection of the dead in the plain and ordinary sense of that phrase—that is, a resurrection by which the living man

[1] Matt. xxii 23-32. Cf. Mark xii 18-27; Luke xx 27-38.
[2] John v 28-29. [3] John vi 39-40. [4] John xi 23-26.

is reconstituted in the everlasting life in the integrity of his human nature, body as well as soul. That was what the resurrection meant to his contemporaries, those Jews who so warmly debated it among themselves. That was the sort of resurrection exemplified in our Lord's own miracles, when he raised the daughter of Jairus, the widow's son of Naim, and Lazarus. That was the power given to his Apostles in the commission : " Heal the sick, raise the dead, cleanse the lepers, cast out devils. Freely you have received, freely give." [1] Throughout the Gospels, throughout the New Testament, " raising the dead " means nothing less than this bodily resurrection, a real restoration of physical life. Some opponents of this bodily resurrection would have it, because the phrase " resurrection of the body " does not occur in the New Testament, that therefore they may interpret the resurrection in a purely spiritual sense. But this is bad exegesis. It is bad exegesis because it takes the phrase " resurrection of the dead " out of its context and gives it a meaning at variance with that context. Of the doctrine of a purely spiritual resurrection there is no hint in the New Testament.

The Resurrection of Christ

So far we have considered the specific teaching of the Gospels concerning the doctrine, but have not considered the most striking evidence for the doctrine which is contained in these same Gospels—namely, the evidence of the Incarnation, Death and Resurrection of our Lord himself. As was suggested in a previous section of this essay, the Incarnation of our Lord, his literal assumption of our human nature, raises the dignity of that nature, and forbids the Christian philosopher from following the path of the Platonist or the Manichee in his rejection of one-half of that nature. The Incarnation of our Lord consecrates the complete human nature, body and soul together, and gives that integral nature, so to say, a second charter. It was divine in its creation, it receives now a reaffirmation of that primeval sanction. Not only so, but the whole Christian dispensation as instituted by our Lord is incarnational, and is inspired throughout by this conception of an integral human nature, a complete unity of body and soul.

But especially does the Resurrection of our Lord himself, the central fact of the Gospel and the climax of his mission, enforce the doctrine of a true bodily resurrection. The Gospels all record this Resurrection, and it is the Resurrection of his identical body in true physical reality. When our Lord appeared to his disciples in the evening of the first Easter Day, St Luke tells us that they were troubled and afraid, supposing that they saw a spirit. But Jesus, to convince them that it was really himself, in perfect physical reality, said to them : " See my hands and feet, that it is I myself ; handle, and see : for a spirit hath not flesh and bones, as you see me to have. And when he had said this, he shewed them his hands and feet. But while they yet believed not and wondered for joy, he said : Have

[1] Matt. x 8.

you here anything to eat? And they offered him a piece of a broiled fish, and a honeycomb. And when he had eaten before them, taking the remains he gave to them."[1] A like demonstration of the physical reality of our Lord's Resurrection is given by St John: "He shewed them his hands and his side. The disciples therefore were glad when they saw the Lord"[2]—that is, knew from this tangible proof that it was really he. And, for St Thomas: "Put in thy finger hither, and see my hands, and bring hither thy hand and put it into my side; and be not faithless, but believing. Thomas answered: My Lord, and my God."[3]

If it be said of this that our Lord's Resurrection is a thing apart and bears no relation to ours, it is answered that the New Testament does not regard it so. To St Paul our Lord's Resurrection is the exemplary type and the guarantee of ours. The Resurrection of our Lord figured so largely in the preaching of the Apostles,[4] not only because it was the supreme proof of Christ's mission, but also because it was itself a book of doctrine, throwing a clear light upon the eternal destiny of man.

§ VI: THE TESTIMONY OF ST PAUL

PASSING now from the Gospels to consider the teaching of St Paul, it is proper to point out in the first place that his Epistles represent the belief of the first generation of the Christian Church. Some of the Epistles are earlier than the earliest of the Gospels, and their testimony has therefore a special value. St Paul claims to represent fully the mind of Christ, and the elaborate attempts of Protestant criticism to construct a Pauline Christianity alien from Christ's teaching have been singularly unsuccessful. Concerning this special doctrine of the resurrection of the body, St Paul's teaching is particularly explicit—it was for this in particular that he incurred the hostility of his compatriots—and we shall now consider his teaching in detail.

Christ's Resurrection and ours

St Paul places the general resurrection on the same level of certainty as Christ's Resurrection: "If Christ be preached that he rose again from the dead, how do some among you say that there is no resurrection of the dead? But if there be no resurrection of the dead, then Christ is not risen again, then is our preaching vain and your faith also is vain."[5] He preached the resurrection of the dead as one of the fundamental doctrines of Christianity before the quick-witted Athenians, and by his teaching aroused their special interest.[6] The same doctrine formed part of his discourse at Jerusalem,[7] of his preaching before Felix,[8] and before Agrippa.[9] He insists on it often in his Epistles.[10] And it is clear that he intended a real bodily

[1] Luke xxiv 39-43. [2] John xx 20. [3] John xx 27, 28.
[4] See Acts, *passim*. [5] 1 Cor. xv 12. [6] Acts xvii.
[7] Acts xxiii. [8] Acts xxiv. [9] Acts xxvi.
[10] Rom., 1 Cor., 2 Cor., Phil., 1 Thess., 2 Tim.

resurrection. If we would have his clearest and fullest exposition of the doctrine, it is to our hand in the "classic source," which has already been cited, the fifteenth chapter of the First Epistle to the Corinthians. So clear, indeed, and full is the exposition of the doctrine in that chapter, that it must be given a detailed notice.

As has been observed already, St Paul argues the doctrine of our resurrection from the fact of the Resurrection of Christ, teaching that the two beliefs stand or fall together:

> "Now if Christ be preached that he rose again from the dead, how do some among you say that there is no resurrection of the dead? But if there be no resurrection of the dead, then Christ is not risen again. And if Christ be not risen again, then is our preaching vain, and your faith also is vain. Yea, and we are found false witnesses of God, because we have given testimony against God, that he hath raised up Christ, whom he hath not raised up if the dead rise not again. For if the dead rise not again, neither is Christ risen again. And if Christ be not risen again, your faith is vain, for you are yet in your sins. Then they also that are fallen asleep in Christ are perished. If in this life only we have hope in Christ, we are of all men most miserable" (12-19).

See how close he makes the connection between Christ's Resurrection and ours—so close that we may fairly argue that in St Paul's mind our resurrection was to be not only as real as Christ's, but also as complete; that it was in its own measure to be like to Christ's, in being a complete resurrection of the whole man, body and soul.

Proceeding with his argument, St Paul indicates that death was the punishment of original sin, and that the resurrection is one of the fruits of Christ's redemption.

> "But now Christ is risen from the dead, the firstfruits of them that sleep. For by a man came death, and by a man the resurrection of the dead. And as in Adam all die, so also in Christ all shall be made alive" (20-22).

The manner of the resurrection

And now we may pass to that part of his argument where he undertakes to define the manner of the resurrection. Although we cannot, if we deny the resurrection of the body, speak properly of any resurrection at all—for the continued existence of the soul is not to be called a resurrection—yet there are those who use words thus and who would interpret "resurrection of the dead" in a purely spiritual sense. We may expect, then, that when St Paul addresses himself to the explanation of the manner of the resurrection, he will give us the means of deciding this question. This is the way in which he approaches the problem:

> "But some man will say: how do the dead rise again? or with what manner of body shall they come? Senseless man, that which thou sowest is not quickened, except it die first. And that which thou sowest, thou sowest not the body that shall be; but bare grain, as of wheat, or of some of the rest. But God giveth it a body as he will: and to every seed its proper body" (35-38).

An analogy

St Paul begins with an analogy from nature. The apparent death of the seed, and then its manifest resurrection into the new life of the plant or tree, provide us with an illustration of man's resurrection from the grave. The analogy has been a favourite one with all writers on the resurrection, and we find it developed by them with great elaboration. It is clear already that St Paul is supposing a real continuity and identity of nature between the dead man and his risen self. But he passes on from this introductory analogy to come to closer grips with the question. God gives this human seed its proper body, as he gives its appropriate body to the acorn or the grain of wheat ; but of what nature, in the case of man, is the body which he gives ? It is not, says St Paul, just the natural body which he had in this world, but a spiritual body. Does he mean by this to empty " body " of all meaning ? Assuredly not. We shall see later what are the special characteristics of the risen body and how this may be called a spiritual body. Yet it remains body none the less. Here are St Paul's words :

" So also is the resurrection of the dead. It is sown in corruption, it shall rise in incorruption. It is sown in dishonour, it shall rise in glory. It is sown in weakness, it shall rise in power. It is sown a natural body, it shall rise a spiritual body. . . . In a moment, in the twinkling of an eye, at the last trumpet : for the trumpet shall sound, and the dead shall rise again incorruptible : and we shall be changed. For this corruptible must put on incorruption, and this mortal must put on immortality. And when this mortal hath put on immortality, then shall come to pass the saying that is written : Death is swallowed up in victory. O death, where is thy victory ? O death, where is thy sting ? " (42-44, 52-55).

Such is the final testimony of St Paul. It will rise a body—he does not cast aside that word—but a body which is spiritual, glorious, powerful, incorruptible, immortal. Had St Paul intended any mere immortality of spirit, was this the way in which to inculcate such a doctrine ? " *It* is sown in corruption ; *it* shall rise in incorruption," and so throughout his argument. What is this mortal that puts on immortality, and this corruptible that puts on incorruptibility, but the real human body ? We may fairly summarise his faith under two main heads. The first is this : that there will be a real bodily resurrection of men, and that in their own bodies. The second is this : that this bodily resurrection is not to be conceived in a crude and material manner, but that the risen body is, as later theology puts it, a " glorified " body. It should be noted also that St Paul fixes the time of this resurrection : it is to be at the last judgement.

" Spiritual " body

Here, then, we have the *locus classicus* for the doctrine ; nowhere else in the New Testament is it so explicitly stated. Nor can it be claimed that St Paul's words teach no more than a " spiritual " resurrection. Such an interpretation is precluded by two considerations. In the first place, as has been indicated already, we must take account of the meaning which the resurrection of the dead would bear for his hearers. There is no hint that St Paul was teaching any new kind of resurrection, and he emphatically correlates our resurrection with the true bodily Resurrection of Christ. In the second place, if we admit this "spiritual" interpretation, we shall have to conclude that the Church from its earliest days embraced an erroneous doctrine, and that it has been obstinate and pertinacious in error for the twenty centuries of its existence. This conclusion cannot be harmonised with our Lord's promise that he would be with his Church "all days, even unto the consummation of the world," nor with his assurance that the gates of hell would not prevail against it.

But it may be objected further that the teaching of the New Testament, whatever its purport, is certainly not so precise and detailed as the teaching of later theology. The objection is true, but unimportant; for the precision of later theology adds nothing to the substance of the doctrine, but is occupied in defining its circumstances and consequences. It is to be remembered that scientific theology was yet far distant when St Paul wrote, and, on the other hand, that exact formulation does not imply distortion or misrepresentation. It is to be remembered also that the written documents of the New Testament do not contain, or profess to contain, a complete and scientific account of the Christian revelation. The Church existed before any part of the New Testament was written, and the Church possessed already and was already teaching the revelation committed to her by her Founder. The Church has never intermitted this teaching office. From her, as from one who lived with Christ and whose continuity of life has never through all the centuries suffered interruption, we learn the full teaching of Christ. She speaks as one having authority to teach. The testimonies from the New Testament which have been adduced in these pages receive from her their full explanation and exposition, and her teaching is the true canon of their interpretation.

Little now remains to be said about the witness of the Scriptures, and this section may end with that vision of the resurrection which is given in the last book of the New Testament. The Seer of the Apocalypse "saw a great white throne, and one sitting upon it, from whose face the earth and heaven fled away, and there was no place found for them. And I saw the dead, great and small, standing in the presence of the throne, and the books were opened, and another book was opened, which was the book of life: and the dead were judged by those things which were written in the books, according to their works. And the sea gave up the dead that were in it, and death and hell gave up their dead that were in them: and they were judged every one according to their works." [1]

[1] Apoc. xx 11-13.

§ VII: THE TESTIMONY OF TRADITION

THE tradition of the Church—so far as it is a written tradition—is embodied in the Creeds, in the decrees of the Councils, in the sacred liturgy, and in the consentient teaching of the Fathers and the theologians. Upon this subject of the resurrection of the body the witness of tradition is so abundant, that to assemble it would require not an essay but a library. The present treatment will attempt only the briefest of summaries.

Creeds and Councils

The most ancient document of the faith is undoubtedly the familiar statement of belief which is denominated the "Apostles' Creed." This Creed was probably first formulated in Rome in the first century of Christianity for use in the ritual of baptism. The exact date of its composition cannot be determined precisely, but it has been traced back to the end of that first century, and we are free to hold that it is, what its title implies, of apostolic date and origin. The early Church in Rome was Greek-speaking, and this Creed in its earliest form was therefore in Greek. Now it is important to observe that here, at the earliest point at which we can test tradition, our doctrine is expressed in the most explicit and unquestionable form. For this earliest Creed expressed the doctrine in the two Greek words *σαρκὸς ἀνάστασιν*, of which the exact Latin equivalent is *carnis resurrectionem*, and the English "resurrection of the flesh." There is no ambiguity here, but a plain and explicit assertion of the bodily resurrection. Tradition, therefore, at its earliest point, is clear and unmistakable.

Besides the Apostles' Creed, the Church recognises two others as of primary authority, those known as the Nicene and Athanasian respectively. It is unnecessary for our purpose to discuss the history of these Creeds, and we shall be content to give their evidence for our doctrine. The Nicene Creed says: "And I look for the resurrection of the dead." This Creed, in the form in which it is used in the Mass, is supposed to date from the Second Oecumenical Council, held at Constantinople in A.D. 381. It will be observed that the formula is not so clear and unmistakable as that of the Apostles' Creed, but there is no ground for supposing that it may be understood in any different sense. Whatever truth there may be in the hypothesis that the vaguer expression was chosen under the influence of Origenist teaching—a mere hypothesis—the article did not in fact suffer any change of meaning, but was understood by the Church throughout in one and the same sense. If any proof were needed of this, it would be sufficient to point to the fact that the Apostles' Creed maintained its position alongside the Nicene, its "resurrection of the flesh" marching harmoniously with the Nicene "resurrection of the dead"; nor is there the least evidence that the Church recognised any difference of meaning in the two formulas.

The third of the three primary Creeds is that which goes by the name of the "Athanasian" (fourth or fifth century). In this Creed, again, the doctrine is presented in unmistakable form. Christ our Lord, affirms the Creed, is to come to judge the living and the dead. At his coming "all men are to rise again with their own bodies."

Confirming the witness of these Creeds is the Canon of the Fifth Oecumenical Council (Constantinople, A.D. 553) condemning the opinion of Origen that the risen body shall be "ethereal and spherical" and that neither Christ our Lord nor men shall have material bodies.

Leaving these Creeds and passing from the era of the Oecumenical Councils, we reach the Eleventh Council of Toledo (A.D. 675) and the explicit pronouncement: "We confess the resurrection of the flesh of all the dead. And we believe that we shall rise again, not in any ethereal or different flesh (as some have foolishly supposed), but in this flesh in which we live and move and are." The Creed of Pope Leo IX (A.D. 1050), still used in the ritual for the consecration of bishops, says: "I believe in the true resurrection of that same flesh which I now bear." The Profession of Faith prescribed by Pope Innocent III for converts from the errors of the Waldenses (A.D. 1210) has the clause: "We believe with the heart and profess with the mouth the resurrection of this flesh which we bear and not of any other." And, most definite of all, the Fourth Lateran Council (A.D. 1215), in its decree against the Albigenses and other heretics, declares that men "shall all rise again with their own bodies, which they now bear, to receive according to their works."

There is no need to produce further evidence from Creed or Council. The doctrine is clear and unmistakable: the true resurrection of all men in true bodies.

When we pass to the witness of the Fathers and theologians we are met with such an abundance of testimony for this particular doctrine that it is very difficult to represent it at all in a brief summary. All that shall be attempted here is to give a few examples of traditional teaching at widely different dates in the Church's history.

Apostolic Fathers

At the very beginning and before the era of the apologists, we have St Clement of Rome (who died about A.D. 99) in his Epistle to the Corinthians teaching the doctrine quite explicitly, basing it on the authority of Scripture, on the example of our Lord's Resurrection, and on some curious analogies from natural history. The Epistle of St Polycarp to the Philippians, as also the authentic Acts of his martyrdom (A.D. 155), provide further testimony. But we are now in the second century and the era of the first Christian apologists. The philosopher and martyr St Justin in his *First Apology* thus states the Christian faith: "We expect to receive again our own bodies, though they be dead and cast into the earth, for we maintain that with God nothing is impossible." He expects, we may note, a literal identity of bodily substance.

Athenagoras

The apologist Athenagoras (*c.* A.D. 180) devoted a special treatise to the resurrection, and goes very thoroughly into the matter. In him we meet the famous problem that was afterwards to exercise the minds of the Scholastics: What if certain particles of matter have served several persons? He is content to appeal to the omnipotence of God.

Irenaeus

We come next to the testimony of St Irenaeus, and it is testimony of the first importance. Irenaeus was born in Asia Minor, and had when young seen and heard the martyr St Polycarp, himself a disciple of St John. He is thus closely linked with the apostolic age, and as one born in the East, familiar with the Church in Rome, and then bishop of the great Christian see of Lyons, he had an exceptional acquaintance with the Church of his day. His teaching may be safely regarded as representative of the faith of the Church in the second century. Unfavourable critics describe it as "materialistic," a very literal raising again of the flesh. Such, then, was the belief of the Church in the second century. Out of very many passages that might be quoted from Irenaeus, here is one brief sample of his teaching:

"Just as a cutting from the vine planted in the ground fructifies in its season, or as a corn of wheat falling into the earth and becoming decomposed, rises with manifold increase by the Spirit of God, who contains all things, and then, through the wisdom of God, serves for the use of men, and having received the Word of God becomes the Eucharist, which is the body and blood of Christ, so also our bodies, being nourished by it and deposited in the earth, and suffering decomposition there, shall rise at the appointed time, the Word of God granting them resurrection to the glory of God, even the Father, who freely gives to this mortal immortality, and to this corruption incorruption." [1]

Passing over the emphatic witness of Tertullian and the doubtful speculations of Origen, it is sufficient to say that the recognised theologians both of East and West in the succeeding centuries, such men as St John Chrysostom, St Epiphanius, St Gregory of Nyssa, St Cyril of Jerusalem, St Ambrose, St Jerome, St Augustine, devote themselves to the exposition and defence of the orthodox belief in a bodily resurrection. From St Augustine alone enough might be quoted to form a treatise on the doctrine; but there is really no need to assemble this abundant witness. There is no question that the Fathers of the Church, with complete unanimity, teach the true resurrection of the body.

The scholastic theologians

When we turn to the scholastic theologians we find that they accept this orthodox teaching and discuss its implications with elaborate care. St Thomas Aquinas, for instance, devotes to it thirteen Questions of his *Summa Theologica* [2] and eleven chapters of his

[1] *Adversus Haereses*, Book V, chap. 2.

[2] Suppl., QQ. lxxv-lxxxvii.

Summa contra Gentiles.[1] The modern critic recognises in this exposition, and in that of the scholastic theologians generally, a complete acceptance of the traditional belief; his only complaint is that these theologians discuss the implications of the resurrection with a too elaborate nicety. However that may be, a quotation from the first article of St Thomas's first question [2] will show clearly the nature of his belief. After setting forth some objections to the doctrine he proceeds as follows:

"But against (these objections) is the text of Job: 'I know that my redeemer liveth and in the last day I shall rise from the earth and again be clothed in my skin,' etc. Therefore there will be a bodily resurrection. Furthermore, the gift of Christ is greater than the sin of Adam, as is clear from the fifth chapter of the Epistle to the Romans. But death was introduced by sin, for if there had been no sin, there would have been no death; therefore by the gift of Christ man shall be restored again from death to life. Furthermore, the members of Christ's mystical body ought to be conformable to the Head. But our Head lives and shall for ever live in body and soul, because 'Christ rising from the dead dieth now no more' (Rom. vi 9). Therefore men also, who are his members, shall live in body and soul. And so there must be a resurrection of the flesh.

"I reply generally that the opinions of those who affirm or deny this resurrection vary with their views on man's last end. The last end of man is happiness. Now some have maintained that a man can attain this end in this life, and so they were under no necessity to posit another life after this in which a man should attain his final perfection. They therefore denied the resurrection. . . . Others have required another life after this, in which man should live after death, but in his soul only; and they held that this soul life was sufficient to meet the natural desire of happiness. . . . And so they also denied the resurrection. For this opinion some had one false reason, others another. Certain heretics, for instance, held that all bodily things were from an evil principle, and spiritual things from a good principle. Wherefore the soul could not attain blessedness unless it was separated entirely from body. So all those heretical sects, who believe bodily things were created or formed by the devil, deny the resurrection. We have shown the falsity of this fundamental theory elsewhere. Others again have held that the soul was the whole man and the body a mere instrument which the soul employed, as a sailor uses a ship. And so with them too the man is perfectly blessed if his soul is blessed. Therefore they also had no use for the resurrection. But their opinion is refuted by Aristotle, when he shows that the soul is the form of the body, and is united to it as form is united to matter. And so it is evident, that if a man cannot attain beatitude in this life, we must necessarily assume the resurrection."

[1] Lib. IV, cc. 79-89.

[2] Suppl., Q. lxxv.

In the specific answers to objections with which he concludes the article, St Thomas argues (*inter alia*) that man is a real unity of body and soul, no fortuitous or accidental compound; that all his deeds are the deeds of this unitary agent; and that therefore the complete man, both body and soul, should receive the meed that his deeds have earned. And further, that the soul's state is more perfect when it is in the body, because it belongs to a whole of which the body also is an integral part; that this is its nature as assigned to it by God; and that therefore it is more conformable to God, more fully in his likeness, when it is united to the body.

With this brief extract in illustration of the teaching of St Thomas, this section may conclude. The evidence of tradition is overwhelmingly plain and does not need further emphasis. Creeds, Councils, Fathers, Liturgy: all these agree in proclaiming the doctrine in its literal sense. The ancient belief of the Church in the bodily Assumption of the Mother of God stands out as a practical affirmation of it. And such as was the doctrine to St Irenaeus, to St Augustine, to St Thomas, such is it to the Catholic Church of the present day. With the modern tendency outside the Church to interpret it in a "spiritual" fashion she has no sympathy. She would belie her claim to divine guidance were she thus to reverse the teaching of the centuries.

§ VIII: IN THE SAME BODIES

Identity of bodily substance—the common view

HITHERTO these pages have dealt with the doctrine of the resurrection of the body in a general way, setting forth its meaning and reasonableness, and assembling the scriptural and traditional evidence for it. It has been seen that the doctrine implies no mere immortality of the soul, or persistence of personal life in some purely spiritual mode of existence, but a real and complete resurrection of man in the fulness of his nature. It has been seen that only such a rising again can properly be called a resurrection, and that reason persuades this redintegration of the human whole. But nothing has been said so far about a matter which would seem to be of great importance in the interpretation of the doctrine—viz., the question of the identity of the risen body. The voice of tradition appears to be unanimous in favour of a very literal identity of material substance. The texts have been assembled in the previous pages, and all, it would seem, are of the same tenor as the profession which every Catholic bishop has to make in his consecration: "I believe in the true resurrection of that same flesh which I now bear." What do these formularies mean? What are we by the rule of faith required to believe regarding this point? Certainly, and obviously, the formularies imply that there is a relation of identity between the earthly and the risen body. But what sort of identity? That is the question.

Two rival views

For there are, among Catholic theologians, two rival views on this matter. There is the classical view, the view of the vast majority of the theologians, which maintains a real identity of bodily substance; and there is the view of a minority, which regards such material identity as unnecessary. Both parties agree, of course, that there is complete identity of soul; and both parties agree that the soul is the " predominant partner " and is the chief factor in the determination of personal identity. But, while the minority would make it the sole factor and effective cause of personal identity, the majority require along with it a coefficient of identical material substance. Let us illustrate the matter from ordinary human life.

Spiritual and vital identity

A man preserves, throughout his life, his personal identity. That identity rests, in the first place, on identity of soul. The conscious life, knit together by memory, is continuous from beginning to end, and the man himself recognises in this continuous experience his identity with himself. But such *spiritual identity* is not the whole of the matter, just as man is not a pure spirit, but a being composed of body and soul. So that there is also a psycho-physical identity, based on the life of the senses and on every vital process of the organism. Let us call this, to distinguish it from the other, *vital identity*. It is true, of course, that the soul vitalises and controls the whole human energy, and yet it will be useful here to distinguish between purely spiritual activity and the mixed activities of the human complex. We recognise, then, in a living man, not merely an identity of soul, but an identity of his complete self, an identity not only in the functions of his mind, but in every function of his sensitive organism. Physiologists say that the substance of which the body is composed is continually changing, and St Thomas Aquinas also recognises a constant flux of matter. But it is a plain fact of experience that this process, however constant and however complete, does not interrupt the vital identity. Though atoms and molecules may change, yet the unitary life persists, and the organism goes on uninterruptedly to the dissolution of death, preserving a continuous vital identity, while apparently wholly indifferent to the material " stuff " which it now appropriates and now discards.

Thus there are spiritual identity and vital identity, these two being in effect in the human life no more than distinct aspects of the same force. But, of the two, that which we call vital identity is the more characteristically human. For we are not disembodied spirits, or spirits using a physical mechanism in a merely external and instrumental way. On the contrary, the spiritual principle is enmeshed in a complex train of sense activity. The soul functions thus in the sense organism, and it is intimately and necessarily conjoined with it. Moreover, in each man as he lives his life, it is not any pure activity of soul that distinguishes him from his fellows, but rather this manifold psycho-physical activity. He is born with a sense life and already with certain characters which distinguish him from his fellows.

The cells which form his body, in their mysterious and wonderful fashion, strive towards and achieve a living structure which is original and unique. A vital formula or pattern dominates the process. And then the man acquires further characteristics, and the experience of life registers itself upon his organism, as well as in his memory. And so we get the unique person of unmistakable individuality, unique not only in the outward and visible features of his body, not only in the central life of the spirit, but in every pulsation of his vital energy. Such an identity and continuity of bodily life is a matter of everyday experience. To the scientist who knows nothing of soul, this vital energy in its manifold manifestations is all that he understands by life, and he recognises fully this vital identity.

Atomic identity

But there is conceivable yet a third component of personal identity, which we may be allowed to call *atomic identity*. Natural science, it is true, has discovered elements more ultimate than the atom, and even the latest ultimates, proton and electron, now find their position threatened ; but *atomic* identity will serve to convey what we intend, an identity of material substance.

For though the substance of our bodies is in constant flux, and though the organism would appear to be indifferent to the stuff which it uses, yet this change and alteration in our material composition is not catastrophic and instantaneously complete, but gradual and piecemeal. A man does not suddenly change his whole material substance. Take him at periods wide apart and there may be no atomic identity whatever, although this is one of those assertions which are far from proven. But even if we grant that the boy has no atomic identity with the man, or that our bodies—according to the current opinion—change entirely in a space of seven years, this does not dispose of the necessity of atomic identity in the personal life. For that life is a continuous process, and the material transformation is continuous also. It is not sudden and abrupt, but gradual. So that we cannot say that atomic identity, because of this flow of matter, has nothing to do with a man's personal identity. On the contrary, it would appear more reasonable to suppose that this identity makes its contribution to the complete human identity. And such is the spontaneous view of common sense, which, while quite ready to accept the metabolism of the physiologist, yet is not disturbed in its belief that there is a real continuity of material substance. The fire of life is passed on from day to day, until it is extinguished in death. And if the torch which carries that fire—the human body—is from day to day repaired and renewed by a marvellous vital chemistry, yet it remains really one and the same to the end of the race.

Such is human identity, not a thing of soul life alone, nor of soul and sense life, but the complex product of three : of soul and sense and body.

The majority view

Now this is the sort of identity which the majority of theologians suppose to obtain in the resurrection. They point to the fact that the resurrections recorded in the Gospels were of this sort: the widow's son of Naim, the daughter of Jairus, Lazarus. Each of these rose from death to life in a body which had this full identity with the body of his previous life. And our Lord's Resurrection, which is the model of ours, was just such a resurrection, in his own body in the full sense of identity. The theologians do not suppose that there need be any absolute atomic identity, because such a condition is not verified in the successive stages of the earthly life. But they ask for such an identity as is certainly characteristic of the earthly life. They suppose that God will make good any defects in the body and remedy all imperfection. They conjecture that all men will rise again in the age of perfect youth, so that a child will be brought forward to this and an old man back. But in this process they believe that God will make use of the material substance which has been the man's in his earthly life. There is no need that he should use all of this, nor is there any objection, where such substance is lacking, to its being supplied from elsewhere. For exact material identity is not necessary. Ferrariensis, commenting on St Thomas's *Contra Gentiles*, speaks thus of this identity: "A man remains one and the same man throughout his life on account of a numerical identity of form (the soul) and on account of some identity of matter. For though there is continual change in his material constituents, yet there remains always some matter in hand to which the new is added. And so it is with the risen body. If by God's power there be given to this some substance that was lacking, yet absolutely and simply speaking the man remains one and the same, though he may be considered as different in an accidental way because of this foreign substance." [1]

And the theologians maintain this theory of identity, not because they suppose that the matter which may have formed our bodies retains in itself any natural inclination to one human body rather than another, but because they believe that God wishes our resurrection to have this completeness. It is his will, and he has the power to carry it out. Nor is it more difficult for him to raise in identical bodies those who have been dead for centuries, and whose bodies have long been dissolved into dust, than it was so to raise Lazarus or the son of the widow of Naim. And they believe that God wills this sort of resurrection, because it appears to them that the documents of the faith, Scripture and Tradition, persuade this resurrection and no other. It is not necessary again to refer to these documents, for they have been assembled in previous pages, but the reader will admit that this teaching regarding the identity of the risen body is the apparent meaning of the very explicit conciliar decrees, as for example the decree of the Fourth Lateran Council which declares

[1] On *Contra Gentiles*, IV, 81.

that men " shall all rise again with their own bodies which they now bear, to receive according to their works."

But it is argued by the theologians who do not accept this view that the decrees of the Councils are patient of another interpretation. It is urged that these definitions are concerned primarily with the reality of the bodily resurrection as against those who either denied this resurrection outright, or contended for such a " spiritual " body as emptied the doctrine of meaning ; but that they do not give unquestionable and decisive testimony regarding the identity of the risen body. It is true that they use such phrases as " that same flesh which I now bear," and that these phrases seem plain enough ; but they may be interpreted, it is urged, not of identity, but of similarity of flesh, as asserting, that is (in scholastic terms), not a numerical, but a specific identity. Such is the argument. However, if we compare these definitions with the teaching of tradition in the Fathers and schoolmen, it would appear that the plain meaning of the formularies is the true one. Some of this teaching has already been cited, but we may here assemble a few definite and explicit sentences.

The authority of the Fathers

St Justin Martyr says : " We expect to receive again our own bodies, though they be dead and cast into the earth, for we maintain that with God nothing is impossible." Athenagoras says : " It is impossible for the same man to be reconstituted unless the same bodies are restored to the same souls." Tertullian teaches that the particles of the body, wherever they may be, will be collected again and the man's proper body thus reproduced. Moreover, when the apologists grapple with the famous problem of the cannibal, the son of cannibals, we get plain evidence of their belief that identity of bodily substance was required for the resurrection.

Again, the Fathers (*e.g.*, St Jerome) commonly point to our Lord's Resurrection in an identical body as the type of our resurrection. As was the resurrection of the Head, so shall the resurrection of the members be. Our Lord was at pains to demonstrate to his disciples the reality of his body, and he showed that it was that body which had suffered and died for us. Our resurrection shall be like to his, in those bodies with which we have lived in the world, and with which we have merited either reward or punishment.

The weighty witness of St Augustine is entirely on the side of this bodily identity. He argues that it is not necessary that the material of which the body has been composed should in the reconstitution of the body occupy the same parts and perform the same functions as before. But he is quite clear that the body will be reconstituted from the same material. He likens the process to the melting down and recasting of a metal statue. All the metal is used again, and the new statue is identical in material with the original one, but the material is bound to be " shuffled " in the process and so differently arranged.

When we turn from the Fathers to the Scholastics we find no

difference of belief. St Thomas discusses the point with considerable care and pronounces definitely for the resurrection of an identical body.[1] After discussing Platonic and Pythagorean views regarding the relation and fate of soul and body, and pronouncing these and all similar views contrary to the teaching of Scripture, he affirms that the resurrection, since it means "rising again," demands that the soul return to the same body. If the soul does not return to the same body, then we ought not to speak of resurrection, but rather call the fact the assumption of a new body.

In his *Summa contra Gentiles* St Thomas considers at greater length the objections to this manner of conceiving the resurrection of the body. One objection is that, if this be true, we must suppose that all matter that has at any time belonged to a man must rise with him, so that he would be of a portentous magnitude. Another is that some men have no other food than human flesh, and beget children who also eat this food. So several men will have a right to the same flesh. St Thomas is not dismayed by these objections. Pointing to the fact of metabolism in the earthly life and the continual change that takes place in the material substance of the body, he argues that a man preserves his identity of body in spite of this flux and reflux of its elements: "What does not bar numerical identity in a man while he lives on uninterruptedly can clearly be no bar to the identity of the risen man with the man that was." So there is no need to suppose that the risen body must have all the matter that has belonged at any time to the man; it is sufficient that it have as much of it as will make a perfect body, repairing loss or mutilation and perfecting the aged or the immature. To the second objection he answers that it is based on the same false supposition, that a man must receive again all the matter that has ever been his. He adds that, if there should be any lack of bodily matter, we may trust God to supply the deficiency.

It is abundantly clear from these citations—which could be multiplied indefinitely—that traditional teaching favours a real identity of bodily substance. It might indeed be urged against this conclusion that the Fathers and Scholastics, had they possessed our modern knowledge of the constitution and behaviour of matter, would have spoken differently. But that is a rather doubtful supposition. For in the course of their arguments they faced objections which anticipated the difficulties of the scientist, and they were not turned away thereby from their insistence on corporeal identity. To all such objections they were content at the last to oppose the omnipotence of God as the all-sufficient solution. Nor is the attitude of the generality of modern theologians any different.

[1] Suppl., Q. lxxix; *Contra Gentiles*, IV, 81.

§ IX: OBJECTIONS AND ANOTHER VIEW

But if the resurrection of the body seems to the modern objector a hard doctrine, the resurrection of an identical body seems to him quite impossible and incredible. Indeed, it may be said, roughly speaking, that most of the "scientific" objections brought against the doctrine are objections to the theory of material identity, and concern this special aspect of the doctrine, rather than the doctrine in itself. The difficulty is not in any sense a new one, for it was evidently felt in every period of the history of the doctrine. But since the modern objections as they are commonly stated appear to many to persuade another view of the resurrection, and since such a view has been propounded, this section must set forth some of these objections, the view in question, and the general theological criticism of the whole.

"The indifference of the atom"

The chief objections to the theory of material identity may be reduced to three and stated as follows. The first objection is based upon what may be denominated the indifference of the atom. It is not an objection of great weight, for the theologians are quite prepared to admit this indifference, and they set the determining cause that requires material identity not in matter but in God. Yet since this objection is urged and is plausible, let it be here set down. Our bodies, then, are composed of atoms of various elements: carbon, oxygen, nitrogen, etc., in various number and proportion. These atoms are taken up into the cell life, are controlled by what may be called the psycho-physical formula of each individual man, and thus the individual, living body is formed. But of themselves these atoms have no personal characteristics or differences whatever. One atom of carbon is exactly like another atom of carbon, and one atom of nitrogen exactly like another atom of nitrogen and so on. (We refrain from carrying the analysis as far as the further ultimates, the proton and electron, though the absence of differentiating character becomes there more evident still.) Therefore when the body dies and the cell life is extinct, there would seem to be no satisfactory ground whatever for identifying any particular atoms with any particular body. It would seem, therefore, to be a matter of indifference what atoms were chosen to form the material substance of the risen body. And so the theory of material identity would seem unnecessary. And if miracles should not be multiplied without cause, why insist on this atomic identity?

The circulation of matter

The second objection is based on the doctrine of the incessant circulation of matter. The particles of matter of which our bodies are composed, it is alleged, have previously belonged to other bodies. And this matter is now, and has been from the beginning, in constant circulation. As the theologian Billot quaintly expresses it, this is a process *per quam ex quolibet quidlibet fit, et rursus quidlibet transit in quodlibet.*

Moreover, since man appeared on the earth untold generations have lived and died, and the question of property in particular atoms of matter has been rendered infinitely complex. And then there is the ancient, yet not unreal objection, based on the practice of cannibalism. So, in the general resurrection, it is asked, how can this universal problem of disputed ownership be settled ?

Metabolism

And a third objection, which is really a particular case of the last, points to that metabolism which is an admitted phenomenon of the individual bodily life. The physiologists do not allow any constant material identity in the living man. To them the fundamental fact of life is the incessant transformation of living substance. Life, they say, is constant decomposition and reconstruction. There is really no stability of material substance, and therefore no such thing as material identity. My body to-day may be substantially the same as what it was last week ; but it is wholly different, in its material constituents, from the body which I had some years ago. So that it would appear that a genuine identity of bodily life in this world does not require any such material identity. Why, then, insist upon it in the resurrection ?

Such are some of the objections raised against the theory of material identity. The general answer to them has already been made when it was said that all such difficulties will not be difficulties to the omniscience and omnipotence of God. And if we grant that the documents of revelation require such material identity, then there is nothing more to be said. But we may press these objections and refuse to make such appeal to God's power. To this the theologian would answer that all the difficulties may be reduced to one, namely to the supposed case where a man can claim no material substance as his own, because it has previously belonged to others. This is the crucial question, and it is a difficulty which is almost as old as the doctrine. What is the solution ? We may either deny the probability of the hypothesis—certainly it cannot be shown to occur —or again we may leave the matter to God.

The view of Durand and Billot

But some few theologians have met these difficulties in another way, and it is only fair to the reader that we should expound their view. It is rather an eccentric view and has not received great countenance among the general body of theologians ; but it has been propounded both in the Middle Ages and in our own day, and it therefore deserves mention. According to this view, then, we are wrong to insist on material identity of bodily substance. That may be characteristic of the resurrection, but it is entirely unnecessary. It is sufficient that there should be identity of soul. Such is the view propounded in the scholastic period by Durand (died 1332), known from the quality of his temper and opinions as the *Doctor Resolutissimus*, and such is the view propounded more recently by the distinguished Jesuit theologian and former Cardinal, Billot.

This opinion has the advantage that it destroys the force of the objections which have just been considered: they no longer apply. It is argued further, in its favour, that St Thomas himself pointed the way to this solution when he observed that a man preserved his numerical identity throughout his life, although the elements of his body were in a constant state of flux. From this Billot argues that the real principle of identity in a man, when we consider him at successive points in his life, is his soul and not the changing body; and therefore also in the resurrection the soul can provide all necessary identity. If it be said that this view is contrary to the plain sense of the formularies, Billot's answer is that they do not contradict it. What the formularies insist on is reality of bodily substance and not identity. They are concerned to condemn errors such as that of Origen, but not to insist upon atomic identity. They wanted to make sure of *flesh*, but not of this particular flesh. And, argues Billot, if their words are to be pressed so as to connote material identity, then this identity ought to be complete. What ground, he asks, is there for saying that there must be some identical matter, but not all? And if we adopt this complete material identity, then all the old problems face us: With what body shall a man rise, for he has tenanted many in the course of his life? And what of the resurrection of cannibals?

But if we neglect this atomic identity and cease to pursue it, how much easier everything becomes. Even in the earthly life how unimportant it is compared with the vital identity of the animated organism. The personal identity of the living body, with all its vital endowment, depends very little, if at all, upon an identity of atomic substance. And shall we insist upon it for the risen body? That body will be identical with the earthly body with the vital identity of which we have spoken. When God raises up a living body in the resurrection, when he restores the bodily life, and sets up again the living organism, he does not restore any bodily life, a sort of standardised product; but he restores that personal and individual life which you had on earth and which was arrested by death. When the soul takes up that life again it returns to intimate union with a familiar vital organism, and does not start a fresh life in a new environment. Your organism with all its special characters and individual traits, with all its experience of life, and with its unique history and unique achievement as the partner of your soul: this is the living body that God will restore to you at your resurrection. And with this vital identity—a very true and genuine identity—why ask for a further and unimportant identity of atomic substance? You have not such identity in your earthly career, why demand it in the resurrection?

Critique

Such, in brief, is the argument of those who deprecate insistence on material or atomic identity, and prefer to hold that identity of soul is sufficient; for from soul identity flows that full vital identity which is proper to man. And, undoubtedly, their theory has its advantages. It is obvious that, by dispensing with a literal identity of bodily substance, it does remove some of the difficulties which are brought against the bodily resurrection. It is definitely an "easier" view; nor can we say that it is not a permissible view. But, if it is more acceptable to the scientist, it is not so attractive to the theologian. For it is not, in spite of all argument to the contrary, in harmony with the tradition. It is at best a forced interpretation of the language of the formularies. And, if our whole business in this matter is to interpret the tradition truly, then it would seem that we must abandon this theory and hold to material identity. While as for the argument that material identity is not characteristic of the earthly life, this is untrue. For although the matter of the body is in constant process of change, yet there is a real continuity of material substance.

Conclusion

And so the view of Durand and Billot, with all its advantages, has not been generally adopted and cannot be said to enjoy great favour among the theologians. It is true that some Scholastics have admitted the possibility of a resurrection in which there should be no material identity, but they have done so only by way of exception and hypothesis. The general attitude towards the view is well stated by Suarez:

"Therefore, although that manner of imperfect resurrection imagined by Durand may be conceived and understood as possible, yet the true resurrection, as the Scripture and the Church speak of it, requires an identity not only of soul, but also of body." [1]

To the "scientific" difficulties which are alleged against material identity, it is answered that there is nothing very new about them. The difficulty arising out of the circulation of matter was contained, in a crucial form, in the old cannibal problem. Nor was St Thomas, for instance, unaware that the matter of our bodies is in a continual state of flux, and we may claim for him that he anticipated the metabolism of the physiologist.

So a man may well prefer to disregard these objections, reflecting that he has hardly any greater difficulties to face than those which were faced by the apologists, the Fathers and the Scholastics. And what was their general answer to all such objections? In its ultimate form it was simply this: that difficulties which seem to us, with our limited knowledge and limited intelligence, almost insuperable will be no difficulties to the omniscience and omnipotence of God. There is really nothing more to be said.

So that our conclusion is this: that, of the two modes of conceiving the true bodily resurrection, that more precise mode which requires some material identity is the one generally taught by the theologians, and is the one which best accords with the tradition. It may be said further, in favour of this view, that this is the sort of bodily resurrection which the ordinary Christian man has always

[1] *De mysteriis vitae Christi*, Disp. 44.

expected. St Thomas aptly expresses the attitude of the plain man when he says that if there be no material identity, we ought not to call the occurrence a resurrection of the body, but the assumption of a new body.

§X: THE RISEN BODY

THIS essay has now dealt with the resurrection of the body and the manner of this resurrection ; it remains to say something about the qualities of the risen body.

The work of theologians on the subject

The subject is a highly speculative one, and there is very little certainty about it. We know that we shall rise again in true bodies, and that these bodies will be in some way spiritualised. So much is the teaching of Holy Scripture and Tradition, and it is the faith of the Church ; more than this is theological deduction and speculation. It may seem to some readers of this essay that it is idle to attempt any further precision in this matter, and that it would be far better to abstain from speculation and abide by the grand, if mysterious, language of St Paul. But Catholic theologians in general and the schoolmen in particular have not so regarded the matter. And indeed, apart from the fact that the subject of itself provoked the scholastic temper to exercise its gift for metaphysical speculation, these theologians had a very practical purpose. For the doctrine of the resurrection had encountered from the earliest times a criticism which sought to empty the risen body of all corporeality. Origen, for example, so emphasised the spirituality of the risen body that he was understood to deny to it any bodily character. Hence the condemnation of the Fifth Oecumenical Council : " If anyone shall say that the future judgement signifies the total abolition of bodies, and that the end of the story is immateriality, and that there will be nothing material in the future world, but only naked mind : let him be anathema." [1]

Therefore the task before the Catholic theologian was to insist on the corporeal reality of the risen body, and at the same time to assert those spiritual characteristics which are proper to it in its glorified state. He had to construct such a theory of the glorious body as would preserve its bodily character and yet emphasise its spiritual transformation. It is obviously an exceedingly difficult thing to do, and the theologians would not claim to have achieved it satisfactorily or finally. Let us consider their tentative conclusions.

Resurrection of the reprobate

To begin with we must note that although we shall be chiefly concerned—as was St Paul—with the bodies of the blessed, yet the wicked also rise again. The wicked too shall live for ever, though it be to be punished everlastingly. So the bodies of all men, both good and bad, are now immortal and incorruptible. But that which is the foundation of the blessedness of the good is the supreme

[1] Canons against Origen, No. 11.

torment of the wicked, that they shall know no respite in their pains. For the rest, apart from this attribute of incorruptibility, the bodies of the blessed and the wicked differ as glory from utter dishonour, as beauty from vileness, as joy from misery. Their very incorruptibility is, in St Augustine's phrase, an incorruptibility of continuous corruption.

Immortality and incorruptibility

Turning from their lamentable state to consider the condition of the blessed, we set it down as the fundamental quality of their bodies that they are now immortal and incorruptible. In this especially does the risen body differ from the earthly body. The earthly body is subject to change and corruption; the risen body is immutable and incorruptible. When the Sadducees confronted our Lord with difficulties against the resurrection, he answered them: "The children of this world marry and are given in marriage. But they that shall be accounted worthy of that world and of the resurrection from the dead shall neither be married nor take wives. Neither can they die any more; for they are equal to the angels, and are the children of God, being the children of the resurrection." [1] From these words of our Lord, reported also in St Matthew and St Mark, we see that the life of the world to come is not a repetition of the life of this world, and that the risen body is body with a difference. To those who think otherwise, "You err," says our Lord, "not knowing the Scriptures nor the power of God." In the resurrection we become like unto the angels of God.

Starting, then, from these data, that we have true bodies and that these bodies are now immortal and quasi-angelic, and basing their exposition upon St Paul's description in First Corinthians, the Scholastics attribute to the risen body four chief qualities—namely, impassibility, clarity, agility and subtlety. Let us consider these separately, and first the quality of impassibility.

Impassibility

We have already said that immortality is the first essential characteristic of the glorified state and that it is intrinsic and fundamental. "This corruptible must put on incorruption, and this mortal must put on immortality." Following directly from this quality, and indeed hardly more than an aspect of it, is the quality of impassibility. By this it is meant that all defect is excluded from the glorified body. Incorruption reigns supreme, and the forces of corruption, waste and change have no more power. From this it follows that all the activities of generation and nutrition, or whatever others are bound up with the nature of a mortal and passible body, are excluded from the glorified body. St Thomas says that the risen body is perfectly subject to the soul and the soul to God. The body, therefore, is assimilated to the nature of the soul and shares its impassibility: it is as the angels of God.

We may revolt against this doctrine as contradicting all our conceptions of the nature of "body," of which constant change,

[1] Luke xx 34-36.

waste and repair, seem necessary characteristics. Yet we know very little of the real nature of body and its inherent possibilities; and we know less of the power of God. But here is the explicit doctrine, imparting to us a piece of divine knowledge, and from this doctrine the impassibility of the risen body is a necessary deduction.

In connection with this quality we may refer briefly to the speculations of the Scholastics with regard to minor points. St Thomas lays it down that men and women will rise with bodies which are perfect in every member and every organ, although the functions of the physical life are no longer performed. If there were defects in the earthly body, these will be repaired in the risen body. And, furthermore, all will rise "in juvenili aetate," in the state of youth. The child who has died before attaining this state, and the old man who has passed through it to decrepitude: both alike will be established in the perfect age. And so they will remain, without change or alteration, immortal and impassible.

Clarity

The second quality of the risen body, according to the Scholastics, is "clarity"—that is to say, beauty, glory and splendour. "It is sown in dishonour," says St Paul, "it shall rise in glory. It is sown in weakness, it shall rise in power. It is sown a natural body, it shall rise a spiritual body." Our bodies, he says, become celestial and possess the glory proper to the celestial. For "one is the glory of the sun, another the glory of the moon, and another the glory of the stars. For star differeth from star in glory." And even so our bodies, when risen and glorified, shall possess a proper glory and beauty. Of this glory we can say little. The soul enjoys the beatific vision, and that infinite beauty irradiates and transforms it. "Eye hath not seen, nor hath ear heard, neither hath it entered into the heart of man to conceive, what things God hath prepared for them that love him." The glory possessed by the soul in the beatific vision overflows, says St Thomas, and transforms the body. "Then shall the just shine as the sun in the kingdom of their Father." [1] St Thomas says that the glory of the soul shines through the body, even as a glass vessel shows the colour of that which is contained in it. So the whole body will be lightsome (*lucidum*), and display in every part the glory of the soul.

Subtlety

The third quality of the risen body is the quality of subtlety, by which is meant that the body, while remaining a true body, is yet assimilated to the spiritual soul, to which it is now utterly docile. "It is sown a natural body: it shall rise a spiritual body"—that is to say, like to a spirit; and this quality of subtlety is especially characteristic of spirit. Yet we must not, with some ancient heretics, push the "rarefaction" of body so far as to abolish the distinction between body and spirit. Body cannot be transformed into spirit, however "subtle" it may become. The risen body shall remain as true a body as was our Lord's when he said, "See my hands and

[1] Matt. xiii 43.

feet, that it is I myself; handle and see: for a spirit hath not flesh and bones as you see me to have."[1] The risen body, says St Thomas, is subtle through completest perfection of bodily nature, and not through lack of that nature. And he derives this perfection from the dominance of the glorified soul over the body, which is now entirely subject to it.

And we are not to think that this quality violates in any way the proper nature of body. Some theologians suppose that this subtlety enables the risen body to pass through other bodies, just as our Lord entered the room, "the doors being shut." But St Thomas regards this as a special exercise of divine power, as a miraculous event, and not as the natural behaviour of a glorified body. For he holds that the glorified body must still have dimensions and must still have its own exclusive locality. And not even two spirits, though infinitely subtle, can be in the same place at one and the same time.

Agility

The fourth quality of the risen body, as specified by the theologians, is denominated "agility." By this is meant again that the body becomes a perfect instrument for the glorified soul. It is able to pass from place to place with great quickness, according to the will of the soul, and to move other bodies with a like velocity. "It is sown in weakness, it shall rise in power." St Thomas here, as in the case of the other qualities, derives this agility from the perfect subjection of the risen body to its soul. The body becomes a perfect instrument, alert and quick to obey the spirit in all the activities of the blessed life.

Dominance of soul over body

Such, then, are the qualities of the risen body as expounded in theological speculation. There is no need to regard this exposition as exhaustive, or to claim for it any finality or absolute certainty. But some such speculation is certainly legitimate and no unreasonable illustration of the effort of faith to seek fuller understanding of its object. And let those note, who impute to the Catholic theology of the resurrection the character of crude materiality, that the whole effort and trend of this exposition is to emphasise the spirituality of the glorified body. The keynote of the whole teaching is the dominance of the risen soul over the whole man. In the earthly life the spirit was trammelled and thwarted by its partner. There was a continual conflict. The balance of man's nature had been upset by original sin, and as a consequence he found "another law in his members fighting against the law of the spirit." But the effect of the resurrection, won for us by Christ our Lord, is to restore the integrity of human nature and to make the body the perfect instrument of the soul. If in the earthly life it was very really and unmistakably an animal body, subject to the necessities and the desires of the animal life, now it is as really and unmistakably a spiritual body, completely obedient to the soul and perfectly fulfilling its behests. In the life of glory, therefore, all conflict and friction have ceased.

[1] Luke xxiv 39.

The soul now expresses itself in a perfect medium, and being most intimately one with the body and with every part of it, is able now, as never before, to exert its proper psychical energy to a degree only limited by the limitations of a finite being. It is here, in this enfranchisement of the soul's energy, in this enlargement and intensification of its power, that we must find the dominant characteristic of the glorified state. And the purpose of the qualities which have been specified above is no other than to depict and emphasise this dominance of spirit.

Preservation of the glorified body

Let us say one word more about the potency of the glorified spirit and its efficiency in the glorified state. The glorified body, as has been said already, preserves every part and every organ of the earthly body. Yet cells and tissues and organs are to be conceived as maintaining their perfection without those processes of waste and repair, that metabolism, which is characteristic of the earthly organism. This is a hard saying, and what scientist can hear it ? To justify it, we may be content to appeal to that omnipotent power which is the cause of the resurrection itself. But is it not possible also, short of invoking the omnipotence of God, to set forth this effect as the direct result of the dominance of spirit ? Modern psychology has come back from its mechanistic wanderings to admit a real psychical force, a force which dominates and controls the material coefficients with which and through which it works. It is shy of using the word " soul," but none the less it has returned to a belief in some such thing. Now modern psychology on its experimental side has also made it more and more clear that the mind exercises a very powerful influence over the body. It has shown that this influence extends even to very profound modifications of the organism. The controlling influence of mind is clear even in the normal functioning of the organism, but it has become especially manifest in those abnormal states which have been elaborately studied by modern investigators, as in the phenomena of hysteria. We now know that there are many bodily affections which are mental in their origin and that they yield to skilled treatment. The mind has the power to disturb and alter the physiological functions of the body, and it can produce all the material effects of genuine bodily disease. This power of mind is admitted by the psychologists.

Now if such is the power of mind in this life, if it so permeates and controls the bodily organism, what will be its power in the future life, when, according to our faith, the soul is raised to such a height of power and glory ? It is a source of energy here and directs the body, though with difficulty and interruption ; in the future life it will exercise a higher power, and will have no obstacles in its path. This soul-action, therefore, this effective psychical energy, is to be conceived as the cardinal fact of the glorified life.

The Beatific Vision and the glorified body

Nor should we omit another word about the effect of the " beatific vision " upon the glorified body. In the Gospel account of our

Lord's Transfiguration we read that he was "transfigured before them. And his face did shine as the sun: and his garments became white as snow."[1] It is the traditional teaching of Catholic theology that this splendour was the normal quality of Christ's body. His human soul, by reason of its hypostatical union with the Eternal Word, enjoyed the beatific vision. But the connatural effect of this vision is the glorification, the transfiguration of the body. However, Christ as man, for the purposes of his Incarnation, restrained this effect, and once only, in his Transfiguration, allowed that glory to be seen.

So is it with the risen body as it was with the body of Christ in his Transfiguration. By virtue of the gift of glory the Blessed enjoy the beatific vision, and the power and splendour of the vision embrace not the soul only, but also the body. St Paul says: "We all, beholding the glory of the Lord with open face, are transformed into the same image from glory to glory, as by the Spirit of the Lord."[2]

And now enough has been said about our doctrine. It will be abundantly evident that Catholic theology is wholly faithful to tradition. It insists on a genuine resurrection of body. It inculcates a complete view of human nature, and provides for a truly human immortality, an immortality of the whole human person. Firm in the faith once delivered to the saints, the Church looks forward confidently to a resurrection which is promised and prefigured in the Resurrection of her Lord.

JUSTIN MCCANN, O.S.B.

[1] Matt. xvii 2. [2] 2 Cor. iii 18.

XXXV

HEAVEN, OR THE CHURCH TRIUMPHANT

§ I: INTRODUCTORY

For God the creation and the final consummation of all things are ever present to his eternity. For men who exist in time, their creation and their consummation are separated by the slow sequence of change measured by many days, many years, and many ages. God created us by an act of thought; he willed, he spoke, and we were. We are, because he knows us. On the impossible supposition that we should ever pass out of his sight, we should instantaneously cease to be and sink back into nothing from which we came. Our creation meant that we entered into the sight of God, and our continued existence means that he keeps us in sight; our very being depends on his mind. Our consummation will be when we know God even as we are known, when we see him, who has ever seen us, and whose sight is our life. God knew us in order that one day we might know him; such is the alpha and omega, the beginning and end of all human history.

The Church of God, in the full sense of the word, is the multitude of those whom God has called to eternal life. "We know," said St Paul, "that to those who love God all things co-operate unto good even to those who, according to his purpose, are called to be saints. For those whom he foreknew, he also predestined to become likened unto the image of his Son, that he might be the first-born among many brethren. But those whom he predestined, he also justified, but those whom he justified, he also glorified." [1] In this sense there is but one Church of God from the days of Adam and Eve until the day when the whole multitude of the saved will be glorified around the throne of God. The Church of God began in Paradise and continues in heaven. On earth it is divided into the church of the primitive covenant, that of the Mosaic and that of the New or Christian covenant, but these three divisions can be united under the one name of Church Militant, for man's life on earth is a warfare, as the Scripture says. To this warfare there is but one final alternative, either heaven or hell.

Hell is complete defeat and everlasting loss. Those that enter hell completely pass out of the communion of the Saints and the church of the Redeemed; they are outside the bond of charity and the benefit of the Atonement of Christ. Those who enter Purgatory not only remain within the Church and the communion of the

[1] Rom. viii 28-30.

Saints, but are its holy and privileged members, who have made their salvation sure. Their state, however, is not a permanent one, and while it lasts it combines the joys of security and the calm of resignation with the most intense pain of being deprived of the sight of God. Hence the multitude of those waiting souls is called the Church Suffering.

Heaven is the only decisive and ultimate victory of which man is capable, hence the company of those who have fought the good fight, won the battle, and entered into the land of their conquest, is called the Church Triumphant.

We shall study the nature of that ultimate triumph, that celestial consummation which awaits those who persevered unto the end and have received from the eternal King the reward that never passes away. In heaven man will achieve the perfection of his manhood in the supernatural order as God intended it. This will mean the complete satisfaction of his faculties of mind and will by the sight and possession of God himself; it will mean the glorification also of his body and its faculties, because the body will be the handmaid of his soul in the perfection of his celestial life.

We must therefore consider his heavenly happiness first in regard to his mind, then in regard to his will, and finally in regard to his body. We shall conclude by considering some of the consequences and implications of his eternal bliss, and by studying some special questions concerning heaven.

§ II: THE VISION OF GOD THE SATISFACTION OF THE MIND

The essence of heaven

HEAVEN is essentially the sight of God face to face.

Almost eighteen hundred years ago St Irenaeus wrote: "The things which are impossible with men are possible with God. For man indeed of himself does not see God. But God of his own will is seen by those whom he wills, when he wills, and as he wills. For God is mighty in all. He was seen then (by the Prophets in the Old Testament) through the Spirit of prophecy, he is now seen in the New Covenant, by adoption also, through the Son; but in the kingdom of heaven he will be seen even as Father. Man will be prepared by the Spirit in the Son of God. Man will be brought to the Father by the Son: man will be endowed with incorruption by the Father unto everlasting life, which comes to everyone by the fact of his seeing God. For as those who see the light are in the light and perceive its brightness, thus also those who see God are in God, perceiving his brightness. This brightness gives them their life; hence they that see God, see life. God is beyond created grasp, intelligence, and sight, but he will put himself within human sight, intelligence, and grasp for the purpose of giving life to those who perceive and see him. God's greatness is indeed unsearchable, but so also is his loving kindness unutterable, even that loving kindness by which, being seen, he gives life to those that see him."[1]

Joy of the Beatific Vision

At first it may seem difficult to realise that our happiness in heaven can possibly consist in an act of contemplation and love. On earth the common idea of enjoying oneself consists in some gratification of the senses : a sumptuous banquet, sweet music, healthy exercise, a beautiful landscape ; or the company and praise of our fellow men, the achievement of some great work through the exercise of our brain and skill, the discovery of something fresh and new, the travelling through unknown and sunlit lands. These and a thousand other things flit before the human mind when it imagines supreme happiness, for this happiness is thought of as an endless variety of such things as our own experience on earth suggests. A life of contemplation may seem a pale and attenuated existence, holding little attraction for us. On reflection, however, it becomes more and more evident that the highest and happiest life must be the complete satisfaction of mind and will in the sight and possession of an infinite personal Being.

Even on this earth the greatest known joy is intimacy—*i.e.*, knowledge and nearness with another intelligent being. Imagine a mother, after the Great War, gazing again on the face of her son, and hearing his voice, and then clasping him in her embrace, and holding him as her very own possession, of which the battlefield had almost robbed her ! The first moments of their mutual happiness contain a joy so intense that all other so-called enjoyments are as nothing in comparison.

Or imagine a husband and a wife, who have been long parted by strange misfortunes, and after years of separation meet again. As a matter of fact, this theme has ever been elaborated in all human literature, and we may rest assured that it will remain so as long as man lives here below. No doubt this theme of story-tellers, poets, and songsters has been degraded times out of number because of the carnal and sexual element which so often is intruded or, rather, intrudes itself. But nobler minds, at least, can realise that the sensual side of this earthly affection ought not and need not be the dominant factor in true human love, that the knowledge and spiritual possession of one another can be the source of a quasi-delirium of pure joy even on earth. True, this does not often last long, but at least as long as it lasts it is supposed to outweigh all other things. Pain, poverty, and distress only provoke a smile, and the very comparison of such joy with other earthly goods is disclaimed as a degradation. " Strong as death is love and many waters cannot quench its fire." Given the infinity of God, God must be infinitely beautiful and infinitely lovable. So far from a pale and extenuated existence, heaven is the romance, the never-ending love story of the soul and God.

[1] *Adv. Haeres.*, iv 20, § 5.

Holy Scripture certainly makes it perfectly plain that our eternal happiness will consist in seeing God.

"We know in part: and we prophesy in part. But when that which is perfect is come, that which is in part shall be done away. When I was a child, I spoke as a child, I understood as a child, I thought as a child. But, when I became a man, I put away the things of a child. We see now through a glass in a dark manner: but then face to face. Now I know in part: but then I shall know even as I am known."[1] "We are now the sons of God; and it hath not yet appeared what we shall be. We know that when he shall appear we shall be like to him: because we shall see him as he is."[2] "Father, I will that where I am, they also whom thou hast given me may be with me: that they may see my glory which thou hast given me, because thou hast loved me before the creation of the world."[3] "Despise not one of these little ones: for I say to you that their angels in heaven always see the face of my Father who is in heaven."[4] "In the midst . . . was the tree of life . . . , the throne of God and of the Lamb shall be in it. And his servants shall serve him. And they shall see his face, and his name shall be on their foreheads. And night shall be no more. And they shall not need the light of the lamp, nor the light of the sun, because the Lord God shall enlighten them. And they shall reign for ever and ever."[5]

Its supernatural character

Some people speak as if the sight of God after death were the natural reward for those who have led good lives. This is a great mistake. It is not natural to any created being, however good, to see God. God is infinite: a created being is finite, limited, circumscribed, and it is not natural to the finite to perceive the infinite. Not that the infinite merely exceeds the finite in extent, and that therefore the finite could only see a part or a portion of it. The infinite has no parts. The infinite cannot be divided. One cannot see the half of it, or a third, or a tenth; one either sees it as a unity in its entirety or one does not see it at all.

The infinite exceeds the finite not in extent, but in innermost being. God does not belong to the same category of being as the creature—in fact, he does not belong to any category of being at all: he is unique. There is nothing with which to compare him. He stands utterly by himself. His essence, his life infinitely exceeds ours. Hence it cannot be natural to any creature to see God—that is, to know him as he is. We are indeed like God, but not as one human being is like another; we are like him, as the image in a mirror is like the man who stands in front of it. God is the Reality, we the image. Created reality consists in this very imagehood, and is of necessity infinitely distant from the self-subsistent Infinite Reality that is its Creator. So far is it from being natural for a

[1] 1 Cor. xiii 9-12.
[2] 1 John iii 2.
[3] John xvii 24.
[4] Matt. xviii 10.
[5] Apoc. xxii 2-5.

created being to understand, to grasp God, to see him face to face, to know him in the way in which he knows himself, that the human mind could never have known, but for divine revelation, that such vision was possible.

Nature of the Beatific Vision

Even after divine revelation, the human mind cannot understand how it is, though it humbly believes God's word. The "how" of it, I mean the core of this mystery of the Beatific Vision, completely escapes us; it remains as utter a secret as the Blessed Trinity, or the Incarnation, or the Blessed Sacrament. The Beatific Vision is the crowning mystery of Christianity, a mystery which leaves the human mind aghast, and is acceptable only by the power of faith. The Beatific Vision is a free gift of God to man exceeding all natural merit of virtue by an absolute measure, and not only the merit of human virtue, but that of any angels and archangels, cherubim or seraphim; nay, even of Mary the Mother of God. God, infinite though he be, could not, even by an exercise of his absolute omnipotence, create a being to whom it should be *natural* to enjoy the Beatific Vision.

Let us study the workings of our mind a little.

Here on earth we have one and only one definite mode according to which we know things. By our five senses we come in touch with the outer world, and through them we form sense-images. These sense-images we have in common with the animal world, but, being men, and not animals only, by the action of our spiritual soul or mind we abstract the essence of things from them—that is, we regard not merely *this* tree, *this* house, *this* dog, *this* man, but transcending their concrete individuality we refer to a tree, a house, a dog, a man, abstracting completely from all those special characteristics by which they are constituted as concrete units; in other words, we form their concept, or general idea. Moreover, we can conceive their abstract relations; we conceive length and breadth and height and measure, and we compare them. Nay, we ascend to such high abstractions as right or wrong, virtue or vice, holiness or sin. Then we can combine our many ideas into judgements, and chain these together into arguments, and reason from truth to truth.

In this way we come to the supreme conclusion that God is, that some infinite, eternal, self-existent cause must have made this world, and thus in a supereminent way contain within himself all the highest perfections of the world he has made. During this life we have no other means of knowledge, no other means of access to reality except the way we have thus described. It is an indirect and discursive way, incapable of leading us to God directly, incapable of bringing us to God as he is in himself.

Now after death, though our body is separated from our soul, our mind does not change its nature. Some are under the impression that death acts like magic and changes our innermost being; but this is not so. If God did not intervene, if God left nature merely to itself, the human mind would possess no further knowledge beyond what it had gained by inference and reasoning. It would know God in an abstract and merely analogous way ; it would never know God directly and immediately ; never by sight. It might still have been rewarded by some happy life in reward for its virtue ; this life would have been endless, but it would not have been the Beatific Vision. There would have been a quasi-infinite difference between that state and the blissful direct sight of God.

What, then, will this vision be ? It will be a vision without any sense or any thought-images. Obviously no sense-image can intervene, for God is in no way corporeal. Moreover, there will be no thought-image or idea. What do we mean by this ? The mind will not form an abstract representation or idea of God ; it will have no " mental picture " as it has in the case of all other things here on earth. The sense-image on the brain is grasped by the mind. It sinks into the mind ; the mind grips it and holds it and transforms itself accordingly : it conceives it, as we say. A thought is a concept, a mental impression, by means of which the thing that is without us is seen by the mind. It is, as it were, a lens between our mental eye and the reality. We know a thing by the idea we form of it ; without such ideal medium our mind knows nothing.

Or perhaps instead of the comparison of a lens it may be better to use that of a seal imprinted upon wax. The schoolmen speak of a *species impressa* and a *species expressa*. Every act of thought modifies the mind. It is as if external reality impressed itself on the mind and shaped and moulded it. There is, however, this difference. The metal die forces itself upon the wax and causes its conformity with the engraving on its surface. In thinking it is the mind which is the active principle and which holds and conforms itself to the external reality and absorbs it, in a sense, by taking it into itself. Now a created thing is understood by us precisely because we thus mentally grasp its outlines, those limitations of a being which make it that being and not another. It is clear that God cannot be understood in this way, because God is essentially infinite and has no limitations. No " idea," since it is necessarily limited, can adequately represent the infinite God.

It remains, therefore, that God should, in some mysterious way, fulfil the role which, in our natural cognitive processes, is played by the " idea." God will render himself immediately present and intelligible to our minds.

In this way we have never as yet known anything on earth. All things remain, as it were, outside us ; they only enter into our minds by way of an " idea." God will not remain outside us. He will be within our mind itself, and there we shall see him. The nearest approximation to such knowledge on earth is our knowledge of ourselves. We know ourselves because we are ourselves ; we are present to ourselves in our innermost being. Hence Holy Scripture uses this knowledge as a means of comparison : " Then I shall know even as I am known."

We must not, therefore, imagine God in the Beatific Vision as some outside Object to look at, but as dwelling within the very essence of our soul, and thus being perceived from within by direct contact. Of course, even of our earthly life it is true that " in him we live, we move, we have our being." God not only created us in the past, but maintains us in being in the present ; our whole being continually rests upon him. We exist only because he incessantly inwardly sustains us. We are kept in being by God as the image in the mirror is kept in being by the person continuing to stand in front of it. Our innermost self is in God and by God, but we do not realise it. We do not perceive God. Our being is in contact with him, but not our knowledge ; when our knowledge also attains him directly, then we shall possess the Beatific Vision.

The principle that rules all intelligence and understanding is that we can know things only in the measure in which we are similar to them. A thing which has nothing in common with us, we could never understand, but inasmuch as we resemble them can we grasp them with our mind. So is it also with regard to our understanding God. We shall know him, and therefore, says the Scripture, " we shall be like unto him." Our life will be in conscious contact with his, and his life will, as it were, overflow into ours and pervade us through and through, and thus we shall know him.

A humble comparison may help us : throw a bar of iron into a blazing furnace and leave it there till it is molten metal in the midst of the fire, and the eye can no longer see the fire. As that iron knows the fire, so shall we know God. Our innermost being will thrill and throb in unison with God's life, and we shall be fully conscious of it. True, by grace we are on earth already " sharers of the divine nature," as St Peter tells us, but the effect of that participation of divine life is in some sense suspended, because our soul is still in our mortal body. Its mode of knowledge is restricted and restrained by our earthly conditions. Set it free from this mortal body and grace changes into glory ; the soul enters into its supernatural birthright.

The Light of Glory

God, in order to make this apprehension possible, creates in us a new faculty, which we call by the technical name of *lumen gloriae*, " the light of glory." By this our cognitive faculty is raised to a supernatural state, being thus enabled to perform an act which exceeds not only the normal human mode and measure of knowing, but the mode and measure of any creature whatever.

But here we are faced with the difficulty that the finite can never grasp the infinite. The difficulty would be insuperable if the Beatific Vision involved that the human mind encompassed God with its knowledge. This indeed would be impossible. The Blessed will see the whole of God—for God has no parts—yet they will not exhaust his infinite intelligibility. God alone can know himself as fully as he can be known.

As in heaven faith and hope cease and only charity remains, the Blessed in heaven will cease to *believe* the Blessed Trinity; they will cease to accept it on faith, for faith will be replaced by vision. The great mystery will be mystery no longer, for they will see the Father, the Son, and the Holy Ghost face to face.

The Blessed contemplate not merely the divine nature as such; by a mental abstraction distinguishing it from the threefold personality as we do on earth, they see God as he is, therefore they see the Three Persons in the Trinity. Their understanding of the mystery will, of course, not be infinite and comprehensive; it will be only finite apprehension, the intensity and depth of which varies with the measure of the *lumen gloriae* which they receive. Their understanding of it will be none the less direct and intuitive, and thus completely satiating their intelligence, so that all further searching into the truth as into a mystery entirely ceases.

Thus will be fulfilled the words of Christ: "No one knows the Father except the Son and he to whom the Son wills to reveal him." The Blessed know the Father through the Son in the Holy Ghost. They see the Unbegotten Source of the Godhead, who is the Father, through the Son whom he eternally begets. They perceive him through his Word and Utterance, through him who is "the splendour of his glory and the figure of his substance." They see both Father and Son in the Holy Ghost, who dwells within them, and in whose light they participate through the light of glory.

The Blessed are adopted sons of God, brothers and co-heirs of Christ, and will therefore rejoice in eternity in love and worship of the Second Person of the Trinity as united to them in a brotherhood through grace and glory. They rejoice in the indwelling of the Holy Ghost, whose temple they are. They rejoice in the adoration of the First Person from whom all good things flow and to whom they have learnt from Christ to say: Abba, Father.

As by baptism they were baptised in the name of the Father and of the Son and of the Holy Ghost when first they received the gift of sanctifying grace, so when grace is changed into glory, they will be hallowed and sanctified in that Name. Their heavenly life will be one continual *Gloria Patri et Filio et Spiritui Sancto*.

In the souls of the just on earth the three Divine Persons dwell, according to the promise of Christ: "If any man love me . . . we will come to him and will make our abode with him." [1] Of this indwelling, however, the just on earth are not normally conscious. In heavenly glory this indwelling will be consciously perceived and enjoyed by the Blessed. In consequence the Blessed stand in a threefold conscious relation to God whom they contemplate and possess within themselves. When they re-echo the threefold "Holy, Holy,

[1] John xiv 23.

Holy" of the Cherubim they will understand the full meaning of the Trisagion, and ascribe this triple song of praise by love and adoration to the Triune God within them whose unveiled presence they hold and embrace.

§ III: THE LOVE OF GOD THE SATISFACTION OF THE WILL

Embrace of God by knowledge and love

THOUGH we describe our eternal reward as "blissful sight," yet this description does not exhaust the reality; it is not, as it were, a definition, a complete designation of it. Even in eternity we shall have not merely mind, but also will. Not only our intelligence, but our human desire will be totally satiated, for in knowing him who is the fount of all truth we shall possess him who is the Infinite Good. As God is infinite he can belong to endlessly many creatures, but still be to each one of them totally his. "I am thy reward exceeding great," said God to Abraham, the patriarch; but this saying in strictest truth is applicable to each one of the Blessed.

Seeing God and possessing God are in a sense the same thing, or, rather, they are the obverse and reverse of a medal. To see is to enjoy; to enjoy is to possess. God is infinite beauty, but to embrace infinite beauty by knowledge is to possess it. God will give himself to us. A friend gives himself to a friend by throwing himself into his arms and being pressed to his bosom. A spirit embraces not with material fleshly arms, but by the power of thought. We shall clasp God to our bosom spiritually, and we shall be united to him with closer bonds than ever joined a lover to his beloved.

These are not mere expressions of poetical exaggeration or mere emotional piety; they are endorsed by strict philosophy and theology, they are almost technical in their value. To possess God is supreme happiness, for God is infinite beauty and lovableness.

If a man wishes to call his imagination to aid—and it is not unlawful in this matter—he should recall the greatest and grandest scene of beauty he has ever gazed upon, the most entrancing melody he ever heard, and remember that God created nature, and that nature is a feeble reflection of God. He should think of the person he most dearly loves or loved on earth, the dearest face, the tenderest heart he knows of, and then say to himself that all human goodness, the sum of all human lovableness is as a drop in the ocean of God's love and magnificence.

Mutual love

A further thought which will aid us is that the love between God and ourselves will be mutual. God is not merely a picture to be looked at, a scene to be contemplated; God is personal, and he returns the gaze we cast upon him. God is a living God, not a mere effulgence of impersonal glory, however great. Our soul will be joined to God in mutual affection; he will ever whisper in our ears: "I have chosen you," and we shall answer, however humbly, "and

I have chosen you." Our union in heaven is the outcome of our free deliberate acts on earth, continued in eternity. These transports, of course, will be mental, spiritual, without any physical emotion, and without that exhaustion which on earth follows the outpouring of mere natural human affections; but they will on that account be only the more intense. When after the Resurrection we shall possess our bodies again, even our glorified flesh will no doubt share in the exaltation of our spirit, and experience a sweetness, indescribable to us now but corresponding to our state of soul, and unaccompanied by that fatigue which is caused by continued emotion here.

No selfishness

All love is essentially an act that goes out from one being to another. It is the precise opposite of selfishness or self-centredness. It is benevolence towards another; it is complacency in the good of another; it is return of affection for a good received from another. All love is union of some kind, but union is impossible except there be at least two parties, and each of these communicates with the other, or gives itself (or at least something of itself) to the other. The more perfect the love the more complete the surrender of the lover to the loved. In consequence the love by which the Blessed love God is one of supreme altruism. On earth we often say that the more a man goes out of himself, the more he leaves himself behind and forgets himself, the more perfect is his love. This is true in the highest manner of the love of the Blessed in heaven.

It is sometimes objected against the Christian conception of an eternal reward in heaven that it is a selfish ideal. This objection rests on a complete misunderstanding. The Blessed in heaven are indeed supremely happy. But this happiness is the necessary consequence of their love of God. They are happy, not in loving themselves, but in loving God. Heaven is the highest act of self-surrender of which a creature is capable. Each one of the Blessed is eternally conscious that he belongs to another, and this very consciousness is the source of his happiness. Heaven is the absolute cessation of self-love, if by self we understand something separate and independent of God.

The love of the Blessed for themselves

Do the Blessed, then, "forget" themselves in God? Have the Blessed no love for themselves? Of course. The Blessed know that they are themselves the objects of divine love, and in loving God, they love all that God loves, including themselves. The precise reason why the Blessed love themselves lies in that they are conscious of being the objects of God's love. They know themselves as the image and likeness of God, and they see in themselves a partial mirroring of the infinite perfection of God. They love God in themselves, for whatever perfection or excellence they possess is a gift of God, and the effect of his creative will. They love it because it is his work. They love themselves because they are his. Heaven is no home for mock humility. St Paul wrote: "By the grace of God I am what I am, and the grace of God in me has not been void." So the Blessed say: "By the glory of God I am what I am, and the glory of God in me is not void." This is not in discord with their former song on earth: "To the King, immortal and invisible, to God alone be honour and glory throughout the ages of ages." The only difference is that the King once invisible is now seen face to face. To him alone indeed be glory, for our glory is his.

Imagine for a moment that a sculptor could make statues, not of dead marble, but endowed with life and thought; imagine, further, that the life and thought of these statues remained continually dependent on the active will of the sculptor who first fashioned them. Imagine, thirdly, that each of these statues was a self-portrait of the sculptor, portraying him in different attitudes and with different charms. Imagine, lastly, that these living statues knew and loved the sculptor who made them and keeps them in being. You will have then imagined something resembling the Blessed in heaven. The more these living statues loved the sculptor the more they would love themselves as portraying one or other of his perfections. The Blessed love themselves, but their love does not rest ultimately there, but in God, whom *alone* they love for himself. Their self-love is but an aspect of their love for God. A very telling though imperfect parallel of this celestial love is sometimes found in the utterance of lover to beloved: "The only reason why I care for myself is that you love me."

Complete satisfaction

The sight and love of God will constitute the complete satisfaction of all our desires. During our mortal life we are beings in progress, in process of evolution towards our final state. The Beatific Vision is that final state. Our mortal life is a tending towards the perfection of our being.

We Catholics are, as a matter of fact, great believers in evolution, but we do not trouble ourselves so much about the evolution of the past, for, whatever it has been, it has only historical interest; we cannot change it now. What has been, has been. We believe in the only evolution that really matters, the evolution which we are actually undergoing, and in which our own freewill plays a part. Because on this earth we are evolving beings, evolving according to God's supernatural plan towards a life in union with him, our mortal life is essentially imperfect. Because we are imperfect, our life here is one of longing, seeking, hoping for the future. All this will one day end. We shall not always be dissatisfied with what we have and are. Our eternal existence will not be one of endless craving, and not yet possessing, a waiting for something beyond; the fulness of our being will come at last, and our life will be one of tranquil possession. That sacred restlessness which necessarily marks even the holiest life on earth, precisely because it has not reached the term and purpose of its existence, will pass away. We cannot picture to ourselves a life without some unfulfilled desires, yet reason tells us that, in the consummation of all things, unfulfilled desires are an impossibility for those who have received their reward exceeding great, in the possession of God. Their whole being is satiated. The question: "Do you lack anything? Is there still anything you need?" would, if put to the lowliest of the saints, provoke a smile and the answer, "How could I, since I have God!"

Repose in intense activity

In heaven we are at the end of life's journey; we are in God's Paradise; we need not, indeed we cannot, travel beyond. Heaven therefore is in a sense something stationary, since it is the complete fulfilment of our being. We have reached God, and we can reach no further. Striving is over; there is now only the unchangeable joy of possession, of repose in God. It is, indeed, the "eternal rest" which we so often pray that God may give to the souls in Purgatory.

Yet this complete repose and satisfaction of our being is no mere passive state. It is the most intense activity. God himself, as we know, is called in Catholic philosophy "pure activity," and in the measure in which we approach God the intensity of our life increases. Heaven is all activity.

The Love of the Blessed is always active. On earth our acts of love towards our neighbour last for a while; they last while we think of them; they cease when the necessities of our daily life force us to think of something else. Even our love of God, which we exercise on earth, is manifested by intermittent acts. Great saints may, indeed, in their waking moments, make an almost continuous act of the love of God, but even they must occasionally interrupt their communion with God to attend to other things. In heaven, as the Beatific Vision is but one unceasing act, so likewise the act of love is one single uninterrupted act which lasts throughout eternity. This act of blissful love not only never ceases, but it never varies, whether in intensity or in the object to which it is directed; for the soul's power of loving is unchangeable and always exercised to the utmost, and God, the object loved, is always clearly seen in all his lovableness as far as the particular soul can apprehend it. On earth we can exercise our love for God on different grounds, loving him now for his justice, now for his mercy, now for his wisdom, now for his tenderness. In heaven we shall see that all God's attributes are identical with his being. This one act of supernatural human love will contain within itself all aspects of love: love of benevolence, love of complacency, love of gratitude—*i.e.*, the will that God should be what he is, the Infinite Good, a pure delight begotten of the contemplation of his infinite goodness, and a realisation that our share in his happiness is due to his generous bounty.

Shall we never tire of the very intensity of our love towards God? Will the transports of joy and love never create any fatigue throughout eternity? No. All fatigue arises from the use of bodily organs by the thinking subject; spiritual activities in themselves are not subject to any fatigue, hence the act of loving will not engender any weariness in the Blessed throughout eternity.

Heaven is "life"

Since our ultimate happiness consists in this perfect satisfaction of the faculties of our spiritual life, we can well understand why the term most commonly used in the Scriptures for heaven is "life." It occurs in this sense about one hundred times in the New Testament, in the majority of cases followed by the adjective "everlasting." It is remarkable that it occurs in this sense in every book or epistle of the New Testament, even in the short letter of St Jude, with the sole exception of the Epistle to Philemon. It must have been the standing expression on the lips of Christ and his Apostles. In St Matthew, St Mark, and St Luke the term "kingdom of God" is more usually employed, whereas St John almost exclusively uses "life," and only speaks twice of the kingdom. St Paul uses "life" more frequently than "kingdom." What is the origin and the bearing of this term "life" for heavenly bliss, and why is it so often characterised as "everlasting"? The origin lies beyond doubt in the Old Testament. In the Garden of Eden was planted the tree of life. The penalty for sin was death, and after the fall God sent Adam out of paradise "lest perhaps he put forth his hand, and take also of the tree of life, and eat, and live for ever."

The New Testament closes with a distinct reference to the opening of the Old: "The Blessed are they that wash their robes in the blood of the Lamb: that they may have a right to the tree of life." In the Psalms the way of the just is called the way of life. In our Lord's day the current expression for man's celestial reward was already "everlasting life." This current expression was used by Christ and the Apostles, and endowed with greater fulness of meaning. St John especially, and also St Paul, elaborate this theme of life everlasting. The Fourth Gospel says of the Word: "In him was life, and the life was the light of men: and the light shineth in the darkness, and the darkness did not comprehend it." This life which is in God the Word will be bestowed on men. "He who heareth my word and believeth him that sent me hath life everlasting, and cometh not into judgement, but is passed from death to life. Amen, amen, I say unto you, that the hour cometh, and now is, when the dead shall hear the voice of the Son of God: and they that hear shall live. For, as the Father hath life in himself, so he hath given to the Son also to have life in himself." [1] "As the living Father hath sent me and I live by the Father: so he that eateth me, the same also shall live by me. This is the bread that came down from heaven." [2]

According to the Gospel of St John this life has indeed already begun in the hearts of the faithful on earth, though it comes to completion only when Christ raises those that believe in him on the

[1] John v 24-26. [2] John vi 58-59.

last day. It consists in sharing the very life which the Father has in himself and gives to the Son, who bestows it on those that are united to him. This life is light, mental light. "This is everlasting life that they should *know* thee, the only true God and Jesus Christ whom thou hast sent."[1] The knowledge of the Father and the Son is the light of men, their ultimate end and everlasting life. It is called everlasting life, clearly, not merely on the ground that it will never come to an end, but that from its very nature it cannot come to an end. It is the fulness of life without the germ of death. The Greek adjective *aionios*, which is translated "everlasting," implies more than that it never ends; it suggests another kind of life than that which we naturally live on earth. It is the life of the *aion* ("the age") to come; it is eternal life or the life in eternity, as Christ promised: "There is no man who hath left house or brethren or sisters or father or mother or children or lands, for my sake and for the gospel, who shall not receive an hundred times as much, now in this time . . . and in the world (*aion*) to come, life everlasting" (*aionios*).[2]

It is distinctly stated that the life hereafter will be not only endless, but timeless. "The angel lifted up his hand to heaven and swore by him that liveth for ever and ever: that time shall be no longer."[3] The reward therefore foretold in the New Testament is a timeless and changeless life akin to that of God, who "dwelleth in eternity (*aiona*)"[4] and who said: "Yea, I lift up my hand to heaven and say: I am living for ever" (unto the *aion*).[5] This timeless divine life is in Christ, and Christ communicates it to others through the truth, which, when possessed, issues in life. Hence Christ said of himself: "I am the way, the truth, and the life. I am the light of the world: he that followeth me walketh not in darkness, but shall have the light of life."

§ IV: SECONDARY SOURCES OF HAPPINESS IN HEAVEN

Christ in his Human Nature

In heaven we shall see Christ, not merely in his Godhead, but also in his manhood. Christ in his human nature will constitute, after the Beatific Vision, or, rather, in the Beatific Vision, the chief delight of the Blessed. The three years' companionship of the Apostles with Christ on earth will be as nothing compared to the companionship of the Blessed with Christ in heaven. In meditating on heaven one is apt to think of Christ as some great King in his glory sitting at the right hand of God the Father, a King to be worshipped with all due honour. No doubt in a sense this is true. The Angels and the Blessed hold court around his throne. In a way of which we cannot now form any conception, all the host of heaven will pay obeisance

[1] John xvii 3. [2] Mark x 29. [3] Apoc. x 5.
[4] Isa. lvii 15. [5] Deut. xxxii 40.

and homage to Christ as King. Some analogy to what on earth we call ceremonial is certainly suggested by the description of heaven in the Apocalypse of St John. But these state occasions, if such one may dare to call them, do not exhaust celestial delights. Though Christ is the Great King, he will also be the intimate personal friend of each of the Blessed.

How this will be achieved we cannot say. On earth in Holy Communion each recipient receives him whole and entire, though thousands receive him at the same time. If this multiplication of Christ's real presence is a fact during the state of our probation here below, we may infer that in heaven Christ will find some means, now unknown to us, to be in close intimacy and individual companionship with each person in that multitude that no one can number. In Holy Communion we only perceive his presence through the act of faith ; hereafter, when faith has ceased, the real presence of his manhood in immediate proximity to each one of the Saints must be immediately perceptible, and after the General Resurrection, no doubt in some way sensible to human eyes. We have Christ's promise : " If any man hear my voice and open to me the door, I will come in to him and will sup with him and he with me." [1] If this is true during our mortal life, it must be truer still in our glorified state.

Christ himself compared the kingdom of heaven to a wedding-feast prepared by a king for his son, and on several occasions Christ refers to himself as the bridegroom. It is plain from the Scriptures that Christ's bride is the Church, which he loves and for which he delivered himself to death. This is true of the Church whether suffering, militant or triumphant, but especially so of the Church Triumphant. St John in the Apocalypse [2] heard one of the Seven Angels say to him : " Come, and I will show thee the bride, the wife of the Lamb " ; whereupon the Angel showed him the holy city, Jerusalem, coming down out of heaven from God. The Lamb signifies beyond doubt Christ in his humanity, for only in his humanity was he slain and became the victim for our sins. Heaven is therefore described as the eternal nuptials of Christ in his humanity with the community of the redeemed.

This close union, however, is fully achieved only by the union of Christ to the individual Blessed. On earth the Church has always designated the individual soul as the spouse of Christ, for the kingdom of God is within us. The banquet of this wedding-feast is here below the reception of the Body and Blood of Christ in the Blessed Sacrament. This is a pledge of future glory when Christ in his humanity will be united with each of the Saints in an everlasting intimacy and mutual friendship. We may, perhaps, have envied Mary the thirty years of hidden life that she spent with Jesus in the holy house of Nazareth, but in a sense this

[1] Apoc. iii 20. [2] xxi 9-10.

privilege will be surpassed when we are risen with Christ and possess the things that are above, where Christ is sitting at the right hand of God; when we mind the things that are above and no longer the things that are on earth; when we have died to this mortal life and our life is hid with Christ in God, though we appear with him in glory.[1] This hiddenness does not involve any secrecy towards our fellow-Saints, but it means a uniqueness, a separateness of our own intercourse with Christ, an intercourse which is in no way troubled by the intrusion of others. The Humanity of Christ is hypostatically united to the Person of God the Son, and the Beatific Vision, which shows us God the Son, shows us the glory and lovableness of the manhood which he assumed. The intercourse with the Sacred Humanity of Christ is the first and foremost thing mediated through the Beatific Vision. After the General Resurrection, even our bodily eyes will rejoice in the sight of God incarnate, and our ears delight in his voice. By what divine ingenuity this Sacred Humanity will be rendered quasi-omnipresent in heaven we cannot at present say. We know only that the Saints will " stand before the throne (the unveiled Godhead) and before the Lamb " (God incarnate), that their songs will perpetually rise " to God and to the Lamb," that the Lamb, standing before the throne, " will shepherd " the Saints. We know that the heavenly city has no temple—*i.e.*, no limited or in any way defined or circumscribed place—in which God wishes to be worshipped. " For the Lord God Almighty is the temple thereof and the Lamb. And the city hath no need of the sun or the moon to shine in it. For the glory of God hath enlightened it and the Lamb is the lamp thereof." [2]

Mary, the Angels, and the Saints

After the sight of God in his divine and in his human nature comes the joy of eternal companionship with the citizens of heaven. To enter into heaven is to enter into a real community life, into social intercourse and permanent association with Mary, the Mother of Jesus, and with the angels and the Saints. Conceivably God might have made the eternal happiness of all spirits a merely personal, self-contained, and isolated state of bliss; he might have left celestial joy and eternal life a merely individual joy and individual life. But he has not done so.

It is the deep conviction of all Catholics that Mary, the Mother of God, was on Calvary made the mother of all the faithful whom her Son redeemed. This spiritual motherhood is exercised not merely by her perpetual intercession for us, while we are working out our salvation in fear and trembling, but continues in heaven, when our love for her and her love for us is the cause of our principal joy, after that of loving her Son. The whole angel world also will enhance our happiness.[3] It is commonly accepted that the Blessed will

[1] Col. iii 1-3. [2] Apoc. xxi 22-23.
[3] See also Essay viii, *The Angels*, pp. 282-285.

occupy the thrones left vacant by the fall of Lucifer and his followers; this means that we shall enter into fraternal intercourse with Cherubim and Seraphim and all the members of the heavenly host. Our contemplation of these mighty first-born sons of God, the splendour of their intelligence and the greatness of their love for him and for us, will fill us with joy.

According to Catholic teaching each of the faithful on earth has his Guardian Angel. This angel, by perpetual guidance and intercession, is a ministering spirit to the soul entrusted to him for everlasting salvation. The bond of affection and intimacy between this celestial guardian and his ward will surely be transformed into a bond of special love and gratitude during eternity.

We know that God has arranged the angel host in "choirs." This means they are related one to another in some definite ordered way, having different and distinct rank and status, dignity, and special powers. They combine together into one great harmony of divine praise. They are not mere units; they are fellows in a divine college. So it is likewise with the blessed Redeemed. They form "a church," the Church Triumphant. They are not a crowd, but a heavenly army. Each redeemed soul has its post and position assigned. Heaven is a commonwealth where divine order reigns. "The Jerusalem which is above" is a city-state, and its inhabitants are citizens. "Our citizenship is in heaven," wrote St Paul. Amongst the Blessed themselves there will be the fellowship begotten of mutual respect, admiration, and intimate intercourse.

Moreover, human nature in heaven is still human nature, however glorified. There will be ties of friendship between the Saints. St Augustine has met St Ambrose and rejoiced. St Francis has met St Clare, and found delight in converse with her. We also shall find among the Saints in heaven our friends whom we loved and venerated on earth. Christ on earth formed friendships, though he possessed the Beatific Vision. He loved John, and Mary and Martha and Lazarus. So, too, among the Blessed friendships will persist. And again: after the Resurrection the Blessed will possess their bodies. This implies that they will have eyes to see, ears to hear, lips to speak, and so on. There must therefore be in heaven something to see, to hear, and some persons to speak to, and these faculties are best and most fully exercised in a community which will enjoy heavenly bliss in fellowship. The unbroken comradeship with those of our own nature and race is part of the complete development of our manhood. In the centre of this fellowship is Christ in his human nature, for the Incarnation remains for ever the link by which men are bound together. In Christ we are all brethren, not merely on earth, but throughout eternity.

The wonders of Creation

Besides the sight and love of God and Christ, the company of Mary, Angels, and Saints, the Blessed will enjoy all the wonders of creation. Until the last day they will know this present world;

after the last day, when this heaven and this earth shall have passed away, they will know the new heavens and the new earth that will be the everlasting abode of the Saints of God. In the Revelation of St John we find set forth in exuberant imagery the glories of the New Jerusalem, the city of God. Perhaps the streets of gold and the crystal sea before the throne of God, the gates and the walls of precious stones, the crowns and the palms, and the costly robes are metaphors, and not to be taken literally. But, if so, they must be metaphors for a reality that far exceeds our greatest expectations. St Paul says that "all creation groaneth and travaileth in pain . . . waiting for the adoption of the Sons of God." [1] The material creation which will be the eternal home of the Blessed will be a universe at least not less marvellous than the vast universe in which we now live. God has in Christ united with himself a material body, in which for ever Christ will sit at the right hand of his Father. God has decreed the resurrection of man's body, and thereby determined the eternal existence of a material universe in which the Redeemer and the redeemed will live and move for all eternity.

If it may be said of this present world: "The heavens show forth the glory of God, and the firmament declareth the work of his hands. Day unto day uttereth speech and night unto night showeth knowledge"; [2] this must be true in an unspeakably higher degree of the world to come. Questions have been asked about this new earth, whether it will have a silvery sea and a starry sky; whether it will contain rivers and mountains, animals and plants. To all these questions we have no answer, for God has not deigned to reveal it to us. But one thing we know, that it will be a real world and a fit abode for men and women to whom are restored the days of Paradise when God walked with man in the Garden of Eden in the cool of the evening. Though the essential happiness of heaven lies in the sight and enjoyment of God, we may also say of such lesser joys as the enjoyment of the marvels of creation that "no eye hath ever seen, nor ear heard, neither hath it entered into the heart of man, what God has prepared for those that love him." [3]

We must remember, however, that our enjoyment of the glories of nature will differ in heaven from our enjoyment of natural beauties now. Now we find it difficult to see the Creator in the things he has created. Our reason, indeed, tells us that all creation is but a manifestation of God, but owing to the limitation of our minds and our natural inability directly to see God, our very attention to the grandeurs of nature may obscure our realisation of God. It will be different in heaven. All things will be seen and admired in the Beatific Vision as in a mirror. The thought of God will never be absent from our minds even for a second, though our mind and body may be occupied with the beauty of the things he made. The whole of creation will be as a constant song praising him, who called it out of

[1] Rom. viii 22, 23. [2] Ps. xviii 2-3. [3] 1 Cor. ii 9.

nothing into being. Every created thing will be as the fragment of crystal in which a ray of the infinite light is reflected.

The glorification of the body

The glorification of man's body has been treated of in greater detail in another essay of this volume. Suffice it here to say that its glory will be the natural consequence of the glory of the soul. The body was intended to be the handmaid of the soul, ministering in every way to its spiritual life. This relation between body and soul was disturbed through the Fall. The dominion of spirit over matter was rudely shaken, and the flesh became the unwilling partner of the mind. Its sluggishness and its passions were a continual hindrance to the full development of the soul's life. This will completely cease in heaven. Man's body will then be a furtherance to his spiritual joys. The joys of the soul will overflow and fill the material side of his being with the most exquisite happiness. Great mental happiness sometimes even on earth buoys up man's physical frame, and gives it a feeling of vigour and lightsomeness, and is the cause of maintenance or restoration of bodily health, even as sorrow is the cause of disease and death. The supreme bliss of heaven proceeding from the soul will pervade the body to such an extent that its physical well-being will exceed anything we have known on earth. Moreover, by special ordinance of God the body will be so exalted that it will become a worthy companion to the soul in possession of the sight of God. As Christ was transfigured on Mount Thabor, so that his face shone as the sun and his garments were white as snow, so shall all those, who are co-heirs with Christ, be glorified in body as well as in soul. The body will receive those preternatural gifts, of which the gifts to Adam in Paradise were but a foretaste. But the description of these gifts will be found in the essay on the Resurrection of the Body.[1]

§ V: IMPLICATIONS OF LIFE IN HEAVEN

Heaven a kingdom

HEAVEN is frequently described in the Scriptures as a kingdom. " I dispose to you, as my Father hath disposed to me, a kingdom ; that you may eat and drink at my table, in my kingdom." [2] " Come, ye blessed of my Father, possess you the kingdom prepared for you from the foundation of the world." [3] " At the end of the world the Son of man shall send his angels, and they shall gather out of his kingdom all scandals and them that work iniquity, and shall cast them into the furnace of fire : and there shall be weeping and gnashing of teeth. Then shall the just shine as the sun in the kingdom of their Father." [4] " The Lord God shall enlighten them and they shall reign for ever." [5] " To him that shall overcome, I will give to

[1] Essay xxxiv, *The Resurrection of the Body*, above, pp. 1242-1247.
[2] Luke xxii 29-30.
[3] Matt. xxv 34.
[4] Matt. xiii 40-43.
[5] Apoc. xxii 5.

sit with me in my throne: as I also have overcome and am set down with my Father in his throne." [1] "In Christ all shall be made to live, but every one in his own order: the first-fruits Christ: then they that are of Christ, who have believed in his coming. Afterwards the end: when he shall have delivered up the kingdom to God and the Father: when he shall have brought to nought all principality and power and virtue. For he must reign until he hath put all his enemies under his feet. When all things shall be subdued unto him, then the Son also himself shall be subject unto him (the Father) that put all things under him, that God may be all in all." [2] Hence also St John in his vision of heaven saw thrones set, and the ancients with crowns on their heads, and he said: "The prince of the kings of the earth . . . hath made us a kingdom and priests to God and his Father, to him be glory and empire for ever and ever." [3]

This kingship promised to the Blessed in the Scriptures involves first of all a manifest triumph and undoubted victory over all adverse powers, over the devils and the damned that tempted them and endeavoured to hinder them in the attainment of their final end, over the obstacles that stood in their way through the frailty of their own nature and the greatness of their task. The Blessed will be like Alpine travellers, who have at last reached the dazzling heights. They have attained the very summit of their desires notwithstanding the storms that raged, the foes that waylaid them, and the steepness of the path they climbed. It includes, further, an untrammelled freedom during eternity, a full liberty and immediate fulfilment of their wishes, and a complete disposal of all the riches of their royal inheritance without any possibility of being thwarted or gainsaid. It includes, lastly, a real dominion over all creation. At the final consummation, after the resurrection of the body, they will have a complete mastery over all material things, and all nature will obey them, and submit to their sovereignty. Even in the spiritual world of Angels and fellow-saints they will reign, for they will be as princes amongst princes, all of whom in celestial courtesy will pay honour one to another. With utter spontaneity and eagerness all will serve God, to serve whom is to reign.

When St Paul says that at the end Christ will deliver up the kingdom to the Father and be subject to him, he means that Christ in his manhood, as head of the human race, with all his brethren, with all those redeemed by his Blood, with all those who were saved in him and through him, will proclaim the full achievement of the Father's will. Before his Passion Christ declared: "Father, I have finished the work which thou gavest me to do; and now glorify thou me, Father, with the glory which I had with thee before the world was made. I pray for them, whom thou hast given me out of the

[1] Apoc. iii 21.
[2] 1 Cor. xv 22-25, 28.
[3] Apoc. i 5-6.

world; I pray for those who through their word shall believe in me that they all may be one, as I in thee and thou in me." [1] At the final consummation Christ will proclaim in regard to his celestial life what he said at the end of his mortal life: "I have finished the work which thou gavest me to do, and now glorify thou me." This handing over of the Kingdom means the public acknowledgement of the completed work of Christ. The first petition of the Lord's prayer: "Hallowed is the Father's name, his kingdom has come," has now been fully granted.

After the final consummation one phase of Christ's activity will cease. Christ's life in heaven is now one of perpetual intercession for us.[2] Then no more intercession will be needed. Christ's daily sacrifice of the altar is one of propitiation and impetration for the living and the dead; in heaven, it will be offered for those purposes no longer. The sacraments are the channels of Christ's Precious Blood to the souls of men; they will require these channels no longer. Christ is on earth the teacher of men through the infallible authority of the Church; they will need that authority no longer. Christ is the Captain of salvation in the great warfare of the militant Church, but the soldiers will then need their general no longer, for the war is now over. In one sense, therefore, the final consummation is an abdication of Christ, and a handing back of the emblems of office to his heavenly Father.

On the other hand, Christ continues to reign in a higher sense. Christ continues eternally the head of the human race, and in their life of glory he is their leader. All the Blessed are what they are through him. On earth to be in grace means to be in Christ; in heaven to be in glory means to be in Christ in an even more complete sense. The Church Triumphant is still Christ's mystical body. The Blessed are in glory through their unbroken union with him. What Christ said on earth remains true in heaven: "I am the vine, you are the branches." [3] The Beatific Vision is given to the Saints because of Christ and in Christ. They need a mediator of propitiation or intercession no longer, for they are eternally sinless and have no wants for which such prayer need be offered. But if they are heirs of God, they are also co-heirs of Christ, and their inheritance is not bestowed upon them independently of Christ. They are heirs of God—that is, they possess the light of glory because their human nature is the same as that of Christ and supernaturally united with it.

The hypostatic union of God the Son with the human nature of Christ is the fountain of all honour and blessings that come upon men, who are brethren according to the flesh of God incarnate. Christ, on the eve of his Passion, said to his Father: "I also have given unto them the glory which thou hast given unto me, that they may

[1] John xvii 4 ff.
[2] Rom. viii 34; Heb. vi 25. [3] John xv 5.

be one, as we also are one : I in them and thou in me ; that they may be perfect in one." [1] The glory which the Father gives to Christ is the glory of divine Sonship. This glory the Father gives to the Son in the Blessed Trinity by the communication of his divine nature, for the Son is the splendour of the Father. This glory the Father gives to the humanity of Christ by the hypostatic union of Christ's human nature to the Son of God. And, again, the Father gives it to the human mind of Christ by the Beatific Vision. Neither the divine Sonship in the Trinity nor the hypostatic union is communicable to us creatures, but the Beatific Vision is. This is the glory which Christ obtained for us from the Father. It is given to us both by the Father and the Son, hence the words of Christ : " I also have given " ; for in giving them sanctifying grace Christ had already given them the seed of glory. Christ could say this not merely as God but also as God incarnate, for his human nature is the link which binds us to him and him to us ; hence he could say, " I in them and thou in me," that thus through Christ we may be perfected into one and God may be all in all.

Heaven a place

Is heaven a real place ? Yes. Christ ascended into heaven and from thence he shall come to judge. Numerous texts of Scripture, which it would be tedious to quote, make it plain that heaven is a locality into which one enters and from which one can depart. The description of heaven as a city with walls given by St John in the Apocalypse is no doubt imaginary and metaphorical, but it would be altogether deceptive unless heaven were a place in some way circumscribed and limited. Moreover, Christ, who has a real material body, is in heaven. This body, however glorified and capable of moving with the speed of light, is a real extended, measurable, visible body, and therefore in some physical relation to space.

Now Christ has prayed : " Father, I pray that where I shall be they may also be." He said to Peter : " You cannot follow me now, but you shall follow hereafter." It is therefore, and always has been, the universal conviction of Catholics that heaven is a definite place in the universe. In this place at present are at least two material bodies, those of Jesus and of Mary his mother, and there will be the saved in their glorified bodies after the General Resurrection. A difficulty naturally arises with regard to the presence of the Angels and of the disembodied souls of the saved previous to the Resurrection. For an explanation of the presence of angels in a particular place we must refer our readers to the treatise on the angels ; [2] with regard to the presence of disembodied souls this may be said : they cannot be localised by material extension, as if they could be measured and had length, breadth, or depth, or could be divided into parts. For these souls, although they are the animating principle of material bodies, are themselves spiritual. They are therefore in a place in a similar way to that in which angels are in a place : they

[1] John xvii 22, 23. [2] See p. 261.

are present in virtue of their activity. The Blessed, therefore, even before the Resurrection, are with Christ who is in heaven. This has to be understood in a local and spatial sense. How precisely that presence is effected and what it implies escapes our experience and knowledge.

Ties of kinship in heaven

In heaven the Blessed will see all things in God and God in all things. They will see all things in that divine order in which they stand in God's mind. Their place and position in the universe that God created will be understood, for the outlook of the Saints on all things will resemble that of God.

The same principle governs also the love of the Blessed for all the creatures of God's hand. They love them in God, and for God's sake. Their love for them is only a particular mode and application of their love for God. Now in this divine law of charity they observe due order. On earth there is a double principle which rules the due measure of charity towards one's neighbour. First, the neighbour's own goodness—that is, his own share in the goodness of God or his proximity to God. Secondly, his proximity to ourselves; thus we must love parents, children, our kith and kin, our countrymen more than strangers. Such is the law of nature and the law of God. In that Beatific Charity, which is the counterpart of the Beatific Vision, there can be but one principle which rules the measure of love, and that is the share in divine goodness which each Saint possesses in his own particular degree. But this Beatific Charity is supernatural, and the supernatural does not destroy the natural, but perfects it. Hence the Blessed will feel greater natural affection towards some persons than towards others. A son will be moved with love towards his mother, a mother will thrill with joy at the sight of her child. Nature in heaven is hallowed and made perfect in charity which, as a simple proverb says, "begins at home."

Our Lord on earth ever possessed the Beatific Vision in a higher degree than any of the Saints; yet he had a disciple "whom he loved"; he had a home at Bethany where lived Mary, Martha, and Lazarus, who were above others beloved. Our Lord now in heaven loves his mother supremely in the Beatific Vision for her holiness, since, indeed, she is the holiest of all creatures. But in addition to this, he also loves her with a perfect natural love because she is his mother, and in the natural order also his love for her is supreme. Our Lord will be the example for all the Saints; they also will love their parents, their brethren, as he loves his.

The Blessed, then, will still love creatures, but their love will be as pure and as sinless as Christ's own. The Saints are of necessity impeccable. They can sin no more. To sin would be to prefer some created good above God, and this is utterly impossible to them. They actually see and possess the Sovereign Good itself. Their will clings to him as a magnet to iron. Once in heaven they leave all sin and all consequence of sin behind; their wills are confirmed in glory; every act, word, and deed must needs be holy, and holy with absolute ease and spontaneity.

The Saints, then, will love their fellow-Saints with an intensity and tenderness beyond any love we can experience on earth, and they will love them each in his proper degree and be loved by them in return to the utmost extent conformable to their sanctity and kinship.

Degrees of happiness

Heaven will not be the same for all. As in the firmament star differs from star in glory, so also is it in the heavenly abode of the Blessed. The principle of celestial happiness will always be the same—viz., the sight of God face to face—and the happiness even of the lowliest Saint will immeasurably exceed what we can now imagine. Yet their glory and happiness will differ.

The gift of the Beatific Vision will be bestowed on the Blessed in unequal measure, according to their merits. It is sometimes asked whether those who upon earth were gifted with great intelligence or who possessed great erudition, and therefore great stores of knowledge, will in heaven have some advantage above those who on earth were dull and ignorant. The answer is not far to seek. Neither natural genius nor acquired knowledge will in itself have any influence upon the degree of glory bestowed by God as a supernatural gift. Our Blessed Lady, as far as her mere natural powers go, is far inferior to the Angels of God—the angelic nature is higher than the human—yet no one, not even the highest of the Seraphim, has such a deep knowledge of God as his Blessed Mother, for her knowledge is the fruit of the grace received. St Thomas well remarks: "He shares more fully in the light of glory who possesses the greater love; for where love is greater, there is greater desire, and desire in some way renders him who desires apt and ready to receive the object desired. Hence he who has more love will see God more perfectly and be more blessed." [1] This inequality of heavenly glory has been solemnly defined by the Council of Trent [2] against the Reformers, who sought the root of justification in the imputed merits of Christ and, as these are equal for all, could not admit varying degrees of reward in heaven.

Moreover, the knowledge of creatures obtained here on earth, even by the greatest mind, is of an inferior kind to that obtained by the humblest Saint in the Beatific Vision. In the Beatific Vision they are seen in a higher and more perfect way: they are seen in the cause which produces them, in God who conceived them and gives them existence. In comparison with this intuitive knowledge, earthly sense knowledge and discursive reasoning will be as a candle-light in the presence of the noonday sun.

If the glory of the Saints is unequal, will not regret enter the hearts of those Saints who have received less because they merited less?

[1] *Summa Theologica*, I, Q. xii, art. 6.
[2] Sess. vi, can. 32.

Will they feel no pang and bitterness of soul in having through their own fault lost a higher degree of eternal happiness ? No, for each will receive to the utmost of his own capacity. They will all drink from the fountain of life, though some will have but a tiny cup and others an ampler vessel. Regret and sorrow is possible only where there is frustration of desire. There can be no such disappointment in heaven, for God will make every soul happy to the utmost of its power, though the power of one soul for happiness will be greater than that of another. Even the humblest Saint will so love God that he will rejoice that God is known and loved by another Saint with greater love than his own.

The Blessed and those on earth

First of all, do the Blessed know what happens on earth ?

We must distinguish the state of the Blessed before and after the General Resurrection. Before the Resurrection these souls are without their bodies, and therefore without the natural means of communication with the outer world. Whether a soul purely in the natural order would, by its own power, be able to know something outside itself during its separation from the body, we cannot say with any certainty. We are dealing, however, not with the natural order, but with the supernatural ; we are dealing with souls that have received the Beatific Vision.

What knowledge does God, as a matter of fact, grant them according to his good pleasure ? We have to guide us, first of all, the fact that the Church authorises and encourages prayers to the Saints, not only to Saints canonised by the Church, but to any persons of whom we have reasonable hope that they are in heaven. This directly involves the truth that those in heaven know when they are addressed by those on earth ; it also implies that they have sufficient cognisance of all those circumstances which alone can make those prayers intelligible to them. When a person on earth utters a cry for help to any Saint, it is obviously not required that he should first mentally or verbally explain what particular distress is the cause of his cry. We have, further, to guide us the fact that the angels know in detail what happens on earth. " There is more joy before the angels of God upon one sinner that does penance than upon ninety-nine who need not penance." [1] Christ threatened those who gave scandal to the little ones, " for their angels ever see the face of my Father who is in heaven." The angel-world, therefore, has cognisance of earthly affairs, as they are " ministering angels sent to help those who have received the inheritance of salvation." As the Blessed share the Beatific Vision with the angels and are their companions, it is unnatural to suppose that they should be in ignorance of what their companions in heaven know. It is an axiom in theology that grace does not destroy nature. It is true still more that glory does not destroy but exalts and sanctifies nature. It would be unnatural if the departed had no wish to know at least some

[1] Luke xv 10.

matters connected with those they loved and still love on earth. It cannot be supposed that God, who grants them the Beatific Vision, would hide from them what they must naturally desire to know.

The Saints, therefore, know, and the Saints care for the welfare of those on earth. They care for their temporal welfare, their health and their sickness, their poverty and their well-being, their honour and dishonour. But they care for these things only as a means to an end. That end is the eternal salvation and the higher glory of those whom they love. The Saints see all things from the standpoint of eternity. If bitter sufferings, even in those who are nearest and dearest to them, are God's instruments for the purification and sanctification of their souls, the Saints will not ask for their removal, lest the everlasting happiness of their future companions be lessened. The Saints love their own, but with a spiritual, supernatural love, that does not shrink from seeing suffering, if suffering is the path to glory.

The Saints, then, desire the good of the souls of those who are their kith and kin on earth. What if they see them in spiritual danger—if they see them sin? They continue their intercession for them at the throne of God. But is there anxiety and sorrow in heaven on account of temptation and of sin on earth? No, there cannot be. God has wiped all tears from their eyes; they can feel sorrow no longer. They have so completely surrendered to God's blessed will, their resignation is so complete, their loving jubilant adoration of God's Will so perfect, that nothing can disturb their souls' happy calm. Perhaps a reader might think: But Christ suffered; Christ had his agony in the Garden, though his resignation was utterly perfect. Why, then, cannot Saints suffer still at the sight of sin on earth? The answer lies in the mystery of the Incarnation. Though Christ's soul ever saw the face of his Father in heaven, yet his body was still mortal and passible on earth. Christ, then, as regards the fulness of his manhood—I mean body and soul together—was still a wayfarer on earth, though his soul saw God in the Beatific Vision. The Saints are no longer wayfarers; they have reached the land of the living where sorrow cannot enter.

Let us remember, however, that though the Saints cannot suffer, they can, until the final consummation after the Last Day, still increase in what theologians call their "accidental happiness." They can truly and really long and intensely wish for the salvation of those who are near and dear to them—in fact, for the salvation of all men. Hence they can pray, they can plead with God, and the doctrine of the communion of the Saints makes us certain that they do. When men sin on earth, do the Saints feel angry with them and call down punishment on the offender? They indeed hate sin, but they do not hate the sinner, for the sinner on earth, however vile, is never beyond God's mercy, and until the moment when God himself has uttered the verdict of eternal damnation against the sinner, the Saints cannot but continue their prayers for those for whom the blood of Christ still speaks better things than that of Abel.

The Blessed and the reprobate

It is often asked how the Saints can be happy when they know that some, even perchance those who were near and dear to them, are in hell. Will a mother lose the love for her son, and be indifferent to his loss ? The difficulty is one not so much of logic and reason, but of sentiment.

The love of mother for child has its first beginnings in mere animal nature. Even the beast of the field "loves" its young. This instinctive tendency in man is lifted to the rational plane. A human mother loves her son because, though his soul was directly created by God, yet his human nature, a compound of body and soul, is derived from her. She collaborated in the building up of that manhood, and his very substance is derived from her. He is her own image and likeness, committed for many years to her care, and thus in another way also her own handiwork. This natural rational love can remain, as we have seen, even in eternity. But as the Blessed are sinless, all their rational acts are in perfect conformity with God's Will. The love of God is the one dominating power in their eternal life. The very greatness of that love casts out every sentiment incompatible with it. Nothing can become the object of love except in as far as it is good and lovable. Now the damned have nothing good or lovable in them, since they deliberately and everlastingly reject God, the Sovereign Good. Hence they have ceased to be possible objects of anyone's love. They are utterly unlovable. Perhaps it will be pleaded that at least mothers do not cease to love ugly and unlovable children, however repugnant to strangers. But in this objection lurks an ambiguity. True, a mother loves a child in spite of its external ugliness, because looking below the surface she sees some lovable characteristics which escape the notice of others. When, however, we deal with moral depravity the case is somewhat different. The knowledge of inner moral depravity normally lessens even a mother's love. Agrippina's love for her son Nero, when she succumbed to his second attempt of assassination, had obviously lessened.

However, it is true that on earth even the moral depravity of the son does but rarely extinguish a mother's love completely. The reason of this is twofold. The depravity is never total. A mother's ingenuity will discover a redeeming trait even in a monster of iniquity. Furthermore, the depravity is not beyond the possibility of change. The mother hopes that her son's better self will one day triumph, be that hope ever so faint, that day ever so distant. Make the depravity total, make it everlasting, and even a mother's love dies, for there remains nothing more to love. The damned are outside the bond of charity.

Opponents of Christianity often consider it horrible that the Saints are said to rejoice in the punishment of the damned. But here, again, we are dealing with an ambiguity. The Saints do not rejoice in the pains of the damned as such. The agony of the lost, viewed in itself, cannot be the cause of pleasure to any right-minded creature, least of all to the Saints in heaven. But they rejoice in the fact that justice is being done, that God should withdraw himself from those that hate him, and thus cause the pain of loss; that those who prefer the creature to the Creator should find in the creature their torment and undergo the pain of sense. They see in this the manifestation of infinite holiness, and they rejoice that it is so. God wills it, and they will it with him, for all that God wills is right and everlastingly to be praised. Moreover, they, the Blessed, know that they themselves were once on trial and in danger of being lost. Having triumphed, and being in everlasting light, they are not afraid to gaze into that darkness from which they are saved. Lastly, the damned are not merely the foes of God. In hating God they hate all the good, because they are good and united to God. Hence the good in union with God are united with him in eternal opposition to the wicked.

§ VI: THE BLESSED BEFORE THE GENERAL JUDGEMENT

Millenarism

In earliest times there were some who, misled by certain texts in the Apocalypse and by the strange fancies of Jewish-Christian circles, exemplified in Papias, early in the second century, imagined that after the General Resurrection a reign of Christ with the risen Saints would be established here on earth for a thousand years. Only after the expiration of this period would the Saints enter heaven in consummated bliss. At the first resurrection only the just would rise and enter this earthly kingdom, in which they would be prepared by Christ for the final consummation, when they would contemplate the Father in his divine glory. These ideas were held by some in East and West. Tertullian, Victorinus, and Lactantius amongst the Latin Fathers, St Irenaeus amongst the Greeks, were affected by them; but their very words betray that these fancies were not shared by all Christians. In fact, they were strongly opposed by many from the very beginning, and after some intermittent vogue during the first four centuries, were universally and definitely set aside within the Church. They would have been for ever relegated to the curiosities of ancient literature, were it not for some revival of them amongst Protestant sects in recent years.

Felicity before the Resurrection

Quite apart, however, from this question of "the thousand years," or Millenarism, as it is called, there remains the uncertainty and ambiguity of some of the Fathers regarding the state of souls between death and the General Judgement. It was indeed realised that neither their punishment nor their reward was full and complete until the Last Day, but wherein this incompleteness consisted was not clearly understood. The incompleteness of the punishment is discussed in the treatise on Eternal Punishment ;[1] here we deal only with the incompleteness of the heavenly Reward.

The point is not whether a definite judgement on the soul's eternal future immediately succeeds death—on this all were agreed—but whether this judgement is forthwith completely carried out. In reading the early Fathers, who speak of a delay after death, even for the Saved, before they enter eternal bliss, we must remember that in many instances they are speaking of the Holy Souls in Purgatory, though they may not use this technical term, but refer to them as the Saints, the Blessed, or the Saved. Still, even after making allowance for such cases, there remain undoubted instances, especially of Greek Fathers, who postpone the bliss of heaven for the Saved till after the General Judgement. They are not unanimous in their description of this state, whether it be a sleep, a rest, or some beginning of celestial happiness.

The bulk of Christian writers has always admitted some beginning of celestial happiness for the Blessed immediately after death. The majority, again, of these admitted that this happiness consisted in the sight of God face to face ; but even amongst these there remained the question whether the Beatific Vision was of equal intensity before the resurrection of the body as it will be afterwards. This question is not peremptorily settled even to-day. St Augustine, and after him St Bernard, St Bonaventure, and also St Thomas in his earlier writings, held that before the General Resurrection the natural craving of the Blessed for the possession of their bodies, and for the reconstitution of their complete human nature, involved some inhibition or retardation of the completeness of their union with God. Their soul not being completely at rest within itself is supposed to lack its utmost concentration upon God ; the attention of the mind and the fervour of the will are supposed to be in some degree still capable of increase and lacking perfection. St Augustine, in his *Retractationes*, towards the end of his life felt not so certain about an affirmative answer to this question as he was in his younger years. So likewise St Thomas seems to have changed his mind in later years. The Beatific Vision, he finally held, was always of equal intensity. The increase of happiness after the resumption of the risen body was one of greater extent, not intensity. The soul rejoiced that its glory extended also to the body. The fact remains, acknowledged by all theologians, that the happiness of the Blessed increases in some way after the General Resurrection, though they possess the substance of their eternal bliss before.

Question of the deferment of the Beatific Vision

Altogether apart from these questions debated amongst orthodox theologians, there was a minority of Christian writers, especially in the East, who did not even grant to the Blessed the enjoyment of the Beatific Vision previous to the General Judgement. Some

[1] Essay xxxiii, p. 1197.

few of these would use language which would suggest a state of sleep, or unconscious rest for the Saved until that day. They wrongly transferred the rest or sleep of the body in the grave to a supposed rest or sleep of the soul. The greater number, on the other hand, would admit a real active life in these disembodied souls, but they invented a kind of intermediate state between earth and heaven, consisting not in the Beatific Vision, but in the enjoyment of the company of Christ. The dead were in Christ and with Christ, possessing a happiness far exceeding any happiness known on earth, yet not in possession of the Beatific Vision in heaven. Moreover, in the Liturgy of St Chrysostom and in the Syriac liturgy, an ambiguity of expression occurs which would easily lead to the mistaken conviction that prayers were offered for the Saints, and even for our Blessed Lady, in company with the other faithful departed. This verbal ambiguity seems to have existed even in St Augustine's time, who, in Sermon 159, says: "According to the discipline of the Church, as the faithful know, when the names of the martyrs are recited at the altar, no prayer is offered up for them, but prayer is offered for the other deceased whose names are mentioned. It would be an insult to pray for a martyr, by whose prayers we ourselves have to be commended to God." Our prayer for the Saints, therefore, asks not that they may obtain eternal happiness, but that their glory amongst men on earth may increase, that everywhere they may be recognised and honoured as Saints. For this "accidental glory" we may pray. Perhaps also we pray for the glorification of their bodies, which they will possess in the General Resurrection. This last prayer we may offer in the sense in which we say in the Lord's Prayer: "Thy kingdom come." The Father's kingdom has not come until all are glorified in heaven in body as well as in soul.

Unsound views, however, about the state of the Blessed previous to the Judgement increased to a great extent in the Greek-speaking world. At the Council of Lyons, held in 1274 for the reunion of the Greeks with the Catholic Church, the opinion that heaven is delayed till after the Judgement had become predominant amongst those schismatic Christians. They were required to subscribe the following dogmatic formula: "The souls of those who, after receiving sacred baptism, have incurred no stain whatever of sin, and also those who, after contracting the stain of sin, have been purified either while still remaining in their bodies or divested of them, will be received forthwith into heaven." [1]

John XXII and Benedict XII

The question, however, was not completely settled by this decision, for it remained possible to discuss the precise meaning of the word "heaven" in the decree. Forty years later it was Pope John XXII who raised this question, and for a short time it was fiercely debated in Western Christendom. It was maintained by some that the souls of the Saints were indeed with Christ in heaven,

[1] *The Profession of Faith proposed to Michael Paleologus*, Denzinger, 464.

and that their heavenly happiness had begun, but that until the Last Day they saw God only in the Sacred Humanity of Christ, and knew him only as in a mirror, and by abstraction. The vision of God face to face was reserved to the final consummation after the General Judgement.

For two or three years the Pope himself seemed inclined to favour this view, though, even as a private teacher, apart from his supreme teaching office, he never held it or taught it definitely. He did, indeed, gather patristic opinions in favour of it; he often referred to it in public sermons, and for a time regarded it as the more probable alternative. As this roused the bitterest opposition in Europe, he seems gradually to have changed his mind, and on his deathbed, on December 3, 1334, he called the Cardinals together, and told them that he had drawn up a bull, of which this was the vital passage: "We confess and believe that the souls separated from the body and fully purified are in heaven, in the kingdom of heaven, in Paradise and with Jesus Christ in the company of the angels, and that according to the common law they see God and the divine Essence face to face and clearly, in so far as is in accordance with the state and condition of a separated soul." His successor, Benedict XII, in an Apostolic Constitution issued January 29, 1336, set the whole matter at rest by defining as follows: "They (disembodied souls) see the divine Essence with intuitive vision and face to face, no creature acting as a medium by way of object of vision; but the divine Essence shows itself to them directly, nakedly, clearly, and plainly, and thus seeing they enjoy this very divine Essence, and through such vision and fruition the souls of the dead are verily blessed and have life and rest eternal."

The reader will note that the qualifying final clause, which John XXII still thought it necessary to add in his dying declaration, is omitted. Benedict XII no longer says: "In so far as is in accordance with the state and condition of a separated soul." He states it absolutely and without qualification whatsoever. There is, in fact, no reason for any qualification, as the soul, even without the body, is completely capable of receiving the Beatific Vision.

The "souls under the altar"

In the light of this question, the following text of Scripture requires some elucidation: "I saw under the altar the souls of them that were slain for the word of God and for the testimony which they held. And they cried with a loud voice, saying: How long, O Lord, holy and true, dost thou not judge and revenge our blood on them that dwell on the earth? And white robes were given, to every one of them one. And it was said to them that they should rest for a little time till their fellow-servants and their brethren, who are to be slain even as they, should be filled up." [1]

The martyrs here referred to, having died for Christ, are in heaven and in enjoyment of the Beatific Vision, yet they are portrayed as

[1] Apoc. vi 9-11.

praying that God may vindicate their blood. They are told to wait and to rest till the number of martyrs is filled up. What does this mean? Are they in some distress, or is anything lacking to their happiness? Why are they under the altar? No altar, indeed, is mentioned in the preceding text, yet the meaning is not far to seek. Before the throne stands the Lamb, as it were, slain. This divine victim is Christ, the Lamb that took away the sins of the world. The martyrs are slain because of him. He is portrayed as standing, though slain, because, having died a victim for sin, he is risen and his glorified body, still carrying the wounds, stands on the altar before the throne. The martyrs, like him, are slain, and slain for his sake, but not as yet risen from the dead. Hence they are portrayed as under his altar awaiting the resurrection of the body. Though dead in the body they are living in soul, hence a robe of glory is given to each one of them, the "light of glory" of the Beatific Vision. They are told to rest and wait till the final consummation of all things, when the last martyrs shall have died for Christ, and, entering into heaven, complete the number of the Saints. Then at the General Resurrection their bodies, once slain for Christ, shall enter also into glory, and their blood be fully vindicated. It would be a mistake, therefore, to see in this text an indication of the delay of the Beatific Vision till after the day of the General Judgement. The judgement here prayed for and the vindication of martyrs' blood is indeed the Last Judgement, and the manifest triumph of all the martyr-host on the Last Day. But it is not a request for their own personal and essential reward. This is symbolised by the white robes at once bestowed upon them, and by the "rest" into which they enter. This "rest" is evidently the living, active rest of those who have entered everlasting life, that rest of which the Epistle to the Hebrews speaks (iv 7-10), when the Blessed rest from their works as God did from his on the seventh day.

Beatific Vision immediately after death

It is quite true that some Scripture texts imply that the bestowal of the final reward or punishment takes place at the Second Coming of Christ in the General Judgement.[1] They do not, however, show that the Beatific Vision, and therefore the essence of heavenly bliss, is not granted to disembodied souls. It is indeed true that final blessedness and consummated glory are bestowed only when the soul rejoins the body. Only then, and not before, will our complete humanity receive its ultimate perfection and joy, and our blessed Lord's words will be fulfilled: "Come, ye blessed of my Father, possess ye the kingdom prepared for you from the foundation of the world." On the other hand, it must be remembered that Christ on Good Friday was asked: "Lord, remember me when thou shalt come into thy kingdom," and answered: "To-day thou shalt be with me in Paradise." It is noteworthy that Christ did not use in his reply the phrase "in my kingdom," as the request of the

[1] See Matt. xxv. 31.

Penitent Thief suggested. The fulness of Christ's kingship and the complete establishment of his kingdom takes place when, as Man, he will rule over men in heaven. His sway over disembodied souls is not the full manifestation of his royalty. Nevertheless, before that day the Blessed will be with him in Paradise. The precise extent of this paradisial bliss with Christ the Scriptures do not define, though they suggest that it includes substantially and in essence man's great reward.

The immediacy of the celestial reward after death for those who are free from sin and its penalties clearly results also from these words of St Paul: "If our earthly house of this habitation be dissolved, we have a building of God, a house not made with hands, eternal in heaven . . . we groan, desiring to be clothed upon with our habitation that is from heaven, yet so that we be found clothed, not naked. . . . We, who are in this tabernacle, do groan, being burthened; because we would not be unclothed, but clothed upon, that that which is mortal may be swallowed up by life . . . we have confidence knowing that while we are in the body we are absent from the Lord, for we walk by faith and not by sight; but we are confident and have a good will to be absent rather from the body and to be present with the Lord." [1]

The passage becomes clear when once the somewhat unusual phraseology is understood. Our earthly house is this mortal body; our heavenly house our glorified body; the naked soul is the disembodied soul, possessing neither its earthly nor its celestial body. Here on earth we groan at the thought of death because we would wish to exchange our mortal body straightway for our glorified one, and not to pass through our naked state, divested of any body at all. Yet though we dread death, we have "a good will to be absent rather from the body and to be present with the Lord." It is better for us to be with Christ, though in a disembodied state, than to be in our bodies here away from Christ. To be away from Christ is to walk only by faith, to be with Christ is to walk by sight. The disembodied soul, therefore, has ceased to walk by faith, and sees God face to face.

Hence St Paul could write: "Christ shall be magnified in my body, whether it be by life or by death, for to me, to live is Christ and to die is gain. And if to live in the flesh, this is to me the fruit of labour; and what I shall choose I know not. But I am straitened between two: having a desire to be dissolved and to be with Christ, a thing by far the better. But to abide still in the flesh is needful for you." [2] St Paul did not know what to desire, whether to die and be with Christ or to remain on earth where he was so much needed by the infant Church. Clearly he expected immediate heavenly bliss after death. The same thought is embodied in those famous words, which it were well that we might all make our own when the

[1] 2 Cor. v 1-8. [2] Phil. i 20-24.

course of life is over: "The time of my dissolution is at hand. I have fought a good fight: I have finished my course: I have kept the faith. As to the rest, there is laid up for me a crown of justice, which the Lord the just judge will render to me in that day: and not only to me, but to them also that love his coming."[1]

APPENDIX—THE SEVEN HEAVENS

A QUESTION has been raised regarding the plurality of heavens, which at first sight seems indicated in some texts of Scripture. Christ is said to have ascended above all heavens.[2] St Paul was taken up to the third heaven.[3] Christ is said to have passed through the heavens, and been "made higher than the heavens."[4] Christ and the faithful are to be together "in the superheavens," for such is the real meaning of the Greek word *epourania* in Eph. i 3, 20; ii 6; iii 10; vi 12. In the Old Testament also God dwells in the heaven of heavens.[5]

In medieval times the theory of the three heavens was commonly accepted. These heavens were called either the aerial, sidereal, and the empyrean, or the sidereal, the crystalline, and the empyrean. According to the first theory, the first heaven is the air in which the birds and the clouds move; the second is the firmament of the stars; the third the heaven in which God and the Blessed dwell. According to the second theory the starry sky or sidereal heaven is the lowest; upon this follows the crystalline—*i.e.*, the blue transparent dome, apparently beyond the stars; and finally the empyrean or "fiery" heaven of God and the Angels. Neither of these explanations of the term "third" heaven can be traced to the first century, and they give the impression of being suggested by the text of St Paul rather than being genuine explanations of it. St Thomas and the Scholastics suggested purely philosophical explanations of the third heaven. It might be an intellectual vision, as distinguished from a mere corporeal or even an imaginative one. It might be a knowledge of God himself, as distinguished from the knowledge of celestial bodies or celestial spirits. It might be a vision equal to that of the third and highest hierarchy of Angels. These speculations, however, have no root in tradition or history.

Some of the very early Fathers imagined that the sevenfold division of the heavens was a fact and by implication taught in Holy Scripture. The idea of Seven Heavens is certainly one which goes back to extreme antiquity. It probably arose in early Babylonian or even Sumerian times, and was connected with the sun, the moon, and the five planets then known. This purely material conception of seven concentric revolving spheres developed apparently in Jewish

[1] 2 Tim. iv 6-8.
[2] Eph. iv 10.
[3] 2 Cor. xii 2.
[4] Heb. iv 14, vii 26.
[5] Deut. x 14; 3 Kings viii 27; Ps. cxlviii 4.

circles of our Lord's time into a sevenfold abode of spirits and superterrestrial beings. The third heaven is not always described in the same way in Jewish literature ; it was certainly sometimes described as Paradise or the Garden of Eden. It is remarkable that St Paul, having spoken of the third heaven, immediately afterwards refers to the same place as Paradise. It must be remembered also that our Lord himself used the term " paradise " for the unconsummated bliss promised to the penitent thief on the Cross. It seems most likely, therefore, that St Paul makes use of a current expression without necessarily endorsing contemporary Jewish fancies, out of which the use of the word had grown ; in the same way as we ourselves speak of being " in the seventh heaven " without in any sense thereby expressing approval of any theory of seven heavens. The third heaven and Paradise were simply terms commonly understood of a state and place of bliss bestowed by God on the just after death. Our Lord on the Cross used toward the common brigand by his side a word which he would readily understand.

So likewise St Paul, in speaking of a third heaven, may have used a phrase intelligible to those whom he addressed, without in any way endorsing the theory of seven or of any other number of heavens. The question whether St Paul on that occasion received a momentary glimpse or some approximation to the Beatific Vision has been variously answered, and cannot be settled through lack of information. It is, however, more commonly held that the Beatific Vision as such is withheld from those who are sojourners on earth.

J. P. ARENDZEN.

INDEX

(*Roman numerals refer to the Analytical List of Contents*)